AN INTRODUCTION AND SURVEY

JESUS AND THE GOSPELS

CRAIG L. BLOMBERG

BROADMAN
& HOLMAN
PUBLISHERS

Nashville, Tennessee

for
Elizabeth
and
Rachel

Ten-Digit ISBN: 0-8054-1058-9
Thirteen-Digit ISBN: 978-0-8054-1058-7

Published by Broadman & Holman Publishers, Nashville, Tennessee
Acquisitions and Development Editor: John Landers

Dewey Decimal Classification: 226.1
Subject Heading: BIBLE. N.T. GOSPELS/JESUS CHRIST—BIOGRAPHY
Library of Congress Card Catalog Number: 97-5288

Unless otherwise stated, all Scripture citation is from the Holy Bible, New International Version,
copyright © 1973, 1978, 1984 by International Bible Society.

Library of Congress Cataloging-in-Publication Data
Blomberg, Craig L.
   Jesus and the Gospels : an introduction and survey / by Craig L. Blomberg
     p. cm.
   Includes bibliographical references and indexes.
   ISBN 0-8054-1058-9 (hardcover)
    1. Bible.   N.T.   Gospels—Criticism interpretation, etc.   2. Jesus Christ—Biography.
I. Title.
BS2555.2.B586   1997
232—dc21   97-5288
                                                         CIP

21 22 23 24 25 26 27 28 29 30 31 12 11 10 09 08 07 06

CONTENTS

LIST OF ABBREVIATIONS

A ll the standard abbreviations for books of the Bible, apocrypha, pseudepigrapha, and Dead Sea Scrolls are used. Other ancient sources are written out in full. In addition, the following abbreviations are utilized.

ABD	*Anchor Bible Dictionary*
AJT	*Asia Journal of Theology*
b.	Babylonian Talmud
BA	*Biblical Archaeologist*
BAR	*Biblical Archaeology Review*
BBR	*Bulletin for Biblical Research*
BI	*Biblical Interpretation*
BIP	Biblical Institute Press
BJRL	*Bulletin of the John Rylands Library*
BSac	*Bibliotheca Sacra*
BTB	*Biblical Theology Bulletin*
BZ	*Biblische Zeitschrift*
CBQ	*Catholic Biblical Quarterly*
chap(s).	chapter(s)
CSR	*Christian Scholar's Review*
CUP	Cambridge University Press

DJG	*Dictionary of Jesus and the Gospels*, ed. Joel B. Green, Scot McKnight, I. Howard Marshall (Leicester and Downers Grove: IVP, 1992)
EQ	*Evangelical Quarterly*
ExpT	*Expository Times*
GTJ	*Grace Theological Journal*
IDB	*Interpreter's Dictionary of the Bible*
ISBE	*International Standard Bible Encyclopedia, Revised*
IVP	InterVarsity Press
JAAR	*Journal of the American Academy of Religion*
JBL	*Journal of Biblical Literature*
JETS	*Journal of the Evangelical Theological Society*
JRH	*Journal of Religious History*
JSNT	*Journal for the Study of the New Testament*
JSOT	Journal for the Society of the Old Testament Press
JTS	*Journal of Theological Studies*
Neot	*Neotestamentica*
NIDNTT	*New International Dictionary of New Testament Theology*
NovT	*Novum Testamentum*
NTS	*New Testament Studies*
OUP	Oxford University Press
p.	Palestinian Talmud
par(s).	and parallel(s)
PEQ	*Palestine Exploration Quarterly*
PRS	*Perspectives in Religious Studies*
SCM	Student Christian Movement
SJT	*Scottish Journal of Theology*
SPCK	Society for the Promotion of Christian Knowledge
s.v.	sub verbum (under the word)
SWJT	*Southwestern Journal of Theology*
TDNT	*Theological Dictionary of the New Testament*
TPI	Trinity Press International
TS	*Theological Studies*
TynB	*Tyndale Bulletin*
v(v).	verse(s)
WTJ	*Westminster Theological Journal*
ZNW	*Zeitschrift für die neutestamentliche Wissenschaft*

ACKNOWLEDGMENTS

I need to thank many people who played a part in the production of this book. It was Dr. Douglas Moo's class on the Synoptic Gospels at Trinity Evangelical Divinity School in 1978 that first organized my thoughts on many of these topics. My Ph.D. mentor at the University of Aberdeen, Prof. I. Howard Marshall, helped clarify them even further. I am grateful to three years of undergraduate students at Palm Beach Atlantic College and nine years of graduate students at Denver Seminary who worked through this material in previous form, helped me to see additional questions I needed to address, and regularly reminded me when I was still not clear! I appreciate the invitation to teach a combined undergraduate/graduate level class in 1996 as a visiting professor at the University of Denver on the Life and Teaching of Jesus. That experience convinced me that much of the material in this book could be used and appreciated even in the less theological environment of a university religious studies department, although there I assigned a wider variety of readings.

I also thank Dr. David Dockery, who was the academic books editor at Broadman Press when this book was first conceived. He and Dr. Trent Butler, also of Broadman, encouraged me to pursue the type of textbook I envisaged. In more recent years Dr. John Landers and Dr. Steve Bond were very helpful in the processes of editing and marketing. On the other side of the Atlantic, Rev. David Kingdon and Mr. Frank Entwistle of InterVarsity Press were most supportive. Drs. David Garland, David Wenham, and William Klein read and commented on the entire manuscript and helped me improve it in numerous ways. A student, Beverly Durham, called numerous typographic errors and stylistic infelicities to my attention. And as always, my wife, Fran, was my most thorough critic, as she too went over the whole work with a fine-tooth comb and made countless helpful suggestions.

Although this is my fifth singly-authored book, I have never yet dedicated one to my two girls. This was intentional; in the past both were not old enough to read and understand such a dedication. Now they can. So, to Elizabeth and Rachel, I say thank you. Thank you for playing so happily on your own and with each other so many times when I was supposed to be watching you but was also reading, writing, or typing this book. Thank you for loving Jesus with a childlike faith. My biggest prayer is that as you grow up, your faith will grow too. I also hope that you come to understand why I spent so much time working on this project. My life's greatest desire is that as many people as possible will come to know the Jesus of the Gospels, which is not always quite the same as the pictures of him we get in church or school. To God be all the glory!

INTRODUCTION

This book is designed to be a "one-stop shopping" textbook for courses on the Gospels. It is hoped that it will be of interest to thoughtful lay-persons who desire to deepen their biblical roots, as well as to pastors and scholars looking for a current summary of the state of a wide swath of scholarship. But the book is written first of all with theological students in mind. It is the outgrowth of twelve years of my teaching on the topic, although my interest in the scholarly study of the Gospels goes all the way back to my first undergraduate course in religion. As I have studied on the Gospels first as an undergraduate and then as a graduate student, and as I have taught similar courses at both levels, I have discovered five topics that lecturers consistently want to introduce: (1) a brief history of the period between Old and New Testaments as a historical backdrop for studying Jesus and first-century Israel; (2) the critical methods that scholars use to study documents like Matthew, Mark, Luke, and John; (3) an "introduction proper" to each Gospel, that is, a discussion of who wrote it, when, where, to whom, with what kind of structure, under what circumstances, and with what distinctives; (4) a survey of the life of Christ, with comments on Jesus' primary teachings and actions; and (5) a synthesis of the major issues surrounding the historicity and theology of Jesus himself. But I am aware of no textbook that sets out systematically to treat all five of these topics. Hence, I have been assigned and have had to assign to others readings from a variety of sources, never entirely compatible one with another.

This type of pedagogy, of course, has its place. Many instructors make the heart of a course their own lectures with the assigned readings more supplementary or peripheral. I began teaching that way, too, but there are so many interesting and worthwhile topics to study in the Gospels that I quickly became frustrated with such a method. To avoid lecturing at dictation speed and to ward off students' frustrations with trying to take notes from my normal, rapid-fire conversational speech, I began to produce detailed, printed outlines of the major topics I wanted to cover. These eventually turned into a spiral-bound, photocopied notebook that students purchased at the start of term and read in advance of class. In this fashion, I could be much more selective about which topics I highlighted in class, I could provide supplementary "mini-lectures," and there was actually time for questions and discussion.

Still, I was not satisfied. Outlines communicate only so much, and I still had to clarify many of my cryptic entries in class. In addition, it is arguable that one of the major gaps in theological education today is helping students make connections from theory to application. For too long lecturers have simply left it up to their students to figure out how a given topic applies, if at all, to the real world of life and ministry. Connections that seem obvious to learned scholars do not necessarily come naturally to someone else's mind. And with the growing maturity and diversity of typical student bodies, students themselves have much more to share from their own experiences than was once the norm. Yet students must be taught to think theologically and analyze real-life problems from a biblical perspective, a rare feat in Christian circles that are dominated these days by a free-wheeling pragmatism. But when is there time to do all this?

As a result, I committed myself to writing out word for word everything I most wanted my students to know—in other words, to writing this book. Now I tell my classes that if they master nothing other than this one book, they still will have the heart of a very solid introduction to the four Gospels. I create weekly quizzes based on the review questions at the end of each chapter to facilitate careful reading. (Italicized expressions highlight foreign words and important terms and concepts to further help the reader, as do numerous subtitles.) I still use some in-class time to highlight and emphasize the most important concepts in each section that I want to stress, but I have considerable time left for additional brief lectures, questions and answers, discussion, application, and case studies. I have tested the book in manuscript form with two years of students now and am pleased with the results thus far. I am hopeful, therefore, that many other instructors will find it similarly useful.

In fact, I envision several ways the book may be used in conjunction with the classroom or lecture hall. I pitched the level so that it may be read by upper-division college and introductory seminary students alike (in Great Britain, the rough equivalent respectively of first-degree university students in general and B.D. students more particularly). In the United States many colleges and seminaries offer quarter- or semester-long courses only on the Synoptic Gospels or the Life of Christ. Others cover all four Gospels. A few combine the Gospels and Acts. I hope this book will be equally usable by teachers of all such courses. In most cases it will need to be supplemented by other readings; in some instances certain chapters may be skipped. Although there is a logic to the sequence of sections and chapters, one need not assign the material in the order in which it appears. I tried to make each chapter relatively self-contained, while at the same time employing an abundance of cross-references to material elsewhere in the book on the topic at hand. As a result, there is occasional overlap between discussions, but hopefully not so much as to distract someone reading sequentially through the work.

Attempting to cover so much material in a manageably-sized volume by definition means that each discussion must be brief and introductory. Still, I tried to get to the heart of what I think students need to know most about each topic. That, of course, also means that detailed defense of the numerous positions I articulate is impossible. I tried not to overwhelm the reader with footnotes but included enough so that interested students can pursue the most important and controversial topics further. The bibliographies at the end of each chapter also serve this objective and include works from a considerable diversity of points of view. With only rare exceptions, I limited myself to citing English language works, although I have also read in some detail from Spanish-, French-, and German-language sources.

The perspective I adopt is broadly evangelical. This is not an approach I was taught in my initial formal theological education. It is a viewpoint I have come to through my scholarly study of the Gospels, and it has been reinforced in numerous ways over the years. I do not write according to some prior doctrinal constraint imposed on me by my publisher or the institution at which I teach. Instead, I serve these communities because their views are compatible with my previously arrived-at perspectives. Much of that prior scholarly pilgrimage first found a published outlet in my book, *The Historical Reliability of the Gospels*, to which I refer readers for a further defense of the approaches adopted here.[1] A short update appears in "Where Do We Start Studying Jesus?" in *Jesus under Fire*.[2] I hope that teachers and students who do not always agree with me can concur that I have represented a broad cross-section of scholarship in my survey and that this present textbook can be of use even among many who come to more conservative or more liberal conclusions at certain points.

In an age of extreme reactions both for and against various forms of political correctness, I owe the reader a brief comment about certain features of my writing style. Except when quoting a source,[3] I have tried to use inclusive language in referring to human beings. In the case of deity, I have retained the traditional masculine pronouns. I do not think it appropriate to defend either of these choices here, although I have my reasons for them. I simply ask readers to excuse me if I have offended them in either case. Primarily for the sake of variety, that is, to avoid repeating the name "Jesus" over and over again, I have used "Christ" as an equivalent proper noun. Its original use as a title ("the Christ") is elucidated in chapter 19. In other cases, I vary terminology to let readers know I am aware of options, without rigidly confining myself to one form of speech: "intertestamental" or "second temple" period; Hebrew Bible, Torah, or Old Testament; heathen, pagan, Gentile, or Greco-Roman; and so on. Again, I am not trying to pursue any agenda or offend anyone through this use of language.

---

1. (Leicester and Downers Grove: IVP, 1987).

2. Ed. Michael J. Wilkins and J. P. Moreland (Grand Rapids: Zondervan, 1995), 17-50.

3. Unless otherwise noted, biblical quotations are taken from the New International Version (NIV). Although an inclusive language edition is being produced, it was not accessible to me for this work.

I invite constructive critique from my readers, particularly with respect to this book's usefulness as a text. If it enables readers better to understand the Jesus of the Gospels, it will have served its purpose, and I will be grateful.

PART ONE

HISTORICAL BACKGROUND FOR STUDYING THE GOSPELS

An understanding of any religion depends heavily on the historical circumstances surrounding its birth. This is particularly true of Judaism and Christianity because of the uniquely historical nature of these religions. Centered on Scriptures that tell the sacred stories of God's involvement in space and time with unique communities of individuals called to be his people, the Judeo-Christian claims rise or fall with the truthfulness of those stories. For Christianity, the central story is about the life, death, and resurrection of Jesus—the story that forms the topic of the four New Testament Gospels.

Because many courses on the life of Christ or the Gospels are the first in a series of classes surveying the entire New Testament, part 1 of this book includes some historical background relevant to the New Testament more generally (i.e., including Acts, the epistles, and Revelation). Still, its primary focus is to prepare students for an intensive study of Matthew, Mark, Luke, and John and the events they narrate. The three major chapter divisions—covering political, religious, and socioeconomic background—obviously overlap, especially when studying a world that knew nothing of the separation of church and state. Still, the divisions are a convenient way of arranging the major topics of historical background to prepare one for a sensitive and informed reading of the Gospels.

HISTORICAL BACKGROUND FOR
STUDYING THE GOSPELS

CHAPTER ONE

POLITICAL BACKGROUND—
An Overview of the Intertestamental Period

F or centuries Christian scholars have referred to the period from the last quarter of the fifth century B.C. to the first century A.D. as the *intertestamental period*.[1] One might just as naturally study this period as the culmination of or sequel to the Old Testament era. However, since surveys of the Old Testament have much more material to cover than studies of the New, textbooks on the New Testament or the Gospels have usually been the place where an overview of these five centuries appears. Furthermore, any informed reading of the New Testament requires some familiarity with the events of this era.

The primary ancient source for the political developments in Israel during the centuries leading up to and including the life of Christ is Josephus's *Jewish Antiquities*, a twenty-volume work on the history of the Jewish people. For the decades immediately after Christ, Josephus's *Jewish War* is most useful. *Josephus* (A.D. 37–about 100) described himself as a one-time Pharisee and a military general in the war against Rome (66–70), who subsequently became a loyal supporter of Rome and wrote voluminously under the patronage of the imperial court. Although clearly writing with pro-Roman biases, Josephus may be regarded as a relatively reliable historian; for some periods his works are all we have.[2]

---

1. This is clearly a Christian term based on the belief that the New Testament is a second collection of revelations from God following the Hebrew Scriptures (the Christian Old Testament). In ecumenical circles "the Second Temple era" is often preferred. This term refers to the period beginning with the rebuilding of the Jewish temple in the late sixth century B.C. and ending with its destruction in A.D. 70. The abbreviations B.C. (before Christ) and A.D. (*Anno Domini*—"in the year of our Lord") are often replaced with B.C.E. (before the Common Era) and C.E. (the Common Era—i.e., when Judaism and Christianity coexisted).

2. For a good survey of Josephus's life and work, see Tessa Rajak, *Josephus: The Historian and His Society* (London: Duckworth, 1983; Philadelphia: Fortress, 1984). The standard editions of his writings are found in the Loeb Classical Library series of ancient Greek and Latin authors.

Other information can be gleaned from the Old Testament *apocrypha* and *pseudepigrapha*. The apocrypha (from the Greek word for "hidden") refers to a collection of fifteen short books that have traditionally been accepted by Roman Catholics as part of the Old Testament canon.[3] These include additions to older canonical works such as Daniel and Esther, books of wisdom literature similar to Proverbs (e.g., The Wisdom of Solomon and Ecclesiasticus), edifying novels (Tobit, Judith), and historical narratives (1 and 2 Maccabees). The pseudepigrapha (from the Greek for "false writings") include more than sixty additional works.[4] Some of these were written in the name of very ancient Jewish heroes (e.g., Enoch, Moses, Levi, Abraham)—hence the name pseud-epigrapha. But none of these books was ever accepted as inspired or canonical by any official segment of Judaism or Christianity. They include apocalyptic literature, the last "testaments" of dying leaders, expansions of Old Testament narratives, wisdom and philosophical literature, psalms, prayers and odes, and various other miscellaneous works. Few of these books even claim to be historical narratives, but their themes captured the interests of the Jews during the various time periods in which they were written. The most significant of these documents for reconstructing the history of intertestamental Israel are 1 and 2 Maccabees (from the apocrypha). These books narrate the events leading up to and including the Jewish revolt against Syria in the mid-second century B.C., with 2 Maccabees viewed as a little less reliable than 1 Maccabees.

Many Jews came to believe that after Malachi, the last of the Old Testament prophets, prophecy ceased to exist in Israel and would arise again only in connection with the events surrounding the arrival of the Messiah and his kingdom.[5] A reasonable date for the writing of Malachi is 433 B.C.,[6] and Josephus claimed that no Scriptures were written after the reign of Artaxerxes, who died in 424 (*Against Apion* 1.8.40–41). So a survey of the intertestamental period begins where the Old Testament leaves off, with various repatriated Jews having returned from exile to Israel, rebuilding the temple, and seeking once again to serve their God in their land.

Why is this era important to study as background for the Gospels? Politically and socioeconomically, key developments occurred, an understanding of which is essential to a correct interpretation of the situation of the Jews in the time of Jesus. Religiously, Judaism was transformed into a set of beliefs and practices often quite different from Old Testament religion. And for those inclined to see the hand of providence in history, numerous events occurred that prepared the way for the first-century world to be more receptive to the message of the gospel than in many other periods of history.

---

3. A standard English translation and edition is *The Oxford Annotated Apocrypha*, ed. Bruce M. Metzger (New York: Oxford, 1977).

4. A standard collection in English translation, with commentary, is *The Old Testament Pseudepigrapha*, ed. James H. Charlesworth, 2 vols. (Garden City: Doubleday, 1983–85). A brief introduction to the types of literature in both apocrypha and pseudepigrapha, along with their significance for New Testament studies and a select bibliography, appears in Craig A. Evans, *Noncanonical Writings and New Testament Interpretation* (Peabody, Mass.: Hendrickson, 1992), 9–47.

5. This claim has been challenged, but see Benjamin D. Sommer, "Did Prophecy Cease? Evaluating a Reevaluation," *JBL* 115 (1996): 31-47.

6. Pieter A. Verhoef, *The Books of Haggai and Malachi* (Grand Rapids: Eerdmans, 1987), 160; for discussion of other options see 156–59. Many critics, of course, often date other Old Testament books even later.

THE BEGINNING OF THE TIME BETWEEN THE TESTAMENTS: JEWS CONTINUE UNDER PERSIAN RULE (CA. 424–331 B.C.)

From the perspective of a secular historian, this is no point at which to begin a new era. Nothing earth-shattering happened with the death of Artaxerxes. Life continued much as it had during the time of Nehemiah, Haggai, and Malachi. The Persian rulers, with varying degrees of consistency, continued the policy inaugurated under Cyrus in 539 B.C. of allowing Jews in exile to return to their homeland and to worship their God freely and obey the laws of Moses. The Jews, of course, did not reestablish a kingship but began to look to future days when they could. An increased preoccupation with the Law was based on the convictions that their past exiles were punishment for disobedience and that God would grant them complete freedom when they achieved a substantial measure of obedience to his Word.

Three important new developments did take place, however, during the Persian period that sowed the seeds for the transformation of Judaism by the first century. The first two of these were the rise of the *synagogue* and the beginning of the *oral Law*. In fact, no one knows for sure the origins of either institution; some would date one or both much earlier or later. But it is reasonable to assume that the events of exile and return had a formative influence on both. Without access to a temple in which to gather or a divinely authorized place to offer sacrifices, Jews began to congregate in local places of worship. They drew on biblical texts such as 1 Samuel 15:22 ("To obey is better than sacrifice") and substituted prayers of repentance and good works as means of atonement for sin. They sought to apply the *Torah* (Law) to every area of life, so that a body of oral tradition—interpretation and application—began to grow up around the written Law of Moses to explain how to implement its commandments in new times and places. Both the synagogue and the oral Law featured prominently in Jesus' interaction with Judaism centuries later.

The third development was the establishment of Aramaic as the main language for business and international relations throughout many parts of the Persian empire, including Israel. A cognate language to biblical Hebrew, Aramaic became and remained the native tongue for everyday use among Jews in Palestine well into the first century. Indeed, by the time of Christ, many Jews were probably not fluent in Hebrew, as it had become a language largely limited to the reading of Scripture.[7]

ALEXANDER THE GREAT AND THE HELLENISTIC PERIOD (331–167 B.C.)

The first major new era of Middle Eastern history after the end of the Old Testament period began with the defeat of the Persians by the Greeks. Winds of change were heralded by the defeat of Athens by Philip II of Macedon in 338 B.C. This small kingdom in the north of what today is Greece had

---

7. A small group of Christian and Jewish scholars centered in Jerusalem vigorously disputes this claim, even arguing that the Gospels were first written in Hebrew. Their arguments can be found in a variety of articles published in the journal *Jerusalem Perspective*, but they have not persuaded many.

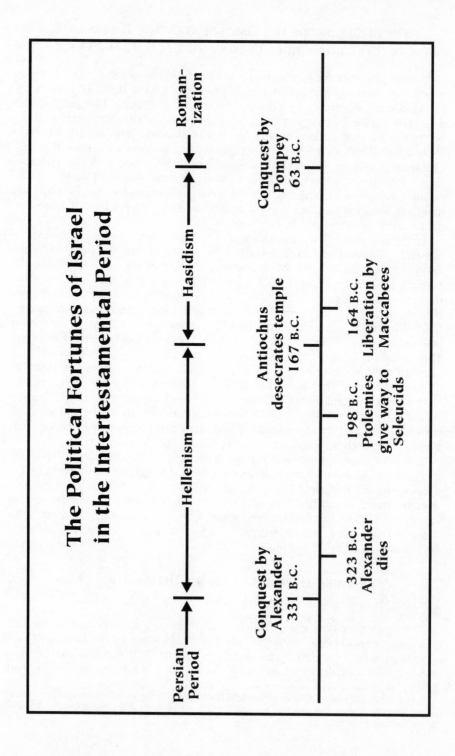

The Political Fortunes of Israel
in the Intertestamental Period

expansionist designs. The Greek historian-philosopher Isocrates challenged Philip with his famous declaration: "Once you have made the Persian subject to your rule, there is nothing left for you but to become a god."[8] Philip was assassinated two years later, however, and it fell to his son, Alexander, to strive for those goals.

Born in 356 B.C., taught by Aristotle, and inspired by Achilles (the warrior in the *Iliad*), Alexander has been considered by many the greatest military ruler ever. In only thirteen years (336–323) he conquered and controlled virtually all of the former Persian empire, plus some territories not previously under its control. His rule extended from Greece to India, from southern Russia to northern Africa.[9]

Greek Rule under Alexander (331–323 B.C.)

Israel came under Greek rule in 331 B.C. as Alexander's armies swept eastward. Like most of the peoples conquered, the Jews were given the same relative freedoms of worship and government as under the Persians, so long as they remained loyal subjects of Greece. Alexander apparently hoped to unite the eastern and western parts of his empire and create a new hybrid of cultures, religions, and peoples, all, however, permeated by *Hellenistic*[10] culture and influence. His turn-of-the-first-century biographer Plutarch, for example, claims that he founded as many as seventy new cities (*Life of Alexander* 1), though most historians think this number is seriously exaggerated.

The voluntary dispersion of many of the Jews continued, as under Persia, since greater economic gain was to be had in many parts of the empire outside Israel. In fact, the largest Jewish community not in Palestine developed in one of Alexander's newly founded cities (in Egypt) named for himself—Alexandria. This city became an important Christian center by the second century A.D. Jews, under the influence particularly of the mid-first-century writer Philo, as well as Christians, especially following the late-second-century theologian Origen, developed in Alexandria an allegorical form of exegesis that sought to harmonize the best of Greek philosophy with Jewish or Christian religion.

In Greece, Alexander and his armies had come from Greek cities with a history of democratic ideals. As he marched eastward, he encountered peoples used to acclaiming or even worshiping their rulers as gods and saviors, most notably the Egyptians with their Pharaohs. At first Alexander was shocked by the inclination of his new subjects to grant him similar acclaim, but eventually he accepted it and even came to demand it, to the horror and disgust of many of his own countrymen. Alexander's morals also decayed toward the end of his life, which ended prematurely just before his thirty-third birthday when, after a heavy bout of drinking, he caught a fever, possibly malaria, and died.

Numerous results of Alexander's conquests lasted well into the Roman period and the time of the rise of Christianity: (1) Greek rule brought improved standards of living and administrative efficiency in an empire that came to be urban- rather than rural-centered. This facilitated mass communication; and

---

8. Helmut Koester, *Introduction to the New Testament*, vol. 1 (Berlin and New York: de Gruyter; rev. 1995), 8.

9. For an excellent biography, see Robin Lane Fox, *Alexander the Great* (Boston: Little, 1980).

10. I.e., Greek—from *Hellas*, the Greek word for Greece.

news, including the gospel, could be spread rapidly by focusing on the major cities in each territory.

(2) Hellenization spread as the result of imperialism. Greek culture and influence could be found everywhere. For Jews, this provided significant enticements to disobey their Law. All the subjugated peoples were exposed to the breadth of Greek religion and philosophy. Major libraries (especially in Alexandria) and universities (especially in Tarsus) were founded. Jews divided among themselves as to whether or not it was acceptable to study, learn from, and incorporate Hellenistic elements into their lifestyles. Second Maccabees 4:10–17 describes some of the temptations of Hellenism a century and a half later in the late 170s B.C.: Greek forms of dress, with idolatrous associations attached to them; male athletic competition in the Greek gymnasia, often in the nude, contrary to Jewish scruples; and so great an interest in sports that worship and sacrifice were neglected! Other pressures on Jews to compromise their ways that began from early on under Hellenistic influence included attendance at or participation in the religiously explicit Greek theater and the availability and attractiveness of nonkosher food. The tensions of this era may perhaps be compared to the mutual pressure Western secularism and Islamic fundamentalism exert on people in various Arab countries today.

(3) No doubt the most pervasive result of Alexander's conquests was the spread of the Greek language itself. Almost everyone who had to do business with the Greek soldiers and merchants who came to be located in every urban center had to learn to speak a little Greek. A simplified form of Attic (Athenian) Greek developed, now known simply as Hellenistic Greek. It was less flowery and semantically precise than its classical predecessors. The Greek of New Testament times became known as *koinē* (Greek for "common") and reflected what Romans called the *lingua franca* (Latin for "common language"). Thus many Jews in Palestine even through the first century may well have been at least marginally trilingual, with some knowledge of *Hebrew* (probably limited in use to religious literature), *Aramaic* as their common vernacular, and *Greek* as the language of business, commerce, and relations with the military and political authorities.[11]

The extent of the spread of the Greek language is perhaps best illustrated by the need of *diaspora* Jews (i.e., outside Israel) to translate the Hebrew Bible into Greek as early as the mid-third century B.C., because of the disuse into which Hebrew was falling even among the generally closed and tightly-knit Jewish communities. This translation of what we call the Old Testament became known in Roman times as the *Septuagint*, from the Latin word for "seventy." Traditions developed that seventy (or seventy-two) scholars were commissioned to produce this translation, and one late legend claimed that all worked independently to produce word-for-word identical copies![12] The latter claim is demonstrably false—the surviving manuscripts demonstrate the same

---

11. It is regularly and rightly assumed that most of Jesus' words in the Gospels reflect the evangelists' translation and paraphrase of his original Aramaic into Greek. Still, we must not underestimate the possibility that on occasion the Gospels have preserved original Greek dialogues. See esp. Stanley E. Porter, "Jesus and the Use of Greek in Galilee," in *Studying the Historical Jesus: Evaluations of the State of Current Research*, ed. Bruce Chilton and Craig A. Evans (Leiden: Brill, 1994), 123–54. More generally, cf. M. O. Wise, "Languages of Palestine," in *DJG*, 434–44.

12. The oldest account is found in the pseudepigraphal Letter of Aristeas. The later legend appears in Philo, *Life of Moses*, 2.7.

complex history of formation and development of textual variants and traditions as do the Hebrew Bible and Greek New Testament.

The importance of the Septuagint for New Testament studies, though, can scarcely be overestimated. In a substantial majority of cases, the LXX (as it is customarily abbreviated) is often the version quoted in the New Testament, even when the Greek rendering varies from the Hebrew in some significant way. The Septuagint was clearly "the Bible" for most first-century diaspora Jews. An important area of scholarship which is only beginning to receive the attention it deserves involves the relationship among the different versions of the Septuagint and the ancient copies of the Hebrew Old Testament. Until the discovery of the Dead Sea Scrolls, the oldest known Hebrew versions were copies of the *Masoretic text* (MT) from the ninth and tenth centuries after Christ, while portions of the Septuagint were half a millennium older. Now, however, we have copies and fragments from pre-Christian times of most Old Testament books in Hebrew. Occasionally, these older readings differ from the MT but support the LXX. So not every instance of a New Testament author apparently taking liberties with the Old Testament text is that at all; in some cases the LXX seems more accurately to translate the underlying Hebrew than we first thought. But there are many other reasons for the distinctive uses of the Old Testament by New Testament writers and much profitable study yet to be undertaken in this field.[13]

Egyptian Rule under the Ptolemies (323–198 B.C.)

When Alexander died he left no living heir to his kingdom, so a struggle for succession ensued among his generals. From 323–301 B.C., the outcome of this power struggle was uncertain; this time frame is known as the period of the *Diadochi* (Greek for "successors"). Initially, the empire was divided into four parts, then three; finally two dynasties that controlled most of the land Alexander had previously held were established by Seleucus and Ptolemy. The northern half, based in Syria, came under *Seleucid* control, and its rulers generally took the names either of Seleucus or Antiochus. The southern half, based in Egypt, was *Ptolemaic*, and its leaders consistently adopted the title of Ptolemy. Because Israel was precariously perched in the only stretch of fertile ground exactly between these two powers, it was consistently vulnerable to expansionist designs on the part of either.

From 311 B.C. on, Israel was securely in the hands of the Ptolemies. The Ptolemaic period seems to have been one of relative peace and freedom for the Jews, with a fairly good standard of living, but sources of information about this time are scarce. One source that has survived is the Zenon papyri that

---

13. For introductions to Old Testament textual criticism, see Ralph W. Klein, *Textual Criticism of the Old Testament: From the Septuagint to Qumran* (Philadelphia: Fortress, 1974); and Ernst Würthwein, *The Text of the Old Testament* (Grand Rapids: Eerdmans, rev. 1994). For *A Comparative Study of the Old Testament Text in the Dead Sea Scrolls and in the New Testament*, see the book with that title by J. de Waard (Leiden: Brill, 1965), though a comparable, up-to-date work is acutely needed in light of the ongoing translation of the Dead Sea Scrolls. For brief surveys of the diverse ways the New Testament writers use the Old, cf. Darrell L. Bock, "Evangelicals and the Use of the Old Testament in the New," *BSac* 142 (1985): 209–23, 306–19; and Moisés Silva, "The New Testament Use of the Old Testament: Text Form and Authority," in *Scripture and Truth*, ed. D. A. Carson and John D. Woodbridge (Grand Rapids: Zondervan, 1983), 147–65. In detail, cf. D. A. Carson and H. G. M. Williamson, eds., *It Is Written: Scripture Citing Scripture* (Cambridge: CUP, 1988).

describe the development in the first half of the third century B.C. of the institution of tax-farmers—local people, including Jews, co-opted into collecting taxes as go-betweens for the Hellenistic authorities. This practice continued into Roman and New Testament times, fueling the Jewish hatred for tax collectors that we see on the pages of the Gospels. During the second half of the third century, a rivalry also grew up between the households of two men named Onias and Tobias. The Oniads were high priestly families who objected to the growing Hellenism of Jewish life; the Tobiads were wealthy supporters of the Ptolemies and were more favorably disposed to Greek culture. This tension, too, continued for several centuries.

The most famous and powerful ruler during this century was Ptolemy III (246–222 B.C.),[14] who promoted scientific investigation. Some of his astronomers even proposed that the earth was spherical, rather than flat, and computed its circumference with relative accuracy. But this information was not widely believed until the discoveries of Galileo in the early 1600s.

Syrian Rule under the Seleucids (198–167 B.C.)

In 198 B.C., the Seleucid ruler Antiochus III conquered and occupied Israel, shifting the balance of power from south to north. For the next several decades Jews were subject to Syria rather than Egypt. Antiochus III (who ruled from 222–187) and Seleucus IV (187–175) continued the Ptolemaic policy of limited freedom and self-government for Israel. But they also wished to keep on friendly terms with the growing power to their west—Rome. A peace treaty by Antiochus in 188 B.C. promised Rome substantial annual tribute, forcing the Seleucids to impose increasingly heavier taxation on their subjects.

Antiochus IV came to power in 175. He began significantly to alter the previously cordial relationship between the Seleucids and the Jews in Israel. At first his motives seemed strictly economic. He severely increased taxation to try to keep up with the payments to Rome. But he also began more actively to promote Hellenization, eventually to the extent of proclaiming himself a god—Antiochus *Epiphanes* (from the Greek for "manifest"). The later historian Polybius commented that his detractors referred to him instead as *Epimanes*—a "madman" (*Histories* 26.1a)!

Relationships progressively deteriorated between Antiochus and the faithful Jews who objected to the growing Hellenism. These Jews were increasingly called the *Hasidim* (Hebrew for "pious ones"). Conflict seemed inevitable when a man named Jason, the brother of the rightful heir to the high priesthood (Onias III), paid a large bribe to Antiochus to receive appointment to that office. The problem worsened when Menelaus, a Benjaminite and thus not lawfully a priest at all, in turn outbid Jason and was installed as high priest shortly afterwards. After a military campaign by Antiochus in Egypt, a false rumor spread throughout Jerusalem that Antiochus had been killed, leading to public rejoicing and celebration. This prompted Antiochus, on his way home to Syria, to enter the temple sanctuary and carry off the equivalent of millions

14. Or 221 B.C. The dates given for many events from the ancient world often vary by a year or so in one direction or the other in different modern textbooks because of uncertainties in the calendars and other ancient forms of dating used. For the most part, this book will not note instances of these discrepancies but merely adopt widely held dates.

of dollars of sacred objects and treasury monies. He also allegedly massacred forty thousand Jews in one day.

After Antiochus's next Egyptian expedition, he again looted Jerusalem, set fire to parts of the city, and slaughtered many—all on a Sabbath, when the Jews would not resist. In addition he made virtually all of Judaism's distinctives illegal and transgressed its holiest laws by renaming the temple for Zeus Olympius, setting up a pagan altar there on which swine were sacrificed (the most unclean of animals in Jewish eyes), prohibiting circumcision and Sabbath observance, banning and burning copies of the Torah, and ordering sacrifices to pagan gods at various altars around the country. Because Daniel 11:1–30 predicted in detail the political events from the time of the Persian empire to Antiochus IV (though without mentioning him by name), many Jews understandably took verses 31–35—Daniel's famous "abomination of desolation"—to refer to Antiochus's desecration of the temple.[15] First Maccabees 1:54 specifically relates this to the events on 15 Chislev (roughly December) in 167 B.C. when "they erected a desolating sacrilege upon the altar of burnt offering," though its specific nature is not described. Jesus later reapplied this imagery to the destruction of the temple by Rome in A.D. 70 (Mark 13:14 pars.), and some interpreters take the imagery of Revelation 11:2 to refer to a similar desolation at the end of human history just prior to Christ's return.

THE MACCABEAN REVOLT AND THE HASMONEAN DYNASTY (167–63 B.C.)

Needless to say, little further provocation was necessary to start a Jewish revolt. An aged priest, Mattathias, was ordered to sacrifice on one of the unlawful altars Antiochus had erected in a small town in northwest Judea called Modein. He refused, and when a fellow Jew came forward to obey the king's orders, Mattathias slew both his countryman and the soldier overseeing the sacrifice. Soon the priest and his five sons fled to the Judean hill country and organized a band of rebel Jews. They repeatedly surprised and defeated outposts of the much larger Syrian armies through the otherwise little-used tactics of guerilla warfare, including nighttime attacks from their mountain hideouts and a willingness to defend themselves and fight on the Sabbath.

Mattathias died in 166 B.C., but his son Judas, nicknamed *Maccabeus* (from the Greek for "hammerer"), continued leading the attacks. The Syrian commander Lysias was unable to devote his whole attention to the Jewish insurgents because of internal divisions among the Seleucids and attacks from the Parthians to the north, so the Maccabees continued to win victories, despite being outnumbered by as many as six to one (cf. 1 Macc. 4:28–29). By 25 Chislev in 164 B.C., Judas succeeded in regaining control of the temple precincts and "purifying" the sanctuary. This crucial stage in the liberation of Israel from foreign rule is still celebrated today by the Jews each December as *Hanukkah* (the feast of "dedication"). John 10:22 introduces one account of Jesus' teaching in the temple at precisely this festival.

---

15. A popular critical interpretation of Daniel sees it as written entirely after the events of Antiochus's reign in the guise of ancient prophecy. For a critique of this view, see, e.g., Stephen R. Miller, *Daniel* (Nashville: Broadman & Holman, 1994), 22–43.

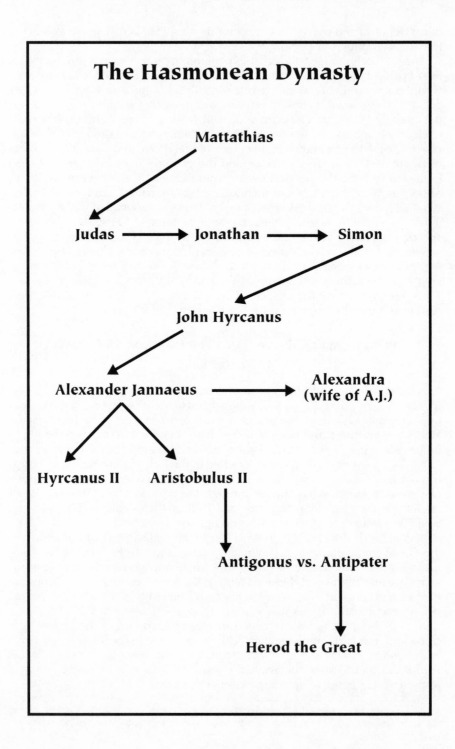

Though Judas did not remove the Syrian forces from the Acra fortress in Jerusalem, a temporary peace was negotiated. Fortunately for the Jews, Antiochus IV died in 164, and his successor, Antiochus V, was prepared to treat the Jews more favorably. Rome, too, sent a letter promising friendship (2 Macc. 11:34–38). Still, as opportunity arose, Judas and his brothers continued to fight Syrian troops until the Seleucid presence was entirely removed from Israel in 142. This ushered in roughly eighty years of independence, still heralded as a golden age of Jewish nationalism. After Rome ended this period in 63 B.C., Jews would never again live in Israel as a free, entirely self-governing people until the reestablishment of the nation after World War II.

The Maccabean revolt, like the events that led up to it, intensified Jew-Gentile hatred to a degree not typically found in Old Testament times. This enmity, with its accompanying Jewish nationalism, is an important phenomenon for understanding New Testament events. Consider, for example, Paul's speech to the Jerusalem crowd in Acts 22:3–21. Paul had almost been beaten to death because of the false rumor that he had brought Greeks into the temple and had been rescued from the Jewish mob by the Roman soldiers who arrested him (21:27–29). When he spoke to the crowd in Aramaic, they quieted down and heard his defense (21:40–22:2). They could patiently listen to his claims about Jesus of Nazareth and to the story of his dramatic conversion. What they could not tolerate was his account of the Lord's commission: "Go; I will send you far away to the Gentiles" (22:21). With this they raised their voices and shouted, "Rid the earth of him! He's not fit to live!" (v. 22).

The era of Jewish independence also reinstituted long dormant hopes of a restored kingship. Increasingly, certain strands of Judaism couched these in messianic language. When the Romans later overran Israel, the author of the pseudepigraphal Psalms of Solomon expressed this hope by echoing words from the canonical Psalms:

> Behold, O Lord, and raise up for them their king, the son of David,
> At the appointed time which, O God, you did choose,
> That he may reign over Israel, your servant.
> And gird him with strength, that he may shatter unrighteous rulers,
> And may cleanse Jerusalem from the Gentiles that trample her down
>   in destruction.
> Wisely and righteously let him expel sinners from the inheritance,
> And destroy the sinner's pride as a potter's vessel,
> With a rod of iron may he break in pieces all their resources.
> Let him destroy the lawless Gentiles by the word of his mouth.
>   (Ps. Sol. 17:21–24)[16]

By the first century A.D., these hopes reached a fever pitch in certain circles and spawned a variety of revolutionary movements.

Judas Maccabeus died around 160 B.C. and was succeeded by his brothers Jonathan (160–143) and Simon (143–34). While the Syrians still controlled part of Israel, they appointed Jonathan high priest, even though everyone recognized

---

16. The translation is taken from Ralph P. Martin, *New Testament Foundations*, vol. 1 (Grand Rapids: Eerdmans, 1975), 110–11, who also provides a brief commentary on the larger passage in which these verses are embedded (109–14).

that he was not the legitimate successor to the office. The move was generally accepted as a stopgap measure in light of the extraordinary circumstances. When Jonathan died and Simon succeeded him as military and political leader, ridding the nation of the final vestiges of Syrian presence, "the Jews and their priests decided that Simon should be their leader and high priest forever, until a trustworthy prophet should arise" (1 Macc. 14:41). What eventuated instead was a new hereditary succession of "priest-kings" that became known as the *Hasmonean* dynasty (after the name of Mattathias's great-grandfather).

After Simon died, Jewish rule finally passed to the next generation, to Simon's son John Hyrcanus (134–104 B.C.). Little by little the ideals of the original Maccabees were lost sight of, as Hyrcanus devoted his reign primarily to territorial expansion and forced conversions, most notably of the Idumeans, south of Judea, from whom Herod the Great would later emerge. Hyrcanus also set the stage for the increased antagonism between Jews and Samaritans that carried over into New Testament times (John 4:9), as he destroyed a temple the Samaritans had built in their territory on Mount Gerizim. This alternate site for worship reflects the same theological debate mentioned by the Samaritan woman at the well in John 4:20. The Samaritans were the descendants of the foreigners who settled in Israel after the Assyrian invasion in 722 B.C. and with whom the Jews had often unlawfully intermarried. In New Testament times, they considered themselves believers in the God of Israel but limited their Scriptures to the Pentateuch, which existed in a slightly different version in their own dialect. They looked for a Messiah, called a *Taheb* (a "restorer"), who was arguably somewhat more of a teacher and a little less of a warrior-king than in the expectations of the Psalms of Solomon.[17]

The Hasidim, who had supported the Maccabean revolt on religious grounds, now reemerged to protest the corruption of the original ideals and the growing Hellenization, which even the Hasmoneans had begun to promote. Probably it was this group from which the Pharisees emerged, calling the Jews back to faithful obedience to their Law. After an aborted one-year rule of Hyrcanus's son Aristobulus (103 B.C.), a second son, Alexander Jannaeus, began a lengthy reign (103–76 B.C.), in which he virtually obliterated the Maccabean ideals. On one occasion he had more than eight hundred of the Pharisees who protested his policies crucified. Pro- and anti-Hellenization positions thus solidified, a polarization that remained unresolved in New Testament times.

Jannaeus determined that his wife, Alexandra, should succeed him. She ruled from 76–67 B.C. and was much more supportive of Jewish law and well liked. After her death a power struggle ensued between her sons Hyrcanus II and Aristobulus II. The former was the older son who had been supported by his mother, but the latter was the stronger and more ambitious. Both appealed for assistance to Rome, by now the strongest political power in the area. Rome indeed intervened; its general Pompey invaded Jerusalem in 63 B.C., profaned the temple by entering the Holy of Holies, and put an end to the century of Jewish independence.

---

17. For more on the Samaritans, see John Macdonald, *The Theology of the Samaritans* (Philadelphia: Westminster; London: SCM, 1964); and John Bowman, *The Samaritan Problem* (Pittsburgh: Pickwick, 1975).

THE ROMAN PERIOD
(63 B.C. THROUGH THE ENTIRE NEW TESTAMENT ERA)

From at least 280 B.C. onwards, Rome had slowly been growing by deliberate expansionist policies. By 148 B.C., for example, Macedon had fallen to the Romans. A subsequent near-century of civil war kept Rome from conquering far more territory more quickly, yet by the time of Pompey's invasion, Rome was already knocking on Israel's door. Egypt fell in 30 B.C., and the Roman empire continued to grow well into the second century A.D., by which time it embraced the largest geographical expanse ever unified by one political administration in antiquity, including major sections of what today are Britain, France, Spain, and Germany, as well as the former Persian and Hellenistic empires.

When Pompey entered Jerusalem, Aristobulus II decided to resist but was defeated. Pompey recognized that Hyrcanus II would likely prove more loyal to Rome and so installed him as the high priest. An Idumean by the name of Antipater, the son of a man with the same name whom Jannaeus had made governor over Judea, was given the local political leadership. In general, Rome established "client-kings" at the provincial or regional levels. Antipater ruled from 63–43 B.C. The Roman emperor during these years was Julius Caesar. Because of Antipater's crucial help for imperial troops in 47 B.C. in Alexandria, Julius reduced Israel's taxes, gave her permission to rebuild Jerusalem's walls and fortify other cities, and supplied Judaism with unique freedoms of religion. This was the origin of Judaism as a *religio licita* (Latin for "legal religion"), which later exempted it from the requirement of sacrificing to those emperors who came to believe themselves to be gods.

From 42–40 B.C. another power struggle ensued, this time between Herod, Antipater's son, and Antigonus, son of Aristobulus II and rightful heir to the Hasmonean throne. From 40–37 Antigonus gained the upper hand, but by 37 B.C. Herod had finally triumphed. He ruled as client-king over Israel for the next thirty-three years. The high priesthood remained a separate institution; its occupants were Roman appointees. This explains, for example, why the Gospels depict hearings of Christ before both Annas and his son-in-law Caiaphas (John 18:13). Although in Jewish law the high priesthood was for life, political fortunes under Rome were less secure. Annas had been appointed in A.D. 6 and deposed in 15. Caiaphas followed a short time later after three brief appointees and held his office until 37.

Herod is the second personality surveyed in this chapter to whom historians have given the title "Great." He ruled in Israel from 37–4 B.C.[18] His reign was marked by massive building projects funded by heavy taxation in addition to his ample private means. The most astonishing of all was the temple in Jerusalem, rebuilt from ground up after the old remains were entirely razed. Although Herod's temple was completely destroyed by Roman armies in A.D. 70, the western retaining wall around the temple precincts was allowed to stand. It became known as the "wailing wall," where faithful Jews to this day

---

18. For the explanation of the anomaly that Herod, ruler in Judea when Christ was born, died four years "before Christ," see below, p. 188.

go to pray. Other projects, the ruins of which are still visible, include fortresses at Herodion just south of Jerusalem and at Masada atop a huge natural outcrop of rock overlooking the Dead Sea, and an amphitheater (now restored) and aqueduct at Caesarea Maritima. Herod also rebuilt the capital city of Samaria and renamed it Sebaste (from the Greek equivalent of "Augustus").

Before the start of Herod's reign, Julius Caesar had been assassinated (44 B.C.). Originally allies, Octavian, Caesar's nephew, and Mark Antony eventually vied for power. Octavian's defeat of Antony at Actium in 31 B.C. led to the suicide of both Antony and his wife Cleopatra. Taking the title of Augustus, Octavian reigned as the new emperor until A.D. 14. Herod had originally been a staunch supporter of Antony, but he quickly convinced Augustus that he could prove equally loyal to him. Most historians credit Herod's success to his good relations with Rome. Indeed, he pursued an active policy of Hellenization and Romanization in Israel, but more subtly than some of his predecessors, all the while insisting that he was a genuine and obedient convert to Judaism. Though never well liked by the masses of Jews, he did gain a significant number of close followers who continued to support the dynasty of his descendants. They appear on two occasions in the Gospels and were known simply as Herodians (Mark 3:6; 12:13 par.).

Toward the end of his life, however, Herod became increasingly paranoid about potential coups and had several of his sons and his most beloved wife, Mariamne, executed to forestall what he feared were attempts to overthrow him. At one point, Augustus ironically remarked that he would rather be Herod's pig (which a Jew would not kill) than his son (whom Herod would kill). Although recorded in Latin, the remark probably preserves a play on words in Greek because of the similarity between *hus* (pig) and *huios* (son).[19] Thus, although there is no independent confirmation of the story in Matthew 2:16 of Herod ordering the massacre of the young children of Bethlehem, the account is entirely in keeping with his character and actions at the end of his time in office.[20]

After changing his will several times in his dying days, Herod finally bequeathed his kingdom to three of his surviving sons: Archelaus, Antipas, and Philip. When Herod died, Archelaus instigated several oppressive measures against the Judeans that led the Jews to send an embassy to Rome to appeal the disposition of the will. All three sons eventually appeared as well, with Augustus deciding to give Judea (including Idumea) and Samaria to Archelaus. Antipas received Galilee and Perea; and Philip, the remaining provinces to the north and east of the Sea of Galilee (cf. Luke 3:1). Jesus' parable of a nobleman who went to a distant land to receive a kingdom and was opposed by an embassy of citizens (Luke 19:11–27) may reflect these events. Archelaus's cruel treatment of the Jews continued, however, and subsequent appeals to Rome led to his banishment in A.D. 6. Little wonder that Matthew 2:22–23 describes Jesus' family avoiding Judea and returning to Galilee after Archelaus replaced his father as ethnarch in the south.

---

19. See Macrobius, *Saturnalia*, 2.4.11.
20. For details, see esp. Richard T. France, "Herod and the Children of Bethlehem," *NovT* 21 (1979): 98–120.

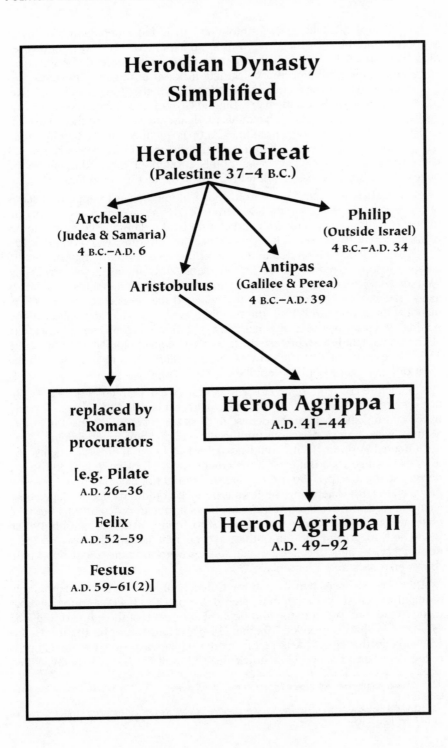

Herodian Dynasty Simplified

Herod the Great
(Palestine 37–4 B.C.)

Archelaus
(Judea & Samaria)
4 B.C.–A.D. 6

Aristobulus

Antipas
(Galilee & Perea)
4 B.C.–A.D. 39

Philip
(Outside Israel)
4 B.C.–A.D. 34

replaced by Roman procurators

[e.g. Pilate
A.D. 26–36

Felix
A.D. 52–59

Festus
A.D. 59–61(2)]

Herod Agrippa I
A.D. 41–44

Herod Agrippa II
A.D. 49–92

Antipas's rule in Galilee was far more benign and included the rebuilding of Sepphoris and the construction of a new capital city on the shores of the Sea of Galilee named Tiberias in honor of the emperor who succeeded Augustus.[21] Since Sepphoris experienced a construction boom in the early twenties, just five miles or so from Nazareth, scholars wonder whether Joseph and Jesus may have plied some of their trade there. But the Gospels never mention either city; perhaps Jesus, at least during his ministry, deliberately avoided these bastions of Hellenization and Romanization.[22] Antipas retained his "tetrarchy" until A.D. 39, when he too finally fell into Roman disfavor and was banished. Antipas is the Herod who appears at several points throughout Jesus' adult life on the pages of the Gospels (esp. Mark 6:14–29 pars.; Luke 13:31–33; 23:6–12).

After Archelaus's banishment from Judea, Rome began to appoint a series of procurators or prefects in the southern half of Israel—Roman governors sent to ensure a more direct link with and control by the empire. The most famous of these today, because of his appearance in Scripture, was Pontius Pilate (A.D. 26–36). Pilate succeeded in alienating the Jews more than all his predecessors. Josephus records three key incidents surrounding his governorship (*Jewish Antiquities* 18.3.1–2; 18.4.1–2): installing military standards and shields in Jerusalem with imperial images that violated the second of the Ten Commandments; taking funds from the temple treasury to build an aqueduct; and putting down an uprising of Samaritans. The first incident ended peacefully after a nonviolent Jewish protest; the latter two, in mass bloodshed. While Luke 13:1–2 does not exactly match any of these incidents, it is in keeping with the spirit of Pilate that Josephus describes.

The picture of Pilate in the Gospels as more weak than cruel does not conflict with Josephus's portrait. If Christ's crucifixion is dated to A.D. 33, it would have occurred shortly after the demise in 31 of the praetorian prefect in Rome, Sejanus, whose previous actions unofficially branded him as anti-Semitic. Without imperial support, Pilate could not afford to be as repressive against the Jews as he once was. But even if the crucifixion took place in A.D. 30 (on the debate, see below, pp. 190–191), Pilate still would not have been in a position of great strength. Alienating the Jews too much could have led to deposition, as in the case of Archelaus. At the same time, a Judean procurator had to take quite seriously any charge that he was "no friend of Caesar" (John 19:12). Being sent to govern the out-of-the-way and rebellious Judea was no great Roman honor, and one senses that such governors were regularly caught "between a rock and a hard place."

After Antipas was banished from Galilee, all of Israel was temporarily reunited under Antipas's nephew, Herod Agrippa I (41–44). Agrippa, sympathetic to Judaism, was a friend and political appointee of the emperor Caligula (37–41) who had succeeded Tiberius (14–37). Herod Agrippa I is the Herod who appears throughout Acts 12, first martyring James the apostle, then imprisoning Peter, and finally being struck dead himself for his blasphemy. When

---

21. An important major work that ranges widely over the entire Herodian family is Harold W. Hoehner, *Herod Antipas* (Cambridge: CUP, 1972).

22. Cf. further Richard A. Batey, *Jesus and the Forgotten City: New Light on Sepphoris and the Urban World of Jesus* (Grand Rapids: Baker, 1991).

Agrippa died, the emperor Claudius (41–54) returned Judea and Samaria to the hands of procurators. Acts mentions two of them in conjunction with the imprisonments of Paul: Felix (52–59) and Festus (59–61 or 62). Agrippa II, however, eventually succeeded his father as client-king in Galilee and ruled for nearly half a century (49–92), gradually regaining territory until he controlled about as much land as Herod the Great originally had.

Until the Roman emperor Nero (54–68) instigated a short-lived but intense persecution of Christians in Italy in 64–68, the period of Roman rule over Israel, and indeed the rest of the empire, was primarily a positive one for the spread of Christianity. Seven major factors may be listed: (1) Greek continued as the *lingua franca* of the empire. A politically unified realm preserved a linguistically unified people. No attempt was made to impose Latin on the masses outside Italy, though some would have been used in military and trade relations. When one compares the dozen or more major languages spoken in the same territory today that Rome once occupied, one understands the boon to communication of having a common language. (2) The *pax Romana* (Roman peace) gave the heart of the empire freedom from warfare over an expanse of time and space previously unparalleled in Middle Eastern history. True, Rome continued to fight skirmishes with Parthia to its northeast and Germany to the north, but these battles did not directly affect the daily life of most people in the lands depicted in the New Testament.

(3) A direct outgrowth of the first two points was the development of the most advanced transportation and communication systems of the ancient world, perhaps never again matched until the time of Reformation Europe in the 1500–1600s. "It has been estimated that the Roman government's mail service covered 75 km per day; messengers on horseback using relay stations, could cover as much as 100 km per day. Soldiers were expected to march 30 km daily."[23]

(4) A cosmopolitan spirit grew, particularly in the cities, that transcended national barriers. Old tribal distinctions and identities were breaking down, leaving people ripe for new religions or ideologies to fill the gaps. The gospel would meet many felt needs in this climate. (5) Closely related was the elimination of many cross-cultural barriers to dialogue and the dissemination of new worldviews because of the cultural and political unification that was increasing.

(6) As long as Christianity was viewed as just another Jewish sect, it too received protection as a *religio licita*. Throughout the events of Acts, all of which were completed by about 62 (before Nero's persecution) Roman rulers consistently came to the rescue of Christians, particularly Paul. Only by the decade of the 60s was it clear to all that Christianity was significantly transcending its Jewish roots and becoming a major world religion, at which point it was no longer granted the legal status it previously enjoyed.

(7) Finally, Rome implemented perhaps the most enlightened and advanced judicial processes of antiquity. It had its tyrants and despots to be sure, along with various breaches of conduct, but due process of law brought justice, at least for citizens, more consistently than in other ancient empires. Jesus of course was not a Roman citizen, but Paul was, and one repeatedly reads of him

---

23. Koester, *Introduction*, 314.

receiving the legal benefits of his citizenship (esp. Acts 16:35–39; 22:23–29; 25:10–11).[24] Little wonder that many Christian historians have seen not only a theological but a historical application of Galatians 4:4: "When the fulness of the time was come, God sent forth his Son" (KJV).

Already this overview of the intertestamental period has gone beyond the time of the life of Christ and even the events of the Book of Acts. But it is worthwhile to continue briefly sketching major developments of Israel under Roman rule; first, because the logical terminus of this period does not come until at least the early second century; and second, because the *writing* of the Gospels and of the rest of the New Testament was probably not complete until at least the end of the first century.

Following the time of Felix and Festus in Judea, two particularly repressive and ruthless procurators were appointed who brought Israel to the brink of revolt: Albinus (62–64) and Gessius Florus (64–66). Taxation had steadily increased, although Galilee to the north remained relatively prosperous. But many farmers had lost their fields to absentee landlords who held vast tracts of property and in turn hired their employees for irregular work at minimal wage, much like migrant workers today. Increasing indebtedness created foreclosures and, in extreme cases, jail sentences in debtors' prisons.

Despite Judaism's protection as a *religio licita*, not all had proceeded smoothly between Jews and Romans. In 41, Caligula tried to erect a statue of himself in the temple in Jerusalem. The fierceness of the protests would almost certainly have led to a horrible massacre had word not reached Israel that Caligula had suddenly died. Under Claudius, in the late 40s, the empire experienced a famine that seems to have been most severe in Judea (cf. Acts 11:27–30; 2 Cor. 8–9). In 49, Claudius expelled all Jews from Rome (many returned after his death in 54) because of frequent "disturbances," which the Roman historian Suetonius described as coming at the instigation of a man named Chrestus (Suet., *Claudius*, 25.4). Most scholars believe that this is a garbled reference to *Christus* (Latin for "Christ") and that conflicts between Christian and non-Christian Jews had provoked the riot. Then in 64, after the great fire of Rome, the emperor Nero looked for a scapegoat on whom to blame the destruction, particularly in view of rumors that he had started it. What resulted was the first persecution of Christians (Jewish or Gentile), now viewed as distinct from the historic Jewish community per se.

Meanwhile, tensions were building between Jews and Romans in Judea. In 61, the Greek residents of Caesarea erected a building partially walling in the local Jewish synagogue, and Nero replied to Jewish protests by revoking their status as legal equals to the Gentile inhabitants of the city. By 66 there was fighting in the streets. Gessius Florus ordered that the temple treasury be raided for political purposes. A combination of military, religious, and socioeconomic factors thus sparked the Jewish War with Rome, which lasted until A.D. 70. Nero's general Vespasian probably would have squelched the rebellion even faster were it not for Nero's death in 68 and the uncertainty of imperial succession. Eventually in 69, Vespasian himself became emperor—after the very

---

24. Cf. further the important studies of Harry W. Tajra, *The Trial of St. Paul* (Tübingen: Mohr, 1989); and Brian Rapske, *The Book of Acts and Paul in Roman Custody* (Grand Rapids: Eerdmans; Carlisle: Paternoster, 1995).

short-lived tenures of Galba, Vitellius, and Otho—and left his commander, Titus, to complete the invasion of Israel and the recapture of Jerusalem. Titus destroyed the temple, burned various parts of the city, and took numerous prisoners of war captive back to Rome. The year 70 marked a decisive turning point in Jewish and Christian history. Never again were the Jews a credible political or economic force in Israel (until today), and if anyone still confused Jews and Christians, Christian refusal to join the Jewish revolt clearly separated the two religions from that point onward. Sporadic fighting continued at Zealot outposts until 73 or 74 when Rome besieged Masada, constructing a huge earthen ramp so as to storm the rocky stronghold, only to discover that the 960 Jews defending it—men, women, and children—had committed mass suicide rather than surrender to the Romans. Or at least that is the way Josephus tells the story as part of his *Jewish War*, a detailed account of the exploits of those years.

Casualties in Jerusalem were enormous and the numbers of those deported sizable. D. A. Carson claims that "the savagery, slaughter, disease and famine (mothers eating their own children) were monstrous," and that "there have been greater numbers of deaths—six million in the Nazi death camps, mostly Jews, and an estimated twenty million under Stalin—but never so high a percentage of a great city's population so thoroughly and painfully exterminated and enslaved as during the Fall of Jerusalem."[25] This could partly explain Jesus' extravagant language in Matthew 24:21: "For then there will be great distress, unequaled from the beginning of the world until now—and never to be equaled again" (but see also below, p. 325). The temple tax was now to be paid directly to Rome, and Roman troops were headquartered in Jerusalem.

While the war was still raging, one nonparticipating rabbi, Johanan ben Zakkai, requested and received permission to found a rabbinical school at the coastal town of Jamnia (Javneh). Following the war, Judaism as a religion largely survived thanks to the study and leadership provided from this academy. Jamnia is probably best known for its late first-century discussions about the biblical (i.e., Old Testament) canon and for its increasing dissociation from Christians. By the 80s or 90s, synagogue liturgies in various parts of the empire had added an eighteenth "benediction" to those regularly recited. But this "blessing" was a euphemism for a curse—on all heretics, with *Christian* Jews prominently included.[26] The Sanhedrin(s) (see below, p. 44) were replaced by the *beth din* ("house of judgment") as the new court of law for Jewish religious affairs. *Rabbinic* Judaism as a movement had begun, and the seeds were planted for a uniformity of belief and practice that was not in existence in the days of the diverse sects of the pre-70 era or during the birth of Christianity.

A final Jewish revolt in Palestine took place in 132–35 under a man named Simeon, who was given the title *bar Kokhba* ("son of a star") and proclaimed

---

25. D. A. Carson, "Matthew," in *Expositor's Bible Commentary*, ed. Frank E. Gaebelein, vol. 8 (Grand Rapids: Zondervan, 1984), 501.

26. The Hebrew expression was the *birkath ha-minim* ("a blessing [i.e., curse] on the heretics"). Translated, it read, "Let the Nazarenes and the heretics perish as in a moment, let them be blotted out of the book of the living and let them not be written with the righteous." Modern scholarship has often seen this as one decisive rejection by Judaism of Christianity toward the end of the first century, but more recent studies increasingly agree that these developments took place more sporadically. For a survey of these studies, see Pieter W. van der Horst, "The Birkath Ha-minim in Recent Research," *ExpT* 105 (1994): 363–68.

the Messiah by Rabbi Akiba. This uprising was also decisively squelched. Historians disagree over whether two edicts were the cause or the result of this rebellion: a ban on circumcision and plans to make Jerusalem a major center of pagan worship named Aeolia Capitolina. Economic conditions had also again deteriorated under the emperor Hadrian (117–38). At any rate, Jews were evicted from Jerusalem and forbidden to enter on pain of death except for one day a year when they could lament their fate at the wailing wall. From this point on, Jewish Christianity also largely disappeared from view, although the factors behind its demise are complex and beyond the scope of this survey.[27]

FOR FURTHER STUDY

Introductory

Cate, Robert L. *A History of the Bible Lands in the Interbiblical Period.* Nashville: Broadman, 1989.
Niswonger, Richard L. *New Testament History.* Grand Rapids: Zondervan, 1988.
Pfeiffer, Charles F. *Between the Testaments.* Grand Rapids: Baker, 1963.
Roetzel, Calvin J. *The World That Shaped the New Testament.* Atlanta: John Knox, 1985.
Rogers, Cleon L., Jr. *The Topical Josephus.* Grand Rapids: Zondervan, 1992.

Intermediate

Bruce, F. F. *New Testament History.* London: Nelson, 1969; Garden City: Doubleday, 1971.
Jagersma, Henk. *A History of Israel from Alexander the Great to Bar Kochba.* London: SCM, 1985; Philadelphia: Fortress, 1986.
Russell, D. S. *Between the Testaments.* Philadelphia: Fortress, 1965.
Scott, J. Julius, Jr., *Customs and Controversies: Intertestamental Jewish Backgrounds of the New Testament.* Grand Rapids: Baker, 1995.
Surburg, Raymond F. *Introduction to the Intertestamental Period.* St. Louis: Concordia, 1975.

Advanced

Grabbe, Lester L. *Judaism from Cyrus to Hadrian.* 2 vols. Minneapolis: Fortress, 1992.
Hengel, Martin. *Judaism and Hellenism.* 2 vols. London: SCM; Philadelphia: Fortress, 1974.
Horsley, Richard A. *Galilee: History, Politics, People.* Valley Forge: TPI, 1995.
Koester, Helmut. *Introduction to the New Testament.* Vol. 1. Berlin and New York: de Gruyter, rev. 1995.
Smallwood, E. Mary. *The Jews under Roman Rule.* Leiden: Brill, 1981.

Bibliography

Noll, Stephen F. *The Intertestamental Period: A Study Guide.* Madison, Wis.: InterVarsity Christian Fellowship, 1985. (Also covers the historical background material treated in chaps. 2 and 3.)

---

27. For an analysis of its latter days, see, e.g., Ray A. Pritz, *Nazarene Jewish Christianity* (Jerusalem: Magnes; Leiden: Brill, 1988).

QUESTIONS FOR REVIEW

1. What are the historical sources we have for reconstructing the intertestamental period? How reliable are they?

2. Why is this period of time important for understanding the New Testament? Consider both overall trends as well as developments unique to a particular portion of this history.

3. What are the major sections of time into which this period may be broken? What key dates and events occurred to mark the beginnings and ends of each section?

4. Who are the key historical figures who influenced the course of events for Israel? Consider both foreign rulers and internal, Jewish figures. How was each significant? Try to distinguish the most significant from the more peripheral individuals.

5. Be sure you can define any foreign or technical terms (particularly those in italics) in this chapter (and throughout the book).

CHAPTER TWO

RELIGIOUS BACKGROUND—
Hellenistic and Jewish Religion

T he world into which Christianity was born contained a cornucopia of religious options. We have already seen the temptations that Jews faced to give in to various unlawful Greco-Roman practices. Yet we have only scratched the surface when it comes to describing the bewildering diversity of belief systems and rituals that pervaded the Hellenistic world. Judaism, too, was diverse, much more so before the fall of Jerusalem in A.D. 70 than afterwards. Intriguingly, almost every religious option of the first century has its counterpart in today's world; only the names have changed. Careful readers will want to look for such parallels as they proceed. Each has its strengths and its weaknesses and a variety of similarities and differences with Christianity.

HELLENISTIC RELIGION

The Greco-Roman world in the age of Jesus Christ was in substantial religious flux. The first century has been seen as a time of "crisis of conscience." Old worldviews and ideologies became increasingly outmoded. New cults abounded. People were uprooted from their traditional homes and lands and encountered conflicting truth claims as they resettled. Mixtures and combinations of beliefs and behaviors created a pluralism often intolerant only of a narrow, exclusive religion such as Judaism or Christianity. We can sketch only the rough contours of the most prominent movements here.[1]

---

1. Two excellent anthologies of primary sources for the study of ancient Greco-Roman religious and philosophical writings are David G. Rice and John E. Stambaugh, *Sources for the Study of Greek Religion* (Missoula, Mont.: Scholars, 1980); and Howard C. Kee, *The New Testament in Context: Sources and Documents* (Englewood Cliffs, N.J.: Prentice-Hall, 1984).

Traditional Mythology

The classic pantheon of Greek gods had reached its height in popularity during the fourth and fifth centuries B.C.—Zeus and Hera ("king" and "queen" on Mt. Olympus), Hermes (the messenger god), Apollo (the sun god), Poseidon (god of the sea), Aphrodite and Artemis (goddesses of love and fertility), and many, many more. After conquering Greece, Rome adopted most of the Greek gods and gave them Latin names: Jupiter and Juno (for Zeus and Hera), Mercury (for Hermes), Neptune (for Poseidon), and so on.[2] The origins of these gods and the mythological adventures surrounding them are debated. Probably they were the outgrowth of primitive animism or spiritism, in which objects and forces of nature were deified and worshiped. Later the gods were seen as distinct beings, described in very anthropomorphic (humanlike) categories, dwelling on the loftiest peak of the Greek mountains. They no doubt formed a primitive substitute for scientific understanding as people sought to explain both the regular and erratic behavior of heavenly bodies and the powers of nature. One had to know which god to pray to in order to receive rain for crops, safety in sea travel, or a large family.

By the Christian era, however, belief in the traditional mythology was seriously declining. As scientific understanding developed, people realized, for example, that the sun was a fiery ball in the sky and not a god with a personality. The geographic limitations of the gods also hindered their staying power. The fact that Rome was able to overrun the land of the Greek gods demonstrated something of their impotence. Indeed, emperors from Alexander to Augustus regularly exceeded the accomplishments of the gods in their conquests. Urbanization, population mobility, the mingling of cultures, and the upheaval of stable, local traditions throughout the Roman world all led to the loss of appeal of the gods and goddesses of old. To be sure, Augustus attempted a renaissance of sorts of the traditional myths by building numerous temples to the gods in Rome and encouraging their use for worship, but this was largely politically motivated. Stable traditions led to a stable, unified empire, and on several occasions Augustus hinted that *his* was the spirit (Lat. *genius*) that infused the powers or qualities the gods had traditionally represented.

The majority of first-century Greeks and Romans probably still gave lip service to the old mythology. For example, families poured out food and drink on their hearths or fireplaces (named after the Greek goddess *Hestia*) as the sacred center of protection in each home. Nevertheless, there were only three prominent areas in which the myths still had substantial influence. First, they remained particularly tenacious in rural or insulated areas. Paul and Barnabas, for example, were mistaken for Zeus and Hermes at Lystra in Acts 14:12—a superstitious identification unlikely to have occurred in first-century Athens or Rome. Second, the gods were consulted and believed to appear to people, particularly in their dreams, at healing shrines and oracles of prophecy. The Asclepian shrines combined elements of medicine, recreation, and religion in a kind of ancient health spa. The oracle at Delphi, Greece, was consulted by

---

2. For comparative lists of the most prominent gods and goddesses in both Greek and Roman pantheons, see Everett Ferguson, *Backgrounds of Early Christianity* (Grand Rapids: Eerdmans, rev. 1993), 143.

thousands of pilgrims seeking guidance for planning political or religious events, while priests and priestesses at the Sibylline oracles claimed the ability to predict future events, particularly surrounding the end of the world. Third, seasonal and annual festivals and temple rituals still persisted, often bringing great socioeconomic benefit to the local merchants or temple keepers. Two prominent New Testament examples surround the worship of Artemis in Ephesus (Acts 19:23–28) and the "sacred prostitution" practiced at the temple of Aphrodite in Corinth.[3]

Philosophies

Although today we think of philosophy as distinct from religion, it was not so in antiquity. All the major philosophers articulated worldviews about correct behavior as well as belief. Most of the major strands of Greco-Roman thought current in New Testament times were in some measure indebted to the fourth- and fifth-century B.C. philosophers Socrates and Plato, but the actual schools of thought they founded were no longer widespread. Platonism, however, bequeathed to the later empires a pervasive *dualism* between matter and spirit. Following Plato's famous allegory of the cave, the material world was viewed as a mere shadow of the unseen spiritual world of ideas. True reality was immaterial reality. Thus salvation was escape from the unreal world of matter to the real world of spirit by means of knowledge of the highest good or Supreme Mind. Sin was ignorance. Salvation produced a disembodied immortality of the soul, not a resurrection of the body. Plutarch (a "middle Platonist") tried, largely unsuccessfully, to reawaken interest in Plato's thought in the late first century A.D. The thought of Socrates was to a certain degree preserved in the emphasis on rhetorical training of the movement known as the Sophists, though at times, unfortunately, it valued style above substance. Paul probably combated some form of Sophistry in his epistles to the Corinthians, but this is less of a full-fledged religious worldview than the other philosophies.[4]

Other groups, however, do merit further consideration. For the most part, full-fledged devotees to the various philosophies were rare, since whole-hearted study often required an itinerant or peripatetic lifestyle. Only the elite, or those prepared to abandon normal occupations and beg for provisions, could afford this level of involvement. But the ideas of the major philosophies were far more widespread in their influence.

Stoicism. The original Stoic was Zeno, an early third-century B.C. philosopher who came to Athens and taught on outdoor porches (Greek, *stoa*). He was essentially a materialist, believing that all that exists is matter, except that he saw all matter infused with a "world-soul" which he called reason or *logos*. Stoicism was therefore also "pantheistic" (God is everything) or at least "panentheistic" (God is a part of everything). The key to contentment in life was to realize what humans could control and what they could not. Where inexorable natural or moral law exists, one must simply accept it, do one's best to fit in,

---

3. For more on this practice and other Greco-Roman religious influences in Corinth, and their relevance for interpreting 1 Cor. 6–7, see Craig L. Blomberg, *1 Corinthians* (Grand Rapids: Zondervan, 1994), 18–27 and *ad loc.*

4. For details, see Bruce Winter's forthcoming Society of New Testament Studies Monograph Series volume on the Sophists (Cambridge: CUP).

and remain in harmony with the cosmos. Zeno believed that in all apparent external evil there was some greater good. One's goal, where possible, was to avoid all extremes of emotion or passion and to seek self-control, calmness, and stability in all circumstances. This was accomplished by focusing on reason and rationality. As the power of the mind was cultivated, one prepared oneself for death and unification with the Mind that fills all the universe.

The most famous early first-century Stoic was Seneca, Nero's tutor as a boy and later adviser to the adult emperor early in his reign. The most famous late first-century Stoic was Epictetus, who taught that happiness was attainable only by the conscious restriction of one's ambition. One must concentrate on cultivating inward virtues and distance oneself from the accumulation of external possessions. Paul encountered Stoics in Athens in Acts 17:18 and even quotes some of their own poets (Epimenides and Aratus—v. 28), stressing that God is *immanent* (cf. v. 27—"He is not far from each one of us"). But, against Stoicism, he balances God's presence with his transcendence; God is distinct from his creation (vv. 24–26). The description of the conflagration of the universe and its re-creation in 2 Peter 3:10 has reminded some commentators of the Stoic belief in the periodic destruction and rebirth of the cosmos, but this view seemed to have been abandoned by first-century Stoicism.

Epicureanism. Epicurus also taught in Athens and founded his rival school of philosophy about the same time that Zeno was establishing Stoicism. If, from a Christian perspective, the "god" of Stoicism was too immanent, then the gods of Epicureanism were too *transcendent*. Epicurus, too, was a materialist, but he saw all the universe as made up of tiny invisible particles (a view foreshadowing atomic science). He did not deny the existence of the traditional gods but saw them as of a similar substance as the world and so removed from its affairs as to have no influence over it. Gods, thus, were unknowable, and death ended one's conscious existence.

The key to this life, therefore, was to maximize pleasure and minimize pain. This philosophy generated the famous slogan, "Eat, drink, and be merry, for tomorrow we die." But far from promoting hedonism, Epicurus was a somewhat sickly, retiring person who was seeking long-term peace of mind and happiness, not the immediate or wanton indulgence of bodily appetites. Epicureans placed a premium on cultivating friendship and enjoying cultural activities. Their philosophy clearly left the door open, however, to abuse and excess by those unprepared to delay gratification of bodily appetites for greater long-term pleasure. Paul encountered Epicureans in Athens in conjunction with the Stoics (Acts 17:18) and agreed with them, against the Stoics, that God is distinct from his creation. But he made it abundantly plain that God is also intimately involved with human affairs and one day will judge the whole world (vv. 24–31).[5]

Cynicism. Antisthenes (early fourth century B.C.) was probably the first philosopher to articulate Cynic thought, but the name of the movement itself comes from one of his followers, Diogenes of Sinope. Diogenes was called a "dog" (Greek, *kuon*—hence the term "cynic") by his detractors because of his

---

5. A plausible case has been made that the false teachers combatted throughout 2 Peter were, in fact, Epicureans. See Jerome H. Neyrey, *2 Peter, Jude* (New York and London: Doubleday, 1993).

vulgar, unkempt lifestyle. He was known for deliberately violating social convention by using abusive language, wearing filthy clothing, and performing acts of sex or defecation in public. Cynicism as a movement was generally not so extreme. It evolved into a philosophy in which "the supreme virtue" was "a simple, unconventional life in rejection of the popular pursuits of comfort, affluence, and social prestige."[6] A later Cynic writer summed up his creed this way: "Take care of your soul, but take care of the body only to the degree that necessity requires" (Pseudo-Crates, *Epistle* 3). Cynics largely objected to wealth and relied on begging to survive, limiting their traveling possessions to a cloak, bag, and staff. The similarities between this aspect of their lifestyle and Jesus' teaching, especially his commands to the Twelve and the seventy in Mark 6:7–13 and Luke 10:1–8 have led some scholars to liken Jesus to a Cynic, but the differences outweigh the similarities.[7]

Skepticism. Founded by Pyrrho of Ellis (about 360–270 B.C.), skepticism sought to challenge "dogmatism"—the traditional claim that absolute truth could be known. A plausible case was made in certain circumstances for denying any absolute claims. Morality involved merely living according to the accepted norms of a given society. Skeptics did not absolutely deny God; that would have been inconsistent with their system. But they were the agnostics of the ancient world. Their resulting lifestyle was remarkably indifferent or apathetic to supporting any causes; it merely sought the suspension of judgment, the practice of peace and gentleness, and freedom from disturbance.

Neo-Pythagoreanism. The first century saw a revival of interest in the teachings of the sixth-century B.C. mathematician and philosopher Pythagoras. Thus, Neo-Pythagoreans formed communal groups that devoted themselves to a combination of mathematical investigation, mysticism, numerology, vegetarianism, and a belief in reincarnation. They emphasized harmony, the resolution of opposites, and the discovery of the divine within oneself. A famous late first-century Neo-Pythagorean, Apollonius of Tyana, gained a considerable reputation as a miracle-worker. Some of the accounts of his miracles in the later biography of his life by Philostratus (early third century) are remarkably similar to Gospel narratives about Jesus, leading scholars to question whether one tradition influenced the other in any way.[8]

Mystery Religions

With mythology on the wane and the philosophies largely reserved for the elite few, a major part of first-century Hellenistic life that increasingly filled the religious void for numbers of people involved the so-called mystery religions. This is a term for a wide variety of secret organizations or cults often largely unrelated to each other. But several common features can be observed. They sought to bring the initiate into communion with the god or goddess the cult worshiped. They often promised conscious, eternal life, in union with the gods, which so many other religious alternatives did not. They offered equality

---

6. Robert H. Gundry, *A Survey of the New Testament* (Grand Rapids: Zondervan, rev. 1994), 61.
7. For the similarities, see F. G. Downing, *Christ and the Cynics* (Sheffield: JSOT, 1988). For a more accurate comparison, see Gregory A. Boyd, *Cynic, Sage or Son of God?* (Wheaton: Victor, 1995).
8. For details, see B. F. Harris, "Apollonius of Tyana: Fact and Fiction," *JRH* 5 (1969): 189–99.

across the greatly stratified society that rigidly determined one's lot in so many other realms of life. At night in a forest, senator and slave could worship together as spiritual equals, even though by day the one might rule over the other. Also, they held out hope for transforming one's pilgrimage through life in a world beset with many seemingly arbitrary terrors because their gods were not localized but had pioneered worldwide journeys themselves.

Some of the mystery cults arose out of ancient tribal and even fertility rituals. Some were indigenous to Greece; others were foreign imports, especially from Persia and Egypt. Several had periodic times of public pageantry, when the myths of their gods were reenacted. In addition, all had more regular, private meetings, with membership reserved for those who had gone through various initiatory rites. Sacramental meals, detailed rules for participation, and strong internal leadership characterized most mystery religions. A typical gathering involved a purification ceremony for members, mystical instruction, contemplation of sacred objects, the enactment of the divine story, and a crowning of new initiates.[9]

Ritual practices could vary dramatically, from the serene to the grotesque. The former category included meditations on an ear of corn or stalk of wheat in the cult of Demeter (corn god), a quiet river bath as part of the Isis cult (goddess of the Nile), or fellowship meals of bread and water in Mithraism. In the latter category were the Cybele cult's "blood baptism," in which the high priest stood in a pit beneath a wooden latticework, over which a bull was slaughtered so that the blood ran down and covered the face and garments of the priest.[10] Lower-level priests devoted to Atargatis castrated themselves, and the drunken orgies associated with the worship of Dionysus (god of wine) were well known and less a secret or mystery than many of the other cults' practices!

In post-New Testament times, Mithraism (originally from Persia) amalgamated with the Roman worship of *Sol Invictus* (the unconquerable sun), and a festival to *Sol* was celebrated every December 25. Christians took advantage of this "day off" to protest against Mithraism by worshiping the birth of Jesus instead. After the Roman empire became officially Christian (fourth century), this date turned into the legal holiday we know today as Christmas. The celebration of the annual death and rebirth of the nature gods finds parallels and contrasts, too, with Christian teaching about the death and resurrection of Christ.

Some historians have called the mysteries the most characteristic type of religion during the Hellenistic period. Many of the people who would have been attracted to them also would have found Christianity appealing. Scholars thus continue to debate the relationships among the different religions, especially with their various forms of baptism and sacred meals.[11]

9. John B. Noss, *Man's Religions* (New York and London: Macmillan, rev. 1980), 49.

10. For a vivid description of this ceremony, see the later Christian writer Prudentius, as quoted in Joseph B. Tyson, *The New Testament and Early Christianity* (New York and London: Macmillan, 1984), 119.

11. For more details, see Ferguson, *Backgrounds*, 235–82.

Magic

Overlapping the mystery religions, but found in combination with many forms of belief and ritual, was the practice of magic. Magic, as phenomenologists of religion use the term, has to do with the attempt to manipulate God or the gods into doing what a person wants by means of incantations, spells, formulas, or various ritual techniques. Magic provided an alternative to the capricious behavior of the goddesses Fate and Fortune, who otherwise seemed so omnipotent. Often people wanted to make someone fall in love with them or to receive healing of illness or good weather for harvest. Hundreds of "magical papyri" with such spells and incantations have survived from centuries just after the New Testament era.[12] Many of them involve long lists of nonsense syllables or names of deities; occasionally people tried to mix in Jewish or Christian names for God and Jesus into their lists. For example, the *Greek Magical Papyri* 12.270–307 includes the following invocation:

> Greatest god, who exceeds all power, I call on you, IAO SABAOTH ADONAI EILOEIN SEBOEIN TALLAM CHAUNAON . . . Abraham, Isaac, Jacob, CHATHATHICH ZEUPEIN NEPHYGOR. . . . I have called on you, greatest god, and through you on all things, that you may give divine and supreme strength to this image and may make it effective and powerful against all [opponents] and to be able to call back souls, move spirits, subject legal opponents, strengthen friendships, produce all [sorts of] profits, bring dreams, give prophecies, cause psychological passions and bodily sufferings and incapacitating illness, and perfect all erotic philters.

In their most sinister forms, ancient magicians were akin to sorcerers, while magic was similar to what we would today call the occult, including spells designed to curse people. Acts 19:19 describes a huge bonfire of magical scrolls at first-century Ephesus as a result of the preaching of the gospel.

Gnosticism

Another increasingly prominent religious movement roughly coinciding with the birth of Christianity was Gnosticism.[13] Based on the Platonic dualism of matter and spirit, Gnostics argued that the material world was inherently evil; only the spirit world was potentially good. This led to one of two ethical systems. Some engaged in *hedonism*, indulging their bodily appetites since they were irredeemable anyway. More commonly, Gnostics practiced *asceticism* and attempted to deny themselves normal bodily satisfactions since the flesh was inherently corrupting. Both approaches may have been present in Corinth (cf. 1 Cor. 6 and 7).

Salvation for the Gnostic thus involved the attempt of the soul to escape the fetters of the body by recognizing and liberating the divine spark that dwells within every person. This salvation became possible through *gnosis* (Greek for

---

12. The standard collection in English is Hans Dieter Betz, ed., *The Greek Magical Papyri in Translation* (Chicago and London: University of Chicago Press, 1986).

13. For an excellent and balanced summary of what we can know about Gnosticism in general, see Robert McL. Wilson, *Gnosis and the New Testament* (Oxford: Blackwell; Philadelphia: Fortress, 1968). For an update in light of recent research, see Pheme Perkins, *Gnosticism and the New Testament* (Minneapolis: Fortress, 1993).

"knowledge"), not of an intellectual nature but by a secret revelation known only to members of a given Gnostic sect. The relevant knowledge usually involved understanding one's divine origin, one's current state of slavery, and the redemptive possibilities of the future. One could then be said to have attained to the resurrection already in this life; all that remained was for one to die and be fully liberated from the material world. Second Thessalonians 2:2 may reflect such a claim that Paul had to combat.

To articulate their theology, Gnostics developed an elaborate mythology. Each sect had its own distinctive twists, but a composite account of generally common features might read as follows: The original god of the universe is remote and largely unknowable. He did not directly create the heavens and the earth. Rather, from him came forth *aeons*—impersonal emanations usually described as abstract virtues or entities (e.g., love, light, truth, justice). Together these aeons formed the "fullness" *(pleroma)* of the Godhead or Deity—the same expression Paul applied to Christ in Colossians 2:9. One of these aeons rebelled against God's designs by creating the material world; hence, matter is by nature evil. Another aeon thus had to be sent to redeem the world. This is usually *Sophia* (Greek for "wisdom"), though occasionally she is seen as the culprit rather than the savior. The ultimate goal of redemption is the restoration of all things to their pristine perfection.

Like the mystery cults, Gnosticism tended to be more "charismatic" and "egalitarian" than institutionalized forms of religion. As part of the process of freeing oneself from the constraints of the body, Gnostics sometimes promoted androgyny—a blurring of the distinctions between male and female—as the ideal form of human existence. All this, coupled with the personification of the divine Sophia as a woman, has led many modern feminist scholars to study ancient Gnosticism with great interest, and at times even to promote it.[14]

Information about Gnosticism became much more abundant just after World War II with the discovery of the "Nag Hammadi Library" in Egypt—a collection of more than sixty mostly Gnostic documents, many of them in Coptic, generally dating from the mid-second to mid-fifth centuries A.D. Some are complete editions of works that had previously been preserved only in Greek fragments; some had been referred to by early Church Fathers, and many were brand new to modern scholars. They include "Gospels" attributed to various disciples, including Mary, which usually comprise little more than lengthy discourses of the risen Jesus (supposedly given in private to different groups of his followers), articulating Gnostic thought. Other documents are more like epistles, treatises, or apocalypses.[15] Consistently in these works, the Gnostic redeemer is equated with Jesus, even though little else resembling New Testament thought may survive.

Undoubtedly the most significant find for New Testament studies, and for Gospel scholarship in particular, was the *Coptic Gospel of Thomas*. This docu-

---

14. For a well-known survey, see Elaine Pagels, *The Gnostic Gospels* (New York: Random House, 1979). Nevertheless, on balance, there are more texts in the Gnostic literature that denigrate the feminine as an inferior gender than those that exalt it.

15. The standard English translation and edition is James M. Robinson, ed., *The Nag Hammadi Library in English* (Leiden: Brill, rev. 1988).

ment, falsely ascribed to the apostle Thomas, contains 114 separate sayings attributed to Jesus, largely without any narrative framework connecting them. Roughly one-third of the sayings are clearly Gnostic in outlook, between one-third and one-half are paralleled fairly closely in the canonical Gospels, and the rest are not demonstrably unorthodox but could lend themselves to Gnostic interpretations. Although there is no hard evidence to date any of these sayings to earlier than the mid-second century, and although it seems likely that most of the paralleled sayings are revisions or distortions of canonical forms, some scholars have speculated that Thomas might consistently reflect an independent witness to the teachings of Jesus, older than the canonical Gospels.[16] More careful analysis renders this highly improbable, though it is not impossible that isolated sayings not previously known reflect authentic teachings of Christ (see also below, p. 376).[17]

Indeed, larger questions of dating and chronology surround the origins of Gnosticism itself. Although it was popular a generation or two ago to assert that Christianity had borrowed its views of Jesus from a Gnostic "redeemer myth," it is now widely recognized that such mythology *post*dates the birth of Christian thought and more likely derived from earlier, more orthodox theology.[18] On the other hand, non-Christian and even Jewish forms of Gnosticism do seem to *pre*date or at least be contemporaneous with the composition of the New Testament. Clearly, several of the heresies Paul combats in his various epistles bear resemblance to later, more fully-developed Gnostic thought. Most scholars therefore use terms like "proto-Gnosticism" or "incipient Gnosticism" to speak of the various Gnostic-like ideas that developed throughout the first century. They then reserve "Gnosticism" proper for the schools of such second-century teachers as Basilides and Valentinus, and perhaps the late first-century Ephesian teacher Cerinthus, whose false teachings may have precipitated the writing of 1 John.[19]

Emperor Worship

Inasmuch as the new world rulers of the time of Christ seemed greater than the traditional gods themselves, it is not surprising that they should have eventually been deified. By the middle of the first century, most Greeks and Romans gave some lip service to emperor worship, but those from the western parts of the empire, unused to taking such beliefs too seriously, probably viewed this as little more than an act of patriotism or an acknowledgment of the emperors'

---

16. See, e.g., Stevan L. Davies, *The Gospel of Thomas and Christian Wisdom* (New York: Seabury, 1983). This perspective has heavily influenced the well-known Jesus Seminar's approach to evaluating the authenticity of the sayings of Jesus in the four canonical Gospels and the Gospel of Thomas. See Robert W. Funk, Roy W. Hoover, and the Jesus Seminar, *The Five Gospels: The Search for the Authentic Words of Jesus* (New York: Macmillan, 1993).

17. On the general illegitimacy of using Thomas as background material for historical Jesus research, see John P. Meier, *A Marginal Jew: Rethinking the Historical Jesus*, vol. 1 (New York and London: Doubleday, 1991), 123–39. For a balanced assessment of the relationship of Thomas to Gnosticism, see Robert M. Grant and David N. Freedman, *The Secret Sayings of Jesus* (London: SPCK, 1958; New York: Doubleday, 1960). For an evangelical response to the Jesus Seminar more generally, see Michael J. Wilkins and J. P. Moreland, eds., *Jesus under Fire* (Grand Rapids: Zondervan, 1995).

18. See esp. Edwin Yamauchi, *Pre-Christian Gnosticism: A Survey of the Proposed Evidences* (Grand Rapids: Baker, rev. 1983).

19. A good overview of the major Gnostic sects and teachers and their literature appears in Jack Finegan, *Myth and Mystery: An Introduction to the Pagan Religions of the Biblical World* (Grand Rapids: Baker, 1989), 217–58.

great powers (and, occasionally, virtue). Precedent for such practice could also be found in the deification of ancient Greek or Roman warriors (e.g., Hercules) or healers (e.g., Asclepius). In the eastern parts of the empire, where rulers had been deified for centuries, emperor worship was probably taken somewhat more seriously.

The first emperor to be deified was Julius Caesar, acclaimed after his death in 27 B.C. as a god by Augustus. This of course legitimized Augustus as a "son of a god." But Augustus generally repudiated attempts, usually from the East, to worship him as a god during his lifetime (though recall our comments about his "genius" above, p. 29). The precedent he established, however, was continued by Tiberius, who declared Augustus to be divine when he died in A.D. 14. Gaius Caligula (37–41) was the first emperor to seek acclamation as a god during his lifetime, and his increasingly bizarre behavior led some to think he had gone mad. The Roman Senate denied him deification at his death. Not until Nero (54–68), and then only toward the end of his reign, did an emperor seek to enforce worship of himself, and then only sporadically and largely as part of the persecution of Christians in and around Rome (64–68). Domitian in the mid-90s finally sought to establish the practice on a more widespread scale, though even then it was short-lived. Christian refusal to call the emperor "Lord and God" (*Dominus et Deus*) and to offer a pinch of incense in sacrifice to him must have struck the average Roman in somewhat the same way as the refusal by Jehovah's Witnesses to pledge allegiance to the flag strikes the average American today. But Christians saw in the sacrifice a blasphemous attribution to Caesar of the divine honors worthy of God alone, and thus, for the most part, they refused to participate. Jews, of course, were exempt because they were still under the protection of being a *religio licita*.

JUDAISM

The study of ancient Jewish thought is both easier and harder than the study of Hellenistic religion. It is easier because in most cases we have far more primary source material available. For that same reason, however, it is harder, because it is virtually impossible for anyone to master it all who was not raised in those branches of orthodox Judaism that still require schoolchildren to study a vast amount of their ancient literature. And in each case, one must try to filter information from the rabbinic material through the grids of its diverse historical contexts and theological biases.

Sources

In addition to the works of Josephus, the apocrypha, and the pseudepigrapha (on which, see above, pp. 7–8), the vast corpus of rabbinic literature sheds much light on ancient Judaism. Almost all of this material, together occupying the same space as several sets of major encyclopedias, originally circulated in oral form before being committed to writing. The written editions all postdate the first century, so one must exercise great care in trying to sift those traditions that are old enough to be relevant to a study of

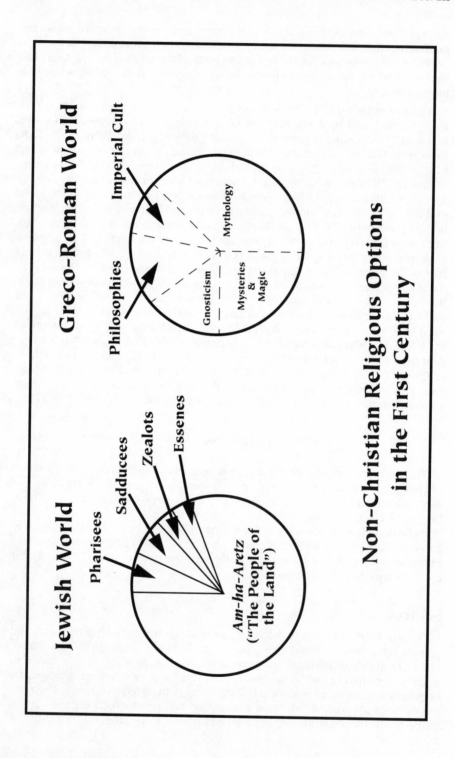

the New Testament or the life of Jesus from the majority of traditions that are considerably younger.[20]

The oral laws that had been developing over the centuries (see above, p. 9) were first codified in the *Mishnah* (from the Heb. for "repetition"), a book slightly thicker than the Bible, by Rabbi Judah Ha-Nasi in about A.D. 200.[21] Its major divisions include *Zeraim* ("seeds"), *Moed* ("set feasts"), *Nashim* ("women"), *Nezikin* ("damages"), *Kodashim* ("hallowed things"), and *Tohoroth* ("cleannesses"). Sixty-three tractates or subdivisions reflect the Mishnah's preoccupation with minute legal matters. For example, the tractates of *Zeraim* deal with "gleanings," "produce not certainly tithed," "heave offerings," "fruit of young trees," and so on. Some of the tractates of *Nashim* treat "sisters-in-law," "marriage deeds," "vows," "suspected adulteresses," and "bills of divorce." Most all of the Mishnah's contents reflect the rulings by named and unnamed rabbis over legal disputes concerning these various topics. Legal material in the rabbinic literature is often called *halakah* (from the Heb. verb "to walk"). Supplementary tractates in subsequent years were added to the Mishnah and called *Tosefta* (from the Heb. for "addition" or "supplement"). An example of a halakah that preserved one of the many traditions about keeping a "kosher" table is found in the Mishnaic tractate *Hullin* 8.1: "No meat may be boiled with milk save meat of fish and locusts. It is also forbidden to bring it to table together with cheese, save meat of fish and locusts. He who vows to abstain from meat is still free to partake of fish and locusts."

Not all of the oral tradition was halakhic, however. Much was *haggadah* ("story" or "narrative"), illustrating the various legal principles often by parables or anecdotes from the lives of famous rabbis. What is more, the oral tradition continued to develop in both halakhic and haggadic form even after the Mishnah was first compiled. Additional commentary on the topics of many of the tractates of the Mishnah and Tosefta was called *Gemara* (Heb. "completion"). This greatly expanded material was first codified in the fourth century A.D. The encyclopedic results were called *Talmud* (Heb. "studying"). The first known edition of the Talmud came from Palestine, sometimes but probably falsely attributed to Jerusalem. Traditions and commentary continued to grow so that an even longer edition of the Talmud, the one orthodox Judaism eventually came to treat as authoritative, was produced in Babylonia in the late fifth century, with further editing and additions even beyond that date. An example of a Talmudic parable (haggadah), commenting on Ecclesiastes 9:8, appears in *b. Shabbat* 153a:

> Rabbi Johanan ben Zakkai said, "A parable. It is like a king who summoned his servants to a banquet without appointing a time. The wise ones adorned themselves and sat at the door of the palace; they said, 'Is anything

---

20. No one has stressed this point and illustrated possible means for going about the sifting process more than Jacob Neusner, a prolific Jewish scholar who has written over five hundred books, mostly on ancient Judaism. His work is impossible to keep up with, but much of it is repetitive. His programmatic study, setting out the appropriate methodology, in what is among the most useful of his works, is *The Rabbinic Traditions about the Pharisees before 70*, 3 vols. (Leiden: Brill, 1971). The highly-touted work of a century ago by Alfred Edersheim, *The Life and Times of Jesus the Messiah* (Grand Rapids: Eerdmans, 1971 [orig. 1883]), is a gold mine of information from ancient Jewish sources but makes no attempt to distinguish what actually dates to the first century from what may at times have arisen up to half a millennium later.

21. The standard English translation is by Herbert Danby, *The Mishnah* (Oxford: OUP, 1933).

lacking in a royal palace?' The fools went about their work, saying, 'Can there be a banquet without preparations?' Suddenly the king desired the presence of his servants. The wise entered adorned, while the fools entered soiled. The king rejoiced at the wise but was angry with the fools. He said, 'Those who adorned themselves for the banquet, let them sit, eat and drink. But those who did not adorn themselves for the banquet, let them stand and watch.'"

The parallels with Matthew 22:10–13 and 25:1–13 are striking.

Rabbinic Judaism also produced detailed commentaries on a large number of the books of its Bible (the Christian Old Testament). These commentaries are known as *midrashim* (plural of *midrash*—Heb. for "searching out"). The oldest perhaps date as far back as the second century; others, from five hundred years or more later. These proceed sequentially through a book, but usually select only key verses for comment. Often the commentary involves the text only as a jumping off point to discuss numerous marginally related topics.[22] For example, in a midrash (*Genesis Rabbah*) on Genesis 12:1 (Abraham's call to leave for Canaan), the commentary begins with a parable of a man fleeing a burning building; quotes Song of Solomon 1:3 to compare Abraham to a tightly closed flask of myrrh opened to give fragrance at just the right time; allegorizes Song of Solomon 8:8 to liken Abraham to one who would unite the whole world; and continues by discussing Ecclesiastes 7:19, Jeremiah 51:9, and so on.

Additionally, there are the *targums* (originally from an Akkadian word for "interpretation"). Already in pre-Christian times, the practice had developed in the synagogues of reading the texts for the week from the Hebrew Bible, followed by an oral translation and paraphrase into Aramaic. Periodically, particularly in the most theologically significant portions of an Old Testament passage, the targumist inserted some of his own commentary in the form of an expanded narrative. Many of these targums on various biblical texts have survived, some from as far back as the first century.[23] A targum on Psalm 45, for instance, adds words to make its interpretation explicitly messianic:

> Your beauty, O king Messiah, is better than that of the children of men; the spirit of prophecy has been placed upon your lips; this is why God has blessed you forever and ever. Gird your sword on your thigh like a valiant warrior so as to slay kings with princes; it is your honor and your prestige, and your prestige is great. Thus you shall succeed in riding upon the royal horses.

Predating the rabbinic literature (which by definition refers to documents written down after A.D. 70) is the entire library of Dead Sea Scrolls. These range in age from nearly 200 B.C. to A.D. 70. In addition to all the ancient copies of biblical books preserved at Qumran on the shores of the Dead Sea (see above, p. 12), the caves containing the scrolls also yielded up dozens of books pre-

---

22. The standard overview of Mishnah, Talmud, and Midrashim, complete with references to various modern translations and studies of each, is Hermann L. Strack and Günter Stemberger, *Introduction to the Talmud and Midrash*, trans. and ed. Markus Bockmuehl (Edinburgh: T. & T. Clark, rev. 1991).

23. An excellent introduction to sample extracts from some of the most theologically interesting expansions of the Old Testament appears in Pierre Grelot, *What Are the Targums? Selected Texts* (Collegeville, Minn.: Liturgical Press, 1992).

Rabbinic Literature

The Talmud

Mishnah **(mostly halakah)**	**Targums** **(Aramaic paraphrase** **of the Bible)**
Tosefta **(additional tractates)**	
Gemara **(halakah & haggadah)**	**Midrashim** **(commentaries on** **biblical books)**

sumably produced by the Jewish community that lived there. It is generally agreed that most of these books reflect a distinctively Essene perspective (see below, pp. 48–50), so that they cannot be taken to be typical of all Second Temple Judaism. But there are remarkable parallels and contrasts with early Christian thought, and they provide crucial background information on at least one important strand of Jewish belief and practice in Jesus' day.[24]

Finally, there is *Philo* of Alexandria. A voluminous writer, Philo was a Hellenistic Jew who wedded Jewish religion to Hellenistic philosophy. He wrote commentary on much of the Pentateuch as well as other philosophical and apologetic works, seeking to demonstrate by means of allegorical interpretation that Moses' teaching was compatible with, and indeed anticipated, the best of Greek thought. He is known for developing further Plato's dualism between earth and heaven (sometimes thought to lie behind Heb. 8) and for his discourse on the *logos* (also prominent in John 1:1–18).[25]

General Characteristics

Although pre-70 Judaism was far more diverse than the rabbinic movement that developed out of the ashes of the destruction of Jerusalem, one can still identify numerous consistent trends and developments with significant import for New Testament and Gospels studies.

1. Perhaps as a result of Persian influence, there was a noticeable increase in interest in *angelology* and *demonology*. Supernatural beings other than God are present but relatively rare in the Old Testament; they proliferate in intertestamental Jewish literature. Angels ministered to Jesus, too (Mark 1:13 pars.), and exorcisms played a prominent role in his ministry (e.g., Mark 1:21–28; 3:20–30; 5:1–20 pars.).

2. A large quantity of poetry and wisdom literature emerged between the testaments—psalms, proverbs, and theodicies (reflections on the problem of evil). Building on the *personification of Wisdom* in Proverbs 8, much of this literature represented Wisdom (Heb. *hokhma*; Greek *sophia*) as a quasi-divine emissary from God to humanity. Jesus, too, is portrayed as divine Wisdom in a variety of ways (see below, pp. 130, 163).[26] The combination of developments (1) and (2) meant that while Judaism remained staunchly monotheistic, it became possible to talk about beings other than Yahweh himself (both angels and great human beings) in categories closely resembling deity. After all, Daniel 7:9, with its reference to plural "thrones" in heaven where "the Ancient of Days took his seat," left the door open for much speculation about "two powers in heaven." The New Testament writers who directly equate Jesus

24. For state-of-the-art surveys of the contents and contributions of the Dead Sea Scrolls against the often inaccurate and sensationalist claims of the media and popular writers, see Joseph A. Fitzmyer, *Responses to 101 Questions on the Dead Sea Scrolls* (New York: Paulist, 1992); and James C. VanderKam, *The Dead Sea Scrolls Today* (Grand Rapids: Eerdmans; London: SPCK, 1994). The most recent official translation of the scrolls and their fragments is Florentino García Martínez, ed., *The Dead Sea Scrolls Translated: The Qumran Texts in English* (Leiden: Brill, 1994).

25. An English translation of all of Philo's works is now conveniently accessible in one volume: C. D. Yonge, trans., *The Works of Philo*, ed. David M. Scholer (Peabody: Hendrickson, 1993).

26. For a complete outline of this development in Jewish thought, see Ben Witherington III, *Jesus the Sage* (Minneapolis: Fortress, 1994).

with God go beyond any of these developments, but such trends may have made the transition somewhat easier for them.[27]

3. An increasingly *positive view of human nature* began to develop. Less was heard about the "original sin" of Adam and Eve that left all people in need of redemption and more about each person's two impulses or natures (Heb. *yetser*)—one good and one bad. This in turn prepared the way for the emergence of "merit theology": the belief that one's good works and one's bad deeds would be weighed at the final judgment and whichever won out would determine one's eternal destiny. Other rabbis went even further and believed that the merits of the patriarchs, especially Abraham, could be imputed to later Jews. On the other hand, we must beware of claiming that this trend was overly influential. Since E. P. Sanders' groundbreaking work, *Paul and Palestinian Judaism*, was published in 1977,[28] scholars have recognized that one dominant framework of first-century Jewish thought was "covenantal nomism"—the Law was given to be obeyed as a response to the covenant God established with Moses (and before him, with Abraham). Just as Sinai came *after* the salvation experience of the Exodus, so obedience to the Law is the proper *response* to God's grace. In short, one does not obey the Law to get into God's covenant; one obeys it to *stay* in. Nevertheless, this position, too, can be overemphasized.[29] One must be alert to the diversity within ancient Judaism so that one neither dismisses the accounts of Jesus' (or Paul's) disputes with certain Jews as historically improbable nor assumes that all Jews would have believed or acted the way those specific individuals and groups did.

4. *Prayer and good works* came to be viewed as an adequate substitute for animal sacrifice. This was required if forgiveness of sins was to be obtained at all when the Jews were in exile or in the diaspora, since access to the temple in Jerusalem became impossible. After the destruction of the temple in A.D. 70, this approach ensured Judaism's survival. Old Testament precedent was found in such passages as Hosea 6:6 ("I desire mercy, not sacrifice") and Psalm 51:16 ("You do not delight in sacrifice, or I would bring it"). Even in pre-70 Israel, the center of worship for the average Israelite had become not the seasonal pilgrimages to the temple but the weekly Sabbath synagogue service, along with one's daily recitation of fixed prayers and confessions (particularly the *Shema*—Deut. 6:4–6) and times of family devotions.

5. A massive interest in *apocalyptic* themes and literature developed. Instead of looking for the establishment of the kingdom of God on earth in all its fullness through ordinary, historical developments, more and more Jews came to believe that only supernatural intervention by God would usher in the messianic age. This belief easily led to a second: that it was the responsibility of a select group of Jews within the nation to prepare the way for the advent of that coming age by intense obedience to the Law. Both the Essenes at Qumran and

---

27. See esp. Larry W. Hurtado, *One God, One Lord: Early Christian Devotion and Ancient Jewish Monotheism* (Philadelphia: Fortress, 1988); and Alan F. Segal, *Two Powers in Heaven* (Leiden: Brill, 1977).

28. (London: SCM; Philadelphia: Fortress).

29. For a survey of some of the key texts that support merit theology and for a brief but balanced assessment of Sanders, see D. A. Carson, *Divine Sovereignty and Human Responsibility* (London: Marshall, Morgan & Scott; Atlanta: John Knox, 1981), 84–109. Cf. Charles L. Quarles, "The Soteriology of R. Akiba and E. P. Sanders' *Paul and Palestinian Judaism*," *NTS* 42 (1996): 185–95.

the disciples of Jesus may be viewed as apocalyptic sects. In the latter case, though, the expectation is revised to allow for *two* messianic advents, and obedience to the Law is replaced by following Christ.[30]

6. *Synagogue worship* and study took on forms that became central in the development of the Christian church. The order of the Sabbath service was largely taken over by early Christian worshipers. Prayers and hymns opened and closed each service. In between came the reading of the Torah, Prophets, and Psalms (eventually in a fixed lectionary cycle), with the targum and homily (sermon) by one of the synagogue elders, based on the texts for the day. Assistants to the elders may have provided a model that later inspired the Christian office of deacon. The synagogue was also used for community gatherings of various kinds, most notably elementary school education for boys from about ages five to twelve or thirteen. It is a myth that most first-century Jewish men were illiterate—an idea sometimes based on a mistranslation of Acts 4:13, which declares only that the first disciples were not formally apprenticed to a rabbi beyond the age of thirteen.[31] Jews were also forbidden to use secular courts to solve their own civil disputes, so the synagogue leaders functioned as a local judiciary when necessary (cf. 1 Cor. 6:1–11; James 2:1–13).

7. *Scribes* took on an increasingly more prominent role in society. Originally they were mere copyists of Scripture, but their familiarity with its contents led them to become experts in and teachers of the Law. Indeed, the terms "lawyers" and "scribes" in the Gospels usually refer to the same group of individuals. They were found in any of the Jewish sects, though most probably came from the Pharisees. The two most famous scribes of the early first century were the Pharisees Hillel and Shammai, the former usually more liberal and the latter usually more conservative on various disputes about Torah. Jesus' teaching on divorce offers a good example of his response to one of these intra-Pharisaic debates (Matt. 19:1–12). These scribes were the forerunners of the more formal post-70 office of rabbi. In Jesus' time, "rabbi" was still a more informal title for a "teacher," whether trained or untrained (cf. Matt. 23:7–8; John 1:38, 49; 3:2, 26; 6:25).

8. The *Sanhedrin* played an increasingly prominent role in Jewish life, at least in Judea. This "supreme court" and legislative body wrapped into one, composed ideally of seventy-one members led by the high priest, included both Pharisees and Sadducees and perhaps other nonaligned elders of the people. Although Pharisees seem to have outnumbered Sadducees in general and been more popular with the people, the distribution of court appointments usually led to a Saducean majority on the Sanhedrin. After all, Rome appointed the high priests and wanted to ensure that the court remained loyal to the empire, and this came more easily for the Sadducees (see below, p. 48). Otherwise, Rome largely permitted the Sanhedrin freedoms of self-government, while reserving the death penalty in at least certain cases for itself (cf.

---

30. For a brief treatment, cf. D. S. Russell, *Divine Disclosure: An Introduction to Jewish Apocalyptic* (Minneapolis: Fortress, 1992). For thorough studies, see David Hellholm, ed., *Apocalypticism in the Mediterranean World and the Near East* (Tübingen: Mohr, 1983); and Christopher Rowland, *The Open Heaven* (London: SPCK; New York: Crossroad, 1982).

31. Rainer Riesner, *Jesus als Lehrer* (Tübingen: Mohr, 1981), 182–236. There is no comparable English-language presentation of this information.

Major Annual Jewish Festivals

Rosh Hashanah
(New Year) — — — — — 1 Tishri
(Sept. - Oct.)

Yom Kippur
(Day of Atonement) — — — — — 10 Tishri
(Sept. - Oct.)

Sukkoth
(Tabernacles) — — — — — 15–22 Tishri
(Sept. - Oct.)

Hanukkah
(Dedication) — — — — — 25 Chislev
(Nov. - Dec.)

Purim — — — — — 14 Adar
(Feb. - Mar.)

Pesach
(Passover &
Unleavened Bread) — — — — — 14 Nisan
15–21 Nisan
(Mar. - Apr.)

Pentecost — — — — — 6 Sivan
(May - Jun.)

John 18:31).[32] Smaller sanhedrins (lower courts) also dotted the landscape, and it is not entirely certain if in Jesus' day there was one permanently appointed Great Sanhedrin, as later described in the Mishnah, or merely a variety of temporarily convened sanhedrins, including those directly under the high priest.

9. Judaism increasingly commended itself as *a religious option for the Gentile world.* Scholars dispute just how active Jews were at proselytizing (cf. Matt. 23:15). Some believe this activity was largely limited to "following up" interested "God-fearers"—Gentiles who had already come to worship the God of Israel and obey much of his Law.[33] At any rate, monotheism was increasingly accepted in the Hellenistic world.

A good summary of the way in which first-century Judaism presented itself involves the three badges of national identity and the three symbols of that nationalism that permeated the corner of the world into which Christ was born.[34] Whatever else a Jewish man did or did not obey, three practices were virtually inviolable if he wanted to remain a member of the community in good standing—the *dietary laws* (keeping a "kosher" table), observing the *Sabbath*, and *circumcision.* Tellingly, Jesus challenged the first two of these head on (e.g., Mark 7:1–23 pars., 2:23–3:6 pars.), and Paul later spoke of the third as a matter of moral indifference (Gal. 5:6)!

The three symbols that went along with these badges of national identity were *temple, land,* and *Torah.* The temple was the political, religious, and economic center of Israel, wielding enormous influence as home to hundreds of daily animal sacrifices and to thousands of seasonal pilgrims attending the annual festivals of Passover, Pentecost, New Year's (with the Day of Atonement) culminating in Tabernacles, and, of a much lesser scope, Hanukkah and Purim. Living in the land of Israel freed from foreign oppressors remained the dream of most, inasmuch as Scripture had promised the land to the Jews in perpetuity. But it was contingent on achieving adequate obedience to the Law; hence the third symbol, the Torah. All truth was contained in this book, if one knew how to find it; therefore, the Bible became the object of enormous amounts of study and exposition. Again Jesus challenged the adequacy of all three of these institutions as they stood, seeing them instead as fulfilled in himself (cf., e.g., John 2:13–22; 4:19–24; Matt. 5:17–48).

Individual Groups or Sects

The vast majority of Jews in Israel were not aligned with any special group. They were ordinary farmers and fishermen, craftsmen and merchants, trying to eke out a living. They no doubt believed in the God of Israel and tried to follow the primary laws of the Old Testament faithfully, offering sacrifices in the temple in Jerusalem for the forgiveness of sins when they were able to make

---

32. The evidence both inside and outside of Scripture on this last point is confusing and seemingly contradictory. One intriguing reference from the Palestinian Talmud (*p. Sanhedrin* 1:1 [cf. 7:2]), if accurate, would explain some of the discrepancies and coincide strikingly with the time of Jesus' crucifixion: "Forty years before the destruction of the temple the right to inflict the death penalty was taken away from Israel."

33. Thus Scot McKnight, *A Light among the Gentiles: Jewish Missionary Activity in the Second Temple Period* (Minneapolis: Fortress, 1991). Defending the view that proselytizing was far more widespread is Louis H. Feldman, *Jew and Gentile in the Ancient World: Attitudes and Interactions from Alexander to Justinian* (Princeton: Princeton University Press, 1993).

34. Cf. further N. T. Wright, *The New Testament and the People of God* (London: SPCK; Minneapolis: Fortress, 1992), 224–32.

the trip there. But they did not concern themselves with the numerous oral traditions and additional legislation that had grown up around the Bible. They probably longed for the redemption of Israel, and it was from this group of ordinary, faithful, at times even impoverished, Jewish folk that Jesus found almost all of his first followers. Ancient Jewish sources refer to this group at times as the *Am-ha-Aretz* ("the people of the land").[35]

The special groups probably comprised no more than 5 percent of the population in Jesus' day. These were the members of four different parties or groups that played a prominent role in first-century Jewish life: Pharisees, Sadducees, Essenes, and Zealots.

Pharisees. According to Josephus, the Pharisees emerged at least as early as the reign of John Hyrcanus, opposing the combination of kingly and priestly power in the Hasmonean rulers. Their name probably means "separatists." They may well have grown out of the earlier *Hasidim* (see above, p. 14). From early on they were consistently opposed by the Sadducees, who had made their peace with the Hasmonean dynasty. The Pharisees were a generally popular and prominent group of laymen who sought to apply the Torah to every area of life.[36] Their primary domain was the synagogue, and their foremost concern was to create "a fence around the Torah," that is, to explain what various Mosaic laws meant and how they applied so that devout Israelites would know exactly how to obey God in any situation they might confront. Hence they developed the so-called oral laws (the "traditions of the elders" in, e.g., Mark 7:5 and Matt. 23:2), which were later codified in the Mishnah and which often brought them into conflict with Jesus.

The Pharisees' popularity continued into first-century times, except among the upper classes who feared them because of their ability to sway the masses. They remained staunchly anti-Roman but usually opposed violence as a means of ridding the land of its foreign oppressor. Instead they sought to teach people to obey God's laws so that God himself would provide a savior in response to his people's obedience. Other distinctives that set them apart from the Sadducees in particular were their beliefs in an immortal soul, a bodily resurrection, future rewards and punishments according to one's works, the existence of angels and demons, and a combination of predestination and free will (or moral responsibility). Pharisees may have been the primary participants in a smaller group of first-century Jews known as the *haberim*, scrupulous law-keepers who were noted for communal fellowship and sharing meals together. It was out of the Pharisaic movement more than any other single group that later Rabbinic Judaism emerged.

Christians, of course, know the Pharisees best as one group of Jewish leaders whom Jesus frequently denounced for hypocrisy and legalistic excess (see esp. Matt. 23). But this is not the entire picture, even in the Gospels. Luke presents the Pharisees in a more favorable light on at least a couple of occasions

---

35. On which, see esp. Aharon Oppenheimer, *The 'Am-ha-Aretz'* (Leiden: Brill, 1977).

36. Modern scholars have frequently described them as applying the laws of priestly and temple purity to all of life, particularly in the areas of eating, tithing, Sabbath, and vows. See, e.g., Jacob Neusner, "Mr. Sanders' Pharisees and Mine," *SJT* 44 (1991): 73–95. For a balanced mediation of the contemporary debate over the Pharisees between Neusner and E. P. Sanders (who sees them as less influential and distinct from other Jews than most scholars do), see Douglas R. de Lacey, "In Search of a Pharisee," *TynB* 43 (1992): 353–72; Martin Hengel and Roland Deines, "E. P. Sanders' 'Common Judaism,' Jesus, and the Pharisees," *JTS* 46 (1995): 1–70.

(Luke 7:36; 13:31), and, in John, Nicodemus is said to be a Pharisee (John 3:1). As a member of the Sanhedrin (Mark 15:43), Joseph of Arimathea may well have been one too. Modern study of ancient Jewish sources has rightly stressed that the composite picture of Pharisaism is highly diverse. It is simply not fair—and it smacks of anti-Semitism—to tar all the Pharisees with the same brush. In many ways Jesus was closer to the Pharisees than to any of the other Jewish sectarians; their quarrels were internecine or "family" disputes. Pharisees were the upstanding "conservative evangelical pastors" of their day, strongly convinced of the inerrancy of Scripture and its sufficiency for guidance in every area of life, if only it could be properly interpreted.[37] Yet it is precisely such an environment in which a balanced perspective on the Bible can easily give way to legalism. Even the Mishnah and Talmud, reflecting back from a later era on the diversity of types of Pharisees, admit more bad types than good.[38]

Sadducees. The Sadducees supported the Hasmoneans, as they reversed earlier policies of protesting the Hellenization of Israel. They were a small group composed almost entirely of the aristocracy and the well-to-do elite. Many were from priestly families; indeed the name Sadducee probably comes from the priestly family of "Zadokites" (cf. 2 Sam. 8:17). Evidence about them is more scanty than for any of the other sects, but it suggests that in the years immediately before Christ's ministry, particularly under Caiaphas, they had amassed great wealth in and around Jerusalem and had become particularly corrupt in their use of it in administering the temple. For example, the policy of introducing money changers into the temple precincts instead of housing them in the nearby Kidron Valley may have been a relatively recent innovation, against which Jesus protested (Mark 11:15–18 pars.).[39]

Sadducees rejected the oral law. Indeed, they held that although all of the Old Testament was God's word, only doctrine that could be demonstrated to be taught in the Pentateuch was binding. Hence they denied immortality, resurrection, angels, and demons. They strongly emphasized the freedom of the human will and living as God's people in this life. They did not protest Roman occupation of Israel, and they largely benefited from this stance by being able to administer and profit from the temple ritual. Jesus repeatedly criticized the Sadducees without the balancing factors noted above in our discussion of the Pharisees. And, on one occasion, in response to their skepticism, he demonstrated the resurrection even from the books of Moses (Mark 12:18–27 pars.,

37. See, e.g., Asher Finkel, *The Pharisees and the Teacher of Nazareth* (Leiden: Brill, 1964); Harvey Falk, *Jesus the Pharisee* (New York: Paulist, 1985), though the latter exaggerates the parallels somewhat.

38. Combining the accounts of Sotah 22b in both Palestinian and Babylonian Talmuds yields the following (somewhat tongue-in-cheek?) description of seven types of Pharisees: the "shoulder" Pharisee—who carries his religious duties upon his shoulder; the one who says "Spare me a moment that I may perform a commandment;" the one who in his anxiety to avoid looking upon a woman dashes his face against the wall; the "pestle" Pharisee whose head is bowed like a pestle in a mortar; the Pharisee who constantly exclaims, "What is my duty that I may perform it?" the Pharisee from love; and the Pharisee from fear. *Shabbat* 7:2 in the Mishnah gives a classic example of the kind of legalism into which the oral Law at times could degenerate, with its list of 39 prohibitions of various types of work on the Sabbath. But the possibility that these statements do not entirely reflect the condition of first-century Judaism must always be acknowledged.

39. Cf. Markus Bockmuehl, *This Jesus: Martyr, Lord, Messiah* (Edinburgh: T. & T. Clark, 1994; Downers Grove: IVP, 1996), 109–12, and the literature there cited.

citing Exod. 3:6). Because the Sadducees were so tied to the temple and its cult, they did not survive the fall of Jerusalem in A.D. 70.[40]

Essenes. Although Josephus describes this group alongside the Pharisees and Sadducees, they appear nowhere by name in the New Testament. Still, their presence on the shores of the Dead Sea near the Judean wilderness, in one quarter of Jerusalem, and in other major cities around the empire makes it probable that Jesus and his disciples interacted with them at times. The name Essene may come from the Aramaic *hasya*—pious or holy. Like the Pharisees, they may be descendants of the *Hasidim.* In fact, they reflect an even more radical protest against the Hellenization and Romanization of Israel than the Pharisees. Evidence from Qumran suggests the existence of a group at that site from mid-second century B.C. until just after the fall of Jerusalem.

The Essenes were apocalyptically oriented. They were founded by an anonymous leader known from their literature as the "Teacher of Righteousness." They believed that Jerusalem and its temple had become hopelessly corrupt, especially under an individual called simply the "wicked priest" (probably Jonathan or Simon, brothers of Judas Maccabeus). They opposed those who taught Israel its Law as "seekers after smooth things" (probably the Pharisees). The present age had become so wicked that its end was surely at hand. But neither social action nor revolution could bring about the messianic age, only withdrawal from society, intense devotion to the Law, and patient trust that God would intervene supernaturally with the armies of heaven to establish his kingdom. The Essenes placed strong emphasis on God's sovereignty and predestination. Needless to say, they saw themselves as the elect subgroup within Israel that would be present to fight for God when he began the "war between the sons of light and the sons of darkness"—described in detail in their document known as the War Scroll.

Most Essenes lived in separate neighborhoods in the main cities. Qumran is the only completely monastic site of Essene life that we know about, therefore it is precarious to generalize from the Dead Sea sect's literature to all Essenes. We know, for example, that elsewhere Essenes married and had children, whereas a vow of celibacy was required for Qumran initiates. Nevertheless, there were probably various parallels in urban Essenism to some of the other major characteristics of the Dead Sea sect: (1) a communal lifestyle, involving daily prayers, work, study, and ritual (including daily baths or baptisms to wash away the previous day's sins); (2) an extensive period of probation before being granted full-fledged membership (up to three years), followed by strict discipline and policies for excommunication of the recalcitrant; (3) a perception that they were fulfilling biblical prophecy, with (a) the Teacher of Righteousness as the prophet like Moses predicted in Deuteronomy 18:18, (b) the entire sect as "a voice of one calling . . . in the wilderness" (Isa. 40:3) and as inaugurating God's new covenant with his people (Jer. 31:31–34), and (c) the events of their day as the fulfillment of numerous "end-time prophecies."[41] In

---

40. A small group of the political supporters of the Herods were known as *Herodians.* Many, though not all, of them were Sadducees.

41. The various commentaries on the prophets repeatedly introduce their discussions with the term *pesher,* rendered in English as "this is that which [is fulfilled in . . .]" In other words, each prophecy is identified with some current event—the coming of the Romans, the apostasy of Israel, and so on.

addition, (4) the Qumran sectarians looked for the coming of two messiahs—one priestly and one kingly (since each had to come from different tribes). (5) They foreshadowed the messianic banquet of Isaiah 25:6 in the communal meals that they shared. (6) Significant interest in Melchizedek as a kind of archangel may provide some of the background for similar imagery in the Epistle to the Hebrews. (7) One entire scroll outlines a blueprint for a new temple, but short of its construction the Essenes would not offer sacrifices. (8) The Copper Scroll refers to the burial of a vast hoard of wealth in the desert; if its account was true, the ability to rediscover the treasure has long since been lost.

Of great fascination to contemporary readers are the various manuals of discipline and communal organization, hymns, psalms, liturgical texts, calendars, Old Testament commentaries, and apocalyptic literature that make up the Dead Sea Scrolls. Inaccurate but sensationalist claims have fueled this interest. The truth is that the vast majority of all the scrolls and their fragments have been translated. There is no conspiracy to hide information damaging to Christianity from the public. There are no Christian documents among the finds at Qumran and no references to Jesus or any Christian disciples anywhere in the literature.[42] A recently published fragment allegedly describing a slain Messiah is more probably to be translated as the Messiah slaying his enemies.[43] Interesting new fragments have emerged with apparent references to Messiah as Son of God, with beatitudes resembling some of Jesus' (including the equation of the "poor" with the Qumran community), and with language similar to Paul's expression "the works of the Law." None of this in any way threatens Christian faith or rewrites Christian origins; we are simply learning more and more about the diversity of the Jewish world into which Jesus emerged. Tantalizing parallels between Jesus and Qumran, and even more so between John the Baptist and Qumran (see below, p. 216), are balanced by an equally impressive list of differences.[44]

Zealots. Josephus refers to this group as the "fourth philosophy." They are the most loosely knit group of the four and probably should not be thought of as a formal party until the Jewish rebellion in the late 60s. But there were important precursors. In A.D. 6, Judas of Galilee led an uprising against a Roman census and registration of property under the Syrian governor Quirinius (cf. Acts 5:37). Throughout subsequent decades numerous self-appointed prophets and rebels emerged, some little more than bandits or terrorists, others commanding more of a following for a time. Acts 5:36 refers to one by the name of Theudas, and 21:38 mentions an unnamed Egyptian who "led four

---

42. Indeed, most all of the writings are in Hebrew, not Greek. One miniscule Greek fragment, with numerous holes in it, has been allegedly identified with a part of Mark 6:52–53, but it is in so bad a state of preservation that most scholars are not convinced that they can identify its contents at all. The most vigorous recent advocate of taking it as part of Mark is Carsten P. Thiede; see, e.g., his *Rekindling the Word: In Search of Gospel Truth* (Leominster: Gracewing; Valley Forge: TPI, 1995), 37–57, 169–97. For a rebuttal, cf. Graham Stanton, *Gospel Truth? New Light on Jesus and the Gospels* (London: HarperCollins; Valley Forge: TPI, 1995), 20–32. For a good overview and refutation of sensationalist claims about Qumran more generally, cf. Otto Betz and Rainer Riesner, *Jesus, Qumran and the Vatican* (London: SCM; New York: Crossroad, 1994).

43. Markus Bockmuehl, "A 'Slain Messiah' in 4Q Serekh Milhamah (4Q285)?" *TynB* 43 (1992): 155–69.

44. James H. Charlesworth, "The Dead Sea Scrolls and the Historical Jesus," in *Jesus and the Dead Sea Scrolls*, ed. James H. Charlesworth (New York and London: Doubleday, 1992), 1–74.

thousand terrorists out into the desert some time ago." Josephus describes many more.

Simon the Canaanite is also called a "Zealot" in the Gospels (Luke 6:15; cf. Acts 1:13). The "thieves" on the crosses next to Jesus were called *lestai* (Mark 15:27 pars.), perhaps better translated "insurrectionists." In the 50s and 60s, the *sicarii* ("dagger men") emerged, killing by stealth prominent local Jews who collaborated with Rome. An intriguing eccentric named Jesus ben Ananias made such a nuisance of himself for several years in the mid-60s, predicting first the destruction of the temple and ultimately his own demise, that he was flogged. He was later accidentally hit by a stone and killed (*Jewish War* 6.5.3). The story of the failure of the Jewish revolt against Rome is described briefly above (pp. 24–25). The Zealots had hoped they could repeat the Maccabean miracle and were convinced that God would honor military efforts to overthrow Rome, but they turned out to be tragically mistaken. In striking contrast, Jesus' preaching was consistently nonviolent.[45]

By way of summary, one may think of first-century Judaism as a diverse collection of responses to the theological "contradiction" involved in living under foreign occupation in a land God had promised to give Israel forever. Pharisees sought to rectify the situation by internal reform; Sadducees benefited from the status quo and so rejected attempts to change the situation; Essenes saw no hope apart from complete withdrawal and a fresh start; and Zealots strove to overthrow the oppressors by military might. The average "person of the land" was too busy simply trying to survive to join any of these parties. But many of them no doubt looked for a messianic deliverer of some kind (cf. also below, pp. 409–411).

CONCLUSIONS

The first-century religious world offered a potpourri of possibilities for Greeks, Romans, and Jews alike. The Hellenistic options could be mixed together in various combinations (what is known as *syncretism*). A Roman equestrian, for example, might give lip service to emperor worship and the traditional myths at the appropriate times for doing so each year, study a little philosophy on the side, and participate in a mystery cult one night each week. Astrology, mixed with primitive astronomy, while not an entire religion or worldview, was often added on to whatever other religious beliefs and practices one followed. By Judeo-Christian standards, the general level of morality was abysmal. Religious ritual was generally divorced from ethical living. Far more prominent and accepted than even in our deteriorating Western world were the practices of homosexuality, heterosexual promiscuity, divorce, abortion, infanticide (especially of baby girls), slavery, and "sacred" prostitution.[46]

---

45. The most balanced treatment of Jesus and the Zealot movement is Martin Hengel, *The Zealots* (Edinburgh: T. & T. Clark, 1989). On the diversity of individuals and groups that fed this movement, see Richard A. Horsley and John Hanson, *Bandits, Prophets, and Messiahs* (Minneapolis: Winston, 1985).

46. The famous quote from the ancient Greek Demosthenes still often applied to the first-century Roman empire: "Mistresses we keep for the sake of pleasure, concubines for the daily care of our persons, but wives to bear us legitimate children and to be faithful guardians of our households" (*Against Neaera*, 122).

The one well-known modern religious option that was extremely rare in the ancient world was pure atheism.

Judaism's monotheism and morality stood out in sharp contrast, as did Christian life and thought as it emerged. But these religions, too, succumbed at times to syncretism, especially in their Gnostic varieties. In an age dominated by pluralism, when Greeks and Romans were willing to add anyone's god to their pantheon, the intolerance for polytheism by Jews and Christians was striking. And to the extent that many Jews had come to believe that God would find his own ways of "saving" righteous Gentiles, early Christian insistence that Jesus was the only way (including for Jews!) seemed even more intransigent. The problems of pluralism and immorality that increasingly afflict our world today are not new; for appropriate responses to them we need to turn again and again to the New Testament.[47]

FOR FURTHER STUDY

See the literature cited at the end of chapter 1. In addition, consult:

Introductory

ABD, s.v. "Cynics," "Epicureanism," "Gnosticism," "Mystery Religions," "Myth and Mythology (Greco-Roman)," "Pythagoreanism," "Roman Imperial Cult," and "Stoicism."

DJG, s.v. "Apocalyptic," "Dead Sea Scrolls," "Judaism," "Pharisee," "Scribes," "Revolutionary Movements," and "Sanhedrin."

Freyne, Séan. *The World of the New Testament*. Wilmington: Glazier, 1980.

Martin, Luther H. *Hellenistic Religions: An Introduction*. Oxford: OUP, 1987.

McNamara, Martin. *Palestinian Judaism and the New Testament*. Wilmington: Glazier, 1983.

Nash, Ronald H. *Christianity and the Hellenistic World*. Grand Rapids: Zondervan, 1984.

Intermediate

Cohen, Shaye J. D. *From the Maccabees to the Mishnah*. Philadelphia: Westminster, 1987.

Ferguson, Everett. *Backgrounds of Early Christianity*. Grand Rapids: Eerdmans, rev. 1993.

Finegan, Jack. *Myth and Mystery: An Introduction to the Pagan Religions of the Biblical World*. Grand Rapids: Baker, 1989.

Murphy, Frederick J. *The Religious World of Jesus*. Nashville: Abingdon, 1991.

Nickelsburg, G. W. E. *Jewish Literature between the Bible and the Mishnah*. Philadelphia: Fortress, 1981.

Rowland, Christopher. *Christian Origins*. London: SPCK; Minneapolis: Augsburg, 1985.

Wright, N. T. *The New Testament and the People of God*. London: SPCK; Minneapolis: Fortress, 1992.

Advanced

Safrai, S. and M. Stern, eds. *The Jewish People in the First Century*. 2 vols. Assen: van Gorcum; Philadelphia: Fortress, 1974–76.

---

47. For helpful, practical guidance, see Tom Wright, *New Tasks for a Renewed Church* (London: Hodder & Stoughton, 1992 [= *Bringing the Church to the World* (Minneapolis: Bethany, 1993)]).

Saldarini, Anthony J. *Pharisees, Scribes and Sadducees in Palestinian Society: A Socio-logical Approach*. Wilmington: Glazier, 1988; Edinburgh: T. & T. Clark, 1989.

Sanders, E. P. *Judaism: Practice and Belief, 63 BCE-66 CE*. London: SCM; Philadelphia: TPI, 1992.

Schürer, Emil. *The History of the Jewish People in the Age of Jesus Christ*. 3 vols. Ed. and rev. Geza Vermes, Fergus Millar, Matthew Black. Edinburgh: T. & T. Clark, 1973–87.

Stemberger, Günter. *Jewish Contemporaries of Jesus: Pharisees, Sadducees, Essenes*. Minneapolis: Fortress, 1995.

QUESTIONS FOR REVIEW

1. Give a brief synopsis of each of the major religious alternatives in both Hellenistic and Jewish religion of the first century. Who are the key characters involved?

2. From your own experience, identify some of the closest parallels to each of these alternatives in the contemporary religious world. How did (how does) authentic Christianity resemble and differ from each of these different options? How did they impact the rise of Christianity?

3. What is the Nag Hammadi Library? What are the Dead Sea Scrolls? What is the significance of both of these finds for our understanding of Christian origins?

4. What other general trends in intertestamental Judaism are important for understanding the birth of Christianity? What other sources do we have for identifying these trends?

CHAPTER THREE

SOCIOECONOMIC BACKGROUND—
Everyday Life in New Testament Times

SOCIAL AND ECONOMIC HISTORY

U ntil recently, historians focused primarily, if not exclusively, on the deeds of the political or military leaders of a society. Church historians also scrutinized church leaders. But historians paid little attention to the everyday life of ordinary people. Today there has been a renaissance of interest in such everyday life. An overview of the social world of early first-century Palestine under Roman domination will help us read the Gospels better. We can visualize the events described and avoid importing anachronistic ideas of living conditions from our world back into a quite different time and place.

Geography

Israel was (and is) made up of four quite different kinds of terrain. (1) The fertile coastal plain contained port cities for seafaring and trade with the rest of the empire. Fruits and vegetables grew in abundance there. (2) The central hill country, which included farmable foothills as well as more rugged, rocky terrain primarily producing timber, divided the country in two from north to south. The less rugged parts were home to shepherds and their flocks, vineyards (esp. for grapes and olives), orchards (esp. for fig trees), small terraced plots for other crops, and numerous small villages (Jerusalem being the much larger exception). (3) The valley of Jezreel in southern Galilee and the entire Jordan River valley formed the country's breadbasket where many grains, especially wheat, were grown, along with the other crops already noted. (4) In southern Judea and into Idumea, the great desert or wilderness area was used for little more than nomads and their various herds of sheep, goats, and camels.

Most of the central ridge "mountains" varied in altitude from roughly 1,500–3,500 feet above sea level, although Mt. Hermon in the far northeast topped out at over 9,200 feet. In striking contrast, the Dead Sea is the lowest place above ground on earth at 1,296 feet below sea level. With roughly one hundred miles separating the two, it is still possible to go from below-freezing, snow-covered terrain to hot, dry desert land with 90–100°F temperatures in a short span of time. Winter was the rainy season; summer, the dry season, and different crops were rotated accordingly through two harvests a year.[1]

In New Testament times, Jerusalem was the largest city in Israel. It was a city dominated by the temple and its precincts, occupying roughly one-quarter of the walled-in portion of the city, itself little more than one-half mile long on any given side. Other major edifices included Herod's Antonia Fortress, and an amphitheater and horse-racing stadium he had constructed for Hellenistic entertainment.[2]

Population

Although many ancient censuses were taken, most of the records have been lost. Very rough estimates can be made based on what data do remain plus archaeologists' computations of the number of people that could have fit into various living spaces. We know that cities were extremely crowded, with many people living in small homes right on top of each other. Even the countryside was often filled with lots of people working small plots of land. It has been estimated that the entire Roman empire contained 50 million inhabitants, of which 4 million were Jews. Perhaps about 700,000 Jews lived in Israel with more than 3 million scattered throughout the diaspora. Alexandria and Antioch were Gentile cities with large Jewish populations.

Rome itself may have topped one million residents, with people constantly leaving the countryside and moving to the urban center of the empire in hopes of a better life. As many as one-third of the inhabitants were slaves, including numerous runaways. Alexandria may have had 750,000 and Antioch 500,000 people. Athens and Tarsus were somewhat smaller but were important university towns. Ephesus, Philippi, Thessalonica, and Corinth were four other major cities, whose inhabitants possibly numbering more than 100,000. Jerusalem was somewhat smaller, with perhaps as few as 25,000 individuals within its walled-in portion, no more than 100,000 in the entire "metropolitan" area of three to four square miles, and perhaps considerably less.[3] The larger vicinity may have swelled to 200,000 or more, however, at festival times, particularly Passover, as Jews who could do so made pilgrimage to Jerusalem from

---

1. An excellent introductory student's Bible atlas is Harry T. Frank, ed., *Hammond's Atlas of the Bible Lands* (Maplewood, N.J.: Hammond, 1977). For physical terrain, rainfall, and crops, see B-4, B-6, and B-7. For more detail, the standard scholarly atlas is Y. Aharoni and M. Avi-Yonah, *The Macmillan Bible Atlas* (New York and London: Macmillan, 1968).

2. The authoritative study on *Jerusalem in the Time of Jesus* is the book so entitled by Joachim Jeremias (London: SCM; Philadelphia: Fortress, 1969).

3. Josephus gives substantially larger figures, but he is known to exaggerate with respect to numbers. Archaeologists' calculations of the number of people that could fit in the various portions of Jerusalem, even given the high density of ancient cities, place more reliable upper limits on our numbers.

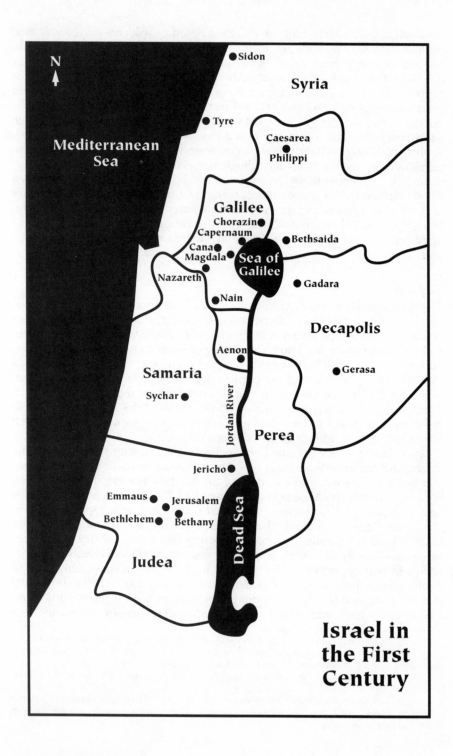

throughout the empire. Most probably stayed in tents on the hilly country surrounding the city.

Although it is disputed, some argue that Galilee had as many or more Gentiles living in it as Jews—hence the name, "Galilee of the Gentiles" (cf. Matt. 4:15). Many lived in the two cities Herod Antipas (re-)built—Sepphoris and Tiberias. Yet the majority of Galilee was made up of as many as two hundred small villages, few as large as Capernaum, which had possibly one thousand inhabitants.[4] We must therefore avoid stereotyping Jesus and his disciples as roaming through largely uninhabited regions with large farms. Galilee was in some respects much more urban than we imagine it. Jew-Gentile tension, coupled with the fact that Jerusalem housed a huge pro-Herodian priestly bureaucracy, could have led to strong rural-urban animosities. Yet, interestingly, except for the annual festival pilgrimages to Jerusalem, we have no record of Jesus ministering in any of the larger, pro-Roman cities.

Transportation and Communication

As previously noted, Rome had by far the best system of travel and communication in the ancient world, never again replicated until the seventeenth century or later. Main roads linked all major towns. Roman highways were paved with cobblestone and were wide enough for a pair of two-horse chariots to pass each other. Many people traveled in simpler ox-drawn carts, by donkey, or on foot. Most roads were simply dirt. A soldier or courier on horseback could average twenty-five to fifty miles a day, and double that in an emergency if fresh horses were available periodically. A wagon averaged seven to eight miles a day; on foot, people often traveled twenty. Nazareth to Jerusalem was thus about a three-day walk for someone in good health. The main roads were relatively safe, but the less well-traveled ones in desolate regions were favorite hideouts for thieves (cf. Luke 10:29–37).

Inns dotted the landscape, providing lodging for travelers, but many were notorious as hangouts for pirates and prostitutes. More reputable people preferred to stay in private homes with relatives, friends, or people who were recommended to them. Hospitality for traveling disciples was therefore highly prized in the early Christian world (cf. Matt. 10:11–13; 3 John 5–8). Sea travel was popular, especially for trade, though it was always potentially dangerous. In winter, the high seas were generally impassable. Cargo boats measured up to 180 feet in length and could carry up to 1,200 tons of goods or 600 passengers and their provisions.[5] (Paul's prison boat carried 276 people—Acts 27:37.) A trip between Rome and Alexandria took as little as ten days going east or as long as three months traveling west, depending of course on wind and weather conditions.[6]

Boats also carried mail, as did overland couriers, but the most reliable form of delivery was through a personal acquaintance. Public news was often posted on notice boards in town squares or announced aloud by "heralds" at

---

4. Richard A. Horsley, *Galilee: History, Politics, People* (Valley Forge: TPI, 1995), 193–94.

5. A. C. Bouquet, *Everyday Life in New Testament Times* (London: Batsford, 1953), 103.

6. John E. Stambaugh and David L. Balch, *The New Testament in Its Social Environment* (Philadelphia: Westminster, 1986), 39.

the marketplace or other public center of activity. The Greek word for herald
(keryx) is related to the word that was frequently used for the early Christian
proclamation (kerygma). Merchants traveling overland usually formed cara-
vans with numerous carts and beasts of burden, both because of the quantity
of merchandise and for the safety that numbers afforded.

Municipal Facilities

Privacy was almost impossible in ancient cities, as crowded as they were.
People deliberately spent most of their waking hours outside of or away from
their houses. The Roman baths were a cross between a modern country club
and a community recreation center. They included "hot tubs," exercise areas,
libraries, and chapels. Similarly multifaceted were the Greek gymnasia—home
to physical exercise for members and schooling for young boys. The town
marketplace was the center for trade and conversation. Excavations have
revealed the rough ancient equivalent to our shopping malls—stoa—laid out
in a square with pillars supporting roofs extending out over various stores.
Extensive night-lighting has been uncovered in places too. Antioch, for example, had over two and one-half miles of oil-lit lamp poles.[7] The library at Alexandria housed over 500,000 volumes, but for the most part only the wealthy
owned books privately.

Homes

The well-to-do, particularly in and around Rome, might own large multi-
story, freestanding brick villas with inner atria where up to fifty people might
gather. A large dozen-room house with three courts has been excavated in
Capernaum, which some think may have been Peter's.[8] The upper room where
the disciples met in Jerusalem would have formed part of one of the larger
homes in that city. For the lucky few (i.e., the rich), Rome had constructed pip-
ing to provide hot and cold running water and sewage removal. In most parts
of the empire, including Israel, among the vast majority who were not wealthy,
houses were much smaller and amenities much plainer. Adobe and hewn
stone were more common building materials. Most ordinary people lived in
one-room, two-level dwellings with living quarters separated from and raised
above the animal stalls. They were usually built with plain exteriors, one
adjoining the next to form three sides of a rectangle with a shared inner court-
yard. Tenement buildings in the larger cities were laid out like small multi-
storied apartment complexes. Roofs of buildings were made of tile, thatch, or
mud. In Palestine roofs were flat, and people socialized there and slept on
them to cool off a little during hot weather.

For all but the handful of rich, furniture was minimal: some kind of bedding,
perhaps no more than mats on the ground; outdoor ovens for cooking; and a
few chairs or benches. Indoors, a depressed area in the middle of a dirt floor
could house a small, covered charcoal fire, which also heated the house during
cool weather. Archaeologists have unearthed a wide variety of pottery, kitchen

---

7. And equally elaborate paved roads, marble-lined streets, and other similar amenities. See Bouquet, Everyday Life, 27.
8. E.g., Virgilio C. Corbo, "Capernaum," in ABD, vol. 1, 866–69.

utensils, glassware among the wealthier homes, and other household tools. Lighting was by olive-oil lamps and torches. Ordinary folk availed themselves of chamber pots dumped outdoors into designated areas for refuse and runoff gutters in the middle of streets for sewage, leaving a generally foul-smelling and unsanitary environment. Local wells, cisterns for storing rainwater, and intercity aqueducts provided most of the water supply. Every house, however modest, was usually equipped with a bolt and lock and shut up for the night. Windows were small, both for security and insulation purposes. The typical solitary aperture would have made searching for a lost coin (Luke 15:8–10) difficult with a small candle or oil lamp.

Meals and Daily Schedules

Farmers worked from sunup until sundown; craftsmen and artisans almost as long. The well-to-do merchants worked much shorter hours, largely from early morning until just before noon and then perhaps for a short time again after a midday siesta.[9] Wealthier Romans enjoyed four meals a day and regularly ate meat and dairy products. Less well-to-do Jews were often limited to two meals. Bread formed the staple of their diet, supplemented by various fruits, nuts, and vegetables. Fish, especially near Galilee, were plentiful; most could afford to eat meat only on festivals and other special occasions. An invitation to a banquet thus gave ordinary folk a rare opportunity to eat food they might otherwise sample only at religious ceremonies (cf. Luke 14:12–14; 1 Cor. 10:27–30). Wine was the basic drink and generally healthier than water or milk, but as much as three times as diluted as it is today.[10] Olive oil was a primary ingredient in cooking; honey, the main sweetener. Salt, sprinkled plentifully on meat, helped to preserve it in a world without refrigeration.

For most, the evening meal culminated a hard day's work, ended daylight hours, and offered a regular opportunity for more intimate socialization. People normally invited only good friends to join them in table fellowship. With little else to do after dark, they ate leisurely over as long as a two- to three-hour span of time and engaged in extensive conversation. For formal gatherings, one "reclined" at the table (cf. John 13:23). Cushions were provided alongside the benches on which the food was served, sometimes arranged in a square-cornered U, on which one placed one's elbow and lay on one side, eating with the free hand. One's legs thus extended out perpendicular to the table. This explains, for example, how the disreputable woman at the house of Simon the Pharisee, coming in from the outside, had access to Jesus' feet to anoint them (Luke 7:38). It was also important to assume one's place at table according to status (Luke 14:7–11).

---

9. For elaboration, see Albert A. Bell, Jr., *A Guide to the New Testament World* (Scottdale and Waterloo: Herald, 1994), 200–2.

10. The views that ancient wine was unfermented and that Jesus and his disciples did not drink alcoholic beverages, however mild, are simply false. See, e.g., Norman L. Geisler, "A Christian Perspective on Wine-Drinking," *BSac* 139 (1982): 46–56, who nevertheless argues for abstinence as an important strategic choice for Christians to make today.

Clothing and Styles

The main garment for the average Jewish man was a linen or cotton "tunic" (Greek *chiton*), a loose-fitting, knee-length shirt, with a girdle or sash that could be tied around the waist while working or walking. In cooler weather a cloak (Greek *himation*), sometimes of wool, was worn over this (cf. Matt. 5:40). Sandals or shoes, some form of head covering, and underwear rounded out a man's attire. For prayer, a Jewish man donned the distinctive shawls with fringes that were fingered, much like later Catholic rosary beads, along with the phylacteries—leather head and arm bands containing key Scriptures written in them. The Roman man wore the longer, distinctive toga—a form of dress forbidden to foreigners.

Women wore simpler but often more colorful robe-like garments. Many women probably wore a shawl over their hair in public, but not the full face veil we often think of.[11] When they could afford it, Middle Eastern women also wore large quantities of jewelry, perfume, and cosmetics. Jewish men were usually bearded, with longer hair than the average Roman. Women in both cultures usually had long hair, often worn in a bun, especially after getting married.

Social Classes

The ancient Roman empire, like most traditional aristocratic empires in largely agrarian societies, concentrated more than half of the total wealth of all its subjects in the top 1 or 2 percent of its populace. This included the emperor and his court, other key political and military leaders, the landed aristocracy, and at times, the most influential religious leaders. The bureaucracy necessary to serve these people, nationally and locally, swelled the ranks of the "rich" to perhaps 5 to 7 percent. A small "middle class"—people who earned enough to have modest savings and not live a merely day-to-day existence—comprised at most another 15 percent and included many priests and Pharisees in addition to the more fortunate merchants and traders, artisans and craftsmen, bankers and toll collectors. Up to 70 percent of the population were struggling farmers and fishermen or subsistence laborers working for others in fields or "factories." A denarius was a standard day's wage (cf. Matt. 20:2) and enabled a laborer to buy food for himself and his family for the day with a little left over. Hired hands resembled modern migrant workers; their employment was seasonal. Any surplus they received had to be carefully saved. By any modern standards, these 70 percent lived in poverty. A bottom 10 percent, and sometimes more, made up the class of outcasts and expendables. They were often below even the subsistence level, with starvation a real threat.[12]

Most of Jesus' disciples and other followers seem to have come from the poor majority. Still, if Joseph's carpentry shop benefited from the boom in the construction industry near Nazareth in Sepphoris, Jesus and his family might have moved up the ladder from the poor people they clearly were at his birth

---

11. On the veiling of women in the New Testament world, see esp. James B. Hurley, *Man and Woman in Biblical Perspective* (Leicester: IVP; Grand Rapids: Zondervan, 1981), 254–71.

12. For a succinct summary of these social classes and how they functioned, see William R. Herzog II, *Parables as Subversive Speech: Jesus as Pedagogue of the Oppressed* (Louisville: Westminster/John Knox, 1994), 53–73.

(see Luke 2:24; cf. Lev. 12:8) into the lower end of the "middle class." Even relatively poor people often had at least one servant (cf. Luke 17:7–10), but the fact that Zebedee and sons had more than one (Mark 1:20) may single them out as slightly more prosperous. Whatever wealth their business gave them, however, Jesus' disciples left it behind for itinerant ministry with Christ. Jesus and his traveling troupe relied on the support that others offered, including considerable help from a strategic group of well-to-do women (Luke 8:1–3).[13]

A social class that cut across all the above economic distinctions was the class of slaves. Most ancient slaves were not the victims of racism but of conquest—prisoners of war, so to speak. Others were born slaves or sold themselves into slavery, to pay debts, for example. Unlike pre-Civil War America, in the Roman world slaves could own property, earn money, and often save enough to buy their own freedom.[14] A slave in a wealthy household was sometimes more prosperous than most freedmen and exercised important responsibilities, including managing his master's estate and teaching his children. At the opposite end of the socioeconomic spectrum were large numbers of slaves who worked in appalling conditions in various mines throughout the empire.

Economic Indebtedness and Its Relief

The first half of the first century offered increasing financial challenges to most Israelites, although Galilee remained relatively prosperous until the decade before the Jewish revolt. For many, however, taxation placed a heavy burden on all of one's earnings. The Jewish triple tithe—10 percent to priests and Levites, 10 percent for temple sacrifice, and 3⅓ percent for the poor—came on top of the sales taxes, customs, and annual tribute paid to the Roman government, much of which went to fund its vast military machine. Tax to Rome varied from about three weeks' earnings per year to 30 percent of all one's income. The annual temple tax for Jerusalem amounted to a half-shekel—or two denarii (cf. Matt. 17:24–27). No doubt, some Jews paid half or more of all their wages in tax of some form. The burden of unpayable taxes led to a lucrative business for loan sharks. Foreclosing on property followed inability to repay loans and led to people being sold into slavery or, worse, languishing in debtors' prisons.[15] Little wonder that the tax collectors, whether the chief Roman "publicans" or the more common Jewish middlemen (the "toll collectors"), were disliked!

In the more Hellenistic parts of the empire, the institution of patronage alleviated the needs of many seasonal laborers or other poor. Well-to-do aristocrats were expected to give generously to the needy through *patron-client* relationships, and the poor were expected to support their benefactors politically, give them public honor and acclaim, and perform various odd jobs for

---

13. On the theme of the socioeconomic level of Jesus and his first followers, see further John P. Meier, *A Marginal Jew: Rethinking the Historical Jesus*, vol. 1 (New York and London: Doubleday, 1991), 278–85.

14. For more details on slavery in the Roman world, see S. Scott Bartchy, *MALLΩN XRHΣAI: First-Century Slavery and 1 Corinthians 7:21* (Missoula: SBL, 1973).

15. For more conservative estimates of the typical Jew's financial plight, see Thomas E. Schmidt, "Taxes," in *DJG*, 804–7. For less conservative ones, with information on indebtedness, cf. Douglas E. Oakman, *Jesus and the Economic Questions of His Day* (Lewiston: Mellen, 1986), 57–77. Exact records of amounts of Roman taxes are generally lacking; questions about how rigidly the Jewish taxes were enforced further complicate our ability to make precise calculations.

them.[16] No developed system of welfare existed in first-century Rome, save for the corn dole and some disaster relief after earthquakes or famines. The Jewish world had more developed systems for distributing food or money to the poor on a daily or weekly basis, but many people still "fell through the cracks."

Kinds of Work

Engaging in honest work was a high priority for Jewish men. Even rabbis had to be "bivocational" and earn their keep from some trade rather than from their religious activity. We have already spoken of the major crops raised by the farmers. Tilling the fields was done with ox-drawn plows; harvesting, by sickle; and sifting wheat from chaff, with a winnowing fork. Donkeys pulled huge millstones around and around in a circle to grind grain, winepresses turned grapes into pulp, and olive presses squeezed out the precious oil. Fishermen used dugoutlike canoes with large dragnets. All of these details crop up in the imagery used in the teachings of John the Baptist and Jesus throughout the Gospels.

Those engaged in more urban work or "industry" included cloth makers, potters, metal workers, the members of the building trades, basket weavers, and dyers. Villages and cities alike required bakers, butchers, and water sellers. A suspect industry among Jews was leather working, since it involved the handling of pigskin. Luxury trades, often to help the rich in Rome grow richer, included gold- and silversmithing, ivory carving, and dealing in ointments, spices, costly jewelry, silks, and expensive dyes.[17] Bankers increasingly practiced what today would be considered a very limited form of capitalism—using savings to give out loans, make modest investments, and grant interest to their customers. Money changing produced a profit as well—at times at extortionary levels. But quite commonly inflation was nonexistent; people stored their metals in strongboxes at home, and exchanging products and services instead of hard currency sufficed for the purchase of goods.[18]

Teaching was "a humble, even despised occupation in classical antiquity because it meant running after customers asking for money and working long hours."[19] Not surprisingly, schoolteachers were often former slaves with no other trade to which to turn, and respect from both pupils and the public at large was low. "Juvenal bitterly calculates that musicians and popular athletes earn more in a day than the teacher does in a year (*Sat.* 7.175–177, 240–243). Some things change little over time!"[20] "University" level education involved study with master philosophers; a rough Jewish equivalent involved would-be rabbis learning from older, established sages. Here, at least, the circumstances were not usually so desperate.

---

16. On patron-client relationships, see Bruce W. Winter, *Seek the Welfare of the City* (Grand Rapids: Eerdmans; Carlisle: Paternoster, 1994), esp. 41–60.

17. The lament of Revelation 18, with its long list of cargoes no longer available to greedy shoppers, mirrors the drain on the empire that first-century commerce created to supply the demands of the wealthy in Rome. For a concise list of Roman imports and policies, see Helmut Koester, *Introduction to the New Testament*, vol. 1 (Berlin and New York: de Gruyter, rev. 1995), 313–14.

18. For a detailed study of the coinage and monetization of that day, see Richard Duncan-Jones, *Money and Government in the Roman Empire* (Cambridge: CUP, 1994).

19. Everett Ferguson, *Backgrounds of Early Christianity* (Grand Rapids: Eerdmans, rev. 1993), 100.

20. Bell, *Guide*, 238.

Family

The family was the basic social unit in Israel in New Testament times. Children were a blessing from God and barrenness a curse, but children had no voice in the larger social world. Crucial to godly living was to know one's place within one's household and function honorably in it. Men were the "breadwinners"; women worked hard in the domestic realm. It was expected that men would marry, and it was assumed something was wrong if they didn't. Later rabbis often quoted the saying, "He who has no wife dwells without good, without help, without joy, without blessing, and without atonement" (*Genesis Rabbah* 17.2)! Throughout the empire, arranged marriages were still practiced; but, particularly under Roman influence, young men increasingly chose their own brides. Change in Israel took place much more slowly. Polygamy was extremely rare; few men could afford it![21]

Jewish men regularly married by eighteen, Romans by twenty-five, but Greeks often not until thirty. Girls of all three cultures, however, were usually wed soon after puberty, in their early to mid-teens. There is no reason to doubt, for example, that Mary was just such a teenage bride. The Jewish groom took his bride back to his father's house to live with the extended family, often in an additional room built on. Extended families might include other relatives as well, along with any slaves the household might have. Divorces were common, though somewhat less so in the Jewish world than in Greece or Rome. But it was almost always only the man who had the right to initiate proceedings.

Jewish boys were sent to school, if one was available (usually in a synagogue), from ages five to twelve or thirteen. Greek boys usually began school at age seven. Jews studied the Bible exclusively; Greeks concentrated on Homer and rhetoric. Rote memorization predominated in both cultures. At the beginning of adolescence, education usually ended and boys learned a trade, often their father's, though sometimes they worked as an apprentice to another man. Few girls had access to formal education; the one primary exception was among the well-to-do in Greco-Roman circles. Role relationships and differentiation remained very traditional throughout adulthood.[22]

Entertainment and Leisure

For Jews, religious holidays provided a prominent opportunity for celebration. Sabbath was a joyous occasion as well as a day of rest. Festival worship was raucous by modern standards, though filled with times of reflection as well. For Greeks and Romans, who had no weekly days off, numerous annual holidays, temple rituals, and patriotic celebrations provided relief from daily routines. Throughout the ancient world, weddings and funerals often lasted up to a week, during which time whole villages rejoiced or mourned. Throughout

---

21. Despite popular misconceptions, even in the Old Testament polygamy was almost exclusively limited to kings and other very wealthy aristocrats. See Walter C. Kaiser, Jr., *Toward Old Testament Ethics* (Grand Rapids: Zondervan, 1983), 182–90.

22. For detailed surveys of women's roles, see, for the Jewish world, Leonard Swidler, *Biblical Affirmations of Woman* (Philadelphia: Westminster, 1979); for the Greco-Roman world, Sarah Pomeroy, *Goddesses, Whores, Wives and Slaves: Women in Classical Antiquity* (New York: Schocken, 1975); and Eva Cantarella, *Pandora's Daughters: The Role and Status of Women in Greek and Roman Antiquity* (Baltimore and London: Johns Hopkins, 1987).

the Hellenistic world and among more Hellenized Jews, sporting events were popular, including the Olympic games, chariot races, and gladiatorial shows—initially limited to men killing wild beasts. Most major cities had large theaters where comedies and tragedies were frequently performed. These were off-limits to more traditional Jews because of the (pagan) religious themes and associations, but all Jews enjoyed music—especially singing and dancing— storytelling, and various forms of recreational "board games."

Science and Medicine

Again, the Roman world was remarkably advanced for its day. Mention was made above of the discoveries of scientists under Ptolemy III (p. 14). Eratosthenes, the librarian at Alexandria during this period, also calculated relatively accurately the distance of the earth from the sun and conjectured the existence of the American continents. Botanists created detailed taxonomies of plants; geographers mapped the known world with considerable accuracy; and mathematicians such as Pythagoras and Archimedes had already developed many of the principles of modern geometry several centuries B.C. Architects and engineers planned and erected state-of-the-art buildings. Physicians and dentists had all manner of sophisticated surgical instruments, but there was no anesthesia apart from strong drink or mild drugs. (Ancient sources describe a good physician as more or less immune to the screams of his patients!) Doctors were paid very poorly but were generally held in good repute. Druggists were far more suspect. All in all, there were still many chronically ill and disabled, for whom the medicine of the day could do nothing, and who often had to resort to begging.

CULTURAL ANTHROPOLOGY AND SOCIOLOGY

A second major aspect of the socioeconomic background of any historical period is a recognition of the shared cultural values and the forms of interaction between social groups, networks, and institutions. We may consider each of these in turn.

Cultural Values

The cultural values of the ancient Mediterranean, as in many parts of the non-Western world today, were often quite different from those we are accustomed to in North America or Europe. To understand the significance of Jesus' ministry at numerous points, an awareness of those values proves crucial.[23]

Honor/Shame. Perhaps the most dominant of all the cultural values was the extent to which honor and shame permeated ancient society. It did not matter nearly so much how much money one made or what trade a person practiced, but it mattered immensely if one acquitted himself or herself honorably in all

---

23. The following discussion is heavily indebted to Bruce J. Malina, *The New Testament World: Insights from Cultural Anthropology* (Atlanta: John Knox, 1981; London: SCM, 1983); and John J. Pilch, *Introducing the Cultural Context of the New Testament* (New York: Paulist, 1991).

things.[24] Honor was either ascribed or acquired. Repeatedly, the Jewish leaders challenged Jesus' honor by asking him questions designed to trap him (most notably, see Mark 11:27–12:34 pars.). Jesus not only avoided the traps but asked questions in reply that they could not answer (e.g. Mark 12:35–37 pars.). In so doing he was honored and they were shamed. The size of following a teacher had also related directly to his honor in society's eyes. So when the multitudes stopped following Jesus because of the difficulty of his teaching, it is little wonder that he asked the disciples if they, too, were leaving (John 6:60–67). His honor was at stake. So was Herod's at the banquet during which he rashly promised up to half his kingdom to his stepdaughter. Mark, in his Gospel, nicely captures the dynamic when he explains why Herod acquiesced to the gruesome request for John the Baptist's head on a platter: "because of his oaths and his dinner guests" (6:26)!

Individual vs. Group Personality. The ancient Mediterranean personality was far more group-centered than we are with our rugged, Western individualism.[25] One owed responsibilities to one's extended family, neighborhood, trade guild or religious association, and other close acquaintances. A true friend was fiercely loyal in responding to any reasonable request with the understanding that reciprocal favors were then owed. In this context, Mark 3:31–35 and parallels prove highly countercultural—Jesus rejected his biological family in favor of his disciples as his closest "kin."[26] Conversely, by calling his disciples his "brother and sister and mother," he implied that they must be devoted to each other to the same degree that blood relatives normally were—a principle the Western church has rarely implemented.

Perception of Limited Good. In a world seventeen and eighteen centuries before the theoretical development of capitalism and socialism, respectively, most people assumed that unless one was a member of the tiny percentage of well-to-do elite, any significant increase in one's standard of living was at someone else's expense. In other words, there was a limited-sized "pie" of material resources to be divided up. Therefore a farmer who had a sudden windfall of crops was expected to share with the needy, unlike the "rich fool" in the parable of Luke 12:13–21. Moreover, when fellow villagers or friends did give one money or other material assistance, one was honor bound to repay them. People did not necessarily say "thank you" in the ancient world; they just returned the favor. In fact, thanking people could imply that one was not going to do anything more and hence would end the relationship of mutual give-and-take. Thus the Samaritan leper of Luke 17:11–19 who returns to give thanks to Jesus was perhaps not the man people would have expected Jesus to praise. Christ, however, was trying to teach that God's grace is given without the possibility of repayment. Equally countercultural was Jesus' insistence that banquet-givers invite those who could not invite them in return (Luke 14:12–14). Paradoxically, God will reward such people in the life to come, but

---

24. Cf., e.g., Halvor Moxnes, "Honor and Shame," *BTB* 23 (1993) 167–76; with W. R. Domeris, "Honour and Shame in the New Testament," *Neot* 27 (1993) 283–97.

25. For a helpful survey of important recent literature, see Stephen C. Barton, "The Communal Dimension of Earliest Christianity," *JTS* 43 (1992): 399–427.

26. See also David M. May, "Mark 3:20–35 from the Perspective of Shame/Honor," *BTB* 17 (1987): 83–87.

only when the motivation for their behavior is not that of wanting such a reward.

Character Plus Performance. Unfortunately in today's corporate business environment, performance or productivity is often the "bottom line"—the only criterion for success. Yet in most non-Western cultures one's character and integrity have been at least as important and usually more so. Good deeds were important to ancient Jews, and they were important to Jesus as well—but only to the extent that they disclosed one's true character. So, in the Sermon on the Mount, Christ taught that one's "fruit" reveals who a person is (Matt. 7:15–20). It is not enough merely to hear his words; words must also be put into practice (7:21–27). On the other hand, performance without godly character is worthless; hence Jesus insisted that his disciples' righteousness exceed that of those scribes and Pharisees who typically opposed him (5:20).

Purity and Uncleanness. Because of all the ritual laws in the Old Testament, ancient Jews were constantly careful not to find themselves in a position of impurity or uncleanness and thus unable for a time to worship with God's people. Without any close modern equivalent, it is difficult for us to imagine living with these cultural values. A woman was more often unclean than a man, due to her monthly cycles. Various kinds of sicknesses, disabilities, or bodily discharges could render one more or less permanently unclean, so the social ostracism became a worse malady than the physical discomfort. When Jesus healed the woman who had suffered from a flow of blood "for twelve years" (Mark 5:25), we realize it was no physiological emergency. To have survived that long with so chronic a problem meant that, medically speaking, her symptoms were not life-threatening—she clearly could get "up and around." But because the woman was unclean for most of that time, her healing was probably an even greater relief socially and culturally than physically.

Another form of impurity resulted from a curse. One interesting belief widely held in ancient Mediterranean cultures was that certain people had the ability to cast a spell on others merely with the power of a malignant stare—known as "the evil eye." In several places in the Gospels, the literal translation of the text makes reference to this belief. For example, in Matthew 6:23 Jesus speaks of those whose eyes are evil, corrupting their entire selves. To avert the curse, one must seek to look at the world in wholesome ways, not coveting "mammon" (material goods), and then one's entire life will be pure (vv. 22, 24).[27]

Present, Past, and Future. Modern Westerners are primarily future oriented. The present is of secondary importance, and the past matters least of all. In the ancient world the present was most important, then the past, and lastly the future (except for the handful of sufficiently wealthy people who could really plan ahead). In general, Jesus affirmed the value of living in the present—praying only for "daily bread" (Matt. 6:11) and not worrying about tomorrow because of the sufficient troubles of today (v. 34). It is not wrong to plan ahead, but we had better leave room in our planning for God's will to overrule ours (cf. James 4:13–17).

---

27. Cf. further John H. Elliott, "The Evil Eye and the Sermon on the Mount," *BI* 2 (1994): 51–84.

Sociological Models

Sociologists characteristically study the interrelationships among social *groups*. This is the hardest aspect of socioeconomic background study to apply to the ancient world because of the nature of the data that have survived. Oftentimes sociological studies of Scripture rely on applying theories or models that have proven true in societies other than those of Bible times because there is reason to believe the social dynamics would have been similar. But sometimes the theories have a bias against the supernatural or have outrun the evidence, or the supposedly analogous cultures are simply too far removed in time or geography from the first-century Roman empire to be helpful.[28] Five of the most popular areas for sociological investigation into the Gospels are treated briefly here.

The Millenarian Cult. It has been observed that small, religious sects often believe that the world as we know it is ending very soon, to be replaced by a golden age or "millennium" in human history. Some even set dates. When the time passes and the end of the world has not come, those groups that survive and even flourish often do so by a vigorous burst of evangelism. It is as if they seek to legitimize their existence by recruiting more people to join them, despite the "disconfirmation" of their prophecies. They then recompute their dates and once again announce that the end is imminent. Early Christianity has been compared to just such a millenarian cult.[29] However, the passages some take to imply that Jesus mistakenly taught his return within the lifetime of his disciples are probably meant to be interpreted differently. And the primary model for modern sociological study from which this theory derives was the Melanesian "cargo cult" (from the South Seas islands), which is probably not close enough in time and space to early Christianity to be sufficiently analogous.

The Meaning of Miracles. Jesus and his followers were by no means the only people in the ancient world who believed they worked or experienced miracles. Sociological analysis of other ancient texts suggests that reports of miracles predominated in situations of intense belief in a sacred dimension of life that revealed itself in situations of hostility, oppression, or social upheaval. Belief in the existence of God or the gods maintained order and stability in times of great change or transience. Miracles were, in a sense, enacted metaphors of God's sovereignty.[30] This kind of analysis neither requires nor rejects the historical reliability of such reports; it concentrates rather on their social function. Given that understanding, these descriptions surely apply well enough to the Gospel miracles.

Wandering Charismatics vs. Nonviolent Protesters. Because of Jesus' sayings about leaving all and going on the road with him (e.g., Luke 9:57–62 par.), one influential theory draws on "structural functional" sociology to argue that Jesus' first followers continued a lifestyle of itinerant teaching, dependent on the support of others, even after the resurrection. This was unrealistic for most,

---

28. On these distinctions, see esp. Edwin Yamauchi, "Sociology, Scripture and the Supernatural," *JETS* 27 (1984): 169–92.

29. See esp. John G. Gager, *Kingdom and Community: The Social World of Early Christianity* (Englewood Cliffs, N.J.: Prentice-Hall, 1975).

30. See esp. Gerd Theissen, *The Miracle Stories of the Early Christian Tradition* (Philadelphia: Fortress; Edinburgh: T. & T. Clark, 1983); Howard C. Kee, *Miracle in the Early Christian World* (New Haven and London: Yale, 1983).

however, so a second tier of discipleship emerged that brought greater stability to the young religious movement—more settled followers provided a support system for the "wandering charismatics."[31] More recently, this perspective has been challenged head-on and a quite different claim put forward: "conflict theory" suggests that the early "Jesus movement" was a nonviolent peasant revolt or prophetic protest against the corruption of society.[32]

Two additional approaches to studying Scripture in general and the Gospels in particular employ a variety of methods that go well beyond mere sociology (and beyond the scope of this book). But a sociological critique of belief systems and institutional structures lies at the heart of these approaches, so they may be profitably mentioned here.

Liberation Theology. Emerging initially out of post-Vatican II Roman Catholic circles, particularly in Latin America, liberation theology has often applied Marxist theories of economics to the Gospels. At one extreme, Jesus is seen as promoting Communism.[33] Christian thought is said to be compatible with violent revolution. Jesus and his followers are viewed as uniformly poor, and God is said to have a "preferential option" for the marginalized of society. But as we have noted above (pp. 60–61), this overlooks the fact that the band of disciples, like the people to whom they ministered, probably encompassed a greater diversity of socioeconomic classes.[34] Indeed, the whole vocabulary of "classes" in society, which we have also employed, is somewhat anachronistic. More crucial to whether one was in the mainstream or on the margins of society was whether or not one had honor, good relationships with friends or villagers (however economically poor one was), and ritual purity. Tax collectors, for example, often were well-off economically but were still considered outcasts in Jewish society because they collected tribute for the foreign oppressor (Rome). The average peasant (farmer or fisherman) was probably very poor, yet was aligned more with the "haves" than the "have-nots" of his community. Nevertheless, Jesus had an undeniably greater concern for the poor and the social outcasts of his world than many in the contemporary West do.[35]

Feminism. Feminist scholarship may be seen as one branch of liberation theology, though it has been dominated by the interests of North American or European women more than those of the Third World. Some feminist analysis focuses primarily on reading the stories of Scripture, in this case of the Gospels, through women's eyes. The Samaritan woman at the well then emerges as one whom Jesus treated with great dignity, as an unexpected heroine in contrast to the great Jewish male teacher, Nicodemus, who merely became increasingly

31. Gerd Theissen, *Sociology of Early Palestinian Christianity* (Philadelphia: Fortress [= *The First Followers of Jesus* (London: SCM)], 1978).

32. Richard A. Horsley, *Sociology and the Jesus Movement* (New York: Crossroad, 1989).

33. See esp. José P. Miranda, *Communism in the Bible* (Maryknoll: Orbis, 1982).

34. Evangelical critics, however, have too often stereotyped liberation theology along the lines of its most extreme practitioners. Far more balanced and exegetically nuanced, e.g., is Juan L. Segundo, *The Historical Jesus of the Synoptics* (Maryknoll: Orbis, 1985). For more recent syntheses of liberationist exegesis of the Gospels, see Christopher Rowland and Mark Corner, *Liberating Exegesis: The Challenge of Liberation Theology to Biblical Studies* (London: SPCK; Louisville: Westminster/John Knox, 1989). For an example of a close reading of an entire Gospel (Mark) with materialist concerns in view, see Ched Myers, *Binding the Strong Man* (Maryknoll: Orbis, 1988).

35. See further Craig L. Blomberg, *Give Me Neither Poverty Nor Riches: A New Testament Theology of Material Possessions* (Leicester: IVP; Grand Rapids: Eerdmans, forthcoming).

confused at Jesus' message (John 3–4). Jesus' praise for the widow's sacrificial giving of her mite (Mark 12:41–44 par.) can also be read as an implicit condemnation of the wealthy male Jewish leaders who allowed her to give a portion of her income that went beyond the 20 percent their laws stipulated. In other cases, as with liberation theology, feminism becomes more of an advocacy movement, arguing for the liberation of women based on Jesus' radically positive affirmation of them. Not to be quickly stereotyped, feminist scholars cover a huge theological spectrum, ranging all the way from conservative evangelicals to antireligious atheists.[36]

CONCLUSION

Clearly a certain degree of social-scientific sophistication is necessary to evaluate these varied hypotheses and any new ones no doubt soon to emerge. The sociological and anthropological study of Scripture is still in its infancy but is clearly on the rise. Some theories are obviously reductionistic, that is, they do not allow for the supernatural or even for the uniqueness of every human agent. But many may be viewed simply as additional components of bettering our understanding of the historical background of the Bible and the nature of the incarnation. Sensitive readers of the Gospels will want to raise such questions as these: To what groups do various individuals in the text belong? What are the social dynamics of those groups? What are their goals? How might they be accomplished? What are the roles of power within the group and the means of attaining them? Are age groups or sex roles defined? What are the boundaries of acceptable behavior? Perhaps most important of all, to what extent does Jesus either affirm or critique the dominant patterns of social interaction in his world? And in moving to our day, how would he respond to our world? Where do we need to be countercultural to be faithful disciples? Which specific details of his teaching remain timelessly applicable, and which need to be applied differently today?[37]

FOR FURTHER STUDY

Social and Economic History

Introductory

Bell, Albert A., Jr. *A Guide to the New Testament World.* Scottdale and Waterloo: Herald, 1994.

---

36. The pioneering study of the birth of Christianity from a modern feminist perspective is Elisabeth Schüssler Fiorenza, *In Memory of Her: A Feminist Theological Reconstruction of Christian Origins* (New York: Crossroad, 1983). To compare and contrast evangelical feminism with more radical versions, one may consult, respectively, two recent anthologies in commentary format: Catherine C. Kroeger, Mary Evans, and Elaine Storkey, eds., *Study Bible for Women: The New Testament* (Grand Rapids: Baker; London: HarperCollins, 1996); and Carol A. Newsom and Sharon H. Ringe, eds., *The Women's Bible Commentary* (Louisville: Westminster/ John Knox; London: SPCK, 1992).

37. These and many similarly helpful questions are raised in Howard C. Kee, *Knowing the Truth: A Sociological Approach to New Testament Interpretation* (Minneapolis: Fortress, 1989), 65–67. Some of the material in this chapter draws heavily on William W. Klein, Craig L. Blomberg, and Robert L. Hubbard, Jr., *Introduction to Biblical Interpretation* (Dallas and London: Word, 1993), 443–57.

Bouquet, A. C. *Everyday Life in New Testament Times.* London: Batsford, 1953.
Gower, Ralph. *The New Manners and Customs of Bible Times.* Chicago: Moody, 1987.
Jenkins, Ian. *Greek and Roman Life.* London: British Museum Trustees; Cambridge, Mass.: Harvard, 1986.
Thompson, J. A. *Handbook of Life in Bible Times.* Leicester and Downers Grove: IVP, 1986.

Intermediate

Ferguson, Everett. *Backgrounds of Early Christianity.* Grand Rapids: Eerdmans, rev. 1993.
Koester, Helmut. *Introduction to the New Testament.* Vol. 1. Berlin and New York: de Gruyter, rev. 1995.
Meeks, Wayne A. *The First Urban Christians.* New Haven and London: Yale, 1983.
Stambaugh, John E., and David L. Balch. *The New Testament in Its Social Environment.* Philadelphia: Westminster, 1986.

Advanced

Freyne, Séan. *Galilee from Alexander the Great to Hadrian.* Wilmington: Glazier; Notre Dame: University of Notre Dame Press, 1980.
Hamel, Gildas. *Poverty and Charity in Roman Palestine, First Three Centuries C.E.* Berkeley and Oxford: University of California Press, 1989.
Horsley, Richard A. *Galilee: History, Politics, People.* Valley Forge: TPI, 1995.
Rostovtzeff, M. *The Social and Economic History of the Hellenistic World.* 3 vols. Oxford: Clarendon, 1941.
Rostovtzeff, M. *The Social and Economic History of the Roman Empire.* 2 vols. Oxford: Clarendon, rev. 1957.

Cultural Anthropology and Sociology

Introductory

Elliott, John H. *What Is Social-Scientific Criticism?* Minneapolis: Fortress, 1993.
Osiek, Carolyn. *What Are They Saying about the Social Setting of the New Testament?* New York: Paulist, rev. 1992.
Schmidt, Thomas E. "Sociology and New Testament Exegesis." In *Introducing New Testament Interpretation,* ed. Scot McKnight, 115–32. Grand Rapids: Baker, 1989.
Tidball, Derek. *An Introduction to the Sociology of the New Testament.* Exeter: Paternoster (=*The Social Context of the New Testament.* Grand Rapids: Zondervan), 1984.

Intermediate

Esler, Philip F. *The First Christians in Their Social Worlds: Social-Scientific Approaches to New Testament Interpretation.* London and New York: Routledge & Kegan Paul, 1994.
Holmberg, Bengt. *Sociology and the New Testament: An Appraisal.* Minneapolis: Fortress, 1990.
Malina, Bruce J. *Windows on the World of Jesus.* Louisville: Westminster/John Knox, 1993.
Malina, Bruce J. and Richard L. Rohrbaugh. *Social-Science Commentary on the Synoptic Gospels.* Minneapolis: Fortress, 1992.

Advanced

Kee, Howard C. *Christian Origins in Sociological Perspective.* Philadelphia: Westminster; London: SCM, 1980.
Lenski, Gerhard E. *Power and Privilege: A Theory of Social Stratification.* New York: McGraw-Hill, 1966.

Malina, Bruce J. *Christian Origins and Cultural Anthropology.* Atlanta: John Knox, 1986.
Oakman, Douglas E. *Jesus and the Economic Questions of His Day.* Lewiston: Mellen, 1986.

Bibliography

May, David M. *Social Scientific Criticism of the New Testament: A Bibliography.* Macon, Ga.: Mercer, 1991.

QUESTIONS FOR REVIEW

1. Choose several passages from the Gospels and discuss how your enhanced understanding of Jesus' social and cultural world illuminates the text. Consider, for example, the parable of the friend at midnight (Luke 11:5–8), Jesus' encounter with the Samaritan woman (John 4:1–42), or the story of the rich young ruler (Mark 10:17–31 pars.). Review each main subsection of the chapter and see how many applications you can find for each passage.

2. Can you think of any passages in the Gospels where you have previously visualized an anachronistic social or cultural setting? Discuss. Consider particularly how our modern, Western individualism distorts the group-centered mind-set of the biblical cultures.

PART TWO

CRITICAL METHODS FOR
STUDYING THE GOSPELS

T hus far we have surveyed background information relevant to the entire New Testament, though with primary attention to the Gospels. From here on our comments will be directed exclusively toward a better understanding of Matthew, Mark, Luke, and John.

INTRODUCTION TO CRITICAL METHODOLOGY

There are numerous "critical" (i.e., analytical) tools that scholars use to help them understand how these four Gospels came to be in the form we now know them. One major division among the methods distinguishes "lower criticism" from "higher criticism." *Lower criticism* is also known as textual criticism and is the science of sorting and comparing the existing manuscripts of an ancient document with a view to reconstructing the text of the original as accurately as possible. *Higher criticism* involves the various disciplines that seek to explain how that original document was composed—what sources the author used, how he put them together, under what circumstances he wrote, and so on.

Higher criticism can in turn be subdivided into two largely discrete disciplines: historical criticism and literary criticism. *Historical criticism* studies the prehistory of a text—all of the influences leading up to and including the final assembling of a finished product by the author or editor. *Literary criticism* analyzes the features of the text in the final form in which an author publishes it. In the case of the Gospels, there is also the interesting phenomenon that Matthew, Mark, and Luke are more similar to each other than different, whereas John's contents differ more. This means that many issues in the formation of Matthew, Mark, and Luke can and should be treated together, whereas the unique issues surrounding John's Gospel merit separate treatment.

The two chapters of part 2 thus treat the various branches of historical and literary criticism in turn. Issues common to the first three Gospels are also treated in these chapters, while topics unique to a particular Gospel are largely reserved for part 3. The rest of this introduction will make some brief remarks about the textual criticism of the Gospels; fuller treatments will have to be sought elsewhere.[1]

TEXTUAL CRITICISM

The existing texts of the Gospels are generally in as good a shape as any portion of the ancient copies of Scripture and in better shape than many parts. We, of course, have none of the autographs—the original documents themselves. But the oldest known fragment of any section of the New Testament that can be reliably dated is p52, the John Rylands papyrus, containing portions of John 18:31–33, 37–38 from approximately A.D. 130—barely forty years after the original was first composed. Another two dozen papyri containing part or all of one or more of the Gospels date from the second, third, and fourth centuries and are housed in various museums and libraries around the world. The five oldest and most reliable complete (or mostly complete) New Testaments date from the fourth and fifth centuries and all contain the Gospels quite well preserved.

Most modern English translations of the New Testament, particularly in "study Bibles," give footnotes (or marginal notes) listing the most significant alternate readings in the ancient manuscripts (called "textual variants") so that readers can know when part of a passage is in doubt. The modern editions of the Greek New Testament (UBS and Nestle-Aland) give a much fuller selection of these variants. In addition to numerous minor transmissional errors that can quickly be identified, there are a number of places in the Gospels in which a passage has been modified to make it more closely match parallel accounts in another Gospel (called "harmonistic variants"). Only rarely are entire sentences in dispute. Two well-known examples that probably reflect later scribal additions are the doxology to the Lord's Prayer (Matt. 6:13b) and the legend of the angel stirring up the water of the pool of Bethesda (John 5:3b–4). On the other hand, Luke 22:19b–20 is missing from some early texts but is probably original.

Only two lengthy passages in the entire New Testament are textually disputed; both of these come from the Gospels. The longer ending of Mark

---

1. Most of which involve the textual criticism of the whole New Testament, inasmuch as the principles remain constant throughout. At the introductory level, see J. Harold Greenlee, *Introduction to New Testament Textual Criticism* (Peabody: Hendrickson, rev. 1995). The best intermediate level treatment is Bruce M. Metzger, *The Text of the New Testament: Its Transmission, Corruption, and Restoration* (New York and Oxford: Oxford University Press, rev. 1993). For more comprehensive detail, see Kurt Aland and Barbara Aland, *The Text of the New Testament* (Grand Rapids: Eerdmans; Leiden: Brill, rev. 1989).

(16:9–20) is almost certainly not what Mark wrote. The two oldest and most reliable complete copies of the Gospel do not contain it (Codexes Sinaiticus and Vaticanus). The style is quite different from the rest of Mark's Gospel, and some of the theology is potentially both heretical and fatal (see v. 18)! These verses themselves contain an inordinately large number of textual variants, and several manuscripts reveal still other alternate endings. Either the original ending of Mark was lost or the author deliberately ended abruptly with verse 8. Either way, early scribes tried to compensate for the abruptness by giving the Gospel a "proper" ending (see further below, pp. 355–356).

John 7:53–8:11 is missing from even more of the oldest and most trustworthy texts. But whereas this story of the "woman caught in adultery" is again not at all likely to have been in the original Gospel of John, a good case can be made that it preserves an account of something Jesus actually did. It fits Jesus' nature, teaching, and ministry, and may well have been handed down by word of mouth until some scribe copying the Gospel decided it was too good to leave out.[2] None of this should alarm the Christian reader; historically, the church's doctrine of Scripture has almost always stressed that it is only the contents of the original manuscripts that are authoritative, inspired, or inerrant. For whatever reason, God did not see fit to ensure that those documents were inerrantly *preserved*.[3] Nevertheless, our ability to reconstruct what the originals looked like is exceedingly high. The contents of 97 to 99 percent of the text are certain beyond any reasonable doubt—far better than for any other documents of the same age. Furthermore, no doctrine of the Christian faith hangs on any disputed text.

---

2. See esp. Gary M. Burge, "A Specific Problem in the New Testament Text and Canon: The Woman Caught in Adultery (John 7:53–8:11)," *JETS* 27 (1984): 141–48.

3. Occasionally some Christians still insist that God did inerrantly preserve the original autographs, in the so-called Textus Receptus tradition of New Testament manuscripts on which the KJV translators relied heavily. But at every stage of the history of the transmission of the text there have been revisions and variant forms that have competed for authoritative acceptance. Belief in inerrant preservation is an act of sheer fideism in defiance of virtually all the relevant evidence, including the fact that there is no "Textus Receptus" for the *Old* Testament. For details, see D. A. Carson, *The King James Version Debate* (Grand Rapids: Baker, 1979); James R. White, *The King James Only Controversy* (Minneapolis: Bethany, 1995).

CHAPTER FOUR

HISTORICAL CRITICISM
OF THE GOSPELS

T
he unique fact that we have four different accounts of the life of Jesus
has generated interest throughout church history.[1] At the end of the
second century, Irenaeus, bishop of Lyons in France, likened the presence of four Gospels to the existence of four winds or zones of the earth. He
believed that theological distinctives accounted for the differences: John wrote
of the divine Word of God; Luke, about Jesus' priestly role, Matthew, of his
humanity; and Mark, of Christ as prophet (*Against Heresies*, 3.11.8). Today,
scholars agree that various theological distinctives characterize each Gospel
but concur with Irenaeus only on his description of John.

A SURVEY OF VIEWS THROUGHOUT HISTORY

During the first seventeen centuries of church history, the most common
way of approaching the phenomenon of having four Gospels was that of producing a "harmony" of the four. In other words, a life of Christ was reconstructed with every text from each Gospel fitted into a possible place in one
larger, composite whole. The first known Christian harmony of the Gospels

---

1. Cf. the relevant material scattered throughout Werner G. Kümmel, *The New Testament: The History of the Investigation of Its Problems* (Nashville: Abingdon, 1972; London: SCM, 1973); and Stephen Neill and Tom Wright, *The Interpretation of the New Testament 1861–1986* (Oxford: OUP, 1988). Much more briefly, see Ralph P. Martin, *New Testament Foundations*, vol. 1 (Grand Rapids: Eerdmans, 1975), 30–49, 119–60.

came from the late second-century Syrian, Tatian, and was called the *Diatessa-ron* (from the Greek, "through four"). Church greats for more than a millennium followed suit, though the details varied. Augustine and Calvin both wrote commentaries on a harmony of the Gospels as well.

Church Fathers generally assumed that Matthew, Mark, and Luke were written in that order, with Mark and Luke both knowing and using Matthew's Gospel, thus accounting for their similarities. It was often assumed that John, too, knew the other three but consciously chose to supplement them and not repeat much of the information already contained in the works of his predecessors.

The principles of the Enlightenment of the 1700s led to quite different approaches to Scripture. The Bible was studied by people, at first primarily in Germany, who were not necessarily believers or who bracketed their faith in order to leave the door open for historical conclusions quite at odds with traditional dogma. They studied the Bible like any other ancient document, not assuming in advance that everything in it was necessarily true, much less inspired. With respect to the Gospels, the accounts of miracles came under close scrutiny. Late eighteenth-century and early nineteenth-century scholars such as Samuel Reimarus and H. E. G. Paulus developed *rationalist* or naturalistic interpretations of the miracle narratives: the feeding of the five thousand involved rich people in the crowds sharing their lunches after seeing the model of generosity by Jesus and the young man; Jesus only appeared to walk on the water—he was actually wading close to shore—and so on.

In the 1830s, D. F. Strauss ushered in a new era in dealing with the Gospels. He rejected both the traditional attempts to harmonize them and the rationalist school of thought in favor of an understanding of Jesus' more spectacular deeds and claims as *myths*—pious but fictitious legends that couched theological beliefs about Jesus in narrative form. In the middle of the nineteenth century, F. C. Baur built on the dialectical philosophy of G. W. F. Hegel (who also inspired Marx) and described the origins of Christianity in terms of "thesis-antithesis-synthesis." Following the description of Paul's confrontation with Peter at Antioch (Gal. 2:11–15), Baur divided all of the New Testament writings into three divisions: conservative Jewish Christianity (like Peter), liberal Law-free Gentile Christianity (like Paul), and later syntheses attempting to reconcile the two. As far as the Gospels were concerned, Matthew was the most Jewish (and thus most authentic); Luke, the most Gentile or Pauline; and Mark, a second-century attempt to reconcile the two.

Throughout the nineteenth century numerous scholars also composed "lives of Jesus." Believing that the Gospels were a blend of fact and fiction, they sought to strip away the later theological interpretations of the early church from the "historical Jesus." Tellingly, however, the "Jesuses" they produced all strikingly resembled whatever philosophy or ideology the given author himself propounded—whether revolutionary or pacifist, romantic or mystic. At the beginning of the twentieth century Albert Schweitzer, the theologian and musician who later became a famous missionary doctor to Africa, wrote a devastating exposé of how the authors of all these "lives" simply re-created Jesus in their own likenesses. Schweitzer's own understanding of Jesus, however, proved equally truncated: an apocalyptic prophet who believed the kingdom would come in all its fulness during his lifetime but who was sadly mistaken.[2]

Throughout the eighteenth and nineteenth centuries, scholars also became increasingly fascinated with the "Synoptic problem," as J. J. Griesbach first named it in the late 1700s. The Synoptic Gospels are Matthew, Mark, and Luke, so named because their similarities enable them to be set side by side in parallel columns in a *synopsis* (from the Greek for "together look").[3] The Synoptic problem, then, is the question of their literary interrelationship. Griesbach broke from the tradition that had persisted since Augustine of seeing Mark and Luke each dependent on Matthew and argued that Mark was the last of the three Synoptic Gospels to be written, as an abridgment of Matthew and Luke. In the 1800s, particularly under the influence of C. H. Weisse and H. J. Holtzmann, a third explanation became dominant: Mark wrote first; then Matthew and Luke both used and expanded Mark's Gospel.

The development of twentieth-century Gospels scholarship has been characterized by successive interest in different critical tools, each building on its predecessor. For the first quarter of the century, *source criticism* predominated as further defense and elaboration of "Markan priority" flourished. Today there has been a revival of interest in the Griesbach hypothesis, largely due to the tireless crusades of and international conferences organized by William R. Farmer.[4] Still, it shows no signs of supplanting Markan priority among the majority of scholars. For the second quarter of the century, interest shifted to *form criticism*—an analysis of the period before the Gospels were written when stories and excerpts of Jesus' life and teachings circulated almost entirely by word of mouth.

After about 1950, *redaction criticism* came to the fore. This discipline concentrates on the Gospel writers as redactors or editors. Redaction criticism seeks to determine why they chose what they did to include or omit, how they arranged their material, and what distinctive theological emphases each wanted to stress. Since about 1975, interest has increasingly shifted to *literary criticism*—treating the Gospels as works of literature and analyzing their plots, themes, characterization, figures of speech, and so on.

During the last fifty years the "quest of the historical Jesus" has reemerged too. After reaching an all-time low during the era of the prolific Rudolf Bultmann, who said that all we can know about Jesus is *"that"* he lived and died,"[5] several of his students in the 1950s embarked on a "new quest" that admitted a fairly significant amount of Jesus' *teachings* as historical, at least in the

---

2. Albert Schweitzer, *The Quest of the Historical Jesus* (London: A & C Black; New York: Macmillan, 1910).

3. The student will find the study of the Gospels (and an understanding of this chapter) greatly enhanced if he or she consults such a synopsis periodically. A standard English edition, using the RSV, is Kurt Aland, *Synopsis of the Four Gospels* (New York: United Bible Societies, 1982). A Greek-English edition is also available.

4. Farmer's foundational work was *The Synoptic Problem* (New York and London: Macmillan, 1964). Most recently, cf. his *The Gospel of Jesus: The Pastoral Relevance of the Synoptic Problem* (Louisville: Westminster/John Knox, 1994). The objections Farmer raises to the radical historical and theological conclusions of many Markan priorists involve their numerous additional hypotheses and not the mere supposition of Markan priority.

5. Roy A. Harrisville and Walter Sundberg, *The Bible in Modern Culture: Theology and Historical-Critical Method from Spinoza to Käsemann* (Grand Rapids: Eerdmans, 1995), 223. When fleshing out this statement, however, Bultmann did affirm a small core of information about Jesus' ministry that could be accepted as historical; see his magnum opus, *The History of the Synoptic Tradition* (Oxford: Blackwell; New York: Harper & Row, 1963 [Germ. orig. 1921]).

Synoptic Gospels.[6] Since the mid-1970s, that quest has taken an even more conservative turn, buttressed primarily by a resurgence of interest in Jesus as a Jew. This so-called "third quest" for the historical Jesus finds some historically accurate material in almost all major categories of Synoptic teachings and *deeds* of Jesus, although John is still seen as far more theological than historical.[7]

What do we make of this potpourri of perspectives that has emerged over the centuries, particularly in recent years? To begin with, we must admit that much of modern scholarship has adopted presuppositions that are not readily compatible with historic, Christian faith. Indeed, many proponents of "the historical-critical method" have defined it to include three quite skeptical principles of the nineteenth-century philosopher Ernst Troeltsch: (1) "methodical doubt," whereby one is suspicious of any historical narrative unless strong corroborating evidence is found to support its claims; (2) the use of "analogy," so that events without precedent in history are inherently impossible; and (3) the principle of "correlation," which posits a closed continuum of natural causes and effects in the universe.[8] On the other hand, every one of the disciplines surveyed has relied on painstaking analysis of the actual data of the Gospels and has been used to varying degrees with profit by conservative scholars in ways that are compatible with orthodox faith.

The remainder of this chapter examines in more detail the three dominant methodologies of the period from about 1900 to 1975, all of which still are firmly entrenched in Gospel scholarship—source, form, and redaction criticism. *The order of our survey this time will correspond to the chronology of the events each method studies in the life of the early church*: first, form criticism with its focus on the period of oral tradition; next, source criticism with its analysis of the first written accounts about Jesus; finally, redaction criticism with its concentration on the role of the evangelists in producing the Gospels as we know them. A brief concluding section will scrutinize "canon criticism," which flows logically from redaction criticism. It is the study of the canonizing process and canonical form of all of the Gospels put together.

Luke, with the information he provides in his prologue (Luke 1:1–4), seems to have anticipated this threefold division of study of the formation of the Gospels. He speaks of "the things that have been fulfilled among us" as being "handed down to us by those who from the first were eyewitnesses and servants of the word" (vv. 1b–2)—*the period of oral tradition*. He also states that "many [including at least Mark and Matthew?] have undertaken to draw up an account" of these things (v. 1a)—language in the Greek that most naturally refers to written narratives—*the oldest Gospels or Gospel sources*. But he, too,

---

6. Beginning with Ernst Käsemann, "The Problem of the Historical Jesus," in *Essays on New Testament Themes* (London: SCM; Naperville: Allenson, 1964 [Germ. orig. 1954]), 15–47. In the U.S. the key impetus came from James M. Robinson, *A New Quest of the Historical Jesus* (London: SCM; Naperville: Allenson, 1959).

7. Key works include E. P. Sanders, *Jesus and Judaism* (London: SCM; Philadelphia: Fortress, 1985); James H. Charlesworth, *Jesus within Judaism* (New York and London: Doubleday, 1988); and John P. Meier, *A Marginal Jew: Rethinking the Historical Jesus*, 3 vols. (New York and London: Doubleday, 1991–). Evangelicals are involved as well, esp. N. T. Wright, *Jesus and the Victory of God* (London: SPCK; Minneapolis: Fortress, 1996) and Ben Witherington III, *The Christology of Jesus* (Minneapolis: Fortress, 1990). A prominent aberration, swimming against this more conservative tide, has been the work of the Jesus Seminar, to date best summarized in Robert W. Funk, Roy Hoover, and the Jesus Seminar, *The Five Gospels: The Search for the Authentic Words of Jesus* (New York: Macmillan, 1993). Cf. further, below, pp. 184–185.

8. See further Edgar Krentz, *The Historical-Critical Method* (Philadelphia: Fortress, 1975).

having functioned as a careful historian (v. 3a), wanted to write his own distinctive account (v. 3b) in order to commend the truth of the Gospel (v. 4)—*the stage of final redaction for theological purposes.*

If some readers wonder if all this "criticism" really is compatible with belief in the Gospels as inspired books, the answer is clearly yes. Of course, we must carefully examine any given practitioner's use of each method, for at times much "chaff" is mixed in with the "wheat." Nonetheless, the basic principles are not only sound, they are demanded if one believes in the accuracy of Luke's description of how he wrote. Given the similarities among Luke, Mark, and Matthew, and, to a lesser degree, John, it stands to reason that the other evangelists proceeded somewhat similarly. Gospel criticism is not inherently an alternative to belief in the inspiration of the texts, though it has been used that way by some radical critics. Rather, it is a study of the ordinary human means of writing that God's Spirit superintended so as to ensure that the final product was exactly what God wanted to communicate to his people (cf. 2 Pet. 1:21).

FORM CRITICISM OF THE SYNOPTIC GOSPELS: THE PERIOD OF ORAL TRADITION[9]

The Method

The rise of Gospel form criticism is associated primarily with three early twentieth-century German scholars: K. L. Schmidt, Martin Dibelius, and, above all, Rudolf Bultmann.[10] Analogous to work already being done in Old Testament studies, these scholars proposed three major stages to the analysis of the period of oral tradition behind the Gospels. First, they believed that the Gospels could be subdivided into discrete "pericopae" (passages) and analyzed according to the *form* of each (almost a "mini-genre"). Forms included parables, miracle stories, pronouncement stories (short controversial episodes climaxed by a key saying of Jesus), proverbs, wisdom sayings, "I-sayings," lengthier discourses, and so on.[11] Some of the labels also involved historical judgments: myths, legends, or utterances of early Christian prophets in the name of Jesus.

Second, form critics assigned each form to a *Sitz im Leben* ("situation in life") in the history of the early church. Pronouncement stories, it was believed, were widely used in popular preaching; miracle narratives, in apologetic interaction. Legends were supposedly created to glorify Jesus as a great hero. Parables were transmitted by popular storytellers, and so on.

---

9. Cf. further Craig L. Blomberg, "Form Criticism," in *DJG*, 243–50; Darrell L. Bock, "Form Criticism," in *New Testament Criticism and Interpretation*, ed. David A. Black and David S. Dockery (Grand Rapids: Zondervan, 1991), 173–96; and Stephen H. Travis, "Form Criticism," in *New Testament Interpretation*, ed. I. Howard Marshall (Exeter: Paternoster; Grand Rapids: Eerdmans, 1977), 153–64.

10. K. L. Schmidt, *Der Rahmen der Geschichte Jesu* (Darmstadt: Wissenschaftliche Buchgesellschaft, 1969 [orig. 1919]); Martin Dibelius, *From Tradition to Gospel* (Cambridge: James Clarke, 1934; New York: Scribner's Sons, 1965 [Germ. orig. 1919]); Bultmann, *History*.

11. The most complete English-language analysis appears in James L. Bailey and Lyle D. Vander Broek, *Literary Forms in the New Testament* (Louisville: Westminster/John Knox, 1992). The most comprehensive treatment of all is Klaus Berger, *Formgeschichte des Neuen Testaments* (Heidelberg: Quelle und Meyer, 1984).

Third, form criticism developed "laws" of the *transmission of tradition*. As bits and pieces of information about Jesus were passed along orally, it was claimed, stories tended to get longer, be embellished with additional unhistorical detail, be given explanatory clarifications and interpretations, have names supplied for previously unnamed characters, be given new contexts and new applications, and be grouped together with other individual teachings. It was the responsibility of the form critic, therefore, to try to strip away all these "secondary accretions" and find the historical kernel, if any, in each passage that represented what Jesus actually did or said.

Several assumptions fueled the form-critical agenda. First, critics assumed that no one wrote down anything Jesus said while he was alive, and that the early Christians relied at first entirely on oral tradition. Second, oral tradition was always viewed as composed of discrete units of material circulating independently of each other. Third, the material that was preserved must have proved useful for some specific purpose in the life of the early church. Fourth, little biographical, geographical, or chronological information about the events and teachings of Jesus' ministry was preserved; this all had to be "created" later. Fifth, analogies from the oral folklore of other countries—from as far away as Europe or Africa—were used to reconstruct how the early Christian oral tradition would have developed. Sixth, it is unlikely that more than a handful of authentic Jesus texts survived this process unscathed. After all, who today, playing the child's game of telephone, expects a whispered message transmitted around a room of thirty or more people to come out the same at the end? One can hardly imagine numerous Jesus traditions passed around for a generation throughout the ancient Middle East to fare any better. Or so the critics claimed.

Critique

Although form criticism developed primarily as a *historical* tool, one of its major strengths came as a by-product—its potential for *interpretation*. In this sense, form criticism does for individual passages what literary criticism does for entire books (see chap. 5). It recognizes that the Gospels are not monolithic wholes but are composed of sub-units of many different literary forms. Parables should not be interpreted in the same way as straightforward history; proverbs are not identical to absolute truths; and pronouncement stories focus all attention on their climactic (and controversial) pronouncements. In several places the Synoptic writers seem to have organized their Gospels by grouping together stories of like form. Therefore an understanding of the different forms can help us recover the evangelists' outlines and discover, for example, when *not* to assume that certain events are recorded in chronological order. In other words, the hermeneutical value of form criticism is enormous.[12]

As a historical tool, many tenets and assumptions of form criticism must be seriously questioned. There is nothing inherently improbable about each form being particularly useful for a given life-situation in the early church, but the

---

12. Cf. further William W. Klein, Craig L. Blomberg, and Robert L. Hubbard, Jr., *Introduction to Biblical Interpretation* (Dallas and London: Word, 1993), 336–44. We will comment briefly on the significance of the major forms as they appear in our study of the life of Christ, below, chaps. 11–17.

Form Criticism

Analysis of Form	**INTERPRETATION**
Sitz im Leben	**HISTORY**
Transmission of Tradition	

actual data available to recover these are virtually nonexistent. The so-called tendencies of the tradition—to embellish and become increasingly "distinct"—find some support in how later apocryphal traditions dealt with the canonical Gospels. But *within* the canon, as one proceeds from Mark to Matthew and Luke, more often than not there is a tendency to abbreviate and streamline.[13] Many of the other assumptions about the lack of historical interest or care with which the tradition preserved details about Jesus' life and teaching are also questionable. Analogies from other continents and the development of oral folklore over a period of centuries are not as relevant as studies of first-century Jewish oral culture and what likely developed over only a few decades. In fact, a good case can be made that the oral tradition of Jesus' words and deeds was extremely conservative and painstaking in preserving historical truth accurately. We may list seven pieces of evidence:

1. *Memorization* was highly cultivated in first-century Jewish culture. As we have seen above (p. 63), it was the predominant method of elementary education for boys. The disciples of the prophets had memorized and passed on their founders' words. Venerated rabbis had at times committed the entire Bible (our "Old Testament") to memory. It would have been quite normal and expected for Jesus' disciples, revering their teacher, to commit to memory significant portions of his teaching and even brief narratives of his great works, and to have remembered those accounts accurately for a considerable span of time. As much as 80 percent of Jesus' teaching seems to have been cast in poetic form, which would have made its memorization that much easier. In addition, the technical language of receiving and passing on traditions in 1 Corinthians 11:2, 23, and 15:3 suggests that Paul recognized that he was delivering to the Corinthians fixed pieces of information he had been given by those who preceded him in Christ. Still, none of this would have precluded the disciples from paraphrasing, interpreting, and rearranging the material they had learned; that, too, was the convention of the day.[14] To varying degrees, prodigious feats of memorization, but with the "gist" of an episode rather than verbatim accuracy as the goal, characterized all of classical antiquity.[15]

2. The continuing presence of *eyewitnesses* to the words and works of Christ, including hostile ones, throughout the entire period of the oral tradition, would have acted as a check to stories running wild or being created out of thin air. Also, within the Christian community there would have been limits placed on the way the Gospel traditions were narrated. Traditional Middle Eastern villagers even today exercise considerable flexibility in orally transmitting cherished traditions, but the entire community knows the boundaries that cannot be transgressed and will correct a storyteller if he or she crosses over them.[16] The center

---

13. See esp. Leslie R. Keylock, "Bultmann's Law of Increasing Distinctness," in *Current Issues in Biblical and Patristic Interpretation*, ed. Gerald F. Hawthorne (Grand Rapids: Eerdmans, 1975), 193–210. Overall in ancient Christianity, no consistent patterns predominate. Thus esp. E. P. Sanders, *The Tendencies of the Synoptic Tradition* (Cambridge: CUP, 1969).

14. Birger Gerhardsson, *Memory and Manuscript: Oral Tradition and Written Transmission in Rabbinic Judaism and Early Christianity* (Lund: Gleerup, 1961); Rainer Riesner, *Jesus als Lehrer* (Tübingen: Mohr, 1981); and Samuel Byrskog, *Jesus the Only Teacher* (Stockholm: Almqvist and Wiksell, 1994).

15. Jocelyn P. Small, "Artificial Memory and the Writing Habits of the Literate," *Helios* 22 (1995): 159–66.

16. Kenneth E. Bailey, "Informal Controlled Oral Tradition and the Synoptic Gospels," *AJT* 5 (1991): 34–54 (reprinted in *Themelios* 20 [1995]: 4–11). Cf. Albert B. Lord, "The Gospels as Oral Traditional Literature," in *The Relationships among the Gospels*, ed. William O. Walker, Jr. (San Antonio: Trinity University Press, 1978), 33–91.

of apostolic leadership in Jerusalem with its various delegations and councils probably functioned in somewhat similar fashion (cf. Acts 8, 10–11, 15).

3. Although sacred traditions were handed down primarily by word of mouth, rabbis and their followers often took *private notes* of important material, which they consulted from time to time to refresh their memories. It would be unusual if Jesus' followers did not do the same.[17] One may also point to the prevalence of wax notebook tablets (cf. Luke 1:63) and to the concern among the Essenes at Qumran to record in writing their Scriptural interpretations (unlike the Pharisees who kept written and oral Law more distinct). As a similar breakaway movement from more orthodox Judaism, Christianity probably had more in common with the Essenes than the Pharisees at this point.[18]

4. There was a *Sitz im Leben* already during the ministry of Jesus for his followers to have formulated *succinct summaries of his words and works*—the missions of the Twelve and the seventy—so that the first attempts to formulate the material that would later form part of the Gospels probably took place within months or weeks of the very events described.

5. Despite all the flexibility in narration and apparent "contradictions" among the Gospels, these documents do not naturally read as though they included information created for the first time after Jesus' death and resurrection. If the early church felt free to "play fast and loose" with the Gospel tradition, why do there remain so many problem passages, the so-called *hard sayings* of Jesus? Why do we read that Jesus claimed not to know the time of his return (Mark 13:32 pars.)? Or what of the three passages that have misled some into thinking that he did claim to know—and predicted his return within the lifetime of his followers (Mark 9:1 pars.; Mark 13:30 pars.; Matt. 10:23)? Conversely, if later Christian prophets spoke in the name of the risen Lord and had their teachings attributed to the earthly Jesus, why do we find *no* sayings of Christ in the Gospels to clear up major early church controversies—the dispute between Jews and Gentiles over whether or not to keep the Law, the role of circumcision in the Christian life, or a proper approach to speaking in tongues?[19] 1 Corinthians 7:10 and 12 testify to Paul's care not to create a word from the historical Jesus to solve sticky matters about divorce when he didn't have one.

6. Why, on the other hand, do we find *major emphases in the Gospels that are not stressed by the later church*? Perhaps the most striking of these is Jesus' characteristic reference to himself as "Son of Man." Our final chapter discusses the meaning of this title, but a point to be made here is that, except from one reference apiece in Acts and Revelation, this title never recurs throughout the rest of the New Testament even though it was Jesus' favorite. If distinctions between the pre-Easter and post-Easter Jesus were blurred, this omission would be inexplicable.[20]

---

17. Cf. E. Earle Ellis, "New Directions in Form Criticism," in *Jesus Christus in Historie und Theologie*, ed. Georg Strecker (Tübingen: Mohr, 1975), 299–315.

18. Alan R. Millard, "Writing and the Gospels," *Qumran Chronicle* 5 (1995): 55–62.

19. Against the view, more generally, that early Christian prophets created sayings of Jesus *de novo*, see David Hill, *New Testament Prophecy* (London: Marshall, Morgan & Scott; Richmond: John Knox, 1979); and David Aune, *Prophecy in Early Christianity and the Ancient Mediterranean World* (Grand Rapids: Eerdmans, 1983). For a more recent defense of that view, cf. M. Eugene Boring, *The Continuing Voice of Jesus: Christian Prophecy and the Gospel Tradition* (Louisville: Westminster/John Knox, 1991).

20. For a more detailed list of similar contrasts, see Eugene E. Lemcio, *The Past of Jesus in the Gospels* (Cambridge: CUP, 1991).

7. It has sometimes been said that even if Jesus did not explicitly predict his return within one generation, his first followers were clearly looking for it (cf., e.g., 1 and 2 Thess.). What is more, people who think the world will soon end are not interested in writing literature, much less history. But the *massive production of literature at Qumran*, including the retelling of Old Testament history, despite the Essenes' belief that they were living very near to the end, belies this skepticism.

Nevertheless, despite all these criticisms, the dominant presupposition of form criticism—that of an initial period of oral tradition for the Gospel material—is well founded. Mark and Luke in particular, as noneyewitnesses of the events they narrated, would have depended on it extensively. When we come to dating the Gospels, we will see that this period may have lasted only twenty to forty years rather than the forty to sixty years some posit (see chaps. 6–9), but any illumination on this first phase of Christian origins is to be welcomed. But then we must pass to the next phase—that of the first extensive written accounts of Jesus' life.

SOURCE CRITICISM OF THE SYNOPTIC GOSPELS: THE SYNOPTIC PROBLEM[21]

From time to time in the history of the church, various people have suggested that there is no literary relationship among the Synoptic Gospels.[22] They argue that the similarities can be explained because the Gospels describe the same events and because God inspired them. The vast majority of careful students of the Gospels reject these conclusions, however. In addition to Luke's testimony (cited above, pp. 80–81), four other features are not adequately accounted for by this approach. First, the parallelism between two Gospels is often *verbatim* for entire clauses or sentences, and even more commonly, identical except for an occasional substitution of a different word from the same root, a synonym, or a slight change in word order. Although statistics vary from textbook to textbook based on how exact the wording of two verses in two different Gospels must be for them to be labeled "parallel," a rough estimate of the amount of parallelism is as follows: Of the 661 verses in Mark, 500 recur in Matthew in parallel form and 350 recur in Luke. In addition, there are another 235 verses common to Matthew and Luke that are not found in Mark.[23] This parallelism occurs not only with Jesus' teachings, where one might argue that the early church simply memorized them, but also with the narrative descriptions of what Christ did. Given the diversity of ways that two different authors can describe the same episode, such verbal parallelism virtually

---

21. Cf. further Robert H. Stein, *The Synoptic Problem: An Introduction* (Grand Rapids: Baker, 1987), 29–157; and Donald Guthrie, *New Testament Introduction* (Leicester and Downers Grove: IVP, rev. 1990), 136–208.

22. The most recent (and virulent) example is Eta Linnemann, *Is There a Synoptic Problem?* (Grand Rapids: Baker, 1992). Linnemann stresses the differences among the Gospels, arguing that the exact amounts of verbal parallelism have been overestimated. Be that as it may, it is the similarities that remain (which she herself acknowledges) that have to be explained. Even a relatively few instances of identical wording betray some cross-fertilization of written sources, particularly when Luke himself expresses reliance on them (Luke 1:1–4).

23. These statistics are taken from H. Wayne House, *Chronological and Background Charts of the New Testament* (Grand Rapids: Zondervan, 1984), chart 9.

requires that one copied from the other or that both copied from a common source. A professor encountering a similar phenomenon on two students' term papers, even occasionally, would certainly agree!

Second, even with Jesus' sayings, it is noteworthy that this verbal parallelism occurs *in Greek*, that is, in translation of the Aramaic that Jesus originally spoke. Anyone who has studied a foreign language knows that there are often numerous ways to translate a given sentence or paragraph from one language to another. Repeated examples of identical translations suggest literary dependence of some kind, unless one posits the unlikely hypothesis that the first *Jewish* Christians circulated accounts of Jesus' teaching in fixed form in *Greek* translation.

Third, the agreement among the Synoptics extends to *parenthetical comments* or explanatory asides added by a particular author. For example, both Mark 13:14 and Matthew 24:15 insert the remark, "let the reader understand," in the middle of their accounts of Jesus predicting the setting up of the "desolating sacrifice" in the temple. Both Mark 2:10 and Matthew 9:6 break off Jesus' words to the onlookers on the occasion of his healing the paralytic at exactly the same place: "But (so) that you may know that the Son of Man has authority on earth to forgive sins. . . . " Both then go on to write, "(Then) he said to the paralytic," and continue with Jesus' words. These would be extraordinary coincidences if Matthew and Mark had no knowledge of each other or some common written document.

Fourth, the parallelism also involves the *order of episodes* that are not linked together chronologically. For example, Mark 2:1–3:6 combines a series of five controversy stories between Jesus and the Jewish leaders without ever indicating the sequence in which they took place. Yet Matthew and Luke both preserve this exact sequence of episodes, although Matthew does insert intervening material (see Luke 5:17–6:11; Matt. 9:1–17; 12:1–14). Or, on a smaller scale, Mark "sandwiches" the story of Peter's denial around his account of Jesus before the Sanhedrin (Mark 14:53–54, 55–65, 66–72). But Matthew employs the identical stylistic device (Matt. 26:57–58, 59–68, 69–75), an unlikely coincidence, particularly given the fact that Luke more conventionally rearranges the material into two discrete stories (Luke 22:54–62, 63–71).

If the overwhelming probability, then, is that the Synoptics are related at a literary level, what is the nature of that relationship? We will consider the most common and most probable answer to that question in three stages, in decreasing order of certainty: Markan priority, the Q-hypothesis, and additional sources distinct to Matthew and Luke.

Markan Priority

Strengths. Numerous arguments of varying weights have cumulatively suggested to a majority of modern scholars that Mark was the first Gospel to be written and that Matthew and Luke both drew heavily on his work:

1. At many points Mark's details are the most vivid, while Matthew and Luke omit what seem to be the touches of an eyewitness report: for example, "after sunset" in Mark 1:32 (cf. Matt. 8:16), the "green" grass in Mark 6:39 (cf. Matt.

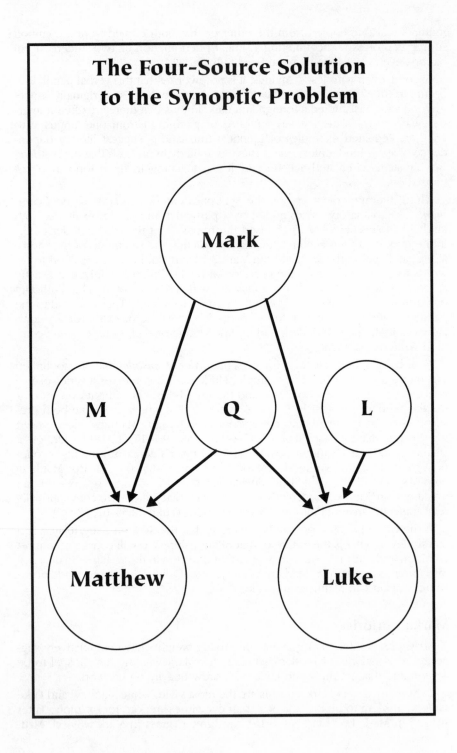

The Four-Source Solution
to the Synoptic Problem

14:19; Luke 9:14), or the "three hundred denarii" of Mark 14:5 (NKJV) (cf. Matt. 26:9).[24]

2. Mark's grammar and style is often the roughest, whereas Matthew and Luke make it more smooth. Mark has a fondness for asyndeton (leaving out conjunctions), parataxis (using merely "and" when he does connect clauses), the historical present tense, redundancies, double negatives, and convoluted order of clauses.

3. Mark narrates potentially embarrassing or misleading details that the other evangelists omit or reword: for example, the apparent "error" (on which see below, p. 238, n. 15) in referring to Abiathar as high priest in 2:26 (cf. Matt. 12:4; Luke 6:4); the statement that Jesus "could" work few miracles in Nazareth in 6:5 (cf. Matt. 13:58; Luke 4:24); and Jesus' reply to the rich young ruler in 10:18: "Why do you call me good? No one is good—except God alone" (cf. Matt. 19:17).

4. Mark's is the shortest of the Gospels, yet within the passages he narrates, his is typically the fullest form. Of 92 passages that Mark and Luke have in common, Mark is longer 71 times. Of 104 he shares with Matthew, he is longer in 63. It makes sense for Matthew and Luke to have abbreviated Mark's characteristically detailed accounts to make room for other information about Jesus they wanted to add; both Gospels occupy about the maximum length of material that could conveniently fit on an ancient scroll. But if Mark were abridging Matthew and Luke, as Griesbach claimed, it would make little sense for him to lengthen those accounts that he did choose to include.

5. There is very little in Mark not reproduced in Matthew and Luke (less than 10 percent of his Gospel overall). Unless Mark were the first to write, why would he bother, with so little new or distinctive to say?

6. Matthew and Luke only rarely deviate from Mark in sequence of passages or nature of wording in the same way at the same time, whereas Matthew and Mark frequently agree against Luke, and Luke and Mark frequently agree against Matthew. What this demonstrates is that Mark must be the "middle term" of the three, that is, he was either the first on which the other two drew, the last (abridging the first two, as with Griesbach), or the Gospel that drew on either Matthew or Luke and was in turn drawn on by the other one (as with Augustine's sequence of Matthew-Mark-Luke). "With the Augustinian hypothesis, we would have to think that Luke almost always chose to use Mark's wording rather than Matthew's; with the two-gospel hypothesis [Griesbach], we would have to assume that Mark almost never introduced any wording of his own. While possible, both procedures are unlikely."[25]

7. Mark contains the highest incidence of Aramaic words preserved in Greek transliteration: for example, *Boanerges* (3:17), *talitha koum* (5:41), *Corban* (7:11), *ephphatha* (7:34), and *Abba* (14:36).[26]

---

24. These examples are taken from Guthrie, *Introduction*, 151.

25. D. A. Carson, Douglas J. Moo, and Leon Morris, *An Introduction to the New Testament* (Grand Rapids: Zondervan, 1992), 33. The other logical possibility of Luke-Mark-Matthew has been defended by the "Jerusalem school" (see above, p. 9, n. 7) led by Robert Lindsey and David Flusser, but it is based on the unlikely view that the one Gospel written by a Gentile, explicitly after other narratives had been compiled, is actually the most Hebraic. These scholars have claimed that Luke translates back into Hebrew more easily than Matthew or Mark, but few others who have replicated the experiment agree with them (except perhaps for chaps. 1–2, on which see below, p. 202).

26. These examples come from Stein, *Synoptic Problem*, 55–57.

8. There seems to be no other explanation for why Mark would have omitted all of the material common to Matthew and Luke if he had known about it, since this includes much of Jesus' most beloved teaching (the Sermon on the Mount, numerous parables, instructions for establishing the church, etc.).

9. When one assumes that Matthew and Luke each redacted Mark, consistent patterns of theological emphasis emerge; on other theories, the patterns of editorial activity prove far less consistent.[27]

Weaknesses. The most important arguments against Markan priority are:

1. Certain minor agreements of Matthew and Luke against Mark do exist. But these may be attributed to overlap between Mark and "Q" (see below), to natural changes in style or detail that writers might be expected to make independently of each other, or to reliance on other oral traditions.

2. A large chunk of Mark is missing from Luke (Mark 6:45–8:26), often called Luke's "Great Omission." But Luke probably had geographical reasons for leaving this out (see below, p. 142).

3. The changes in the Gospel tradition are not as drastic if Mark wrote last rather than first. This may be true, but one dare not favor a view just because it is apologetically convenient. Our response to form criticism has demonstrated that there are plenty of other reasons for supporting the general trustworthiness of the Gospel tradition.

4. Markan priority is a hypothesis that was created primarily by modern, liberal scholars eager to find a miracle-free Jesus. This may well be true, but they did not succeed. Mark still has plenty of miracles, and the primary reasons for adopting Markan priority are independent of whatever motives may have prompted the exercise in the first place.

5. Strong patristic testimony supports Matthean priority. This is the one weighty objection to seeing Mark as having written first. Indeed, this external evidence fits certain internal evidence: Matthew's parallels to Mark do not as consistently seem to be later, editorial revisions as do Luke's. We will suggest in our introduction to Matthew that there is a way to harmonize this evidence with the arguments for Markan priority, and that Matthew may have composed his Gospel in stages, partly before reading Mark and partly afterwards.

The Q-Hypothesis

In the early 1800s, Friedrich Schleiermacher first created the symbol Q (from the German *Quelle*, meaning "source") to designate a hypothetical document on which Matthew and Luke drew. This would account for the material not found in Mark that they shared—almost exclusively sayings of Jesus. Although scholars have not accepted this hypothesis quite as strongly as they have Markan priority, it still finds a fair consensus of support.

Strengths. Why not simply assume that Luke used Matthew or vice versa? The most important reasons include:

1. Although sufficient verbal parallelism occurs in places to suggest a literary relationship, the parallels are not as consistently close to each other as in the

---

27. For proof, one has but to read those who have tried. Most notably, in defense of the Augustinian model, see Michael D. Goulder, *Luke: A New Paradigm*, 2 vols. (Sheffield: JSOT, 1989); following Griesbach, see C. S. Mann, *Mark* (Garden City: Doubleday, 1986).

"triple tradition" (material found in all three Synoptics). This would be accounted for if both Matthew and Luke drew on a common source and redacted it independently of each other.

2. Sometimes Matthew seems to preserve the most literal account of Jesus' words; other times Luke does. Often, too, Matthew's style is more Semitic (most notably, in preserving Hebrew parallelism), whereas Luke's order seems more original. Who, for example, would have actually taken Matthew's long sermons (like the Sermon on the Mount) and scattered parallels to it throughout his Gospel the way Luke would have had to if he were directly dependent on Matthew?[28]

3. The oldest testimony about the formation of Matthew, from the early second-century Christian writer Papias, as quoted by Eusebius in the early 300s (*Ecclesiastical History* 3.39.16), says that "Matthew collected the oracles [of Jesus] in the Hebrew language [or "dialect"] and everyone translated [or "interpreted"] them as best he could." The Greek word for "oracles" (*logia*) most naturally means "sayings," not a full-fledged narrative Gospel. So perhaps Matthew himself was the author of something like "Q" before he (or a translator?) turned it into Greek.[29]

4. There is a general theological and stylistic homogeneity to a reconstructed Q. Recurring themes include teaching about wisdom, the more radical demands of itinerant ministry for the kingdom, the power and authority of Jesus, and a lively hope for the end of the age to come soon. Form critics have even given Q a plausible *Sitz im Leben*—the wandering preachers who continued the tradition of Matthew 10 and Luke 9–10 (the sending of the Twelve and seventy) throughout Galilee after Jesus' death.[30]

Weaknesses. Above all, Q has never been discovered; it is a purely hypothetical document. Still, the genre of a collection of Jesus' sayings is known to have existed, at least in heterodox circles, with the Gospel of Thomas. Too, in many instances the parallels are not close enough to prove a written source; perhaps a common oral tradition was all that Matthew and Luke had. There is also little agreement on the exact delineation of Q's contents, its order, or its purpose. Some scholars prefer, therefore, to speak of a combination of shorter written and/or oral sources rather than one definite document.[31]

---

28. For a table of the Q material, thematically arranged, see Guthrie, *Introduction*, 167–68.

29. This was the view Schleiermacher proposed. Although not widely held in recent times, defenders can still be found, most notably Matthew Black, "The Use of Rhetorical Terminology in Papias on Mark and Matthew," *JSNT* 37 (1989): 31–41.

30. See, e.g., John S. Kloppenborg, *The Formation of Q* (Philadelphia: Fortress, 1987); and Leif E. Vaage, *Galilean Upstarts: Jesus' First Followers according to Q* (Valley Forge: TPI, 1994). For a balanced treatment of the possible contents and theology of Q, see David R. Catchpole, *The Quest for Q* (Edinburgh: T. & T. Clark, 1993). It is irresponsible, however, to write as if Q were an actual document with precisely identifiable contents, as, e.g., in Burton L. Mack, *The Lost Gospel: The Book of Q and Christian Origins* (San Francisco: HarperCollins, 1993). Particularly important in showing the compatibility of Q with Mark (and with Jesus himself) is Edward P. Meadors, *Jesus the Messianic Herald of Salvation* (Tübingen: Mohr, 1995).

31. It is also important to stress that scholarly study of Q has nothing to do with popular writers of fiction who from time to time co-opt the same symbol to refer to imaginary, newly discovered documents that allegedly discredit Christianity, as, e.g., in Irving Wallace's celebrated novel (and film), *The Word* (New York: Simon & Schuster; London: Cassell, 1972).

M, L, and Proto-Luke

The most prominent twentieth-century proponent of Markan priority and the Q-hypothesis was B. H. Streeter, an Englishman writing in the 1920s.[32] Streeter, however, went beyond the widely accepted "two-source hypothesis" to champion what came to be called the "four-source hypothesis." Streeter believed that, in addition to using Mark and Q, Matthew and Luke each had written sources of their own on which they drew; Streeter labeled these two additional sources "M" and "L" respectively. These supposed sources could account for much of the material unique to each of these two Gospels (333 verses in Matthew; 564 in Luke). Streeter also speculated that Luke wrote a first draft of his Gospel before seeing a copy of Mark ("proto-Luke") and then revised and expanded it considerably after reading Mark. This would account for the alternation of Markan and non-Markan material in Luke in large blocks (see below, p. 140) and for the larger percentage of non-Markan, non-Q material in Luke than in Matthew. But this is the most tenuous of Streeter's proposals and does not currently command consensus acclaim.

As for M and L, some scholars have claimed to see a theological homogeneity in this material,[33] but often it corresponds merely to the redactional interests of Matthew and Luke. What is more, if Matthew was written by the apostle of that name, the material unique to his Gospel could simply reflect his personal reminiscences.[34] A plausible case can be made for Luke having relied on a Semitic source for chapters 1–2: this information about the conceptions and births of John and Jesus is written in a very Hebraic style quite different from the rest of his Gospel.[35] It is also possible that a parables source accounts for the large percentage of parables unique to Luke clustered in the central section of his Gospel (see below, p. 289).[36] But beyond this, "M" and "L" remain highly speculative. The heavy reliance of ancient historians on multiple sources leads us to assume that a comprehensive solution to the Synoptic problem may be quite complex and irrecoverable.

To the beginning student, all this discussion of Gospel source criticism often seems irrelevant, but it is actually crucial in several respects. For those interested in the question of the historical reliability of these documents, it is important to understand as best as possible how they were formed. For example, if Q existed, it would probably be dated to the 40s or 50s. This puts us within ten to twenty years of the crucifixion and considerably shortens the period in which the Gospel traditions circulated exclusively by word of mouth. For those interested in the theological distinctives of the different evangelists, it is equally crucial to know who wrote first and who edited which document. Then one can separate tradition from redaction and have a better grasp of the unique

---

32. See his classic work, *The Four Gospels: A Study of Origins* (London: Macmillan, 1924).

33. E.g., Stephenson H. Brooks, *Matthew's Community: The Evidence of His Special Sayings Material* (Sheffield: JSOT, 1987); Gerd Petzke, *Das Sondergut des Evangeliums nach Lukas* (Zürich: Theologischer Verlag, 1990).

34. Nevertheless, evidence from the Church Fathers, esp. Ignatius, suggests that there may have been an "M," since a disproportionately large percentage of their quotations of Matthew come from the unparalleled portions of Matthew's Gospel.

35. See esp. Stephen C. Farris, *The Hymns of Luke's Infancy Narratives* (Sheffield: JSOT, 1985).

36. Craig L. Blomberg, "Midrash, Chiasmus, and the Outline of Luke's Central Section," in *Gospel Perspectives*, vol. 3, ed. R. T. France and David Wenham (Sheffield: JSOT, 1983), 217–61.

emphases of each writer. That brings us naturally to phase three of the developing Gospel tradition: redaction criticism.

REDACTION CRITICISM:
THE EDITORIAL CONTRIBUTIONS OF THE SYNOPTIC EVANGELISTS[37]

Again a trio of Germans is responsible for vaulting this discipline into prominence: Günther Bornkamm on Matthew, Willi Marxsen on Mark, and Hans Conzelmann on Luke.[38] A good working definition of the method they pioneered explains that redaction criticism "seeks to lay bare the theological perspectives of a Biblical writer by analyzing the editorial (redactional) and compositional techniques and interpretations employed by him in shaping and framing the written and/or oral traditions at hand."[39] One may subdivide redaction criticism into two complementary tasks: *reading horizontally* and *reading vertically*.[40] Reading horizontally involves looking *across* a gospel synopsis to compare the differences among parallels and to determine how later writers altered their sources. Reading vertically refers to looking *down* the given column of a synopsis (and hence throughout the larger context of a specific Gospel) to see what themes and other editorial distinctives repeatedly recur and whether or not they are paralleled in the other Gospels. It also involves looking for editorial seams, summaries, introductions and conclusions, and the outline or arrangement of material. All told, one can get a good feel for a given writer's emphases through these procedures.

As with form criticism, redaction criticism has often been used by more radical critics to deprecate the historical reliability of the Gospels. Some falsely assume that what is told for theological purposes is less likely to be historical than is a mere recitation of facts. Indeed, often the opposite is the case, as people passionately committed to a cause want the facts to be known. Post-holocaust Jews insisted the story of the atrocities in Nazi Germany be told and retold so that such horrors might never recur. They had a much greater vested interest in the truth than those "revisionist" historians who argued that the holocaust had been vastly exaggerated. Redaction critics also often allege that what the Gospel writers added to their sources cannot be historical, ruling out the possibility of additional written or oral sources beyond Mark and Q, or in Matthew's case, personal memory. Others exaggerate the extent to which minor stylistic variations reflect theological motives. Some use a fairly atomistic form of analysis, counting word frequencies to determine characteristic vocabulary and confidently pronouncing on the traditional or redactional origin of almost

---

37. For conservative introductions, see D. A. Carson, "Redaction Criticism: On the Legitimacy and Illegitimacy of a Literary Tool," in *Scripture and Truth*, ed. D. A. Carson and John D. Woodbridge (Grand Rapids: Zondervan; Leicester: IVP, 1983), 119–42; Grant R. Osborne, "Redaction Criticism," in *DJG*, 662–69; for much more liberal introductions, cf. Norman Perrin, *What Is Redaction Criticism?* (Philadelphia: Fortress, 1969); and Joachim Rohde, *Rediscovering the Teaching of the Evangelists* (London: SCM; Philadelphia: Westminster, 1968).

38. Günther Bornkamm, Gerhard Barth, and Heinz J. Held, *Tradition and Interpretation in Matthew* (London: SCM; Philadelphia: Westminster, 1963); Willi Marxsen, *Mark the Evangelist* (Nashville: Abingdon, 1969); Hans Conzelmann, *The Theology of St. Luke* (New York: Harper & Row; London: Faber & Faber, 1960).

39. Richard N. Soulen, *Handbook of Biblical Criticism* (Guildford: Lutterworth; Atlanta: John Knox, rev. 1981), 165.

40. Cf. Gordon D. Fee and Douglas Stuart, *How to Read the Bible for All Its Worth* (Grand Rapids: Zondervan, rev. 1994), 121–26.

Two Kinds of Redaction Criticism

	Reading	Vertically
John	Reading	Vertically
Luke	Reading	Vertically
Mark	Reading	Vertically
Matthew	Reading	Vertically

READING HORIZONTALLY

every word or phrase in a passage. This in fact goes far beyond anything we can know for sure. And with all the attention to diversity, one can lose sight of the substantial amount of agreement among the three Synoptics.

The value of redaction criticism, stripped of these methodological impropri- eties and excesses, however, remains great, perhaps even more than that of source or form criticism. As an interpretive tool, it is equivalent to asking the question of each passage in the Gospels: "Why did the Gospel writer choose to include this in precisely the way he did?" Readers of the Gospels from the beginning of church history have recognized that the different writers had dif- ferent theological emphases. But the church's preoccupation with constructing harmonies of the life of Christ generally blurred these distinctions. Ironically, it is often those more conservative Christians who insist most strongly on the inspiration and inerrancy of the very texts the evangelists penned who pay least attention to the form in which those texts were inspired, opting instead to study an artificial, man-made synthesis of the four.

Surely there is a legitimate place for such harmonies and, indeed, our survey of the life of Christ below will make cautious use of them.[41] But we dare not lose sight of the fact that God inspired four Gospels, not one, and presumably for a reason! Every preacher choosing a text from the Gospels should therefore want to stress what the original author intended. For example, if one deter- mines to preach on the feeding of the five thousand (a passage occurring in all four Gospels), the sermon should sound slightly different depending on which account one follows. The preacher must research that author's emphases and make the sermon correspond accordingly. Sadly, this is not often done. In our introductions to each of the four Gospels, however, we shall highlight a variety of these distinctives and point out others at the conclusions of most major sec- tions of our survey of the life of Christ.

CANON CRITICISM AND THE FORMATION OF THE CANON

Canon Criticism

The work of two American scholars, Brevard Childs and James Sanders, in the 1970s through the 1990s, bequeathed yet one more brand of criticism to our array of scholarly methods.[42] Disenchanted with the increasing sterility of source, form, and redaction criticisms—especially in the hands of their more radical practitioners—Childs in particular argued in a series of impressive and lengthy works that more attention should be paid to the final or canonical form of the text. At times, this closely overlaps redaction criticism and simply attempts to recover the intention of the evangelists in "packaging" their Gos- pels as they did. In other cases, however, canon criticism takes seriously the

---

41. Indeed, harmonization and redaction criticism can actually work hand in hand: the former demonstrating that passages are not contradictory; the latter explaining why they *do* differ in the ways they do. See Craig L. Blomberg, "The Legitimacy and Limits of Harmonization," in *Hermeneutics, Authority, and Canon*, ed. D. A. Carson and John D. Woodbridge (Grand Rapids: Zondervan, 1986), 135–74.

42. Most directly relevant to a study of the Gospels is Brevard S. Childs, *The New Testament as Canon* (London: SCM, 1984; Phil- adelphia: Fortress, 1985), 57–209. More generally, cf. James A. Sanders, *From Sacred Story to Sacred Text* (Philadelphia: Fortress, 1987).

intentions of the early Christian communities in the fourth and fifth centuries as agreement was finalized on exactly which books belonged in the New Testament and in which order.

Thus, for example, canon criticism looks beyond the diversity on which redaction criticism focuses to highlight the unity of themes between, say, Matthew's and Luke's infancy narratives (chaps. 1–2 of each Gospel). Presumably, each original audience had, at first, only its one Gospel, so that highlighting this unity goes beyond what can be ascribed to the evangelists' intentions. Again, canon criticism may focus on a passage like the Sermon on the Mount and observe its long history of interpretation in light of Paul's later teaching about the inability to keep the Law. Although Jesus did not demonstrably mean for the Sermon to be taken this way, canon criticism grants a certain legitimacy to using later texts to interpret earlier ones, a kind of "halfway house" on the road to full-fledged systematic theology. In still other cases, canon criticism focuses on the significance of the order of the books in the Bible (John's interrupting the original unity of Luke-Acts because it, too, is a Gospel) or on the way different books' contributions to different themes balance each other out (Matthew and James on the need for works of righteousness vs. Luke and Paul on salvation by grace). In the case of Sanders, canonical criticism focuses much more on the "intertextual" echoes between Old and New Testaments.

There is much in all this to be applauded. Any focus on the final form of a text in its integrity is to be welcomed. But at the points where the results of canon criticism stand opposed to what would be derived from analyzing one biblical book by itself in its original, historical setting, we must demur. If the locus of the inspiration or authority of Scripture is in what the first-century biblical writers themselves penned rather than in the fourth- or fifth-century Christian communities that completed the canonizing process, then we must choose the meaning implied by the former over that attributed to the texts by the latter. Given this caveat, it is not clear that canon criticism offers anything very distinctive from certain forms of redaction or literary criticism. Scholarship as a whole seems to agree—the method has not widely caught on outside a handful of committed followers,[43] and it may not long outlive its vigorous advocacy by Childs and Sanders.

The Formation of the Canon

Although the topic of the development of the New Testament canon goes far beyond an introduction to the Gospels, it is one of those issues that often falls through the cracks in a curriculum and gets overlooked altogether. Other works will have to be consulted for details,[44] but a few introductory remarks germane to Matthew, Mark, Luke, and John seem in order here. Already by the mid–second century there was wide agreement that there were four and only four narratives that accurately portrayed the life of Jesus. All the existing lists

---

43. In evangelical circles, see esp. the various works of Robert W. Wall and Eugene E. Lemcio, several of which are collected in their anthology entitled *The New Testament as Canon: A Reader in Canonical Criticism* (Sheffield: JSOT, 1992).

44. See esp. David G. Dunbar, "The Biblical Canon," in *Hermeneutics, Authority, and Canon*, 315–42; F. F. Bruce, *The Canon of Scripture* (Leicester and Downers Grove: IVP, 1988); and Bruce M. Metzger, *The Canon of the New Testament: Its Origin, Development, and Significance* (Oxford: Clarendon, 1987).

for the next three hundred years, until the various councils that finalized the New Testament canon once and for all, agreed that Matthew, Mark, Luke, and John were the Gospels to be included, even though they occasionally disputed some of the epistles or the Apocalypse. To be sure, the Gnostic sects had their additional texts (see above, pp. 35–36), but we are not sure just how authoritatively they functioned even for those communities. No existing record ever suggests that any apocryphal Gospel was put forward for inclusion alongside the other four in any multivolume collection of "Scripture."

The criteria used for including Matthew, Mark, Luke, and John, to the extent that we can recover them, are the same as for the rest of the New Testament: *apostolicity* (authorship by an apostle or a close associate of an apostle during the first century), *orthodoxy* (not contradicting the apostolic testimony that was handed down from earliest times), and *relevance* (widely used throughout the early church rather than being limited to one or a few small groups). The canonical sequence—Matthew, Mark, Luke, John—was no doubt developed partly because of the belief that they were written in that order. But at least as important in putting Matthew first were the links between his work and the Old Testament: the most Jewish of the Gospels, containing the most quotations of the Old Testament and the greatest comparisons and contrasts with it. The early church did not create a new canon of only Christian books when it formed a "New Testament." Rather, by using that label, it affirmed its belief that the authority of these books equaled that of the Hebrew Bible, now to be interpreted in light of its fulfillment in Jesus Christ.

FOR FURTHER STUDY

Because this chapter has surveyed several different disciplines, key bibliography for each individual discipline has already appeared in the footnotes. Here we will simply list several key works that treat most or all of the critical methods surveyed here. Several treat the literary methods discussed in chapter 5 as well. A distinctive of the volume by Green is that all writers illustrate the methods they discuss with reference to the same texts: Luke 3:1–20; John 4:1–42; 1 Corinthians 11:2–34; James 4:13–5:6; and Revelation 5.

Introductory

Black, David A., and David S. Dockery, eds. *New Testament Criticism and Interpretation*. Grand Rapids: Zondervan, 1991.

Blomberg, Craig. *The Historical Reliability of the Gospels*. Leicester and Downers Grove: IVP, 1987.

Dockery, David S., Kenneth A. Mathews, and Robert B. Sloan, eds. *Foundations for Biblical Interpretation*. Nashville: Broadman & Holman, 1994.

McKnight, Scot. *Interpreting the Synoptic Gospels*. Grand Rapids: Baker, 1988.

Intermediate

Green, Joel B., ed. *Hearing the New Testament: Strategies for Interpretation*. Grand Rapids: Eerdmans; Carlisle: Paternoster, 1995.

Guthrie, Donald. *New Testament Introduction.* Leicester and Downers Grove: IVP, rev. 1990.

Marshall, I. Howard, ed. *New Testament Interpretation.* Exeter: Paternoster; Grand Rapids: Eerdmans, 1977.

Porter, Stanley E., and David Tombs, eds. *Approaches to New Testament Study.* Sheffield: Sheffield Academic Press, 1995.

Sanders, E. P., and Margaret Davies. *Studying the Synoptic Gospels.* London: SCM; Philadelphia: TPI, 1989.

Stein, Robert H. *The Synoptic Problem: An Introduction.* Grand Rapids: Baker, 1987. (Also includes discussion of form and redaction criticism.)

Advanced

Bultmann, Rudolf. *The History of the Synoptic Tradition.* Oxford: Blackwell; New York: Harper & Row, 1963 [Germ. orig. 1921].

France, R. T., and David Wenham, eds. *Gospel Perspectives.* Vols. 1–3. Sheffield: JSOT, 1980–1983.

Gerhardsson, Birger. *Memory and Manuscript.* Lund: Gleerup, 1961.

Taylor, Vincent. *The Formation of the Gospel Tradition.* London: Macmillan, 1933.

QUESTIONS FOR REVIEW

1. What are source, form, and redaction criticism? How does each method work? From an evangelical perspective, what are the strengths and weaknesses of each?

2. Specifically with regard to form criticism, what evidence must temper various theories of unbridled creativity among those who first handed down traditions about Jesus?

3. Why is Markan priority the most common solution to the Synoptic problem? Which arguments in its favor seem strongest? Which arguments against it seem strongest? What are the Q, M, and L hypotheses? What are their relative merits?

4. Why is it important to understand the literary interrelationship of the Gospels? Why is it necessary to postulate such a relationship at all?

CHAPTER FIVE

LITERARY CRITICISM
OF THE GOSPELS

The term "literary criticism" has been used to refer to just about any kind of analysis of a work of literature. Earlier in this century it was sometimes used synonymously with source criticism. As we discussed in the previous chapter, from the late-1970s on, a number of scholars began calling for a paradigm shift in biblical studies away from detailed focus on the historical circumstances of an author and the historical processes involved in creating a text. Instead, the kind of literary criticism put forward as the primary model was an analysis of the text, as written, without reference to any information gleaned outside of the text concerning its formation or purposes. This shift was often linked to a shift in the hermeneutics of literature more generally, away from the conviction that meaning was determined by an author's intent. An intention, after all, is a mental process largely irrecoverable, especially when one is dealing with the texts of ancient authors from foreign cultures. Rather, meaning was said to reside in the texts themselves. Whatever an author may have desired, the only thing a reader could be expected to comprehend was the sense of the words that were actually written.

The more scholars focused on the process of understanding by the reader, the more a second phase in modern literary criticism emerged: reader-oriented theories of meaning. It became commonplace to argue that meaning did not reside in either authorial intention or texts themselves but in readers. At a more conservative end of this spectrum, meaning was said to emerge from the

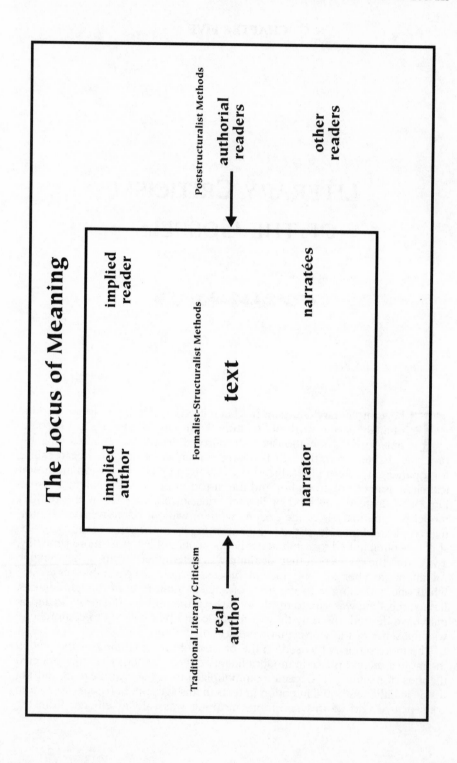

The Locus of Meaning

Traditional Literary Criticism

real author

implied author

implied reader

Formalist-Structuralist Methods

text

narrator

narratées

Poststructuralist Methods

authorial readers

other readers

product of the interaction between text and reader. The text, as well as the "interpretive communities" to which readers belonged, put definite constraints on interpretation. At a more radical end of the spectrum, meaning was believed to be almost entirely "in the eye of the beholder." Cleverness and consistency in interpretation overshadowed truth or correspondence to any external world of realities.

We will briefly survey two phases of modern literary criticism—*formalism-structuralism* and *poststructuralism*—and sample ways in which each has been applied to the Gospels. Then we will discuss another branch of analysis of the finished form of any literary product—*genre criticism*—to try to determine what genre of literature the Gospels are. This will clarify our hermeneutical expectations of these documents—for example, what kind of history and theology to look for in them. In turn, it will set the stage for our more detailed analysis of the four Gospels individually and the life of Christ himself.

FORMALIST-STRUCTURALIST METHODS

The Bible as Literature/Narrative Criticism

Early in the twentieth century, secular literary criticism developed what became known as "formalism" or "new criticism." Emerging particularly out of a study of poetry, formalism dispensed with the gathering of information about authors' historical circumstances and what they might be trying to teach about the world in which they lived. Instead, it encouraged a meticulous analysis of the poems themselves as works of art with integrity of their own. Today, in biblical circles, the discipline of *narrative criticism* often reasonably approximates the designs of formalism more generally.[1] From one perspective, the development is not new. With the historic separation of church and state in America, English classes in public schools have long studied "The Bible as Literature." To avoid promoting religion through this exercise, teachers often focused primarily on such literary characteristics of biblical narratives as plot, characterization, symbolism, point of view, figures of speech, and so forth. Certainly one does not have to deny either the historicity or the theological significance of the Scriptures to recognize that they are filled with many of the artistic devices of great works of literature.

An application of this analysis of the "surface features" of a text to the Gospels can, in fact, prove quite instructive. Major programmatic works have been penned in the United States by Jack Kingsbury, David Rhoads and Donald Michie, Robert Tannehill, and Alan Culpepper.[2] Among evangelicals, Leland Ryken, long-time English professor at Wheaton College, has been especially prolific.[3] Following these scholars' lead, one may concentrate, for example, on *plot* and note that the Gospels are not disinterested biographies selecting a

---

1. See esp. Mark A. Powell, *What Is Narrative Criticism?* (Minneapolis: Fortress, 1990).

2. Jack D. Kingsbury, *Matthew as Story* (Philadelphia: Fortress, 1986); David Rhoads and Donald Michie, *Mark as Story* (Philadelphia: Fortress, 1982); Robert C. Tannehill, *The Narrative Unity of Luke-Acts*, 2 vols. (Philadelphia and Minneapolis: Fortress, 1986–1990); R. Alan Culpepper, *Anatomy of the Fourth Gospel* (Philadelphia: Fortress, 1983).

3. See esp. Leland Ryken, *How to Read the Bible as Literature* (Grand Rapids: Zondervan, 1984); idem, *Words of Life: A Literary Introduction to the New Testament* (Grand Rapids: Baker, 1987).

representative sample of everything Jesus did in every major stage of his life. Rather, they highlight those events that created a growing conflict with the Jewish leaders and ultimately led to his death. Individual stories, like the parables, also contain plots. Some are "comic," that is, they have a "happy" ending—for example, the good Samaritan. But many are "tragic," ending on a note of judgment—for example, the parable of the talents or pounds.[4] Because the *climax* of a story usually comes near its end, how these stories culminate helps us determine which elements in them are stressed most.

Characterization distinguishes, among other things, between "flat" and "round" characters. In Matthew in particular, the Jewish leaders are mostly flat—one-dimensional—in this case portrayed in an unrelentingly negative light. However, the Jewish crowds, like the disciples, are more round or complex, sometimes siding with Jesus, sometimes opposing him, and on occasions simply remaining confused. Matthew sees more hope for them than for Jesus' opponents, who remain implacably antagonistic. In John, Nicodemus approached Jesus as though he were an exceptional, positive model from within the Jerusalem leadership (John 3:1). Yet his increasing bewilderment and diminishing role as a dialogue partner with Jesus suggests that, at that stage in his life at least, he just didn't understand (vv. 2–15).[5] This characterization is reinforced by John's use of symbolism—Nicodemus came by night (v. 2), but those who turn to God through Jesus do not love the darkness but come into the light (vv. 19–21).

Indeed, John's Gospel uses a greater amount of *symbolism* and *double-entendre* (double-meanings) than the other three Gospels. In that conversation with Nicodemus, Jesus told him that to enter the kingdom of God a person must be born *anōthen*. This Greek word can mean "from above" or "again," and most commentators suspect that John implied both concepts when he chose this term to translate Jesus' original Aramaic words. Also in the early chapters of John, Jesus tells Mary at Cana, "My time [literally, "hour"] has not yet come" (John 2:4). In the immediate context, this appears to mean simply, "I'm not quite ready yet to work the miracle you've requested." But the expression turns up again (e.g., John 7:6), until eventually Jesus' "hour" does come (12:23), and it becomes clear that "hour" refers preeminently to the time of his death and resurrection. Probably John saw a hint of this meaning already in chapter 2 in the Cana narrative.

This last example of symbolism leads directly to another literary device—*foreshadowing*. Well-crafted stories often leave clues for readers to help them anticipate what will come later. Matthew 2:1–12 describes surprising opposition to the birth of the Messiah by Herod and his Jewish supporters in Jerusalem and surprising acceptance, even worship, by the Magi—pagan astrologers! But by the end of his Gospel, Matthew makes it clear that Jesus is a king for all peoples (28:16–20) and that "the kingdom of God will be taken away from you [the Jewish leadership] and given to a people [Jesus' followers from any ethnic background] who will produce its fruit" (21:43). In both Matthew and Mark, John the Baptist plays the role of a forerunner to Christ, not

---

4. See esp. Dan O. Via, Jr., *The Parables: Their Literary and Existential Dimension* (Philadelphia: Fortress, 1967).

5. Cf. esp. F. Peter Cotterell, "The Nicodemus Conversation: A Fresh Appraisal," *ExpT* 96 (1985): 237–42.

only in his ministry but also in his death (Mark 6:14–29 pars.). Matthew makes this point in a particularly striking way by juxtaposing the description of Jesus' rejection in Nazareth with John's arrest, imprisonment, and beheading (Matt. 13:53–58; 14:3–12), even though John was arrested before the major events of Jesus' ministry (see 14:1–2; cf. Luke 3:19–20).

The *point of view* of a narrator may be limited to what is known by a particular character in the story or it may reflect "omniscience"—the perspective of someone who understands all the events with the insights of everyone in the narrative. Appropriately, the Gospel narrators are omniscient, in this technical sense, though the more theological omniscience of God stands behind them too. We recognize that the evangelists claim to present God's perspective on the events they describe. What they put forward as positive models we are to imitate; what they criticize we are to reject. They accept a supernatural worldview, the possibility of miracles, the existence of angels and demons; and they want us to follow suit.

Narrative time can play a significant role in indicating what is important to an author. Years may speed by in a matter of a few pages, whereas brief incidents may be narrated at great length. All four Gospels, though Mark and John in particular, are dominated by their passion narratives. That is to say, time slows down considerably as one approaches the death of Jesus. Literary criticism reinforces what we know theologically from the later New Testament writings: the most important thing about Jesus' life was his death and resurrection. Narrative time can build suspense within an individual story as well. Why did Jesus delay leaving for Bethany when told that Lazarus was gravely ill (John 11:6)? He knew what no one else around him did, that he was going to raise Lazarus from the grave (vv. 38–44). But John also offers a foreshadowing of that miracle with Jesus' cryptic remarks in verse 4: "This sickness will not end in death. No, it is for God's glory."

We noted that formalism began primarily as a method of studying poetry, a form of literature that often seems to have "a life of its own" apart from original authorial intent. It is interesting that the written form of the majority of Jesus' teaching is at least semipoetic. Various studies have profitably analyzed the Semitic parallelism in which it is often couched, along with numerous figures of speech—hyperbole (rhetorical exaggeration), irony or satire, simile and metaphor, paradox, and riddle.[6] We dare not interpret literally a passage that employs one of these devices, lest we maim ourselves (cf. Matt. 5:29–30) or take up arms when we are not supposed to (cf. Luke 22:35–38 with vv. 49–51)!

Narrative criticism in modern biblical studies also goes one step beyond older formalism and distinguishes among the *real author* of a text, the *implied author* (the image the text discloses of the author apart from external historical information), and the *narrator* (the personality in the text that actually tells the story). So, too, one may distinguish among the *authorial readers* (whom the text was first intended to address), the *implied readers* (the image the text discloses of the intended audience apart from external historical information), and the *narratées* (the people to whom the story is told within the story line itself).

---

6. For an excellent, brief introduction, see Robert H. Stein, *The Method and Message of Jesus' Teachings* (Louisville: Westminster/John Knox, rev. 1994), 7–32.

For those who accept the traditional claims of authorship for the four Gospels, these distinctions seem less significant than they do for others. But, for example, in Luke's Gospel a good case can be made that while the narratée is merely Theophilus (Luke 1:3), the authorial readers are an entire Christian church (see below, p. 150).

Reading the Gospels as literature can prove quite valuable. We recognize their artistic merit—their ability to affect our emotions as well as our intellects—as they captivate, encourage, and convict us. We are more sensitive to what is more central and what is more peripheral in individual stories. We understand how they function to create multiple levels of meaning—main themes, subordinate motifs, and allusive echoes to other well-known traditions, not least in the Old Testament. But we run across pitfalls as well. Much literary criticism assumes that the Gospels are not necessarily historical or else it plays down their theological or religious content. However, these assumptions are not inherent in the method; a well-crafted piece of historical writing also promotes certain ideological concerns in an artistic and aesthetically pleasing way. Indeed, it has been argued that the features of a text that an approach to the Bible as literature stresses are often those aspects of the reading process that come most naturally to first-time Bible readers not yet taught to treat Scripture atomistically (e.g., verse by verse).

Structuralism

In the 1970s and 1980s a much more esoteric branch of formalist analysis developed that did not scrutinize the obvious surface features of a text but sought to disclose primordial "deep structures" allegedly inherent in all narratives. In biblical scholarship, this method was closely associated with Daniel Patte and a school of his associates at Vanderbilt University,[7] however already it has waned considerably. Growing disinterest can probably be attributed to two major factors: a highly technical vocabulary and methodology that were tedious to master, combined with little exegetical "payoff" not discernible through other methods. For example, "actantial analysis" sought to plot six major "actants" (characters or objects) that potentially formed the plot of every narrative, however otherwise complex it may have been: a "sender" tries to communicate an "object" to a "receiver" by means of a "subject," who may be aided by a "helper" or hindered by an "opponent."

One might thus reduce the parable of the rich man and Lazarus to its basic constituent elements: God wants to bring happiness and ultimately Paradise to the rich man by means of the man's proper response to Lazarus according to the commands of Moses and the prophets, but the man's reception of this good is thwarted by his own self-indulgence and luxurious living.[8] An advantage of such analysis is that it turns attention away from potentially distracting but peripheral details and debates (the nature of the afterlife, the reason for Lazarus' salvation, whether or not the closing verse of the parable hints at Jesus' resurrection, etc.). But it is not clear that one would have to have developed

---

7. See esp. Daniel Patte, *What Is Structural Exegesis?* (Philadelphia: Fortress, 1976); idem, *Structural Exegesis: From Theory to Practice* (Philadelphia: Fortress, 1978).

8. Cf. Pheme Perkins, *Hearing the Parables of Jesus* (New York: Paulist, 1981), 69.

this particular grid to recognize the main emphases of the story. Still other far more complex developments of structuralism go well beyond the scope of this brief introduction.[9]

POSTSTRUCTURALIST METHODS

Deconstruction

The French philosopher Jacques Derrida is undoubtedly the most prominent figure behind this most avant-garde of modern literary developments. Deconstruction believes that all language is inherently unstable, that all attempts to communicate successfully are hindered by features in language that work against the understanding of meaning, and that any attempt to interpret a text discloses more about the condition of the interpreter than any inherent significance of the text itself. Deconstructionists, therefore, revel in deriving conflicting meanings from a given text and playing them off against each other.[10]

Parables have been the most frequent part of the Gospels used for such deconstruction because the more cryptic forms of literature naturally lend themselves to "polyvalent" (multiple and diverse) readings. One author applied deconstruction to the parable of the hidden treasure (Matt. 13:44) and concluded that its theme of abandoning everything for the sake of the kingdom ultimately meant abandoning the parable and then abandoning abandonment![11] Another writer began with the wordplay (in English!) between the names "Mark" and "Luke" and "mark" as the stroke of a letter on a piece of paper and "look" meaning to see. He then proceeded to discuss Mark and Luke in association with a wide range of modern literature as two Gospels that stress written marks and the art of seeing, respectively.[12]

Of course, no deconstructionist consistently employs this method. The method is inherently unstable. Sooner or later all communicators want to be understood for their actual intentions as expressed through spoken and printed words! Not surprisingly, there are clear signs that interest in deconstruction, like structuralism before it, is dissipating (dare we say deconstructing?).

Reader-Response Criticism

A second poststructuralist development in literary criticism will likely have a longer life. "Reader-response criticism" describes a loose collection of approaches that are united by the common feature of focusing on the act of reading in interpretation.[13] Some highlight how meaning changes during the

---

9. A particularly concise and readable survey of the major methods that have been applied to the New Testament appears in Raymond F. Collins, *Introduction to the New Testament* (Garden City: Doubleday, 1983), 231–71.

10. A standard introduction to the method is Jonathan Culler, *On Deconstruction: Theory and Criticism After Structuralism* (Ithaca: Cornell, 1982).

11. John Dominic Crossan, *Finding Is the First Act* (Philadelphia: Fortress, 1979).

12. Stephen D. Moore, *Mark and Luke in Poststructuralist Perspectives* (New Haven and London: Yale, 1992).

13. Most credit Stanley E. Fish with providing the greatest impetus for this movement. See esp. his *Self-Consuming Artifacts* (Berkeley: University of California, 1972); and idem, *Is There a Text in This Class?* (Cambridge, Mass. and London: Harvard, 1980). For a sampling of the diversity of methods included, see Jane P. Tompkins, ed., *Reader-Response Criticism* (Baltimore and London: Johns Hopkins, 1980).

reading process—the more we understand about the development of a plot, the more earlier details take on new significance. Or critics may study the effects of reading a work for the second or third time—after one already knows the ending or acquires additional information about the events described in the text. Does John deliberately intend his audience to reflect back on Jesus' words about eating his flesh and drinking his blood (John 6:54) in light of their later reading of his Farewell Discourse (chaps. 13–17) and their knowledge of the Last Supper from Christian tradition? Is Mark's cryptic reference to a young man who fled naked from the Garden of Gethsemane (Mark 14:51–52) a kind of literary signature and self-reference? Do Mark and Matthew both want their readers to think about how ridiculous the disciples' question about how to feed the four thousand appears (Mark 8:4; Matt. 15:33) after they have already experienced the feeding of the five thousand?[14]

Reader-response criticism has helpfully stressed how much meaning readers really do create and import into texts based on their backgrounds, presuppositions, and, in Christian circles, theological traditions. Undoubtedly we must admit that some of this is inevitable in a fallen world. Because of our limited perspectives, we may never fully grasp the potential meaning inherent in a text. In addition, reader-oriented theories of interpretation go a long way toward explaining why people in different cultures or communities hear various acts of communication differently or reach varying conclusions about what they think a text means. Yet we dare not choose simply to celebrate the diverse meanings we create and stop trying to overcome the distorting effects of "eisegesis"—reading in meanings that are foreign to a text. Unless we acknowledge limits to the interpretive process, anything can be made to mean anything and successful communication becomes impossible. Such a conclusion is incompatible with the Christian conviction that God in Jesus and in his Word has spoken to humanity in ways that it can truly understand. It is better to recognize that fixed *meaning* is present in an author's intentions disclosed through the symbols that remain in a written text, however partial our ability to recover that meaning may be. Only the *significance* or *application* of that unchanging meaning may vary from one individual to another.[15] In a "postmodernist" as well as poststructuralist age in which belief in absolute truth is rapidly vanishing, we neglect these important distinctions at great cost.[16]

---

14. The most thorough survey of reader-response criticism applied to the Gospels is Stephen D. Moore, *Literary Criticism and the Gospels* (New Haven and London: Yale, 1989), 71–170. From an evangelical perspective, cf. James L. Resseguie, "Reader-Response Criticism and the Synoptic Gospels," *JAAR* 52 (1984): 307–24.

15. This approach is particularly associated with E. D. Hirsch, *Validity in Interpretation* (New Haven and London: Yale, 1967). Hirsch has been rightly criticized at points, but the gist of his thesis can stand, esp. as nuanced by Anthony C. Thiselton, *New Horizons in Hermeneutics* (Grand Rapids: Zondervan, 1992).

16. *Postmodernism* is an increasingly common term used to refer, among other things, to the conviction (*contra* modernism) that objective, scientific criteria are lacking in the quest for truth in the historical, philosophical, or religious spheres. An important critique of Stanley Fish thus appears from P. R. Noble under the title, "Hermeneutics and Post-Modernism: Can We Have a Radical Reader-Response Theory?" *Religious Studies* 30 (1994): 419–36; 31 (1995): 1–22.

THE GENRE OF THE GOSPELS

So what *is* encoded in the texts of Matthew, Mark, Luke, and John to help us know how to interpret them on the "macro-scale"? Are they unadorned works of history or biography? Are they extended myths? historical fiction? In short, how do we assess the *genre* or literary form of an entire "gospel"?

When one compares the Gospels with modern biographies, vast differences emerge. Mark and John tell us nothing of Jesus' birth, childhood, or young adulthood. They devote almost half of their narratives to the events of the last few weeks of his life. Matthew and Luke add a few details from Christ's birth, while Luke narrates one event that occurred when Jesus was twelve, but nothing else appears before his adult ministry. In all four Gospels, to varying degrees, material is arranged topically as well as chronologically. The words of Jesus are paraphrased, abridged, explained, and recombined in a variety of ways. Little wonder that many modern scholars have looked for something other than "history" or "biography" to characterize the Gospels' genre.

Some of the suggestions that have been made involve "aretalogies"—Greco-Roman accounts of the life of a "divine man" that embellish or exaggerate the feats of a famous hero or warrior of the past. Others use language of the theater and label the Gospels as "comedies" or "tragedies." Some focus on the extensive use of the Old Testament (or the use by later Gospels of earlier ones as if they were sacred Scripture equivalent to the Old Testament) and identify individual Gospels as "midrash" (see above, p. 40). The particularly cryptic character of parts of Mark has suggested to a few that the whole Gospel genre be considered a "parable" or an "apocalypse," while John's divergence from the Synoptics has led others to label his work a "drama."[17]

These and related suggestions capture certain dimensions of the Gospels, but none accounts for a majority of their features. An increasing number of scholars, therefore, recognizes that the list of traits setting the Gospels apart from *modern* biographies does not distinguish them nearly so much from *ancient* Greco-Roman biographies or Greek and Jewish "historiography" (history-writing). Ancient writers were more highly selective, ideological, and artistic in narrating the great events of their day or the lives of key individuals. There are unique features of the Gospels, to be sure, generally related to the unique events they narrate and the distinctive nature of the person of Jesus of Nazareth. But this makes them no less historical or biographical by the conventions of their day. Perhaps it is best, then, to refer to the Gospels as *theological biographies*.[18]

At any rate, what is important to conclude at the end of this two-chapter survey of modern methods of Gospel study is that there is a legitimate place for historical, theological, *and* literary study of Matthew, Mark, Luke, and John.

---

17. The last two paragraphs are an abbreviation of material covered in Craig Blomberg, *The Historical Reliability of the Gospels* (Leicester and Downers Grove: IVP, 1987) 235–40; and William W. Klein, Craig L. Blomberg, and Robert L. Hubbard, Jr., *Introduction to Biblical Interpretation* (Dallas and London: Word, 1993), 323–25.

18. Cf. Robert Maddox, *The Purpose of Luke-Acts* (Edinburgh: T & T Clark, 1982), 16, who identifies the overall genre of Luke-Acts as a "theological history." For a similar conclusion after a detailed comparison of the Gospels with other works of their day, see Richard A. Burridge, *What Are the Gospels?* (Cambridge: CUP, 1992).

Despite attempts of various scholars to pit one method against the other two, all three actually go hand in hand. Indeed, unless we approach the Gospels expecting to find historically reliable information, theologically motivated emphases, and delightful literary artistry, we shall overlook important dimensions of the texts and run the risk of misinterpreting them as well.

APPLICATION

The three Synoptic versions of the parable of the wicked tenants are printed on the facing page. Look for ways that each of the critical methods discussed in the last two chapters might apply to this passage. One sample application of each method is given by way of illustration:

1. *Source Criticism.* Mark 12:6 finds the landlord predicting that the tenants will respect his son, whereas Luke 20:13 reads, "It may be that they will respect him." Once the landlord is viewed as God, Mark's wording is subject to the misunderstanding that God did not know that his son would be rejected. Luke takes pains to clarify this. It is inconceivable that Mark would introduce this problem, but it makes perfect sense that Luke would try to alleviate it. Thus Mark seems clearly prior to Luke at this point.

2. *Form Criticism.* Only Luke clearly organizes the missions of the various servants into an enumerated, threefold sequence. In Luke 20:10, the master sends one servant, in verse 11 another, and in verse 12 "a third." The mistreatments of each also build toward the climax of the sending of the son who is killed. This stylistic streamlining was characteristic of ancient oral tradition and was likely a product of the frequent repetition of this story during the period before it was written down.

3. *Redaction Criticism.* Only Matthew includes the verse in which Jesus declares that the kingdom will be taken away from the wicked tenants and given to a nation that will produce appropriate fruit (Matt. 21:43). Once we recognize that Matthew understands the tenants as the Jewish leaders and the new nation as the church, we can see why he in particular would wish to include this part of the story. Of all the evangelists, we discover that Matthew was the most interested in highlighting the Jewishness of Jesus' message *and* the break that Christianity underwent from Judaism.

4. *Canon Criticism.* When Jesus first spoke this parable, some of his listeners might have had an inkling that he was referring to himself as the son and perhaps even predicting his violent death. But they would not have known that he would be crucified *outside* the city walls of Jerusalem. Many commentators, however, speculate that Matthew and Luke (unlike Mark) worded their descriptions of the tenants taking the son and casting him out of the vineyard *before* killing him as an allusion to the subsequent fate of Jesus (Matt. 21:39; Luke 20:15). From a canonical perspective, this could be justified as bringing out the significance of Jesus' original story in light of later developments.

5. *Narrative Criticism.* Formal literary analysis will observe that this is a tragic parable. The climax in all three versions comes with the judgment pronounced against the Jewish leaders, followed by the observation that they realized Jesus had told this parable against them. The central thrust of judgment

The Wicked Servants

Matthew 21:33-46, RSV

"Hear another parable. There was a householder who planted a vineyard, and set a hedge around it, and dug a wine press in it, and built a tower, and let it out to tenants, and went into another country. When the season of fruit drew near, he sent his servants to the tenants, to get his fruit; and the tenants took his servants and beat one, killed another, and stoned another. Again he sent other servants, more than the first; and they did the same to them. Afterward he sent his son to them, saying, 'They will respect my son.' But when the tenants saw the son, they said to themselves, 'This is the heir; come, let us kill him and have his inheritance.' And they took him and cast him out of the vineyard, and killed him. When therefore the owner of the vineyard comes, what will he do to those tenants?" They said to him, "He will put those wretches to a miserable death, and let out the vineyard to other tenants who will give him the fruits in their seasons."

Jesus said to them, "Have you never read in the scriptures:

'The very stone
    which the build-
    ers rejected
has become the head
    of the corner;
this was the Lord's
    doing,
and it is marvelous in
    our eyes'?

Therefore I tell you, the kingdom of God will be taken away from you and given to a nation producing the fruits of it."

When the chief priests and the Pharisees heard his parables, they perceived that he was speaking about them. But when they tried to arrest him, they feared the multitudes, because they held him to be a prophet.

Mark 12:1-12, RSV

And he began to speak to them in parables. "A man planted a vineyard, and set a hedge around it, and dug a pit for the wine press, and built a tower, and let it out to tenants, and went into another country. When the time came, he sent a servant to the tenants, to get from them some of the fruit of the vineyard. And they took him and beat him, and sent him away empty-handed. Again he sent to them another servant, and they wounded him in the head, and treated him shamefully. And he sent another, and him they killed; and so with many others, some they beat and some they killed. He had still one other, a beloved son; finally he sent him to them, saying, 'They will respect my son.' But those tenants said to one another, 'This is the heir; come, let us kill him, and the inheritance will be ours.' And they took him and killed him, and cast him out of the vineyard. What will the owner of the vineyard do? He will come and destroy the tenants, and give the vineyard to others. Have you not read this scripture:

'The very stone
    which the builders
    rejected
has become the head
    of the corner;
this was the Lord's
    doing,
and it is marvelous in
    our eyes'?"

And they tried to arrest him, but feared the multitude, for they perceived that he had told the parable against them; so they left him and went away.

Luke 20:9-19, RSV

And he began to tell the people this parable: "A man planted a vineyard, and let it out to tenants, and went into another country for a long while. When the time came, he sent a servant to the tenants, that they should give him some of the fruit of the vineyard; but the tenants beat him, and sent him away empty-handed. And he sent another servant; him also they beat and treated shamefully, and sent him away empty-handed. And he sent yet a third; this one they wounded and cast out. Then the owner of the vineyard said, 'What shall I do? I will send my beloved son; it may be they will respect him.' But when the tenants saw him, they said to themselves, 'This is the heir; let us kill him, that the inheritance may be ours.' And they cast him out of the vineyard and killed him. What then will the owner of the vineyard do to them? He will come and destroy those tenants, and give the vineyard to others." When they heard this, they said, "God forbid!" But he looked at them and said, "What then is this that is written:

'The very stone
    which the builders
    rejected
has become the head
    of the corner'?

Every one who falls on that stone will be broken to pieces; but when it falls on any one it will crush him."

The scribes and the chief priests tried to lay hands on him at that very hour, but they feared the people; for they perceived that he had told this parable against them.

that permeates the parable must not be lost in any exposition or application of it.

6. *Structuralism.* The three main characters or groups of characters in this parable are the landlord, the wicked tenants, and the new tenants. Corresponding to a frequently recurring structure in Jesus' parables elsewhere, these characters stand, respectively, for God, his enemies, and his true people. Perhaps other details are to be allegorized, but even if so, they remain subordinate to these three foci. If Jesus meant the son to stand for him, he has kept the son in a subservient role to the other main characters. This may actually argue for the passage's authenticity because later Christian reflection would probably have given the son a more prominent role.

7. *Poststructuralism.* The differences among Matthew 21:40–41, Mark 12:9, and Luke 20:15b–16 are striking. Who asked the question about what the owner would do? Who gave the answer? And what was the answer? Historically, it is unlikely that Jesus posed the question to a diverse crowd and received one answer from everyone as if from a choir replying in unison. He would have had to repeat the answer he endorsed. Ironically, this traditional kind of "harmonization" is actually given greater credence by reader- (or listener-) response approaches that remind us that different people will interpret the same story quite differently. So it is not surprising that some were ready to condemn the tenants, while others were appalled at their fate.

FOR FURTHER STUDY

As in chapter 4, the following list includes only those works that cover a broad sweep of the issues raised in this chapter. Several of the works listed for further study at the end of chapter 4 also include various dimensions of literary criticism.

Introductory

Adam, A. K. M. *What Is Postmodern Biblical Criticism?* Minneapolis: Fortress, 1995.

Longman, Tremper, III. *Literary Approaches to Biblical Interpretation.* Grand Rapids: Zondervan, 1987.

Petersen, Norman R. *Literary Criticism for New Testament Critics.* Philadelphia: Fortress, 1978.

Ryken, Leland. *Words of Life: A Literary Introduction to the New Testament.* Grand Rapids: Baker, 1987.

Intermediate

Alter, Robert, and Frank Kermode, eds. *The Literary Guide to the Bible.* Cambridge, Mass.: Harvard, 1987.

Aune, David E. *The New Testament in Its Literary Environment.* Philadelphia: Westminster, 1987.

McKnight, Edgar V. *The Bible and the Reader: An Introduction to Literary Criticism.* Philadelphia: Fortress, 1985.

Ryken, Leland, and Tremper Longman III, eds. *A Complete Literary Guide to the Bible.* Grand Rapids: Zondervan, 1993.

Advanced

Frye, Northrop. *The Great Code: The Bible and Literature.* New York: Harcourt, Brace, Jovanovich, 1982.
Malbon, Elizabeth S., and Edgar V. McKnight, eds. *The New Literary Criticism and the New Testament.* Sheffield: JSOT, 1994.
Moore, Stephen D. *Literary Criticism and the Gospels.* New Haven and London: Yale, 1989.
Thiselton, Anthony C. *New Horizons in Hermeneutics.* Grand Rapids: Zondervan, 1992.

Bibliography

Powell, Mark A., et al. *The Bible and Modern Literary Criticism: A Critical Assessment and Annotated Bibliography.* Westport, Conn.: Greenwood, 1992.

QUESTIONS FOR REVIEW

1. Choose several passages from the Gospels and discuss how each of the various branches of literary criticism might illuminate the text. Consider, for example, the parable of the prodigal son (Luke 15:11–32), Jesus' conversation with Nicodemus (John 3:1–15), or the end of Mark's Gospel (Mark 16:1–8).

2. Can you think of passages in the Gospels where literary criticism helps us recognize what is (or is not) to be stressed *theologically?*

PART THREE

INTRODUCTION
TO THE FOUR GOSPELS

B iblical scholars often use the word "introduction" in a fairly narrow, technical way to refer to the study of the circumstances surrounding the formation of a particular portion of Scripture. Typically, discussions proceed from a determination of the author and his circumstances (date, place of writing, audience) to a discussion of the theology and structure of his work. In the case of the Gospels, strictly speaking, all four works are anonymous. That is to say, there is no chapter or verse that gives the name of the author in any instance. The headings on the existing manuscripts are not likely original. Four scribes probably would not have independently decided to entitle their documents, "The Gospel according to *X*." These titles were most likely added when the fourfold Gospel collection first began to circulate, at least by the early second century, to distinguish one document from another. Although we must take these early claims about authorship seriously, we dare not elevate them to the level of inspired Scripture. Even less certainty surrounds issues of date, destination, and place of origin.

In light of the above information, we will invert the typical sequence of discussing introductory topics in the following four-chapter section. Structure and theology will be discussed first based on the data that *are* observable in the texts themselves. Then we will see if that information helps us narrow down the options on the more speculative considerations of setting and author.

CHAPTER SIX

THE GOSPEL OF MARK

STRUCTURE

Ancient Middle Eastern writers were not as bound by logical, linear thinking as modern Western ones are. The Gospels, like most documents of their day, would have been written to be read aloud. Many listeners might never see or know how to read a written copy, so writing had to include repetition for emphasis and rhetorical markers that would make connections between sections clear. The modern commentator always runs the risk, therefore, of imposing too much structure or symmetry when trying to outline these books. A second pitfall assumes that ancient historians or biographers were consistently concerned to write in chronological sequence; they were not. Many modern outlines of the Gospels simply divide the material according to an assumed historical or geographical progression of the life and ministry of Christ. There are too many places, however, where it is clear that an evangelist grouped materials together not for chronological reasons, but because they contain the same literary "form" or because they share a similar theme or topic. The words "then" and "now" in English versions often translate Greek words (*tote, nun*) which, like their English counterparts, can mean "therefore" or "so," rather than "later" or "at the same time." Many times successive stories in the Gospels are simply connected by Greek words for "and" (*kai* or *de*). A comparison of parallels in a synopsis shows how often events are narrated in a different order from one Gospel to the next. Therefore we are safest in *not* assuming any chronological connection between individual passages unless the writer uses a term that unambiguously requires such a connection or unless some other cause-and-effect relationship demands it.

There is fairly widespread agreement concerning the general structure of Mark, but considerable disagreement as to exactly where specific sections begin or end.[1] This suggests that several passages may have been designed as transitions or "seams," bringing one stage of the narrative to a close and introducing a new stage. Still, we observe that Mark's Gospel falls into two main sections. Most of the first eight chapters use action-packed narratives to focus on the powerful ministry of Jesus, particularly as he gathers disciples and amazes crowds with his mighty deeds.[2] Following Peter's confession of Jesus as the Christ on the road to Caesarea Philippi (8:27–30), Jesus abruptly begins teaching about his coming suffering and death. From there on, all events move inexorably toward the cross. This disproportionate amount of attention to the last events of Jesus' life reflects the centrality of the crucifixion in early Christian thought. It also prompted Martin Kähler, a century ago, to give one of the more famous descriptions of the structure of the Gospels: "passion narratives with extended introductions."[3]

The first half of the Gospel frequently groups a series of stories of like form (healings, controversies, parables, etc.), with a particular emphasis on Jesus' miracles. There are also two literary seams in which Mark has just described significant opposition to Jesus, appears to bring a section to a close, and then starts afresh with Jesus withdrawing from hostility and calling or commissioning his disciples for further service in a new location (3:7; 6:6b). In the second half of Mark, events proceed much more chronologically, with more emphasis on Jesus' teachings. But the narrative again seems to move to new scenes at two key points—with Jesus' triumphal entry into Jerusalem, and when the fateful Passover that would claim his life was approaching (11:1; 14:1). From 11:1 on, as noted above (p. 103), narrative time slows down considerably. Additional thematic groupings lead us to propose an outline that, following an introduction, divides each half of Mark's Gospel into three main sections with three main subsections apiece.[4]

I.   Introduction: The Beginning of the Gospel (1:1–13)
II. The Ministry of Christ (1:14–8:30)
     A. The Authority of Jesus and the Blindness of the Pharisees (1:14–3:6)
        1. Introduction (1:14–20)

---

1. For a helpful, recent survey of approaches, see Joanna Dewey, "Mark as Interwoven Tapestry: Forecasts and Echoes for a Listening Audience," *CBQ* 53 (1991): 221–36.

2. This sense of action is enhanced by Mark's forty-two uses of "immediately" (Greek *euthus*), at times virtually equivalent to little more than "the next, important thing I want to tell you is. . . ." The word appears only seven times in Matthew, once in Luke, and three times in John. Mark also delights in using the "historical present"—present tense verbs for past tense action—particularly with verbs introducing Jesus' speech, for the sake of emphasis and vividness. See, e.g., Mark 1:12, 21, 40; 2:3; etc.

3. Martin Kähler, *The So-Called Historical Jesus and the Historic, Biblical Christ* (Philadelphia: Fortress, 1964 [Ger. orig. 1896]), 80, n. 11.

4. A few of the section headings are adopted or adapted from Eduard Schweizer, *The Good News according to Mark* (Richmond: John Knox, 1970; London: SPCK, 1971), 7–10. Vincent Taylor (*The Gospel according to St. Mark* [London: Macmillan, 1952], 107–11) is particularly helpful in stressing the smaller groupings according to form. In general agreement with the overall structure discerned here, with slight verse modifications at points, are the commentaries by Robert A. Guelich (*Mark 1–8:26* [Dallas: Word, 1989]) and William L. Lane (*The Gospel according to Mark* [Grand Rapids: Eerdmans, 1974; London: Marshall, Morgan & Scott, 1975]).

2. Healing Miracles (1:21–45)
3. Controversy Stories (2:1–3:6)
B. The Parables and Signs of Jesus and the Blindness of the World (3:7–6:6a)
1. Discipleship and Opposition (3:7–35)
2. Parables (4:1–34)
3. More Dramatic Miracles (4:35–6:6a)
C. Jesus' Ministry to Gentiles and the Blindness of the Disciples (6:6b–8:30)
1. More Mission, Opposition, and Miracles (6:6b–56)
2. Clean and Unclean: Withdrawal from Israel (7:1–8:21)
3. Physical and Spiritual Eyesight (8:22–30)
III. The Passion of Christ (8:31–16:8)
A. Predictions of Death and the Meaning of Discipleship (8:31–10:52)
1. Cross and Resurrection Foreshadowed (8:31–9:29)
2. On True Servanthood (9:30–50)
3. Ministry in Judea in Light of the Cross (10:1–52)
B. Jesus and the Temple (11:1–13:37)
1. Entry and Judgment (11:1–25)[5]
2. Teaching and Debate (11:27–12:44)
3. Prediction of Destruction and Christ's Return (13:1–37)
C. The Climax of Jesus' Life (14:1–16:8)
1. Preparation for Suffering (14:1–72)
2. Crucifixion (15:1–47)
3. Resurrection (16:1–8)

It has also been frequently observed that the main contours of this outline correspond to early Christian preaching as reflected in Acts. For example, in Acts 10:36–41 Peter describes the good news (cf. Mark 1:1) as God anointing Jesus through the Spirit (cf. 1:10); Jesus then begins his ministry in Galilee, doing good and healing many (cf. 1:16–8:26), moves on to Jerusalem (cf. chaps. 10–14), and climaxes his career with his death and resurrection (cf. chaps. 15–16). It may well be that Mark's Gospel is the narrative expansion of a common outline used by many in the early church to tell the story about Jesus.[6]

THEOLOGY

Views of Jesus
What was Mark trying to do by sharply juxtaposing Christ's "successes" and his "failures"? Why does half of this Gospel focus on his mighty deeds and half on his suffering and death? Presumably the answer to this question is crucial for unlocking Mark's theological perspectives on the person and work of Jesus. A common modern suggestion (associated esp. with Theodore Weeden) is that

5. Verse 26 is not in the oldest and most reliable manuscripts. If it were to be accepted, it would go with vv. 1–25.

6. This view is particularly associated with C. H. Dodd, *The Apostolic Preaching and Its Developments* (London: Hodder & Stoughton, 1936), 54–56.

early attempts to tell the story of Jesus in Greek and Roman circles focused on portraying him as a "divine man" (Greek, *theios aner*), akin to the semi-legendary heroes of Greco-Roman history who were deified upon their deaths. Mark, however, viewed this as a one-sided account of Jesus. While appropriating the emphasis on Jesus the wonder-worker, he then substantially qualified it by highlighting the ignominy of Christ's death.[7] Quite recently, Robert Gundry has stood this argument on its head, insisting that Mark was tempering a traditional emphasis on Jesus' suffering and death with a more triumphalist stress on his glory. Gundry finds a powerful Jesus even in chapters 9–16, inasmuch as he consistently predicts his suffering and fate, demonstrating that he is in control of his own destiny and not a victim of circumstance.[8]

Both approaches, however, seem too one-sided. A writer wanting to play down a distorted emphasis in one direction would probably not devote a full half of his book to reinforcing that position. More likely Mark is trying to keep two essential truths in balance: Jesus' glory and the centrality of the cross, both in Jesus' life and in the lives of his disciples (see esp. 8:31–9:1). Analogously, Ralph Martin refers to Mark's Gospel as the one that best *balances an emphasis on Jesus' divinity with his humanity.*[9] This seems best, although if Mark was trying to achieve this balance by correcting a previous imbalance, the climactic role of Jesus' death and the amount of attention Mark devotes to it compared to the other Gospels suggest that Weeden is more on target than Gundry.[10]

Mark's distinctive christological titles line up with this balance between Jesus' divinity and humanity. Although not used often, *Son of God* (or just *Son*) occurs at strategic places in the Gospel to highlight Jesus' exalted role.[11] "Son of God" forms part of Mark's "headline" to the Gospel (1:1)[12] and recurs again as part of the Roman centurion's climactic confession at the time of Jesus' death (15:39). In between, the heavenly voice refers to Jesus as "Son" at both his baptism and his transfiguration (1:11; 9:7). Elsewhere the title occurs only on the lips of demons, reflecting their supernatural knowledge of Jesus' identity (3:11; 5:7).

The other title Mark introduces in his opening verse is *Christ* (the Greek equivalent to the Hebrew, "Messiah"). This title is not common either; it does not recur until Peter's dramatic confession in 8:29 (and then six times thereafter). But all of chapters 1–8 seem to build toward that confession, only to have

---

7   Theodore J. Weeden, *Mark—Traditions in Conflict* (Philadelphia: Fortress, 1971). Among others, however, Barry Blackburn (*Theios Aner and the Markan Miracle Traditions* [Tübingen: Möhr, 1991]) has demonstrated that there was no one, uniform "divine man" concept for early Christians even to consider appropriating. Another influential treatment that pits Mark against tradition is that of Werner H. Kelber (*The Oral and the Written Gospel* [Philadelphia: Fortress, 1983]), who finds Mark criticizing the *ecclesiastical* interests of the original apostles and substantially altering the course of the Gospel tradition by committing it to *writing*.

8.   Robert H. Gundry, *Mark: A Commentary on His Apology for the Cross* (Grand Rapids: Eerdmans, 1993).

9.   Ralph P. Martin, *Mark: Evangelist and Theologian* (Exeter: Paternoster, 1972; Grand Rapids: Zondervan, 1973). Martin's work is also an excellent overview and critique of modern Markan studies more generally. For updating through the eighties, see Larry W. Hurtado, "The Gospel of Mark in Recent Study," *Themelios* 14 (1989): 47–52.

10.   Cf. further Paul J. Achtemeier, "'He Taught Them Many Things': Reflections in Marcan Christology," *CBQ* 42 (1980): 465–81. One does not have to see early Christians as formulating an explicit divine-man Christology, however, to imagine them at times becoming overly triumphalist. Paul certainly combats that general trend in both 1 and 2 Corinthians.

11.   See esp. Jack D. Kingsbury, *The Christology of Mark's Gospel* (Philadelphia: Fortress, 1983).

12.   One important early manuscript (along with several later ones) lacks this title in 1:1, but the majority of early texts and the majority of texts overall contain it, so it is most probably what Mark originally wrote.

Peter's expectation subsequently redefined. What *is* prominent is a motif that has often been called the *Messianic secret*. More so in Mark than in any other Gospel, Jesus frequently commands people not to tell anyone about his identity. In 8:30 he abruptly silences Peter without any of the praise or promises so well known from Matthew's version (Matt. 16:17–19). Insight into parables is not to be given to "outsiders" (Mark 4:10–12); demonic confessions are rebuked (1:25, 34; 3:12); and spectacular miracles are to be reported to no one (1:44; 5:18–19, 43; etc.). William Wrede first promoted an influential view that Mark created this motif to justify his conviction that Jesus was the divine Christ and Son of God, when in fact Jesus himself had made no such claims. In other words, by creating both the claims and the "cover-up," Mark could account for why earlier stages of Christianity had not believed in Jesus as Messiah, and yet Mark himself could still promote the notion.[13]

It is far more probable that Jesus did indeed believe himself to be the Christ but was very cautious about accepting the title or allowing premature enthusiasm to overwhelm his mission because popular christological expectation did not leave room for a *suffering* Messiah (see further below, pp. 409–411). After the crucifixion and resurrection, Christ's more glorious nature could be described without as much fear of misunderstanding (9:9).[14] For Mark, however, 10:45 may be the most important verse in the Gospel in summarizing his emphasis on Jesus' road to the cross: "For even the Son of Man did not come to be served, but to serve, and to give his life as a ransom for many." The term "ransom" calls to mind the redemption of slaves in the marketplace and highlights the need for Jesus to die a substitutionary, atoning death. Jesus' words over the cup at the Last Supper point in the same direction: "This is my blood of the covenant, which is poured out for many" (14:24). Although Mark never uses the exact expression, the concept of *suffering servant* (as in Isa. 52:13–53:12) perhaps best encapsulates this very human side of Jesus' nature and mission. In short, the Gospel of Mark is about why Jesus died.[15]

Other Distinctive Themes

Disciples and Discipleship. At first glance, Mark's portrayal of the disciples is as surprising as the Messianic secret motif. Often in dramatic contrast with their responses in the other Gospels, we read in Mark of their frequent failure and misunderstanding. They do not grasp Jesus' parables (4:11–13, 33–34), their hearts are hardened, they have little faith, they are perplexed after crucial miracles (4:40; 6:51–52; 8:4, 14–21), and they are unable to fulfill Christ's commission to exorcise (9:14–29). As already noted, Peter is rebuked immediately after his confession for failing to leave room in it for a suffering Messiah (8:33). The account of the disciples' spiritual blindness is contrasted with two miracle-stories about the literally blind receiving their sight (cf. 8:22–26 and 10:46–52 in context). Ultimately, Peter denies Jesus; Judas betrays him; and all flee (chaps. 14–15). (We can even say that Mark's whole Gospel is a parable, confounding

---

13. William Wrede, *The Messianic Secret* (London: J. Clarke, 1971 [Ger. orig. 1901]).

14. For a survey of approaches to the Messianic secret, see Christopher Tuckett, ed., *The Messianic Secret* (London: SPCK; Philadelphia: Fortress, 1983). Most persuasive of these is that of James D. G. Dunn, "The Messianic Secret in Mark," 116–31.

15. Morna D. Hooker, *The Gospel according to Saint Mark* (London: A & C Black; Peabody: Hendrickson, 1991), 22.

those who look only on a material level rather than a spiritual one.) Yet even while they fail to understand, Jesus' disciples remain those who responded to his initial call (1:16–20; 2:13–14; 3:13–19), are given truths that outsiders are not (4:14–20; 7:17–23), and receive special privileges and promises about the future (14:28; 16:7). Thus their ultimate role seems ambivalent.[16]

At first glance, the women followers appear to fare better than the inner circle of the twelve men. They exemplify tenacious faith (5:28, 34; 7:29), sacrifice (12:41–44), and love (14:3–9). They stay at the cross, watch to see where Jesus is buried, and go to the tomb to tend to the corpse after the Sabbath has passed (chaps. 15–16). But the most probable end of the Gospel relativizes these successes as the women respond to the angelic announcement of the resurrection with trembling and bewilderment, fleeing from the tomb and saying nothing to anyone because of their fear (16:8).[17]

Imminent Eschatology. As the first Gospel written, Mark still preserves a lively hope in Christ's near return, whereas later Gospels at times reflect a sense of delay.[18] The climactic promise that "He is going ahead of you into Galilee" (16:7), coupled with the emphasis on Christ's earlier ministry there, has led some to see Galilee as the place of revelation for Mark and the promised location of Christ's return that his followers are to anticipate.[19] It is also noteworthy that, although Mark has fewer teachings of Jesus than the other three Gospels, the one extensive "sermon" that he preserves is Christ's eschatological discourse (chap. 13).[20] One plausible analysis of Mark's narrative flow sees the entire Gospel building towards and foreshadowing the structure of this major sermon.[21]

The Message about Jesus as Good News. Mark may well have been the first Christian to use the term *gospel* (Greek *euangelion,* "good news") as a term for the story about Jesus rather than for the message Jesus himself brought (though cf. Rom. 1:1–4 for a possible antecedent). That is the way the NIV interprets Mark 1:1 (taking "of" to mean "about"), and in several places Mark adds the term "gospel" in this same sense into his narrative (e.g., 8:35; 10:29). The word occurs seven times in Mark, four times in Matthew, and never in Luke or John. Mark's literary product then naturally was given the identical label.[22]

16. Cf. esp. Ernest Best, *Following Jesus* (Sheffield: JSOT, 1981); idem, *Disciples and Discipleship* (Edinburgh: T. & T. Clark, 1986). Various hypotheses about rival factions within Mark's church have at times been put forward to explain Mark's ambivalence about the disciples, but none of these is really based on any solid evidence.

17. Cf. further, Mary Ann Beavis, "Women as Models of Faith in Mark," *BTB* 18 (1988): 3–9; Joseph A. Grassi, "The Secret Heroine of Mark's Drama," *BTB* 18 (1988): 10–15. A provocative but often insightful Japanese feminist reading is now available in Hisako Kinukawa, *Women and Jesus in Mark* (Maryknoll: Orbis, 1994).

18. This has been exaggerated by those who misinterpret texts like 9:1 and 13:30 (and Matt. 10:23) as Christ's "mistaken" belief that he would return within his disciples' lifetimes. Cf. also Albert Schweitzer, *The Quest of the Historical Jesus* (London: A & C Black; New York: Macmillan, 1910), 330–97.

19. This view is particularly associated with Willi Marxsen, *Mark the Evangelist* (Nashville: Abingdon, 1969).

20. Though this is balanced somewhat by the observation that references to Jesus as a teacher are frequent. Vernon K. Robbins latches on to this dimension of Mark in a one-sided but otherwise helpful study of *Jesus the Teacher: A Socio-Rhetorical Interpretation of Mark* (Philadelphia: Fortress, 1984).

21. Timothy J. Geddert, *Watchwords: Mark 13 in Markan Eschatology* (Sheffield: JSOT, 1989).

22. Cf. further Ralph P. Martin, *New Testament Foundations*, vol. 1 (Grand Rapids: Eerdmans, 1975), 23–27.

CIRCUMSTANCES

What occasion in the life of the early church most probably elicited a Gospel with the structure and theological distinctives of Mark? The bulk of the external evidence (the testimony of the early Church Fathers) that has been preserved associates Mark's Gospel with Rome or "the regions of Italy" (see the Anti-Marcionite Prologue to Mark, Irenaeus [*Against Heresies* 3.1.2], and Clement of Alexandria [quoted by Eusebius *Ecclesiastical History* 6.14.6–7]—all near A.D. 200). Chrysostom (near A.D. 400) ascribes Mark's writing to Egypt, and the apocryphal "Secret Gospel of Mark," apparently cited by Clement of Alexandria, could also support an Egyptian provenance.[23]

The Roman origin is clearly the better attested and fits well with the internal evidence of the Gospel. The negative portrait of the disciples prior to the formation of the church, along with Mark's emphasis on the way of the cross as the precursor to glory, suggests a concern *to reassure a struggling community that it too could eventually cope and that victory comes only through suffering.* Given the Jewish Christians' expulsion from Rome in A.D. 49, growing tensions within the community and with the government after their return in the mid-50s, and the Neronic persecution from A.D. 64–68, *Roman Christians would have formed an audience much in need of such comfort and encouragement.* In other words Mark's concerns may have been first of all *pastoral* in nature.

Other evidence that would fit Mark's writing to Roman Christians includes the various Latinisms he uses (e.g., *quadrans* for "penny" in 12:42), his frequent explanation of Jewish concepts and terms (e.g., ritual handwashing and *corban* in 7:3–4, 11), the apparent combination of mostly lower-class with a few more upper-class concerns, the mixed ethnicity of the people with whom Jesus interacts, his repeated dealings with people in houses (cf. the Roman house churches), and the like.[24] However, since these data could be harmonized with many different settings, we dare not put too much weight on them.

The external evidence concerning the date of the Gospel seems divided. According to Eusebius, Clement declared that

> When Peter had preached the word publicly in Rome and announced the gospel by the Spirit, those present, of whom there were many, besought Mark, since for a long time he had followed him and remembered what had been said, to record his words. Mark did this, and communicated the gospel to those who made request of him. When Peter knew of it, he neither actively prevented nor encouraged the undertaking. (*Ecclesiastical History* 6.14.6–7)

---

23. In 1958, Morton Smith discovered an ancient letter apparently by Clement of Alexandria which quoted twenty lines of Greek text from an allegedly secret Gospel that Mark wrote in Alexandria after penning his original Gospel. The three excerpts quoted involve Jesus resurrecting a young man, teaching a young man at night who comes to him wearing only a linen cloth, and refusing to receive three women who come to him in Jericho. Although, with Smith (*Clement of Alexandria and a Secret Gospel of Mark* [Cambridge, Mass.: Harvard, 1973]), some scholars go so far as to argue that this secret Gospel of Mark is an earlier, more original, and more heterodox version of Mark, we do not even know for sure if this letter attributed to Clement was actually written by him, much less if it describes a complete Gospel, less still if such a "secret" Gospel actually existed. Least probable of all is that, contrary to "Clement's" claim, it predates our Mark. See John P. Meier, *A Marginal Jew: Rethinking the Historical Jesus*, vol. 1 (New York and London: Doubleday, 1991), 120–23.

24. For details, cf. C. Clifton Black, "Was Mark a Roman Gospel?" *ExpT* 105 (1993): 36–40. For the most compelling, recent alternative proposals, see esp. Joel Marcus, "The Jewish War and the *Sitz im Leben* of Mark," *JBL* 111 (1992): 441–62 (supporting a Palestinian provenance); and Pieter J. J. Botha, "The Historical Setting of Mark's Gospel: Problems and Possibilities," *JSNT* 51 (1993): 27–55 (there is simply too little evidence to know).

Irenaeus, on the other hand, can be interpreted as believing that Peter had already died when Mark wrote, as he maintains that after Peter's and Paul's "departure" (Greek, *exodos*), "Mark the disciple and interpreter of Peter also transmitted to us what he had written about what Peter had preached" (*Against Heresies* 3.1.38–41). Peter's "departure" may, however, refer to his leaving Rome (or some other location) to travel somewhere else prior to his death. It is also important to observe that Irenaeus claims only that the *transmission* of the Gospel occurred after Peter's death, not necessarily its *composition*.[25] But if Mark wrote during Peter's lifetime, and if the early church tradition can be trusted that Peter was martyred under Nero before A.D. 68, then Mark must have composed his Gospel at some still earlier date (perhaps 64–65, when Nero's persecution was beginning).[26]

One piece of internal evidence often said to contradict a pre-70 date involves Jesus' prophecy of the destruction of the temple in Mark 13:14–23—an alleged creation by the evangelist after A.D. 70. Three factors make such a creation improbable: (1) These verses form a very muted reference to the destruction of the temple, if indeed that is what they refer to at all. "Twenty-twenty hindsight" would surely have made the allusion more explicit. (2) Jesus commanded his followers to flee to the Judean hill country, but what actually occurred during the Jewish war was Christian flight to Pella in the Transjordan. (3) Only an unwarranted antisupernaturalism would deny to Jesus the powers of predictive prophecy. Given the volatile days in which Jesus lived, even an uninspired person might have successfully predicted such sacrilege!

A fair number of scholars across a variety of theological traditions thus dates Mark to the mid to late 60s during Neronic persecution in Rome.[27] But a complicating factor intrudes at this point: we have already given reason for believing that Luke wrote later than and in partial dependence on Mark (see above, pp. 87–90). When we come to the introduction to Luke (below, p. 151), we will see that a plausible case can be made for dating his Gospel to about A.D. 62. This, therefore, would require Mark to have been written earlier still, though perhaps by only a year or two. Paul reached Rome in about A.D. 60, and Peter may well have too. He was there at least by 63 or 64, with Mark (1 Pet. 5:13), according to the most common dating of Peter's first epistle (on the assumption that it is authentic). Since Peter's whereabouts throughout the 50s are almost entirely unknown, there is no reason that Peter and/or Mark could not have come sooner.[28] If Mark's Gospel stems from the late 50s or early 60s, then its qualification of a theology of glory with a theology of the cross would not be as direct an antidote to widespread persecution as if Mark were

---

25. See esp. Gundry, *Mark*, 1042–43.

26. As noted above p. 50 n. 42, Carsten Thiede has resurrected the argument of José O'Callaghan (originally published as "¿Papiros neotestamentarios en la cueva 7 de Qumrán?" *Biblica* 53 [1972]: 91–100) that a fragment of Mark 6:52–53 is to be found at Qumran, which, if true, would virtually guarantee a pre-70 date because the Essene community there vanished after the Jewish War. But, also as noted above, this identification is highly improbable.

27. See esp. Martin Hengel, *Studies in the Gospel of Mark* (London: SCM; Philadelphia: Fortress, 1985), 1–30.

28. On the other hand, John Wenham's attempt to date Mark to the mid-40s (*Redating Matthew, Mark and Luke* [Leicester and Downers Grove: IVP, 1992], 146–72, 230–38) depends on seeing Luke written in the mid-50s (on the basis of equating "the brother who is praised by all the churches for his service to the gospel" in 2 Cor. 8:18 with Luke and the "service" being the writing of Luke's Gospel) and on Peter's departure to "another place" in Acts 12:17 being a reference to Rome. But Wenham's interpretation of the former passage is highly speculative, and his interpretation of the latter, while plausible, is based only on fairly late church tradition.

writing a few years later. But it might be an attempt to rebut triumphalist attitudes that were challenging and discouraging Christians in Rome, much like the views promoted by the Judaizers who were unsettling the Corinthians in about 56 (see 2 Cor. 10–13).[29] On the other hand, Luke may have been written after A.D. 70 (see below, p. 150), in which case the Neronic persecution could be the best *Sitz im Leben* for Mark's Gospel. A date of *somewhere in the 60s* is probably our safest guess, without trying to narrow things down any more than that.

AUTHORSHIP

All of the traditions already cited, indeed all that have been preserved from antiquity, support *John Mark, companion of Peter and Paul, as author* (see Acts 12:12, 25; 13:5, 13; 15:37; Col. 4:10; 2 Tim. 4:11; Phm. 24; 1 Pet. 5:13). Mark is best known for his falling out with Paul, but Paul's greetings in the later epistles demonstrate that this was remedied. Presumably a Judean and Jewish Christian, it was Mark whose mother's home was one of the meeting places for the early church in Jerusalem (Acts 12:12), so the family may have been relatively well off. Those who held to Mark as author included Irenaeus, Tertullian, Clement of Alexandria, Origen, Jerome, and the Muratorian canon. These sources also consistently associated the information in Mark's Gospel with Peter's preaching. But the oldest and most important testimony, from very early in the second century and recorded by Eusebius in the early 300s, is that of Papias. Papias himself cites an elder named John, presumably the apostle, as having taught that

> Mark became Peter's interpreter and wrote accurately all that he remembered, not indeed, in order, of the things said or done by the Lord. For he had not heard the Lord, nor had he followed him, but later on, as I said, followed Peter, who used to give teaching as necessity demanded but not making, as it were, an arrangement of the Lord's oracles, so that Mark did nothing wrong in writing down single points as he remembered them. For to one thing he gave attention, to leave out nothing of what he had heard and to make no false statements in them. (*Ecclesiastical History* 3.39.15)

On the assumption that "in order" means in chronological order, this testimony also corroborates our observations about the frequently thematic nature of Mark's outline. It also fits our earlier conclusions about redaction criticism, that the evangelists were deliberate and highly selective in what they chose to include, without thereby falsifying the material that was included.

Many contemporary scholars nevertheless dispute the reliability of this tradition for several reasons: (1) The author could not have been Jewish because of the Latinisms, a lack of Jewish coloring, the explanation of Hebrew terms

---

29. E. Earle Ellis, "The Date and Provenance of Mark's Gospel," in *The Four Gospels 1992*, ed. F. van Segbroeck, and others, vol. 2 (Leuven: University Press and Peeters, 1992), 801–15, makes a plausible case for stages of composition, with Petrine or Markan input throughout, culminating in a final product composed in Caesarea in the mid-50s and delivered to Rome in the mid-60s. For a date at the beginning of the 60s, see Gundry, *Mark*, 1043. Interestingly, Gundry's hypothesis that Mark tempers a theology of the cross with a theology of glory could fit equally well into this time frame, a further reminder that Mark keeps the two themes in balance and that all dates must be tentative.

and customs, and allegedly confused topography (cf. Mark 7:31, which has Jesus traveling to Galilee and the Decapolis, southeast of Tyre, by means of Sidon to the north). (2) The author could not have been Mark, the companion of Paul, because the Gospel shows no contact with Pauline theology. (3) The material could not have come from Peter because of the disparaging way the author treats the disciples, including Peter. (4) The material could not have come from any single, primary witness of the life of Christ because of the complex history of tradition that source, form, and redaction critics have demonstrated for the Gospel.[30]

In response, however, we must note: (1) The Gentile coloring of the Gospel is sufficient to demonstrate a primarily Gentile audience for whom the book was designed to be intelligible, but it cannot prove that its author was non-Jewish. Given the Hellenization of Palestine and plentiful apostolic travels and ministry outside of Israel, it is extremely difficult to pontificate as to what Mark could or could not have written. Mark 7:31 reflects a circuitous itinerary to be sure, but this would have been natural for an itinerant preacher. (2) An emphasis on the cross is in fact one of Paul's theological centerpieces (cf., e.g., 1 Cor. 2:2). (3) It is arguable that no one but Peter could have authorized so negative a treatment of the disciples, given how quickly the early church began to exalt them, and Peter in particular. He may have wanted to be more modest or to combat an inflated view of himself. (4) Dependence on Peter in places does not rule out Mark's use of numerous other sources, oral and/or written, nor does it preclude his having edited source material and imposed his own stylistic imprint on each passage. (5) Given that Mark was not one of the Twelve but a relatively obscure character with a mixed record of ministry during his lifetime, it is unlikely that anyone unfamiliar with the true author of this Gospel but desiring to credit it to an authoritative witness would have selected Mark as his man. Little of interpretive significance depends on whether or not Mark was the author, but modern objections scarcely outweigh the unanimous testimony of the early church.

FOR FURTHER STUDY

Commentaries

Introductory

Cole, Alan. *The Gospel according to Mark.* [rev. TNTC] Leicester: IVP; Grand Rapids: Eerdmans, 1989.

English, Donald. *The Message of Mark.* [BST] Leicester and Downers Grove: IVP, 1992.

Garland, David. *Mark* [NIVApplComm] Grand Rapids: Zondervan, 1996.

Hurtado, Larry. *Mark.* [NIBC] Peabody: Hendrickson, 1989.

Williamson, Lamar, Jr. *Mark.* [Int] Atlanta: John Knox, 1983.

Intermediate

Brooks, James A. *Mark.* [NAC] Nashville: Broadman, 1991.

Cranfield, C. E. B. *The Gospel according to St. Mark.* [CGT] Cambridge: CUP, rev. 1977.

Hooker, Morna D. *The Gospel according to Saint Mark.* [BNTC] London: A & C Black; Peabody: Hendrickson, 1991.

---

30. Although Mark is typically viewed as the first Gospel written, so that we have no written sources of his with which to compare his final edition, plausible suggestions have been made about pre-Markan units of tradition: controversy stories, parables, cycles of miracles, and so on. And detailed studies of Markan style confidently dissect numerous passages, dividing them into Markan and pre-Markan wording. Cf. esp. E. J. Pryke, *Redactional Style in the Marcan Gospel* (Cambridge: CUP, 1978).

Lane, William L. *The Gospel according to Mark.* [NIC] Grand Rapids: Eerdmans, 1974; London: Marshall, Morgan & Scott, 1975.

Schweizer, Eduard. *The Good News according to Mark.* Richmond: John Knox, 1970; London: SPCK, 1971.

Advanced

Guelich, Robert A. *Mark 1–8:26.* [WBC] Dallas: Word, 1989. Vol. 2 forthcoming by Craig A. Evans.

Gundry, Robert H. *Mark: A Commentary on His Apology for the Cross.* Grand Rapids: Eerdmans, 1993.

Taylor, Vincent. *The Gospel according to St. Mark.* London: Macmillan, 1952.

Other Key Studies of Markan Introduction or Theology More Generally

Best, Ernest. *Mark: The Gospel as Story.* Edinburgh: T & T Clark, 1983.

Cunningham, Phillip J. *Mark: The Good News Preached to the Romans.* New York: Paulist, 1995.

Hengel, Martin. *Studies in the Gospel of Mark.* London: SCM; Philadelphia: Fortress, 1985.

Kealy, Séan P. *Mark's Gospel: A History of Its Interpretation from the Beginning until 1979.* New York: Paulist, 1982.

Kee, Howard C. *Community of the New Age: Studies in Mark's Gospel.* Philadelphia: Westminster; London: SCM, 1977.

Mack, Burton L. *A Myth of Innocence.* Philadelphia: Fortress, 1988.

Martin, Ralph P. *Mark: Evangelist and Theologian.* Exeter: Paternoster, 1972; Grand Rapids: Zondervan, 1973.

Stock, Augustine. *The Method and Message of Mark.* Wilmington: Glazier, 1989.

Telford, William R., ed. *The Interpretation of Mark.* London: SPCK; Philadelphia: Fortress, 1985.

Tolbert, Mary A. *Sowing the Gospel: Mark's World in Literary-Historical Perspective.* Minneapolis: Fortress, 1989.

Trocmé, Etienne. *The Formation of the Gospel according to Mark.* London: SPCK; Philadelphia: Westminster, 1975.

Bibliography

Neirynck, F. *The Gospel of Mark: A Cumulative Bibliography 1950–1990.* Leuven: University Press and Peeters, 1992.

QUESTIONS FOR REVIEW

1. What is a plausible overall outline for the Gospel of Mark? That is, how many main sections may it be divided into and by what criteria? What theology may be inferred from this structure?

2. According to typical evangelical reconstructions, who wrote this Gospel, when, where, to whom, and under what circumstances (to the extent that this information may be reasonably inferred)?

3. What are several of the major theological distinctives of this Gospel?

4. Take a passage from a Gospel synopsis that appears in all three Synoptics, and identify the probable theological emphases of Mark. Consider both the "horizontal" and the "vertical" dimensions of redaction criticism.

5. Given the emphases and probable circumstances of Mark's Gospel, in what settings in contemporary Christian living might it be even more acutely relevant than the other Gospels?

CHAPTER SEVEN

THE GOSPEL OF MATTHEW

STRUCTURE

Matthew is considerably longer than Mark. Whereas Mark begins with the ministry of John the Baptist and the adult Jesus, Matthew prefaces his narrative with two chapters about Jesus' ancestry, conception, and infancy (chaps. 1–2). Whereas Mark ends abruptly without a formal resurrection appearance, Matthew has a full chapter about Jesus' return from the grave and his final commissioning of the disciples (chap. 28). Whereas Mark has very few sections of extended teaching by Jesus, Matthew has five large blocks of discourse material ("sermons"). The first and last of these span three chapters; the middle three comprise one chapter apiece (chaps. 5–7; 10; 13; 18; 23–25). In the second, third, and fifth of these, Mark has much shorter blocks of corresponding teaching; in the first and fourth, he has virtually no parallels at all.

That Matthew intends these five major sermons of Jesus to be viewed as unified discourses punctuating his historical narrative is clear from the recurring refrains with which he concludes each of them: "When Jesus had finished saying these things . . ." (7:28; 11:1; 13:53; 19:1 and 26:1—which adds "all" before "these things"). Early in this century, B. W. Bacon popularized the view that these five sermons were the key to Matthew's structure and that Matthew was creating a new Law or Pentateuch of sorts, with the five sermons corresponding to the five books of Moses.[1] More recently, a second structural observation, promoted particularly by Jack Kingsbury, has been added to this. Twice,

---

1. B. W. Bacon, "The 'Five Books' of Matthew against the Jews," *Expositor* 15 (1918); 56–66.

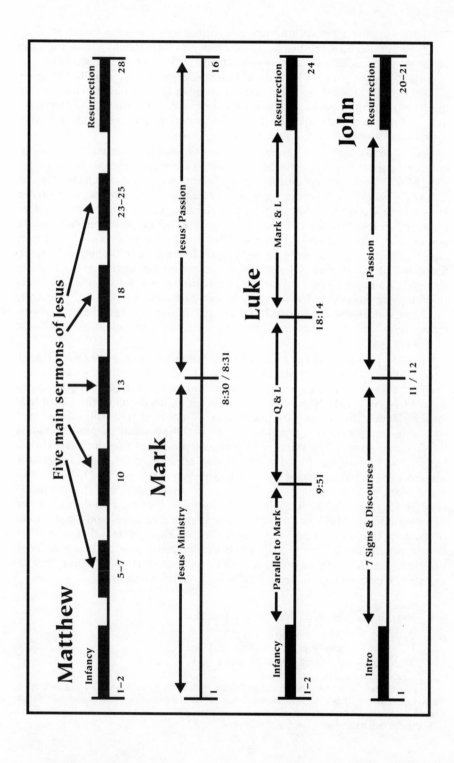

Matthew uses the identical formula, "From that time on Jesus began to . . . "
(4:17; 16:21). Because the first appearance of this formula introduces the main
phase of Jesus' adult ministry, beginning in Galilee, while the second corresponds to the pivot in Mark's Gospel that sets Christ on the road to the cross,
it is probable that Matthew inserted these comments to divide his narrative into
thirds: introduction, body, and extended conclusion or climax.[2] It is then common to find each of these subsections subdivided in terms of Matthew's alternating blocks of discourse and narrative.

One attractive way of outlining Matthew's Gospel is to see each pair of dis-
course-plus-narrative segments as highlighting a common theme. At the beginning of the "body" of the Gospel, Matthew stresses two main facets of Jesus'
ministry—his preaching-teaching and his healing (4:23). The Sermon on the
Mount clearly illustrates his authoritative teaching (cf. 7:29); chapters 8–9 go
on to group together ten miracle stories (mostly healings) to demonstrate his
authority in that realm too. Matthew 9:35 repeats the language of 4:23 very
closely, confirming that chapters 5–9 belong together as a unified section. To
this point in the narrative, Jesus has not experienced significant opposition,
though the attitude expressed in 9:34 foreshadows what is to come. In his second sermon, however, Jesus calls and commissions the Twelve, preparing
them to expect substantial hostility (chap. 10). In the next two chapters of narrative, Jesus and his followers begin to experience that animosity (11:20–24;
12:1–14, 22–49).

Chapter 13 has long been seen as a turning point in Matthew's Gospel.
Unlike Mark's chapter of parables (chap. 4), Matthew's divides evenly into
one-half addressed to the crowds in public and one-half to the disciples in private (13:1–35; 36–52). Increasingly, Jesus is sifting his listeners into "outsiders"
and "insiders." This progressive polarization is repeated in his subsequent ministry as his rejection among the Jews increasingly gives way to ministry among
the Gentiles and teachings that go beyond the bounds of Jewish convention or
territory (13:53–14:36; 15:1–16:20). In the conclusion to the Gospel, the
sequence of narrative and discourse is reversed. Matthew 16:21–17:27 finds
Jesus repeatedly clarifying the implications of discipleship, and the sermon in
chapter 18, delivered exclusively to the disciples, lays the foundation for the
fledgling church. Matthew 19:1–25:46 is comprised of small and large blocks
of teaching that increasingly warn about God's judgment on unbelief, particularly in Israel. The final three chapters describing Jesus' passion, death, and resurrection balance the opening chapters of introduction. Putting this all
together, we may propose an outline along the following lines:[3]

I.   Introduction to Jesus' Ministry (1:1–4:16)
     A. Jesus' Origin (1:1–2:23)
     B. Jesus' Preparation for Ministry (3:1–4:16)
II. The Development of Jesus' Ministry (4:17–16:20)

---

2. Jack D. Kingsbury, *Matthew: Structure, Christology, Kingdom* (Philadelphia: Fortress, 1975). One of Kingsbury's students,
David R. Bauer, has surveyed all the major structural options for Matthew's Gospel and refined his teacher's approach still further (*The
Structure of Matthew's Gospel* [Sheffield: Almond, 1989]).

3. Cf. further Craig L. Blomberg, *Matthew* (Nashville: Broadman, 1992).

THEOLOGY

Views of Jesus

Teacher. Already it is clear that one of Matthew's distinctive portraits, at least over against Mark, is that Jesus is the consummate Teacher. Most scholars have not accepted Bacon's proposal regarding the sermons as five books of new Law, but many have seen as prominent the theme of Jesus as a new Lawgiver, or as a new Moses more generally.[4] Like Moses, Jesus has miracles surrounding his infancy, causes turmoil among the rulers of the land, survives when babies his age are massacred, and retraces the journey of the Exodus to and from Egypt (chaps. 1–2). He remains in the wilderness forty days and forty nights in preparation for his ministry and then gives his programmatic teaching from a mountain (chaps. 4–5). Indeed, mountains remain significant places of revelation throughout the Gospel, both in the paralleled story of the transfiguration (17:1–9) and in the unparalleled finale of the Great Commission (28:16–20).[5] It must be stressed, however, that Jesus' teaching is considerably different from pure "Law" for Matthew; it is a higher-order "righteousness" (5:20), which brings rest rather than a burden (11:28–30). Put another way, with Jesus' moral demands comes a new empowerment for obedience not previously available.

Son of David, King, and Royal Messiah. One of the most distinctive titles for Jesus in Matthew is "Son of David." It occurs nine times, eight of which are

---

4. See esp. Dale C. Allison, Jr., *The New Moses: A Matthean Typology* (Minneapolis: Fortress, 1993).
5. Cf. further Terence L. Donaldson, *Jesus on the Mountain* (Sheffield: JSOT, 1985).

unparalleled in any other Gospel. Elsewhere the term appears in Luke four times and in Mark three times, but it is absent from all other New Testament documents. The title fits Matthew's Jewish orientation (see below, p. 132) and the conventional expectation of a Messiah from the house of David who would exercise regal functions. Thus Herod and his followers in Jerusalem fear a literal king who will usurp their power (2:1–12), and Pilate wonders if Jesus is "king of the Jews" (27:11). Interestingly, whereas the people in power who should have been able to recognize a true Messiah cannot, the individuals who address Jesus as "Son of David" are consistently the powerless ones in need of healing (9:27; 15:22; 20:30).[6]

A Heightened Son of God? Mark 1:1 indicated that "Son of God" was an important title for Mark, but several scholars suggest that Matthew's use of the term even more closely approaches the full-fledged divinity that later creeds and confessions make explicit.[7] Again, key references frame Matthew's text (2:15; 26:63). The devil assumes Jesus to be God's Son at the temptation (4:3, 6). Only in Matthew do the disciples confess him as the Son of God after he walks on the water (14:33). Only in Matthew does Peter use this title as well as "Christ" in his climactic confession (16:16). And in another framing device, Jesus is introduced as *Immanuel* (God with us) at his conception (1:23) and then promises his followers, "I will be with you always," as part of the Gospel's closing words (28:20).

Wisdom Incarnate? In 12:42 and 13:54, Jesus' wisdom is highlighted. In 11:19, he and John the Baptist are said to vindicate God's wisdom. In 11:25–30, Jesus calls the lowly to himself and promises them rest, similar to the role of God's Wisdom personified in the intertestamental book of "wisdom literature" attributed to Jesus, son of Sirach. These phenomena have suggested to some a distinctively Matthean concern to portray Jesus as God's Wisdom incarnate, building on the model of Proverbs 8–9.[8]

Lord. Perhaps the most important of Matthew's titles for Jesus is not one of his most distinctive. Numerous people call Jesus "Lord," and in many instances it need mean little more than "Master." But in several places the context suggests that Lord is the correct title for full-fledged disciples to use, particularly when they are in need of aid that only one who has divine power can supply (e.g., 8:2, 6, 25; 9:28).[9] Then it would seem appropriate to speak of people "worshiping" the Lord even during his lifetime (cf. also 2:2, 8, 11; 14:33).[10]

Other Distinctive Themes

Particularism and Universalism in the Gospel Offer. One of the most striking distinctives, apparent already from the structure of Matthew's Gospel, is that

---

6. Cf. further W. R. G. Loader, "Son of David, Blindness, Possession, and Duality in Matthew," *CBQ* 44 (1982): 570–85.

7. See esp. Kingsbury, *Structure;* cf. idem, *Matthew as Story* (Philadelphia: Fortress, 1986).

8. M. Jack Suggs, *Wisdom, Christology, and Law in Matthew's Gospel* (Cambridge, Mass.: Harvard, 1970); Celia Deutsch, *Hidden Wisdom and the Easy Yoke* (Sheffield: JSOT, 1987).

9. Cf. further Günther Bornkamm, Gerhard Barth, and Heinz J. Held, *Tradition and Interpretation in Matthew* (London: SCM; Philadelphia: Westminster, 1963), 41–43.

10. The verb that appears in these passages is *proskuneō.* It can mean to "fall down before" someone and/or to "worship" a person. The verb is a favorite of Matthew's, appearing thirteen times, compared to only twice in Mark and twice in Luke.

Matthew is perhaps the most Jewish of all the Gospels, and yet at key places it also foreshadows the Gentile mission as clearly as any of the other three.

Approximately twenty times Matthew cites a particular Scripture as fulfilled in the events of the life of Christ. Roughly half of these are unique to his Gospel. Five of them are found in the first two chapters as Matthew describes the events surrounding Christ's birth (see further below, p. 199). The unparalleled quotations tend to follow the original Hebrew a bit more closely than the LXX, which is the version of choice for most of the paralleled citations.[11] Jesus' teaching can also be said to fulfill the whole of the Scriptures more generally (5:17–20). And although Jesus demands a greater "righteousness" than that of the Jewish leaders (v. 20),[12] the context of this claim (vv. 21–48) makes it clear that he is not just telling his followers to do a better job of keeping the Law. There are both continuities and discontinuities between the Old Testament and Jesus' teaching, but Christ's fulfillment of the Law, analogous to his fulfillment of Old Testament prophecies, suggests that he is the one to whom all of the Scriptures pointed and for whom they prepared. God's will can now be understood only by following Jesus and adhering to his teaching.[13]

Three famous passages in Matthew have provoked much controversy as they all seem to limit Jesus' mission to only the Jews. He commands his followers to go nowhere among the Samaritans or Gentiles, seems to say that he will return before their ministry to the Jews is completed, and tells the Syrophoenician woman he was sent only to Israel (10:5–6, 23; 15:24). Matthew's Jewish flavor is further reinforced by his distinctive use of the term "kingdom of heaven," a typically Semitic circumlocution to avoid pronouncing the holy name of God. This expression appears thirty-three times in Matthew but nowhere else in the New Testament, and parallel passages in Mark and Luke regularly have "kingdom of God" instead.

At the same time it is only in Matthew that Gentile Magi come and worship the Christ Child (2:1–12) or that a series of three parables is found predicting the demise of the current Jewish leadership (21:18–22:14). In the one parable of this cluster that is found in Mark and Luke (the wicked tenants), Matthew alone includes Jesus' prediction that the kingdom would be "taken away from you and given to a people who will produce its fruit" (21:43). Only Matthew recounts Christ's "parable" of the sheep and the goats, with its emphasis on universal judgment of the world's peoples (25:31–46). And only Matthew includes Jesus' Great Commission, commanding the Twelve to make disciples of all people groups (Greek, *ethne*, the same term used in chap. 25).

The best resolution of this apparent tension between Jewish particularism and multiethnic universalism sees Jesus' ministry unfolding in two stages. Before the cross and resurrection, Jews, as God's chosen people, deserved to hear Christ's message first. Inasmuch as many of them, particularly Israel's leadership, rejected the Gospel offer, Jesus' followers were to go out after his resurrection and proclaim his offer of salvation to everyone. Jesus' occasional

---

11. On which, see esp. Robert H. Gundry, *The Use of the Old Testament in St. Matthew's Gospel* (Leiden: Brill, 1967).

12. "Righteousness," too, is a key theme for Matthew. See esp. Benno Przybylski, *Righteousness in Matthew and His World of Thought* (Cambridge: CUP, 1980).

13. John P. Meier, *Law and History in Matthew's Gospel* (Rome: BIP, 1976); Robert Banks, "Matthew's Understanding of the Law," *JBL* 93 (1974): 226–42; Douglas J. Moo, "Jesus and the Authority of the Mosaic Law," *JSNT* 20 (1984): 3–49.

contact with Gentiles during his lifetime foreshadowed this worldwide mission. Interestingly, Paul later recognized a priority of going to the Jews first, even during the church age, but he became the consummate apostle to the Gentiles (cf. his pattern of ministry throughout Acts—e.g., 13:46; 18:6; 19:9). Romans 1:16 captures the sequence succinctly: The gospel "is the power of God for the salvation of everyone who believes: first for the Jew, then for the Gentile."[14] And, like Paul, Matthew wishes to ground both stages very firmly in the Old Testament and Jewish expectation.

   Discipleship and the Church. Although it has been overstated, there is nevertheless a perceptible difference between the fairly negative portrait of the disciples in Mark and a somewhat more positive picture of them in Matthew. In several key places where Mark emphasizes their lack of faith, Matthew focuses on the fledgling belief that they do have (e.g., Matt. 8:26; 13:51; 14:33).[15] Matthew is also the only gospel ever to use the word "church" (Greek, *ekklesia*)—three times in 16:18 and 18:17—or to include teaching about community discipline and forgiveness (18:15–35). Matthew's distinctive term for followers of Jesus is "little ones" (10:42; 18:6, 10, 14; 25:40), stressing their humble position before God. And Matthew may reflect ongoing roles or even offices in the church to which he is writing with his distinctive references to wise men, prophets, and scribes (10:41; 13:52; 23:34). Matthew may further be concerned to oppose false teachers in his midst, who rely on their own "antinomian" (lawless) and "charismatic" claims to spiritual authority (cf. esp. 7:15–23).[16]

   Conflict with Jewish Authorities. For a Gospel that is so thoroughly Jewish, it is surprising not only to discover Matthew's universalism but also to see how he portrays Jesus' encounters with the scribes, Pharisees, and Sadducees in so unrelentingly hostile a fashion. The woes of chapter 23 illustrate this in greatest detail, and 27:25 has been called by some the most anti-Semitic statement in the New Testament (as the crowds at Jesus' crucifixion cry out, "Let his blood be on us and on our children"). Matthew and Jesus refer to Jewish houses of worship as "their" synagogues (4:23; 9:35; 10:17; 12:9; 13:54), as if these men were not also Jewish. And Matthew refers to the Sadducees in seven passages, always negatively, whereas they appear in all of the rest of the Gospels only twice.

   Yet a passage like 23:39 demonstrates that Matthew does not write off all Jews for all time. All Jesus' first followers remain Jewish, and missionary work must continue to include them and even give them priority (28:19, 10:23). Still, God's people are now being constituted as all those who follow Jesus in discipleship, not merely one chosen ethnic group.[17]

---

   14. Cf. Amy-Jill Levine, *The Social and Ethnic Dimensions of Matthean Social History* (Lewiston: Mellen, 1988).

   15. See, classically, Bornkamm, Barth, and Held, *Matthew*, 52–57. On discipleship more generally, see esp. Michael J. Wilkins, *The Concept of Disciple in Matthew's Gospel* (Leiden: Brill, 1988).

   16. Particularly helpful on these topics is Eduard Schweizer, "Matthew's Church," in Graham N. Stanton, ed., *The Interpretation of Matthew* (Edinburgh: T & T Clark, rev. 1995), 149–77.

   17. Cf. further D. A. Carson, "The Jewish Leaders in Matthew's Gospel: A Reappraisal," *JETS* 25 (1982): 161–74.

CIRCUMSTANCES

What situation in the life of the early church would give rise to such a bewildering combination of seemingly pro- and anti-Jewish positions? External evidence helps us to confirm our suspicion that Matthew wrote primarily to *Jewish Christians*. But most of the testimony states merely that Matthew wrote "to the Hebrews," although occasionally a place in Palestine is suggested (see Irenaeus, *Against Heresies* 3.1.1; Eusebius, *Ecclesiastical History* 3.24.5–6; Jerome, *Lives of Illustrious Men* 3). Modern scholars have often suggested Syria, especially its central city of Antioch, which was up to one-seventh Jewish. At any rate, Jewish Christianity was always strongest in the eastern part of the empire.

More fruitful is discussion of the type of situation within Judaism that would have provoked this Gospel. Some have argued for a predominantly Gentile audience, and interpreted Matthew's Jewish emphasis as teaching Gentile Christians how to appropriate their Jewish heritage and Scriptures. A few have seen the Gospel as an evangelistic tract to non-Christian Jews. But most interpreters recognize Matthew's audience as a Jewish-Christian community *either on the verge of or just recovering from a substantial break from Judaism as a whole.* Graham Stanton helpfully suggests the concept of the church having broken from but still in vigorous debate with "the synagogue across the street."[18] Recent studies of "formative Judaism" point out how diverse Jewish thought and practice were before A.D. 70. After the destruction of the temple, however, only two primary branches emerged: Rabbinic Judaism, carrying on to a certain degree the legacy of the Pharisees, and Jewish Christianity, which would survive in significant numbers only into the mid–second century. Needless to say, the tensions would have become quite high as each of these groups competed in the same communities to defend the claim that they alone were the true heirs to their religious heritage.[19] A situation like this very plausibly explains how Matthew could be so concerned to show Jesus as the fulfillment of all things Jewish and yet stress the rebellion of Israel's leaders, comparable in Matthew's mind to the hostility of the synagogue leadership in his day.

The common critical approach to Matthew has deduced from these observations that Matthew must have been written after A.D. 70. Some would insist that the Gospel must be dated to 85–100, after the so-called *birkath ha-minim* (see above, p. 25, n. 26). The end of the first century seems to be the latest possible date because the Apostolic Fathers, beginning already at the turn of the century, were quoting Matthew on a regular basis. But, as we saw earlier, it is doubtful if one clear break ever occurred between Judaism and Christianity, and already in the events of Acts in the 40s and 50s, synagogues were expelling Paul and persecuting Jewish Christians who joined him. So it is not at all clear that Matthew must have been writing after 70.

---

18. Several of his helpful studies on this topic are now collected and augmented in Graham N. Stanton, *A Gospel for a New People: Studies in Matthew* (Edinburgh: T & T Clark, 1992; Louisville: Westminster/John Knox, 1993). Archaeologists have actually discovered communities in which church and synagogue were very close to each other.

19. See esp. J. Andrew Overman, *Matthew's Gospel and Formative Judaism: The Social World of the Matthean Community* (Minneapolis: Fortress, 1990); Anthony J. Saldarini, *Matthew's Christian-Jewish Community* (Chicago and London: University of Chicago Press, 1994).

Scholars also frequently appeal to Matthew's versions of Jesus' predictions concerning the destruction of the temple. Matthew's Eschatological Discourse is little different from Mark's at this point (Matt. 24:15–24; cf. Mark 13:14–23), but in the parable of the wedding banquet (Matt. 22:1–14) only Matthew includes the details that the originally invited guests "seized his servants, mistreated them and killed them. The king was enraged. He sent his army and destroyed those murderers and burned their city" (22:6–7).

This has struck many readers as a patently transparent reference to the Jewish rebellion against Rome, followed by the imperial burning and destruction of Jerusalem. For those who do not believe in the possibility of predictive prophecy, this passage ensures that Matthew was written after 70. And even for some who are not philosophically prejudiced in this way, the explicitness of detail convinces them that these words were written after the fact to make Jesus' original prophecy clearer. On the other hand, it is not true that most of Jerusalem was burned; it was primarily the temple that was set on fire. And the imagery of a city's fiery destruction was frequently used in Jewish literature for warfare (cf., e.g., Judg. 1:8, 1 Macc. 5:28, Test. Jud. 5:1–5), so it need not be so specific a reference to the events of A.D. 70 at all.[20] In this event, its value for helping us date the Gospel disappears altogether.

One can become so eager to defend a pre-70 date, however, that one jumps on the bandwagon of inconclusive evidence. Carsten Thiede, for example, has gone against most of the scholarly world by dating the Magdalen papyrus of Matthew, known as p64 and housed in Oxford University, to the mid-first century. Yet a comparison of this manuscript with Gospel papyri housed in Barcelona and Paris make it highly likely that all three documents formed a codex (book) from about A.D. 200.[21]

The external testimony of the early Fathers may prove more helpful at this point. Irenaeus (again in *Against Heresies* 3.1.1), endorsed by Eusebius (*Ecclesiastical History* 5.8.2), believed that Matthew wrote "while Peter and Paul were preaching the gospel and founding the church in Rome," a reference that most naturally fits a date within the 60s. This could mesh with our conclusion concerning the Synoptic problem that Matthew relies in part on Mark (though Irenaeus himself thought Matthew wrote *before* Mark; see p. 122). If Mark was written in the early to mid-sixties and a copy soon fell into the hands of Matthew, he could have penned his Gospel shortly thereafter. Of course, those who find compelling internal evidence to place this Gospel after 70 will not imagine one early Church Father's testimony sufficient to challenge it.

Various data within Matthew's Gospel might also support an earlier dating.[22] Why would only Matthew include references to the temple tax (17:24–27), offerings (5:23–24) and ritual (23:16–22), or to Sabbath-keeping in Judea (24:20) in an era (after 70) in which none of these was practiced any longer? Why would he stress Jesus' antagonism against the Sadducees in an age in

20. Cf. John A. T. Robinson, *Redating the New Testament* (London: SCM; Philadelphia: Westminster, 1976) 19–21.

21. Cf. Carsten P. Thiede, *Rekindling the Word: In Search of Gospel Truth* (Leominster: Gracewing; Valley Forge: TPI, 1995), 20–32; with Graham Stanton, *Gospel Truth? New Light on Jesus and the Gospels* (London: HarperCollins; Valley Forge: TPI, 1995), 11–19.

22. See esp. Robert H. Gundry, *Matthew: A Commentary on His Handbook for a Mixed Church under Persecution* (Grand Rapids: Eerdmans, rev. 1994), 599–609.

which they had died out? One answer, of course, is that these things happened that way during Jesus' lifetime. But given the evangelists' consistent pattern of selecting episodes from Jesus' life that were theologically meaningful for their communities, one wonders if these data are not indirect pointers to a pre-70 date. The evidence is finely balanced, but we believe there is a slight weight in favor of opting for *a date in the 60s, sometime after the composition of Mark.*

AUTHORSHIP

A generation or more ago many critics believed "Matthew" was a Gentile writing for Gentiles. The dominant Jewish orientation of the Gospel coupled with the above survey of the probable circumstances of its composition lead a majority today to conclude that the author was a Jewish Christian.[23] Tradition, of course, beginning with the superscription placed on early copies of this document, attributes the Gospel to *Matthew, also called Levi, a converted tax collector and one of Jesus' twelve apostles* (cf. Matt. 10:3; 9:9–13; Mark 2:14–17). The most important early external evidence is again attributed to Papias, quoted by Eusebius (*Ecclesiastical History* 3.39.16). There are several possible ways to translate different words in Papias' testimony, as reflected by the bracketed expressions in the following quote: "Matthew composed [compiled] his Gospel [sayings] in the Hebrew [Aramaic] language [dialect, style], and everyone translated [interpreted] as they were able."

This testimony allows for several variables: (1) Matthew could have functioned as a conservative editor or he could have composed material more creatively. (2) Matthew may have written what we know as his Gospel or he may have collected a group of Jesus' sayings together that formed the nucleus of a later full-fledged Gospel. (3) Matthew could have written in either Aramaic or Hebrew. (4) Others after Matthew might have translated his work into the Greek we now have, or Matthew might have translated the work himself with others later debating its interpretation.[24]

Perhaps the most significant of these variables is (2). The Greek *logia* in Papias's remarks is a term that normally refers to "sayings" or "oracles" and is not naturally attached to an entire narrative Gospel. Some assume that Papias *was* referring to a whole Gospel because in his earlier testimony about Mark he had used the term there also. But a careful reading of that text suggests that the *logia* refer back to Jesus' "oracles" (i.e., teachings) which Peter gave "as necessity demanded," even though Papias recognizes Mark wrote both about "the things said or done by the Lord." We should then consider the possibility that what Matthew first wrote down in Hebrew was something along the lines

---

23. For comprehensive detail of options and for advocates of the various positions on this issue and on the other introductory concerns surveyed in this chapter, see W. D. Davies and Dale C. Allison, Jr., *A Critical and Exegetical Commentary on the Gospel according to Saint Matthew*, vol. 1 (Edinburgh: T & T Clark, 1988), 1–148.

24. Gundry, in the first edition of his commentary (entitled *Matthew: A Commentary on His Literary and Theological Art* [1982]), caused quite a stir in evangelical circles by arguing in detail that Papias refers to a Hebraic "style" of writing, and that the style is one of "midrash," in which Matthew embellished his sources (Mark and Q) with fanciful, unhistorical, but theologically edifying detail, much like certain intertestamental Jewish sources treated Scripture. The full-blown theory has been accepted by almost no subsequent writers, inside or outside evangelicalism, and has been well critiqued, whatever elements of truth it may contain here or there. Gundry has now responded to his critics in the newer edition (see n. 22), however, xi–xxx.

of the reconstructed Q source. Indeed, although it goes beyond anything we can demonstrate, it has been plausibly suggested that this "first draft" of Matthew *was* what scholars call Q.[25] Then either Matthew himself or some other Greek-speaking Christian would have later incorporated into this first draft elements of Mark along with more distinctive traditions ("M") to create the Greek version of Matthew we now possess.

The truthfulness of Papias's testimony, whatever the *logia* refer to, remains in doubt, however, so long as no ancient copy of any portion of Matthew *in Hebrew* is discovered. Yet the testimony of early Church Fathers that Matthew wrote something in Hebrew, often allegedly prior to Mark, is widespread and persistent (cf. esp. Irenaeus, *Against Heresies* 3.1.1; Eusebius, *Ecclesiastical History* 5.10.3). In addition, one fourteenth-century Hebrew manuscript of Matthew shows some evidence of being not just a translation of our canonical Greek text but reflects certain independent renderings of an older Hebrew tradition. It is not inconceivable that it preserves a few traces of what Matthew originally wrote.[26]

It is also objected that Matthew does not read like a literal Greek translation from an underlying Hebrew text. But Matthew's "Q" passages regularly show signs of careful Semitic parallelism; Matthew is not without his Semitisms; and we need not argue that Matthew (or whoever) translated literally. Where we know that ancient sources have been translated from Hebrew into Greek (e.g., with some of Josephus's writings), there are also clear signs that the translator at times rendered his text freely and paraphrastically. What is more, as we have seen already in our discussion of Mark, it is difficult to claim that the Jewish Matthew, especially if he were a tax collector who needed to be literate and well conversant with the Gentiles for whom he worked, could not have produced a document based on prior Hebrew and Greek sources in reasonably good Greek style.

There are other objections that critics raise to Matthew as author of this Gospel. The most important include (a) the anti-Jewishness already noted; (b) theological incompatibility with other Jewish-Christian sources; (c) the possibility that 13:52 is a self-reference to the author as a Christian "scribe," not a tax collector;[27] (d) the improbability of Matthew living beyond A.D. 85; and (e) the unlikelihood of an apostle borrowing from a nonapostolic author like Mark. Of these, only (e) proves at all serious.

To respond to each of these charges: (1) If many scholars can agree that a Jew wrote this book in a situation of tension and polemic with non-Christian Judaism, then Matthew, already once alienated from his contemporaries by his former profession, surely could have done so. (2) The Gospel of Matthew is actually quite compatible with the epistle of James, another probable early Jewish-Christian document, and all Jewish Christianity was not monolithic in its beliefs. (3) It is not at all clear that 13:52 is the author's self-reference, but

25. T. W. Manson, *The Sayings of Jesus* (London: SCM, 1949; Grand Rapids: Eerdmans, 1979) 15–20; Matthew Black, "The Use of Rhetorical Terminology in Papias on Mark and Matthew," *JSNT* 37 (1989): 31–41; Donald A. Hagner, *Matthew 1–13* (Dallas: Word, 1994), xlvi.

26. George Howard, *The Gospel of Matthew according to a Primitive Hebrew Text* (Macon: Mercer; Leuven: Peeters, 1987).

27. See esp. O. Lamar Cope, *Matthew: A Scribe Trained for the Kingdom of Heaven* (Washington: Catholic Biblical Association of America, 1976).

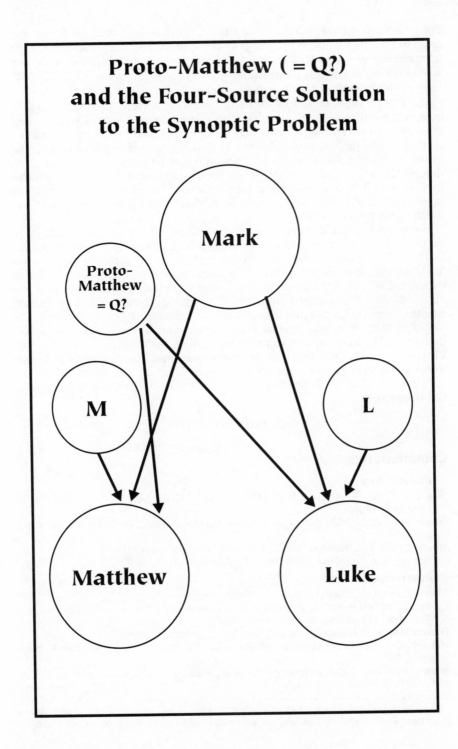

Proto-Matthew (= Q?)
and the Four-Source Solution
to the Synoptic Problem

Mark

Proto-
Matthew
= Q?

M

L

Matthew

Luke

even if it were, what would be more natural than a former tax collector to continue to use his writing skills and consider himself a Christian scribe? (4) We
have already seen that Matthew's Gospel may be as early as the 60s, but if not,
we do not have enough information, even in more legendary Christian writings, to surmise when Matthew died or how old he was at the time.

(5) The problem of Matthew's dependence on Mark is substantially eased
by accepting the early traditions that Mark carried the authority of Peter's teaching with him (see above, pp. 121–122). Peter, James, and John formed the inner
core of Christ's three closest followers. Put simply, Peter was present for certain
events in Jesus' ministry when Matthew was not (cf., e.g., 17:1; 26:37). Even
though Matthew did observe much that Mark described, it is surely conceivable
that he would be curious to see how a Gospel based on Peter's preaching
would look. Matthew scarcely depends on Mark slavishly and feels free to add
much of his own material.

Some commentators have noted that Matthew does seem to include more
details in his story related to money matters (e.g., the story of the temple tax
in 17:24–27 or parables like the unforgiving servant in 18:23–35). But it is not
likely we can prove much from this. In short, there is no compelling reason to
overturn the unanimous testimony of antiquity that Matthew/Levi was the
author of the Gospel attributed to him. Even though Matthew was an apostle,
he came from a disreputable background. No apocryphal works are attributed
to him as they are to apostles like Peter, James, John, Thomas, Andrew, or Bartholomew. He seems an unlikely candidate, even among the apostles, for later
Christians to have selected in an attempt to give this Gospel greater authority,
if indeed he were not the author. On the other hand, as with Mark, little of our
ability to interpret the Gospel's historical context or exegetical detail hangs on
this decision.[28]

FOR FURTHER STUDY

Commentaries

Introductory

France, R. T. *The Gospel according to Matthew.* [rev. TNTC] Leicester: IVP; Grand Rapids:
    Eerdmans, 1985.
Green, Michael. *Matthew for Today.* London: Hodder & Stoughton, 1988; Dallas: Word,
    1989.
Mounce, Robert H. *Matthew.* [NIBC] Peabody: Hendrickson, 1991.
Ridderbos, H. N. *Matthew.* [BSC] Grand Rapids: Zondervan, 1987.

Intermediate

Blomberg, Craig L. *Matthew.* [NAC] Nashville: Broadman, 1992.
Carson, D. A. "Matthew." In *Expositor's Bible Commentary.* Vol. 8. Edited by Frank E.
    Gaebelein. Grand Rapids: Zondervan, 1984.
Garland, David E. *Reading Matthew.* New York: Crossroad, 1993.
Hill, David. *The Gospel of Matthew.* [NCB] London: Oliphants, 1972; Grand Rapids: Eerd-
    mans, 1981.
Morris, Leon. *The Gospel according to Matthew.* [Pillar] Grand Rapids: Eerdmans; Leices-
    ter: IVP, 1992.

---

28. Even as staunch a conservative as D. A. Carson ("Matthew," *Expositor's Bible Commentary,* vol. 8, ed. Frank E. Gaebelein
[Grand Rapids: Zondervan, 1984], 19) leaves the question open (and also notes that any date from 40–100 is possible [p. 21]).

Schweizer, Eduard. *The Good News according to Matthew*. Richmond: John Knox, 1975;
London: SPCK, 1976.

Advanced

Davies, W. D., and Dale C. Allison, Jr. *A Critical and Exegetical Commentary on the Gospel according to Saint Matthew*. 3 vols. Edinburgh: T & T Clark, 1988–.

Gundry, Robert H. *Matthew: A Commentary on His Handbook for a Mixed Church under
Persecution*. Grand Rapids: Eerdmans, rev. 1994.

Hagner, Donald A. *Matthew*. 2 vols. [WBC] Dallas: Word, 1993–95.

Other Key Studies of Matthean Introduction or Theology More Generally

Balch, David L., ed. *Social History of the Matthean Community*. Minneapolis: Fortress,
1991.

Bornkamm, Günther, Gerhard Barth, and Heinz J. Held, *Tradition and Interpretation in
Matthew*. London: SCM; Philadelphia: Westminster, 1963.

France, R. T. *Matthew: Evangelist and Teacher*. Exeter: Paternoster; Grand Rapids:
Zondervan, 1989.

Kingsbury, Jack D. *Matthew: Structure, Christology, Kingdom*. Philadelphia: Fortress,
1975.

Luz, Ulrich. *The Theology of the Gospel of Matthew*. Cambridge: CUP, 1995.

Meier, John P. *The Vision of Matthew: Christ, Church and Morality in the First Gospel*.
New York: Paulist, 1979.

Overman, J. Andrew. *Matthew's Gospel and Formative Judaism: The Social World of the
Matthean Community*. Minneapolis: Fortress, 1990.

Powell, Mark A. *God with Us: A Pastoral Theology of Matthew's Gospel*. Minneapolis: Fortress, 1995.

Saldarini, Anthony J. *Matthew's Christian-Jewish Community*. Chicago and London: University of Chicago Press, 1994.

Stanton, Graham N. *A Gospel for a New People: Studies in Matthew*. Edinburgh: T. & T.
Clark, 1992; Louisville: Westminster/John Knox, 1993.

Stanton, Graham N., ed. *The Interpretation of Matthew*. Edinburgh: T. & T. Clark, rev.
1995.

Stock, Augustine. *The Method and Message of Matthew*. Collegeville, Minn.: Liturgical
Press, 1994.

Bibliography

Mills, Watson E. *The Gospel of Matthew*. Lewiston and Lampeter: Mellen, 1993.

QUESTIONS FOR REVIEW

1. What is a plausible overall outline for the Gospel of Matthew? That is, how
many main sections may it be divided into and by what criteria? What theology
may be inferred from this structure?

2. According to typical evangelical reconstructions, who wrote this Gospel,
when, where, to whom, and under what circumstances (to the extent that this
information may be reasonably inferred)?

3. What are several of the major theological distinctives of this Gospel?

4. Take a passage from a Gospel synopsis that appears in all three Synoptics,
and identify the probable theological emphases of Matthew. Consider both the
"horizontal" and the "vertical" dimensions of redaction criticism.

5. Given the emphases and probable circumstances of Matthew's Gospel, in
what settings in contemporary Christian living might it be even more acutely
relevant than the other Gospels?

CHAPTER EIGHT

THE GOSPEL OF LUKE

STRUCTURE

The structure of Luke closely resembles parts of Mark's outline and parts of Matthew's. Where Luke narrates events contained in Mark, he follows Mark's sequence even more faithfully than Matthew does. Yet, like Matthew, Luke is about half-again as long as Mark, with significant material added from "Q" (material shared with Matthew but not found in Mark) and "L" (material unique to Luke). Like Matthew, too, Luke begins with two detailed chapters of the events surrounding Christ's birth and ends with a lengthy chapter highlighting resurrection appearances. Luke, however, is not characterized by the lengthy sermons of Matthew. As we noted in discussing Streeter's hypothesis about proto-Luke (above, p. 92), Luke alternates between large blocks of Markan and non-Markan material. Chapters 1–2 are wholly unparalleled in Mark. Luke 3:1–9:50, especially from 4:14 on, follows Mark's outline very closely for the bulk of Jesus' Galilean ministry, with occasional modifications. Luke 9:51–18:14 contains primarily teachings of Jesus from his itinerant ministry and includes almost exclusively Q and L material. From 18:15 on, Mark's outline is followed again but with more insertions of distinctively Lukan texts than in chapters 4–9.

Whatever source-critical conclusions one draws from this, these major sections seem also to correspond to Luke's thematic structure. At first glance Luke seems to be the hardest Gospel to outline. A survey of commentators certainly reveals the least amount of agreement compared with treatments of Matthew, Mark, and John. Yet at the same time, we must always keep in mind when

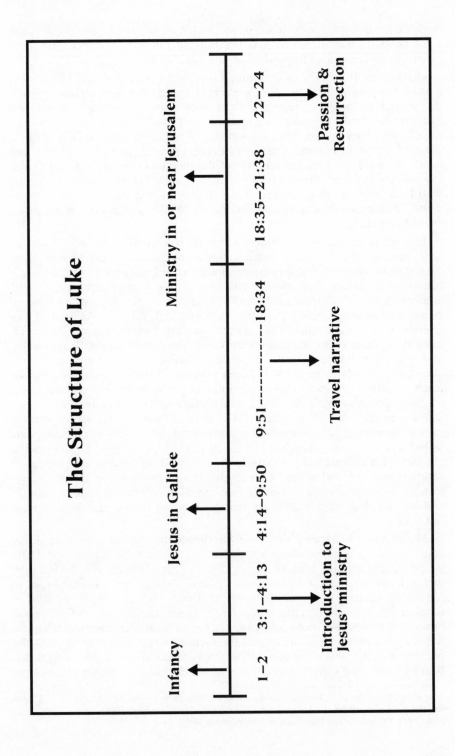

The Structure of Luke

Infancy
1–2

Introduction to Jesus' ministry
3:1–4:13

Jesus in Galilee
4:14–9:50

Travel narrative
9:51 ----------- 18:34

Ministry in or near Jerusalem
18:35–21:38

Passion & Resurrection
22–24

studying Luke that he wrote a sequel to his Gospel, the book of Acts. Although a full-fledged introduction to Acts lies beyond the scope of this text, some observations are crucial for understanding Luke's Gospel.

One observation involves structure. It is widely agreed that Acts 1:8 presents a rough geographical outline for the events narrated in Luke's second volume: the gospel progresses from Jerusalem ever outward, through Judea and Samaria, eventually reaching "the ends of the earth." Thus Acts 1–7 describes the church in Jerusalem. After the stoning of Stephen, many believers move out, and Acts 8–12 narrates a variety of events explicitly in Judea, Samaria, and nearby areas. Then with the ministry of the newly converted Saul (Paul), the Gospel begins to travel throughout the known world (chaps. 13–28). Acts ends with Paul finally having reached Rome, the heart and capital of the Gentile world. Within one generation, an exclusively Jewish sect has become a major "worldwide" religion.

This exact geographical sequence can be discerned in Luke's Gospel as well, only in reverse order. Interestingly, the sequence corresponds fairly closely to the source-critical divisions already noted, suggesting that the organization is deliberate. The opening chapters include a significant cluster of references to various Roman rulers and Roman appointees in power when the events surrounding Christ's life begin to unfold (1:5; 2:1; 3:1). As he does frequently in Acts, Luke situates his narrative within "empire history." As he follows Mark, Luke omits the entire section on Jesus' "withdrawal" from Galilee and adjoining material (Mark 6:45–8:26), leaving 3:1–9:50 narrating events almost exclusively from Jesus' Galilean ministry. We will discuss the significance of 9:51–18:14 more later (a section that probably extends at least to vv. 31–34, which read like a conclusion and transition). But two interesting observations are that the only geographical references in this section place Jesus in or near Samaria (9:52; 17:11) and that immediately after this section he appears in Judea, en route to Jerusalem (18:35; 19:1, 11, 28, etc.). Christ, of course, is crucified and resurrected just outside the city walls of Jerusalem, but what is striking about the end of the Gospel is that Luke narrates none of Christ's later resurrection appearances in Galilee but several in or near Jerusalem. Luke 24 and Acts 1 also overlap in that each narrates the resurrection and the ascension of Christ.

All this strongly suggests that Luke was designing a two-volume, chiastically structured account of the life of Jesus and the growth of the early church.[1] The gospel begins with the birth of Jesus in the context of Roman history and rule, then follows Jesus as he travels from Galilee, through Samaria and Judea to Jerusalem, zeroing in on the holy city of God's chosen people. In light of Israel's fateful decision on the whole to reject Jesus, the ministry of God's good news now progresses outward again via the same steps: from Jerusalem, to Judea and Samaria, and throughout the Gentile world, culminating with the preaching of the gospel by Paul extending as far as Rome. If one objects that "Galilee" and "the Gentile world" do not match, one has only to recall that,

---

1. Kenneth Wolfe, "The Chiastic Structure of Luke-Acts and Some Implications for Worship," *SWJT* 22 (1980): 60–71. Cf. Sidney Greidanus, *The Modern Preacher and the Ancient Text* (Grand Rapids: Eerdmans; Leicester: IVP, 1988), 283; Luke T. Johnson, *The Writings of the New Testament: An Interpretation* (Philadelphia: Fortress, 1986), 204–5.

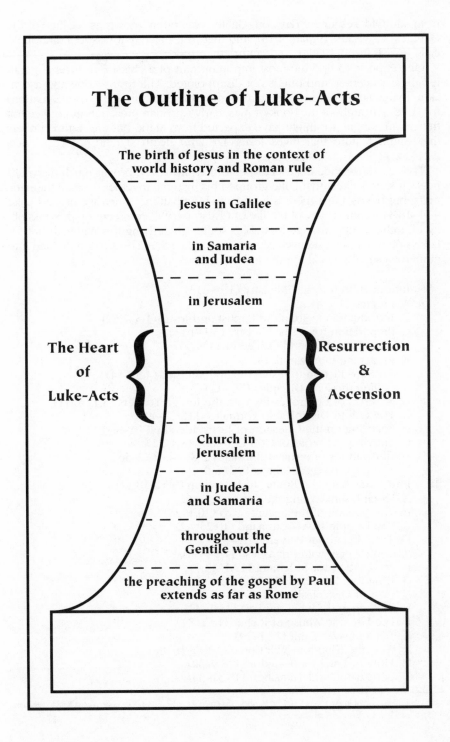

The Outline of Luke-Acts

The birth of Jesus in the context of world history and Roman rule

Jesus in Galilee

in Samaria and Judea

in Jerusalem

The Heart of Luke-Acts

Resurrection & Ascension

Church in Jerusalem

in Judea and Samaria

throughout the Gentile world

the preaching of the gospel by Paul extends as far as Rome

from late Old Testament days on, Galilee was often known as "Galilee of the Gentiles" (cf. Isa. 9:1; Matt. 4:15), and that in Jesus' day it was less monolithically Jewish in population and culture than Judea.

One expects to find the most important part of a chiasm, or inverse parallelism, at its center, and one is not disappointed. The resurrection and ascension, twice narrated, form the heart of the Christian "kerygma" (proclamation) for Luke. Throughout the book of Acts, early Christian preachers announce not the crucifixion, as we might have expected from Mark, but the resurrection as the central feature that gives Jesus' life *and* death significance (e.g., Acts 2:24–36, 13:30–37, 17:18, 23:6).

Trying to subdivide Luke's Gospel further, however, proves much more difficult. It seems likely that Luke grouped his material together in small thematic units, but beyond that there is no overarching pattern. When we discuss Luke 9:51–18:34 in our survey of the life of Christ, we will comment on the possibility of a chiastically arranged parables source underlying this material, but for Luke's final outline it seems best simply to see each major division divided into numerous small units along the following lines:[2]

I.   Introduction to Jesus' Ministry (1:1–4:13)
     A. Preface (1:1–4)
     B. Introduction to John the Baptist and Jesus (1:5–2:52)
     C. Preparation for Jesus' Ministry (3:1–4:13)
II. Ministry in and around Galilee (4:14–9:50)
     A. Preaching in Nazareth (4:14–30)
     B. An Introduction to Jesus' Healing Ministry (4:31–44)
     C. Calling the First Disciples (5:1–11)
     D. A Series of Controversies with the Jewish Leaders (5:12–6:11)
     E. The Call to Discipleship Formalized (6:12–49)
     F. Focusing on the Question of Jesus' Identity (7:1–8:3)
     G. Hearing the Word of God Correctly (8:4–21)
     H. Illustrations of Jesus' Authoritative Word (8:22–56)
     I. The Christological Climax (9:1–50)
III. Jesus' Teaching "En Route" to Jerusalem (9:51–18:34)
     A. Discipleship Eyeing the Cross (9:51–62)
     B. The Mission of the Seventy-two (10:1–24)
     C. The Double Love Command (10:25–42)
     D. Teaching about Prayer (11:1–13)
     E. Controversy with Pharisees (11:14–54)
     F. Preparation for Judgment (12:1–13:9)
     G. Kingdom Reversals (13:10–14:24)
     H. Cost of Discipleship (14:25–35)
     I. Seeking and Saving the Lost (15:1–32)
     J. The Use and Abuse of Riches (16:1–31)
     K. Teachings on Faith (17:1–19)
     L. How the Kingdom Will Come (17:20–18:8)
     M. How to Enter the Kingdom (18:9–30)
     N. Conclusion and Transition (18:31–34)

2. Particularly helpful in this task is I. Howard Marshall, *The Gospel of Luke* (Exeter: Paternoster; Grand Rapids: Eerdmans, 1978), which I have followed at several points.

THEOLOGY

Views of Jesus

Jesus' Humanity and Compassion for the Outcasts of Society. Although Luke preserves several of the key events that Mark and Matthew use to highlight Jesus' exalted nature, they do not dominate his narrative as much. None of the titles such as "Christ," "Son of God," or "Lord" is nearly as prominent. Rather, what strikes most readers of Luke's Gospel is how Jesus' humanity shines through, particularly in his association with and compassion for numerous categories of social outcasts. Four groups stand out in particular: (1) Samaritans and Gentiles; (2) tax collectors and sinners; (3) women; and (4) the poor.

1. Samaritans and Gentiles. Only Luke records the parable of the Good Samaritan (10:25–37) and the story of the ten lepers who were cleansed, with only the Samaritan leper returning to give thanks (17:11–19). Although Jesus does not leave Jewish territory in Luke, many commentators see foreshadowings of the later Gentile mission in such details as the sending of the servant further afield to bring more to the master's banqueting table in the parable of the great supper (14:23). Certainly, by the time we reach Acts the Gentile mission becomes a dominant theme.

2. Tax collectors and sinners. Readers who do not sense how unusual this combination of "tax collectors and sinners" is, found in texts like 5:30, 7:34, and 15:1, have probably been in church too long! "Sinners" in this context refers to those who flagrantly violated the cultural and religious norms of Judaism. The parable of the prodigal son offers a classic example (15:11–32). As another paradigm of the lawless, tax collectors are listed—Jewish tollhouse keepers who collected customs and duties for the occupying Roman empire. They may not have been among the "down and out," but they were, in the minds of their contemporaries, at least "up and out." Not only does Luke use the phrase, "tax collectors and sinners," to characterize those who gathered around Jesus to hear him and were welcomed by him, but Luke alone tells two stories in which tax collectors were heroes—the parable of the Pharisee and the publican (18:9–14) and the conversion of Zaccheus (19:1–10).

3. Women. Luke has far more women in his account than do the other Gospels. The birth narratives are told from the perspectives of Elizabeth and Mary (chaps. 1–2). The prophetess Anna appears alongside her male counterpart Simeon (2:25–38). Pairs of parables balance men's and women's characteristic roles—the mustard seed and leaven (13:18–21) and the lost sheep and lost coin (15:3–10). Both a woman and a man are healed of their crippling diseases on

different Sabbaths (13:10–17; 14:1–6). Jesus affirms the notoriously sinful woman who anoints him with oil despite the complaints of his Pharisaic host (7:36–50). He praises Mary's devotion to his teaching, against the cultural norms of the day (10:38–42). And only Luke describes Jesus' itinerant ministry as being funded in part by the contributions of several well-to-do women who traveled with him (8:1–3).[3]

4. The Poor. Whereas Matthew's Jesus blesses the poor in spirit, Luke's blesses "you who are poor" (6:20). Jesus' programmatic manifesto in Nazareth, brought to the front of his Galilean ministry in Luke's outline, claims that he fulfills the mission of Isaiah's servant who was anointed by God "to preach good news to the poor" (Luke 4:18). The various teachings in 14:7–24 all demonstrate God's concern for the sick and dispossessed who are unable to help themselves or return favors. The parable of the rich man and Lazarus vindicates the poor beggar at the expense of his counterpart wallowing in luxury (16:19–31).

Savior. Perhaps the title that best sums up the themes of Jesus' humanity and compassion is "Savior." In 2:11 the angel announces, "Today in the town of David a Savior has been born to you; he is Christ the Lord." Interestingly, "Savior" is the most distinctive title for Jesus in Luke. The Greek words for Savior and salvation (*sotēr, sotēria, sotērion*)occur eight times in Luke, nine times in Acts, and nowhere else in the Synoptic Gospels. Luke 19:10 arguably provides a one-verse summary of the entire Gospel: "For the Son of Man came to seek and to save what was lost." Interestingly, however, the title "Lord" features more prominently in Acts even than "Savior," as if Luke were trying to stress different emphases in Jesus' ministry before the cross and resurrection than afterward.[4] I. H. Marshall, nevertheless, makes a compelling case for seeing "salvation" as the unifying theme for all of Luke's theology.[5]

Prophet. Unique to Luke is Jesus' revivification of the widow's son in Nain, a passage strikingly similar to Elisha's re-animation of the Shunammite woman's son (2 Kings 4:8–37). Luke seems to recognize this similarity with his comment that the crowd responded by declaring, "A great prophet has appeared among us" (7:16). In another uniquely Lukan passage, Jesus apparently refers to himself as a prophet (13:33). Several scholars have seen the whole of Luke's central section (9:51–18:34) as paralleling topics found in a similar sequence in Deuteronomy,[6] or at least echoing themes characteristic of Deuteronomy's theology: (a) Jesus sent as God's messenger, (b) to warn a stiff-necked generation, (c) of its coming destruction, (d) only to be rejected.[7] Luke's use of the Old Testament is best summed up as a prophetic and christological use—all of the Scriptures point to Jesus and must be fulfilled by him (Luke 24:25, 44).[8]

---

3. Cf. esp. Jane Kopas, "Jesus and Women: Luke's Gospel," *Theology Today* 43 (1986): 192–202.

4. C. F. D. Moule, "The Christology of Acts," in *Studies in Luke-Acts*, ed. Leander E. Keck and J. Louis Martyn (Nashville: Abingdon, 1966), 159–85.

5. I. Howard Marshall, *Luke: Historian and Theologian* (Exeter: Paternoster; Grand Rapids: Zondervan, rev. 1988), esp. 77–102.

6. E.g., John Drury, *Tradition and Design in Luke's Gospel* (London: Darton, Longman & Todd; Atlanta: John Knox, 1976), 138–64.

7. See esp. David P. Moessner, *Lord of the Banquet* (Minneapolis: Fortress, 1989).

8. Darrell L. Bock, *Proclamation from Prophecy and Pattern* (Sheffield: JSOT, 1987).

Teacher of Parables. Twenty-eight of the forty passages most commonly classified as parables appear in Luke, fifteen of these found only in this Gospel. All but one of these fifteen appear in the central section (9:51–18:34). For the most part, Luke's parables do not include Jesus' more enigmatic narratives, designed to weed outsiders from insiders (à la Mark 4 and Matt. 13) but down-to-earth, simple, illustrative stories for Jewish peasant folk. Four of them have often been called example-stories because they seem to have a less symbolic nature than most: the good Samaritan (10:25–37), the rich fool (12:13–21), the rich man and Lazarus (16:19–31), and the Pharisee and the publican (18:9–14).

The Resurrected and Exalted One, Benefactor. As already noted, when studying Acts Christian preachers focus primarily on the resurrection and exaltation, not the crucifixion. This ties in with Luke's omission of the teaching about Christ's substitutionary atonement in Mark 10:45. Luke's parallel account, uniquely placed in the context of the Lord's Supper, focuses instead exclusively on the need for Christ's followers to imitate their master's servanthood. They must not expect reciprocity for the good deeds they do (Luke 22:24–30). Instead of imitating the Hellenistic patrons (see above, p. 61), they can trust in Jesus as their ultimate benefactor who will pay them back in the ways the people they help cannot (cf. 14:12–14).[9]

Other Distinctive Themes

Stewardship of Material Possessions. Closely related to Jesus' concern for the poor in Luke is the emphasis on the need for Jesus' followers not to accumulate or hoard riches for themselves. Only Luke balances his beatitudes with woes—against those who are rich, well fed, laughing, and well spoken of (6:24–26). Only Luke includes the "hymns" of Mary and Zechariah, who speak of "the great reversal"—the powerful being rendered powerless and the lowly in Israel exalted (1:46–55, 67–79). Again the parables of the rich fool and the rich man and Lazarus carry pointed implications for those who spend all their riches simply improving their own lifestyles. The unjust steward is commended for using his wealth shrewdly; believers must do the same for kingdom purposes (16:1–13). Not all Christians are called to give up everything as the rich young ruler was (18:18–30); but Zaccheus voluntarily gives up half (19:1–10), and the faithful servants invest all they have for their master's work (19:11–27). Some liberation theologians have seized on Luke and exaggerated his teaching on stewardship to the point of arguing that it is impossible to be both rich and Christian. Nevertheless, Luke certainly knows nothing of rich Christians who are not generous in giving of their wealth to the needy (cf., e.g., 12:33; 14:33; and Acts 2:44–47)![10]

9. See esp. Frederick W. Danker, *Jesus and the New Age* (Philadelphia: Fortress, rev. 1988).

10. Numerous well-balanced studies of this theme have appeared: Walter E. Pilgrim, *Good News to the Poor* (Minneapolis: Augsburg, 1981); David P. Seccombe, *Possessions and the Poor in Luke-Acts* (Linz: Studien zum Neuen Testament und seiner Umwelt, 1982); Halvor Moxnes, *The Economy of the Kingdom* (Philadelphia: Fortress, 1988); Warren Heard, "Luke's Attitude Toward the Rich and Poor," *Trinity Journal* n.s. 9 (1988): 47–80; Joel B. Green, "Good News to Whom? Jesus and the 'Poor' in the Gospel of Luke," in *Jesus of Nazareth: Lord and Christ*, eds. Joel B. Green and Max Turner (Carlisle: Paternoster; Grand Rapids: Eerdmans, 1994), 59–74.

The Jewish People and Obedience to the Law. Until recently, most commentators took it for granted that Luke was the Gospel with the greatest Gentile
orientation. Recently, however, various writers have challenged this consensus.[11] They have pointed out that it is only Luke that at times has a moderately
positive view of the Jewish leaders. For example, they invite Jesus to their
homes (7:36–50; 14:1–24) and warn him about Herod (13:31). We have already
noted how the Gospel climaxes (and Acts begins) in the temple in Jerusalem,
as though Luke acknowledges it as God's holy place. Most strikingly, Luke
seems to go out of his way to describe how various individuals during Jesus'
ministry and the life of the early church still obey the Jewish law (e.g., Luke
1:6, 59; 2:21–24), even as Christians (e.g., Acts 3:1; 18:18; 21:21–24). A whole
spectrum of views has now emerged as to how Luke saw Jews and Gentiles
related in Christ and as to whether or not part or all of the Mosaic Law was still
incumbent on believers.[12] How the apostolic decree of Acts 15 is interpreted
plays a crucial role in this debate. But a good case can still be made that while
Luke is faithful to history by reporting how Jesus' first followers did not immediately break away from Judaism and its Torah, Luke's redactional emphases
time and again point to a law-free Christianity as the desired goal to which God
was ultimately guiding first-century events. Christ is the *fulfillment* of Judaism,
not its preservation (see esp. Luke 24:44); the religion of God's people does
not merely continue unchanged.[13]

Writing Christian History. The pioneering redaction critic of Luke was Hans
Conzelmann.[14] Although virtually every one of his major tenets has been challenged, his views still remain influential. Conzelmann saw Luke as the first
Christian historian, that is to say, the first Gospel writer to tell the story of Jesus
as a part of the ongoing history of the world, or more precisely, of the history
of God's dealings with his people. The latter has often been called "salvation
history" (German, *Heilsgeschichte*). Clearly Luke is the only one who wrote an
Acts, a sequel to the Gospel, and at least to this extent Conzelmann's observation is on target. But "salvation history" for scholars has often meant inaccurate
history in that Luke embellished his sources with unhistorical detail and at
times fabricated sayings or events that were not what Jesus actually did or said.
Other writers have therefore suggested terms such as "theological history" or
"empire history" as less misleading.[15] Luke's details may well be accurate, at
least by the historiographical standards of his day, but they were chosen
because of their theological or spiritual significance in the context of the
Roman empire.

Conzelmann became well known also for his interpretation of Luke as dividing history into three periods—the period of Israel, the time of Jesus, and the

---

11. The pioneer in this movement was Jacob Jervell, *Luke and the People of God* (Minneapolis: Augsburg, 1972).

12. For a survey, see Joseph B. Tyson, ed., *Luke-Acts and the Jewish People: Eight Critical Perspectives* (Minneapolis: Augsburg, 1988).

13. Craig L. Blomberg, "The Law in Luke-Acts," *JSNT* 22 (1984): 53–80; idem, "The Christian and the Law of Moses," in *The Book of Acts in Its First-Century Setting*, vol. 6, ed. I. Howard Marshall and David Peterson (Carlisle: Paternoster; Grand Rapids: Eerdmans, forthcoming).

14. *The Theology of St. Luke* (New York: Harper & Row; London: Faber & Faber, 1960).

15. See, respectively, Robert Maddox, *The Purpose of Luke-Acts* (Edinburgh: T. & T. Clark, 1982), 16; and Richard J. Cassidy, *Jesus, Politics, and Society: A Study of Luke's Gospel* (Maryknoll: Orbis, 1978), 1–19.

subsequent life of the early church. The German title of his work reflects this scheme—*Die Mitte der Zeit* ("The Middle of Time"). Whereas Mark and Matthew maintained the typical Jewish division of history into "this age" and "the age to come," while differing from conventional Judaism by seeing "the age to come" as having dawned with the ministry of Jesus, Luke separates the period of Jesus as a special, ideal age, distinct also from the life of the early church. For example, Conzelmann saw this period as a "Satan-free period," with the devil departing after Jesus' temptations (4:13) and not returning until just before the crucifixion. The book of Acts, on the other hand, reflected the era of *Frühkatholisizmus* ("early Catholicism"), in which the church was becoming increasingly institutionalized and less dependent on the Spirit than at first.

Closely tied in with all of this is the idea that Luke, of all the Gospel writers, most stresses the delay of the Parousia (Christ's return). Luke 12:35–38, 19:11, and 21:20–24 play down the possibility of an immediate return, while 12:20, 16:19–31, and 23:43 show that Christians need to reckon more with the possibility of their deaths *before* the Parousia. This too is part of the "early Catholic" trajectory of Luke.

Whatever one makes of all this, Conzelmann certainly described the church as it very quickly became and has often remained. It is more doubtful that it was so already in Luke's day and that Luke wanted to promote such a picture. While not stressing the immediacy of Christ's return, Luke does still retain a hope for its near arrival. Luke 17:20–21 and 22–37 nicely balance present and future eschatology, but the latter, lengthier passage certainly stresses the need to be ready for the end to happen at any time after Christ's death.[16] The number of parallels that can be drawn between the ministries of Peter and Paul in Acts and Jesus in Luke belie the notion that Luke tries to paint a picture of the church era with significantly different strokes than the period of Jesus.[17] Nor is it clear that Satan was absent during most of Jesus' ministry (cf. 11:14–26; 22:31). But a key theme for Luke is "the demise of the devil" (cf. 10:18–19). Luke even describes certain miracles as if they were a kind of exorcism (cf., most notably, 8:24).[18] All of Luke-Acts, to be sure, is pervaded by a progression of events that leaves no doubt that God, with a sovereign plan, is in charge.[19]

The Holy Spirit, Prayer, and Joy. The Spirit appears considerably more often in Luke than in Matthew or Mark. A characteristic expression of Luke's in both of his volumes is that someone is "filled with the Spirit," a recurring phenomenon that always leads to bold proclamation and service of the Gospel (e.g., Luke 1:15, 41; Acts 2:4; 4:31). The Holy Spirit empowers Jesus and his followers for many other kinds of ministries as well.[20] One of these is prayer. Prayer is the focus of three parables unique to Luke (11:5–8; 18:1–8, 9–14) and features distinctively in critical moments in Christ's own life (e.g., 5:16; 6:12; 9:18, 28).[21]

---

16. See esp. E. Earle Ellis, *Eschatology in Luke* (Philadelphia: Fortress, 1972); John T. Carroll, *Response to the End of History: Eschatology and Situation in Luke-Acts* (Atlanta: Scholars, 1988).

17. For details on these and numerous other parallelisms within sections of Luke or Acts, see Charles H. Talbert, *Literary Patterns, Theological Themes, and the Genre of Luke-Acts* (Missoula: Scholars, 1974).

18. Susan R. Garrett, *The Demise of the Devil: Magic and the Demonic in Luke's Writings* (Minneapolis: Fortress, 1989).

19. Cf. further John T. Squires, *The Plan of God in Luke-Acts* (Cambridge: CUP, 1993).

20. For details, see Roger Stronstad, *The Charismatic Theology of St. Luke* (Peabody: Hendrickson, 1984).

21. Cf. Peter T. O'Brien, "Prayer in Luke-Acts," *TynB* 24 (1973): 111–27.

Another distinctive aspect of life in the Spirit in Luke is joy. The infancy narratives are filled with joyful poems or songs of praise, and the word "joy" itself is unusually common throughout the Gospel (e.g., 1:14; 2:10; 10:17; 15:7, 10). "Rejoice" and "praise" are also more frequent in Luke than in other Gospels.

CIRCUMSTANCES

The above survey clearly demonstrated a richness and diversity to Luke's theology that does not readily lead to a narrowly defined community or set of circumstances in which Luke must have been writing. The dominant concern about material possessions, furthered in Acts with its models of communal sharing (Acts 2:43–47; 4:32–37), suggests to many that Luke was addressing a Christian community at least somewhat more well-to-do than many, though not without poor people in its midst. *He would then be calling the better-off Christians to give generously and share with needier brothers and sisters in the Lord.* Jesus' compassion for outcasts, coupled with the progress of the Gospel from distinctively Jewish to predominantly Gentile contexts, also supports the traditional idea of Luke as *a Gentile writing to a mostly, if not exclusively, Gentile-Christian community.* Beyond this, details become hard to pin down.

If the motif of the delay of the Parousia is not so prominent as to rule out a balancing concern for Christ's imminent return, then nothing about the date of the Gospel may be deduced from it. It has been fashionable to assume that Luke must be late because of this motif, written probably between 80–100, but questions over the delay of Christ's return were surfacing already at the beginning of the 50s in Thessalonica (see the balance Paul tries to strive for between 1 and 2 Thessalonians). In the nineteenth century, the hypothesis associated with Ferdinand Baur and the so-called Tübingen school was popular. According to this view, Luke-Acts was a mid-second-century attempt to gloss over the severity of early Christian debate about the relationship of Law and Gospel. This view has now been rightly abandoned.

The question of the fall of Jerusalem comes back to haunt commentators again in Luke. Luke 21:20–24 differs substantially from its parallels in Matthew and Mark and seems at first to require a post-70 date. The city would have been destroyed, so Luke could interpret for his readers what the "desolating sacrilege" was—"Jerusalem surrounded by armies" and "trampled on by the Gentiles until the times of the Gentiles are fulfilled" (vv. 20, 24). This view does not require Luke to have invented these sayings after the fact. And it fits our outline of Acts whereby Rome is the zenith of the progress of the Gospel thus far and a fitting climax to the book, even if written some years after the events of its final chapter.[22]

On the other hand, many readers of Acts have puzzled over why Luke would emphasize Paul's arrest, imprisonment, and trials for eight chapters (Acts 21–28)—more than a quarter of his book—yet never give the outcome of Paul's appeal to Caesar or an account of his martyrdom, paralleling Jesus' fate.

---

22. Thus evangelical commentators like David Williams, *Acts* (Peabody: Hendrickson, 1990), 13; and Ralph P. Martin, *New Testament Foundations*, vol. 2 (Exeter: Paternoster; Grand Rapids: Eerdmans, 1978), 66, defend exactly this position (supporting dates of ca. A.D. 75 and 80, respectively).

All this becomes even more perplexing inasmuch as a fair amount of early church tradition supports the claim that Paul was indeed released after his two years of house arrest in Rome, only to be rearrested a few years later.[23] This state of affairs has convinced many conservative commentators that Acts must have been written immediately after the events it narrates, so that the reason Luke does not give the results of Paul's appeal is because the emperor had not yet rendered his verdict. *This would require a date for Luke's Gospel of sometime before the book of Acts and no later than about A.D. 62* (the probable date of the end of Paul's house arrest in Rome).[24] Given that we must leave room for Luke to have received and utilized a copy of Mark's Gospel, it probably could not have been written more than a year or two before this date either.

Other factors make the decision between pre- and post-70 more complicated still. Is Paul's consistently positive view of Roman government throughout Acts a sign that Nero's pogrom has not yet started and that Christianity is still being treated as a *religio licita* (see above, p. 23)? Is Acts 20:25 a sign that Luke in fact does know that Paul has since been (re-) arrested, condemned, and martyred? Or is Paul's understanding that he would never again see the Ephesian elders one that changed later when he hoped to return to Ephesus (1 Tim. 3:14; cf. 1:3—on the assumptions that the Pastoral Epistles are Pauline and dated to the years immediately after Paul's house arrest in Rome)? David Wenham has even created a meticulous reconstruction of what he believes is an original Eschatological Discourse, longer and more detailed than any of the Synoptic accounts, in which Luke 21:20 is not a reinterpretation of Mark 13:14 but stands before it as a part of what Jesus originally uttered: "When you see Jerusalem surrounded by armies and the desolating sacrilege, which was spoken of by Daniel the prophet standing in the holy place, let the reader understand . . ."[25] Darrell Bock argues that Luke's stress on the debate over Jew-Gentile relations fits more naturally in a pre-70 era,[26] but, as we saw with Matthew, this debate persisted, at least in the East, throughout the first century.

The external evidence helps us make little further progress. The only relevant datum is Irenaeus' testimony that Luke wrote after Matthew and Mark (*Against Heresies* 3.1.1). The Anti-Marcionite Prologue claims that Luke came from Syrian Antioch but wrote in Achaia. Plausible suggestions concerning Luke's audience have ranged from Rome to Philippi to Antioch, with little evidence for judging among them. Internally, Luke addresses his Gospel to *Theophilus* (1:1—a name that means "lover of God"). But we know nothing about this individual except that Luke wanted to give him greater certainty about the truth of the faith. He could have already been a Christian or someone quite interested in Christianity (v. 4). Given that Luke's prologue (1:1–4) closely resembles other Greco-Roman prefaces in which a patron's name is mentioned, Theophilus is most likely a well-to-do Greek who funded Luke's writing project.[27] By addressing him, Luke is not implying that he is the only or

23. For details, see F. F. Bruce, *Paul: Apostle of the Heart Set Free* (Grand Rapids: Eerdmans [=*Paul: Apostle of the Free Spirit* (Exeter: Paternoster)], 1977), 441–55.
24. The fullest defense of this position now appears in Colin J. Hemer, *The Book of Acts in the Setting of Hellenistic History*, ed. Conrad H. Gempf (Tübingen: Mohr, 1989), 365–410.
25. David Wenham, *The Rediscovery of Jesus' Eschatological Discourse* (Sheffield: JSOT, 1984) 217.
26. Darrell L. Bock, *Luke 1:1–9:50* (Grand Rapids: Baker, 1994), 18.
27. For a detailed study of Luke's preface and its parallels, see Loveday Alexander, *The Preface to Luke's Gospel* (Cambridge: CUP, 1993).

primary person for whom the book was written. The assumption from early in church history has been that Luke was writing to a Christian community, of which Theophilus may have been a part, just as much as all the other evangelists did. To claim with confidence more certainty regarding the circumstances of Luke's composition would go beyond the data.[28]

Why specifically did Luke write? In Luke 1:3–4 he explains, "Therefore, since I myself have carefully investigated everything from the beginning, it seemed good also to me to write an orderly account for you, most excellent Theophilus, so that you may know the certainty of the things you have been taught." These verses suggest *historical, catechetical, apologetic,* and perhaps also *pastoral motives* behind Luke's work. His concerns to situate events in light of empire history and, in Acts, to portray the Roman government as not a threat to Christians (e.g., Acts 16:35–40; 18:12–17; 26:30–32) have suggested to many that Luke is trying to defend the church before Rome (or vice versa). The ambivalence with which Luke treats the Jews (more positively than in the other Gospels but still as Jesus' and the early church's primary opponents) also suggests some context of Jew-Gentile tensions. We cannot say, as do some older commentators, that the rupture between Luke's church and Judaism is long since past, but neither is there enough evidence to demonstrate recent contentions that Luke's audience and concerns are more Jewish than Gentile.[29] Readers of almost every different walk of life have found in Luke something to cherish; his is often considered the most universal of all the Gospels. Perhaps that is the reason his purposes and circumstances are so hard to pin down; he may have been deliberately trying to reach a wide audience.

AUTHORSHIP

Early church tradition is much more helpful here. The unanimous witness of the Fathers is that *the writer named Luke was the Gentile disciple, Paul's "beloved physician," mentioned in Colossians 4:14, and Paul's companion for several portions of his missionary journeys.* Proponents of this claim include the Muratorian canon, the Anti-Marcionite Prologue, Irenaeus, Clement of Alexandria, Origen, and Tertullian. In favor of this claim are (1) the so-called "we-passages" in Acts: four sections in which the author uses the first-person plural to describe events during Paul's ministry—Acts 16:10–17; 20:5–15; 21:1–18; 27:1–28:16. From Paul's letters we can learn of his main coworkers who accompanied him at various points in his travels. Luke is the only one not otherwise mentioned in Acts who fits all the data. (2) Luke is nevertheless a relatively obscure figure. He was not among the best-known of Paul's companions, nor was he an apostle himself, so it seems unlikely that anyone would have fictitiously attributed a Gospel to him. In the late nineteenth century, W. K. Hobart argued from the allegedly distinctive medical language of Luke-Acts for a doctor as the author of this work, but H. J. Cadbury early in the twentieth

28. The most comprehensive recent introduction, weighing all the various possibilities, appears in Joseph A. Fitzmyer (*The Gospel according to Luke I-IX* [Garden City: Doubleday, 1981], 35–62), who is even more thorough in his survey of Luke's distinctive theology (143–270).

29. As, e.g., in Donald Juel, *Luke-Acts: The Promise of History* (Atlanta: John Knox, 1983).

century demonstrated that this vocabulary was just as frequent in nonmedical writers.[30]

As with the other Gospels, many modern scholars dispute the traditional authorship claims. Those who hold to a very late date for Luke understandably find the theology and historical setting too late for a contemporary of Paul. Some argue that the "we-passages" reflect an eyewitness source that a later author used (a diary perhaps), preserving the original first-person language. Others allege that such language is merely an artificial literary device, though the suggested parallels to this convention in other ancient literature have not proved convincing.[31] No doubt, the strongest argument against Lukan authorship has involved the alleged discrepancies between Luke's portrait of Paul in Acts and the picture of Paul that emerges from his firsthand comments in the undisputed epistles.[32] Such a discussion would take us entirely outside the boundaries of Luke's Gospel and is therefore beyond the scope of this introduction. Suffice it to say that various scholars have quickly agreed that the differences in perspective demonstrate that *Paul* did not write Acts but fall short of proving that one of his followers, with independent interests and contexts, could not have done so.[33]

Given the resurgence of interest in Jewish concerns in Luke, it is not improbable to imagine that Luke was at one time a "God-fearer"—a Gentile who had already begun to worship the God of Israel and follow some or many of its laws.[34] But we cannot prove this. Attempts to equate him with a Jew[35] go well beyond the data and oppose the natural interpretation of Colossians 4:10–11, which seems clearly to distinguish Paul's Jewish supporters from the subsequent names listed in verses 12–14. As with our conclusions concerning Matthew and Mark, we find no compelling reason to reject the unanimous early church tradition[36] but recognize that we can still find much interpretive common ground with those who choose other options.

FOR FURTHER STUDY

Commentaries

Introductory
Bock, Darrell L. *Luke.* [NIVApplComm] Grand Rapids: Zondervan, 1996.
Bock, Darrell L. *Luke.* [NTC] Downers Grove and Leicester: IVP, 1994.

---

30. W. K. Hobart, *The Medical Language of St. Luke* (Dublin: Hodges, Figgis & Co.; London: Longmans, Green & Co., 1882); H. J. Cadbury, *The Style and Literary Method of Luke* (Cambridge, Mass.: Harvard, 1920), 39–72.

31. Contrast Vernon K. Robbins, "By Land and By Sea: The We-Passages and Ancient Sea Voyages," in *Perspectives on Luke-Acts*, ed. C. H. Talbert (Edinburgh: T & T Clark; Danville, Va.: American Association of Baptist Professors of Religion, 1978), 215–42; with Colin J. Hemer, "First Person Narrative in Acts 27–28," *TynB* 36 (1985): 79–109.

32. The classic formulation of this tension appears in Philipp Vielhauer, "On the 'Paulinism' of Acts," in *Studies in Luke-Acts*, 33–50. Vielhauer's four main ways in which he finds Luke differing from Paul deal with his views of natural theology, the Law, christology, and eschatology.

33. Cf. esp. David Wenham, "Acts and the Pauline Corpus II. The Evidence of Parallels," in *The Book of Acts in Its Ancient Literary Setting*, ed. Bruce W. Winter and Andrew D. Clarke (Carlisle: Paternoster; Grand Rapids: Eerdmans, 1993), 215–58.

34. E.g., John Nolland, *Luke 1–9:20* (Dallas: Word, 1989), xxxii–xxxiii.

35. E. Earle Ellis, *The Gospel of Luke* (London: Oliphants, 1974; Grand Rapids: Eerdmans, 1981) 51–53.

36. For a robust and detailed defense of Lukan authorship, see Hemer, *Acts*, 308–64.

Evans, Craig A. *Luke*. [NIBC] Peabody: Hendrickson, 1990.
Wilcock, Michael. *The Message of Luke*. [BST] Leicester and Downers Grove: IVP, 1979.

Intermediate

Ellis, E. Earle. *The Gospel of Luke*. London: Oliphants, 1974; Grand Rapids: Eerdmans, 1981.
Evans, C. F. *Saint Luke*. London: SCM; Philadelphia: TPI, 1990.
Schweizer, Eduard. *The Good News according to Luke*. Atlanta: John Knox; London: SPCK, 1984.
Stein, Robert H. *Luke*. [NAC] Nashville: Broadman, 1992.
Talbert, Charles H. *Reading Luke*. New York: Crossroad, 1982.

Advanced

Bock, Darrell L. *Luke*. 2 vols. [BECNT] Grand Rapids: Baker, 1994–96.
Fitzmyer, Joseph A. *The Gospel according to Luke*. 2 vols. [AB] Garden City: Doubleday, 1981–85.
Marshall, I. Howard. *The Gospel of Luke*. [NIGTC] Exeter: Paternoster; Grand Rapids: Eerdmans, 1978.
Nolland, John. *Luke*. 3 vols. [WBC] Dallas: Word, 1989–93.

Other Key Studies of Lukan Introduction or Theology More Generally

Bovon, Francois. *Luke the Theologian: Thirty-three Years of Research*. Allison Park, Pa.: Pickwick, 1987.
Conzelmann, Hans. *The Theology of St. Luke*. New York: Harper & Row; London: Faber & Faber, 1960.
Esler, Philip F. *Community and Gospel in Luke-Acts*. Cambridge: CUP, 1987.
Fitzmyer, Joseph A. *Luke the Theologian*. New York: Paulist, 1989.
Green, Joel B. *The Theology of the Gospel of Luke*. Cambridge: CUP, 1995.
Keck, Leander E., and J. Louis Martyn, eds. *Studies in Luke-Acts*. Nashville: Abingdon, 1966.
Maddox, Robert. *The Purpose of Luke-Acts*. Edinburgh: T. & T. Clark, 1982.
Marshall, I. Howard. *Luke: Historian and Theologian*. Exeter: Paternoster; Grand Rapids: Zondervan, rev. 1988.
Neyrey, Jerome H., ed. *The Social World of Luke-Acts: Models for Interpretation*. Peabody: Hendrickson, 1991.
O'Toole, Robert F. *The Unity of Luke's Theology*. Wilmington: Glazier, 1984.
Powell, Mark A. *What Are They Saying about Luke?* New York: Paulist, 1991.
Schweizer, Eduard. *Luke: A Challenge to Present Theology*. Atlanta: John Knox, 1982.
Talbert, C. H., ed. *Perspectives on Luke-Acts*. Edinburgh: T. & T. Clark; Danville, Va.: American Association of Baptist Professors of Religion, 1978.

Bibliography

Mills, Watson E. *The Gospel of Luke*. Lewiston and Lampeter: Mellen, 1994.

QUESTIONS FOR REVIEW

1. What is a plausible overall outline for the Gospel of Luke? That is, how many main sections may it be divided into and by what criteria? What theology may be inferred from this structure?

2. According to typical evangelical reconstructions, who wrote this Gospel, when, where, to whom, and under what circumstances (to the extent that this information may be reasonably inferred)?

3. What are several of the major theological distinctives of this Gospel?

4. Take a passage from a Gospel synopsis that appears in all three Synoptics, and identify the probable theological emphases of Luke. Consider both the "horizontal" and the "vertical" dimensions of redaction criticism.

5. Given the emphases and probable circumstances of Luke's Gospel, in what settings in contemporary Christian living might it be even more acutely relevant than the other Gospels?

CHAPTER NINE

THE GOSPEL OF JOHN

A ny reader who has worked carefully through Matthew, Mark, and Luke is immediately struck by how different a Gospel John is. Much that is central to all three Synoptics is entirely absent in John: Jesus' baptism, the calling of the Twelve, the exorcisms, the Transfiguration, the parables, and the institution of the Lord's Supper. John has numerous lengthy discourses of Jesus, but none of them is the same as those found in the Synoptics. Equally distinctive are the miracles of water turned into wine and the reawakening of Lazarus, an account of Jesus' early ministry in Judea and Galilee, his regular visits to Jerusalem, and the lengthy Farewell Discourse on the night before his crucifixion. As our survey of John's distinctive themes will demonstrate later in this chapter, there are equally prominent theological differences. There are also the same kind of apparent discrepancies with parallel passages in the Synoptics as periodically emerge among the Synoptics themselves. To top it all off, John's narrative demonstrates a uniform style, whether or not he is "quoting" Jesus, that differs considerably from the language of Christ that characterizes Matthew, Mark, and Luke.

On the other hand, there is some overlap between John and the Synoptics: considerable attention to the ministry of John the Baptist, the feeding of the five thousand and walking on the water, Sabbath controversies with the Jews (particularly related to healing the lame and giving sight to the blind), Jesus' friendship with Mary and Martha, and numerous events surrounding Jesus' passion. While the actual teachings of Jesus in John rarely repeat those of the Synoptics, the themes often dovetail closely: humility needed to enter the kingdom, an abundant harvest awaiting Christ's laborers, the dishonor a

-156-

prophet receives in his homeland, judgment against unbelievers according to their works, the revelation of the Father through the Son to those the Father has granted him, Jesus as the Good Shepherd, true discipleship as servanthood, guidance through the Spirit for ministry and proclamation, predicted future opposition for the disciples from the world, and authority to forgive or retain sins within the church.[1]

HISTORICITY

Can John be taken seriously as a historically trustworthy account of the life of Jesus in light of this combination of similarities and differences from the Synoptics? Most modern scholars have thought not. However the issue is not so clear-cut. We will look at a selection of the most famous "discrepancies" within specific passages as we survey the life of Christ in the next section of this book. But several general comments are in order here. First, one of the reasons John seems so different is because *Matthew, Mark, and Luke are so similar* to each other. Actually it is the latter observation that should at first glance be the more surprising and significant. It is precisely the similarities among the Synoptics that lead to conclusions about literary dependence. It is arguable, on the other hand, that John is largely independent of the Synoptics, at least in terms of direct literary borrowing (see below, p. 169), and that this accounts for the diverse selection of details. Although clearly a hyperbole, John 21:25 nevertheless encapsulates an important truth: Jesus did so many things that had four writers all written of him independently their Gospels might *all* have produced books as different from each other as John is from the Synoptics.

Second, even though the Fourth Gospel may be for the most part *literarily* independent of the Synoptics, it is hard to imagine its author being ignorant of the core kerygma that they share. He was almost certainly aware of the most common information widely reported about Jesus and could well have consciously chosen not to repeat most of it. Conversely, we have seen a variety of theological and geographical motives for the outlines of the Synoptics. So it is conceivable that *Matthew, Mark, and Luke could have wanted to omit information* about Jesus (however precious it may seem to us) that did not fit their particular agendas (e.g., all of Jesus' visits to Jerusalem before his last Passover).

Third, at least *some* of the differences between John and the Synoptics can be explained on the basis of the *different audiences* within the Gospels' narratives. Only John chooses to record Jesus' "Farewell Discourse" (chaps. 13–17); the very intimate concerns Jesus shared with his disciples on his last night would understandably differ considerably from his more public teaching elsewhere. The same is true for Jesus' teaching in Jerusalem at festival times, which occupies much of John 5–11. Unique concerns and styles of speaking would naturally emerge when Jesus explained the significance of his ministry *vis-à-vis* the sacred institutions of Israel to its authorities in the midst of its holy city.

---

1. For these and other similarities and differences, complete with all the appropriate chapter and verse references, see Craig Blomberg, *The Historical Reliability of the Gospels* (Leicester and Downers Grove: IVP, 1987), 153–59.

Fourth, historical trustworthiness in the ancient world was not defined by the degrees of scientific precision or exact quotation that our modern society relishes. (And even *we* often accept as accurate a report of the "gist" of what someone has said.) We should freely admit that John wrote his entire Gospel *in his distinctive style*, paraphrasing, excerpting, and interpreting Jesus' words in his own language to bring out what he believed were their full and true significance. John's unique emphasis on the role of the Holy Spirit as an interpreter of Jesus' words no doubt explains much of the freedom he felt to do this (14:26; 15:26; 16:12–13). And various scholars have plausibly seen the lengthier discourses in John, at least in part, as the product of several decades of early Christian reflection, preaching, and application of Jesus' authentic words to the needs of the emerging "Johannine community."[2] Indeed, John's genre in places resembles Hellenistic "drama" more than straightforward historical reporting, yet both genres may be effectively used to describe the story of someone's life and faithfully convey its significance.[3] Already in the late second century, Clement of Alexandria explained John's distinctives with these words: "Last of all John, perceiving that the bodily [or external] facts had been set forth in the [other] Gospels, at the instance of his disciples and the inspiration of the Spirit, composed a spiritual Gospel" (cited in Eusebius, *Ecclesiastical History* 6.14.7).

Fifth, although John writes in a fairly uniform style throughout his Gospel—even when Jesus is speaking—there are at least *145 words used only by Jesus* that appear nowhere in John's narrative sections.[4] And even when John's and Jesus' styles seem to merge, it is not impossible that John picked up some of his characteristic vocabulary from Jesus himself. A "Q"-passage that discloses many marks of authenticity (Matt. 11:25–27; Luke 10:21–22) has often been called the "Johannine thunderbolt" in the middle of the Synoptic tradition because of its similarities to otherwise distinctively Johannine language. In these verses Jesus praises God for revealing himself not to the wise but to "little children" to whom he was pleased to make himself known. Matthew 11:27 concludes, "All things have been committed to me by my Father. No one knows the Son except the Father, and no one knows the Father except the Son and those to whom the Son chooses to reveal him."[5]

To the extent that "Jesus the Sage" emerges as a dominant picture of Christ in both the Synoptics and John, this text could account for a number of John's distinctive emphases—on Jesus as the one sent from God to reveal God's purposes to the world—and yet reflect historical tradition.

Sixth, several of John's longer sermons unique to his Gospel show signs of *Jewish midrash*—the homiletical development of Old Testament texts—characteristic of the rabbis of the day but not of early Christian preaching (see esp. John 6:26–59). While admittedly different in style from much of the Synoptic material, it is still easier to believe that this form of discourse stems from the

2. See esp. Barnabas Lindars, *The Gospel of John* (London: Oliphants, 1972; Grand Rapids: Eerdmans, 1981).

3. Cf. further Blomberg, *Historical Reliability*, 162–89; idem, "To What Extent is John Historically Reliable?" in *Perspectives on John: Method and Interpretation in the Fourth Gospel*, ed. Robert B. Sloan and Mikeal C. Parsons (Lewiston and Lampeter: Mellen, 1993), 27–56.

4. H. R. Reynolds, *The Gospel of St. John*, vol. 1 (London and New York: Funk & Wagnalls, 1906), cxxiii–cxxv.

5. On the pervasive influence of this passage in John, see John W. Pryor, "The Great Thanksgiving and the Fourth Gospel," *BZ* 35 (1991): 157–79.

Jewish Jesus than from the Hellenistic milieu in which the Fourth Gospel was written (see below, p. 168).

Seventh, John actually contains *more details of time and place* in the course of Jesus' ministry than do the Synoptics. It is only from John that we are able to determine that Jesus' ministry spanned approximately a three-year period. It is only John who preserves a careful chronological sequence of virtually all the details he narrates. Several studies have demonstrated how John's references to geography and topography prove remarkably accurate, particularly in and around Jerusalem. Archaeologists have identified and excavated the probable sites of such locations as the pools of Bethesda (5:2) and Siloam (9:11) and the "Stone Pavement" of Pilate's judgment seat (*Gabbatha*—19:13).[6] This accuracy of detail is all the more impressive since it appears incidentally. In other words, John does not seem to be trying to supply us with information that will enable us to reconstruct a detailed life of Christ. He is concerned to show Jesus as the fulfillment of the Jewish festivals (see below, p. 167), and so he stresses how Jesus went to Jerusalem at various feast times and narrates what he did there.

Eighth, John is clearly *contextualizing the gospel* for an audience living under quite different circumstances than the communities to which Matthew, Mark, or Luke wrote. This would naturally affect both the style and contents of his writing. Yet in light of the central role of such themes as "witness" and "truth" (cf., e.g., 19:35), it is difficult to imagine him dealing so creatively with the traditions he inherited as to actually distort them.

Finally, we must *avoid overestimating the differences*. It is often said, for example, that only John's Jesus actually claims to be divine. Yet Jesus' characteristic claims in John (the "I am" sayings) regularly invoke metaphorical language ("I am the gate," "I am the living water," etc.) that would not have been as transparent in its original setting as it is to us. John 8:25, 10:25, and 16:29 all remind us that the disciples did not think Jesus was speaking plainly to them until the last night of his life, and even then they misunderstood him! On the other hand, there are implicit claims scattered throughout the Synoptics (see below, pp. 402–405) that suggest there, too, that Jesus was indicating his oneness with God.

STRUCTURE

Like Mark, John falls into two "halves," one stressing Jesus' mighty deeds (chaps. 1–11) and one reflecting the events leading up to and including his death and resurrection (chaps. 12–21). The first eighteen verses reflect theologically on Jesus' preexistence with God as the *logos* ("Word") who becomes incarnate and thus function as a prologue to the entire Gospel. Because 20:31 reads like a closing, many scholars have viewed chapter 21 as a later appendix added to a previous draft of the Gospel. More likely it is a deliberately designed

---

6. Bruce E. Schein, a pastor and tour leader in Israel for many years, was so impressed with this type of information that he wrote an entire commentary on the Gospel of John in travelogue form, an exercise which would have been almost entirely speculative if done with any of the Synoptics. See his *Following the Way: The Setting of John's Gospel* (Minneapolis: Augsburg, 1980). The most detailed accumulation of indirect evidence for John's reliability in matters of chronology, geography, and historical verisimilitude is John A. T. Robinson, *The Priority of John* (London: SCM, 1985; Oak Park, Ill.: Meyer-Stone, 1987).

conclusion to bring closure to certain issues raised in the opening chapter. For example, there we learn of the disciples' first calling (1:35–51); here we read of their reinstatement and further commissioning (21:15–23).[7] John 20:31 also makes the purpose of the Gospel clear: to promote belief in Jesus as the Christ (Messiah) and Son of God. This statement, coupled with the recurring theme of "testimony" throughout John's narrative (e.g., 2:25; 3:32–33; 5:34; 8:17; 15:26; 21:24) makes plausible an outline that understands all of John's information as witnessing to the truth of the Gospel so that people might believe it. One study has likened John's structure to the form of prophetic "lawsuit" (Hebrew, *ribh*) in the Old Testament, in which Scripture calls its readers to render a verdict on the evidence provided for them about God's dealings with his people (e.g., Ps. 50; Isa. 1:2–3; 3:13–15; Jer 2:4–13; Hos. 4:1–3; Micah 6:1–5).[8]

Within the first half of the Gospel, chapters 2–11 are dominated by seven miracles (John calls them "signs") and seven major discourses of Jesus.[9] Several pairs of signs and discourses are clearly related. For example, the feeding of the five thousand (6:1–15) leads into the Bread of Life Discourse (6:25–71). Healing the man born blind (9:1–41) illustrates Jesus' claim to be the Light of the World (7:1–8:59). But not all can be matched so neatly. More noteworthy are the structural indicators that suggest chapters 2–4 and 5–10 are each to be taken as a unit. Chapters 2–4 begin and end with miracles in Cana, the only two explicitly enumerated "signs" of Jesus in this Gospel ("first," "second"—2:11: 4:54). All of the stories in these three chapters illustrate the newness of Jesus' ministry over against the old forms of Jewish religion. Chronologically, all of these events seem to precede Jesus' great Galilean ministry. Chapters 5–10 for the most part describe what Jesus did at festival times in Jerusalem, punctuating what we know from the Synoptics as a primary ministry in Galilee. Here John takes pains to stress Jesus as the fulfillment of the Jewish festivals—Passover, Tabernacles, and the "Dedication" (Hanukkah). Even the one main pair of events in this section not from Jesus' ministry in Jerusalem is explicitly said to take place at Passover time—the feeding of the five thousand and the walking on the water. These events in turn lead to Jesus' sermon about the Bread of Life, which ties in closely with the symbolism of bread at Passover (chap. 6). Chapter 11 ties in with the rest of John's first main section by narrating Jesus' greatest miracle to date.

Chapters 12–21 also contain two major central portions. After the introduction in chapter 12 to the events that will culminate in Christ's death, chapters 13–17 narrate what took place on the night of Jesus' betrayal and primarily comprise Jesus' Farewell Discourse to his disciples. Chapters 18–20 then

---

7. On the unity of chap. 21 with the rest of the Gospel, see Paul S. Minear, "The Original Functions of John 21," *JBL* 102 (1983): 85–98. Cf. also the series of three articles by Franzmann and Klinger, Breck, and Ellis in *St. Vladimir's Theological Quarterly* 36 (1992): 7–15, 17–25, 27–49.

8. A. E. Harvey, *Jesus on Trial* (London: SPCK; Atlanta: John Knox, 1976).

9. Leon Morris uses these as the organizing motifs for subdividing these chapters of John's Gospel, while interspersing other subdivisions as well (*The Gospel according to John* [Grand Rapids: Eerdmans, rev. 1995]). One could in fact outline all of John 2–11 in terms of these seven signs and discourses and material related to them: Sign 1: Water into Wine (2:1–11); Discourse 1: Born Again (1:12–3:36); Discourse 2: Living Water (4:1–42); Sign 2: The Official's Son (4:43–54); Sign 3: Healing the Paralytic (5:1–15); Discourse 3: Imitating the Father (5:16–47); Sign 4: Feeding the Five Thousand (6:1–15); Sign 5: Walking on the Water (6:16–24); Discourse 4: Bread of Life (6:25–71); Discourse 5: Light of the World (7:1–8:59); Sign 6: The Man Born Blind (9:1–41); Discourse 6: The Good Shepherd (10:1–21); Discourse 7: Oneness with the Father (10:22–42); Sign 7: Raising Lazarus (11:1–57).

recount the arrest, trials, crucifixion, and resurrection, containing the most extensive overlap with the Synoptics of any multiple-chapter section in John. Chapter 21 forms the conclusion. Putting this all together leads to a probable outline along the following lines:[10]

I. Introductory Testimony (1:1–51)
   A. Prologue (1:1–18)
   B. The Testimony of John and the First Disciples (1:19–51)
II. The Testimony of Signs and Discourses (2:1–11:57)
   A. Jesus and Jewish Institutions (2:1–4:54)
       1. Water into Wine—A New Joy (2:1–11)
       2. Temple Cleansing—A New Temple (2:12–25)
       3. Jesus, Nicodemus, and the Baptist—A New Birth (3:1–36)
       4. Jesus, the Samaritan Woman, and the Official's Son—A New Universalism (4:1–54)
   B. Jesus and Jewish Festivals (5:1–10:21)
       1. Healing the Paralytic and Imitating the Father (5:1–47)
       2. The True Passover: The Bread of Life (6:1–71)
       3. The True Tabernacles: Living Water and Light of the World (7:1–9:41)
       4. The Good Shepherd and Oneness with the Father (10:1–42)
   C. Jesus as the Resurrection and the Life (11:1–57)
III. The Testimony of Death and Resurrection (12:1–20:31)
   A. Actions in Preparation for Death (12:1–50)
       1. Anointing in Bethany (12:1–11)
       2. Entry into Jerusalem (12:12–50)
   B. Teaching in Preparation for Death (13:1–17:26)
       1. Servant Ministry vs. Betrayal (13:1–30)
       2. Farewell Discourse (13:31–16:33)
       3. High-Priestly Prayer (17:1–26)
   C. Events Surrounding the Death Itself (18:1–20:31)
       1. Arrest, Trials, and Crucifixion (18:1–19:42)
       2. Resurrection (20:1–29)
       3. Purpose of the Gospel (20:30–31)
IV. Concluding Testimony (21:1–25)
   A. The Reinstatement of the Disciples (21:1–23)
   B. Epilogue (21:24–25)

---

10. Cf. esp. Gerald L. Borchert, *John 1–11* (Nashville: Broadman & Holman, 1996). Because the death and resurrection of Lazarus (chap. 11) also foreshadows Jesus' own death and resurrection, a few commentators place the break between the two main halves of John after chap. 10. Because chap. 12 still contains key deeds and Jesus' reflection on them, many writers place the break after chap. 12. A compromise occasionally adopted is to set off chaps. 11–12 by themselves as a transitional section. The division after 11, however, seems to be the best. 12:1 marks a clear shift in time and place. No more miracles ensue, and all events from here on lead inexorably to the Cross.

THEOLOGY

Views of Jesus

Because John is otherwise so different from the Synoptics, it is significant that the two main titles used for Jesus in this Gospel's purpose statement (John 20:31) are identical to those used in Mark's headline verse (Mark 1:1)—the *Christ* and the *Son of God*. But "Son" for John is even more clearly identified with a heavenly figure than in the Synoptics. John 3:31–36 is a key christological passage that sums up important Johannine themes: "The one who comes from above is above all; . . . For the one whom God has sent speaks the words of God; to him God gives the Spirit without limit. The Father loves the Son and has placed everything in his hands. Whoever believes in the Son has eternal life, but whoever rejects the Son will not see life."

Four other emphases are considerably distinctive within Johannine Christology:

Logos. Only John calls Jesus "the Word" (Greek, *logos*), particularly in his prologue (1:1–18). The background and significance of this term have been endlessly debated.[11] It was a term widely used in a variety of ancient Hellenistic and Jewish sources. In Stoic pantheism it could refer to the animating life force or "world soul" that permeated all the universe, while in the Hebrew Scriptures it could refer to God's spoken word. In the targums the Aramaic equivalent *memra* was often substituted for names of God, especially in Genesis 1. What all these and other uses have in common is that the logos was a widely used term to refer to the way God or the gods revealed themselves and communicated with humankind. John may well be exploiting this diverse background to stress that Jesus is the way in which the true, living God reveals himself and communicates with his people. The revelation of true knowledge remains a key function of the Johannine Redeemer. John 1:14 is a crucial verse in this context: "The Word became flesh and lived for a while among us." The logos is no mere vision or phantom; he became incarnate as a genuine human being. Although John is better known for his emphasis on Christ's deity, the doctrine of the logos who became *sarx* ("flesh") is also an important reminder of his full humanity, a theme which John also reinforces throughout his Gospel.[12]

Lamb of God. John is the only New Testament writer to call Jesus the "Lamb of God" (John 1:29, 36; and twenty-seven times in Revelation). John the Baptist links this expression with Jesus' role in taking away the sin of the world (1:29). Undoubtedly, part of the background for the image is the sacrificial lamb of the Jewish Passover. But the victorious, conquering Lamb of Revelation suggests that John may also draw on the motif in intertestamental literature of a sheep or ram who represents a Messianic warrior and deliverer of God's people from their enemies (cf., e.g., Testament of Joseph 19:8–9; Testament of Benjamin 3).[13]

---

11. For a survey of options, see Ed L. Miller, "The Johannine Origins of the Johannine Logos," *JBL* 112 (1993): 445–57.

12. See esp. Marianne Meye Thompson, *The Incarnate Word* (Peabody: Hendrickson, 1993). Another important text in combating docetism (see below, p. 168) is John 19:34, which confirms Jesus' fully human death.

13. George R. Beasley-Murray, *John* (Waco: Word, 1987), 24–25.

Wisdom and Agent. Even more so than in Matthew, numerous parallels emerge between John's portrait of Jesus and personified "Wisdom" in Jewish sapiential literature. In intertestamental works like the Wisdom of Solomon or the Wisdom of Sirach, we find close parallels to the following emphases of John regarding Jesus: coming into the world to enlighten those who had eyes to see (1:9), being written of by Moses and the prophets (1:45; 5:46), being known by Abraham (8:56), and having a glory that Isaiah saw (12:41). Wisdom, like Jesus, was also said to come and go from heaven, supply God's people with bread to eat, and bring the dead to life. She regularly spoke in lengthy discourses.[14] Also prominent in John is the picture of Jesus as the one whom God, his heavenly Father, has sent (e.g., 3:17, 28, 34; 4:34; 5:23, 24, 30; etc.). This language draws on the Hebrew concept of the *shaliach*, a messenger or "sent one" who acts as an agent for his master. Often the agent acts on behalf of the master in ways that begin to blur the distinction between the two (see further, p. 405).

God. The above three sections all prepare the reader for this fourth one. Although no text in John ever has Jesus explicitly declare, "I am God," John does make claims for Jesus that imply his deity. In the prologue, the logos was "with God" and "was God" (1:1). Seven times Jesus makes "I am" statements that describe his exalted nature and reflect wildly arrogant claims if in fact he is not in some sense divine. Thus he calls himself "the bread of life" (6:35), "the light of the world" (8:12; 9:5), "the gate for the sheep" (10:7),"the good shepherd" (10:11), "the resurrection and the life" (11:25), "the way and the truth and the life" (14:6), and "the true vine" (15:1). He claims to be one with the Father in a sense that the Jews interpret as blasphemy—too close an equation with God (10:30–33). After the resurrection, Thomas touches Christ's scars and cries out in worship, "My Lord and my God!" (20:28).[15]

One must be careful not to make either too little or too much of these claims. Many writers find all this "high" Christology so lofty as to be incompatible with the Synoptics.[16] Yet it is Matthew and Luke who describe Christ's virginal conception, and there are clear hints of Jesus' deity scattered around the Synoptics: Jesus claims to forgive sins with divine authority (Mark 2:5 pars.), accepts worship (Matt. 14:33), and announces that people's final destiny before God will be based on their response to him (Mark 8:38; Luke 12:8–10). And he applies further metaphors to himself that in the Old Testament are often reserved for Yahweh (Lord of the harvest, shepherd, sower, vineyard owner, bridegroom, rock, etc.).[17] A few critics, on the other hand, stress that none of the "I am" sayings in John reflects an unambiguously divine self-consciousness on Jesus' part, not susceptible to "subordinationist" interpretations.[18] But their

---

14. For these and numerous other parallels, see Ben Witherington III, *John's Wisdom: A Commentary on the Fourth Gospel* (Louisville: Westminster/John Knox, 1995), 18–27.

15. For a detailed exegesis of John 1:1, 18; and 20:28 in the context of a thorough study of "God" as a christological title, see Murray J. Harris, *Jesus as God: The New Testament Use of* Theos *in Reference to Jesus* (Grand Rapids: Baker, 1992), 51–129.

16. A good example, otherwise helpful in its understanding of John on his own terms, is James D. G. Dunn, *Christology in the Making* (London: SCM; Philadelphia: Westminster, 1980), 213–50.

17. See further Robert L. Reymond, *Jesus, Divine Messiah* (Phillipsburg, N.J.: Presbyterian & Reformed, 1990), 94–126; Philip B. Payne, "Jesus' Implicit Claim to Deity in His Parables," *Trinity Journal* n.s. 2 (1981) 3–23.

18. See esp. Robinson, *Priority*, 343–97.

cumulative effect remains too powerful for us to content ourselves with a picture of Jesus as merely an emissary or spokesperson for God.

Other Distinctive Themes

Realized Eschatology. Whereas the Synoptics stress a future hope and the return of Christ, John defines eternal life and death as beginning now in this age, based on men's and women's responses to Jesus. John 3:18 is representative: "Whoever believes in him is not condemned, but whoever does not believe stands condemned already because he has not believed in the name of God's one and only Son." Or compare 5:24: "Whoever hears my word and believes him who sent me has eternal life and will not be condemned; he has crossed over from death to life" (cf. also 3:36; 9:39; 12:31). Yet this latter passage reminds us also that the future hope is not entirely absent from John, as it goes on immediately to describe the time of the coming resurrection of both the just and the unjust (5:25–29; cf. also 6:39–40; 12:25, 48; 14:3, 28). Whereas "kingdom" texts dominate the Synoptics, they are rare in John. But it is arguable that John uses "eternal life" with the same present and future dimensions as the kingdom (see further below, pp. 384–386) to contextualize the Gospel as it moves out of a Jewish into a more Hellenistic context.[19]

Miracles as Signs and Their Relation to Faith. In the Synoptic Gospels, whenever someone asks for a "sign" (Greek *sēmeion*), Jesus uniformly refuses to give one (e.g., Matt. 12:38–39; 16:1–4 pars.). In John, however, "signs" function positively as reason to believe in Jesus (e.g., John 2:11; 4:53–54), although neither does John's Jesus ever perform a miracle "on demand" merely to satisfy a skeptic. But there is a second set of texts in John that takes a more critical view of signs. In Cana, Jesus seems to speak with exasperation when he laments that "unless you people see miraculous signs and wonders . . . you will never believe" (4:48). And although Jesus praises Thomas's belief based on firsthand evidence, he goes on to add, "Blessed are those who have not seen and yet have believed" (20:29). Robert Kysar helpfully proposes that we understand three stages in John's concept of faith—an embryonic stage that is at least open to faith (which is required before God will grant any sign), preliminary faith based on signs, and a mature faith that no longer requires them.[20]

Incipient Trinitarianism and the Unity of Jesus' Followers. Particularly in his private teaching to the disciples in the Farewell Discourse, Jesus comes as close as anywhere in the Gospels to the type of Trinitarian theology that would later issue from early Christian creeds and councils.[21] He insists that he is "in the Father" and "the Father is in" him (14:11); when he leaves, the Spirit will replace him as *"another* Counselor" performing many of the identical roles he played (v. 16). Jesus' high-priestly prayer speaks of the Father's and Son's

19. George E. Ladd, *A Theology of the New Testament*, rev. Donald A. Hagner (Grand Rapids: Eerdmans, 1993), 290–95. Several writers have observed that "eternal life" may be the best one-phrase summary of the entire theology of the Fourth Gospel. The scholar who is best known for his study of realized eschatology in John is C. H. Dodd. See esp. his *The Interpretation of the Fourth Gospel* (Cambridge: CUP, 1953). Offering an important corrective to Dodd at a few key places is John T. Carroll, "Present and Future in Fourth Gospel 'Eschatology'," *BTB* 19 (1989): 63–69.

20. Robert Kysar, *John, the Maverick Gospel* (Atlanta: John Knox, 1976), 67–73.

21. For a thorough study, see Royce G. Gruenler, *The Trinity in the Gospel of John* (Grand Rapids: Baker, 1986).

reciprocal glorification (17:1–5). Yet Father, Son, and Spirit are not entirely interchangeable in function or status. John 14:28 preserves a classic "subordinationist" strain, with Jesus' declaration, "the Father is greater than I." And John's characteristic language of the Father sending the Son or the Son doing only what the Father commands (see esp. 5:19–42) is never reversed. That is, the Son never sends the Father, and the Father never does what the Son commands. To use the language of later theological reflection, John preserves ontological equality within functional subordination among the members of the Godhead.

Similar comparisons and contrasts emerge from a study of the key Johannine theme of the unity of all true disciples. John never confuses the creature with the creator or says that believers can become gods.[22] But Jesus prays that all of his followers will experience a unity created by their relationship with God in Christ, so "that all of them may be one, Father, just as you are in me and I am in you" (17:21; cf. vv. 11, 23a). This unity is to produce a powerful evangelistic effect, "to let the world know that you sent me and have loved them even as you have loved me" (v. 23b).

The Election and Security of the Believer. John includes several distinctive texts that speak of God's (and Jesus') unique role in choosing, drawing, and preserving those who are his people. Most famous of these are probably 6:39 ("And this is the will of him who sent me, that I shall lose none of all that he has given me, but raise them up at the last day") and 10:29 ("My Father, who has given them to me, is greater than all; no one can snatch them out of my Father's hand"). The disciples did not choose Christ, but he chose them (15:16). Conversely, Judas's betrayal demonstrates that he was not elected to salvation; Christ protected all the Father gave him. The one who was lost was "the one doomed to destruction" (17:12).

Yet balancing this predestinarian emphasis is John's equally prominent use of the word *abide* (or *remain*), particularly in chapter 15. Believers must abide in Christ, and then he will abide in them, so that they can bear much fruit (v. 4). And verse 2 offers a solemn warning that the Father "cuts off every branch in me that bears no fruit." John's own harmonization of these two seemingly contrary strands of thought in his theology is probably provided in 1 John 2:19, when he describes those who abandoned the church to follow false teachers: "They went out from us, but they did not really belong to us. For if they had belonged to us, they would have *remained* with us; but their going showed that none of them belonged to us."[23]

The Death of Christ as Exaltation/Glorification. It is sometimes argued that the death of Jesus in John is "docetic"—Christ is so in control of events that he only seems to be human (see, e.g., John 18:6; 19:11, 30). But 19:33–34 would surely preclude this; here John insists that the man Jesus truly died.

Others argue that John has no theology of atonement, but 1:29 and 36 challenge this claim.[24] What *is* a genuine Johannine distinctive involves several

---

22. On the meaning of John 10:34 in context, see below, pp. 299–300.
23. On the balance between *Divine Sovereignty and Human Responsibility* in John, see the book with that title by D. A. Carson (London: Marshall, Morgan & Scott; Atlanta: John Knox, 1981), 125–98.
24. Cf. further Max Turner, "Atonement and the Death of Jesus in John," *EQ* 62 (1990): 99–122.

references to Christ's crucifixion as exaltation or glorification. John appears to collapse the death, resurrection, and ascension of Christ all into one event, anticipating their final outcome. A key reference is 12:32—"But I, when I am lifted up from the earth, will draw all men to myself," presumably anticipating both his physical crucifixion and spiritual exaltation. John 7:39; 12:16, 23; and 13:31 all anticipate Christ's "glorification" with similar double meanings. In particular, 12:23 reflects the culmination of a recurring motif throughout the Fourth Gospel. After repeatedly insisting that his "hour" had not yet come (2:4; 7:30; 8:20), now Jesus declares "the hour has come for the Son of Man to be glorified."

The Holy Spirit as Paraclete. The Holy Spirit is even more prominent in John than in Luke. Wholly unparalleled elsewhere is John's use of the term *parakletos* in the Farewell Discourse to refer to the Spirit. The word does not have a precise English equivalent; in different contexts it can include such concepts as counselor, comforter, or advocate. Five discrete roles for the Paraclete emerge in John 14–16: helper (14:15–21), interpreter (14:25–31), witness (15:26–16:4), prosecutor (16:5–11), and revealer (16:12–16).[25] One plausible reconstruction of the Johannine church finds it as a "charismatic" holdout (putting Spirit-filled experience at the forefront of the Christian life) against an increasingly institutionalized ecclesiastical world surrounding it.[26]

Anti-Sacramentalism? One of the puzzling features of John's narrative is that he gives more details surrounding the events of Christ's baptism and the institution of the Lord's Supper than do the Synoptics (1:19–34, chaps. 13–17), and yet he never actually describes either of these events. Many scholars have seen his teachings in 3:5 ("No one can enter the kingdom of God unless he is born of water and the Spirit") and 6:53 ("Unless you eat the flesh of the Son of Man and drink his blood, you have no life in you") as cryptic allusions to or foreshadowings of Christian baptism and the Lord's Supper. But in context these make adequate sense as metaphorical references to the cleansing work of the Spirit in bringing new life and to identification with Christ in his suffering and death, respectively.[27] It is at least arguable that again John was trying to play down the role of these two rituals in an era that had already begun to value them too highly, viewing them perhaps as means of grace in and of themselves.[28]

Anti-Baptist Cult? John has also struck readers with the way he plays down John the Baptist's authority. Although in the Synoptics Jesus speaks of the Baptist figuratively as Elijah come again (Matt. 11:14; cf. Luke 1:17), in the Fourth Gospel the Baptist explicitly denies that he is Elijah (John 1:21). He also denies that he is the Christ. The Fourth Gospel goes out of its way to stress that the Baptist recognized that he must decrease in importance while Jesus increased (3:30). Given the presence of a group of John the Baptist's followers in Ephesus in the mid-first century who had a very truncated understanding of the gospel

25. F. F Bruce, *The Gospel of John* (Basingstoke: Pickering & Inglis; Grand Rapids: Eerdmans, 1983), 301–21.
26. Gary M. Burge, *The Anointed Community: The Holy Spirit in the Johannine Tradition* (Grand Rapids: Eerdmans, 1987). This, however, created different tensions of its own *within* the community.
27. See D. A. Carson, *The Gospel according to John* (Leicester: IVP; Grand Rapids: Eerdmans, 1991), 191–96 and 295–98.
28. For a survey and balanced assessment of options, see R. Wade Paschal, Jr., "Sacramental Symbolism and Physical Imagery in the Gospel of John," *TynB* 32 (1981): 151–76.

(Acts 19:1–7) and given later testimony about second-century followers of John who elevated him to messianic status (Pseudo-Clementine *Recognitions* 1.54, 60; cf. also the passing allusion in Justin, *Trypho*, 80), it is at least plausible to suggest that John was trying to dampen any improper enthusiasm some in his church might have had for the Baptist when he was writing to Ephesus at the end of the first century (for place and date, see further below, p. 168).

Relationship to Judaism. Like Matthew, John has often been accused of being anti-Semitic (or, more precisely, anti-Jewish), because of his frequent use of "the Jews" as a seemingly blanket term for condemning all of Jesus' opponents. This expression occurs sixty-eight times in John and only sixteen times in all of the Synoptics. But a careful analysis of contexts shows that sometimes *Ioudaioi* means merely Judeans (as opposed to Galileans), other times it is shorthand for the Jewish leaders, and frequently it refers to the general rejection of Jesus by the bulk of the Jewish people. John recognizes as readily as the Synoptics that Jesus' first followers were all Jewish, so there is no universal indictment of an entire ethnic group here. What John does stress, though, is how Jesus fulfills the purpose of all the major Jewish institutions and rituals, including the Scriptures themselves. Without ever using the explicit language of Jeremiah's new covenant prophecies (Jer. 31:31–34), John has Jesus inaugurating everything that the new covenant anticipated.[29] The church is now the chosen people of God.

Dualisms. John certainly does like to paint pictures in very black-and-white terms. Pairs of opposites characterize various aspects of his theology: light vs. darkness, life vs. death, love vs. judgment, above vs. below, spirit vs. flesh, truth vs. falsehood, those who believe vs. the world. In reality there are many shades and nuances of perspective throughout humanity, but John points to the one central truth that ultimately all people will be judged by God and put into one of only two camps: those who have believed in Jesus and those who have not.[30] Painting these stark contrasts makes sense in light of the "sectarian" context of John's community (see below, p. 169). When one is embattled by hostile forces both inside and outside the church, it is natural to warn against error with strong language, even as it is important, as John does, to stress love and unity. Another kind of dualism also characterizes John: not that of opposing theological concepts but that of intended double meanings in passages that often lead to misunderstandings that were corrected only after the resurrection (e.g., John 2:20–22; 3:5–15; 4:10–14; etc.).[31]

CIRCUMSTANCES

In the first half of the twentieth century, most scholarship assumed John to be very late and Hellenistic in origin. The assumption was common that its exalted Christology could only have been the product of a long, slow evolution away from a more primitive, Jewish understanding of Jesus that did not yet

---

29. John W. Pryor, *John: Evangelist of the Covenant People* (London: Darton, Longman & Todd; Downers Grove: IVP, 1992), esp. 157–80.

30. Cf. further Ladd, *Theology*, 259–72.

31. See esp. D. A. Carson, "Understanding Misunderstandings in the Fourth Gospel," *TynB* 33 (1982): 59–91.

think of him as God. Already back then, conservatives protested that "high Christology" was found as early as the 60s in texts like Philippians 2:5–11. Further, Luke's use in the early sermons of Acts of titles for Jesus like "the Holy and Righteous One" and "the author of life" (terms not characteristic of his writing elsewhere and thus not likely to be redactional) demonstrated that the first generation of Christianity also had a very high view of Jesus. Today, however, particularly in light of the discovery of the Dead Sea Scrolls with its unrelenting dualism (e.g., "the sons of light vs. the sons of darkness"), the Jewishness of John and even of his Christology is much more widely affirmed.[32]

Reasonably strong early church tradition, however, does date the Gospel to *the end of the first century, probably during the reign of Domitian (81–96), when John was a very old man ministering in Ephesus.* This picture results from combining the testimony of such writers as Irenaeus (*Against Heresies* 3.1.1, 3.3.4), Polycrates, Papias, Polycarp, and Clement, all quoted in Eusebius (*Ecclesiastical History* 3.31.3, 3.39.4, 5.20.4–6, 6.14.7), Eusebius himself (3.24.7), and Jerome (*Lives of Illustrious Men* 9).[33] Least secure of these details is the date itself. A few writers have argued for a pre-70 date, in part on the basis of present tense references to Jewish places destroyed in the war with Rome (e.g., John 5:2),[34] but this may simply reflect John's style.

A popular critical reconstruction of the Johannine community has described its development in two main stages (often with numerous, smaller phases identified as well). The first stage is a Jewish-Christian community perhaps in Palestine in the mid–first century, finding itself increasingly in tension with the Jewish authorities and eventually excommunicated from the synagogues (9:22; 12:42; 16:2). The second stage is a Christian community of a more mixed nature but predominantly Gentile, in Asia Minor in and around Ephesus, toward the end of the first century. Both Jewish and Hellenistic features in John's Gospel would then be adequately accounted for.[35]

On the other hand, it is not obvious why both of these strands of thought could not have been present simultaneously, given what we know about Ephesus at the end of the first century. Irenaeus and Eusebius both report on the presence of a heretical teacher named Cerinthus, clearly a *docetist* (believing only in Christ's deity and not his humanity) and probably a *Gnostic*, who ministered in Ephesus at the end of the first century (*Against Heresies* 3.2.1; *Ecclesiastical History* 3.28.6, 3.31.3, 4.14.6). Revelation 2:9 and 3:9, however, refer to Jewish communities that were hostile to Christianity in two cities near Ephesus as "synagogues of Satan." Clearly it was possible that *the church in Asia Minor had to combat both a growing Gnostic and an antagonistic Jewish presence.*[36]

---

32. See Stephen S. Smalley, *John: Evangelist and Interpreter* (Exeter: Paternoster, 1978), esp. 9–40, for a survey of this shift in trends when they were first beginning to flourish.

33. For the texts of the most important of these passages, see J. Ramsey Michaels, *John* (Peabody: Hendrickson, 1989), 5–7. One ancient tradition has John banished by Nero before A.D. 70 (*Syriac History of John*), but it is of dubious historical worth.

34. Most notably, John A. T. Robinson, *Redating the New Testament* (London: SCM; Philadelphia: Westminster, 1976), 254–311.

35. The most nuanced articulation of this evolution, dividing itself into eight phases altogether, appears in John Ashton, *Understanding the Fourth Gospel* (Oxford: Clarendon, 1991), 163–66. The most famous two-stage approach is that of J. Louis Martyn, *History and Theology in the Fourth Gospel* (Nashville: Abingdon, 1979), who argues that the references to excommunication refer to the events of John's day not Jesus'.

36. Similarly, Witherington, *John's Wisdom*, 27–29.

Interestingly, the Johannine epistles seem to reflect a corrective or balancing emphasis to some of the Fourth Gospel's theological distinctives. Raymond Brown notes four in particular: (1) more of an emphasis on Jesus' humanity than on his deity; (2) the importance of keeping God's commandments vs. claims of sinlessness; (3) more future than present eschatology; (4) and an insistence that the community has already learned God's truth through his Spirit vs. the promise of being guided into further truth. All of these contrasts make sense against a backdrop of increasing Gnostic distortion of the Gospel. *It may well be that John originally wrote as he did to try to contextualize the Good News about Jesus for a community beginning to be interested in or influenced by incipient Gnosticism, only to find that the false teachers were picking up on those themes that orthodoxy and Gnosticism had in common and emphasizing them at the expense of balancing themes.* The Johannine epistles, particularly 1 John, would then have been written with slightly different emphases to try to correct the imbalance.[37]

A quite different reconstruction of the circumstances behind John's composition understands the Fourth Gospel as an evangelistic tract to unsaved Jews.[38] This would certainly account for the emphasis on Jesus as the fulfillment of Jewish institutions and festivals, but it is not as clear that a writer would use John's more virulent polemic against Jesus' Jewish opponents if he were trying to win over hostile opponents. Part of this argument also depends on translating John 20:31 as ". . . that you may believe that the Christ, the Son of God, is Jesus," that is, helping people looking for a Messiah to recognize who he is. This translation is possible but not probable.[39] There is a second issue surrounding this verse as well. Slightly better textual evidence supports a reading of the verb "believe" as a present rather than an aorist subjunctive, in which case the Church Fathers' testimony is reinforced that John is writing first of all to those who already believe in Jesus, so that *they might continue to believe*, in the face of this two-pronged opposition.[40] Ben Witherington suggests a plausible compromise: *John is writing to Christians to help them, among other things, be more effective in evangelizing non-Christian friends and relatives, with a special focus on Jews.*[41]

A final issue involves the literary relationship of John and the Synoptics. As noted already, older commentators usually explained John's differences as due to the fact that John was writing last of all the four. He knew what Matthew, Mark, and Luke had already written and for the most part felt no need to repeat their information. In short he went about *supplementing* their material. In the past generation, the pendulum has swung dramatically to the view that John is largely *independent* of the Synoptics.[42] There are relatively few places in which

---

37. Raymond E. Brown, *The Community of the Beloved Disciple* (New York: Paulist, 1979) 109–44. For antidocetic and anti-Gnostic tendencies present (though more muted) already in the Gospel of John, see respectively Udo Schnelle, *Antidocetic Christology in the Gospel of John* (Minneapolis: Fortress, 1992); and Marinus de Jonge, *Jesus: Stranger from Heaven and Son of God*, ed. John E. Steely (Missoula: Scholars, 1977).

38. See esp. D. A. Carson, "The Purpose of the Fourth Gospel: John 20:31 Reconsidered," *JBL* 106 (1987): 639–51.

39. See J. V. Brownson, "John 20:31 and the Purpose of the Fourth Gospel," *Reformed Review* 48 (1995): 212–16.

40. Cf., e.g., Luke T. Johnson, *The Writings of the New Testament: An Interpretation* (Philadelphia: Fortress, 1986), 472.

41. Witherington, *John's Wisdom*, 2, 11, *et passim*.

42. Usually credited with initiating this surge is P. Gardner-Smith, *St. John and the Synoptic Gospels* (Cambridge: CUP, 1938), although it was not until the 1970s that the movement really took hold.

John's wording is so close to that of the Synoptics, even where they run parallel, to prove literary borrowing. But if John is not dependent on the written form of the other three evangelists' compositions, then we can deduce nothing about the date of the Fourth Gospel on the grounds of literary borrowing. A few writers, however, have plausibly suggested a mediating approach: several sets of parallel texts suggest that John may well have known at least Mark but did not feel compelled to follow him closely.[43] So any date from the 60s on is in theory possible. Older views that placed John well into the second century have been discarded, however, with the discovery of the John Rylands fragment—already at least one stage of copying removed from John's original and yet dating from ca. 125–140. *The traditional idea of a date in the 80s or 90s remains best.*

AUTHORSHIP AND SOURCES

The internal evidence points to an individual to whom five passages refer as "the disciple whom Jesus loved" (John 13:23; 19:26; 20:2; 21:7, 20) as the primary witness to the events of this Gospel (21:24). With the "new look on John" recovering an emphasis on the Jewish roots of the Gospel, most commentators today agree that the author could well have been Jewish, and even Palestinian in origin. "Disciple" for John does not necessarily mean one of the Twelve, however, and some have imagined the "beloved disciple" to be Lazarus (cf. 11:3), Thomas,[44] or some other anonymous follower of Jesus. But it is more natural to think of one of Christ's inner circle, probably from the group of three that the Synoptics described as his closest followers (Mark 9:2; 14:33)—Peter, James, and John. The Fourth Gospel knows that Jesus had twelve apostles (John 6:67, 70, 71) but never names them all. It does, however, refer to Peter as separate from and paired with the beloved disciple on two occasions (20:2–9; 21:20–24). James, the son of Zebedee, was martyred too early to be this Gospel's author (A.D. 44—cf. Acts 12:1–2). That leaves only his brother, the apostle John. Interestingly, this John never appears by name in the Gospel, while the John that does appear is always the Baptist, without ever being called by that title. Unless John the apostle were known to be the author of this document, surely this omission of any further clarification as to which "John" was in view would be surprising. All this adds up to strong circumstantial evidence for *equating the beloved disciple with the apostle John.*[45]

The external evidence concurs. Here, however, is the one Gospel for which early Church testimony is ambiguous. Papias (arguably the oldest surviving witness) declared: "If ever anyone came who had followed the presbyters, I inquired into the words of the presbyters, what Andrew or Peter or Philip or

---

43. E.g., C. K. Barrett, *The Gospel according to St. John* (London: SPCK; Philadelphia: Westminster, rev. 1978), 42–54; and numerous, mostly foreign language works from the University of Louvain in Belgium.

44. Note, e.g., how Peter and Thomas are paired in 21:1, and then Peter and the beloved disciple are compared and contrasted in vv. 7–23. This view is defended at length by James H. Charlesworth, who comprehensively surveys all the other proposals and arguments concerning authorship in *The Beloved Disciple: Whose Witness Validates the Gospel of John?* (Valley Forge: TPI, 1995).

45. The detailed evidence for narrowing down the author of this Gospel to a Jew, Palestinian, eyewitness, apostle, and then John is classically stated by B. F. Westcott (*The Gospel according to St. John* [London: John Murray, 1908] x–lii), with important updating by Leon Morris (*Studies in the Fourth Gospel* [Grand Rapids: Eerdmans, 1969], 139–292).

Thomas or James or John or Matthew, or any other of the Lord's disciples had said, and what Aristion and the presbyter John, the Lord's disciples, were saying" (cited in Eusebius, *Ecclesiastical History* 3.39.4).

It is not clear if Papias is referring to one or two different individuals named John here. Some, following Eusebius himself, believe he lists two different groups of Christians—first generation apostles and church leaders of Papias's day ("presbyter" can also be translated "elder"). If there were a presbyter John active in the early second century, one would not have to imagine the eighty- or ninety-year-old apostle still alive and capable of writing the Fourth Gospel at the end of the first century. Martin Hengel recently redefended this interpretation in detail and ascribed authorship of the Fourth Gospel to this John the presbyter (the same title given to the anonymous author of 2 and 3 John in the opening verses of those letters).[46] On the other hand, if the aged John were the only apostle still left alive at the time referred to in Papias's life, it would explain John's inclusion in both lists: the first reference would link him with the other (now deceased) apostles; the second, with a fellow elder in the church of his day. This is the more common understanding of Papias's testimony.

Modern scholars often reject Johannine authorship for several other reasons however. For example, they claim that: (1) the Judean focus of the Gospel is inappropriate for someone of Galilean origin (cf. Mark 1:16–20), especially given this author's apparent connection with the high priest (John 18:15–16); (2) a "Son of Thunder" (Mark 3:17) would have been too volatile to pen this calm treatise; (3) John was illiterate (cf. Acts 4:13); (4) a Jew would not have used the phrase "the Jews" so critically; and (5) the apostle could not have called himself "beloved."

On the other hand, (1) John's focus on Judea and Jerusalem may be due to historical and theological reasons, and he could have accompanied Jesus on all his trips there. His closeness to Mary (John 19:26–27), who herself had priestly relatives (Luke 1:5, 36), could suggest that John also had friends or relations in high places.[47] (2) A simple nickname hardly determines someone's entire personality. (3) The view that John was illiterate is based on a mistranslation of Acts 4:13, which affirms only that John did not have formal rabbinic training. (4) We have already seen Matthew use equally pointed language in situations where Judaism staunchly rejected early Christianity. (5) This witness never calls himself the only disciple Jesus loved or the one he loved most, and his refusal to mention his name could even be seen as a mark of humility. Or the references to the beloved disciple could be redactional insertions by the final editors of the document John largely created (see below, p. 173). On the positive side, the simple but generally accurate *koinē* Greek used in all of the Johannine documents fits well with one who learned Greek as a second language.

---

46. Martin Hengel, *The Johannine Question* (London: SCM; Philadelphia: TPI, 1989). But Hengel's profile of John the presbyter closely matches traditional reconstructions of John the apostle!

47. R. Alan Culpepper (*John, the Son of Zebedee* [Columbia: University of South Carolina Press, 1994], 62) believes that the story of Peter's denial requires the beloved disciple to be relatively unknown. Presumably he means that this disciple, who accompanied Peter, if John the apostle, would have stood equally accused. But the "accusers" are only servants and bystanders. Perhaps they *did* know about John but were unsure of Peter, which is why they questioned him—more out of mockery than overt hostility.

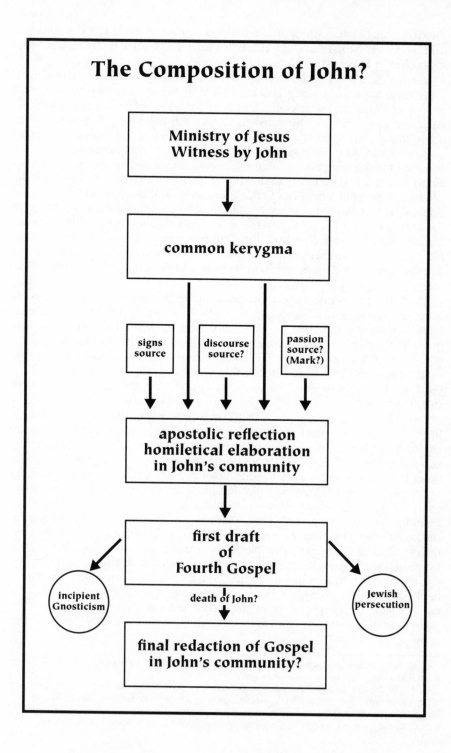

The Composition of John?

**Ministry of Jesus
Witness by John**

common kerygma

signs
source

discourse
source?

passion
source?
(Mark?)

**apostolic reflection
homiletical elaboration
in John's community**

**first draft
of
Fourth Gospel**

incipient
Gnosticism

death of John?

Jewish
persecution

**final redaction of Gospel
in John's community?**

The only serious stumbling block to accepting Johannine authorship is the striking difference in theology between him and the Synoptics. While we must not minimize these differences, we hope that our comments above (pp. 157–159) have demonstrated that these differences can also be exaggerated. Futhermore, one must not underestimate the diversity that existed even within apostolic Christianity.[48]

A related issue is that of Johannine source-criticism. Rudolf Bultmann's ground-breaking commentary argued for three major sources behind the Fourth Gospel: a signs source, discourse source, and passion source.[49] Supporting stylistic and literary evidence appears in a significant amount only for the first of these.[50] There are intriguing "seams" in John's narrative where it appears that material could have been reversed in sequence in some stage of editing or copying. The most noteworthy of these comes at John 14:31–15:1, in which Jesus declares, "Come now; let us leave," and then continues for two more chapters with his discourse. But it may well be that John did intend to portray Jesus as getting up at that point and heading with his disciples from the Upper Room toward the Garden of Gethsemane while continuing to teach.[51] Be that as it may, recent studies have stressed the stylistic and narrative unity of John's Gospel in its finished form.[52] As one writer put it (tongue-in-cheek), "If the author of the Fourth Gospel used documentary sources, he wrote them all himself."[53]

Many commentators have taken a slightly different tack and tried to isolate stages or levels of redaction within the Gospel. The prologue and final chapter are regular candidates for "add-ons" to an original document. Various schemes of two, three, and five stages of editing have proved popular,[54] but again the data are too slippery down to pin any of these with confidence. The closing two verses of the Gospel (21:24–25) support at least some minimal redactional activity, as they distinguish the beloved disciple who wrote down the events of the Gospel from a group of people ("we") who "know that his testimony is true" and an "I" who supposes that the whole world couldn't contain the books that could be written about Jesus. The fact that 21:20–23 debunks a false rumor that had spread that the beloved disciple would live until Christ's return makes the hypothesis attractive that John had just died and a group of his followers or members of his church were now editing his work for final publication.[55]

Such editing could have affected many parts of the Gospel, but we really have no way of knowing for sure. Beyond this, theories of the composition of

---

48. Cf. further Blomberg, "To What Extent?" 30–37.

49. Rudolf Bultmann, *The Gospel of John* (Oxford: Blackwell; Philadelphia: Westminster, 1971 [Germ. orig. 1941]).

50. See esp. Robert T. Fortna, *The Gospel of Signs* (Cambridge: CUP, 1970); idem, *The Fourth Gospel and Its Predecessor* (Philadelphia: Fortress, 1988).

51. Incidental evidence for this may include the shift in 15:1–8 to the metaphors about vines, a common sight in the gardens surrounding the temple that the troupe would have passed as they headed for their place of prayer. Cf. Ernst Haenchen, *John*, vol. 2 (Philadelphia: Fortress, 1984), 128.

52. See esp. Alan Culpepper, *Anatomy of the Fourth Gospel* (Philadelphia: Fortress, 1983).

53. Pierson Parker, "Two Editions of John," *JBL* 75 (1956): 304.

54. See respectively Martyn, *History and Theology*; Rudolf Schnackenburg, *The Gospel according to St. John*, vol. 1 (London: Burns & Oates; New York: Herder & Herder, 1968) 100–4; Raymond E. Brown, *The Gospel according to John*, vol. 1 (Garden City: Doubleday, 1966), xxxiv–xxxix.

55. Smalley, *John*, 120.

the Fourth Gospel tend merely to compound one speculative hypothesis with another. It seems safest to assume that at least a substantial core of the Gospel as we know it goes back to the apostle John, and any editing that may have occurred was done to put it into a form that enabled God's Spirit best to apply the truths of the Gospel to the Johannine community. The story of Jesus may have been contextualized, but it has not been distorted or falsified.

FOR FURTHER STUDY

Commentaries

Introductory

Bruce, F. F. *The Gospel of John*. Basingstoke: Pickering & Inglis; Grand Rapids: Eerdmans, 1983.
Michaels, J. Ramsey. *John*. [NIBC] Peabody: Hendrickson, 1989.
Milne, Bruce. *The Message of John*. [BST] Leicester and Downers Grove: IVP, 1993.

Intermediate

Beasley-Murray, George R. *John*. [WBC] Waco: Word, 1987.
Borchert, Gerald L. *John*. 2 vols. [NAC] Nashville: Broadman & Holman, 1996– .
Carson, D. A. *The Gospel according to John*. [Pillar] Grand Rapids: Eerdmans; Leicester: IVP, 1991.
Lindars, Barnabas. *The Gospel of John*. [NCB] London: Oliphants, 1972; Grand Rapids: Eerdmans, 1981.
Morris, Leon. *The Gospel according to John*. [NIC] Grand Rapids: Eerdmans, rev. 1995.
Talbert, Charles H. *Reading John*. New York: Crossroad, 1992.
Witherington, Ben, III. *John's Wisdom: A Commentary on the Fourth Gospel*. Louisville: Westminster/John Knox, 1995.

Advanced

Barrett, C. K. *The Gospel according to St. John*. London: SPCK; Philadelphia: Westminster, rev. 1978.
Brown, Raymond E. *The Gospel according to John*. 2 vols. [AB] Garden City: Doubleday, 1966–70.
Haenchen, Ernst. *John*. 2 vols. [Hermeneia] Philadelphia: Fortress, 1984.
Schnackenburg, Rudolf. *The Gospel according to St. John*. 3 vols. London: Burns & Oates; New York: Herder and Herder; Seabury, 1968–82.

Other Key Studies of Johannine Introduction or Theology More Generally

Ashton, John. *Understanding the Fourth Gospel*. Oxford: Clarendon, 1991.
Beasley-Murray, George R. *Gospel of Life: Theology in the Fourth Gospel*. Peabody: Hendrickson, 1991.
Brown, Raymond E. *The Community of the Beloved Disciple*. New York: Paulist, 1979.
Cassidy, Richard J. *John's Gospel in New Perspective: Christology and the Realities of Roman Power*. Maryknoll: Orbis, 1992.
Culpepper, R. Alan, and C. Clifton Black, eds. *Exploring the Gospel of John*. Louisville: Westminster/John Knox, 1996.
Hunter, A. M. *According to John*. London: SCM; Philadelphia: Westminster, 1968.
Kysar, Robert. *The Fourth Evangelist and His Gospel: An Examination of Contemporary Scholarship*. Minneapolis: Augsburg, 1975.

Morris, Leon. *Jesus Is the Christ: Studies in the Theology of John.* Grand Rapids: Eerdmans; Leicester: IVP, 1989.
Painter, John. *The Quest for the Messiah: The History, Literature, and Theology of the Johannine Community.* Edinburgh: T. & T. Clark; Nashville: Abingdon, rev. 1993.
Pryor, John W. *John: Evangelist of the Covenant People.* London: Darton, Longman & Todd; Downers Grove: IVP, 1992.
Robinson, John A. T. *The Priority of John.* London: SCM, 1985; Oak Park, Ill.: Meyer-Stone, 1987.
Smalley, Stephen. *John: Evangelist and Interpreter.* Exeter: Paternoster, 1978.
Smith, D. Moody. *The Theology of the Gospel of John.* Cambridge: CUP, 1995.
van Tilborg, Sjef. *Reading John in Ephesus.* Leiden: Brill, 1996.

Bibliography
Mills, Watson E. *The Gospel of John.* Lewiston and Lampeter: Mellen, 1995.

QUESTIONS FOR REVIEW

1. What is a plausible overall outline for the Gospel of John? That is, how many main sections may it be divided into and by what criteria? What theology may be inferred from this structure?

2. According to typical evangelical reconstructions, who wrote this Gospel, when, where, to whom, and under what circumstances (to the extent that this information may be reasonably inferred)?

3. What are some of the unique issues surrounding the authorship of this Gospel that are not present with the Synoptics? What are some of the unique issues surrounding the source and redaction criticism of this Gospel?

4. What are several of the major theological distinctives of this Gospel?

5. In what ways is John more different from the Synoptics than they are from each other? Why might this be?

6. Given the emphases and probable circumstances of John's Gospel, in what settings in contemporary Christian living might it be even more acutely relevant than the other Gospels?

PART FOUR

A SURVEY OF THE LIFE OF CHRIST

I n the modern era, conservative scholars have been preoccupied with fitting all of the details of the four Gospels together into a harmony of the life of Christ. Liberal scholars have been just as preoccupied with stressing the theological distinctives of each Gospel. Each of these approaches, when employed to the exclusion of the other, leads to a distorted understanding of the texts. Theology without harmonization discovers only distinctions and alleged contradictions without seeing how much the Gospels have in common and how they can be combined into a harmonious whole. Harmonization without appreciation for the theological distinctives of the Gospels trades the inspired form of the text for a humanly created one. It is our desire to keep both history and theology in balance in this book.

Related to this balance are the results of the so-called "quest for the historical Jesus." What can we know about Jesus, from the Gospels or elsewhere, following strict historical method? The answers have varied widely from "virtually nothing" to "almost everything." It is our conviction that a fair-minded application of the standard criteria for assessing the historicity of any ancient document can lead to a substantial confidence in the reliability of the Gospel tradition, even though we lack the comparative data to authenticate more than the major themes and contours of that tradition.

The first chapter of part 4 will thus survey the various approaches to the historical Jesus that the last two centuries of scholarship have spawned, followed by a brief chronology of the life of Christ that provides the rationale for the subsequent divisions of Gospel material in the remaining chapters. These chapters will then read the Gospels themselves in a broad chronological sequence, to the extent that it is recoverable. We will watch for the most significant redactional emphases of each Gospel as highlighted previously in part 3. We will assess the historicity of select details and comment on some of the most famous apparent "contradictions" within the texts. But we will focus primarily on the most important and interesting exegetical details. We do not have room for a full-fledged commentary on each episode from Jesus' life and ministry, but we can highlight main themes and patterns, and focus on particularly crucial or controversial texts. We will even try to debunk a few commonly held misinterpretations of passages and suggest occasional applications to contemporary Christian living.

CHAPTER TEN

THE HISTORICAL JESUS—
The Quests and the Chronology

THE QUESTS OF THE HISTORICAL JESUS

The First Quest

I n our survey of Gospel criticism (above, pp. 77–81), we spoke briefly
of the nineteenth-century responses to the question of the miraculous.
We may now review several of these schools of thought with respect
to their portraits of Jesus more generally.[1] At least three main approaches predominated during this first quest of the historical Jesus. *Rationalists and
mythologizers* alike determined that the Jesus of history was a mere man, shorn
of any miracle-working abilities or "divine nature," even though they differed
as to how to explain the miracle-stories in the Gospels (above, p. 78). For
Reimarus, Jesus was very much a Jew of his day, coming to fulfill the revolutionary sociopolitical hopes of his people. He thus waited in vain for the popular uprising he anticipated would help him overthrow Rome. For Strauss,
Jesus was a suffering Messiah who mistakenly believed that his death would
spark the events that would bring about the literal, earthly Jewish kingdom of
God.

Romantics, most notably the French Catholic Ernest Renan, portrayed Jesus
as the consummately gentle teacher of love, beauty, and joy who offered compelling moral precepts for his people. At a later stage in his life, however, Jesus
abandoned this approach in favor of a miracle-working ministry, added an

---

1. The story is told comprehensively in Albert Schweitzer, *The Quest of the Historical Jesus* (London: Black; New York: Macmillan, 1910 [Ger. orig. 1906]), 1–351.

-179-

eschatological urgency to his message, and increasingly longed for martyrdom as an outgrowth of his Messianic consciousness.

Nineteenth-century *liberals*, spearheaded by Adolf von Harnack, promoted a Jesus who fit in with their beliefs in social progress and moral evolution. Jesus was the great ethical teacher who stressed the fatherhood of God, the brotherhood of all humanity, the infinite value of a person's soul, and a higher righteousness by the way of love. For these liberals, the historical Jesus maintained this agenda consistently throughout his life.

The first quest came to an end due to the combined writings of four key scholars. Martin Kähler's influential book discloses its theme in its title: *The So-Called Historical Jesus and the Historic, Biblical Christ (Die sogennante historische Jesus und die geschichtliche biblische Christus).*[2] In German, there are two quite distinct words for history: *Historie* (the actual chronicle of events) and *Geschichte* (the significance of those events). Kähler argued that the early Christian kerygma (faith-proclamation) was so intertwined with the actual life of Jesus that the two kinds of history were inseparable. Christians could believe in the significance of the story, even though it was largely impossible for historians to separate fact from significance. The second scholar, Johannes Weiss, still believing that the historical Jesus could be recovered, persuasively portrayed a consistently eschatological Jesus—one who preached the near arrival of the kingdom—in contrast to the social or ethical Jesuses of the previous "questers."[3] Third, William Wrede advanced his thesis about the messianic secret (see above, pp. 118–119). Whereas previous scholars had assumed that at least Mark, the earliest Gospel, provided a genuine window into Jesus' self-consciousness, Wrede challenged even this much, leaving only a handful of items in Mark that one could trust. Certainly not enough remained to reconstruct a detailed description of the Jesus of history.[4]

Fourth, and most important of all, Albert Schweitzer's detailed exposé of how nineteenth-century portrayals of Jesus regularly re-created him in the image of their authors led to widespread skepticism about the possibility of the undertaking. Schweitzer's own alternative, however, would remain extremely influential. As with Weiss, Schweitzer's Jesus was consistently eschatological, an apocalyptic Jew who became convinced God would supernaturally intervene to establish his kingdom on earth during his lifetime. Jesus sent out the twelve with this expectation (Matt. 10:23), only to have it frustrated. The second stage in his ministry thus followed, as Jesus became convinced that he had to take upon himself the tribulations or messianic woes that many Jews believed had to precede the coming of a new age. This would be accomplished by his death, so he went to Jerusalem as a hidden Messiah, convinced he must become a martyr. Peter and Judas, each in their own ways, disclosed Jesus' messianic claims to the authorities so that he was crucified. That the kingdom did not immediately appear as he had envisioned implies that in one sense he died a failure.[5]

---

2. (Philadelphia: Fortress, 1964 [Ger. orig. 1892]).

3. Johannes Weiss, *Jesus' Proclamation of the Kingdom of God* (Philadelphia: Fortress, 1971 [Ger. orig. 1892]).

4. William Wrede, *The Messianic Secret* (Cambridge: James Clarke, 1971 [Ger. orig. 1901]).

5. Schweitzer, *Quest*, 352–403.

No Quest and the New Quest

The dominant figure in the history of biblical criticism and theology during the first half of the 1900s was Rudolf Bultmann. Bultmann combined and modified the major claims of Kähler and Schweitzer. He consistently set out to demonstrate that we could know virtually nothing about the historical Jesus because of the interweaving of history and faith throughout the Gospels. He agreed that some of what we could know resembled Schweitzer's portrait of a teacher with demanding ethical standards, but he believed that Jesus was looking for someone other than himself when he spoke of the coming Son of Man. Theologically, Bultmann viewed his historical agnosticism as a positive state of affairs because he thought any attempt to ground our faith in history would destroy the cardinal principle of Reformation Christianity—justification by *faith* alone. Building on Strauss, Bultmann developed a "demythologizing" agenda—trying to understand the theological truths that are left when one strips away the mythological husks in which the Gospel texts are wrapped. Following the existentialist philosopher Martin Heidegger, Bultmann saw the essence of Jesus' teaching as calling people to a moment-by-moment encounter with God—learning to live what he called "authentic existence" in the present, given the transience of life and the uncertainty of the future.[6]

Particularly due to Schweitzer's and Bultmann's influence, relatively few writers writing from the 1900s through the 1950s attempted to compose a life of Christ. Then in 1954 at a reunion of Bultmann's students at the University of Marburg, Ernst Käsemann gave a paper entitled, "The Problem of the Historical Jesus." That paper launched what became known as the "new quest" for the Jesus of history. In it, he applied the dissimilarity criterion (see below, p. 186), that Bultmann himself had developed, to argue that one could recover from the Gospels a significant historical core of information. This material showed Jesus to be an apocalyptic Jew who decisively challenged the religious authorities of his day and even the Torah itself.[7]

Two other scholars soon followed suit. James Robinson, an American, argued that an eschatological Jesus—indeed, the entire early Christian kerygma—demanded historical grounding. Robinson appealed to a newer understanding of history in which one does not have to rigidly separate fact from interpretation to determine a historical figure's intentions and commitments.[8] Back in Germany, Günther Bornkamm produced the first book-length treatment of Jesus to come out of the new quest. While still not accepting a messianic self-consciousness for Jesus, and while limiting his study primarily to the sayings material, thematically arranged, Bornkamm nevertheless believed that a large percentage of Jesus' teaching was authentic and disclosed his radically transcendent personality. The kingdom was both present and future. God as Father loved humanity but was calling people, through Jesus, to repent of sin.[9]

---

6. See esp. Rudolf Bultmann, *Jesus and the Word* (New York: Scribner's, 1934); cf. idem, *Jesus Christ and Mythology* (New York: Scribner's, 1958; London: SCM, 1960).

7. More conveniently available in Ernst Käsemann, "The Problem of the Historical Jesus," in *Essays on New Testament Themes* (London: SCM; Naperville: Allenson, 1964), 15–47.

8. James M. Robinson, *A New Quest of the Historical Jesus* (London: SCM; Naperville: Allenson, 1959).

9. Günther Bornkamm, *Jesus of Nazareth* (London: Hodder & Stoughton; New York: Harper & Row, 1960).

All of the initial "new questers" still shared, to varying degrees, Bultmann's commitment to existentialism, emphasizing how Jesus mediated God's divine presence to humanity with a directness that radically differed from the Judaism of his day. However, coming largely out of a Germany only a few years removed from the Nazi atrocities, the portraits of Judaism painted by the "new questers" were often caricatures that bordered on anti-Semitism.

The Third Quest

The 1960s and 1970s made it increasingly clear that the new quest would not advance beyond the old quest as far as its original proponents had thought. Again, historical Jesus research died down—until the early 1980s. Since then it has reemerged with great fervor. This so-called third quest has several distinctives: (a) a rigorous examination and application of historical criteria to determine the authenticity of the various Gospel data; (b) a reclamation of Jesus the Jew, interpreting him clearly against the backdrop of the religious ideas and institutions of his day; and (c) a far more nuanced and detailed understanding of the diversity of early first-century Judaism.[10] Within the third quest one may discern two broad "camps" or approaches.

An Emphasis on the Deeds of Jesus. Quite unlike Bultmann and most of his disciples, many "third questers" focus more on the deeds of Jesus than on his sayings. They stress that one must adequately account for the indisputable fact of Jesus' crucifixion by Pontius Pilate and that his teachings alone were not a sufficient cause of his execution. At least four main views of Jesus result from this approach, along with various combinations.

Jesus was an *eschatological prophet* according to E. P. Sanders, one of the pioneers and, arguably, still the most significant scholar in the third quest. Sanders restores Jesus to his rightful place as a first-century Jew convinced the end of the age was near. But Sanders plays down the Gospels' picture of Jesus in conflict with the Jewish leaders. He believes Jesus offered God's forgiveness to the wicked of his society, without making them first prove themselves by repenting. Sanders places great significance on the incident of the temple "cleansing," which he thinks is better understood as part of Jesus' expectation that the temple would be destroyed and rebuilt. In short, Jesus' agenda was one of restoring Israel to a right relationship with God.[11]

Jesus was a *charismatic holy man* in the view of Geza Vermes. This Jewish scholar has compared and contrasted Jesus with other influential religious leaders of his day who operated outside normal institutional channels, particularly Honi the Circle-Drawer and Hanina ben-Dosa. Both developed reputations for working miracles as a result of the effectiveness of their prayers—Honi for being able to make it rain and Hanina for a variety of healings and exorcisms.[12] From a more liberal perspective, Marcus Borg has developed a view of Jesus that sees him as a "Spirit-person," someone particularly in tune with the divine

---

10. For a thorough survey, see Ben Witherington III, *The Jesus Quest: The Third Search for the Jew of Nazareth* (Downers Grove: IVP, 1995), from which some of the subtitles below derive.

11. E. P. Sanders, *Jesus and Judaism* (London: SCM; Philadelphia: Fortress, 1985); idem, *The Historical Figure of Jesus* (London: Penguin, 1993).

12. Geza Vermes, *Jesus the Jew* (London: Collins, 1973; Philadelphia: Fortress, 1974).

and able to be a conduit of God's Spirit to others.[13] From a more conservative angle, Martin Hengel, too, accepts the label "charismatic" as the best description of Jesus.[14] Common to all of these writers is an emphasis on Jesus as a threat to the religious establishment because he did not accept the official spokesmen for Judaism as appropriate authorities, did not treat the Torah with adequate reverence from their perspective, and emphasized moral rather than ritual holiness.

Other writers have portrayed Jesus as a *social reformer.* In varying ways Gerd Theissen and Richard Horsley have both stressed the impact they believe Jesus wanted to make on the Jewish society of his day. As an itinerant minister who spawned a following of wandering charismatics supported by local sympathizers in various villages, Jesus was developing a renewal movement within Israel. Groups of disciples created countercultural communities based on the principle of loving even one's enemy. Yet they were still perceived as threats to the authorities due to their policies of nonviolent resistance to oppression.[15]

Still other scholars see in Jesus the *marginalized Messiah.* This perspective accepts the greatest amount of the Gospel data as authentic. It recognizes that Jesus did claim to be the Jewish Messiah, however unconventional his concept of that role was. He was a teacher, a miracle worker, a prophet, and a gatherer of Israel, but it was ultimately his Messianic claims and deeds that ran him afoul of the authorities. He who was committed to the marginalized of his society became marginalized himself and was executed. N. T. Wright defends this perspective by means of a detailed mastery of Jewish backgrounds; John Meier, by applying a rigorous critical methodology that Protestants, Catholics, Jews, and atheists could in principle share.[16]

An Emphasis on the Sayings of Jesus. This second main category does not exclude the first; all of the "third questers" deal with deeds *and* sayings, but most clearly place more weight on one area or the other. Again, four main subcategories may be discerned. The first two focus on Jesus and Wisdom; the second two focus on Jesus the teacher of short, subversive sayings.

The most holistic of the four is the view that sees Jesus as the *incarnation of Divine Wisdom,* in continuity with the increasing development in Judaism of Wisdom as a personification for God (cf. Proverbs 9; recall above, p. 42). Ben Witherington surveys Jesus' relationships, deeds, and sayings, but he argues that the sayings are the most important. Supplementing prophetic and messianic categories, Witherington identifies Jesus above all as a sage, a divine emissary (Hebrew, *shaliach*; Greek, *apostolos*), and God's eschatological agent for revealing himself to humanity. Jesus' teachings are often countercultural like those of Job and Ecclesiastes in the Old Testament. Of the views surveyed here,

---

13. Marcus Borg, *Jesus, a New Vision* (San Francisco: Harper & Row, 1987).

14. Martin Hengel, *The Charismatic Leader and His Followers* (Edinburgh: T. & T. Clark, 1981).

15. Gerd Theissen, *The Shadow of the Galilean: The Quest of the Historical Jesus in Narrative Form* (London: SCM; Philadelphia: Fortress, 1987); Richard A. Horsley, *Jesus and the Spiral of Violence* (San Francisco: Harper & Row, 1987).

16. N. T. Wright, *Jesus and the Victory of God* (London: SPCK; Minneapolis: Fortress, 1996); John P. Meier, *A Marginal Jew: Rethinking the Historical Jesus*, 3 vols. (New York and London: Doubleday, 1991–). Much more briefly, cf. Markus Bockmuehl, *This Jesus: Martyr, Lord, Messiah* (Edinburgh: T. & T. Clark, 1994; Downers Grove: IVP, 1996); and Peter Stuhlmacher, *Jesus of Nazareth—Christ of Faith* (Peabody: Hendrickson, 1993).

this one, along with the marginalized Messiah view, most closely approximates historic Christian understanding of who Jesus was.[17]

Elisabeth Schüssler Fiorenza developed this wisdom perspective in portraying Jesus as *a feminist before his time*. She has also vigorously argued for the importance of understanding Wisdom in the Gospels. But she stresses the feminine side of God, through the (feminine) Greek word for "Wisdom" (*Sophia*) that played an influential role in some Jewish and much Greek religious thought of the day. For Schüssler Fiorenza, Jesus himself is not divine Wisdom but rather "Sophia's prophet" and offspring. His teachings about and patterns of interacting with women, when separated from the later "repatriarchalizing" distortions of the early church, demonstrate him to be a true proponent of women's spiritual and social liberation in the best senses of those terms.[18]

John Dominic Crossan's influential and prolific literary output has portrayed Jesus as a *Cynic sage*. Crossan has applied virtually every modern critical method to the Gospels over the years to produce at times complementary, at times contradictory reflections on the historical Jesus. He seems to have come to rest on a view of Jesus that finds him having more in common with itinerant Greek Cynic philosophers (on which, see above, pp. 31–32) than with any clearly Jewish categories of religious leader. Central to Crossan's reconstruction are Jesus' characteristic willingness to eat on equal terms with the outcasts of his day and his ability to work miracles (by psychosomatic powers of suggestion) that were phenomenologically indistinguishable from pagan "magic" (on which, see above, p. 34). Little can be known of the events of his passion, but much can be recovered of his subversive teachings in parables and aphorisms (other short, pithy, and unconventional sayings). Promoting a radical egalitarianism, Jesus stirred up peasant hopes of a better life to a sufficient extent to threaten the Roman authorities of his day, who are alone to blame for his execution. Unlike the other perspectives listed above, Crossan's relies heavily on the improbable assumptions that noncanonical documents (or their sources) can be dated to a period earlier than the canonical Gospels, and that in places they reflect a more historically reliable portrait of the life of Jesus.[19]

The highly publicized Jesus Seminar has popularized Jesus as an *oriental guru*. Over the last decade a small group of mostly quite radical scholars, calling themselves the Jesus Seminar, and cochaired by Crossan and Borg, have met periodically to vote on the probable authenticity of the various sayings and deeds of Jesus. In many ways their Jesus resembles that of Crossan's, but only 18 percent of the Gospel sayings (including Coptic Thomas) survive as closely resembling what Jesus actually said. Among many of their wildly improbable methodological presuppositions is the notion that Jesus could *never* have spoken in more than very short, cryptic utterances.[20] Although they do not use the

---

17. Ben Witherington III, *The Christology of Jesus* (Minneapolis: Fortress, 1990); idem, *Jesus the Sage* (Minneapolis: Fortress, 1994).

18. Elisabeth Schüssler Fiorenza, *In Memory of Her* (New York: Crossroad, 1983); idem, *Jesus: Miriam's Child, Sophia's Prophet* (New York: Continuum, 1994).

19. See esp. John Dominic Crossan, *The Historical Jesus* (San Francisco: HarperSanFrancisco, 1991). Cf. also Burton L. Mack, *A Myth of Innocence* (Philadelphia: Fortress, 1988).

20. Robert W. Funk, Roy W. Hoover, and the Jesus Seminar, *The Five Gospels: The Search for the Authentic Words of Jesus* (New York: Macmillan, 1993).

term, the only conceivable analogy in the religious world of Jesus' day would be the stereotypic Eastern holy man with a reputation for speaking very little, save periodically to utter short profundities. The Jesus Seminar's approach has been widely and severely critiqued,[21] and their claim to speak for a consensus of modern biblical critics is irresponsible. But, unlike most scholars, they have deliberately courted the mass media to promote their views widely and, unfortunately, have convinced many that they represent mainstream scholarship.

Assessment and Criteria of Authenticity

What are we to make of this almost bewildering variety of "Jesuses"? It would be easy to despair of historical methodology and/or to argue that the whole enterprise is ideologically misguided.[22] But in fact, after certain eccentric portraits are bracketed, we find a surprising amount of agreement with respect to both historical method and the results of its application. One of the main reasons scholars disagree as to how much of the Gospel portraits can be corroborated by historical research has to do with initial presuppositions. An anti-supernaturalist worldview will clearly rule out much *a priori*. A second important issue involves the "burden of proof." Does one assume a saying or deed of Jesus to be authentic unless contradictions or inconsistencies with other data emerge? Or does one assume all the data to be inauthentic unless good reasons can be marshalled for accepting them? The former approach is the standard one in the investigation of other ancient historical documents, but the latter approach is the one more often applied to the Gospels.[23]

Why this apparent double standard? The most common answer is because the Gospels are not straightforward accounts of history or biography; they are the products of faith communities that could easily have biased their reporting—intentionally or unintentionally—in order to glorify their founder, Jesus. But at least two replies to this argument need to be stressed: (1) An ideological bias can actually create a greater concern to tell the story "straight." For example, as noted above (p. 93), it has often been the Jewish historians of the holocaust during World War II that have proved the most accurate, precisely because they wanted to do all they could to ensure that such horrors never again occur. (2) In antiquity, *all* history writing was ideologically biased. No one ever thought of recording information merely for information's sake, as we sometimes do. Instead the attitude was one of asking, if history didn't teach certain lessons or morals, why preserve it? Yet our history textbooks are filled with "facts" about the ancient world far less well attested than the Gospel data.[24]

On the other hand, even for those who insist that we begin from a position of methodical doubt, various standard "criteria of authenticity" have been

---

21. Cf. esp. Luke T. Johnson, *The Real Jesus* (San Francisco: HarperSanFrancisco, 1996); with Michael J. Wilkins and J. P. Moreland, eds., *Jesus under Fire* (Grand Rapids: Zondervan, 1995). More briefly, see Craig L. Blomberg, "The Seventy-Four 'Scholars': Who Does the Jesus Seminar Really Speak For?" *Christian Research Journal* 17.2 (1994) 32–38.

22. Ironically, this is a view maintained by many fundamentalists, despite its roots in the Enlightenment's divorce of faith from history.

23. See Stewart C. Goetz and Craig L. Blomberg, "The Burden of Proof," *JSNT* 11 (1981): 39–63.

24. See esp. A. N. Sherwin-White, *Roman Society and Roman Law in the New Testament* (Oxford: OUP, 1963); cf. Paul Merkley, "The Gospels as Historical Testimony," *EQ* 58 (1986): esp. 328–36.

developed that can go a long way toward enhancing our confidence in the reliability of the Gospel record.[25] Four stand out in particular:

1. The *dissimilarity* criterion looks for information about Jesus in which he noticeably diverges both from the conventional Judaism of his day and from the major emphases of the early church (including the redactional emphases of a given evangelist)—as with his use of parables, the kingdom of God, or the "Son of Man" title. Potentially awkward or embarrassing information about Jesus also falls into this category. Such material would not likely have been invented by any Christian, Jew or Gentile. This criterion cannot be used to determine what is *characteristic* of Jesus, merely what is *distinctive*, but it can yield a "critically assured minimum" of historical information. Unfortunately, material that does not pass this criterion has often been labeled unhistorical. This, of course, would require Jesus to have been totally different from every Jew of his day and misunderstood by every one of his followers, a hypothesis which is patently absurd.[26]

2. The criterion of *multiple attestation* takes several forms. That which appears in more than one Gospel, more than one Gospel source, or more than one form stands a better chance of being authentic than that which is singly attested. This, in broad strokes, lends an inherent plausibility to most of the main contours of Jesus' ministry—for example, conflicts with the Jewish leaders, healings and exorcisms, and the events leading up to and including his passion. Again, it is unfortunate that some use this criterion negatively to exclude singly attested material. Material that cannot be corroborated may still be historical; we may simply have no way of knowing for sure.

3. The criterion of *Palestinian environment* or *Semitic language* reminds us that in many ways Jesus was thoroughly a person of his times. Despite the fact that the Gospels were written in Greek in an age when the church was primarily Hellenistic in culture, features unique to Palestinian culture or environment are preserved (details of village life, agriculture, etc.). Language that reads like a fairly literal translation of a distinctively Semitic idiom frequently appears—for example, "the poor" (from Heb. *anawim*) meaning those afflicted with both spiritual and material poverty. When this kind of phenomena occur, we may suspect that we are in touch with tradition at least as old as early Palestinian Jewish Christianity, perhaps dating back to Jesus himself. Again, a negative use of this criterion is not as valid. Distinctive Greek idioms may reflect an evangelist's paraphrase, and occasionally Jesus himself probably spoke in Greek. Non-Palestinian cultural elements may reflect a Gospel writer's desire to "contextualize" his message without falsifying the gist of the account—as when Luke replaces Mark's Palestinian thatched roof with Greco-Roman tiling (cf. Mark 2:4 with Luke 5:19).

4. Finally, the criterion of *coherence* identifies details that do not pass the above criteria in and of themselves but fit in very much with the distinctive style, form, or content of those teachings and actions of Jesus that do pass the

---

25. For the most comprehensive survey of criteria, see Dennis Polkow, "Method and Criteria for Historical Jesus Research," *Society of Biblical Literature Seminar Papers* 26 (1987): 336–56. For the best evangelical analysis, see Craig A. Evans, "Authenticity Criteria in Life of Jesus Research," *CSR* 19 (1989): 6–31.

26. See esp. A. E. Harvey, *Jesus and the Constraints of History* (London: Duckworth; Philadelphia: Westminster, 1982).

criteria (cf., e.g., our argument below that the "nature miracles" fit in closely with Jesus' parables and other teachings about the kingdom of God—pp. 267–268).

Secondary criteria, less conclusive but at times suggestive, include the *tendencies of the developing tradition* (what shows signs of being a later development of an earlier form, or vice versa), *necessary explanation* (what *must* have happened to account for a later historical fact—e.g., the crucifixion or the rise of Easter faith), and *vividness* as a pointer to an eyewitness report of a given account. But for almost every alleged tendency of the tradition, an opposite one can be found,[27] and the latter two criteria are highly subjective.

By now the student who believes in the inspiration of the Bible may be asking, "Where is the Holy Spirit in all of this discussion?" or "Don't we simply accept the trustworthiness of the Gospels on faith?" The answer to the first question is clearly that the Spirit's inspiration has *not* been taken into account by those who have engaged in the quest for the historical Jesus, liberal or conservative. *By definition* the quest involves ascertaining what can be known on purely historical grounds—what results believer and unbeliever alike can affirm. In response to the second question, it is undoubtedly true that the believer will affirm by faith more than what history can demonstrate, but there is much to be said for arguing that such faith *builds on* the evidence that does exist, rather than flying in its face.[28] In part 5 we will return to some of these reflections and synthesize our findings as well as advance further arguments for the trustworthiness of the Gospel tradition.

THE CHRONOLOGY OF THE LIFE OF CHRIST

Dating the details of the life of Jesus is at times an uncertain proposition. The dates of some events in the ancient world are well established, some are reasonable approximations, while others are educated guesses at best. What we call the first century included the years 754–854 for the Romans (reckoning from the supposed date of the founding of Rome) and 3760–3860 for the Jews (counting from the supposed date of the creation of the world). But ancient historians did not use these numbers nearly so much as they referred to the "nth" year of a certain king's reign. Here ambiguities crop up. Some writers reckon from the exact date of a king's accession to the throne; others from the first full calendar year of his reign. Some use "exclusive reckoning" (e.g., the second through fifth years would total three years); others, "inclusive reckoning" (with second through fifth equaling four years by counting "two, three, four, and five"). What is more, Jewish and Roman calendars started at different times of the year. So a comparison of the standard textbooks on biblical chronology will regularly yield a variation of a year in one direction or another for many dates. The encyclopedia articles listed in the bibliography at the end of

---

27. E. P. Sanders, *The Tendencies of the Synoptic Tradition* (Cambridge: CUP, 1969).

28. Cf. G. N. Stanton, *Jesus of Nazareth in New Testament Preaching* (Cambridge: CUP, 1974), 189: "at least some aspects of the portrait of Jesus are essential to faith, for if historical research were ever able to prove conclusively that the historical Jesus was quite unlike the Jesus of the gospels, then faith would certainly be eroded. The gospel is concerned with history: not in that it stands if its claims could be verified by the historian, but in that it falls if the main lines of the early church's portrait of Jesus of Nazareth were to be falsified by historical research."

this chapter present the key references from the ancient writers on which we base our information. For the sake of simplifying matters and not overwhelming the introductory student, our discussion here will not list all that data.

The Birth of Christ

Paradoxical as it sounds, the date of Christ's birth was probably somewhere between 6–4 B.C. Our division of the calendar into B.C. and A.D. is of course a Christian invention. It began to catch on as early as the ninth and tenth centuries but was not formally adopted in Europe until the era of Pope Gregory XIII in the late 1500s. The oldest recorded attempt to fix a date for the birth of Jesus was made in the early sixth century by Dionysus Exiguus, who failed to take the evidence of Josephus into account. The date we call A.D. 1 eventually became so well entrenched that changing the calendar proved impossible. According to Josephus's information about Herod the Great's death and the start of the reigns of his sons, Herod must have died in what we now know as 4 B.C. Because, shortly before his death, he had the babies in Bethlehem slaughtered "who were two years old and under, in accordance with the time he had learned from the Magi" (Matt. 2:16), it may be that Christ had been born up to two years earlier. Attempts to link the star of Bethlehem (2:2, 9–10) with an unusual conjunction of planets (7 and 6 B.C.) or the appearance of a comet or supernova (5 B.C.) have produced more precise suggestions, but if this "star" was a fully supernatural phenomenon, then it cannot be used to further our quest of a date for Jesus' birth.

Complicating matters is Luke 2:2—Jesus was born when Quirinius was governor of Syria. The only governorship of Quirinius we know about for sure began in A.D. 6. Yet the Greek word for "governor" is a very general one that can refer to many leadership roles, and there is some evidence to suggest that Quirinius may have held administrative duties under earlier rulers. It is also possible that we should translate this verse: "This was the census that took place before Quirinius was governor of Syria," though this solution is perhaps less likely.[29]

The day of Jesus' birth is even more uncertain. Christians in the Western part of the Roman empire began to celebrate "Christmas" on December 25, a holiday for worshiping Sol Invictus ("the unconquerable sun"—see above, p. 34); in the East, on January 6. Both dates also coincided at times, in the ancient calendars, with the winter solstice. So it is doubtful if these dates reflect any information about the actual day on which Jesus was born. Some historians point to the fact that shepherds would have watched their flocks *at night* (Luke 2:8) primarily in the springtime when most lambs were born, so perhaps Jesus was born in the spring. Still, we simply have no way of being sure.

Beginning of Christ's Ministry

A number of pieces of data must be assembled and interpreted to try to arrive at a starting point for Christ's adult ministry.

---

29. Cf. further Craig L. Blomberg, "Quirinius," in *ISBE*, vol. 4, 12–13; Darrell L. Bock, *Luke 1:1–9:50* (Grand Rapids: Baker, 1994), 903–9.

(1) According to Luke 3:1, John the Baptist was preaching in the fifteenth year of Tiberius Caesar. Tiberius' rule began in A.D. 14, suggesting a date of either 28 or 29 for the ministry of John. But in 12, Augustus gave Tiberius joint rule in the Eastern provinces, so it is possible, though probably less likely, that Luke calculated from this date, which would yield the year 26 or 27 for John's preaching.

(2) In Luke 3:23, Jesus is said to be "about thirty years old when he began his ministry." This is clearly a rough estimate that would fit any of the above dates, though it is closer to the exact mark if we accept the earlier date.

(3) In John 8:57, Jesus' opponents comment that he is not yet fifty, but this is clearly a round number to stress how few years have elapsed in his life compared to the time since Abraham.[30]

(4) In John 2:20, "the Jews" protest to Jesus that "it has taken forty-six years to build this temple, and you are going to raise it in three days?" According to Josephus, rebuilding of the temple began in Herod's eighteenth year, which, counting from 37 B.C., would give a date of 20 or 19 B.C. for the beginning of the project.[31] Adding on 46 more years (and remembering that there was no year "zero") would then yield either A.D. 27 or 28 for the first Passover of Christ's ministry.

(5) The choice of date for the outset of Christ's ministry is also affected by the number of years one assigns to that ministry and by the date one comes up with for the crucifixion (see below, pp. 190–191). But for now *27 or 28 seems to be the most probable date for the beginning of John's and Jesus' ministries*. How long John ministered before Jesus was baptized we do not know. Most scholars allow for at least a few months; some for up to a year.

The Length of Christ's Ministry

Down through the centuries various Christians have proposed a one-, two-, three-, or four-year ministry for Christ. The most common of these proposals has been a three-year ministry, give or take a few months. The relevant data come primarily from John, since the Synoptics mention only one Passover. (1) John explicitly mentions three Passovers (John 2:13; 6:4; and 12:1). (2) John 5:1 refers to an unnamed feast of the Jews. Some manuscripts call this "the feast" (rather than "a feast"). "The" central feast for the Jews would have been Tabernacles, but for Christian Jews (such as John) it would have been Passover. If this feast were a Passover, another year must be added to John's chronology.[32] (3) It is difficult to decide if the account of Jesus' cleansing the temple at

---

30. George R. Beasley-Murray, *John* (Waco: Word, 1987), 139, suspects it may allude to one possible date for ending the prime working years of a man's life, by analogy with Num. 4:2–3, 39; 8:24–25.

31. The Greek for "build" is aorist, leading Harold W. Hoehner (*Chronological Aspects of the Life of Christ* [Grand Rapids: Zondervan, 1977], 40–43) to argue that it cannot refer to the still incomplete temple precincts as a whole but must refer to the more limited and completed work of building the inner sanctuary. But this took only a year and a half, and the aorist "was built" is even less likely to mean "has been standing for [46 years]." In fact, Hoehner's interpretation of the aorist is too narrow. It frequently appears in Scripture with a durative sense (equivalent to the English perfect tense), meaning to "have been" part of a process.

32. A few have tried to add still another year on the basis of John 4:35 in which Jesus refers to the fields being ripe for harvest, suggesting to some that John is speaking in January or February before the spring harvest. But this fits well with the feast of John 5:1 as being either the spring Passover or the fall Tabernacles of that same calendar year, since Israel had two growing seasons. It is not certain that Jesus intends to make any statement about time of year at all; he is more likely applying a common proverb to the harvest of ripe souls awaiting evangelists.

Passover in John 2:13–25 is a separate event from the temple cleansing during the last week of his life (see Mark 11:12–19 pars.) or if John has moved this account forward as a kind of headline for Jesus' entire ministry.[33] If the latter, then we might deduct a year, although Jesus could have still been in Jerusalem for a Passover early in his ministry *without* having cleansed the temple. (4) In the Synoptics there are two hints of the passing of springtimes. In Mark 2:23–28 and parallels, Jesus and his disciples pick and eat grain from the fields that would have ripened at spring harvesttime. At the feeding of the five thousand, Mark comments on the "green" grass (6:39), a phenomenon unusual in the wilderness (v. 32) except right after the winter rains. *All of this makes a ministry of two to three years, and possibly even a little longer, quite probable.*

For those who see a roughly three-year period, it is common to divide it into three stages: a "year" of obscurity (embracing all of the events prior to Jesus' great Galilean ministry); a "year" of popularity (up until the aftermath of the feeding of the five thousand, when many of Jesus' more loosely associated followers abandoned him—John 6:66); and a "year" of rejection (from after the feeding of the five thousand until his death).[34] These, of course, are broad generalizations that do not characterize every detail of each of these periods, and the first two phases cannot be dated to a set number of months. Each may have been more or less than a year. Still, the labels create a helpful schematic for painting the ministry of Christ in broad strokes.

The Crucifixion of Christ

We know that Christ died during the reigns of the prefect Pilate (A.D. 26–36), the high priest Caiaphas (18–36), and the tetrarch Antipas (4 B.C.–A.D. 37). It would seem that he was crucified on a Friday (the day before the Sabbath—Mark 15:42 par.) and the day after the evening on which the initial Passover meal was celebrated (Mark 14:12, 14, 16 pars.).[35] But John seems to indicate Christ being crucified *on* the day of the Passover celebration, before the initial meal was eaten (John 13:1; 18:28; 19:14, 31). So, was Passover, following the Jewish custom of counting a day from sundown to sundown, from Thursday night to Friday night or from Friday night to Saturday night?[36] Since we know that Passover was celebrated on the 15th day of the month Nisan and

---

33. For arguments for and against, see Craig Blomberg, *The Historical Reliability of the Gospels* (Leicester and Downers Grove: IVP, 1987), 170–73.

34. See, e.g., Robert H. Gundry, *A Survey of the New Testament* (Grand Rapids: Zondervan, rev. 1994), 111–17.

35. Some have argued for a Wednesday crucifixion on the grounds that in Matt. 12:40, Jesus predicts that he will be in the "heart of the earth" for "three days and three nights," thus requiring three full days before Resurrection Sunday. But this interpretation fails to recognize the standard Jewish idiom of using "a day and a night" to refer to any portion of a twenty-four-hour period of time. See Robert H. Gundry, *Matthew: A Commentary on His Handbook for a Mixed Church under Persecution* (Grand Rapids: Eerdmans, rev. 1994), 244, for references.

36. Numerous suggestions have been made: (1) Jesus followed an Essene or Galilean calendar that differed from others (unlikely because of the confusion that would have been caused in Jerusalem by different groups of Jews celebrating the various parts of the week-long festival on different days). (2) Jesus and the Twelve celebrated by themselves a day early, since he knew he was to die (possible, but without any corroborating evidence, and cf. Mark 14:12). (3) The Synoptics are right and John is wrong; John wants to bring out the theology of Jesus as the Passover Lamb by this unhistorical modification (plausible, but elsewhere John seems to bring out the theological significance of Jesus at the various festivals without such falsification of the data). (4) John is right and the Synoptics are wrong (this fits John's concern for chronology but the Synoptic change then seems unmotivated). (5) Both John and the Synoptics actually agree that Jesus ate the Passover meal Thursday night and was crucified on Friday (this seems best; John 13:1–2 does not refer to the Passover meal per se; 18:28 can refer to the *chagigah* lunchtime meal on the day after the initial sacrifice of the lambs; and 19:14, 31 probably refer to the day of preparation for the Sabbath in Passover week (cf. Mark 15:42). For details, cf. Blomberg, *Historical Reliability*, 175–78.

calculated from the appearance of the new moon, we can use astronomical data to determine the years this date fell on a Friday or Saturday.[37] But weather conditions always made it doubtful whether the first sliver of a new moon would be sighted on the first or second day of a new month. As it turns out, *a case can be made for Passover having fallen on either Friday or Saturday in A.D. 30 or 33*, although it is more difficult to date the festival in 33 on a Friday.

Choosing between these dates is extremely difficult. If one equates the cosmic disruptions in Mark 15:33 and Acts 2:19–20 with a *lunar* eclipse, then the year must be 33.[38] Yet if the darkness is a wholly supernatural phenomenon, then this information is of no help. If the earliest plausible date for the beginning of Christ's ministry is 28, and if it could be as late as 29, and if one is convinced that he had about a four-year ministry, then it is natural again to opt for 33. But with all the uncertainties noted above, it is not at all impossible that Jesus' ministry lasted only two years or a little more and that the bulk of it occurred during 28–30. If Sejanus' demise (A.D. 31) put Pilate in a more awkward position, which would account for his behavior at Jesus' trial (see above, p. 22), then once more 33 emerges as the winner. Still, none of this can be demonstrated very conclusively. Also relevant is the dating of the events in the book of Acts and the life of Paul. It is somewhat easier to fit all of those details into a period beginning with A.D. 30; things are a much tighter squeeze if one waits until 33.[39] Among commentators who take the Gospel data seriously enough to reconstruct any kind of a chronology, *30 thus emerges as a slight favorite*. Fortunately, little of great exegetical significance rests on these exact dates.

Further Details of the Life of Christ

From the other festivals mentioned in the Gospel of John we may fill in the details of Jesus' trips to Jerusalem. As for the outset of his ministry, it is customary to assume that all of John 1:19–4:42 preceded the Galilean ministry narrated by the Synoptics because the healing of the nobleman's son in Cana (4:43–54) closely resembles the healing of the centurion's servant near the outset of Jesus' ministry in Galilee (Matt 8:5–13 par.). The preceding events of John 2:13–4:42, which all take place further south, would then have occurred before Christ begins in earnest in Galilee. If John 5:1 refers to Tabernacles, then it would have punctuated the Galilean ministry since chapter 6 proceeds with the feeding of the five thousand and the walking on the water back north. Jesus' climactic journey to Jerusalem in the Synoptics (beginning in Luke 9:51; Mark 10:1 par.) does not seem to allow for any return to Galilee, so it presumably takes place after his penultimate trip to Jerusalem in John 7:1–10:21. After his ministry in Jerusalem at Hanukkah (John 10:22–39), Jesus seems to remain in the southern part of Israel until his fateful entry into Jerusalem a week before

---

37. See the exhaustive compilation of data in Herman H. Goldstine, *New and Full Moons, 1001 B.C. to A.D. 1651* (Philadelphia: American Philosophical Society, 1973).

38. See esp. Colin J. Humphreys' and W. G. Waddington's influential article ("Dating the Crucifixion," *Nature* 306 [1983]: 743–46). But the Gospels speak of a darkening of the *sun*.

39. See, e.g., F. F. Bruce, *Paul: Apostle of the Heart Set Free* (Grand Rapids: Eerdmans [= *Paul: Apostle of the Free Spirit* (Exeter: Paternoster)], 1977), 475 *et passim*.

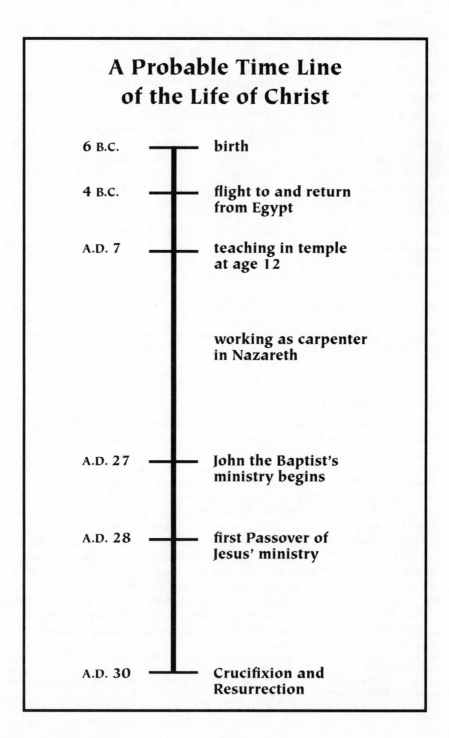

A Probable Time Line of the Life of Christ

6 B.C.	birth
4 B.C.	flight to and return from Egypt
A.D. 7	teaching in temple at age 12
	working as carpenter in Nazareth
A.D. 27	John the Baptist's ministry begins
A.D. 28	first Passover of Jesus' ministry
A.D. 30	Crucifixion and Resurrection

his death (10:40–11:57). All of this, admittedly, is very tentative; nevertheless it may be helpful to lay out these conclusions in chart form:[40]

Date	Event
late 27?	Appearance of John the Baptist
early 28	Baptism of Jesus
	Early events of John 1–2
spring 28	Passover of John 2:13
spring-fall 28	Rest of events of John 3–4
	Ministry in Galilee as in Synoptics
fall 28	Tabernacles (?) of John 5:1
until spring 29	More ministry in Galilee as in Synoptics
spring 29	Passovertime feeding of five thousand
	(John 6:4 pars.)
until fall 29	End of ministry in Galilee, withdrawal and return
fall (Oct.) 29	Tabernacles (John 7:1–10:21) and return to Galilee
Nov-Dec. 29	"Perean ministry"—Jesus' final trip to Jerusalem
late Dec. 29	Hanukkah in Jerusalem (John 10:22)
winter-spring 30	Ministry in and around Judea and Jerusalem
Apr. 2–6, 30	"Triumphal entry," "passion week"
Apr. 7–9	Crucifixion and resurrection

---

40. Cf. esp. John A. T. Robinson, *The Priority of John* (London: SCM, 1985; Oak Park, Ill.: Meyer-Stone, 1987), 157, and the preceding chapter's discussion.

Beyond this, it is difficult to construct an exact account of when and where every detail in Christ's life belongs. In making this observation we must avoid two commonly held but extreme views that prove unwarranted. One is the claim that the reconstruction of a complete harmony of Christ's life, fitting every episode of the four Gospels into a single, connected, coherent narrative, is impossible. It has often been done, and the sequence of events from one scholar's harmony to the next is in many respects strikingly similar. Unreconcilable contradictions in sequence occur only when one reads in chronological order where it is not explicitly affirmed (see above, p. 115) or assumes that all passages remotely similar to each other represent true parallels.[41]

On the other hand, it is precisely the frequent topical grouping and thematic rearrangement of details from one Gospel to the next that makes the opposite conclusion—that there is one and only one way to fit all of the data together—equally unwarranted. Numerous different harmonies have been created that do not agree in every detail, and we simply lack sufficient data in many instances to decide which is the most plausible chronology. For example, which events in Christ's great Galilean ministry took place before the Sermon on the Mount and which ones took place after? In Luke 6:12–16, Jesus calls all Twelve of his disciples just before preaching his great sermon. This has suggested to many that all of the events in Mark 1:1–3:19—that is, up through the calling of the Twelve—should also precede the Sermon. But a number of these events appear in Matthew after the Sermon (see esp. chaps. 8, 11, and 12). Once we realize that both Mark and Matthew are grouping thematically at this point, the chronological question could be decided either way. We simply do not know.

Our outline of the life of Christ for the rest of part 4 will proceed chronologically when we have sufficient information for doing so and thematically when we do not. We will generally follow Mark's outline for these thematic groupings—Jesus' healings, controversy stories, parables, and miracles—while inserting other examples of the same forms from the other Gospels. We will use discrete sections to treat Matthew's, Luke's, and John's material that is unparalleled in Mark, noting thematic patterns there as well. For those who want one plausible harmony of the sequence of events in Christ's life that goes into more detail than the broad chronological outline given above, many synopses are available. The standard scholarly synopsis of all four Gospels is that of Aland, to which the student is encouraged to refer throughout our discussions in the chapters to come.[42] The following is a slight modification of Aland's sequence, complete with section references, which reflects one plausible outline of the major stages of Christ's career. Within each major portion

41. This, too, requires nuancing. It is absurd to assume something happened twice, just to reconcile apparent contradictions among the Gospels, when parallel texts clearly place the event at the same time and place in Jesus' ministry (e.g., two resurrections of Jairus' daughter or two celebrations of the Last Supper). On the other hand, it is gratuitous to assume that every "Q" saying was uttered in one and only one context, even though Luke and Matthew consistently differ on where they place many of these teachings of Jesus (e.g., the Lord's Prayer or the parable of the lost sheep). For an attempt to bring some methodological control to this enterprise for one important sample of Jesus' teachings (the parables), see Craig L. Blomberg, "When Is a Parallel Really a Parallel? A Test Case: The Lucan Parables," *WTJ* 46 (1984): 78–103.

42. Kurt Aland, *Synopsis of the Four Gospels: English Edition* (New York and London: United Bible Societies, 1982).

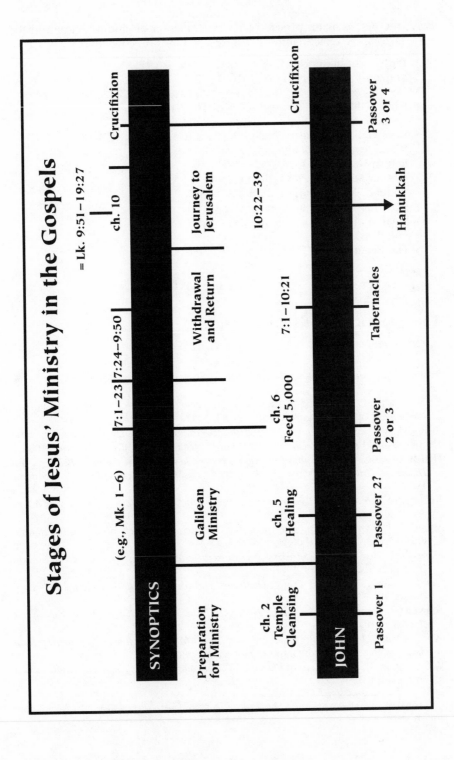

Stages of Jesus' Ministry in the Gospels

SYNOPTICS

(e.g., Mk. 1–6) | 7:1–23 | 7:24–9:50 | = Lk. 9:51–19:27 | ch. 10 | Crucifixion

Preparation for Ministry | Galilean Ministry | Withdrawal and Return | Journey to Jerusalem

ch. 2 Temple Cleansing | ch. 5 Healing | ch. 6 Feed 5,000 | 7:1–10:21 | 10:22–39

JOHN

Passover 1 | Passover 2? | Passover 2 or 3 | Tabernacles | Hanukkah | Passover 3 or 4 | Crucifixion

listed, the details again proceed by a combination of chronological and thematic factors, the exact nature of which is at times irrecoverable.[43]

Birth and Childhood (§2–5, 7–12)
Preparation for Ministry (§13–16, 18, 20)
Beginning of Jesus' Public Ministry (§21–29)
Early Galilean Ministry (§30–32, 34–41, 49)
Sermon on the Mount (§50–83)
Later Galilean Ministry, Including Trip to Jerusalem (§84–86, 89–150)
Withdrawal from Galilee (§151–63)
Return Home (§164–73)
Further Ministry in Jerusalem (§238–50)
"Perean" Ministry (§174–237)
Final Judean Ministry (§251–68)
Final Ministry in Jerusalem (§269–304)
The Passion (§305, 307–51)
The Resurrection (§352–57, 366–67, 364–365)

For Further Study

The Quest for the Historical Jesus

Overviews

Borg, Marcus J. *Jesus in Contemporary Scholarship*. Valley Forge: TPI, 1994.
Brown, Colin, ed. *History, Criticism, and Faith*. Leicester and Downers Grove: IVP, 1976.
Chilton, Bruce D., and Craig A. Evans eds. *Studying the Historical Jesus: Evaluations of the State of Current Research*. Leiden: Brill, 1994.
Evans, C. Stephen. *The Historical Christ and the Jesus of Faith*. Oxford: Clarendon, 1996.
Hagner, Donald A. *The Jewish Reclamation of Jesus*. Grand Rapids: Zondervan, 1984.
Harrisville, Roy A., and Walter Sundberg. *The Bible in Modern Culture: Theology and Historical-Critical Method from Spinoza to Käsemann*. Grand Rapids: Eerdmans, 1995.
Kissinger, Warren S. *The Lives of Jesus: A History and Bibliography*. New York and London: Garland, 1985.
McArthur, Harvey K. *The Quest through the Centuries: The Search for the Historical Jesus.* Philadelphia: Fortress, 1966.
Marshall, I. Howard. *I Believe in the Historical Jesus*. London: Hodder & Stoughton; Grand Rapids: Eerdmans, 1977.
Neill, Stephen C., and Tom Wright. *The Interpretation of the New Testament 1861–1986.* Oxford: OUP, 1988.
Schweitzer, Albert. *The Quest of the Historical Jesus*. London: A & C Black; New York: Macmillan, 1910.
Wilkins, Michael J., and J. P. Moreland eds. *Jesus under Fire: Modern Scholarship Reinvents the Historical Jesus*. Grand Rapids: Zondervan, 1995.
Witherington, Ben, III. *The Jesus Quest: The Third Search for the Jew of Nazareth*. Downers Grove: IVP, 1995.

---

43. Going well beyond what the evidence can demonstrate, e.g., are theories that divide Jesus' Galilean and/or Perean ministries into three separate "tours."

Bibliography

Evans, Craig A. *Jesus*. IBR Bibliographies #5. Grand Rapids: Baker, 1992.

The Chronology of the Life of Christ

Chronology

Caird, G. B. "The Chronology of the New Testament." S.v. "Life of Jesus." In *IDB*. Vol. 1. 599–603.

Donfried, Karl P. "Chronology: New Testament." S.v. "Chronology of the Life of Jesus." In *ABD*. Vol. 1. 1012–16.

Finegan, Jack. "Chronology of the New Testament." S.v. "Chronology of the Life of Jesus." In *ISBE*. Vol. 1. 686–89.

Hoehner, Harold W. *Chronological Aspects of the Life of Christ*. Grand Rapids: Zondervan, 1977.

Vardaman, Jerry, and Edwin M. Yamauchi, eds. *Chronos, Kairos, Christos*. Winona Lake, Ind.: Eisenbrauns, 1989.

Life of Christ

Culver, Robert D. *The Life of Christ*. Grand Rapids: Baker, 1976.

Drane, John. *Son of Man: A New Life of Christ*. Alresford: Hunt & Thorpe; Grand Rapids: Eerdmans, 1993.

Guthrie, Donald. *Jesus the Messiah*. Grand Rapids: Zondervan, 1972.

Harrison, Everett F. *A Short Life of Christ*. Grand Rapids: Eerdmans, 1968.

Stauffer, Ethelbert. *Jesus and His Story*. London: SCM; New York: Alfred Knopf, 1960.

Stein, Robert H. *Jesus the Messiah: A Survey of the Life of Christ*. Downers Grove: IVP, 1996.

Harmonies and Synopses

Aland, Kurt. *Synopsis of the Four Gospels: English Edition*. New York and London: United Bible Societies, 1982.

Pentecost, J. Dwight. *A Harmony of the Words and Works of Jesus Christ*. Grand Rapids: Zondervan, 1981.

Robertson, A. T. *A Harmony of the Gospels*. New York: Harper & Row, 1922.

Thomas, Robert L., and Stanley N. Gundry, eds. *The NIV Harmony of the Gospels*. San Francisco: Harper, 1988.

Throckmorton, Burton H., Jr. *Gospel Parallels: A Synopsis of the First Three Gospels*. Nashville: Thomas Nelson, rev. 1992.

QUESTIONS FOR REVIEW

1. What are the three quests of the historical Jesus? How are they similar to or different from each other?

2. What are the major scholarly options for understanding the historical Jesus? Which one seems most probable to you and why?

3. Explain the criteria of authenticity.

4. To what extent can we confidently reconstruct a chronology of the life of Christ? To what extent can we not? What are the relatively fixed dates and how do we arrive at them?

CHAPTER ELEVEN

THE BIRTH AND CHILDHOOD
OF JESUS

T
he Gospel of Mark begins with Jesus already grown up. Matthew and
Luke, however, each devote two chapters to describing the events surrounding his birth. John's prologue is much more theological, developing the concepts of Jesus' preexistence and incarnation. We will begin by
looking at Matthew and Luke, because even though they differ considerably
on the events they narrate, these two Gospels do actually provide information
about the beginning of Jesus' life. Because there is almost no verbal parallelism
between Matthew 1–2 and Luke 1–2, the two evangelists are probably relying
on their distinctive sources or traditions at this point. The reasons for each
including what they did will become clear as we survey each "infancy narrative." Still we should not lose sight of the fact that there is considerable agreement on the main details: The engaged couple, Mary and Joseph, are the
parents, yet Jesus was conceived while Mary was still a virgin, by the power of
the Holy Spirit, in the time of Herod. Both parents were godly. An angel makes
the announcement of the coming birth and names the child in advance. The
birth occurs in Bethlehem, but the family eventually settles in Nazareth. Jesus'
Davidic heritage and messianic role are stressed in each.[1] Beyond this, Matthew and Luke largely go their separate ways.

---

1. Cf. further Joseph A. Fitzmyer, *The Gospel according to Luke I–IX* (Garden City: Doubleday, 1981), 307.

MATTHEW'S INFANCY NARRATIVE (MATT. 1–2)

The Genealogy of Jesus (1:1–17) [Aland §1, 6]

Matthew stresses the theological significance of Jesus right from the outset. Jesus is the Jewish Messiah—the Christ—and the descendant of King David. He is also the descendant of Abraham, the father of the Jewish nation (v. 1). Yet Abraham's offspring were promised to be a blessing to all nations (Gen. 12:2–3), and this universalist strain is foreshadowed in Matthew's genealogy as well. Unexpectedly, five women's names are included—Tamar, Rahab, Ruth, Uriah's wife (Bathsheba), and Mary. All but Mary had Gentile connections of some kind, and all including Mary had a cloud of suspicion surrounding their sexual behavior, whether or not it was warranted.[2] If the Messiah can be born from this kind of ancestry, he can be a deliverer for all kinds of people, even disreputable ones.

Even though the Old Testament mentions several additional ancestors, Matthew arranges his names into three groups of fourteen, with David as the fourteenth. In Hebrew the *gematria* (the sum of the numerical equivalents of the consonants in a word) for David was 14 (D+V+D = 4+6+4). Given the popularity of various creative uses of gematria in ancient Judaism, Matthew may well have employed this device to stylize his genealogy and stress Jesus as Son of David. The verb "to beget" (NIV "was the father of") can mean "to be one's ancestor," so there was no problem in leaving names out. The word "whom" in verse 16 is feminine, making it clear that Matthew is claiming that only Mary was Jesus' biological parent.

Events Surrounding Jesus' Birth (1:18–2:23) [Aland §7, 8, 10, 11]

Everything else Matthew includes in chapters 1–2 has to do with one of five Old Testament texts he finds fulfilled in the time of Jesus' infancy. From these passages we learn about the "who" and the "where" of Christ's birth: chapter 1 portrays Jesus as the Christ, the Son of David, and Immanuel; chapter 2 describes the significance of Jesus in Bethlehem, Egypt, and Nazareth.[3] As elsewhere with the Gospels' use of the Old Testament, some of these prophecies are fairly literal, straightforward predictions that have now come to pass. For example, 2:6 notes that the Messiah must be born in Bethlehem (Micah 5:2). Choosing his birthplace is not part of the Messiah's "job description" that Jesus could have set out to accomplish, so this kind of fulfillment has considerable apologetic value.

On the other hand, some fulfillments are clearly *typological*. Typology here means "the recognition of a correspondence between New and Old Testament events, based on a conviction of the unchanging character of the principles of

---

2. Jane Schaberg (*The Illegitimacy of Jesus* [San Francisco: Harper & Row, 1987]) goes beyond the evidence in arguing for Jesus as a literal bastard. But *suspicions* of illegitimate births or sexual relations did shroud each of these five women; see Craig L. Blomberg, "The Liberation of Illegitimacy: Women and Rulers in Matthew 1–2," *BTB* 21 (1991): 145–50.

3. Krister Stendahl, "Quis et Unde? An Analysis of Matthew 1–2," in *Judentum, Urchristentum, Kirche*, ed. W. Eltester (Berlin: Töpelman, 1960), 94–105.

God's working, and a consequent understanding and description of the New Testament event in terms of the Old Testament model."[4] Matthew's use in 2:15 of Hosea 11:1, for example, involves a text that is not prophetic in its original context but a past tense reference to God having called Israel out of Egypt. Still, Christians saw a divinely intended coincidence in the fact that Jesus, like the Israelites, had to flee and return from Egypt as part of God's process of inaugurating a covenant with his people. In general, they believed that redemptive history followed patterns that repeated themselves, often on ever grander scales, demonstrating the same God at work in each instance.[5] This logic, too, has considerable apologetic force, even if it is different from straightforward prediction and fulfillment.

In still other cases there may be a combination of literal and typological fulfillments. The famous Isaiah 7:14 prophecy of a virginal conception (Matt. 1:23) is forward-looking, but the fact that the son was to be born in Ahaz's day (Isa. 7:15–16) implies at least a provisional fulfillment in Isaiah's lifetime. Probably "virgin" (Heb. 'almah) meant simply "a young woman of marriageable age," while the promised son was Maher-Shalal-Hash-Baz (8:3). Yet in the larger context of Isaiah 7–9, the son to be born who will be called Immanuel ("God with us"—7:14; 8:8) is also identified as "Mighty God" (9:6). The Septuagint later translated Isaiah 7:14 with a Greek word (parthenos) that more strictly referred to a woman who had never had sex. Doubtless, Matthew felt justified in concluding that Isaiah's prophecy was not exhausted in Ahaz's day, and that the true, ultimate intent of the prediction was to point to Jesus.[6] In fact, the word "fulfill" had a broad semantic range that could include the concepts of "completing" or "filling full" and allowed for multiple fulfillments of prophecy of varying kinds. We will now make further exegetical comments on each of the five passages of Matthew 1:18–2:23 in turn.

The Conception of Jesus (1:18–25). Betrothal was a binding contract, but the marriage was not consummated until after the wedding, often a year or more later. Young Jewish women frequently married in their early teens to men several years older than them. We have no reason to suspect Mary and Joseph were any different. The perspective throughout this passage is primarily Joseph's, suggesting that it may first have been related by him. Joseph's "righteousness," however, reflects a key theme of Matthew's and may be the evangelist's additional emphasis. It does not mean Joseph was sinless, merely godly. The name of the child, "Jesus," a Greek translation of the Hebrew, "Joshua," means "Yahweh saves" or "Yahweh is salvation."

Birth in Bethlehem and Visit of the Magi (2:1–12). Despite popular Christmas cards and carols, Matthew never says that the Magi were kings or that there were three of them (although they do bring three gifts fit for royalty). *Magoi* were astrologers, probably from Persia, who combined a primitive science of stargazing with attempts to understand the signs of the times and of the future.

4. R. T. France, *The Gospel according to Matthew* (Leicester: IVP; Grand Rapids: Eerdmans, 1985), 40.

5. For a detailed study of typology, see Leonhard Goppelt, *Typos* (Grand Rapids: Eerdmans, 1982). On this passage in particular, see esp. Tracy L. Howard, "The Use of Hosea 11:1 in Matthew 2:15: An Alternative Solution," *BSac* 143 (1986): 314–28, who speaks of an "analogical correspondence" between the two passages.

6. For an explanation of these and related concepts and an excellent survey of interpretive options, see John T. Willis, *Isaiah* (Austin: Sweet, 1980), 158–68.

Here is another hint at the universal impact of the Gospel and a striking contrast with the reaction of Herod and the Jerusalemites (dominated by priestly and government families). The people least expected to worship the Christ Child come to do so, while those who should have been awaiting him are threatened by his arrival. The star has often been explained as a comet, a conjunction of planets, or a meteor, but none of these rationalistic attempts to explain the seemingly supernatural succeed in accounting for the element of timing and location. Matthew makes one change in verse 6 to the text of Micah by adding "by no means." Although this seems to negate the original meaning of the prophecy, one must understand Matthew's point to be that although Bethlehem was small and of little significance as a town in and of itself, the birth of the Christ child now gave it great importance.[7] Mary and Joseph have apparently settled into a home there (v. 11), but they will soon be told to flee.

Flight to Egypt (2:13–15). It is sometimes argued that Luke leaves no room in his narrative for this journey, but we do not know how much time is implied by Luke 2:39. Anywhere from a few months to a couple of years might well have elapsed.

Massacre of the Innocents (2:16–18). The same kind of typology seems to be involved here as with Matthew's use of Hosea 11:1. Jeremiah 31:15 refers to women at the time of the exile bemoaning the loss of their children, but already alluding back to Rachel as the personification of the mothers of Israel. Just as her children, Joseph and Benjamin, were threatened with "being no more" in Egypt, so, too, these later women cried when their sons departed, some in exile and some in death. Now Matthew reapplies the motif one more time to the mothers in Bethlehem whose babies were slaughtered by Herod's troops. We must not exaggerate the numbers involved; in a town this small there may have been no more than about twenty children two-years-old or younger.[8] Verse 16 suggests that the Magi may have arrived as late as two years after Jesus' birth; they certainly do not belong in manger scenes next to the shepherds!

Return to Nazareth (2:19–23). There is no Old Testament passage that contains the statement, "He will be called a Nazarene" (v. 23). But this is also the only "quotation" Matthew introduces with a plural reference to *prophets.* Presumably, then, he is summarizing a key theme of various prophecies without actually citing any one of them. But which theme is in view? The two most common suggestions have involved (1) a play on words on the Hebrew *nezer* (branch)—referring to Jesus' regal, messianic role as the "branch" of Jesse (i.e., from David's line; cf. Isa. 11:1); and (2) taking Nazareth as proverbial for a "backwater" or "hick" town (cf. John 1:46) and referring to the theme of the Messiah's obscurity (see esp. Isa. 52:14; 53:2–9).

Matthew, then, is clearly writing not merely as a historian but as a theologian with apologetic motives to show Jesus as the true fulfillment of Old Testament hopes for a perfect, Davidic king. This has implications for contemporary Christian apologetics too. It is sometimes observed that there are over two

7. D. A. Carson ("Matthew," in *Expositor's Bible Commentary*, ed. Frank E. Gaebelein, vol. 8 [Grand Rapids: Zondervan, 1984], 88) calls it a "merely formal" contradiction.
8. See further on all aspects of this episode, Richard T. France, "Herod and the Children of Bethlehem," *NovT* 21 (1979): 98–120.

hundred fulfillments of prophecy in the Gospels and that the odds of all these coalescing around one individual are microscopically small.[9] The problem is that only a handful of the Old Testament texts "fulfilled" in the Gospels are of the straightforward predictive variety. Yet once we enter into the ancient Jewish mind-set, there is still great apologetic value in the broader concepts of fulfillment found on the pages of the New Testament. When key events heralding the salvation of God's people recur in strikingly similar patterns, surely that, too, is testimony to the fact that all is not merely happening by chance.

Conclusion

To sum up, Matthew's infancy narrative stresses three key themes. First, *Jesus is the hope of Israel*, its long-awaited Messiah, and the fulfillment of the Old Testament. Second, through him *blessings will be extended to the Gentiles* and others who are now ostracized. Third, *Jesus is the legitimate king and ruler*, not Herod, not the priests in Jerusalem, nor any other earthly authorities.

LUKE'S INFANCY NARRATIVE (LUKE 1–2)

The Preface (1:1–4) [Aland §1]

We have already alluded to the function of this paragraph in helping to identify the purposes and circumstances of Luke's writing (above, p. 152). Composed in highly elegant literary Greek, it follows the form of preface found in numerous other historical and biographical works of the day.[10] It describes the formation of the Gospel tradition in the three stages analyzed by form, source, and redaction criticism (see above, pp. 80–81). It justifies study of Luke as both a historian and theologian and suggests that he aimed at a level of trustworthiness in both spheres. That he writes an "orderly account" (v. 3) implies deliberate structure, though not necessarily chronological or "consecutive" order (*contra* the NASB).

The Birth Stories (1:5–2:52) [Aland §2–5, 7–9, 11–12]

Abruptly, with 1:5, Luke adopts a very Semitic form of Greek writing. From chapter 3 on, he uses standard *koinē*, though with a bit more literary artistry than the other evangelists, but not as elegantly as the preface or as Hebraic in style as the rest of these two chapters. This has often raised the question of whether Luke might have been translating material written in Hebrew or Aramaic here. Given that much of this information had to have come from the closest relatives of Jesus, the suggestion is not improbable.[11] Indeed, Luke 1–2 reflect the perspectives of Elizabeth and Mary more than the male characters,

---

9. See, e.g., Josh McDowell, *Evidence That Demands a Verdict* (San Bernardino: Campus Crusade for Christ, 1972), 147–84.

10. Loveday Alexander (*The Preface to Luke's Gospel* [Cambridge: CUP, 1993]) finds the closest parallels in scientific treatises, only one step removed from the most literate and classical of Greek styles.

11. The most sophisticated attempt to defend this suggestion is Stephen C. Farris, "On Discerning Semitic Sources in Luke 1–2," in *Gospel Perspectives*, vol. 2, ed. R. T. France and David Wenham (Sheffield: JSOT, 1981), 201–37, which overlaps in part with his more wide-ranging study, *The Hymns of Luke's Infancy Narratives* (Sheffield: JSOT, 1985).

leading one to speculate about Luke having interviewed someone like Mary herself.

Whereas Matthew structures his infancy narrative around Old Testament "prophecies," Luke organizes his to provide an overview of God's plan of salvation and to highlight the similarities and differences between John the Baptist and Jesus. First the birth of John is foretold (1:5–25), then the birth of Jesus is predicted (1:26–38). The two mothers, Elizabeth and Mary, come together, showing how the stories of their two sons intersect (1:39–56). Then the birth and growth of John are narrated (1:57–80), followed by the birth and growth of Jesus (2:1–52). Numerous parallels make it clear that Luke is drawing attention to the similarities between John and Jesus as heralds of a new age: born to godly, Jewish parents,[12] who experienced miraculous conceptions involving the Holy Spirit and outward "signs"; angelic promises of the coming prophetic and redemptive significance of the children; impact first for Israel but then beyond, offering deliverance in both spiritual and socioeconomic realms; initial fear and disbelief on the part of the parents followed by acceptance and praise to God; and details of the circumcision, naming, and subsequent growth of the children.

On the other hand, it is also clear that Luke wants to portray Jesus as greater than John. The miracle of a virginal conception is greater than that of merely opening a once-barren womb. John will be the forerunner who will point others to Jesus. Only Jesus is called "Savior," "Christ," and "Lord" (2:11). Indeed, the sheer amount of space devoted to the birth and growth of Jesus far outstrips that allotted to John.[13]

The Birth of John Foretold (1:5–25). John was born to a priestly family of impeccable credentials. With approximately eighteen thousand priests in first-century Israel, the opportunity that Zechariah received to minister in the Holy Place in the temple was a once-in-a-lifetime experience. The angel's announcement identified the child to be born as special. Teetotaling was uncommon in the Old Testament; for someone permanently to be filled with the Spirit "yet from his mother's womb" (a more literal rendering than NIV's "from birth"—v. 15) was unprecedented. Both of these features reinforce more explicit imagery that links John with a prophetic role of calling people to repentance and preparing the way of the Lord, like Elijah of old (v. 17; cf. further below, p. 216). Zechariah is struck dumb for not believing the angel, presumably on the grounds that a devout student of Scripture such as himself would have been very familiar with the stories of God opening the wombs of women like Sarah, Rachel, and Hannah. But his faith will return, and he will later praise God. Elizabeth, on the other hand, rejoices and immediately credits God with taking away the social stigma that barrenness created in ancient Judaism (v. 25).

The Birth of Jesus Foretold (1:26–38). Mary, too, has an angel come and promise her a miraculous conception (cf. also 3:23). Gabriel addresses her as

---

12. As with the statement about Joseph being righteous in Matt. 1:19, "blameless" in Luke 1:6 does not mean sinless, just generally upright and law-abiding.

13. For more on the similarities and differences between John and Jesus in this context, see John Nolland, *Luke 1–9:20* (Dallas: Word, 1989), 40–41.

The Infancy Stories of Jesus

Matthew

Luke

conceived of a virgin
(1:18–25)

birth of John
the Baptist predicted
(1:5–25)

born in Bethlehem
(2:1–12)

birth of Jesus predicted
(1:26–38)

the two mothers visit
(1:39–56)

out of Egypt
(2:13–15)

birth of John the Baptist
(1:57–80)

wailing in Ramah
(2:16–18)

birth of Jesus
(2:1–40)

called a Nazarene
(2:19–23)

Jesus in the temple at age 12
(2:41–52)

"highly favored" (Greek *kecharitōmenē*, lit. "having been given grace" or "having been treated graciously"—v. 28). The later Latin mistranslation of this verb by the expression "full of grace" led to the traditional Roman Catholic conception of Mary as somehow uniquely meritorious or deserving of this honor. In fact, the original language strongly suggests it was God who simply took the initiative to bestow grace.[14] The child Mary would bear was to be "the Son of the Most High," which in this context is a Davidic, regal, messianic title (cf. v. 32a with vv. 32b–33). Protestants as well as Catholics have been embarrassed by Mary's seeming disbelief in response (v. 34). But instead of trying to exonerate her as initially less skeptical than Zechariah, we should recognize that she was being promised something entirely unprecedented in Jewish history. Verse 38, at any rate, concludes with her humble acceptance of Gabriel's explanation.[15]

Mary Visits Elizabeth (1:39–56). When Mary arrives at the home of her "relative" (cf. v. 36), the older woman, Elizabeth, repeats the angel's blessing (vv. 41–45). Here is the first of Luke's numerous references to someone who boldly proclaims God's word as being "filled with the Holy Spirit." *In utero*, John "leaps" for joy, showing that he, too, is empowered by the Spirit (v. 41). Mary is "blessed" by God and called the "mother of my Lord" (though never the "mother of God"). She responds with a poetic outburst of praise, often referred to as a "hymn," that repeatedly echoes Hannah's psalm in 1 Samuel 2:1–10. It may well be a composition she had carefully crafted soon after Gabriel visited her. The hymn is the first of several in Luke's infancy narratives. Together they point to the Christ Child as the coming salvation of Israel but also as "a light for revelation to the Gentiles" (2:32; cf. 1:54–55). They combine spiritual and socioeconomic dimensions of that salvation, promising to remove the oppressive powerful and rich from their thrones (1:52–53). Mary once more refers to being called blessed, but only because of the great things God has done for her (vv. 48–49). Her "song" (vv. 46–55) has been called the *Magnificat*, after the first word in its Latin translation ("magnified"—NIV "glorified"—v. 46). With the other hymns of Luke 1–2, it occupies a treasured place in the history of the church's liturgy.

The Birth and Growth of John (1:57–80). Events transpire joyfully as predicted, and Zechariah's and Elizabeth's child is born. To everyone's surprise, they choose not to name him after his father, or any other relative, but call him John ("The Lord is gracious"). Zechariah is released from his muteness and is also filled with the Spirit, praising God in hymnic form for bringing his promised salvation. His song (vv. 68–79) has been called the *Benedictus* (Latin for "blessed"; NIV "praise"—v. 68). It, too, combines promise of physical rescue from Israel's enemies with spiritual restoration (forgiveness of sins) and hints at an extension of these blessings beyond the boundaries of Israel. The covenant with Abraham is being fulfilled, including the blessing of all nations, and it will benefit those "living in darkness" (v. 79), a term not naturally limited to

---

14. As is now widely recognized by Catholic as well as Protestant scholars. See, e.g., Raymond E. Brown, *The Birth of the Messiah* (New York and London: Doubleday, rev. 1993), 325–27; Fitzmyer, *Luke I–IX*, 345–46.

15. For a recent Protestant survey of Mary in the New Testament and the apocrypha, addressing a cross-section of historical, theological, and literary questions, see Beverly R. Gaventa, *Mary: Glimpses of the Mother of Jesus* (Columbia: University of South Carolina Press, 1995).

Jewish people. John will be a prophet of God to point the way (v. 76). Verse 80 summarizes John's growth to maturity in one clause and then alludes to his departure to the wilderness, where we will meet him again, baptizing (see below, p. 215).

The Birth and Growth of Jesus (2:1–52). The birth of Jesus took place six months after John came into the world (cf. 1:26), probably in about 6 B.C. (see above, p. 188). The details about the census registration serve to stress Joseph's link with David and the appropriate "pedigree" for the Messiah. Here is the famous "Christmas story" that has generated so many idyllic manger scenes. We ought to read the text again, with a reliable translation, more carefully! The manger is a feed-trough, and the delivery takes place among animals. The word in verse 7 usually translated "inn" (*kataluma*) elsewhere in the New Testament means "guest room" (Luke 22:11; Mark 14:14). Joseph and Mary would have no doubt made arrangements to stay with family or friends in a town overcrowded by the registration, but so would have many others. In a small Palestinian home of one or two rooms, the milking cow and perhaps a few other animals often stayed in a corner on ground level, separated from the raised portion of the rest of the house by the feeding trough.[16] One apocryphal tradition also speaks of Jesus being born in a cave (Protevangelium of James 18–19).

The announcement to shepherds furthers the humble, even humiliating circumstances of Messiah's birth. Shepherds were often despised in the first century for their nomadic lifestyle and reputation for theft. (For their part, Mary and Joseph were poor enough that they would offer the sacrifices for those unable to afford sheep—v. 24; cf. Lev. 12:8.) It was to such lowly people and not to the emperor or his court that God sent still more angels to proclaim, "Today in the town of David a Savior has been born to you; he is Christ the Lord" (v. 11).[17] As noted earlier, Savior is the most distinctive title in Luke; Lord, the most characteristic in Acts (see above, p. 146). Verse 14 (the *Gloria in Excelsis*—Latin for "glory in the highest") has also been much misunderstood. The best textual evidence supports not "on earth peace, good will toward men" (KJV) but "on earth peace to men of good will," with the concept behind "men of good will" being "people on whom God's favor rests" (cf. NIV).[18] Just a few verses later, Mary will be promised that her son's ministry will cause grief as well as joy in Israel (vv. 34–35). Jesus will later proclaim that for some he came not to bring peace but division (Luke 12:51–53 par.).

Jesus' family proceeds to raise the child as a Law-abiding Jewish boy. In taking him to the temple for various rituals, they meet the aged prophet Simeon who was promised he would live to see the Messiah born. He can now die in peace, after he "sings" the final Spirit-led hymn of Luke's infancy narratives (the *Nunc Dimittis*—"Now dismiss . . . "—vv. 29–32). Here appears the most explicit

---

16. See esp. Kenneth E. Bailey, "The Manger and the Inn: The Cultural Background of Luke 2:7," *Near East School of Theology Theological Review* 2 (1979): 33–44.

17. Joel B. Green ("The Social Status of Mary in Luke 1,5–2,52: A Plea for Methodological Integration," *Biblica* 73 [1992]: 457–72) disputes the idea of shepherds as despised but does stress the lowly circumstances of Mary, her family, and the birth, particularly in contrast with Elizabeth's and Zechariah's privileged position.

18. This expression ("men of [God's] good pleasure") finds a particularly close parallel in a recently discovered Dead Sea Scroll. See Al Wolters, "Anthropoi Eudokias (Luke 2:14) and 'NSY RSWN (4Q416)," *JBL* 113 (1994): 291–92.

reference to the Messiah's ministry extending to the Gentiles (v. 32, alluding to Isa. 42:6 or 49:6). Simeon's testimony is matched by that of the elderly prophetess, Anna. Luke is fond of pairing male and female characters in parallel roles. But verses 22–40 break the parallelism between Jesus and John and reinforce the point that the ministry of Jesus will be far greater.

The final part of this section sums up Jesus' growth (vv. 41–52). The only incident Scripture records about Christ between his infancy and his adult ministry is this story of his astounding the Jewish leaders with his answers to questions in the temple at age twelve. The occasion could have been the forerunner to the later *bar mitzvah* ("son of the commandment") ceremony, in which boys, usually at age thirteen, read and expound the Law for themselves and "come of age," religiously speaking. Jesus also hints at his special relationship with God, by referring to the temple as "my Father's house" (v. 49).[19] But the later apocryphal literature goes much farther and turns the child Jesus into a prodigy—fashioning sparrows out of clay and causing them to fly away, miraculously stretching lumber in Joseph's carpenter's shop to help him balance a bed, and withering up a belligerent playmate to the horror of his parents (Infancy Gospel of Thomas 2, 13, 3).[20] The historical truth is that we do not have a shred of solid evidence to determine what else Jesus did before age thirty, except that he no doubt worked diligently as Joseph's apprentice and partner.

In fact, although Jesus amazes the authorities when he is twelve, nothing miraculous is described here. He is never said to be teaching his teachers, as popular conception has so often imagined. And Luke seems intent at the climax of the passage precisely to stress Jesus' full *humanity*. He complied with his parents' wishes, went home with them as an obedient child (v. 51), and grew in the ways all normal children do—intellectually, physically, spiritually, and socially (v. 52).[21]

The Genealogy of Jesus (3:23–28) [Aland §6, 19]

Unlike Matthew, Luke records Jesus' genealogy from Jesus' day back through history and goes well beyond Abraham, all the way to Adam, who is then called "son of God." Luke is the Gospel most stressing Jesus' humanity and universal significance. But Jesus is also Son of God in a unique sense as Luke seems to indicate by placing his genealogy between Jesus' baptism and temptation, two occasions in which Jesus demonstrated that sonship (3:22; 4:3). The names of ancestors closest in time to Jesus diverge considerably from Matthew's list, and not merely because each list is selective. The two most common attempts to harmonize these data have suggested that either (a) Luke gives Mary's genealogy (v. 23b hints that Jesus was not the biological son of Joseph), while Matthew gives Joseph's ancestry; or, perhaps more likely, (b)

---

19. Literally, "the things of my Father." Cf. the KJV's "about my Father's business." Francis D. Weinert ("The Multiple Meanings of Luke 2:49 and Their Significance," *BTB* 13 [1983]: 19–22) argues that the translation "in my father's company" best captures the sense of this expression.

20. See esp. the Infancy Gospel of Thomas (not to be confused with the Coptic Gnostic Gospel by the same name, discussed above, pp. 35–36).

21. Charles H. Talbert, *Reading Luke* (New York: Crossroad, 1982), 38.

Luke gives Jesus' human ancestry through Joseph, while Matthew gives Jesus' legal and royal ancestry through Joseph (the lines diverging when certain men left no biological heirs).[22]

Conclusion

In short, Luke's opening chapters present many of the same themes as Matthew's, albeit by way of an almost entirely different selection of stories. *Jesus is the Davidic Messiah* coming as the consolation of Israel, *but he is also "a light to enlighten the Gentiles." He will be both Savior and Lord, bringing spiritual and socioeconomic liberty*, with special compassion for women, the poor, and other social outcasts, inverting the world's standards and beliefs. As the Gospel of Luke and the Book of Acts unfold, however, it will be clear that, unlike Matthew, Luke's greatest interests involve universal, Gentile themes. Jesus is clearly "the man for all people."

HISTORICITY AND THEOLOGY
OF THE VIRGINAL CONCEPTION AND THE BIRTH OF CHRIST

Historicity

What are modern readers to make of the amazing stories of Christ's virginal conception? How historically reliable are these birth narratives more generally, permeated as they are with miraculous dreams, angels, and a traveling star? Of course if one rules out the supernatural *a priori*, there is much here that will have to be dismissed or radically reinterpreted. For those open to a God who occasionally intervenes miraculously into his universe, however, several arguments favor the trustworthiness of this material.

First, the lack of straightforward correspondence between many of the details of Christ's birth and the Old Testament texts matched with them argues powerfully for the evangelists not having invented these data as pious legends or "midrashic" embellishments of their sources. Had they felt free to invent parts of their stories, they could easily have made them match the Old Testament texts more closely. As it stands, the events of the first century are the non-negotiables; the Gospel writers "mine" the Old Testament looking for parallels.[23]

Second, as already noted, Luke's preface most closely mirrors those of other relatively trustworthy historical works, while the abrupt shift into a more Semitic Greek for chapters 1–2 suggests the use of early Jewish sources, perhaps stemming from Mary herself. Matthew's emphasis on Joseph's perspective might then suggest traditions ultimately coming from *his* side of the "holy family."

---

22. For details of what are actually four different variants of this latter proposal, see Darrell L. Bock, *Luke 1:1–9:50* (Grand Rapids: Baker, 1994), 920–23.

23. Cf. further R. T. France, "Scripture, Tradition, and History in the Infancy Narratives of Matthew," in *Gospel Perspectives*, vol. 2, 239–66. *Contra*, e.g., significant portions of both Brown, *Messiah*; and Robert H. Gundry, *Matthew: A Commentary on His Handbook for a Mixed Church under Persecution* (Grand Rapids: Eerdmans, rev. 1994), who find Matthew creatively inventing material in numerous places.

Third, although it is often observed that no other ancient sources record Herod's "massacre of the innocents," this event may have been on such a small scale and so politically insignificant as not to merit attention. Then again, a passing reference in a section of the pseudepigraphal Testament of Moses that includes after-the-fact "prophecies" about Herod may actually allude to the slaughter (6:4—"He will kill both old and young, showing mercy to none"). The problems with Luke's census have also cast doubt on his trustworthiness, but we have already commented on some possible resolutions of those problems (above, p. 188).

Fourth, and most important, it is unlikely that early Christians would ever have invented the narratives of the virginal conception itself. Its nature is barely described (contrast the later apocryphal Protevangelium of James, which describes Mary's unbroken hymen—even after Jesus' birth! [19.3–20.1]). Mary is told only that the Holy Spirit would "overshadow" her (Luke 1:35), and she apparently believes from this point on (vv. 38, 45). Luke's narrative shows remarkable tact and restraint compared to various Greco-Roman myths of "virgin births"—Alexander's mother being surrounded by a sacred python so that her husband, Philip, could not approach her on the night of their son's conception, or the gods appearing in human form to copulate with mortal women in crass, anthropomorphic fashion.[24] Narrators creating pious legends usually go into much more detail than Luke does here. It is also important not to underestimate the scientific knowledge of the ancient world. People then knew that a human man and woman were needed to produce children, so it will not do to attribute the origin of the Gospel stories to prescientific gullibility. The idea of a virginal conception obviously created a scandal in some circles (cf. John 8:41); consistent post-New Testament polemic alleged that Jesus was an illegitimate child (e.g., Origen, *Against Celsus* 1:32). Finally, very little is made of this doctrine elsewhere in the New Testament (save for possible hints in Gal. 4:4 and Mark 6:3). All of these observations make it highly unlikely that the church would have included these accounts unless there were strong historical reasons for doing so.

Theology

The virginal conception neither proves the incarnation nor is demanded by it.[25] Nevertheless, it is a very fitting way to reinforce the Christian conviction that Jesus is both fully God (divine paternity) and fully man (human maternity). He is thus able to be both an adequate substitute and an adequate representative for us in his "cross-work." In Luke, the emphasis is on Jesus as God's absolute gift, reminding us of salvation by grace. In Matthew, the emphasis is on Jesus as Immanuel, God in solidarity with us. Given how little the New Testament and even the Gospels make of this doctrine, it probably does not deserve

---

24. For these and other parallels, see the discussion in J. Gresham Machen, *The Virgin Birth of Christ* (New York: Harper & Row, 1930), 317–79, whose overall argument remains one of the strongest in defense of the historicity of this event.

25. On both historicity and theology, cf. esp. C. E. B. Cranfield, "Some Reflections on the Subject of the Virgin Birth," *SJT* 41 (1988): 177–89; H. Douglas Buckwalter, "The Virgin Birth of Jesus Christ: A Union of Theology and History," *Evangelical Journal* 13 (1995): 3–14.

to rank among the top five fundamentals of the faith.[26] Yet it remains a cherished truth not to be glibly denied or explained away.

JOHN'S PROLOGUE (JOHN 1:1–18) [ALAND §1]

Background and Form

John's Gospel begins entirely differently than the other three. In modern scholarship this prologue has often been viewed as a classic example of late Hellenistic thought because of its high Christology: equating Jesus with the *logos* (see above, p. 162) and the *logos* with God. The language about "light" shining "in the darkness" (v. 4), about understanding, recognition, and knowledge (vv. 5, 10, 18), along with the expression "fullness" (Greek, *pleroma*—v. 16), suggested to many that these verses more resembled later Gnostic thought than earliest Christian orthodoxy. Other alleged parallels have been identified in Mandaism, Stoicism, and Philo.

Within the last generation, however, it has been increasingly recognized that all of these features are explicable within a thoroughly Jewish milieu. The Aramaic targums often substitute the word *memra* ("word") for God's name, especially in the opening chapters of Genesis. In other words, God created by his word. The Dead Sea Scrolls have revealed numerous dualisms, most notably the description of the War between the Sons of Light and the Sons of Darkness. And John's use of "fullness" appears in the context of contrasting grace and Law. There may be a proto-Gnostic environment in which John is trying to contextualize the Gospel, but in so doing he is opposing Gnostic thought. More climactic and significant in the prologue even than the declaration of the Word being God is verse 14—"The Word became flesh and lived for a while among us"—a fully human incarnation against all docetic denials.

As we have seen previously, John is most likely addressing a diverse audience influenced by many backgrounds, including both Jewish and Gnostic (p. 168). He uses language well known in a variety of religious contexts but invests it with Christian content. He thus dramatically points out that Jesus is the one to whom all general revelation was pointing and whom all human religions were ultimately seeking ("the true light that gives light to every man"—v. 9).

The prologue is poetic in form, but there is little agreement on the number and nature of its stanzas. Some have postulated a pre-Johannine form, but this, too, is largely speculation. In any event, the prologue as it stands is thoroughly Johannine, introducing the key themes and characters of his narrative.

Exegetical Remarks

Verses 1–18 seem to form a chiasmus of at least seven parts. Verses 1–5 and 16–18 both focus on the nature of the Word, verses 6–8 and verse 15 on John the Baptist's testimony to the Word, and verses 9–11 and 14 on the incarnation

26. As in "fundamentalism," stemming from A. C. Dixon and Louis Meyer, eds., *The Fundamentals*, 12 vols. (Chicago: Testimony Publishing, 1910–1915).

of the Word. Verses 12–13 then comprise the climactic center, highlighting the positive reception of the Word.[27]

The Nature of the Word (vv. 1–5, 16–18). In conscious allusion to Genesis 1:1, John begins by proclaiming the *logos* as preexistent with God from before creation (vv. 1a, 2). Not only that, but "the Word was God" (v. 1b). Though not identical to God the Father, the *logos* fully shared in his divinity. The ancient Arian heresy (still reflected in certain modern cults) stressed the fact that "God" in the Greek lacks the definite article. They translated verse 1b as, "the Word was a god," making Christ the first created being, however exalted he may have been. This translation overlooks the grammatical principle that in a vast majority of cases in a sentence of the form "x is y" (two nouns joined by a form of the verb "to be"), if the author wants to distinguish one of the nouns as the subject of the sentence, then only that noun is given the article.[28] In other words, the form of this sentence ensures that we take "the Word" as the subject, rather than translating "God was the Word." No further theological corollaries may be drawn from the grammar.

The Word was also God's agent for all of creation (v. 3). Not only does this allude to God speaking all things into existence in Genesis 1, but it also picks up the theme of God's Wisdom personified as springing forth before all creation and remaining active throughout the entire process (Prov. 8:22–31). In him is spiritual, eternal life, which the *logos* has revealed to all humanity (vv. 4–5a). Nevertheless many continue to reject him, but evil will not triumph (v. 5b). The verb at the end of verse 5 is better translated "overcome" than "understand" (NIV margin). The Word has revealed himself as the ultimate disclosure of the invisible God, a God of grace and blessing, who has moved beyond the Law (vv. 16–18). Not that grace and truth were absent from the Old Testament period, but they characterize the New Testament age much more. Verse 16 reads literally, "We have all received from his fullness, even grace instead of grace." One level of grace supersedes the previous one.[29]

The Testimony to the Word (vv. 6–8, 15). The primary role of John the Baptist in the Fourth Gospel is to testify about Jesus. John the apostle goes out of his way to stress that the Baptist is not the Messiah but merely a witness to him. As suggested above, this was probably in response to a sect or group of people in Ephesus claiming more for John than they should have (see pp. 166–167). This prologue thus alternates between Jesus and John, reminiscent of the structure of Luke 1–2, but for a quite different reason.

The Incarnation of the Word (vv. 9–11, 14). The *logos* came both to fallen humanity in general ("the world"—vv. 9–10) and to Jews in particular ("his own"—v. 11), but he was rejected by a majority of people in both categories. This coming is described as the Word being made flesh and dwelling among us (v. 14). The Greek verb "dwelt" comes from the same root as the "tabernacle" (*skēn-*) and was used in the LXX because it contained the identical

---

27. Cf., with slight modification and elaboration, R. Alan Culpepper, "The Pivot of John's Prologue," *NTS* 27 (1980): 1–31; Jeff Staley, "The Structure of John's Prologue," *CBQ* 48 (1986): 241–64.

28. This rule is often called Colwell's rule, after the detailed examination of it by Greek grammarian E. C. Colwell in "A Definite Rule for the Use of the Article in the Greek New Testament," *JBL* 52 (1933): 12–21.

29. Cf. Ruth B. Edwards, "χάριν ἀντὶ χάριτος" (John 1.16): "Grace and the Law in the Johannine Prologue," *JSNT* 32 (1988): 3–15.

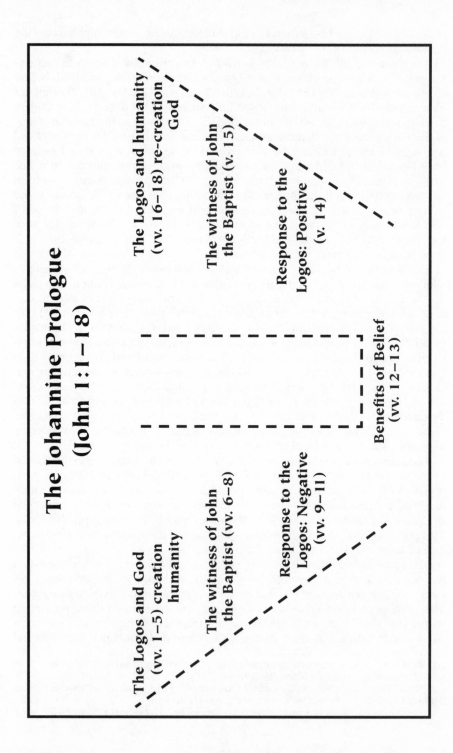

The Johannine Prologue
(John 1:1–18)

The Logos and God
(vv. 1–5) creation
humanity

The witness of John
the Baptist (vv. 6–8)

Response to the
Logos: Negative
(vv. 9–11)

Benefits of Belief
(vv. 12–13)

The Logos and humanity
(vv. 16–18) re-creation
God

The witness of John
the Baptist (v. 15)

Response to the
Logos: Positive
(v. 14)

consonants as the Hebrew for God's *shekinah* glory. The incarnation thus harks back to the days of the Israelites "tenting" in the wilderness and following God's presence, which dwelt among them as a cloud by day and pillar of fire by night. Yet the glory of God revealed in Jesus is the glory of the unique Son, the "One and Only" (a more accurate translation than "Only Begotten").

The Reception of the Word (vv. 12–13). Today it is commonplace to speak of "receiving" Jesus into one's life. This language is relatively rare in the New Testament (though cf. John 13:20 and Col. 2:6), but it is important nonetheless. Reception is defined as "belief in his name," which implies trust in his power or authority. Those who trust in Jesus acknowledge him as their master and become God's spiritual children, with a new authority or status (NIV "right") themselves.

Conclusion

Here then is one of the most important and extensive teaching passages of "high christology" in all of the New Testament—clearly delineating *the preexistence and deity of Jesus*. Yet it is equally insistent on *Christ's genuine humanity*, against any Gnostic docetism. In context, John starts from a point of agreement with his opponents (Christ's deity) and tries to move them on to the point on which they disagree (his humanity). Today, the historic Christian faith usually finds itself combating those who deny Christ's deity, the opposite error. But how many professing Christians really believe in Christ's full humanity? The number of people who have fallen into pronounced or prolonged sin and who then protest that Jesus could not possibly relate to them or forgive them suggests that docetism is not far from any of us.

FOR FURTHER STUDY

Matthew 1–2 and Luke 1–2

Alexander, Loveday. *The Preface to Luke's Gospel.* Cambridge: CUP, 1993.

Boslooper, Thomas. *The Virgin Birth.* London: SCM, 1962.

Brown, Raymond E. *The Birth of the Messiah.* New York and London: Doubleday, rev. 1993.

Brown, Raymond E. *The Virginal Conception and Bodily Resurrection of Jesus.* New York: Paulist, 1973.

Farris, Stephen C. *The Hymns of Luke's Infancy Narratives.* Sheffield: JSOT, 1985.

Gundry, Robert H. *The Use of the Old Testament in St. Matthew's Gospel.* Leiden: Brill, 1967.

Hendrickx, Herman. *The Infancy Narratives.* San Francisco: Harper & Row, 1984.

Horsley, Richard A. *The Liberation of Christmas.* New York: Crossroad, 1989.

Machen, J. Gresham. *The Virgin Birth of Christ.* New York: Harper & Row, 1930.

John 1:1–18

Evans, Craig A. *Word and Glory: On the Exegetical and Theological Background of John's Prologue.* Sheffield: JSOT, 1993.

Harris, Elizabeth. *Prologue and Gospel: The Theology of the Fourth Evangelist.* Sheffield: Sheffield Academic Press, 1994.

Miller, Ed L. *Salvation History in the Prologue of John.* Leiden: Brill, 1988.

QUESTIONS FOR REVIEW

1. What are several of the major structural features that characterize Matthew's and Luke's birth narratives? John's prologue?

2. What is the distinctive theology that each of these three writers wishes to communicate in the opening portions of his Gospel?

3. What kinds of uses of the Old Testament appear in Matthew 1–2? What is the relevance to Christian living of these various kinds of uses?

4. How do the birth narratives of Matthew and Luke differ from common conceptions of Christmas in the culture today? in the church?

CHAPTER TWELVE

THE BEGINNINGS OF JESUS' MINISTRY

THE MINISTRY OF JOHN THE BAPTIST

We next encounter Jesus as an adult. All four Gospels agree that he began his public ministry soon after the rise of John the Baptist's movement. There are many questions we would love to answer about what Jesus and John were doing previously and why John seemed to have so little prior knowledge of his carpenter relative. We have already commented on Jesus' probable socioeconomic standing, education, and work in his father's trade. John's priestly lineage may have left him slightly better off. Beyond this, the reliable sources simply are silent. We may perhaps infer that nothing during this period unusually distinguished Jesus or John.

Background

Traditionally John has been viewed as a lone figure without recent precedent in the Jewish world of his day. Indeed, just as many Jews believed that prophecy had ceased since the time of Malachi, Christians have regularly seen John's ministry as the resumption of that prophecy. But the discoveries of the Dead Sea Scrolls at Qumran have led to widespread questioning of this traditional view. Soon after the discoveries, exaggerated claims were made: John (or even Jesus) was an Essene and had lived with the Dead Sea sect. Occasionally these claims are revived, but an increasing consensus adopts a mediating position. John (more so than Jesus) may well have met the Essenes in Qumran or elsewhere, and his message has significant features in common with them. Ultimately, however, the differences between the two movements outweigh the similarities.[1]

What are those points of comparison and contrast? Similarities include (1) the location of John's primary ministry, at least according to the Synoptics, in the Judean wilderness between Jerusalem and the Dead Sea; (2) belief in the fulfillment of Isaiah 40:3 in each of the two movements (Mark 1:3 pars.; 1QS 8:12–14); (3) an ascetic lifestyle emphasizing repentance and purification from sin; (4) immersion in water as a central ritual to symbolize this purification (at Qumran the "covenanters" took daily ritual baths for this purpose); and (5) prophecy about baptism in spirit or fire with reference to coming salvation and judgment (Matt. 3:11 par.; 1QH 3:29–36; 4:21).

On the other hand, John's ministry was by no means limited to these places and practices. If we accept evidence from the Fourth Gospel, he ministered up and down the Jordan valley. Bethany beyond the Jordan (John 1:28) may well refer to Batanea in the northeast,[2] and Aenon near Salim (3:23) was probably in Samaria.[3] Although, like many of the Essenes, John had a priestly background, the role he adopted much more closely resembled that of a prophet, and specifically a prophet like Elijah. He wore the identical prophetic garb (cf. Mark 1:6a with 2 Kings 1:8) and preached a similar message of imminent judgment for those who failed to repent. As the forerunner, preparing the way of the Lord, John fit in well with the prophecies in Malachi 3:1 and 4:5–6 about Elijah returning before the Day of the Lord. When John denied that he was Elijah in John 1:21 he probably meant only that he was not the literal Elijah returned from heaven whom some Jews awaited.[4] Even John's asceticism (e.g., the desert diet of Mark 1:6b) finds parallels outside Qumran. In particular, Josephus describes a Jewish holy man named Bannus, who led an austere desert life reminiscent of John's (*Life*, 2:11). Other popular prophetic resistance movements also began in the wilderness, though unlike most of them, John's was nonviolent.

Message (Mark 1:2–6 pars.; Luke 3:7–18 par.; John 1:19–51) [Aland §13–16, 21]

Mark: The Key Summary. Mark 1:4 reflects the Synoptic Gospels' epitome of what John was all about: "preaching a baptism of repentance for the forgiveness of sins." Although there are uncertainties about how early the practice

---

1. Leonard F. Badia, *The Qumran Baptism and John the Baptist's Baptism* (Lanham, Md.: University Press of America, 1980). More concise but more wide-ranging is William S. LaSor, *The Dead Sea Scrolls and the New Testament* (Grand Rapids: Eerdmans, 1972), 142–53.

2. See esp. Rainer Riesner, "Bethany beyond the Jordan (John 1:28): Topography, Theology and History in the Fourth Gospel," *TynB* 38 (1987): 29–63.

3. Jerome Murphy-O'Connor ("John the Baptist and Jesus: History and Hypotheses," *NTS* 36 [1990]: 359–74) makes a plausible case for John's having gone to Galilee as well, under the conviction that his message was intended for all Israel. This would account for how he got in trouble with Antipas, tetrarch of Galilee and Perea.

4. Marinus de Jonge ("Jewish Expectations about the 'Messiah' according to the Fourth Gospel," *NTS* 19 [1972–73]: 246–70) notes also that many Jews believed in a "hidden Messiah" who would not know who he was or have any power until Elijah came and revealed him. John may well have wanted to deny this notion too.

began, it is possible that Jews were already familiar with the concept of baptism from the initiatory rite they required of proselytes to their religion. And, as already noted, the Essenes in Qumran practiced daily ritual bathing. The size of baptismal pools excavated demonstrates that these were most likely immersions. John, however, was unique in calling upon *all* Jews to be baptized as a once-for-all action signifying their repentance from sin. "Repentance" in Greek (*metanoia*) referred to a change of mind, but the corresponding term in the Hebrew Bible (*shuv*) indicated a dramatic change of action as well. The genitive case in the expression "baptism of repentance" is probably either subjective ("baptism produced by repentance") or descriptive ("baptism characterized by repentance").

"For the forgiveness of sins" may be a misleading translation. It is unlikely that John taught that the ritual of baptism itself produced forgiveness. Interesting corroboration of this comes from Josephus, who described John's ministry in the context of a later defeat of Antipas's army:

> But to some of the Jews the destruction of Herod's army seemed to be divine vengeance, and certainly a just vengeance, for his treatment of John, surnamed the Baptist. For Herod had put him to death, though he was a good man and had exhorted the Jews to lead righteous lives, to practice justice towards their fellows and piety towards God, and so doing to join in baptism. In his view this was a necessary preliminary if baptism was to be acceptable to God. They must not employ it to gain pardon for whatever sins they committed, but as a consecration of the body implying that the soul was already thoroughly cleansed by right behaviour. (*Antiquities* 18:5.2)

The Greek preposition *eis* ("for") can also be translated "directed towards" or "with reference to," and it is probably one of these looser senses in which baptism is for the forgiveness of sins.[5] In any event, John's message would have proven shockingly radical as he called the complacent in Israel to recognize that their ancestry was not adequate to keep them in God's favor.

John's ministry was not an end in itself, however. He also predicted a "coming one" (possibly a messianic title based on Ps. 118:26 and possibly the Targum to Isa. 5:26–27[6]), whose status would make John seem like a menial slave in comparison (Mark 1:7). John baptized merely in water; the one who was coming would baptize with the Spirit. The Greek expression alternately translated as the baptism "in," "with," or "by" the Spirit occurs seven times in the New Testament, six of them citing this statement of John's (Mark 1:8; Matt. 3:11; Luke 3:16; John 1:33; Acts 1:5; 11:16). In light of Acts 1–2, the expression is at least a reference to the outpouring of God's Spirit on Jesus' followers at Pentecost, initiating the "church age." The seventh reference comes in 1 Corinthians 12:13, in which Paul declares all the Corinthian believers, including many who were quite immature, to have been baptized in the Spirit. This, therefore, must coincide with their conversion experience. There is no biblical warrant for employing this phrase to refer to any subsequent work of the Spirit

---

5. See esp. Murray J. Harris, "Appendix," *NIDNTT*, vol. 3, 1208.
6. See Gordon D. Kirchhevel, "He That Cometh in Mark 1:7 and Matthew 24:30," *BBR* 4 (1994): 105–11.

or so-called "second blessing." Luke has a term for later empowerings, when he refers to people repeatedly being "filled" with the Spirit (see above, p. 149).[7]

The Distinctives in Q. Matthew and Luke go on to add a paragraph in which John warns the Jewish leaders who have come to observe his baptism.[8] Nothing less than a thoroughgoing change of lifestyle will suffice; they must "produce fruit in keeping with repentance" (Matt. 3:8). Otherwise judgment will be imminent: "The ax is already at the root of the trees" (v. 10). Judgment is also depicted by the metaphor of the threshing floor, as the farmer sifts the wheat from the chaff (v. 12). Matthew and Luke each agree that John predicted Jesus' baptism would be not only with the Spirit but also with fire (v. 11). The Spirit's coming is like a refiner's fire, purifying that which can withstand the heat and burning the rest, disclosing its worthlessness.[9]

Luke's Unique Additions. Luke 3:10–14 adds still one more paragraph about John's ethical instructions and radical demands. As is characteristic of Luke, he ties his story in with "empire history" (vv. 1–2). He also includes a longer portion of the Isaiah 40 quotation in verses 4–6. By extending the reference, he has it culminate in the prophecy that "all mankind will see God's salvation" (v. 6). As we have already seen, Luke stresses God's universal offer of salvation in Jesus.

Johannine Distinctives. Although there are significant points of overlap between the treatments of John the Baptist in the Fourth Gospel and in the Synoptics (see esp. John 1:23, 26–27, 30, 32), the distinctives are more pronounced. Above all, John is a witness to Jesus. The Fourth Gospel emphasizes who the Baptist is not (vv. 20–21), possibly to counter a Baptist-worshiping sect (see above, p. 166). The writer has John testify that Jesus is the "Lamb of God"—Passover sacrifice, apocalyptic warrior, and suffering servant all wrapped up into one (vv. 29, 36). He omits any explicit reference to Jesus' baptism but develops at length the accounts of Jesus calling his earliest disciples. One of the first two is Andrew; the other is unnamed. Both transfer their allegiance from John to Jesus (vv. 35–40). Andrew in turn calls Peter. Jesus "finds" Philip (v. 43), who then brings his friend Nathanael (arguably the same person as the Synoptics' Bartholomew). There is no mention of any full-time commitment to itinerant discipleship here; that apparently still awaits the more formal commissioning scenes in Galilee (see below, p. 234).

Perhaps the most noteworthy distinctive of these early verses in John is the remarkable collection of titles with which people address Jesus. He is not only the Lamb of God, but Rabbi (v. 38), Messiah (v. 41), Son of God and King of Israel (v. 49). In verse 45 he is the one written about in the Law and Prophets. Could so many people during their first encounters with Jesus come to such exalted impressions of him? They had heard the Baptist's testimony for some time, and Jesus no doubt had a very "charismatic" personality. But at this stage,

7. Cf. further James D. G. Dunn, *Baptism in the Holy Spirit* (London: SCM; Philadelphia: Westminster, 1970). Dunn's arguments were challenged by the more charismatic Howard M. Ervin (*Conversion-Initiation and the Baptism in the Holy Spirit* [Peabody: Hendrickson, 1984]). For a succinct discussion, cf. Craig L. Blomberg, "Baptism of the Holy Spirit," in *Evangelical Dictionary of Biblical Theology*, ed. Walter A. Elwell (Grand Rapids: Baker; Carlisle: Paternoster, 1996), 49–50.

8. Matt. 3:7 should be translated as in the NIV: the Pharisees and Sadducees were coming "to where he was baptizing," not "for baptism" as in the RSV. Cf. Luke 7:30.

9. Cf. further Craig L. Blomberg, "Baptism of Fire," in *Evangelical Dictionary of Biblical Theology*, 49.

none of these titles needs to mean more than that people were hoping that Jesus was the long-awaited Messiah. As developing events will demonstrate, these fledgling disciples probably still had a very nationalistic conception of that Messiah—one who would come to overthrow Rome and its oppressive armies.

The most enigmatic verses in John 1 may be verses 47–51. Jesus calls Nathanael, literally, "an Israelite in whom there is nothing false"—a play on the two names for the patriarch Jacob/Israel, since "Jacob" meant "deceiver" (v. 47). In reply to Nathanael's surprised question about how Jesus knew him, Christ explains, "I saw you . . . under the fig tree" (v. 48). It has been pointed out that a seat under a fig tree was often a place of prayer, but perhaps more significant are those passages that speak about the coming age of blessing when every Israelite will sit in peace under his own fig tree (e.g., 1 Kings 4:25; Micah 4:4, 1 Macc. 14:12), at least one of which appears in a seemingly Messianic context (Zech. 3:10). Jesus also promises greater wonders than mere insight into Nathanael's character—"You shall see heaven open, and the angels of God ascending and descending on the Son of Man" (v. 51). This clearly alludes to Jacob's dream about the ladder to heaven (Gen. 28:10–12). But how does the order "ascending and descending" apply to Jesus? Perhaps it is a cryptic foreshadowing of the cross and resurrection—angels accompanying Jesus to bear his body to heaven, in keeping with typical Jewish belief, and returning to announce his resurrection (as in Matt. 28:2 par.).[10]

Additional Events in John's Life

Further Testimony to the Christ (John 3:22–36) [Aland §28–29]. For some unspecified period of time, John's and Jesus' ministries overlapped. Both baptized and made disciples (3:22–23), though apparently Jesus let his followers do most of his baptizing for him (4:2). As time went by, Jesus' ministry began to eclipse John's, but John deferred to him with great magnanimity: "He must become greater; I must become less" (3:30). John was still just a witness, a best man for the bridegroom (v. 29).

Imprisonment (Mark 6:17–20 pars.) [Aland §144]. Eventually, John found himself in trouble with Antipas because he had boldly criticized him for marrying his brother Philip's ex-wife Herodias in violation of Leviticus 18:16. Josephus does not identify the brother of Antipas referred to here as Philip the tetrarch but as another Herod (*Antiquities* 18.5.1). He also states that John was imprisoned in Machaerus (18.5.2), a fortress in Perea. Josephus' portrait is also more unrelentingly negative toward Antipas than Mark's. But it is conceivable that these details can be harmonized.[11] Luke describes John's imprisonment much earlier in his narrative than do the other Gospels (Luke 3:19–20), probably to deal with all his material on John the Baptist in a tidy, thematic unit.

10. Cf. F. F. Bruce, *The Gospel of John* (Basingstoke: Pickering & Inglis; Grand Rapids: Eerdmans, 1983), 62–63. Christopher Rowland ("John 1.51, Jewish Apocalyptic and Targumic Tradition," *NTS* 30 [1984]: 498–507) notes that the Targum on Genesis describes the angels going from earth to heaven to invite their companions to come and see the pious man whose features are fixed on God's glorious throne. This would fit Jesus well too.

11. Harold W. Hoehner, *Herod Antipas* (Cambridge: CUP, 1972), 124–49. There is reason to believe that there was a Herod Philip distinct from Philip the tetrarch.

John's Doubts and Jesus' Reassurance (Matt. 11:2–19 par.) [Aland §106–107]. From prison, John sends messengers to Jesus to ask him if he really is the "coming one" (vv. 2–3). Despite John's earlier testimony and association with Christ, the question is entirely understandable. Prison was not part of John's expected plan for the unfolding of redemption. His apocalyptic message of judgment did not seem to be coming to fruition, while Jesus was becoming known much more for his compassion for his enemies. Jesus does not answer John's question directly but tells him to consider the significance of his miracles and concern for the poor (vv. 4–6)—an allusion to his Nazareth manifesto (Luke 4:16–19), which in turn echoed the servant passage of Isaiah 61:1–2 (see further, below, p. 233). In so doing, Jesus not only tacitly acknowledges his messianic ministry but redirects John's attention to its true nature.

As John's disciples return to report to their master, Jesus continues to talk to the crowds about John. He affirms John's ministry with the highest of praise. Verses 7–8 covertly compare him with Antipas, who minted coins with reed insignia and lived in pampered regal luxury.[12] But it is John, not any king, who is the greatest mortal who has lived thus far (v. 11a). Still, John will not live to see the kingdom fully inaugurated with Christ's death and resurrection, and thus every subsequent believer has an advantage on which he misses out (v. 11b). John is the greatest of the Old Testament age prophets and the fulfillment of prophecies about the coming of Elijah (vv. 13–14). But a greater power is now present that causes violent people to attack it, as Herod has already done by imprisoning John (v. 12).[13]

Jesus concludes his address to the crowds with a short parable that laments ironically how neither John's harsh message of judgment nor Jesus' carefree association with "sinners" has met with the approval of the Jewish leadership. Yet he promises that God's wisdom, represented by both of these emissaries, will be vindicated (vv. 16–19).[14]

John's Death (Mark 6:14–16, 21–29 pars.) [Aland §143–144]. The Gospels suggest that Herodias, even more than Herod, is the individual who wants to get rid of John. She gets her chance at a royal party when her daughter's dancing lures Herod into making a rash vow. Drink and sexual innuendoes, though not explicitly mentioned here, were common enough in the Herodian household and may have contributed. Antipas is more concerned not to go back on his word in public than to see justice carried out, so he agrees to John's execution by beheading. As John pointed the way forward to Jesus as Messiah in his lifetime, so his execution prefigures Jesus' own death at Roman hands.

Historicity

Given the early Christian concern to play down the role of John the Baptist and to exalt Jesus, just about everything that places John in a positive light is likely to be historical: the considerable early impact of his ministry, numerically and geographically; the fact that Jesus' first disciples came from John's follow-

---

12. Gerd Theissen, *The Gospels in Context* (Minneapolis: Fortress, 1991), 26–42.
13. Matt. 11:12b is notoriously difficult to translate, but the NIV rendering does not seem as likely as "the kingdom of heaven suffers violence, and violent people attack it." See G. Schrenk, "βιάζομαι, βιαστής," *TDNT*, vol. 1, 609–14.
14. Craig L. Blomberg, *Interpreting the Parables* (Downers Grove and Leicester: IVP, 1990), 208–10.

ers; the possibility that Jesus himself first followed John for a while; and Jesus' praise of John as the greatest of all who had previously lived. The strong contrast between John's austere message and Jesus' joyful ministry (Matt. 11:16–19 par.) must also reflect authentic tradition; Christians would not likely have portrayed Jesus' precursor as so different from Christ himself. John's ministry of baptism further satisfies the "double dissimilarity" criterion in differing from the kinds of baptism practiced by both Judaism and the early church. On the other hand, the strong line of continuity from Judaism through Jesus to Paul and the early church on the need for repentance for the forgiveness of sins in view of the in-breaking kingdom makes it difficult to imagine John teaching anything different. That John uses no well-established titles for Jesus as Messiah (despite the suggestiveness of "coming one" and "lamb of God") speaks for his veracity here too. And his death at the hands of Antipas is corroborated by Josephus.

THE BAPTISM OF JESUS (MARK 1:9–11 PARS.) [ALAND §18]

Just as the Gospels often group material thematically, we have kept all of the story of John the Baptist together except for the accounts of his baptism of Jesus. We now return to pick up this incident and then follow the course of Jesus' ministry as it subsequently unfolds. Here is the key commissioning of Christ for his public years of itinerant preaching, teaching, and healing.

Its Purpose

Matthew and John reflect the most self-consciously on the purpose of Jesus' baptism. If it was related to repentance for the forgiveness of sins, did Jesus think he had sinned? Matthew insists not, inserting the unparalleled verse that John tried to prevent Jesus from going through with the ceremony (Matt. 3:14). Instead, Jesus replied that it was proper to do so "to fulfill all righteousness" (v. 15). Given Matthew's characteristic use of "fulfill" to mean "complete everything to which God's Word has pointed," he presumably understands Jesus' words as a way of identifying with John's baptism and putting his stamp of approval on it. No doubt that is why Matthew summarizes John's and Jesus' ministries with the identical words: "Repent, for the kingdom of heaven is near" (3:2; 4:17). To the extent, however, that repentance in ancient Israel involved a *corporate* confession of the nation's sins, Jesus could participate. In short, he does all that God requires. John's testimony in the Fourth Gospel to Jesus as the Lamb, apparently uttered at this very time (John 1:29), points him out also as the one who would perform God's will in atoning for the sins of humanity.

Accompanying Signs

All four Gospels refer to a dove, but all use a simile to clarify that the Spirit's descent on Jesus was "like" a dove (Matt. 3:16; Mark 1:10; Luke 3:22; John 1:32). We do not know what was literally visible, but something reminded the onlookers of a dove. Doves in the ancient world could symbolize peace, love, and even divinity itself, but the most obvious reference would be to the activity of God's Spirit in creation, just as Genesis 1:2 spoke of him "brooding" or "hovering" over the waters.[15] Jesus now begins a work of re-creation. The voice from heaven also suggests the resumption of divine revelation after the centuries of its cessation.

Its Message

God declares Jesus his beloved Son with whom he is well pleased (Mark 1:11 pars.). Most commentators find allusions in this declaration to Psalm 2:7 and Isaiah 42:1. The former is part of a royal psalm; the latter falls in one of the servant passages of Isaiah. Both "son" and "servant" seem to have been understood in a messianic sense by important segments of pre-Christian Judaism (see 4QFlor 10–14 and Targum Isaiah 42:1, respectively). Therefore it would appear that God is forthrightly declaring Jesus to be both kingly Messiah and suffering servant. There is also an incipient Trinitarianism in this baptism: God speaks and the Spirit descends on the man Jesus.

Its Historicity

Because of the theological problems created by Jesus accepting John's baptism that symbolized repentance of sin, it is inconceivable that the early church would have created this story. In view of the messianic overtones of the account, it is likely that Jesus' baptism would have spawned widespread eschatological fervor, however misguided. Thus the credibility of the rash of exalted titles applied to Jesus in the latter half of John 1 is also enhanced.

THE TEMPTATION OF JESUS (MARK 1:12–13; MATT. 4:1–11 PAR.) [ALAND §20]

So far in the Gospels God has disclosed Jesus' identity from heaven. But will Christ be faithful to his role as his ministry unfolds? One might expect Jesus' baptism to launch him instantly into fame and prosperity. Instead, God allows the devil to test him to see what kind of Messiah he really will be. Mark stresses that the temptations come immediately after the baptism. Many Christians ever since have faced some of their greatest struggles soon after their conversion or some act of recommitment rather than before. We ought not to be quite as surprised as we sometimes are when this pattern continues to recur.

Background and Sources

Only Matthew and Luke narrate the temptation in any detail. Mark records merely that it happened, who was involved, where, and for how long. Interestingly, however, he alone adds that Christ was with the wild beasts. Mark agrees with Matthew that angels served him. Probably both comments are meant to stress Jesus' triumph over temptation and sovereignty over creation.[16]

---

15. A recently discovered Dead Sea Scroll seems to confirm this conclusion. The fragment known as "A Messianic Vision" includes this line: "over the poor will His Spirit hover and the faithful will he support with his strength." This is the first unambiguous ancient Jewish allusion to Genesis 1:2 in a messianic context and suggests that the dove at Jesus' baptism refers to Jesus as the bringer of a new creation. Dale C. Allison, Jr., "The Baptism of Jesus and a New Dead Sea Scroll," *BAR* 18.2 (1992): 58–60.

16. Jeffrey B. Gibson, "Jesus' Wilderness Temptation according to Mark," *JSNT* 53 (1994): 3–34.

The presence of beasts adds to the danger and even to the demonic threat of the desert (cf. Test. Naph. 8:4; Luke 11:24). The forty-day period of Jesus' testing calls to mind Moses' period of preparation for forty days and nights before receiving the Law (Deut. 9:9) as well as the Israelites' wanderings in the wilderness for forty years. Jesus is a new and better Moses and will succeed where Israel as a whole had failed.

Agency and Sequence

Mark stresses that the temptations came immediately after the baptism. There is an important balance in the description in all three Synoptics between God's Spirit initiating the sequence of events and the devil as the direct agent of temptation. A pair of crucial truths is encapsulated here: God is always sovereign and allows no temptation except that which furthers his broader purposes. Yet he never directly tempts anyone (cf. James 1:13) and is wholly dissociated from evil. Matthew and Luke both agree that Jesus was tempted by Satan in three particularly acute ways: to turn stones into bread, to be supernaturally rescued from death after jumping off the temple portico, and to receive all the world's kingdoms in return for worshiping Satan. Luke, however, has the last of these two in reverse order, probably because of the climactic importance of the temple for him. But here is one of those classic cases in which a Gospel writer connects his episodes merely with "ands" or "buts," so that chronological sequence should not be inferred.

Their Nature and Christ's Resistance

There are fascinating parallels between the three temptations of Christ, the three temptations in the Garden of Eden (Gen. 3:6), and the three kinds of temptation 1 John 2:16 lists to summarize "everything in the world."

Jesus' temptations	Adam & Eve's temptations	1 John 2:16
stones into bread	tree was good for food	lust of the flesh
see all kingdoms	pleasing to the eye	lust of the eyes
save life spectacularly	desirable for gaining wisdom (serpent: so as not to die)	pride of life

Whether or not any of these parallels was intentional, together they point out that Jesus did experience representative temptations of all kinds, therefore the writer of Hebrews could declare that Christ was "tempted in every way, just as we are—yet was without sin" (Heb. 4:15).[17]

---

17. Henri J. M. Nouwen (*In the Name of Jesus* [New York: Crossroad, 1993]) sees these three temptations as paradigms of ones all Christian leaders face: the desire to be relevant, popular, and leading at the expense of prayer, ministry, and being led.

In the immediate context of Matthew and Luke, it is significant that the devil recognizes Jesus' sonship. "If you are the Son of God" in Matthew 4:3 should probably be translated, "Since you are the Son of God." The devil knows full well who Jesus is, but he tries to seduce him into being the wrong kind of Son—a triumphant, regal Messiah who foregoes the road to the cross and is unfaithful to his Father's will. The primary weapon Christ uses to defeat the devil is Scripture. In each case, he refutes the tempter by quoting Deuteronomy (8:3; 6:16; 6:13). In the second case, the devil quotes Scripture, too (Ps. 91:11–12), but misapplies.

Christ's temptations may well have been to a certain degree subjective or visionary, though no less real or diabolical.[18] The text gives no locale for the "Mount of Temptation," though tourists are regularly shown one overlooking Jericho! In fact, there is no mountain on earth from which one can literally see all the kingdoms of the world. Nor would it have been possible for Jesus to do arduous mountain-climbing or even temple-climbing after a forty-day period without food, unless he drew on the very supernatural power for self-help that the devil was enticing him to employ. Christ's refusal to succumb to the tempter's snares points out at one and the same time his sinlessness and peccability. Many of the more liberal theologians have often denied the former; many of the more conservative ones, the latter. Yet without the possibility of sinning, his temptation could hardly be said to have been like ours; without the reality of his not sinning, his atonement could scarcely have been vicarious.[19]

Historicity

As with Jesus' baptism, it is hard to imagine any early Christian inventing this story. Here Jesus is at his most vulnerable, reflecting the weakness of his humanity, in contrast with Satan who is depicted as having the power to offer real alternatives to Christ's God-ordained mission. If Christ thought it important to have disciples close enough to him in Gethsemane to hear his prayers there (before they fell asleep!), he would presumably have told his followers about these temptations in the wilderness as well.

FROM CANA TO CANA (JOHN 2–4)

John 1:19–4:42 has often been called Christ's early Judean ministry since he seems to be based near John the Baptist and near Jerusalem. Yet chapters 1 and 3 give no precise location for Jesus' ministry of baptizing, and two of the events in chapters 2 and 4 take place in Galilee and Samaria, respectively. As noted above (p. 190), this has also been called his year of obscurity. But a year passes by only if 2:13 is *not* a transposition of the account of his final Passover and if 5:1 *is* a Passover. Also, this is a period of obscurity only in contrast to the huge crowds that throng around Jesus during his great Galilean ministry to

18. Robert H. Mounce, *Matthew* (Peabody: Hendrickson, 1991), 31.

19. Cf. Millard J. Erickson, *Christian Theology*, vol. 2 (Grand Rapids: Baker, 1984), 720: "while he *could* have sinned, it was certain that he *would* not."

come. We will do more justice to John's intentions in these chapters if we resist the temptation to try to locate every detail chronologically and focus on what he wants to teach us about Christ through these episodes. The overall outline of John (above, p. 161) suggests that these three chapters form one discrete subsection, bracketed by the two references to signs done in Cana as an "inclusio" (a framing device of repetition to mark the beginning and end of a literary unit).

The First Miracle: Water into Wine at the Cana Wedding (2:1–12) [Aland §22–23]

Early in his career, Jesus is invited to a wedding during which the wine runs out. Inability to provide for the festivities would have caused the host of the multiday party acute social embarrassment and shame. Drinking wine in moderation, particularly with meals, was commonplace in the ancient Jewish world. At times it was healthier than the water that was available. Various Scriptures and intertestamental works considered wine a gift of gladness and rejoicing from God (see esp. Sir. 31:27–28; cf. Ps. 104:15; Judg. 9:13). It was considerably more diluted than our modern wines but still could cause drunkenness if someone overindulged (cf. the caricature of Jesus in Luke 7:34 as a "glutton and a drunkard," because of his willingness to join in such merriment).

Mary, too, has been invited to this wedding, and she turns to her son for help in this time of need (v. 3). Jesus' cryptic reply that his hour has not yet come (v. 4), if taken at face value, would imply that he is not prepared to help just now. In light of similar statements throughout John, it suggests also that the climactic hour of his self-revelation still lies in the future. The original idiom of Jesus' reply involves no disrespect[20] but stresses his acquiescence to God's sovereign timing. Mary is not rebuffed and trusts that Jesus can still help in some way. In fact he does work a miracle to help out his host, but it occurs unobtrusively, even secretly, convincing only to those with eyes of faith.

The remaining details in the passage suggest that more is involved than merely compensating for an awkward social faux pas. In an otherwise sparse narrative, the detail of verse 6 stands out. Why bother noting that the water jars were used for Jewish rites of purification? Given, too, that wedding banquets in Jewish literature often symbolized the messianic age, many commentators have seen a symbolic level of meaning here: Jesus is bringing the wine of the new age, a joy that transcends and replaces the old "water" of Jewish ritual. This interpretation is made probable by the fact that in the Synoptics he will tell a parable about not putting new wine in old wineskins to make a very similar point (Mark 2:22 pars.). Verse 10 here reinforces this: Jesus has saved the best wine for last.[21] John adds one of his favorite themes—that this "sign" revealed Jesus' glory and helped to produce faith (v. 11, though recall our balancing comments above, p. 164).

---

20. The NIV translation of v. 4a ("Dear woman, why do you involve me?") is better than many. The Greek reads literally, "What [is it] to me and to you, woman?"—idiomatic language that is easily misunderstood in English.

21. See further Craig L. Blomberg, "The Miracles as Parables," in *Gospel Perspectives*, vol. 6, ed. David Wenham and Craig Blomberg (Sheffield: JSOT, 1986), 333–37, and the literature there cited.

Clearing the Temple in Jerusalem (2:13–25) [Aland §24–26]

Most commentators see this as a chronologically relocated passage whereby John highlights the significance of Christ's coming death and resurrection early on in his Gospel as a kind of headline for what is to come.[22] On the other hand, there are hints in both John and the Synoptics that something like this account may indeed have happened early in Christ's ministry. Most notable are the references to the forty-six years of building the temple (John 2:20), which dates this event to about A.D. 28 (see above, p. 189), and the garbled accusation at Christ's trial that he would destroy the temple and build another "not made by man" (Mark 14:58 par.). This accusation becomes intelligible if Jesus had spoken the words of John 2:19 two or three years earlier and if his claims had become distorted during the time that had since elapsed.[23]

More significant for John is what this event symbolized. It probably should be called a temple clearing rather than a cleansing. To be sure, Jesus rued that his Father's house had been turned into a marketplace (v. 16). But buying and selling animals was necessary if sacrifices were to continue. It is likely, then, that John sees a more radical implication in Jesus' words: the temple and its entire sacrificial system are about to be replaced.[24] Verse 19 corroborates this understanding, as Jesus speaks of substituting his resurrected body for the temple, a prediction that is not understood until after it has been fulfilled (vv. 20–22). John notes that the disciples later saw a fulfillment of Psalm 69:9 as well (v. 17). When God's people have been zealous for true worship, they have often been persecuted. John closes the story with another reference to the positive value of signs, but he adds a cautionary note that belief based merely on signs may often prove fickle (vv. 23–25).

Jesus and Nicodemus: The Gospel in a Nutshell (3:1–21) [Aland §27]

An example of superficial interest in Jesus without true understanding follows. Nicodemus, a leading Pharisee, comes to Jesus praising him as a heaven-sent teacher because of his signs. As the conversation continues, Nicodemus' ignorance simply becomes more pronounced.[25] Here is the context for Jesus' famous declaration that a would-be disciple must be "born again" (v. 3).

---

22. E.g., J. Ramsey Michaels (*John* [Peabody: Hendrickson, 1989], 50) argues that each of the two main sections of John begins with a chronologically dislocated but programmatically emphasized episode—the temple cleansing in 2:13–25 and the anointing of Jesus at Bethany in 12:1–10.

23. Cf. esp. John A. T. Robinson, *The Priority of John* (London: SCM, 1985; Oak Park, Ill.: Meyer-Stone, 1987), 125–31.

24. Cf. Kenneth A. Mathews, "John, Jesus and the Essenes: Trouble at the Temple," *Criswell Theological Review* 3 (1988): 101–26; Charles H. Talbert, *Reading John* (New York: Crossroad, 1992), 96.

25. See F. Peter Cotterell, "The Nicodemus Conversation: A Fresh Appraisal," *ExpT* 96 (1985): 237–42, for a helpful "discourse analysis" of this passage, highlighting how Nicodemus' contributions to the conversation become increasingly shorter, while Jesus increasingly points out the Pharisee's lack of understanding. Nicodemus will reappear in two slightly more positive contexts in John (7:45–52 and 19:38–42), but nowhere are we told that he ever became a full-fledged disciple. Later apocryphal traditions made this claim, but it seems better to follow Jouette M. Bassler ("Mixed Signals: Nicodemus in the Fourth Gospel," *JBL* 108 [1989]: 635–46) in observing that within John, Nicodemus always remains a sufficiently ambivalent character as to represent those who are (just) outside the kingdom.

The Greek can also be translated "born from above" (*anōthen*), and the double meaning may well be intentional.[26] Verse 5 further defines this new birth as "born of water and the Spirit." There are at least four main interpretations of this clause: (a) a reference to Christian baptism as described in Acts and the rest of the New Testament (but historically this will not begin until after Pentecost, and John elsewhere plays down allusions to the baptism and the Lord's Supper—see above, p. 166); (b) a reference to John's baptism as a sign of repentance (but would this leave Nicodemus so incredulous?); (c) a reference to physical birth plus spiritual birth (cf. v. 6; but the use of "water" as a metaphor for physical birth was relatively rare in antiquity); and (d) a reference to the spiritual cleansing predicted in Ezekiel 36:25–27 that would characterize messianic times. Option (d) seems most likely, though perhaps in combination with some form of (a) or (b).[27] This new birth is the result of the Spirit's sovereign, unpredictable activity, just like the wind (v. 8). The Greek *pneuma* can mean both wind and S/spirit. Jesus' ministry blows Nicodemus away by not fitting conventional Pharisaic expectations (v. 9).

Verses 10–21 elaborate further. The last use of the first person ("I" or "we") comes in verse 12, and verse 15 rounds out a paragraph, so it is possible that verses 16–21 are John's own commentary on the dialogue just narrated (see NIV margin). In verses 10–15 Jesus observes that the principles he has enunciated should be simple to understand compared with more esoteric matters that have no earthly analogies (vv. 10–13). But the key to understanding Jesus is accepting him as the Son of Man who must be crucified and exalted (vv. 14–15). John (or Jesus) then stresses that there are ultimately only two options available to people: those who believe in the Son will have eternal life; those who reject him will be condemned. Verse 16, of course, is one of the most precious promises in all the Bible and is often memorized. But verses 17–21 prove equally crucial, stressing also the "dark side" of the gospel. All of God's condemnation remains fair, however, because those who live in "darkness" have chosen rebellion over living in the "light" (vv. 19–20).

John 3:22–36 repeats and reinforces the themes of the Nicodemus dialogue, only now the conversation continues between John the Baptist and his disciples. There is the same ambiguity here as to when the Baptist's words end and when the apostle's begin. Arguably the break comes between verses 30 and 31. For further comments, see above, p. 219.

---

26. There is also a striking parallel with Matt. 18:3, leading several commentators to speculate that the Synoptic saying was the historical kernel on which this Johannine narrative, a homiletic elaboration of the Johannine community, was built. See, e.g., Barnabas Lindars, *The Gospel of John* (London: Oliphants, 1972; Grand Rapids: Eerdmans, 1981), 48, 150–51. Whether or not such a hypothesis can ever be proved or disproved, the point of connection is significant in showing that John's Jesus is not as radically different from the Synoptics as some have claimed.

27. For a thorough survey of options and a defense of (d), see Linda L. Belleville, "'Born of Water and Spirit': John 3:5," *Trinity Journal* n.s. 2 (1981): 125–41. G. R. Beasley-Murray ("John 3:3, 5: Baptism, Spirit and the Kingdom," *ExpT* 97 [1986]: 167–70) ably defends the combination hypothesis.

Jesus and the Woman at the Well in Samaria (4:1–42) [Aland §30–31]

Again the fourth evangelist narrates a lengthy dialogue between Jesus and an "outsider," but the contrasts between this episode and the story of Jesus and Nicodemus could hardly be more striking. He was a powerful, male Jew, probably well off, a religious leader, and a model of piety and wisdom. She was a powerless, female Samaritan, probably poor, unlikely to have had access to any religious education, and an outcast because of her marital history. Yet she is the individual who responds positively to Jesus' claims and winds up being a witness to bring many of her townspeople to the Lord.[28]

Verses 1–9 find Jesus, surprisingly, taking the initiative to talk to this unnamed woman at the well. In so doing, he crosses over three social boundaries that made such conversation surprising—their differences in gender and in religious/ethnic background, along with the taboo against associating with one who carried the stigma of sexual immorality.[29] The narrative overall has often been used as a model of how to do evangelism, and certain relevant principles may be derived from it. But far more central to John's purpose is his concern to present a paradigm of *whom* to evangelize. The gospel breaks down all humanly-erected boundaries that categorize certain people as second-class citizens.

In verses 10–15 Jesus turns the conversation to spiritual matters, referring to his ability to offer the woman "living water." At first she does not grasp the metaphor. "Living water" could simply mean "flowing water" (as opposed to the well water), which was preferred in Jewish purification rites. But once she understands that Jesus means something more than this, she wants an inexhaustible supply. Before responding to her request, Jesus shifts the topic to make the woman confront her marital situation (vv. 16–19). While Jesus displays a remarkable openness to the "sinners" of his society, he also calls all of them to repent. Here his reference is more subtle. Nevertheless, it makes a lasting impression on the woman, who will later insist, with some exaggeration, that she met a man who told her everything she ever did (vv. 29, 39). The setting of Jacob's well (v. 6) and the comparison between Jesus and Jacob (v. 12) again suggest a contrast with Judaism. The old water of the Torah, even in its Samaritan form, must give way to Jesus' new, living water.

It is not clear if verses 20–24 are a red herring on the woman's part to distract attention from the problem. They are certainly an integral part of the conversation for John, who is stressing how Jesus replaces all "holy space." Already the dispute between Jews and Samaritans concerning whether to worship on Mt. Zion (Jerusalem) or Mt. Gerizim in Samaria (all based on a debate over the

---

28. For elaboration of these contrasts and outcomes, see Craig L. Blomberg, "The Globalization of Biblical Interpretation: A Test Case—John 3–4," *BBR* 5 (1995): 1–15. For a good survey of approaches to interpretation, see David S. Dockery, "Reading John 4:1–45: Some Diverse Hermeneutical Perspectives," *Criswell Theological Review* 3 (1988): 127–40.

29. That is not to say that it can be proven that the woman was at fault in this respect. Women rarely had opportunity to initiate divorce, so this woman may have been the victim of numerous conniving men. Who knows but what the last husband left her without even legally divorcing her, so that she now felt forced to live with a man simply for his financial and legal protection? Cf. Alice Mathews, *A Woman Jesus Can Teach* (Grand Rapids: Discovery House, 1991), 24–26.

interpretation of Deut. 12:5) is moot. God's people may now worship him any-where they want, "in spirit and in truth" (v. 24).[30]

Verses 25–26 bring the conversation to its climax. Jesus reveals himself clearly to this woman as the Messiah. Ironically, he is more direct with her than with any of his Jewish contemporaries, at least early in his ministry. This may well be because the Samaritan expectation of a Messiah (*Taheb*—converter or redeemer) was in some respects less nationalistic or militaristic than much Jewish expectation, and thus less susceptible to misinterpretation.[31] The aftermath of Jesus' conversation occupies verses 27–42. The woman and many of her townspeople come to belief. "Savior of the world" (v. 42) invests Jesus with authority claimed by the Roman emperors and may hint at Samaritan animosity to imperial oppression.[32] Jesus encourages his followers to recognize that the fields are "ripe for harvest" (v. 35). The disciples, too, at first fail to grasp his figurative intent (v. 33). But he elaborates, and this passage has become a key text for evangelistic and missionary work in all ages. Verses 37–38 articulate key principles: some sow while others reap, but there is always urgent work to be done regardless of the immediate results.

The details of the miracle of 4:43–54 will be discussed in conjunction with its Synoptic parallels, below, pp. 240–241. We have come full circle to Cana again and are ready to proceed to Jesus' great Galilean ministry.

Historicity

The similarity of the water-to-wine miracle to Jesus' parable of the wineskins speaks for its authenticity. So also does the potentially embarrassing light in which it paints the relationship between Jesus and Mary, along with the possible misunderstanding created by having the Lord produce so much wine for merrymaking! The cleansing of the temple has parallels with Synoptic tradition, and we have already commented on the possible relationships with the similar incident there (above, p. 226). Jesus' dialogue with Nicodemus is not unlike various Synoptic stories that pit Jesus against the Jewish leaders, and his key claim in John 3:3 ("Unless a man is born again, he cannot see the kingdom of God") closely resembles Matthew 18:3 ("Unless you change and become like little children, you will never enter the kingdom of heaven"). John 3:29 contains the nucleus of a small parable about a bridegroom that could easily have generated the dialogue that surrounds it. The encounter with the Samaritan woman places Jesus in numerous compromising positions and ties in perfectly with the Synoptics' emphasis on his role as a "friend of tax collectors and sinners." John 4:35–38 is closely reminiscent of Matthew 9:37–38. Finally, the healing of the nobleman's son is so similar to the miracle involving the centurion's servant in Q (Matt. 8:5–13; Luke 7:1–10) that some take them to be variants of the same event. All these considerations support a general trustworthiness of these episodes, even if John narrates them in his own distinctive style and for his unique purposes.

30. On this theme, see esp. W. D. Davies, *The Gospel and the Land* (Berkeley: University of California, 1974).

31. Raymond E. Brown (*The Gospel according to John*, vol. 1 [Garden City: Doubleday, 1966], 172–73) points out that the Samaritans were looking more for a teacher and lawgiver.

32. Richard J. Cassidy, *John's Gospel in New Perspective* (Maryknoll: Orbis, 1992), 34–35.

Theology

John 2–4 is a very carefully structured unity. It begins and ends with miracles in Cana. In between appear two central discourses that contrast dramatically with each other—Jesus with Nicodemus and the Samaritan woman. The main points of the four main parts of this section all stress the newness of Jesus' ministry. The new age he is ushering in brings *a new joy* (2:1–12), *a new worship and temple* (2:13–25), *a new birth* (3:1–36), and *a new universal offer of salvation* even to the most outcast of society (4:1–54).[33] We begin to understand a little better the contrast John intended in 1:16–17 between the grace of the period of the Law and the greater grace and truth that came through Jesus Christ.

FOR FURTHER STUDY

John the Baptist

Meier, John P. *A Marginal Jew: Rethinking the Historical Jesus.* Vol. 2, 19–233. New York and London: Doubleday, 1994.
Scobie, C. H. H. *John the Baptist.* London: SCM; Philadelphia: Fortress, 1964.
Webb, Robert L. *John the Baptizer and Prophet.* Sheffield: JSOT, 1991.
Wink, Walter. *John the Baptist in the Gospel Tradition.* Cambridge: CUP, 1968.
Witherington, Ben, III. "John the Baptist." In *DJG,* 383–91.

Jesus' Baptism and Temptation

Beasley-Murray, G. R. *Baptism in the New Testament.* London: Macmillan; New York: St. Martin's, 1962.
Blomberg, Craig L. "Temptation of Jesus." In *ISBE.* Vol. 4, 784–86.
Gerhardsson, Birger. *The Testing of God's Son.* Lund: Gleerup, 1966.
Gibson, Jeffrey B. *The Temptations of Jesus in Early Christianity.* Sheffield: Sheffield Academic Press, 1995.

John 2–4

Okure, Teresa. *The Johannine Approach to Mission.* Tübingen: Mohr, 1988.
Olsson, Birger. *Structure and Meaning of the Fourth Gospel: A Text-Linguistic Analysis of John 2:1–11 and 4:1–42.* Lund: Gleerup, 1974.

QUESTIONS FOR REVIEW

1. What are the most important issues of historical background and exegetical or interpretive commentary worth highlighting in order to understand each of the following: (1) the ministry and message of John the Baptist; (2) the baptism of Jesus by John; (3) the temptations of Jesus?

2. What do all the episodes of John 2–4 have in common? What is the main point of each? How can we tell?

3. Compare and contrast Jesus' encounters with Nicodemus and with the Samaritan woman. What is John's purpose in juxtaposing these two episodes as he does?

---

33. This last theme continues in the healing of the nobleman's son in 4:43–54, inasmuch as the man is most likely a Gentile. See A. H. Mead, "'The βασιλικός' in John 4.46–53," *JSNT* 23 (1985): 69–72.

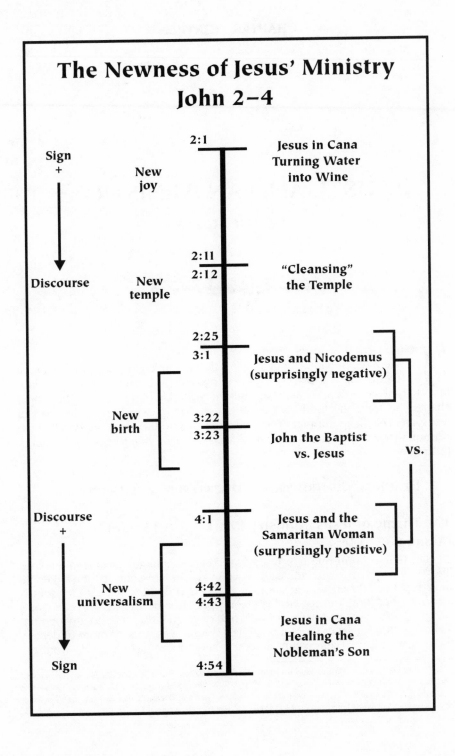

The Newness of Jesus' Ministry
John 2–4

Sign +	New joy	2:1	Jesus in Cana Turning Water into Wine
Discourse	New temple	2:11 / 2:12	"Cleansing" the Temple
	New birth	2:25 / 3:1	Jesus and Nicodemus (surprisingly negative)
		3:22 / 3:23	John the Baptist vs. Jesus
Discourse +	New universalism	4:1	Jesus and the Samaritan Woman (surprisingly positive)
		4:42 / 4:43	Jesus in Cana Healing the Nobleman's Son
Sign		4:54	

vs.

CHAPTER THIRTEEN

JESUS' GALILEAN MINISTRY—

Earlier Stages

T he period of Jesus' greatest visibility and popularity now ensues. As we have previously noted, all of the Synoptic Gospels group material thematically at places, so it is impossible to be sure what took place in exactly what order. We will mostly follow Mark's outline for his first three chapters to trace the kinds of events that were typical of the earlier part of Jesus' great Galilean ministry. Then we will pause to look in more depth at the Sermon that encapsulates the heart of what he was trying to teach throughout this region.

HEALINGS, CONTROVERSIES, DISCIPLESHIP, AND OPPOSITION

The Theme of Jesus' Ministry (Mark 1:14–15 pars.) [Aland §32–33]

After John is imprisoned, Jesus emerges on center stage of Galilean religious life. Mark summarizes his message in language reminiscent of John's. People must repent and believe the good news he is preaching. God's kingdom is arriving. The "kingdom" of God is a concept that is best understood as God's "kingship." It refers primarily to God's rule or reign rather than to a geographical realm. It is a power more than a place.[1] After a century or more of debate, there is widespread agreement among contemporary scholars that from the

---

1. For the current state of research, see Bruce D. Chilton, "The Kingdom of God in Recent Discussion," in *Studying the Historical Jesus*, ed. Bruce Chilton and Craig A. Evans (Leiden: Brill, 1994), 255–80. Although language of God's kingship is relatively rare in the Old Testament, it is more common in the Jewish targums and refers to God acting "in strength." It is not that he was not previously king, but his sovereignty is now being demonstrated in a new, clearer, and more powerful way.

standpoint of Jesus' ministry this kingly power is both present and future.[2] The verb translated "is near" in Mark 1:15 has been the subject of detailed scrutiny. Is the kingdom just very close, or has it in some sense actually arrived? Despite a few demurrals, the latter seems most likely.[3] Jesus' ministry is inaugurating a new era in human history (see further, below, pp. 384–388).

Characteristically, Matthew expands his discussion of Jesus' setting up his ministry in Galilee by pointing out how it fulfills prophecy (Matt. 4:13–17). He also phrases the summary of Jesus' teaching so it exactly matches that of John (v. 17; cf. 3:2). For the most part, however, Matthew avoids using the expression "kingdom of God," substituting instead "kingdom of heaven." This expression occurs thirty-three times in Matthew's Gospel and nowhere else in the New Testament. The numerous occasions on which these expressions appear interchangeably in otherwise parallel passages (including within Matthew himself—see, e.g., 19:23–24) make it clear they are synonyms. Almost certainly, Matthew is following Jewish scruples and using a "circumlocution" or euphemism for the divine name to avoid treating something holy in an overly familiar way.

Luke does not begin his account of Jesus in Galilee with a one-line epitome of his teaching but rather narrates the story of Jesus' preaching in his hometown of Nazareth. Luke 4:14–15 confirms what the parallels in Matthew and Mark suggest—that this incident actually happened quite a ways into the Galilean ministry (cf. Mark 6:6b–13 par.). Yet Luke places it early, as a programmatic "headline" for this section of his Gospel, to make it clear what Jesus was all about and to foreshadow the opposition that would later intensify (vv. 16–30). As was the custom, a distinguished guest is invited to read from the biblical scroll one of the passages designated for a given Sabbath and then to expound it. Jesus reads a text that includes one of Isaiah's servant prophecies (Isa. 61:1–2) and then stuns his audience by declaring it to be fulfilled in *him* at that very moment. Here appear several of Luke's favorite themes—empowerment by the Spirit, reversal of fortune for the socioeconomically disadvantaged, and holistic healing of body and spirit. In essence, Jesus is announcing the arrival of the Jubilee year, when all debts are forgiven (cf. Lev. 25:8–55). Interestingly, Luke's quotation of the Old Testament ends just before Isaiah's words continue with "and the day of vengeance of our God" (Isa. 61:2b), probably because Jesus understood he would be coming twice—now to save and only later to judge. The audience marvels at his "gracious words" (v. 22), but he keeps on speaking and directs attention to Gentiles whom God favored over his chosen people in Old Testament times. This turns their wonder into outrage and leads to a spontaneous attempt to kill Jesus, which seems to be miraculously thwarted.[4]

---

2. For a history of recent developments, see Wendell Willis, ed., *The Kingdom of God in 20th Century Interpretation* (Peabody: Hendrickson, 1987). A minority dissents from this consensus and tries to eliminate the future apocalyptic element from Jesus' teaching in favor of a timeless or "permanent eschatology." In this view Jesus subverts conventional categories of this world's thinking, much as in an older form of existentialism. See esp. Robert W. Funk, Roy W. Hoover, and the Jesus Seminar, *The Five Gospels: What Did Jesus Really Say?* (New York: Macmillan, 1993).

3. G. R. Beasley-Murray, *Jesus and the Kingdom of God* (Exeter: Paternoster; Grand Rapids: Eerdmans, 1986), 72–73. The most convincing version of the former view argues that the kingdom arrives immediately after Christ's death and resurrection. See esp. Chrys C. Caragounis, "Kingdom of God, Son of Man and Jesus' Self-Understanding," *TynB* 40 (1989): 3–23, 223–38.

4. On this whole passage, cf. esp. William W. Klein, "The Sermon at Nazareth (Luke 4:14–22)," in *Christian Freedom: Essays in Honor of Vernon C. Grounds*, ed. Kenneth W. M. Wozniak and Stanley J. Grenz (Lanham, Md.: University Press of America, 1986), 153–72.

Gathering Disciples (Mark 1:16–20 pars.) [Aland §34, 41]

All three Synoptics agree that Jesus called several of his disciples very early in his Galilean ministry. The four specifically named here are Peter, Andrew, James, and John. Levi/Matthew will appear shortly. In light of the previous association of at least some of these individuals with Jesus in Judea (John 1:35–51), we must not overestimate how instantaneous their decisions were to leave family and occupation and join Jesus' itinerant ministry. That they did leave was nevertheless a radical move, given the cultural responsibility to submit to parents and fulfill family obligations. Jesus' behavior stood typical rabbinic practice on its head. Instead of sifting among "applicants," Jesus took the initiative to command people to follow him. And, unlike the prophets who pointed people to God, Jesus pointed people to himself.

Luke includes in this context an account of a miraculous fish-catch (Luke 5:1–11). Jesus uses this object lesson to explain that now his followers will be fishing for people (Luke 5:10; cf. Mark 1:17; Matt. 4:19). "The call to discipleship means also a call to ministry."[5] We also see something of a balance between intentional mission and allowing for the Spirit to act in a sovereign, unpredictable fashion. Although Peter will obey, he fears one who is so holy, and impulsively but tellingly blurts out, "Go away from me, Lord; I am a sinful man" (Luke 5:8).

A Series of Exorcisms and Other Healings (Mark 1:21–45 pars.) [Aland §35–40, 42, 50]

Mark 1:21–34 has been described as a typical day in the life of Jesus the healer. Capernaum is now Jesus' "home base" (cf. also Matt. 4:12–16). Mark groups together representative examples of Jesus' healings, including exorcisms, throughout the rest of this chapter. What stands out in each instance is Christ's authority over the powers of Satan and sickness. Numerous reports of other Jewish and Greco-Roman healers or exorcists have been preserved from the ancient world. But Jesus distinguishes himself from all of them by the directness of his approach. He invokes no lengthy list of deities, recites no formulaic incantations, and uses no magical paraphernalia to cast his spells. A simple word of rebuke is all it takes.[6]

One of the striking features of the Gospel exorcisms is the regular recognition by the demons of Christ's true identity (cf. Mark 1:24 par.). In fact, early on in the Synoptics, *only* the demons grasp Jesus' full identity. Surprisingly to us, Jesus always rebukes these proclamations. But, in fact, this is spiritual warfare at work. One of the keys to gaining supernatural power over an opponent is to invoke his name (cf. Jesus' own strategy in Mark 5:9). "The recognition-formula is not a confession, but a defensive attempt to gain control of Jesus . . . [in hopes that] the use of the precise name of an individual or spirit would secure mastery over him."[7] But, in every instance, the demons' ploys fail, and Jesus casts them out. Interestingly, Mark notes that the synagogue

---

5. Morna D. Hooker, *The Gospel according to Saint Mark* (London: A & C Black; Peabody: Hendrickson, 1991), 60.

6. For a careful sifting of similarities and differences, see Graham H. Twelftree, "EI DE . . . EGΩ EKBALLΩ TA DAIMONIA . . ." in *Gospel Perspectives*, vol. 6, ed. David Wenham and Craig Blomberg (Sheffield: JSOT, 1986), 361–400.

7. William L. Lane, *The Gospel according to Mark* (Grand Rapids: Eerdmans, 1974; London: Marshall, Morgan & Scott, 1975), 74.

worshipers call the exorcism a "new teaching" (1:27), linking Jesus' command to the demon with his more formal exposition for the worshipers.[8] Matthew, too, summarizes Jesus' early ministry as demonstrating unique authority in both preaching/teaching and healing (Matt. 4:23–25).

Although exorcisms and healings are often linked in the Gospels, they are also distinguished from one another (Mark 1:32–34).[9] Mark 1:29–39 relates further examples of each, while verses 40–45 proceed to recount in more detail the healing of a particular leper. This passage illustrates several themes: (a) Jesus' divine power; (b) his compassion for the sick (and/or outrage at the sickness and its effects[10]); (c) his willingness to be considered ritually defiled by touching the man; (d) the miracle as a proof to the people—not merely of the leper's health but also of who Jesus was;[11] and (e) testimony by deed rather than word. On the "Messianic secret" motif that appears in verse 44 (see above, p. 119).

A Collection of Pronouncement Stories (Mark 2:1–3:6 pars.) [Aland §43–47]

Mark next groups together a series of five stories, all of which fall into the category that form critics call "pronouncement stories" (see above, p. 81). They are also sometimes called conflict or controversy stories. In each case the climax of the account is a radical pronouncement by Jesus that challenges Jewish tradition and leads to conflict with the authorities. Mark will balance these five controversies early in his Gospel with five more at its climax (Mark 11:27–12:37). The five here arguably form a chiasm: two that include controversial healings (Mark 2:1–12, 3:1–6); two that involve debates about food—when to harvest it and with whom to eat it (2:13–17, 23–28); and a central climactic pair of metaphors about the joy and newness of the kingdom (2:18–20, 21–22).

The Healing of the Paralytic (2:1–12 pars.). Although this account begins as yet another example of the healing miracles that chapter 1 highlighted, the real focus quickly turns to Jesus' claim to be able to forgive sins (v. 5). Jesus may have been playing off the conventional Jewish belief that sickness was often a punishment for sin, but he arrogates to himself divine authority in pronouncing the man forgiven. To the Jewish leaders, this borders on blasphemy. How can he back up his claim? It is always easier to say that someone is spiritually whole than to declare that person to be physically well because the latter is more quickly disproven. Therefore Jesus performs the harder task to corroborate the easier (vv. 9–12).

---

8. On which, see esp. R. T. France, "Mark and the Teaching of Jesus," in *Gospel Perspectives*, vol. 1, ed. R. T. France and David Wenham (Sheffield: JSOT, 1980), 101–36.

9. *Contra* the claim that the ancients could not tell the difference, and so attributed various physiological maladies to demon-possession when we know better. On the widespread recognition of the distinction in antiquity, see Edwin Yamauchi, "Magic or Miracle? Diseases, Demons, and Exorcisms," in *Gospel Perspectives*, vol. 6, pp. 89–183.

10. A somewhat weakly attested variant substitutes "enraged" for "had compassion" in v. 41. But the former is a less common trait attributed to Jesus and not as likely to be added by later scribes. It also fits in with Jesus' "strong warning" in v. 43.

11. "As a testimony to them" (v. 44) should perhaps even be translated "as a testimony *against* them" Cf. Mark 6:11 and 13:9, and see Edwin K. Broadhead, "Mk 1,44: The Witness of the Leper," *ZNW* 83 (1992): 257–65.

A Chiasmus
of Pronouncement Stories
Mark 2:1–3:6

A 2:1–12
Healing the
paralytic

A' 3:1–6
Healing
on Sabbath

B 2:13–17
Call of Levi/
Eating with
sinners

B' 2:23–28
Plucking grain
on Sabbath

C 2:18–22
Saying on fasting
and on old vs. new

The Call of Levi/Matthew (2:13–17 pars.). Here Jesus' crucial and controversial pronouncement likens his role to a physician's—calling not the spiritually healthy but the sick. His words, "I have not come to call the righteous, but sinners" (v. 17), are ambiguous on two counts. (1) Who are the sinners? Probably not just the *Am ha-aretz*, since Jesus himself is one of them, and the Pharisees could hardly object to his associating with his own kind. More likely these tax collectors epitomize the more notorious wayward in Jewish society because of their treachery in working for Rome. Not only does Jesus eat with such people, against all social taboos, but he accepts them as his followers without first requiring them to pass through a probationary period of penance.[12] (2) Who are the righteous? Presumably, the Jewish leaders. But is Jesus then speaking ironically? Perhaps, though it may be at this stage that Jesus is merely accepting their self-designation at face value for the sake of argument.[13] Matthew again adds a quotation of Scripture (Matt. 9:13; cf. Hos. 6:6), which does not depict an absolute dichotomy (mercy rather than sacrifice) but a statement of relative priorities (mercy much more than sacrifices; cf. Ps. 51:16–19). Luke distinctively adds one of his characteristic references to "repentance" (Luke 5:32).

The Question of Fasting (Mark 2:18–22 pars.). Again Jesus seems indirectly to link himself with God. He rejects the Pharisaic traditions of fasting twice weekly because it is time to celebrate a wedding feast, a common Jewish image for the messianic banquet. The bridegroom, an Old Testament metaphor for Yahweh (e.g., Isa. 61:10; 62:5; Jer. 2:2, 32), is here. But Jesus seems to be referring to himself! One day, though, he will be taken away (a veiled reference to the crucifixion?). Then fasting, as part of mourning, will be appropriate.[14] As the metaphors of the wine and wineskins demonstrate, a joyful new age has arrived demanding new ways and not just a patched-up Mosaic covenant. Matthew has sometimes been taken as disagreeing with this; he adds, "both (covenants?) are preserved" (Matt. 9:17). However, in context, "both" more naturally refers to both the new wine and the new wineskins. Luke adds a cryptic comment as well: "No one after drinking old wine wants the new, for he says, 'The old is better.'" (Luke 5:39). But this should probably be taken as an ironic lament over those who are rejecting Jesus' "new wine."

Sabbath Controversies (Mark 2:23–3:6 pars.). The final two pronouncement stories in this sequence challenge traditional Jewish understandings of the Sabbath. It is not clear that Jesus breaks any laws of Scripture, though he clearly violates the oral Torah. Reaping and threshing were two of the thirty-nine definitions of work forbidden on the Sabbath in the Mishnah (*Shabbat* 7:2). The Mishnah also forbade the healing on the Sabbath of an individual whose life was not in danger (*Yoma* 8:6). But Jesus not only cuts through all this casuistry, he claims to be "Lord of the Sabbath" (Mark 2:28), the one who can decide

---

12. On which, see esp. E. P. Sanders, *Jesus and Judaism* (London: SCM; Philadelphia: Fortress, 1985), 174–211.

13. Cf. R. T. France, *The Gospel according to Matthew* (Leicester: IVP; Grand Rapids: Eerdmans, 1985), 168: "*Righteous* is not entirely ironical: in their sense of the word they *were* 'righteous' (*cf.* Phil. 3:6), but it is precisely the adequacy of such righteousness that Jesus constantly calls in question."

14. Whether that "day" extends on throughout the Christian age is uncertain. Christian fasting appears only twice in the rest of the New Testament, both in contexts of seeking God's guidance for crucial ecclesiastical decisions (Acts 13:2–3; 14:23). Robert H. Gundry (*Mark: A Commentary on His Apology for the Cross* [Grand Rapids: Eerdmans, 1993], 133) comments, "Thus the statement does not point to an ongoing practice of fasting in the church, but centers on the person of Jesus."

how it now applies. And the precedent to which he appeals—David eating the sacred showbread (1 Sam. 21:1–6[15])—involves a case of breaking not just the oral but also the written Law. In Matthew's account, Jesus adds a statement that "one greater than the temple is here" (Matt. 12:6). In the case of the man with the shriveled hand, all three Gospels agree that Jesus believed it was right to "do good" on the Sabbath (Mark 3:4 pars.), and this could include a lot of what even the Old Testament called "work." So it would seem that Jesus was suggesting very far-reaching changes in how his followers were to observe the fourth commandment.[16] Matthew adds a pointed comparison between the Jews' willingness to rescue a sheep in danger, and their objecting to his healing a man (cf. Luke 13:10–17; 14:1–6).[17] Little wonder that, with Mark 3:6 and parallels, we reach a miniclimax of opposition to Christ early in his ministry.

The Formal Call of the Twelve (Mark 3:7–19/Luke 6:12–19) [Aland §48–49]

Following a transitional summary statement about Jesus' ministry thus far (Mark 3:7–12), Mark proceeds to narrate the formal call of the twelve men who would become Christ's closest followers (vv. 13–19). In Luke, the parallel statements immediately precede Christ's Sermon on the Plain. So, to the extent that we can identify a place to locate this sermon chronologically, it should probably be inserted here. But Mark betrays no knowledge of the sermon, and his thematic groupings make it convenient for us to continue following his narrative until the end of chapter 3 before discussing the Sermon. Matthew does not list the names of the Twelve until Jesus' later missionary discourse (Matt. 10), but there he makes it clear that they had already been gathered together for some time (v. 1). The number twelve is theologically significant. Just as twelve tribes of Israel constituted God's people at the institution of the Mosaic covenant, so now twelve disciples will form the foundation for God's people at the beginning of the new covenant. Here, among all those who follow Jesus, is the true or restored Israel.[18] The chart on page 239 gives a very brief synopsis of what we know about each of the Twelve. Much additional legendary material exists, but it is often very difficult to sift out the small portion that may be based on historical fact.[19] The chart summarizes what we can know, primarily from the Gospels.

---

15. On the famous "contradiction" between Abiathar in Mark 2:26 and Ahimelech in the 1 Samuel account, see John W. Wenham, "Mark 2.26," *JTS* n.s. 1 (1950): 156. Mark may be referring to the larger section of the scroll identified by the name of "Abiathar"; the identical Greek construction (*epi* with the genitive) is used in this exact way in Mark 12:26.

16. For a full-blown New Testament theology of the Sabbath, see D. A. Carson, ed., *From Sabbath to Lord's Day* (Grand Rapids: Zondervan, 1982). Sunday is *not* the Christian Sabbath (a day of rest on the *seventh* day of the week), but a day of worship and celebration of the resurrection on the *first* day of the week. More briefly, cf. Craig Blomberg, "The Sabbath as Fulfilled in Christ," in *The Sabbath in Jewish and Christian Traditions*, ed. Tamara C. Eskenazi, Daniel J. Harrington, and William H. Shea (New York: Crossroad; Denver: University of Denver, 1991), 122–28.

17. At Qumran, even helping an animal out of a well that it had fallen into on a Sabbath was forbidden (CD 11:13–14).

18. On which, see esp. Ben F. Meyer, *The Aims of Jesus* (London: SCM, 1979), 153–54, *et passim*.

19. The best source for this task is Edgar Hennecke, *New Testament Apocrypha*, ed. Wilhelm Schneemelcher, vol. 2 (London: Lutterworth; Philadelphia: Westminster, 1965), 35–74. Curiously, most of this information has been omitted or drastically abbreviated in the revised version (Cambridge: James Clarke; Louisville: Westminster/John Knox, 1992).

A Brief Sketch of Jesus' Twelve Disciples

Simon *(Simōn)* from Heb. for "hearing." Called **Peter** *(Petros)* or **Cephas** *(Kephas)*, meaning "rock" in Greek and Aramaic, respectively. Leader and frequent spokesman for the Twelve. Married and resided in Capernaum. Denied Jesus three times but was restored to fellowship (John 21). First leader of Jerusalem church following Pentecost in fulfillment of promises of Matt. 16:16–19. Both 1 and 2 Peter are attributed to him. Tradition claims that he was martyred under Nero in the 60s and crucified upside down.

Andrew *(Andreas)* from Gk. for "manliness." Brother of Peter; both were originally fishermen from Bethsaida and previously disciples of John the Baptist. He appears incidentally in Mark 13:3, John 6:8, and 12:22.

James *(Iakōbos)* from Heb. name "Jacob" (see Gen. 25:26 for its meaning). Another Galilean fisherman. Son of Zebedee, a relatively prosperous fisherman. One of the "Sons of Thunder" (Mark 3:17), possibly explaining his apparent vindictiveness in Luke 9:52–54 and selfishness in Mark 10:35–40. Mother was Salome; he was thus possibly Jesus' cousin. Executed by Herod Agrippa I not later than A.D. 44 (Acts 12:2). Probably therefore not the James who wrote the letter of James nor the leader of the Apostolic Council (Acts 15).

John *(Iōannēs)* from Heb. "the Lord is gracious." Brother of James. With James and Peter, part of the inner circle of three. Special relationship to Mary indicated in John 19:25–27. Peter's "right-hand man" throughout Acts. To him are attributed the Fourth Gospel, three epistles, and Revelation, the last of these while in exile on Patmos. Traditionally viewed as the "beloved disciple" of John 13:23–26; 19:25–27; 20:2–10; and 21:2, 20–23. Tradition also says he ministered in his old age to the church in Ephesus and was the only one of the Twelve not to die a martyr's death for his faith (though a minority tradition disputes this).

Philip *(Philippos)* from Gk. "horse lover." With Simon and Andrew, one of Jesus' first disciples (cf. John 1). From Bethsaida. Appears briefly in John 6:5–7; 12:21–22; and 14:8–9. Not to be confused with Philip the deacon in Acts 6 and 8.

Bartholomew *(Bartholomaios)* from Heb. "son of Talmai." Traditionally viewed as same person as Nathanael *(Nathanaēl)*, from Heb. "God has given"—Philip's companion in John 1—since always paired with Philip in Synoptic lists, and since Bartholomew not a given name but a patronymic.

Matthew *(Maththaios)* from same Heb. phrase as Nathanael. Called **Levi** in parallel passages, after the son of Jacob by that name. A converted tax collector. Traditionally identified as author of Gospel that bears his name. Jesus risked scandal in reaching out to him and his friends. Son of Alphaeus. Later legends describe his travel to Ethiopia and martyrdom there.

Thomas *(Thōmas)* from Heb. "twin." Became famous for doubting the resurrection of Jesus until he personally saw and touched him (John 20:24–29). But also revealed a fierce loyalty to Jesus, irrespective of the cost (John 11:16). Possibly reliable tradition associates him with the later evangelization of India.

James the less *(Iakōbos ho mikros)*. Alternately translated "James the younger." Son of (another?) Alphaeus or Cleopas. His mother, another Mary, was among the women at Jesus' tomb. Little else known.

Judas *(Ioudas)* from Heb. "Judah" ("praise"). Son of a Jacob (James). Also called Thaddaeus and, in some textual variants, Lebbaeus. Only recorded words appear in John 14:22. Little else known.

Simon the Zealot (or Caananite, from the Heb. for "Zealot"). Converted from the sect of Jewish revolutionaries that later rebelled against Rome and was defeated in A.D. 70.

Judas Iscariot *(Iskariōth)*. Infamous for betraying Jesus. Treasurer for the Twelve and a thief. Iscariot is usually interpreted as from Heb. for "man of Kerioth." Other options include a derivation from the word *sicarii* ("assassins")—a radical wing of the Zealot movement—or from "false one." Ended his life by hanging himself and falling from the rope so as to "burst his bowels asunder" (cf. Matt. 27 with Acts 1).

The Healing of the Centurion's Servant (Matt. 8:5–13; Luke 7:1–10; John 4:43–54?) [Aland §85]

One additional healing/pronouncement story occurs in Jesus' early Galilean ministry, apparently just after the Sermon on the Mount/Plain. It is not found in Mark, but it is natural to treat it here along with other episodes of like form from the same period in Christ's ministry. In both Matthew and Luke, Jesus heals from a distance the sick slave of a centurion from Capernaum. In Matthew, the man himself seems to come to request the healing, while in Luke he sends Jewish emissaries to plead on his behalf. The "contradiction" is more apparent than real, since ancient convention permitted one to speak of a person acting through his agents.[20] Matthew's polemic against the Jewish leaders gave him reason to employ this convention (see above, p. 132, and cf. Matt. 8:11–12, verses unique to Matthew's account). Luke is more willing to portray the Jews in a positive light, but primarily these spokesmen function to testify to the worthiness of this good Gentile. Thus Luke's account more clearly prefigures the coming Christian mission to the Gentiles. Indeed, this passage preserves striking parallels to the conversion of a later Gentile centurion, Cornelius (Acts 10). Both versions agree, however, that Jesus' authority is now demonstrated ever more greatly. He does not even have to be physically present with people in order to heal them.

In Matthew, this healing comes as the second in a series of three episodes in which Jesus cures those who were socially ostracized by orthodox Jews: a leper, the centurion, and a woman (Matt. 8:1–4, 5–13, 14–15). With his predilection for quoting the Old Testament, Matthew sees in all this a fulfillment of Isaiah 53:4: "He took up our infirmities and carried our diseases" (8:16–17). In the modern charismatic debate, this quotation has often been used to try to resolve the question of whether or not there is physical healing in the atonement. In context, it probably does not address the issue at all, but points out Jesus' concern to abolish categories of *ritual* uncleanliness.[21]

As noted earlier, John includes a very similar story about a royal official's son whom Jesus heals from a distance of a life-threatening fever (John 4:43–54). The language is vague enough at several points that this could be a variant of the story that Matthew and Luke record. John's *basilikos* could be a Gentile military officer. Matthew's *pais* could be a son as well as a servant, although Luke uses *doulos,* which normally just means a slave. But we do not have enough information to be sure. The two events may also be entirely separate. We must resist the temptation to think that we have anything like an exhaustive account of Jesus' ministry. The types of things the Gospels narrate are no doubt representative selections of many other similar incidents. John's point in narrating this particular story is to stress again that miraculous signs can and should produce faith, but that one ought not be dependent on them (cf. vv. 53 with 48, taking the latter as a cry of exasperation and noting that the man has to go away believing without seeing—v. 50; recall also above, p. 164).

---

20. Cf. our modern convention of reading in a newspaper, "The President announced today that. . .," when in fact the report was written by a speech writer and read by his press secretary.

21. Cf. David E. Garland, *Reading Matthew* (New York: Crossroad, 1993), 107.

Jesus' Family, Critics, and True Followers (Mark 3:20-35 pars.) [Aland §116-121]

The final segment of Mark 1–3 contrasts Jesus' disciples with his opponents. Here is the first of several places where Mark employs a sandwich-like (ABA) structure to compare and contrast two events. By breaking up one narrative into two parts and putting the second one in between, Mark invites the reader to view the two as closely linked in some way. Here the reactions of Jesus' family and relatives (3:20–21, 31–35) are sandwiched around the attacks by the Jewish leaders (vv. 22–30). We realize that even Jesus' biological kin do not understand him, although their hostility is a little less vicious than that of the Pharisees and scribes (cf. v. 21—"He is out of his mind"—with v. 30—"He has an evil spirit"). By way of contrast, his disciples, whether or not biologically related, form his true family as they do God's will (vv. 33–35). In a culture that valued family commitments above all other social obligations, Jesus' call did indeed prove radical and inflammatory.[22]

The scribes' slander (v. 22) remained a common Jewish explanation of who Jesus was, well into later centuries. The Talmud would insist that "Jesus the Nazarene practiced magic and led Israel astray" (b. Sanhedrin 43a, 107b). No record exists of ancient Jews attempting to deny Christ's miracle-working activity; they merely ascribed his power to the devil rather than to God. Jesus' reply to his original critics was twofold. First, their charge was self-contradictory. Satan does not work to destroy his own efforts; it is the Messiah who comes to bind Satan (vv. 23–27). Second, their charge was self-condemning. It was widely acknowledged that there were other Jewish exorcists with God-given powers;[23] would the Pharisees want to accuse all of them of being diabolically inspired (Matt. 12:27/Luke 11:19)? Indeed, such charges border on committing an unforgivable sin—"blasphemy against the Holy Spirit" (Mark 3:28–30).

This intriguing expression has caused needless consternation for countless Christians over the centuries. Could a true believer ever commit such a sin? It is important to keep this reference in context. Jesus' critics here are not his disciples but his most malicious, implacable opponents who would later nail him to the cross. In context, blasphemy against the Holy Spirit means the persistent equation of Christ's power with the demonic by those who refuse to believe him. All other sins—based on more ambiguous evidence—are forgivable (v. 28).[24] There is no evidence anywhere in Scripture that an individual who genuinely desires to repent and turn back to God is denied the opportunity. Indeed, the very consternation that causes some believers to wonder if they

---

22. See esp. Stephen C. Barton, *Discipleship and Family Ties in Mark and Matthew* (Cambridge: CUP, 1994), 67–96; cf. David M. May, "Mark 3:20–35 from the Perspective of Shame/Honor," *BTB* 17 (1987): 83–87.

23. Cf. further A. E. Harvey, *Jesus and the Constraints of History* (London: Duckworth; Philadelphia: Westminster, 1982), 98–119. On the other hand, Robert Shirock ("Whose Exorcists Are They? The Referents of οἱ υἱοὶ ὑμῶν at Matthew 12.27/Luke 11.19," [*JSNT* 46 (1992): 41–51]) makes a strong case that "your sons" refer to Jesus' disciples who will later judge Israel (Matt. 19:28 par.).

24. Notice the imperfect tense in v. 22 (lit., "they kept on saying"). Mark speaks of blasphemies "of men" being forgiven; Matthew and Luke, of blasphemies "against the Son of man." The latter probably reflects the ambiguous nature of this title (see below, pp. 405–407). Rejecting Christ when the evidence is less than crystal clear is always reversible as long as one lives. But without such a reversal, such rejection inevitably leads to spiritual death. With Robert A. Guelich, *Mark 1–8:26* (Dallas: Word, 1989), 185: "One commits the 'unpardonable sin,' therefore, by rejecting God's redemptive overture for humanity in Jesus Christ." But v. 28 "assures whoever seeks God's forgiveness that God's comprehensive amnesty includes all sins committed against others as well as against God."

have committed the unforgivable sin by definition demonstrates that they have not.[25]

Matthew and Luke go on to include in this context additional important teachings of Jesus. If he casts out demons not by Beelzebub but by God's Spirit, then this is a further sign of the presence of God's kingdom. Matthew 12:28/ Luke 11:20 is one of the clearest passages in the Gospels to support "realized eschatology"—the arrival of the kingdom, at least in part, with the person and work of Christ. Matthew 12:38–42/Luke 11:29–32 explains part of the reason the Jewish leaders misunderstand. They are looking for unequivocal signs susceptible to no misinterpretation. God never grants anything that conclusive; he refuses to coerce faith. The sign of the death and resurrection of Christ (analogous to the experience of the prophet Jonah) should be adequate.[26] Finally, it is not enough to expel evil; one must replace it with a positive good. Otherwise a greater number of demons may return (Matt. 12:43–45/Luke 11:24–26).

Historicity

That Jesus came announcing a partly present, partly future kingdom as the centerpiece of his message is widely acknowledged to be at the heart of what we can know about the historical Jesus. The "kingdom of God" is not an expression found in the Old Testament, but the concept of God as king is pervasive. After the Gospels, Christian writers preferred other expressions such as "eternal life" or "salvation" for their summaries of Jesus' proclamation. Jesus' inauspicious beginning in Nazareth is scarcely flattering—able to work few miracles and having to escape from the mob's death threats—and would not likely have been invented. His appeal to Isaiah 61:1 grounds his claims in the Jewish Scriptures, but his declaration to have fulfilled them was unparalleled. Yet later pious fiction would probably have placed more explicit titular claims on Jesus' lips.

Gathering disciples matches other Jewish testimony about Jesus' ministry (e.g., b. Sanhedrin 43a). But, as noted, unlike conventional rabbis, he called his followers rather than "receiving applicants." The number twelve, tying in with the twelve tribes of Israel, also grounds Jesus' behavior in the Judaism of his day, but it was not a number Christians felt had to be preserved after their initial replacement of Judas by Matthias (Acts 1:20–26). The inclusion of Judas, the arch-traitor, virtually guarantees the accuracy of the list; no one playing fast and loose with history would have kept such a villain among the inner core of Jesus' followers.

As already noticed, Jesus' exorcisms are attested to by non-Christian Jewish sources, yet they differ from others of his day by their simplicity and directness (see above, p. 234). Jesus does not even pray to his Father first, as his contem-

---

25. Cf. Larry Hurtado, *Mark* (Peabody: Hendrickson, 1989), 66: "A person doing such a thing would have no concern about Christ's forgiveness for it. So, the very anxiety lest one may have done something that cuts one off from Christ's forgiveness is, ironically, evidence that one believes Christ to be sent from God, and thus proof that one cannot have committed the sin warned against here."

26. Unlike Mark, the Q material has Jesus saying that no sign will be given "except the sign of Jonah"—Christ's death and resurrection—corresponding to Jonah's time in and out of the great fish (Matt. 12:39–40; Luke 11:29–30; cf. also Matt. 16:4). But this is not a material contradiction with Mark, since this kind of "sign" was precisely not the kind of sign requested. See further Jeffrey Gibson, "Jesus' Refusal to Produce a 'Sign' (Mk 8.11–13)," *JSNT* 38 (1990): 37–66.

porary Hanina ben Dosa was known to do. The apostles, on the other hand, exorcise "in Jesus' name" (e.g., Luke 10:17; Acts 16:18). The Gospels' exorcisms appear in multiple sources, including both Mark and Q, and multiple forms, including summary statements (e.g., Luke 8:1–3), other healings (e.g., Mark 9:14–29 pars.), and parables (Mark 3:27 pars.). The fact that the demons engage in spiritual warfare with Jesus and are not always instantly vanquished also speaks against Christian creation. The criterion of coherence, moreover, comes into play as the exorcisms are a key sign of the arrival of God's kingdom (Matt. 12:28 par.).[27]

That Jesus performed physical healings is also widely conceded, again as an important attestation of the kingdom's inauguration and of Jesus' identity (see esp. Matt. 11:4–6 par.), although debate remains over whether they were genuinely supernatural events or psychosomatic cures by the power of suggestion. Again, there is the distinctive directness by which a simple command effected a cure. There are three passages that involved the characteristic ancient use of spittle or mud (Mark 7:33; 8:23; John 9:6), and in one of these a two-stage healing potentially makes Jesus' powers appear deficient (Mark 8:23), so it, too, is not likely to have been fabricated. Several of the healings involve Jesus seemingly going out of his way to cause controversy—risking defilement by touching lepers, healing nonemergency maladies on the Sabbath, and favoring the outcasts as recipients of his miracle-working ministry (women, Samaritans, Gentiles, etc). These features, too, set him off from his contemporaries and were not widely imitated by his followers. (It was holiness, not uncleanness, that Jesus believed was "contagious"[28] —a difficult idea for most religions to accept, much less practice). The closest "parallels" in antiquity come from Philostratus' *Life of Apollonius* (on whom, see above, p. 32), but these seem to be too late to have influenced Gospel accounts of Jesus. Further support for the authenticity of Jesus' healing miracles comes from their appearance in multiple sources and forms, including later Christian testimony in Acts 10:38 and Hebrews 2:4, and from the brief remarks of the Jewish historian Josephus in *Antiquities* 18:63–64.[29]

Jesus' pronouncement stories offer a further example of material that passes the "dissimilarity test." All the debates are thoroughly conceivable within an early Jewish milieu, but in each case Jesus takes a radical perspective—claiming authority to forgive sins, dispensing with traditions about when to fast and with whom to feast, and challenging the prevailing Sabbath laws and the traditional ways of honoring one's biological family. Yet the Christology in the story of the healing of the paralytic is only implicit; no title save "Son of Man"

---

27. The most detailed defense of the historicity of the various exorcisms appears in Graham H. Twelftree, *Jesus the Exorcist* (Tübingen: Mohr; Peabody: Hendrickson, 1993).

28. See esp. Marcus Borg, *Conflict, Holiness, and Politics in the Teaching of Jesus* (New York and Toronto: Mellen, 1984).

29. Cf. further Craig L. Blomberg, "Healing," in *DJG*, 304–5. For considerable detail on the likelihood of Jesus' ministry of healing in general (though coupled with substantial skepticism about the details of several individual passages), see John P. Meier, *A Marginal Jew: Rethinking the Historical Jesus*, vol. 2 (New York and London: Doubleday, 1994), 617–45, 678–772. Meier nevertheless concludes: "Viewed globally, the tradition of Jesus' miracles is more firmly supported by the criteria of historicity than are a number of other well-known and often readily accepted traditions about his life and ministry. . . . Put dramatically but with not too much exaggeration: if the miracle tradition from Jesus' public ministry were to be rejected *in toto* as unhistorical, so should every other Gospel tradition about him" (p. 630).

is used. And the early church quickly reverted to more conservative practices concerning eating and not eating, Sabbath restrictions, and "family values," so again this material would not likely have been invented. Nor would charges of blasphemy against Christ!

Conclusion and Theological Distinctives

Despite the differences in where they place these various events, Matthew, Mark, and Luke all demonstrate widespread agreement about the types of things Jesus did early in his Galilean ministry: he called men and women to repent, gathered disciples, exorcised and healed, challenged conventional Jewish wisdom with the radical newness of the gospel, created a new family out of those who would follow him, and engendered considerable hostility among at least a handful of his nation's leaders. All of this demonstrated a new and vibrant presence of God's reign.

In addition, each evangelist has distinctive emphases of his own. *Mark* stresses the Messianic secret, Jesus' authority, and the radical newness of Jesus' ministry, and he places initial hostility with the Jewish leaders early in his narrative. *Matthew* heightens the focus on who Jesus is and on the requirements of discipleship, particularly by grouping key miracles of healing and related teachings into a two-chapter unit (Matt. 8–9). Together, this section combines with the sermon of chapters 5–7 to disclose Jesus' authority in both preaching/teaching and healing. The conflict stories are postponed until chapter 12 as Matthew portrays a more linear development of official Jewish hostility to Jesus. As throughout his Gospel, he also adds several examples of how various events have fulfilled Old Testament prophecy. *Luke* is less unrelentingly negative in his portrait of the Jewish leaders, stresses Christ's compassion for outcasts, and highlights his calls for repentance. Otherwise he follows Mark's sequence more closely than Matthew does.

THE SERMON ON THE MOUNT

As we noted above (p. 238), not too far along into his Galilean ministry, Jesus went up into the hill country to pray and formally call twelve of his disciples (Mark 3:13–19; Luke 6:12–16). Matthew reserves a list of the Twelve for a later stage in his narrative but knows that a small group of Jesus' followers were recognized as his "disciples" earlier on (Matt. 5:1). On this occasion, he taught those disciples, along with larger crowds thronging about the periphery, what has become his most famous sermon. It is the quintessential teaching of Jesus.

Matthew and Luke each include versions of the address (Matt. 5–7; Luke 6:20–49), though Matthew's is considerably longer. Each begins with beatitudes; moves on to teachings about love, especially for one's enemies; and ends with illustrations about the need to respond correctly to Jesus, including the parable of the wise and foolish builders. Luke has Jesus teaching on a level place (Luke 6:17), leading some to call Luke's version the Sermon on the Plain, and even to postulate that Jesus spoke two different addresses. But Luke knows that Jesus has been in the mountains (v. 12), and he would have stood on some small plateau in order to teach large crowds, so there is no necessary contradiction between the two Gospels, and no need to imagine two entirely separate discourses.

The standard, critical view of the relationship between Matthew's and Luke's sermons is that each writer has drawn a variety of teachings from Q to create the appearance of the one, unified discourse that now exists. Luke may have preserved an original core sermon from Q relatively intact, but Matthew has augmented it greatly. This idea is not inherently implausible or objectionable; something like it was suggested by Calvin centuries before the rise of modern biblical scholarship.[30] But it is no less plausible that Jesus spoke a discourse much longer than either Matthew or Luke has preserved and that each has excerpted from that original.[31] Given the complexity and uncertainty of Synoptic source-criticism, it is even conceivable that the origins of the canonical accounts combine something of both of these approaches.

History of Interpretation

The Sermon on the Mount has been a favorite of Christians over the centuries, and there have been a multitude of approaches to interpreting it; one recent survey counts no less than 36![32] This should come as no surprise, given the strenuous demands of Jesus' message, not least his summary that we are to be "perfect" as our "heavenly Father is perfect" (Matt. 5:48). We can probably simplify matters, however, and itemize eight major schools of thought that have dominated the history of Christian exegesis of the sermon.

Traditional Catholic. Medieval Catholicism solved the problem of the difficulty of Jesus' teachings by postulating two tiers of Christians. They argued that these more strenuous commands for righteousness need be implemented literally only by those in certain clerical or monastic orders. But the Sermon is addressed to all of Christ's disciples and to larger crowds, without any hint of such a division in its original setting.

Lutheran. Martin Luther read the Sermon much like he understood Paul's view of the Law. The Sermon was Law, not Gospel, meant to drive us to our knees in repentance for our inability to keep God's moral standards. By pointing out our need of grace and a Savior, it brings us back to Christ in contrition. But, again, the Sermon is not addressed first of all to those wanting to learn how to enter the kingdom but to those who had already expressed allegiance to Christ in some form.

Anabaptist. Many of the radical Reformers applied the Sermon's ethics in an extremely literal fashion to promote full-fledged pacifism in both personal and

---

30. John Calvin, *A Harmony of the Gospels Matthew, Mark, and Luke*, ed. David W. Torrance and Thomas F. Torrance, vol. 1 (Edinburgh: St. Andrew; Grand Rapids: Eerdmans, 1972 [Latin orig. 1555]), 168.

31. Cf. George A. Kennedy, *New Testament Interpretation through Rhetorical Criticism* (Chapel Hill: University of North Carolina Press, 1984), 67–69. Given that most of the places Luke has sermonic material not found in Mark, Luke is merely extending a series of teachings that are partially paralleled in Matthew, this hypothesis gains probability. E.g., Matthew has eight almost identically structured beatitudes (out of nine); Luke only four. But Luke has four contrasting woes. It is easy to imagine that there was an original sequence of eight matching beatitudes and woes, especially given a similar collection of six contrasting blessings and curses in 2 Enoch 52:11–12. The recently translated Dead Sea fragment, 4Q525, also contains a series of parallel beatitudes reminiscent of some of Jesus' teaching.

32. Clarence Bauman, *The Sermon on the Mount: The Modern Quest for Its Meaning* (Macon: Mercer, 1985).

civil arenas. The later Russian Christian writer Tolstoy promoted a similar perspective. But we will see that the historical background for Jesus' teaching is the environment of village life in Palestine under Roman occupation. Varying circumstances may require different practices. Further, Jesus is addressing his followers with standards for how they should live in community. It is not obvious that all his principles are directly transferrable to the state or government.

Old Liberal and Postmillennial. In the nineteenth century, there was great optimism about the possibility of Christianizing the earth—by both missionary work and the application of Christian principles to the laws of countries. Many believed the fullness of the kingdom would be ushered in prior to Christ's return through the efforts of Christians empowered by the Spirit. Then the ethics of the Sermon could be widely implemented. The numerous wars and genocides of the twentieth century have largely dispelled this optimism, though postmillennialism is making a comeback in certain pockets of Christianity today. A secular equivalent whose heyday seems to have passed has been Marxism.

Interim Ethic. At the turn of the century, Albert Schweitzer promoted his view that Christ thought the end would come within his lifetime. This gave his ethic a greater urgency than it now has, since we realize that world history may continue for centuries. But the texts which Schweitzer took as implying Christ mistakenly thought that the end was immediate (Mark 9:1 pars.; Mark 13:30 pars.; Matt. 10:23) probably do not imply that at all.[33]

Existentialist. Particularly through the writings of Rudolf Bultmann, a major twentieth-century movement has reinterpreted Jesus' kingdom ethics in terms of personal transformation that occurs when one embraces "authentic existence." This approach usually rejects finding any absolute ethics in the Sermon, but views them instead as a profound challenge to personal decision making in light of the consciousness of human finitude and divine encounter. We will see that there are places in the Sermon that dare not be absolutized, but existentialists have not developed a sufficiently convincing hermeneutic by which the entire Sermon may be "demythologized." More often than not, their thoroughgoing relativistic presuppositions are incompatible with historic Christianity.

Classic Dispensationalist. An older dispensationalist view often taught that the Sermon was part of Jesus' kingdom offer to the Jews. Had they accepted it, people would have lived by the ethics Jesus taught. Because they rejected it, the kingdom has been entirely postponed until the millennium, at which point the seemingly impossible ideals of the Sermon will be realized. But it is hard to maintain that these commands are only for a "golden age" of human morality, since they include provisions for responding to evil, persecution, hatred, and rejection. Not surprisingly, this view has been abandoned by "progressive dispensationalists" in the current theological scene.[34]

Kingdom Theology. A widespread consensus of current scholarship thus opts for an eighth view, given particular currency by the numerous writings of W. G. Kümmel and G. E. Ladd.[35] If the kingdom has been inaugurated (par-

33. See Craig Blomberg, *The Historical Reliability of the Gospels* (Leicester and Downers Grove: IVP, 1987), 33–34.

34. A title especially associated with a movement spearheaded by Craig A. Blaising and Darrell L. Bock, and reflected in their *Progressive Dispensationalism* (Wheaton: Victor, 1993).

35. See esp. Werner G. Kümmel, *Promise and Fulfillment: The Eschatological Message of Jesus* (London: SCM; Naperville, Ill.: Allenson, 1957); and George E. Ladd, *The Presence of the Future* (Grand Rapids: Eerdmans, 1974; London: SPCK, 1980). For an important, brief statement of the perspective, see Robert A. Guelich, "The Matthean Beatitudes: 'Entrance Requirements' or Eschatological Blessings?" *JBL* 95 (1976): 415–34.

tially present now but only fully to be realized after Christ's return—see above, p. 233), then it seems best to assume that Jesus' ethics are also meant for believers now. But we must admit that they are only partially realizable in the present age, even though they remain the ideal for which we all should strive, as we yield ourselves to the Spirit. This is not a "works-righteousness" by which we become Christ's disciples, but a "fruit befitting repentance" whereby we demonstrate our continuing allegiance to him.

There is no doubt an element of truth in every one of the perspectives surveyed, but we believe this last one to have captured the correct approach most fully. What is more, while Jesus' ethics clearly apply to individual lives, and while Christians ought to use all legal means in whatever societies they find themselves to promote their ethics in the public arena, Jesus' sermon is not addressed first of all either to the individual or to the state but to the *community* of his followers. As the church of Jesus Christ, corporately, in local communities, learns increasingly to follow his ethics, his will is implemented on earth and men and women are drawn to the faith.[36]

Contents and Exegesis of Matthew 5–7

Matthew's Sermon on the Mount is carefully structured, with a pattern of grouping Jesus' teachings into units of three or multiples of three items. The nine beatitudes plus the salt and light sayings form the introduction (5:3–16). The thesis paragraph follows: Jesus demands a "greater righteousness" (5:17–20). Six illustrations of this ensue, contrasting the Law with his ethic (5:21–48). Three examples of not parading one's piety come next (6:1–18). Then follow three teachings about wealth and worry (6:19–34), followed by three sections on how to treat others (7:1–12), including the Golden Rule as the climax of the body of the Sermon (v. 12). The conclusion of Jesus' classic message uses three illustrations to focus on the only two options open by way of response: acceptance or rejection (7:13–27).[37] Interestingly, there are parallels to almost every saying of Jesus in the Sermon elsewhere in Jewish writing.[38] But the cumulative effect of Jesus' teachings and the context of the arrival of the kingdom into which they are set makes them stand out as radically different (cf. 7:28–29).

The Beatitudes (5:3–12) [Aland §51]. Jesus opens his Sermon with "kingdom blessings" (vv. 3, 10). The Greek word *makarios* means blessed, fortunate, or "to be congratulated."[39] The tenses of the verbs are mostly future, but the first and eighth beatitudes give present tense blessings—"theirs is the kingdom." So we are reminded of the partially present realization of these blessings, coupled with their full manifestation in the age to come.

The first kind of person to be considered blessed is "the poor in spirit" (v. 3). Luke's parallel refers merely to the "poor" (Luke 6:20). Many have viewed this

---

36. See esp. Richard Lischer, "The Sermon on the Mount as Radical Pastoral Care," *Interpretation* 41 (1987): 157–69; James L. Bailey, "Sermon on the Mount: Model for Community," *Currents in Theology and Mission* 20 (1993): 85–94. Cf. also Craig L. Blomberg, "How the Church Can Turn the Other Cheek and Still Be Political," *Southern Baptist Public Affairs* 3.1 (1990): 10–12.

37. This outline is heavily indebted to Dale C. Allison, Jr., "The Structure of the Sermon on the Mount," *JBL* 106 (1987): 423–45.

38. For a detailed compilation, see Dennis Stoutenburg, *With One Voice/B'Qol Echad: The Sermon on the Mount and Rabbinic Literature* (Bethesda, Md. and London: International Scholars Publications, 1996).

39. France, *Matthew*, 108.

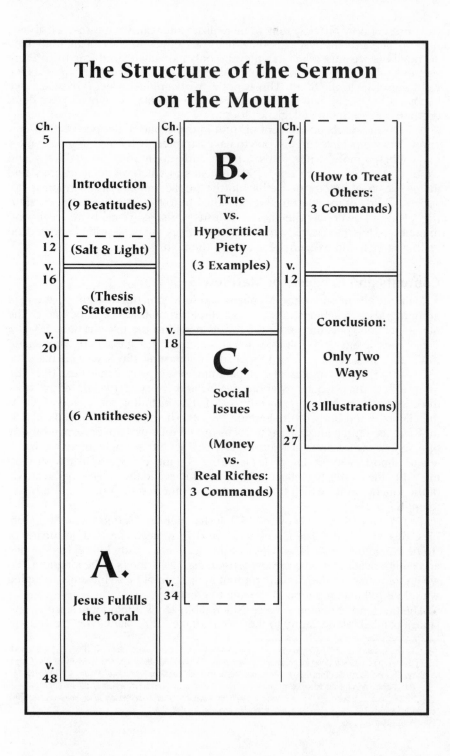

as an outright contradiction between the Gospels. But the probable Hebrew behind the Greek word for poor (*ptōchoi*) is *anawim* , which increasingly in the latter part of the Old Testament came to be used for the materially oppressed or impoverished within Israel who recognized that God was their only hope or refuge (as, e.g., in Isa. 61:1). Although Luke is more interested in the social dimension (see above, p. 147, he recognizes a spiritual side to the oppression as well (6:22–23). So it is best to understand both evangelists' beatitudes as congratulating "those who because of sustained economic privation and social distress have confidence only in God."[40]

This two-pronged focus then runs right through the rest of the beatitudes. Those who mourn may be repenting of sin or lamenting the lack of implementation of God's righteous standards on earth. The meek can be the spiritually humble or the physically oppressed. The righteousness for which we must hunger and thirst is both spiritual and social, and so on.[41] The composite portrait of a follower of Jesus is a stark inversion of what the Greco-Roman world considered admirable. To borrow a term from contemporary Hispanic culture, blessed are all those who are not "macho"!

Metaphors of Salt and Light (5:13–16) [Aland §52–53]. Values as countercultural as those expressed in the beatitudes might suggest to some that Jesus was promoting monasticism. Verses 13–16 dispel that notion. Jesus' disciples must remain effective change agents within the world. Of all the images salt evoked in ancient society, most relevant to this context is its role in arresting corruption and decay. Light, in a world without electricity, was all the more valuable a commodity for illuminating one's way and giving guidance.

Jesus and the Law (5:17–48) [Aland §54–59]. The combination of Jesus' countercultural beatitudes and his commands to model those values within society could easily have led his listeners to question whether he was overthrowing the Law of Moses. Verses 17–20 introduce the body of the Sermon and answer this question in a nutshell. Jesus has not come to abolish the Old Testament. But neither is he preserving all things unchanged. In "fulfilling" the Law, he is bringing to completion all that to which it pointed (v. 18b—"until everything is accomplished"). The later New Testament church would come to the conclusion that major aspects of the Law no longer needed to be literally practiced—for example, the sacrifices. But that is because they are obeyed by Christians when they turn to Jesus, the ultimate sacrifice. Every Old Testament commandment must today be filtered through a grid of fulfillment in Christ to see how its application may have changed.[42] Kingdom standards actually

---

40. D. A. Carson, "Matthew," in *Expositor's Bible Commentary*, ed. Frank E. Gaebelein, vol. 8 (Grand Rapids: Zondervan, 1984), 131. Cf. also Frederick D. Bruner (*The Christbook* [Waco: Word, 1987], 135): "If we say that 'blessed are the poor in spirit' means 'blessed are the rich, too, if they act humbly,' we have spiritualized the text. On the other hand, if we say that 'blessed are the poor' means 'poor people are happy people,' we have secularized the text. . . . Jesus said something incorporating both Matthew's spirituality and Luke's sociality, with the best of each."

41. For a detailed exposition balancing the spiritual and social dimensions of these texts, see Michael H. Crosby, *Spirituality of the Beatitudes: Matthew's Challenge for First World Christians* (Maryknoll: Orbis, 1981).

42. We must avoid two often-held extremes that the text does not justify. One argues that all Old Testament teaching not rescinded in the New Testament is still in force. The other argues that all Old Testament teaching not reaffirmed in the New Testament is no longer in force. 2 Tim. 3:16 requires us to argue that *every* Old Testament law is somehow still relevant for Christians. But *none* of it can be applied until we understand how it has been fulfilled in Christ. See esp. John P. Meier, *Law and History in Matthew's Gospel* (Rome: BIP, 1976). Cf. Robert Banks, "Matthew's Understanding of the Law: Authenticity and Interpretation in Matthew 5:17–20," *JBL* 93 (1974): 226–42.

demand a greater righteousness than that practiced by the Jewish leaders (v. 20), but Jesus also supplies a greater empowerment (cf. Matt. 11:28–30).

Verses 21–48 are known as the six "antitheses." They provide illustrations of Jesus' relationship to various laws by contrasting traditional Jewish interpretations with Jesus' understanding of their significance. Three of the antitheses seem to intensify and internalize the Law's demands (vv. 21–26, 27–30, 43–47), but the other three seem to revoke certain portions of the Torah (vv. 31–32, 33–37, 38–42). The unifying feature of all six is that Jesus shows himself to be the Law's sovereign interpreter, explaining how it applies in the new age he is inaugurating.[43] It is also possible to divide five of the six antitheses (excepting vv. 31–32) not just into two parts but into three: the old prohibitions in the Law that are no longer adequate; Jesus' new set of prohibitions; and positive practices to implement the principles behind the prohibitions.[44]

First, Jesus condemns not only murder but hatred and abusive language. One must instead take positive steps to be reconciled with one's adversary (vv. 21–26). Second, not only is adultery sinful but so is lust. Disciples must take drastic action to remove themselves from situations that would nurture it (vv. 27–30).[45] Third, Jesus takes a more stringent stand on divorce (for details here, see below, pp. 305–307). Fourth, he condemns oath-taking and commands them to be people of unswerving integrity (vv. 33–37). Fifth, he abolishes the *lex talionis* (the Mosaic "law of retaliation") in favor of doing good to one's opponents (vv. 38–42). Finally, he commends loving one's enemy (vv. 43–47). No Old Testament text ever says to hate them, but, given God's commands to exterminate some of them, it was undoubtedly a natural inference for many! The culmination of all of this is the command to be perfect (v. 48). The word here (Greek, *teleios*) is perhaps better translated "mature" or "complete." The Lukan parallel employs synecdoche (a part for the whole) to highlight one key component of this maturity—showing mercy (Luke 6:36).

Throughout Matthew 5:33–42, we find a series of commands, all of which are "contradicted" elsewhere in the New Testament. This is a tip-off that these are not to be absolutized but to be understood in their historical context.[46] Jesus does not abolish all oaths (cf. Gal. 1:20; 2 Cor. 1:23) but condemns the Pharisaic casuistry that permitted oaths in the name of certain sacred objects to be less binding than oaths that directly invoked God's name. Jesus clearly resists evil with his exorcisms, but *anthistēmi* ("resist"—v. 39) often meant to resist in a legal context or to resist with violence.[47] "Turning the other cheek" is not a call to allow oneself or one's loved ones bodily injury. The backhanded slap across the cheek was a characteristic Jewish insult to one's "inferior." Jesus calls us to allow insults without feeling compelled to trade them

---

43. For this understanding and a survey of competing interpretations, see Douglas J. Moo, "Jesus and the Authority of the Mosaic Law," *JSNT* 20 (1984): 3–49. Cf. idem, "Law," in *DJG*, 450–61.

44. Glen H. Stassen, "Grace and Deliverance in the Sermon on the Mount," *Review and Expositor* 89 (1992): 234–35.

45. Vv. 29–30 form an excellent example of hyperbole or rhetorical exaggeration. They cannot be intended literally; a blind or maimed person can still lust! Cf. the helpful comments of John R. W. Stott, *The Message of the Sermon on the Mount* (Leicester and Downers Grove, IVP, 1978), 89.

46. Particularly helpful in this regard is Richard A. Horsley, "Ethics and Exegesis: 'Love Your Enemies' and the Doctrine of Non-Violence," *JAAR* 54 (1986): 3–31.

47. Provocatively developing an entire social ethic from the latter interpretation is Walter Wink, "Jesus and the Nonviolent Struggle of Our Time," *Louvain Studies* 18 (1993): 3–20.

(cf. Rom. 12:14). Giving one's cloak was an action of offering collateral in a law court; going the extra mile meant being conscripted by Roman soldiers to carry their equipment. Jesus tells his listeners to give freely to the one who asks to borrow from them (v. 42; cf. Luke 6:30, 34) because lenders were more reluctant to give loans just before the Jubilee year when all debts were to be forgiven. Jesus' ethics remain radical, but they must be implemented intelligently. The examples in these verses take the form of "focal instances"—extreme commands that attract our attention to a key ethical theme that must be variously applied as circumstances change.[48]

The final antithesis, on enemy love, is arguably the single most distinctive portion of all of Jesus' ethic. This observation dovetails with Jesus' words that if we do not obey him on this count we are no better than the pagans (v. 47). With his reference to perfection following immediately (v. 48), he may also be hinting that loving one's enemies is the clearest mark of Christian maturity. Romans 12:17–21 echoes these words in a context that also gives the state the right to wield the sword (13:4), so it is not obvious that a full-blown doctrine of pacifism can be derived from the Sermon. But, on a personal level, revenge is clearly excluded.

Religious Hypocrisy (6:1–18) [Aland §60–63]. Having stressed in the antitheses that righteousness is not merely external, Jesus now goes on to address the right motives for outward acts of piety. Three examples—almsgiving, prayer, and fasting—all illustrate the same principle: good deeds are not to be done for human praise (6:1). In 5:16 the disciples were told to perform their good deeds in public but so that others might praise the Father. In the context of the second of the three illustrations Jesus adds what has come to be known as the Lord's Prayer (6:9–13), though it might better have been entitled the Model Prayer or the Disciples' Prayer, since it is one prayer Jesus never prayed nor could have ("forgive us our trespasses").[49]

The prayer is carefully structured. The first half focuses on God's desires; the second half, on human needs. The first half also balances God's intimacy with his sovereignty. Jesus' distinctive use of *Abba* (the Aramaic near equivalent of "daddy") for Father (Mark 14:36) probably lies behind the opening clause of the Lord's Prayer. But God is also the heavenly Father whose reign must advance and whose will must be accomplished. The second half of the prayer balances the believer's material needs (daily bread) with his or her spiritual needs (forgiveness of sin and protection from evil). "Lead us not into temptation" is a misleading translation, since God tempts no one (James 1:13). Probably the sense is "do not let us succumb to temptation."[50] The traditional

---

48. Robert C. Tannehill, "The 'Focal Instance' as a Form of New Testament Speech: A Study of Matthew 5:39b–42," *Journal of Religion* 50 (1970): 372–85.

49. Although he could have confessed the corporate sins of Israel. For an excellent treatment of the prayer overall, see Jan M. Lochman, *The Lord's Prayer* (Grand Rapids: Eerdmans, 1990).

50. Cf. W. D. Davies and Dale C. Allison, Jr., *A Critical and Exegetical Commentary on the Gospel according to St. Matthew*, vol. 1 (Edinburgh: T & T Clark, 1988), 612–13. Another option is to translate it, "Do not bring us to the test." This is sometimes tied in with a view that sees the entire second half of the prayer focused on ushering in the end of human history. This view includes translating v. 11 as "Give us today our bread *for tomorrow*," i.e., for the messianic age. But the best lexical evidence is against this translation, and God uses tests for purifying value. Kenneth Grayston ("The Decline of Temptation—and the Lord's Prayer," *SJT* 46 [1993]: 294) offers the intriguing alternative, "Lead us not into a situation where we engage in *provocation*, where we find the hardships so intolerable that we are forced into provocation and into trying your patience."

Matthew 5:33–48
Oaths, Retaliation, and Loving One's Enemies

Jesus' Command	Counterexamples	Historical Background	Church Application
don't swear (take oaths) (v. 34)	Paul uses God's name to assure truth of his claims (Gal. 1:20; 2 Cor. 1:23)	Pharisees got off hook if they swore by something other than God	be so trustworthy and straight-forward that your word can be taken at face value
don't resist evil (v. 39)	exorcisms (Gospels, Acts) spiritual warfare (Eph. 6)	"resist" was legal term; thus don't take to court	believers shouldn't sue other believers (1 Cor. 6)
turn the other cheek (v. 39)	Jesus withdraws from hostility (Matt. 12:15; 14:13)	backhand slap was a typical Jewish insult	allow an insult without retaliation (Rom. 12:14)
give your cloak (v. 40)	those who have nothing to give away (Matt. 10)	collateral in legal proceedings was clothing	be more generous by doing more than just what you are asked/required to do
go the extra mile (v. 41)	the need for rest (Mk. 6:31)	helping Roman soldiers carry equipment on forced marches (conscription)	same as above
give to the one who asks to borrow (v. 42)	don't give pearls to swine (Matt. 7:6)	reluctance to give loans when near to Jubilee	choose wisely how you give but then don't begrudge lack of repayment
love your enemies (v. 44)	hate sin (Rev. 2:6; Jude 23) resist the devil (1 Peter 5:9)	no personal vengeance; leave justice to the law	use due process to air grievances; seek the best interest of those you don't like

ending ("for yours is the kingdom") is not in the oldest and most reliable manuscripts and is probably the pious addition of a later scribe who wanted to give the prayer a "proper" conclusion. It may be based on 1 Chronicles 29:11–13.

Matthew 6:7–8 encourage the disciples to use this prayer to distinguish themselves from the heathen, not just to repeat it thoughtlessly like a magical formula. Ironically, some in the history of the church have done just that, while others have overreacted by refusing ever to pray it! It remains a superb model, but it can become meaningless if used mechanically. The concepts, not the exact wording, are what matter the most.

Wealth and Worry (6:19–34) [Aland §64–67]. The rationale for the sequence of the next two sections of the Sermon is less clear. One influential approach has seen them as unpacking the petitions of the second half of the Lord's Prayer, but the parallels are not consistently close. More likely, the transition is that even when a person's behavior and attitudes are correct, the greater righteousness demanded of disciples is not present unless God and not money is served. Verses 19–21 command us not to accumulate too many possessions—a sure sign that our treasure is on earth and not in heaven. Verses 22–24 stress how decision making in this arena affects all of life. One either serves material possessions ("mammon") or God. Verses 25–34 repeatedly command us not to worry about material needs; God will take care of us. Here is where it is crucial to understand the community focus of the Sermon. Taken as an individual promise, verse 33 is patently false; committed believers have frequently starved to death. But to the extent that God's people as a whole (the verbs are second person *plural* commands) seek God's righteous standards, they will by definition share their surplus with the needy in their midst. Luke's parallel to this verse (Luke 12:31) confirms this interpretation, as it is embedded in a context that commands believers to sell their possessions and give to the poor (v. 33).[51]

How to Treat Others (7:1–12) [Aland §68–71]. The final triad in the body of the Sermon groups together commands about social behavior. Disciples must not be judgmental or censorious (vv. 1–5a), but they must make discerning judgments about the behavior of others (vv. 5b–6). They must pray boldly and persistently for their needs and expect God to answer them (vv. 7–11). Still, Jesus presupposes that we remember the clause from the Lord's Prayer, "your will be done" (6:10). Moreover, God gives only good gifts (7:11), and unfortunately our perspective on what is truly good is often quite warped. Finally, Christ brings the body of the Sermon to a close with an epitome that captures the heart of his ethic: the so-called Golden Rule (v. 12). It is often pointed out that many other Jewish teachers, along with a few from other religions, taught much the same thing, but most of them phrased it negatively—in essence, "Don't treat others the way you wouldn't want to be treated." Jesus is the only

---

51. Cf. Robert A. Guelich, *The Sermon on the Mount: A Foundation for Understanding* (Waco: Word, 1982), 373: "Part of the presence of the Kingdom is indeed material blessings. Therefore, we can hardly live under God's reign, receive his blessings, and not use them to help alleviate the evil of hunger and need elsewhere." On vv. 19–34 more generally, see also Craig L. Blomberg, "On Wealth and Worry: Matt. 6:19–34—Meaning and Significance," *Criswell Theological Review* 6 (1992): 73–89.

person to state the principle in this emphatically positive form.[52] Taking the initiative in doing good is always more challenging than simply avoiding evil.

Conclusion: Only Two Ways (7:13–27) [Aland §72–75]. Jesus' vintage Sermon concludes with three illustrations that all make the same point. Ultimately, there are only two options—to be for Jesus or against him. He hopes we will all hear, obey, and follow. The narrow vs. the wide gate (vv. 13–14) reminds would-be disciples that the road may be fraught with difficulty. The good vs. the bad tree (vv. 15–20) calls on disciples to demonstrate their genuineness by producing proper fruit. As noted above (p. 132), Matthew may have been combating false teachers in his own midst. Clearly, some of those who prove false are nevertheless involved in ministry—preaching, exorcising, or performing miracles. Verses 21–23 make it clear that they have been masquerading, as Jesus declares, "I never knew you" (v. 23). Finally, the wise vs. the foolish builder calls on us to establish a secure foundation by not only hearing but also obeying Jesus' teaching. Many have admired the ethics of the Sermon on the Mount without accepting Jesus' personal claims on their lives (in this century, most notably Mohandas Gandhi), but Christ does not consider that option acceptable.

The Crowd's Reaction (7:28–29) [Aland §76]. Jesus' words elicit amazement because of their unique authority. It is not that the Jewish leaders did not have immense power. But their teaching always had to be grounded in Scripture or in the teaching of previous rabbis. In this sermon, Jesus cites no one to corroborate his views, and he quotes Scripture only to reinterpret it dramatically. Such brashness borders on lunacy unless it reflects a divine mandate.

The Sermon on the Plain (Luke 6:20–49) [Aland §78–83]

Almost all of the teaching in Luke's abbreviated sermon has appeared in Matthew's longer version or is parallel in form to what does appear (extra beatitudes, contrasting woes, etc.). Luke's account is equally carefully structured and divides naturally into three parts: (1) introductory blessings and warnings (vv. 20–26); (2) central teachings about loving one's enemies (vv. 27–36); and (3) three concluding illustrations of an appropriate response to Jesus—rejecting judgmentalism, bearing good fruit, and building wisely (vv. 37–49). Luke, as a Gentile writing to Gentile Christians, understandably omits all of Matthew's material contrasting Jesus' teaching with the Law and challenging the behavior of the Jewish leaders. What remains, however, focuses all the more pointedly on that most distinctive aspect of Jesus' ethic—enemy love.[53] Plus, as noted above, Luke has considerably more interest in the socioeconomic plight of people in this life.

---

52. For a list of twelve of the most commonly cited parallels, see Bock, *Luke 1:1–9:50*, 596–97. Most well known of all is Hillel's so-called Silver Rule (clearly not a Jewish designation!): "What is hateful to you, do not do to your neighbor; that is the whole Torah, while the rest is commentary" (*b. Shabbat* 31a).

53. On this theme, see esp. John Piper, *"Love Your Enemies": Jesus' Love Command in the Synoptic Gospels and in Early Christian Paraenesis* (Cambridge: CUP, 1979).

Historicity

Just about every major theme in Jesus' great sermon passes the "dissimilarity" test. The "ethical perfectionism" outlined here goes beyond that which any religious tradition could be expected to follow—or invent! Jesus blesses the poor, while many in Judaism saw the rich as blessed. The beatitude form was common in Judaism, but Jesus' exaltation of the humiliated was uncommon in any ancient religion. The sayings about disciples as salt and light fit Jesus' characteristic use of metaphor. His transcendence of the Law—fulfilling yet not abolishing it—walks a tightrope rarely maneuvered successfully in Judaism or Christianity.[54] The hyperboles of the antitheses create strenuous commands indeed; yet we have seen that their meanings are clarified once one recognizes the distinctive background of a Palestinian village setting. Nonretaliation and enemy love are among the least paralleled teachings, even in Judaism. The Lord's Prayer echoes Jewish sentiment in almost every clause, yet it creates a distinct package with its "Abba"-intimacy and kingdom theology. Jesus' words on stewardship and judgmentalism are also too demanding for later Christians to have readily created them. The Golden Rule finds numerous parallels, but, as noted, most of them are phrased negatively. The concluding "two ways" section follows an established Jewish form of writing but with a distinct christological focus. Little wonder the crowds marveled at Jesus' unique authority!

FOR FURTHER STUDY

Healings, Controversies, Discipleship, and Opposition

Carson, D. A. *When Jesus Confronts the World: An Exposition of Matthew 8–10.* Grand Rapids: Baker, 1987; Leicester: IVP, 1988.

Dewey, Joanna. *Markan Public Debate.* Chico: Scholars, 1980.

Hultgren, Arland J. *Jesus and His Adversaries: The Form and Function of the Conflict Stories in the Synoptic Tradition.* Minneapolis: Augsburg, 1979.

Kümmel, Werner G. *Promise and Fulfillment: The Eschatological Message of Jesus.* London: SCM; Naperville, Ill.: Allenson, 1957.

Kuthirakkattel, Scaria. *The Beginning of Jesus' Ministry according to Mark's Gospel (1,14–3,6).* Rome: BIP, 1990.

Ladd, George E. *The Presence of the Future.* Grand Rapids: Eerdmans, 1974; London: SPCK, 1980.

Mack, Burton L., and Vernon K. Robbins. *Patterns of Persuasion in the Gospels.* Sonoma, Calif.: Polebridge, 1989.

Sloan, Robert B., Jr. *The Favorable Year of the Lord.* Austin: Schola, 1977.

Twelftree, Graham H. *Jesus the Exorcist.* Tübingen: Mohr; Peabody: Hendrickson, 1993.

---

54. To be sure, a typical "tradition history" of the Sermon has postulated conflicting tendencies represented here and throughout: a radical Jesus toned down and "re-Judaized" by early Jewish Christianity. See esp. Hans Dieter Betz, *Essays on the Sermon on the Mount* (Philadelphia: Fortress, 1985). But Matthew as redactor did not find these tendencies contradictory, or he would have eliminated at least one of them. So there is no reason not to ascribe the balance to Jesus himself, in light of the resulting double dissimilarity.

The Sermon on the Mount

Introductory

Carson, D. A. *The Sermon on the Mount*. Grand Rapids: Baker, 1978; Carlisle: Paternoster, 1994.

Carter, Warren. *What Are They Saying about Matthew's Sermon on the Mount?* New York: Paulist, 1994.

Dockery, David S., and David E. Garland. *Seeking the Kingdom: The Sermon on the Mount Made Practical for Today*. Wheaton: Harold Shaw, 1992.

Stott, John R. W. *The Message of the Sermon on the Mount*. Leicester and Downers Grove: IVP, 1978.

Intermediate

Guelich, Robert A. *The Sermon on the Mount: A Foundation for Understanding*. Waco: Word, 1982.

Lapide, Pinchas. *The Sermon on the Mount: Utopia or Program for Action?* Maryknoll: Orbis, 1986.

Strecker, Georg. *The Sermon on the Mount: An Exegetical Commentary*. Nashville: Abingdon, 1988.

Advanced

Betz, Hans Dieter. *The Sermon on the Mount*. [Hermeneia] Minneapolis: Fortress, 1995.

Davies, W. D. *The Setting of the Sermon on the Mount*. Cambridge: CUP, 1964.

Bibliography

Kissinger, Warren S. *The Sermon on the Mount: A History of Interpretation and Bibliography*. Metuchen, N.J.: Scarecrow, 1975.

QUESTIONS FOR REVIEW

1. According to Mark, what kinds of activity occupied the earlier stages of Jesus' Galilean ministry? How does he summarize the heart of Jesus' message?

2. What does the "kingdom of God" mean?

3. What are we to learn about Jesus through his exorcisms of demon-possessed people? from other miracles of healing?

4. What is a pronouncement story? What else is it called? How does understanding this form help us in interpreting the stories in Mark 2:1–3:6 and elsewhere?

5. Why did Jesus call a special group of twelve disciples? What was unique about their calling?

6. What is the preferred approach to interpreting the Sermon on the Mount adopted in this book? Why is this one preferred? What difference does it make?

7. Identify several of the exegetical highlights of the Sermon. What issues would you most want to explain to the type of people among whom you typically live and work if you were teaching a series of studies on this Sermon? What would you stress and why?

8. What relationship between Jesus and the Law is disclosed in 5:17–20 and the following antitheses (vv. 21–42)? How are we most probably to understand the seemingly impossible demands of the second half of these (vv. 33–42)?

CHAPTER FOURTEEN

JESUS' GALILEAN MINISTRY—
Later Stages

T he Synoptic Gospels all continue to arrange their material topically, and
so will we. Mark resumes his narrative with a group of Jesus' parables
(4:1–34) followed by a series of some of his more spectacular miracles
(4:35–6:6; 6:30–56). The sending of the Twelve (6:7–13) will be discussed later
(below, pp. 285–286) and the death of John the Baptist (6:14–29) has already
been treated (above, pp. 219–220). In 7:1–9:50, Jesus withdraws from Galilee,
both in spirit (by offering his most scathing critique of the Jewish traditions thus
far) and in reality (by traveling to the north and to the east). Only brief periods
of return to Galilee intervene before he begins his climactic journey to Jerusalem. This chapter thus falls naturally into three parts: Jesus' parables, his miracles, and his withdrawal from Galilee. The last of these sections will also treat
his final days of ministry in Galilee before he embarks on the road to the cross.

PARABLES

Interpretive Method

A parable is a brief metaphorical narrative. The Greek *parabolē* comes from
two words that mean "to throw alongside," alluding to the symbolic or analogical nature of a parable. It is a story with two levels of meaning. *Parabolē*, like
its Hebrew equivalent, *māshāl*, could refer to a wide variety of forms, including
proverbs, allegories, prophetic discourses, and enigmatic sayings. Throughout
most of the history of the church, Christians treated the parables of Jesus as
detailed allegories. The most famous example was Augustine's treatment of the
good Samaritan (Luke 10:30–35) as a story about Adam who left the heavenly

city and was attacked by Satan. The Law and the Prophets were unable to save him, but Christ, the Samaritan, did rescue him, taking him to the church for safekeeping until he should return. Such interpretation, however, entirely neglects the point of the story as an answer to the question of the lawyer, "Who is my neighbor?" (vv. 25–29, 36–37).

At the end of the nineteenth century, Adolf Jülicher produced a voluminous work sounding the death knell to this type of interpretation.[1] Pointing out the inconsistencies and absurdities of the competing allegorical interpretations of virtually every parable of Jesus, Jülicher argued that each parable made only one main point and that details within the parables were not to be allegorized. They are merely lifelike reflections of first-century Palestine used in service of the overall point of a story. Thus the good Samaritan is simply an example of compassionate behavior for the needy that we should imitate (v. 37). Most twentieth-century interpretation has followed Jülicher and has stressed that the purpose of Jesus' parables is to illustrate truths about God's kingdom. Thus a lot of ink has been spilled over the question of whether the parables demonstrate God's kingly reign to be primarily future, primarily present, or some of each. The last of these options reflects the consensus that has emerged, particularly through the influential work of Joachim Jeremias.[2]

The most recent phase of research has stressed literary and structural analyses of the parables. Jesus' stories are no mere illustrations but "weapons of warfare." They draw people into a seemingly innocuous story only to confront them with the demands of discipleship in ways that subvert conventional religious tradition and expectation. Not every detail in a parable *is* lifelike. A Samaritan as hero would surely have shocked and even repulsed Jesus' Jewish audiences, but that is exactly the point: even one's mortal enemy is one's neighbor.

A minority view that has remained (and steadily grown) ever since Jülicher now challenges his two main points head-on: Jesus' parables may not be the detailed allegories that the church often made them, but they do have a limited number of allegorical elements. It is not as obvious as Jülicher claimed that they teach only one central truth. If one focuses on the Samaritan, one finds a model of compassion. If one adopts the perspective of the man in the ditch, one learns that even one's enemy can be neighborly. But both of these points could have been made without ever introducing the priest and Levite. Presumably, at least a third lesson is present: religious duty (or whatever other motive may have been in these clerics' minds when they passed by the wounded man) is no excuse for lovelessness.

I have elsewhere argued that a valuable working hypothesis for interpreting the parables may be to look for *one main point associated with each main character or group of characters in the parables*. More often than not this leads to three main points associated, in turn, with a master figure and two contrasting subordinates. This approach seems to fit best with the way ancient rabbinic parables were interpreted, and it corresponds reasonably well to the way many

---

1. Adolf Jülicher, *Die Gleichnisreden Jesu*, 2 vols. (Freiburg: Mohr, 1899). One of the curiosities of modern biblical scholarship is that this immensely influential work has never been translated into English.

2. Joachim Jeremias, *The Parables of Jesus* (London: SCM; Philadelphia: Westminster, rev. 1972).

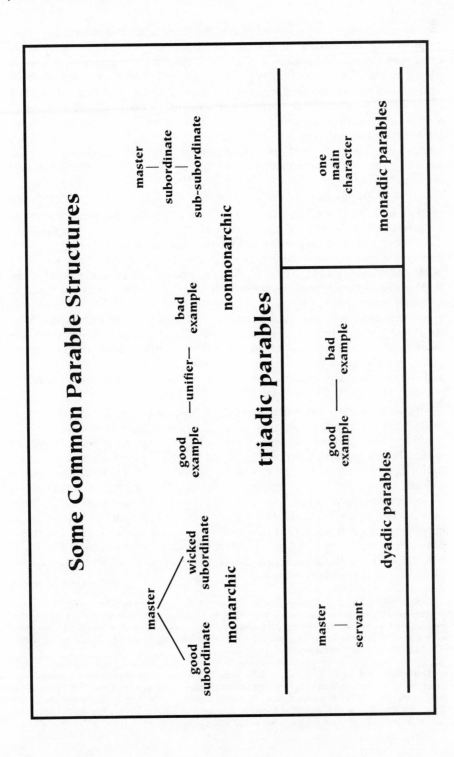

Some Common Parable Structures

triadic parables

nonmonarchic

master
|
subordinate
|
sub-subordinate

good
example —unifier— bad
example

monarchic

master
/   \
good   wicked
subordinate   subordinate

dyadic parables

good   bad
example ——— example

master
|
servant

monadic parables

one
main
character

literary narratives in various cultures communicate truth. The parables are generally lifelike, but usually, in at least one glaring instance in each text, something very unrealistic provides a clue to the spiritual or metaphorical level of truth that Jesus intended to convey. The proper antidote to excessive allegorization is not to exclude allegory from parables altogether but to insist that any claim about a certain detail standing for something else in a given passage fit with what an early first-century Jewish audience could have grasped. Jewish parables contain numerous "stock metaphors"—kings for God, harvests for judgment, servants for God's people, and so on. But labeling the "inn" in the parable of the good Samaritan as the church is clearly anachronistic because the church did not yet exist.[3]

The contexts in which the Gospel parables occur support the mediating perspective advocated here. In two instances the evangelists themselves attribute to Jesus a relatively detailed allegorical interpretation of a given parable—for the sower (Mark 4:13–20 pars.) and for the wheat and weeds (Matt. 13:37–43). The critical consensus since Jülicher has had to argue that these were the unhistorical creations of the early church that had already misunderstood Jesus. But with almost every parable, some brief introductory or concluding remarks by either Jesus or the evangelist narrating the story imply that main characters in the passage carry allegorical freight. For example, the prodigal son clearly stands for tax collectors and "sinners," with the Pharisees and scribes as the older brother (Luke 15:1–2). Or in the parable of the children in the marketplace, the playmates proposing the different games probably stand for Jesus and John, while their recalcitrant friends represent Jesus' and John's contemporaries who rejected them (Matt. 11:16–19).

Of course, many critics will jettison all of these contextual indicators as inauthentic. But if his earliest interpreters all uniformly misunderstood him, then it is rather presumptuous for us to claim to know better what Jesus originally meant. Better to utilize the contexts of the Gospels or else admit sheer ignorance! But if we follow the interpretations of the text, it is virtually impossible to limit a given parable to one single meaning. For example, is Luke 18:1–8 about persistent prayer (so Luke 18:1) or about God's eagerness to vindicate his elect (so vv. 6–8)? Those committed to the one-point rule of interpretation have debated endlessly which of these two truths is more central, but if the passage can make one point per character, the stalemate is resolved. The judge is a foil to teach about the character of God; the widow, about the proper response of his people.[4]

---

3. See further Craig L. Blomberg, *Interpreting the Parables* (Downers Grove and Leicester: IVP, 1990). An excellent resource for sampling some of the oldest and most similar Jewish parables is Harvey K. McArthur and Robert M. Johnston, *They Also Taught in Parables* (Grand Rapids: Zondervan, 1990). From the perspective of literary criticism more broadly, see John W. Sider, *Interpreting the Parables* (Grand Rapids: Zondervan, 1995), though Sider does not believe the multiple lessons from the parables match up quite as predictably with main characters as I do.

4. For brief surveys of the history and principles of interpretation corresponding to the perspective sketched here, see Craig L. Blomberg, "Parable," *ISBE*, vol. 3, 655–59; and Klyne R. Snodgrass, "Parable," *DJG*, 591–601. For an article-length defense of the position adopted in my book, see Craig L. Blomberg, "Interpreting the Parables of Jesus: Where Are We and Where Do We Go From Here?" *CBQ* 53 (1991): 50–78. For an update, cf. idem, "The Parables of Jesus: Current Trends and Needs in Research," in *Studying the Historical Jesus: Evaluations of the State of Current Research*, ed. Bruce Chilton and Craig A. Evans (Leiden: Brill, 1994), 231–54. For homiletical implications, see idem, "Preaching the Parables: Preserving Three Main Points," *PRS* 11 (1984): 31–41.

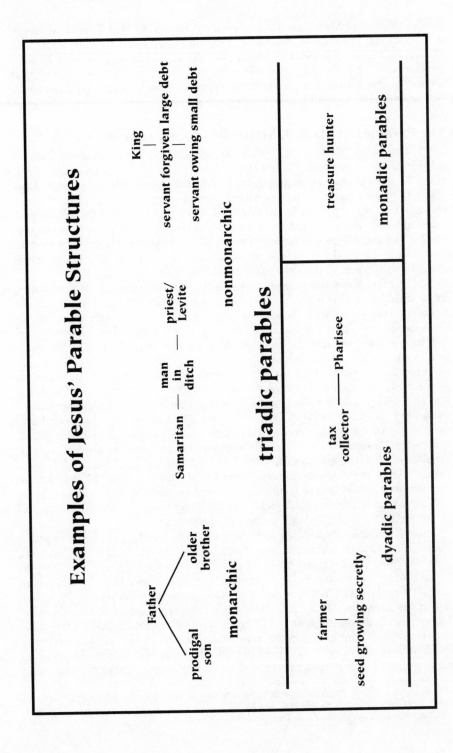

Examples of Jesus' Parable Structures

monarchic

Father
- prodigal son
- older brother

nonmonarchic

King
- servant forgiven large debt
- servant owing small debt

Samaritan — man in ditch — priest/Levite

triadic parables

tax collector —— Pharisee

treasure hunter

farmer — seed growing secretly

dyadic parables

monadic parables

The majority of Mark's parables appear in chapter 4 of his Gospel. Matthew has additional parables in his parallel chapter 13. Luke's parallel section in chapter 8 is more abbreviated. Other parables in Matthew are primarily clustered towards the end of Jesus' life; others in Luke, in his distinctive central section. We will make selected comments about those passages later but focus primarily on Mark 4 and parallel material here.

The Parables of Mark 4, Matthew 13, and Luke 8

The Sower (Mark 4:1–9, 13–20) [Aland §122, 124]. Mark presents his first parable of Jesus' as a "parable about parables" (cf. v. 13). Understanding it will open the door to understanding the rest of Jesus' stories, indeed the rest of his teaching more generally. Here is another reason we must admit at least a limited amount of allegory in Jesus' parables, since this is one of those two passages in which Jesus himself gives a more detailed allegorical explanation (vv. 13–20). But the allegory is natural. Jewish literature provides ample precedent for viewing the seed as God's word (most notably 4 Ezra 9:30–33). Once this is established, then all the other details fall into place.[5]

The story is about the various ways God's word is received. At first glance there seem to be five main "characters" or foci—the sower and four different kinds of soil sown with seed. But it seems clear from the principle of "end-stress" and from the nature of farming that the first three kinds of soil belong together as illustrations of inadequate response. The only harvest a farmer cares about is that which produces mature fruit. So, too, the only true disciples in this story are those who endure and yield an abundant harvest. Simon Kistemaker concisely captures the three main points associated with the sower, the bad soil, and the good soil, along with the three subpoints related to each of the three kinds of bad soil: "The Word of God is proclaimed and causes a division among those who hear; God's people receive the Word, understand it, and obediently fulfill it; others fail to listen because of a hardened heart, a basic superficiality, or a vested interest in riches and possessions."[6] All of these responses are illustrated within the Gospels. But despite the widespread rejection of Jesus, his followers are assured that God's kingdom will advance. A hundredfold yield for an ancient harvest was unusual and points to the surprisingly large growth of God's reign.

Jesus' Rationale for Speaking in Parables (Mark 4:10–12, 21–25, 33–34 pars.) [Aland §123, 125, 130]. In between the parable of the sower and its explanation, Jesus' disciples ask him why he uses this form of teaching. Jesus' reply has perplexed many. He seems to be saying that parables conceal truth rather than reveal it (vv. 11b–12). Yet even Jesus' enemies elsewhere catch on to his meaning in his parables (Mark 12:12 pars.). An adequate answer to this dilemma requires several considerations: (1) True, spiritual understanding in the Bible is never merely cognitive but also volitional. That is, unless one acts on Jesus' teaching by becoming an obedient disciple, one has not *truly* understood his message. (2) Jesus is using a shrewd rhetorical device. Parables, once they

---

5. See esp. Philip B. Payne, "The Authenticity of the Parable of the Sower and Its Interpretation," in *Gospel Perspectives*, vol. 1, ed. R. T. France and David Wenham (Sheffield: JSOT, 1980), 163–207.

6. Simon Kistemaker, *The Parables of Jesus* (Grand Rapids: Baker, 1980), 29.

drive home their lessons, either attract or repel. Those who are not prepared to accept Jesus often become even more hostile against him (again cf. Mark 12:12 pars.), but others are convicted and repent. (3) Jesus is quoting Isaiah 6:9–10 from a context in which the prophet was told to pronounce judgment on an already rebellious nation. Yet the end of the chapter (6:13) promises that a godly remnant will reemerge. God never so exercises his judgment in this life as to prevent anyone who wants to move from becoming "outsider" to "insider" from doing so.[7]

In short, Jesus is revealing secrets not previously understood about God's plans for his people (vv. 11a, 21–23).[8] For those already out of touch with God, his enigmatic yet forceful way of revealing these secrets in parables, to illustrate the coming kingdom of God, will further repel and repulse (cf. vv. 24–25). For those open to Jesus' claims, greater understanding and discipleship will result (cf. v. 33). Still, God is sovereign and is portrayed as choosing some people for different treatment than others.[9]

The Seed Growing Secretly (Mark 4:26–29) [Aland §126]. This parable contains only two foci—a farmer and his seed. From the farmer's perspective, the harvest is always uncertain, dependent on the vagaries of nature. From the perspective of this particular seed, a good crop is guaranteed, thanks to the sovereignty of God. Cranfield captures both of these concepts in his summary of the parable's meaning: "As seedtime is followed in due time by harvest, so will the present hiddenness and ambiguousness of the kingdom of God be succeeded by its glorious manifestation."[10]

The Mustard Seed and Leaven (Mark 4:30–32 pars.; Matt. 13:33 par.) [Aland §128–129]. These short, twin parables arguably do make only one main point, though it may be expressed as the contrast between two foci—great endings out of small beginnings. The mustard seed was proverbial for its smallness and usually grew big enough to be considered only a medium-sized bush. This one becomes "the largest of all (literally 'vegetables')" (Mark 4:32), so that Matthew and Luke can call it a "tree" (Matt. 13:32; Luke 13:19). Luke also contextualizes the story for a Greek audience by specifying the "field" (Matt. 13:31) or "ground" (Mark 4:31) as part of a "garden" (Luke 13:19). The illustration clearly surprises the audience with the size of the plant. So, too, God's kingdom will have a surprisingly large size and effect, considering its inauspicious start with Jesus' "ragtag" band of followers. The reference to the birds of the air nesting in its branches may allude to Ezekiel 17:23 or Daniel 4:12, in which the birds stand for Gentiles. God's reign extends so widely that even non-Jewish people are included.

A few commentators interpret the parable of the leaven differently, with the yeast as a symbol for corrupting influence within the church. Although leaven

---

7. Cf. William L. Lane, *The Gospel according to Mark* (Grand Rapids: Eerdmans, 1974; London: Marshall, Morgan & Scott, 1975), 159: "The citation of Isa. 6:9f. does not mean that 'those outside' are denied the possibility of belief. It indicates that they are excluded from the opportunity of being further instructed in the secret of the Kingdom so long as unbelief continues."

8. The "mystery" of the kingdom is best defined as the fact that God's reign is present but not with irresistible power. See George E. Ladd, *The Gospel of the Kingdom* (Grand Rapids: Eerdmans; Exeter: Paternoster, 1959), 56.

9. Cf. further Craig A. Evans, *To See and Not Perceive* (Sheffield: JSOT, 1989). Evans shows how both the Isaiah and Mark passages contain an unavoidable predestinarian element which later Jewish and Christian interpreters regularly tried to tone down.

10. C. E. B. Cranfield, *The Gospel according to St. Mark* (Cambridge: CUP, rev. 1977), 168.

is often a symbol of corruption in the Bible, most notably in the context of using only unleavened bread for Passover, it is not always so used (cf. esp. Lev. 23:17). The immediate context here makes a negative interpretation highly unlikely. Jesus frequently pairs parables that make the same basic point (e.g., Luke 14:28–32; 15:3–10; Matt. 13:44–46), and the Gospel writers frequently pair examples of balancing concerns for men and women (esp. Luke; see above, p. 145), Similar patterns are probably present in these two passages.

The Wheat and Weeds and the Dragnet (Matt. 13:24–30, 36–43, 47–50) [Aland §127, 131, 133]. The wheat and weeds is the second parable for which Jesus offers a detailed, allegorical interpretation (vv. 37–43). Again the story line is one any first-century Jew could have readily grasped: God and Satan as opponents, each trying to thwart the other's schemes. The three main foci are the farmer, the wheat, and the weeds. The parable can be divided into three episodes, corresponding to which of these three holds, for a time, the upper hand. In the beginning, the weeds seem to have won (vv. 24–28a). Evil at times seems to have thwarted God's purposes in the world. Then it turns out that the wheat survives after all (vv. 28b–30a). God's kingdom will advance despite the seeming indistinguishability of his people from his enemies.[11] Finally, Judgment Day will sort all things out properly (v. 30b). The wicked will be destroyed, and the righteous will enjoy God's presence forever.

The parable of the dragnet (vv. 47–50) has the same triangular structure—fishers, good fish, and bad fish—but without the focus on the period of time preceding judgment. There is also perhaps a hint of the Gentile mission here: the fishers catch "all kinds" of fish (v. 47). The Greek word translated "kind" (*genos*) often refers to a "tribe" of people and is somewhat unusual when used with fish.

The Treasure and the Pearl (Matt. 13:44–46) [Aland §132]. As with the twin parables of the mustard seed and leaven, these short illustrations arguably make only one main point, though it can be expressed in at least two different ways: the inestimable value of the kingdom or the need to sacrifice all in order to obtain it. In the first parable, the man stumbles across the treasure; in the second, he is searching for costly pearls. Whether seeking or stumbling, people who find out about God's kingly reign should do whatever it takes to submit to it.

The Scribe Trained for the Kingdom of Heaven (Matt. 13:51–52) [Aland §134]. As the conclusion to Matthew's "sermon" in parables, Jesus compares the understanding disciple to a householder who brings out of his storehouse things old and new. As we discussed under Matthew 5:17–20, Jesus' kingdom teaching has points of both continuity and discontinuity with the Jewish Law and the Old Testament age. Discerning followers will identify both.

---

11. Augustine's famous interpretation of this feature as justification for a mixed church of believers and unbelievers is unjustified. Jesus explicitly declares that "the field is the world" (v. 38). The confusion results from mistakenly equating God's kingdom (v. 41) with the church. God's kingly reign is exercised in all the world, not just among his people, even if at times in different ways in each sphere.

The Ministries of Various Women (Luke 7:36–8:3)
[Aland §114–115]

The only other parable in all the Gospels not naturally treated in a later section of our book is the short story of the two debtors in Luke 7:41–43. In context, Jesus has been invited to dine with Simon the Pharisee. While there he becomes the subject of lavish attention by a disreputable woman (a prostitute?) who has come in off the street (vv. 36–38). Aware of Simon's displeasure, he tells the story of two debtors, one forgiven a small debt and one forgiven a much larger debt. The answer to the parable's closing question as to who will be more grateful is obvious. But Jesus is intending to compare the woman with the debtor forgiven more and proceeds to declare her sins forgiven (v. 47).

The subsequent rationale, "for she loved much," was used by traditional Catholic thought to justify a kind of works-righteousness. But it is now widely agreed that Jesus is claiming that the woman's love demonstrated her prior forgiveness. Grammatically, "for" (or "because") modifies "I tell you," not "her many sins have been forgiven." In other words, Jesus can *declare* that her sins are forgiven because of this public demonstration of the fact.[12] As in Mark 2:17, Jesus does not question the Jewish leader's estimation of himself as someone in need of less forgiveness. The parable is open-ended and offers Simon continued fellowship as well, though not without challenging his lack of hospitality. The final word of the passage overall is a declaration of the woman's salvation (v. 50). The refrain, "Your faith has saved you," recurs in three other Gospel contexts (Mark 5:34 pars; Mark 10:52 par.; Luke 17:19). In each of these other passages, Jesus has physically healed someone but seems to be pointing out that the individual has also become right with God. A similarly holistic understanding of salvation may be implied in Luke 7:50, although we have no explicit mention of the woman having been previously healed by Christ of any physical affliction.[13]

Luke nevertheless immediately proceeds to describe several women whom Jesus has healed, who in turn provide out of their material resources support for Jesus and his itinerant troupe. Indeed, they, too, go on the road with Jesus (Luke 8:1–3). Most notable among these is Mary Magdalene, who, contrary to popular lore, is not equated with the notorious woman of 7:36–50. At least one of these women (Cuza's wife) would have been quite well-to-do; perhaps they all were. Although these women are apparently not as privileged as Christ's twelve closest (male) disciples, that they would travel with him would have proved scandalous enough in the ancient world. In view of Luke 10:38–42, he probably taught them and treated them as equal to any of the male members of the larger group of crowds and followers that regularly attached themselves to him.[14]

---

12. Cf. Joseph A. Fitzmyer, *The Gospel according to Luke I–IX* (Garden City: Doubleday, 1981), 691–92.

13. See further Craig L. Blomberg, "'Your Faith Has Made You Whole': The Evangelical Liberation Theology of Jesus," in *Jesus of Nazareth: Lord and Christ*, ed. Joel B. Green and Max Turner (Carlisle: Paternoster; Grand Rapids: Eerdmans, 1994), 75–93.

14. For a helpful list of eight key themes present in this short passage, see Ben Witherington III, "On the Road with Mary Magdalene, Joanna, Susanna, and Other Disciples—Luke 8,1–3," *ZNW* 70 (1979): 247–48.

Historicity

It is widely agreed that the parables form the very core of the authentic teachings of Jesus. They reflect his distinctive and characteristic manner of illustrating the kingdom of God. Rabbinic Judaism has bequeathed to us over two thousand parables but almost all are used in service of the exegesis of a text of Scripture, the one thing Jesus almost never does with his parables. Christ uses many of the same stock characters as did the rabbis—kings and masters for God; servants and sons for God's people; banquets and harvests for the final judgment; and so on. And his stories regularly depend on standard features of Palestinian peasant life, but almost always with a surprising twist somewhere in each passage. Purely at the level of aesthetics, many literary critics would consider Jesus' parables unrivaled. Of course, the parables have also been the subject of many hypotheses about the developing tendencies of the tradition, but these have often relied on assuming that pairs of very different parables (e.g., the wedding feast in Matt. 22:1–10 and the great banquet in Luke 14:16–24) were necessarily variations of one original. The undeniably allegorical elements and interpretations have regularly been rejected too. But if our argument for the existence of limited allegory in the parables is valid (see above, p. 258–260), then these objections dissipate.[15]

Theological Distinctives

As elsewhere, the Synoptists' theological distinctives shine through in their unique treatments and arrangements of Jesus' parables. *Mark* highlights the disciples' lack of understanding and the obfuscatory role of the parables. He also sees a correct understanding of the parables as a key for discerning the meaning of his Gospel more generally.[16] *Matthew* has the largest grouping of parables in any one chapter of the Gospels at the exact literary center or pivot of his narrative. Chapter 13 forms the turning point at which Jesus increasingly focuses on his disciples and on people outside of Israel because of his homeland's growing rejection of him. This chapter is thus a key transition from Jesus' self-disclosure to Israel, and, as regularly in Matthew, a fulfillment of the Old Testament appears (Matt. 13:35; cf. Ps. 78:2).[17] *Luke* places the sower into a context of three passages that all deal with how to hear and obey the word of God correctly (Luke 8:4–21; cf. esp. vv. 11, 18, 21).[18] And the parable of the two debtors is embedded in a context that illustrates several of Luke's favorite

15. Cf. further Philip B. Payne, "The Authenticity of the Parables of Jesus," in *Gospel Perspectives*, vol. 2, ed. R. T. France and David Wenham (Sheffield: JSOT, 1981), 329–44. On the so-called tendencies of the tradition, cf. esp. Jeremias' claims (*Parables*, 23–114) with my critique (Blomberg, *Parables*, 79–94).

16. Numerous writers have pointed out ways in which Mark's narrative overall is "parabolic." Most recently, Terence J. Keegan ("The Parable of the Sower and Mark's Jewish Leaders," *CBQ* 56 [1994]: 501–18) shows how the different responses to the parable of the sower match the varying responses of the main characters throughout Mark and help us to decode his overall plot.

17. Even the chapter itself breaks into halves—first Jesus addresses "outsiders," then exclusively "insiders" (13:1–35, 36–52). For the probable chiastic structure of 13:1–52, see David Wenham, "The Structure of Matthew XIII," *NTS* 25 (1979): 517–18. For an excellent treatment of Matthew 13 more generally, cf. J. D. Kingsbury, *The Parables of Jesus in Matthew 13* (Richmond: John Knox; London: SPCK, 1969); and, for the parables throughout Matthew, Jan Lambrecht, *Out of the Treasure* (Grand Rapids: Eerdmans; Louvain: Peeters, 1992).

18. Charles H. Talbert, *Reading Luke* (New York: Crossroad, 1982), 93–94.

themes, most notably Jesus' compassion for women and the moral outcasts of society and his holistic healing of body and spirit.

MIRACLES

Background Considerations

As with the parables, a number of broader issues must be raised before we can proceed immediately to interpreting the miracle stories in Mark 4–6 and elsewhere. Can people in today's scientific world believe in miracles? If there are examples of extraordinary phenomena that science cannot explain, how can we distinguish a genuine miracle from a hoax or a legend? Given that miracle stories proliferated in the ancient world, is it not more likely that the Gospel writers were simply portraying Jesus as yet another divine wonder-worker, deifying their heroes as so many Greeks and Romans had done?

Detailed answers to these and related questions lie largely outside of our scope in this book, but we can suggest directions in which the interested student might proceed. One's overall worldview and presuppositions loom large in this kind of discussion. If one believes in a supernatural God who rules the universe, miracles are a natural (though not necessary) corollary of such *theism*. If one believes in a closed universe where every event is determined by a mechanistic system of cause and effect, the Gospel miracles will be incredible. But in a post-Einstein, post-Heisenberg age, fewer and fewer scientists are making such sweeping pronouncements. Almost every doctor who has been in practice for some length of time can testify to having treated patients who have been inexplicably healed of serious ailments shortly after times of intense prayer. Indeed, many scholars today are prepared to grant that Jesus performed genuine healings, even if they do not accept every detail that the Gospels record about those healings (see above, p. 242–244).[19]

More difficult, however, are the so-called "nature miracles" that tend to be clustered in Mark 4:35–6:56. Can we really believe in Jesus stilling a storm, multiplying the loaves and fishes, walking on the water, or raising the dead? What about all the similar legends from antiquity associated with other religious figures that no one takes seriously as historical fact? Yet, upon closer inspection, the differences between these Gospel miracles and their apparent parallels in other religious literature may outweigh the similarities. Jesus never works a miracle solely to benefit himself. He shows no interest in the merely spectacular and, indeed, regularly refuses to give a sign to satisfy skeptics. He does not first pray to God, mutter some religious incantation, or utilize magical objects. The way in which the miracle occurs is often left altogether unstated.

Instead, each of the more unusual "nature miracles" coheres closely with Jesus' teaching about the kingdom of God, teaching that *is* widely accepted as authentic. Indeed, it is interesting how themes from Jesus' parables, regularly cited as among the most indisputably authentic parts of the Gospels, closely

---

19. Three works that all have passage-by-passage discussions of the credibility of the various Gospel miracles are René Latourelle, *The Miracles of Jesus and the Theology of Miracles* (New York: Paulist, 1988); Leopold Sabourin, *The Divine Miracles Discussed and Defended* (Rome: Catholic Book Agency, 1977); and Hendrik van der Loos, *The Miracles of Jesus* (Leiden: Brill, 1965).

match the points of his nature miracles. We have already seen the similarity between his turning water into wine and his parable of the wineskins (see above, p. 225). We will later highlight the remarkable correspondence between the miracle of withering the fig tree and Jesus' parable on the same topic (see below, p. 317). In this section we will note how the miracles of Mark 4–6 all draw people's attention to Jesus and make them confront the question of his identity. They are *enacted "object lessons" about the nature and arrival of the kingdom of God.* In this light, we should perhaps think twice before automatically dismissing them as impossible.[20]

The Miracles of Mark 4:35–6:56 pars. and Related Passages

In the following passages we see Jesus' power and authority over disaster, demons, disease, and death.

Stilling the Storm (Mark 4:35–41 pars.) [Aland §136]. Countless generations of Christians have applied this passage as if it were a promise that Jesus would "still the storms of this life." In context, all three synoptists agree that it had a very different purpose: to make people address the question, "Who is this? Even the wind and the waves obey him" (Mark 4:41 pars.). All of the details of the story highlight Jesus' sovereign authority and calm in the midst of chaos. In the Old Testament, it is Yahweh who alone has the power to still the raging tempests of the sea (cf. Jonah 1–2; Ps. 104:7; 107:23–32). The gospel writers contrast Jesus' power with the disciples' lack of faith. Mark puts it pointedly: Even after the storms have calmed (unlike Matt. 8:26), Jesus rebukes his followers: "Why are you so afraid? Do you still have no faith?" (Mark 4:40).[21] The miracle is meant to instill greater faith in Jesus as the Son of God. Jesus does not always still the storms of life, but he does promise to preserve spiritually in the midst of those storms those who believe in him.[22]

Exorcising the Gerasene[23] Demoniac (Mark 5:1–20 pars.) [Aland §137]. We have seen Jesus exorcise before, but now he faces a case of multiple demons in a man whom Mark, in particular, goes out of his way to describe as unusually savage and afflicted. Jesus' power to deal with this situation, therefore, magnifies his divine authority all the more. As in Mark 1:24, the demons' knowledge of Christ reflects spiritual warfare, which Christ combats by eliciting their name ("Legion")—v. 9. Their banishment into the pigs reflects the fact that Christ's first coming was not the time of the complete and final judgment of the demonic realm (cf. Matt. 8:29). They are still allowed to destroy life, but in this

---

20. Cf. further Craig L. Blomberg, "The Miracles as Parables," in *Gospel Perspectives*, vol. 6, ed. David Wenham and Craig Blomberg (Sheffield: JSOT, 1986), 327–59.

21. Günther Bornkamm ("The Stilling of the Storm in Matthew," in *Tradition and Interpretation in Matthew*, by Günther Bornkamm, Gerhard Barth, and Heinz J. Held [London: SCM; Philadelphia: Westminster, 1963], 52–57) has made famous the argument that Matthew wants to portray the disciples in a considerably more positive light by limiting Jesus' rebuke to *before* the miracle and by stressing that they have a "little faith." We may grant that there are shades of emphases, but it is hard to see Matt. 8:26 as a compliment under any circumstances!

22. Cf. David E. Garland, *Reading Matthew* (New York: Crossroad, 1993), 158.

23. The best textual evidence has Mark and Luke reading "Gerasene," while Matthew has "Gadarene." Some textual variants in each Gospel opt for "Gergesene." While the towns of Gadara and Gerasa were a considerable distance from the eastern shores of Galilee, Khersa was close by. It is conceivable that either or both of the spellings in Greek, Gerasa and Gergesa, could have resulted from trying to transliterate Khersa, and it is probable that by Gadara Matthew simply means the larger region. Cf. Cranfield, *Mark*, 176.

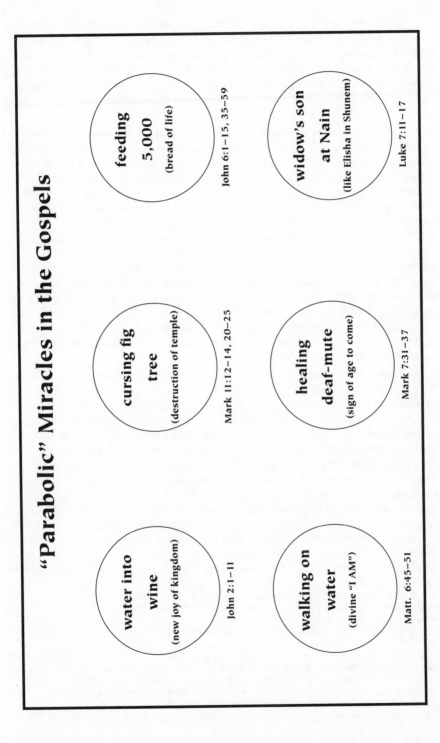

"Parabolic" Miracles in the Gospels

feeding
5,000
(bread of life)

John 6:1–15, 35–59

widow's son
at Nain
(like Elisha in Shunem)

Luke 7:11–17

cursing fig
tree
(destruction of temple)

Mark 11:12–14, 20–25

healing
deaf-mute
(sign of age to come)

Mark 7:31–37

water into
wine
(new joy of kingdom)

John 2:1–11

walking on
water
(divine "I AM")

Matt. 6:45–51

instance not human life. No self-respecting Jew would have bemoaned the loss of these pigs by the (Gentile?) farmers; they knew God's law against eating the pork for which the pigs were presumably being raised.[24] As with the stilling of the storm, one of the purposes of the miracle is to instill faith (Mark 5:19–20), though as with the miraculous fish catch, some of those who come immediately into the presence of one so powerful and holy plead with him to leave (v. 17).

Many people today doubt the reality of demons or demon possession. But Christians who have worked with those caught up in the occult can testify to too many strikingly similar incidents that still take place for such skepticism to prove convincing. Others attribute more to direct demonic activity than is warranted. In Scripture, demon possession is regularly reserved for incidents involving several of the following phenomena observed in Mark 5:1–20 and parallels: (1) a disregard for personal dignity; (2) social isolation; (3) retreat to the simplest kind of shelter; (4) recognition of Jesus' deity; (5) demonic control of speech; (6) shouting; and (7) extraordinary strength.[25] It is sometimes argued that Christians cannot be demon-possessed, only oppressed. However the latter is not a term that ever appears in Scripture, and, indeed, the expression often translated "demon possession" is merely the one Greek word *daimonizō* (literally, "to demonize"). It is certainly true that Scripture gives no grounds for the notion that a person, Christian or otherwise, can be controlled in these bizarre ways by the devil apart from overtly yielding him- or herself to evil influences (cf. 1 John 4:4).

Raising Jairus' Daughter and Healing the Hemorrhaging Woman (Mark 5:21–43 pars.) [Aland §138]. As one of his trademarks, Mark sandwiches together two related stories here. They also belong together chronologically. Jesus is summoned to heal a synagogue ruler's daughter who is at the point of death. Before he can respond, he must also deal with a woman who has had an intermittent flow of blood for twelve years.[26] Both episodes involve Jesus risking defilement by touching the ritually impure. Yet the ministry and message of Jesus bring good news and cleanness for all the socially ostracized. In the case of the hemorrhaging woman, her ritual impurity might have been a more severe problem than the physical malady, given its chronic condition.[27] In the case of Jairus' daughter, Jesus' power is disclosed via the greatest miracle he has worked to date—raising the dead. In both instances, Jesus indicates that the faith of those seeking the miracles is an operative principle in helping to produce what they desire (Mark 5:34, 36). Thus a miracle can be designed to

24. Cf. Robert H. Gundry, *Mark: A Commentary on His Apology for the Cross* (Grand Rapids: Eerdmans, 1993), 262: "Because of their revulsion against pigs, a Jewish audience would find humorous satisfaction in the drowning of the herd as well as in the self-banishment of the unclean spirits."
25. Walter L. Liefeld, "Luke," in *Expositor's Bible Commentary*, ed. Frank E. Gaebelein, vol. 8 (Grand Rapids: Zondervan, 1984), 913.
26. Matthew breaks up Mark's sandwich and narrates each story in its own right (Matt. 9:18–26). This relieves him of the necessity of having to tell of the arrival first of Jairus and then later of messengers who inform him that his daughter has died. As a result he seems to contradict Mark and Luke as to when exactly the girl passed away. But this kind of literary convention was common in antiquity and would not have been viewed as an "error." Moreover, time of death in the ancient world was notoriously imprecise. Cf. further, Robert H. Stein, *Difficult Passages in the Gospels* (Grand Rapids: Baker, 1984), 33–34.
27. See esp. Marla J. Selvidge, *Woman, Cult, and Miracle Recital* (Lewisburg, N.J.: Bucknell University Press, 1990).

produce or strengthen faith (as above, p. 268) or it can be worked in response to faith (as here).

Raising the Son of the Widow in Nain (Luke 7:11–17) [Aland §86]. At some point in his later Galilean ministry, Jesus also performed a second "revivification."[28] It occurs only in Luke's Gospel but is best treated in this survey of nature miracles. It contains striking parallels to the story of Elisha raising the Shunammite widow's son (2 Kings 4:18–37), not least of which is the "coincidence" of Nain occupying approximately the same site as Old Testament Shunem (cf. also a similar miracle by Elijah in 1 Kings 17:17–24). Did the crowd recognize these parallels when it responded by calling Jesus "a great prophet" (Luke 7:16)? It seems likely that at least Luke intends to call attention to the similarities. A later parallel of sorts attributed to Jesus' near contemporary Apollonius of Tyana has suggested to some that Luke sees Christ as fulfilling both Jewish and pagan hopes. But a mid–first-century date for Luke's writings would rule out his awareness of the Apollonius stories.

Healing the Blind Men and the Dumb Demoniac (Matt. 9:27–34) [Aland §96–97]. Like Luke, Matthew's accounts of Jesus' miracles during his Galilean ministry largely duplicate Mark. But Matthew also adds a couple of brief passages unique to his Gospel. They run closely parallel to the kind of miracle that Jesus will perform again later (cf. Matt. 12:22–24; Mark 7:31–37; 10:46–52), so we will reserve comments for those occasions.

Rejection in Nazareth (Mark 6:1–6 pars.) [Aland §139]. As noted above, this is probably the same incident that Luke amplifies and places earlier in his outline (Luke 4:16–30; cf. above, p. 233). The distinctive of Mark's more chronological placement is to highlight that after working so many great deeds elsewhere, Jesus could do few miracles in his hometown because of their lack of faith (vv. 5–6). Matthew rewords Mark's account slightly to make it clear that it was not that Christ was impotent, but that he chose to respond differently because of the Nazarenes' skepticism (Matt. 13:58). This passage also contains the sole references in the Gospels to Jesus as a carpenter and son of a carpenter (Mark 6:3; Matt. 13:55). And it is unique in naming Jesus' brothers and referring to his sisters.[29]

Feeding the Five Thousand (Mark 6:30–44, 53–56 pars.) [Aland §145–146, 148–149]. Here Jesus' motive is neither to instill nor to respond to faith but merely to exhibit compassion (Mark 6:34). However it is not primarily his compassion for the crowd's hunger, but "because they were like sheep without a shepherd," an allusion to Ezekiel 34 (esp. v. 5), in which the prophet laments how Israel languished without adequate leadership. This chapter reverberates with messianic overtones as God predicts a coming day when his people will

---

28. The word "resurrection" is perhaps best reserved for what happened to Jesus and will one day happen to all believers—a reawakening to life that will never again end. Murray J. Harris uses the term cited here in his excellent survey of this category of miracles: "'The Dead Are Restored to Life': Miracles of Revivification in the Gospels," in *Gospel Perspectives*, vol. 6, 295–326. Harris also discusses the similarities and differences with the Elisha and Apollonius stories noted below.

29. Even contemporary Catholic commentators recognize that the older Roman view that the Greek words for "brothers" and "sisters" here were to be translated as "cousins" rested on dogma rather than exegesis. The two major options are that Joseph and Mary had these children through normal human processes *after* Christ's birth or, perhaps less likely, that they were Joseph's children by a *former* marriage (see, e.g., John P. Meier, *A Marginal Jew: Rethinking the Historical Jesus*, vol. 1 [New York and London: Doubleday, 1991], 324–32).

experience proper shepherding. The feeding of the five thousand also harks back to the time of Moses when God first provided bread in the wilderness. In view of Deuteronomy 18:18, many Jews came to expect that the Messiah would reenact this miracle on a grander scale (for further Old Testament parallels, cf. Ps. 132:15; 1 Kings. 17:9–16; and 2 Kings 4:42–44). As with the previous passages, this "gift-miracle" is also fundamentally Christocentric—pointing out Jesus as the Messiah.

John's account brings out this Christology most explicitly as he narrates Jesus' subsequent discourse in the Capernaum synagogue (John 6:25–59) and its aftermath (vv. 60–71). Here Jesus identifies himself as the Bread of Life (vv. 35, 48). He is responding to a request to repeat Moses' miracle (vv. 30–31). What more did they want after the previous feeding? Or is this a different crowd who had not been present on that occasion? In Jesus, God is giving his people true, spiritual bread from heaven (vv. 32–33, 41–42, 50–51).[30] The messianic implications of the feeding miracle were not lost on the crowd present then, but they misinterpreted what kind of Messiah Jesus was, as they were hoping for an earthly king (v. 15).

Five additional themes emerge from Jesus' discourse: (1) Instead of doing *works* to please God, Jesus insists that the solitary *work* needed is to have faith in him (vv. 28–29). (2) Whether or not the questioners in verses 30–31 had seen or heard of the feeding of the five thousand, John's literary juxtaposition of miracle and sermon reinforces his theme that faith based on signs may often prove inadequate (see above, p. 164). If the feeding miracle can't convince, probably nothing will. (3) Jesus preserves his true followers; he will lose none of those the Father has given him (vv. 37–40). Yet God's drawing power in giving people to Christ does not come "with the crude brutality of a rapist, but with the gentle wooing magnetism of a lover" (v. 44).[31] And he knows that Judas was never truly his but is destined to betray him (vv. 64, 70–71). (4) One must eat Christ's flesh and drink his blood (vv. 51–58). These words are often seen as a foreshadowing of the Eucharist, but nothing in John's immediate context would indicate that Jesus' audience could have understood them thus, and the words of the Last Supper consistently relate the bread to Christ's *body*, not to his flesh. Further, on this interpretation, verses 51, 53–54, and 56–58 would seem to demand that the Eucharist itself imparted salvation, a doubtful interpretation in view of verse 63 (in which Christ's "words" give life). The learned Jew would recall that God's Wisdom, too, called out to people to eat of her and her food (Sir. 24:19–21; Prov. 9:5). More likely, consuming Christ's flesh and blood are graphic metaphors for people being associated so closely with Jesus that they also suffer and die for him if necessary.[32] (5) The larger crowd of disciples falls away, leaving only the Twelve (v. 66). In a Johannine equivalent of sorts to Peter's confession on the road to Caesarea Philippi

---

30. On this theme, and on the organization and significance of the sermon more generally, see Peder Borgen, *Bread from Heaven* (Leiden: Brill, 1965).

31. Roy Clements, *Introducing Jesus* (Eastbourne: Kingsway, 1986), 75.

32. C. K. Barrett (*Church, Ministry, and Sacraments in the New Testament* [Exeter: Paternoster; Grand Rapids: Eerdmans, 1985] 74–75), believes that John wrote when the Eucharist was in danger of becoming a mechanical rite believed to secure salvation in and of itself, and so he dissociated these traditions from any overtly eucharistic context to make it clear that faith in Christ alone was salvific. As in John 3:5 with "born of water," however, John's readers may be meant to see a secondary, sacramental allusion.

(Mark 8:27–30 pars.), Peter speaks for the Twelve, confessing Jesus alone as the "Holy One of God" whose words impart "eternal life" (vv. 68–69).

Walking on the Water (Mark 6:45–52 pars.) [Aland §147]. Immediately after his feeding miracle, Jesus sends the disciples on ahead of him to cross back over the lake to Galilee.[33] After a severe storm stalls their progress, he appears to them walking on the lake. Although the storm ceases and the boat reaches its destination, once again the primary point behind the miracle is not one of physical rescue. Rather Christ is revealing the transcendent dimension of his nature. "It is I" (Greek, *egō eimi*) in Mark 6:50 echoes the identical words of Exodus 3:14, with its divine name, "I AM." So, too, the verb "pass by" (v. 48) is the same as used in the LXX of Exodus 33:19 and 34:6 for God "passing by" (i.e., revealing himself to) Moses. Job 9:8 and Psalm 77:19 provide further Old Testament background for Yahweh as the one who treads upon the sea. Christ is here disclosing his divine nature.[34]

Unique to Matthew is the episode of Peter's attempt to imitate his Lord (Matt. 14:28–31). Indeed, Matthew has five distinctive insertions involving Peter in chapters 14–18 (cf. also 15:15; 16:17–19; 17:24–27; and 18:21). None is very flattering; Matthew is arguably trying to combat an overly exalted view of Peter that was beginning to creep into certain circles already in his day.[35] As noted above (p. 130), Matthew ends his version of the miracle far more positively than does Mark, but confession of Jesus as Son of God (14:33) will recur with serious misunderstanding in 16:16–23, showing that "hardened hearts" could still have been present even in this context (Mark 6:52). Mark links this lack of understanding to the feeding of the five thousand. Had the disciples fully captured the christological implications there, they would have caught on better to the point of Jesus' walking on the water as well. Mark 6:53–56 generalizes about Jesus' miracle-working activity and brings this subsection of his Gospel to an end.

Additional Distinctive Material in Matthew and Luke (Matt. 11:20–30 par.) [Aland §108–110]. Understanding and properly responding to Christ's ministry of miracles is no trivial pursuit. Jesus here berates cities in which his ministry was prominent for their failure to repent, and he notes that it will be more tolerable for God's archenemies in Old Testament times (Tyre, Sidon, Sodom, and Gomorrah) than for these (vv. 20–24). On the other hand, those who are responding are the "babes" of this world—those who do not pride themselves in their religious or intellectual credentials (vv. 25–27). As we see consistently in Scripture, these verses balance a predestinarian motif with a clear indication of human free will ("No one knows the Father except . . . those to whom the Son chooses to reveal him" and "Come to me, all you who are weary and burdened"—vv. 27–28). Together these two passages (vv. 20–24, 25–30) stress that God demands much of those to whom much is given, but his yoke (in contrast to those Jews taking upon themselves the "yoke of the Torah"?) is easy and his

---

33. A contradiction has been alleged between Mark 6:45 ("to Bethsaida") and John 6:17 ("to Capernaum"), but if the disciples were setting out from due east of the Sea of Galilee, both cities would be to the northwest, with the former as possibly a stopping point en route to the latter. The storm, as it turns out, blows them far enough south so that they actually land at Gennesaret (Mark 6:53)—more directly to the west.

34. Cf. further John P. Heil, *Jesus Walking on the Sea* (Rome: BIP, 1981).

35. Augustine Stock, "Is Matthew's Presentation of Peter Ironic?" *BTB* 17 (1987): 64–69.

burden light (vv. 28–30). With the greater demand comes a greater empowerment.[36]

Historicity

We have already noted the distinctive problems posed by the nature miracles and tried to reply briefly to certain philosophical, scientific, and historical
objections to their credibility (above, pp. 267–268). We have stressed their
coherence with Jesus' central theme of the kingdom of God. They are not primarily miracles of rainmaking as with Jesus' contemporary, Honi the
Circle-Drawer. They are not myths of fertility as with the cyclical births and resurrections of Greco-Roman religion. They show great restraint in detail compared to the later Christian apocrypha. Their closest parallels are found in the
Elijah/Elisha material of 1 and 2 Kings; Old Testament background should
enhance the case for their authenticity. As with the physical healings and exorcisms, these miracle stories appear in multiple sources and forms, some of
them arguably pre-Markan.[37] And they bear the signs of realism in a Palestinian
milieu, down to minute detail. For example, in Galilee, women mourners
walked in front of a bier rather than behind it as in Judea. Thus it was natural
for Jesus to address the widow of Nain before approaching the casket (Luke
7:13–14).[38] But would Luke have likely "got this right" if he were inventing the
story, given that Judean customs were in general better known? These miracles
also include Aramaic words transliterated into Greek (e.g., *Talitha koum* in
Mark 5:41) and embarrassing details (such as Christ's question "Who touched
my clothes?" in Mark 5:30). And the original christological significance is usually somewhat blurred by later theological overlays (eucharistic motifs at the
feeding of the five thousand, questions about faith and discipleship in the two
miracles on the storm-tossed sea, etc.). All in all, unless one simply rules out
such phenomena *a priori*, a substantial case for their historicity can be
marshalled.

Theology and Conclusion

As with other portions of the life of Christ, each evangelist has his own distinct theological emphases surrounding Jesus' miracles. *Mark* contrasts the
miracle-working Messiah with the suffering Messiah by his relegation of almost
all of his miracles to the first half of his Gospel (chaps. 1–8). *Matthew* consistently abbreviates or omits peripheral details from Mark to streamline his
accounts and focus the christological issues more clearly. *Luke* has been said
to have a slightly more "magical" view of Jesus' miracles (e.g., Luke 8:44–46)
and to stress the conquest of Satan's power and domain (e.g., 10:18–20; cf. also
8:35 with 39; 13:11–12). *John*, as we have seen, links miracles with discourses
as signs to encourage faith. But as faith matures, signs may well prove less
necessary.

36. On 11:25–30, see esp. Celia Deutsch, *Hidden Wisdom and the Easy Yoke* (Sheffield: JSOT, 1987).
37. On which, see esp. Paul J. Achtemeier, "Toward the Isolation of Pre-Markan Miracle Catenae," *JBL* 89 (1970): 265–91.
38. Harris, "Revivification," 298–99.

The purposes of Jesus' miracle-working ministry have been described as "evidential, evangelistic, empathetic, and eschatological."[39] There is no predictable relationship between miracles and faith. Sometimes faith helps to produce a miracle; sometimes a miracle is meant to instill faith where it is absent. Challenging Jewish tradition, breaking down social barriers, and demonstrating compassion for the suffering are all important subordinate themes. But the primary focus is christological—to demonstrate that Jesus is the divine Messiah and that the kingdom of God is now breaking into human history with new force (cf. Matt. 11:2–6 par.; Luke 11:20 par.). Miracles by definition are exceptional events; we should never expect or demand them of God. We cannot predict when he, in his sovereignty, may work one, though there is some slight evidence from history and human experience that they may be more prevalent whenever God's reign is forcefully advancing into an area largely enslaved by the powers of darkness.

WITHDRAWAL FROM GALILEE AND RETURN

After the bulk of his Galilean ministry, Jesus withdraws from his homeland and spends a fair amount of time in provinces to the north and east. Even after his return to Galilee, the Synoptics still describe his repeated departures. It is also during this time that he elicits Simon Peter's dramatic confession that Jesus is the Christ. Still, Peter does not understand that the Christ must suffer, so Jesus increasingly turns to address this topic. This shift in focus is regularly perceived as a major pivot in the life of Christ, as he moves into his third main period of ministry. This period of "rejection" (recall above, p. 191) will culminate in his final journey to Jerusalem and the fate that awaits him there. For the remainder of this chapter we will survey these developments under two main headings: Jesus' withdrawal from Galilee and Peter's confession and its aftermath.

Withdrawal

For this section of Christ's life we are dependent solely on Matthew and Mark. Mark 7:1–8:26 has no corresponding parallels in Luke. This section of Mark forms the bulk of what source critics call Luke's "Great Omission," because Luke does not want to digress from his geographically oriented outline that traces Christ's ministry from Galilee, through Samaria and Judea, to Jerusalem (recall above, p. 142).

Preparation for Ministry Outside Israel: On Defilement (Mark 7:1–23 par.) [Aland §150]. Immediately before Jesus literally departs from Jewish territory we read of an episode that depicts him breaking from Jewish theology as dramatically as at any point thus far.[40] Jewish leaders from Jerusalem have come to Galilee and criticize Jesus for allowing his disciples to violate the ceremonial cleanliness laws of handwashing (vv. 1–5). These were part of the oral but not the written Torah. Jesus replies first by criticizing the hypocrisy of another portion of the Pharisees' traditions, the laws of *corban* (vv. 6–13). Although there

---

39. Douglas J. Moo, "Synoptic Gospels" course notes, Trinity Evangelical Divinity School, Deerfield, Ill., 1978.
40. Now two of the three "badges of national righteousness" (see above, p. 46) have been directly challenged—Sabbath-keeping and the dietary laws. Robert A. Guelich, *Mark 1–8:26* (Dallas: Word, 1989), 362, following Gnilka, remarks: "A spiritual break precedes a geographical break in Jesus' ministry with Israel."

is some uncertainty over the details, the basic practice seems to have been one of dedicating given monies to God for use in the temple after one's death. Meanwhile a person could still gain income from the funds, but no one else was allowed to benefit from them, even if they were in dire need.

Having dissociated himself from the oral laws more generally, Jesus returns to the specific issue of handwashing to declare that it is not food and drink (which go into the body) but evil thoughts, speech, and behavior (which come out of the body) that truly defile (vv. 14–23). The principle enunciated here had the potential of abolishing the entire ritual law of the Old Testament. By Mark's day, the evangelist could add the parenthetical explanation that Jesus' words overturned all the dietary laws (v. 19b). And of course, if all foods are clean, then ritual handwashing is unnecessary and the major barrier to fellowship with the Gentiles is lifted. But it is not clear that the sweeping implications of all this were understood on the spot. Peter later had to experience a three-fold vision from God declaring unclean food clean, followed by his encounter with the Gentile Cornelius who repented in response to Peter's preaching, before the church understood on a widespread basis (Acts 10:1–11:18). Matthew characteristically heightens the polemic with his reference to the Jewish leaders as blind guides (Matt. 15:14).

Exorcising the Syrophoenician Woman's Daughter (Mark 7:24–30 par.) [Aland §151]. Jesus now withdraws from Galilee. At first, his theology seems as nationalist or exclusivist as the Jewish leaders'. A Gentile woman requests healing for her daughter, but Jesus replies that he "was sent only to the lost sheep of Israel" (Matt. 15:24). This verse appears only in Matthew's Gospel and fits his Jewish particularism. In fact, Jesus calls the woman and her daughter "dogs," the standard Jewish epithet used to insult Gentiles (Mark 7:27 par.)! Nevertheless, the woman offers a clever retort, is praised for her faith, and receives the healing she requested. What is going on here? At least three observations may help us reply: (1) Jesus is following the consistent biblical pattern of going to the Jew first and then to the Greek (cf. Rom. 1:16 with Mark's "first" in v. 27 here). The time for wholesale Gentile ministry will not come until after his resurrection. (2) The diminutive form *kunarion* could suggest that Jesus is more affectionate in referring to the woman's child as a household pet—a "little puppy." Or, if he is being more blunt, he may be wanting to test the woman's faith and demonstrate her tenacity. (3) Galileans resented the Syrian provincial leadership that often doled out governmental funds so that Jews received only the "crumbs." Jesus may be seeing how the woman will respond if he suggests the tables be turned for a change.[41]

Healing the Deaf-Mute in the Decapolis (Mark 7:31–37 par.) [Aland §151–52]. Jesus remains in Gentile territory for this next miracle. It is unique in that the recipient of the healing is a person who "could hardly talk" (v. 32). The word used here *(mogilalos)* is found elsewhere in the Greek Bible only in the LXX of Isaiah 35:6, where such a person is said to be able to "shout for joy" when the messianic age arrives. This is also one of three passages in which Jesus uses spit or saliva as part of the healing process. This practice has parallels in primitive medicine and magic. It may be Jesus' way of contextualizing his ministry

---

41. See esp. Gerd Theissen, *The Gospels in Context* (Minneapolis: Fortress, 1991), 61–80.

for a Hellenistic audience in order to communicate to them that he is about to heal a person, even if more supernatural forces are also at work.

Feeding the Four Thousand and Follow-Up Conversations (Mark 8:1–21 pars.) [Aland §153–155]. The geographical sequence suggests that Jesus is still outside Galilee because after the feeding miracle he crosses the lake and lands at Magadan (probably another name for Magdala) on the west bank (Matt. 15:39).[42] The miracle is remarkably similar to the feeding of the five thousand, but this time Jesus' compassion reflects a serious hunger problem among the crowds (Mark 8:2–3). Nevertheless, the abundant provision of food again points to Jesus as the Messiah (cf. above, p. 272). As this episode forms part of Jesus' withdrawal from Galilee, it is attractive to suggest that Jesus is repeating for a mixed or predominantly Gentile audience the type of miracle he previously worked for a more Jewish crowd. Previously they had collected twelve baskets of leftovers (the number of the tribes of Israel); this time they pick up seven (a number of completeness, standing for all of humanity). Even the Greek words for "basket" in the two passages differ (*kophinos* and *spuris*), corresponding, respectively, to characteristic Jewish and Hellenistic bags or sacks. Jesus will be the Bread of Life for both Jews and Gentiles.[43] The disciples' obtuseness seems total (v. 4), given their presence at the earlier feeding miracle. But Matthew 15:33 may suggest that this time they felt the onus was on them to imitate Jesus ("Where could *we* get enough bread?")

Two dialogues follow immediately on the heels of the miracle (Mark 8: 1–10). Back in Galilee, certain Pharisees request a sign from heaven (vv. 11–13). Coming just after the feeding miracle, the request is highly ironic. Clearly they were looking for a sign that could be interpreted in no other way than that God was at work, but what kind of miracle would ever meet this criterion for a die-hard skeptic (cf. Luke 16:31)? Jesus refuses their request. Even were such a sign possible, God does not work miracles "on demand," particularly when they are demanded by his critics.

Second, Jesus again crosses the lake with his disciples (vv. 14–21). In verse 15, they misunderstand his warning about figurative leaven (the corrupting influence of the Jewish leaders[44]) as a rebuke for not bringing enough literal bread. Jesus reminds them of the two feeding miracles to try to get them thinking at the metaphorical level again. He who provided so abundantly can surely meet their physical needs. But they need to recognize who Jesus is and not misunderstand as the Jewish leaders have. One may also hear overtones about Jew-Gentile unity here. Just as Jesus provided bread for both groups, so *one* loaf (v. 14) will be adequate for everyone's needs as they again head across into pagan territory.[45]

---

42. The parallel in Mark 8:10 refers to the otherwise unattested "Dalmanutha." But Magdala may be a variant of the name *Migdal Nunya* ("fish tower"), referring to a village just outside of Tiberias. Removing the first syllable from these two words would then elicit *Dalnunya*, a form that could easily give rise to Dalmanutha.

43. On these parallels and on other examples of Jesus repeating in Gentile territory what he has done at home, see Eric K. Wefald, "The Separate Gentile Mission in Mark," *JSNT* 60 (1995): 3–26.

44. In Mark 8:11, only the Pharisees are mentioned as Jesus' interrogators. Then in v. 15, Jesus warns against the leaven of the Pharisees and "of Herod." In Matt. 16:1, Pharisees and Sadducees together try to trap Jesus, and in v. 12 Jesus warns against the leaven "of the Pharisees and Sadducees." Matthew distinctively adds polemical references to the Sadducees at several points in his gospel. But the Sadducees would have sided with Herod, so there is no contradiction in perspective.

45. So esp. Norman A. Beck, "Reclaiming a Biblical Text: The Mark 8:14–21 Discussion about Bread in the Boat," *CBQ* 43 (1981): 49–56.

Healing the Blind Man in Bethsaida (Mark 8:22–26) [Aland §156]. As Jesus ministers near the boundary of Jewish and Gentile territory, we read about the only "two-stage" healing in the Gospels. As with the use of saliva, we may be meant to recognize God's sovereignty in healing people with whatever methods he chooses.[46] Given the disciples' spiritual blindness in the preceding passage, it is difficult not to see also a deliberately metaphorical meaning in the story. Like this blind man, the disciples begin with only partial sight and require further illumination (see esp. 8:18). This will come in the very next passage, with Peter's confession, but subsequent events will demonstrate that only after the resurrection will the disciples really understand as they should.

Peter's Confession and Its Aftermath

The Pivot of Jesus' Ministry (Mark 8:27–9:1 pars.) [Aland §158–60]. Once again Jesus is traveling outside of Galilee, this time in the vicinity of Caesarea Philippi. It may not be coincidental that here an ancient center of worship of the Hellenistic god, Pan, thrived. The city, Paneas, had also been renamed in honor of the emperor and Herod Philip. Where more appropriate to determine if Jesus' followers understood *his* true, divine identity? In short compass and in sharp juxtaposition to each other, Peter expresses the high and low points of the disciples' christological understanding. Matthew's account here is by far the fullest (Matt. 16:13–28).

On the one hand, Peter confesses that Jesus is "the Christ, the Son of the living God" (v. 16). In context, this is a substantial improvement on the popular belief that Jesus was merely one of the prophets (v. 14). It is a divinely revealed insight (v. 17). It elicits Jesus' promise that he will build his church "on this rock" (v. 18). Extensive medieval debates have made it difficult to read this text as Jesus originally intended it. Roman Catholicism at the time of the Reformation used this passage to support the authoritative ministry of each successive bishop of Rome (i.e., pope) in an unbroken chain of apostolic succession from the days of Peter on. Luther, in turn, argued that the rock was Christ. Various scholars and theologians before and since have adopted a mediating position, that it was Peter's *confession* of Jesus as the Christ that was the "rock" on which the church would be built.

In the original setting, however, it makes little sense to take the rock as anything but Peter himself. Why else make a play on words using Peter's name ("You are 'a rock' [Greek, *Petros*] and on this rock [*petra*]. . .")?[47] Peter has just told Jesus who he is; now Jesus tells Peter who he is. What is more, soon Jesus will call Peter a different kind of rock ("a stumbling stone"—v. 23), which contrasts all the more poignantly with this conversation if he has here directly called Peter a foundational stone. But recognizing Peter as the rock in no way commits us to any doctrines about the papacy or apostolic succession. There

---

46. J. Keir Howard ("Men as Trees, Walking: Mark 8.22–26," *SJT* 37 [1984]: 163–70) observes that this is the closest miracle of Jesus to an actual medical healing, particularly if the blindness was not congenital, the man had severe cataracts, the saliva washed away dried secretions, and the pressure of Jesus' fingers on his eyes was able first to dislodge and then to relodge the lens in the proper position.

47. The inflectional ending of *petra* is feminine and so had to be altered to -*os* to form a masculine proper name. In Aramaic, *Kepha* would have been used for both forms.

is nothing of these Roman traditions in this context, and indeed Matthew 18:18 will apply the identical authority granted to Peter in 16:19 to the entire community of disciples. Peter is foundational in that he was the leader of the early church in Jerusalem and a key figure in opening the door to Samaritan and Gentile missions in Acts 8 and 10.[48] The church he led in its infancy will never succumb to the powers of death ("gates of Hades"). That door-opening ministry of offering forgiveness to all who repent is described in verse 19 as receiving "the keys of the kingdom." Thus God in heaven and Christians on earth mutually agree on who or what is "bound" or "loosed" (cf. John 20:23).[49]

On the other hand, although Peter seems to grasp something of Jesus' unique relationship with God, he is still not prepared for a suffering Messiah who refuses to overthrow Rome or promote Jewish nationalism. That is why Jesus must silence him for the time being (Mark 8:30 pars.) and proceed to instruct his followers about his upcoming death (8:31–9:1 pars.). Here appears the first of three key "passion predictions," as the period of Jesus' rejection begins (8:31–32; 9:30–32; 10:32–34). How quickly Peter turns from "hero" to "culprit"! He "rebukes" Jesus for his predictions (8:32), and Jesus has to "return the favor" (v. 33). In replying, "Out of my sight, Satan!" he is not saying Peter was possessed by demons, but he is very seriously stressing that Peter is reflecting the same perspective as the devil, who wanted to keep Christ from the road to the cross. Jesus goes on to teach the Twelve about the necessary self-renunciation that true discipleship requires (vv. 34–38). This may lead to the shame attached to a criminal's execution by crucifixion (v. 34) or involve denial of the goods or status of this world (vv. 35–37), but it will result in a heavenly glory that far more than compensates (v. 38).[50] Only one who was in some sense divine himself could legitimately make the claims of this last verse.

Mark 9:1 and parallels is one of the most enigmatic sayings in the Gospels, but given the passage that immediately follows, it probably has something to do with the Transfiguration.[51] While Christ's second coming, and with it the full manifestation of the kingdom in all its power, was yet a long way off, a few of Jesus' followers would see glimpses of his transcendent glory within just a few days. Those glimpses and their aftermath are described in the next section.

The Transfiguration and Its Sequel (Mark 9:2–29 pars.) [Aland §161–163]. While for Jesus and his followers, suffering and death must precede permanent glory, both are allowed to experience foretastes in this life. For believers, those foreshadowings often provide the necessary sustenance for perseverance during the difficult times. Jesus' transfiguration contains numerous parallels to the experience of Moses on Mt. Sinai at the time of the receiving of the Law and

---

48. Cf. further R. T. France, *The Gospel according to Matthew* (Leicester: IVP; Grand Rapids: Eerdmans, 1985), 253–54.

49. A grammatical debate about whether the future perfect passive periphrastic constructions should be translated "will be bound/loosed" or "will have been bound/loosed" is probably best resolved with the mediating sense of "will be in a state of boundedness/loosedness." Jesus is not saying that heaven ratifies Christians' decisions or vice-versa, merely that they are in accord when Christians are properly exercising their ministries. See further Stanley E. Porter, "Vague Verbs, Periphrastics, and Matt. 16:19," *Filología Neotestamentaria* 1 (1988): 155–73.

50. Morna D. Hooker, *The Gospel according to Saint Mark* (London: A & C Black; Peabody: Hendrickson, 1991), 208, captures it succinctly: "The cost is comprehensive, but so is the reward."

51. See esp. Cranfield, *Mark*, 285–88. Other suggestions for the kingdom of God coming in power have included the resurrection, Pentecost, the establishment of the church, the destruction of Jerusalem in A.D. 70, and the mistaken belief that Christ would return within the lifetime of some of his hearers.

is doubtless intended to reflect a theology of Jesus as a new Moses, inaugurator of a new covenant, and prophet par excellence: Luke in particular highlights these connections. (1) Jesus is on a mountain.[52] (2) He hears a heavenly voice, giving the same message as at his baptism (on which see above, p. 222). (3) There is an enveloping cloud and an appearance of God's glory. (4) Talk centers on Jesus' "exodus" (Luke 9:31—NIV "departure"). (5) Peter proposes to build "booths" as in the wilderness wanderings. (6) Moses and Elijah, messianic precursors and recipients of mountaintop theophanies, appear with Jesus. (7) The disciples must listen to Jesus (v. 7), in fulfillment of Deuteronomy 18:15–18. (8) All this occurs "after six days" (Mark 9:2; cf. Exod. 24:16).[53]

Again, the disciples fail to grasp what is happening. Peter wants to prolong the mountaintop experience (Mark 9:5), but this is not the time or place to dwell on glory. As they descend, they ask about Elijah (vv. 11–13 par.). His coming as forerunner to restore all things does not seem to leave room for the Messiah's suffering and death (Mal. 4:5–6). But if John the Baptist has fulfilled prophecy and yet been executed, how can the Christ expect anything less?[54] In the valley beneath, the nine disciples who did not accompany Jesus up the mountain have been unable to fulfill their prior commissioning (Mark 6:7 pars.), as they have failed to cast out a demon from an epileptic boy (Mark 9:14–29 pars.). Again, the contrast between Jesus' majesty and the disciples' failure proves striking. Jesus performs the exorcism but castigates his followers for acting like the "unbelieving generation" that is more overtly rejecting him. Their problem was a lack of prayer (v. 29; some late manuscripts add "and fasting"), that is, a failure to trust utterly in God. Matthew goes on at this point to add Jesus' promise about the power of even a little faith (Matt. 17:20–21), but these words must always be balanced with his prior command to leave room for God's will to overrule ours in all our prayers (6:10).

Further Teachings on Discipleship (Mark 9:30–50 pars.) [Aland §164, 166–168]. As with his first passion prediction, Jesus' second meets with a lack of understanding and with distress (vv. 31–32 pars.). So Mark appends a collection of Jesus' teachings, the parallels to which are somewhat more scattered in Matthew and Luke. All focus on the lowliness, service, and life of peace required by a faithful pilgrim on the road to the cross.[55] Jesus' disciples are arguing about greatness (v. 33–34), so he explains that they must (a) have a child- or servant-like attitude (vv. 35–37); (b) recognize as legitimate anyone ministering under Jesus' authority, whether or not in their regular circle (vv. 38–41),[56] (c) avoid possibility of scandal—for others and themselves— in

---

52. The mountain is unnamed. Tradition identifies it as Mt. Tabor in central Galilee. But this "mountain" is only 1900 ft. high, and a fortress was nestled atop it in Jesus' day. Modern scholars often suggest Mt. Hermon (9200 ft. and northeast of Galilee), but it may have been too distant and rugged. Liefeld, "Luke," 929, opts for Mt. Meron, the highest mountain within Israel at nearly 4000 ft., just northwest of the Sea of Galilee.

53. Luke's "about eight days" (v. 28) loses this allusion but does not contradict Matthew and Mark because both expressions were standard references to a week's time.

54. Cf. Craig L. Blomberg, "Elijah, Election, and the Use of Malachi in the New Testament," *Criswell Theological Review* 2 (1987): 100–108, and the literature there cited.

55. Harry Fleddermann, "The Discipleship Discourse (Mark 9:33–50)," *CBQ* 43 (1981): 57–75.

56. Luke 11:23 (par. Matt. 12:30) states the converse of this text ("He who is not with me is against me"), but this claim is equally appropriate in its context: all non-Christians, however benign, are ultimately against Christ. But all true Christians, whether or not they are in *our* elite circles, are ultimately on our side.

light of coming judgment (vv. 42–49); and (d) live at peace among themselves and with others (v. 50).

Discussion about the Temple Tax (Matt. 17:24–27) [Aland §165]. At this point, Matthew alone includes a curious little story about a dispute over paying the annual half-shekel tax for the upkeep of the Jerusalem temple. Jesus makes two main points. First, he and his followers as "sons of the kingdom" should be exempt. This fits his consistent rejection of Jewish civil and ritual law; believers are now free from these Old Testament requirements. Second, however, he refuses to cause unnecessary offense and so encourages a voluntary contribution. But the method of payment—catching a fish with a coin in its mouth—ensures that no hardship for anyone is created in the process![57]

Historicity

The authenticity of several of the themes and literary forms in Mark 7–9 and parallels (e.g., miracle stories or conflicts with the Jewish leaders) has already been discussed in previous sections. In addition we may note the following arguments for the historicity of various passages discussed here: (1) Jesus' implicit challenge to the kosher laws satisfies the double dissimilarity criterion; it differed radically from the rest of Judaism but was not immediately followed by early Christianity.[58] Indeed, Romans 14:14 may preserve an allusion to this very teaching of Christ. (2) Jesus' "insulting" behavior toward the Syrophoenician woman passes the test of "embarrassment," but it is understandable in a Jewish milieu and his cryptic repartee is characteristic. And the form and contents of the passage closely parallel those of the healing of the Capernaum centurion's son (Matt. 8:5–13 par.). (3) *Ephphatha* in Mark 7:34 preserves a rare Aramaic word in the Gospels, and the two healings of blind men (Mark 7:31–37 par. and 8:22–26) describe a kind of miracle unparalleled in ancient Judaism or the early church. (4) Mark 8:11–13, 14–21 and parallels cohere with Jesus' classic unwillingness to respond to his opponents on their terms. He evades their trap and then issues a characteristically metaphorical warning.

The interchange between Peter and Jesus on the road to Caesarea Philippi raises broader historical questions. It has often been disputed whether or not Jesus even intended to found a church. That is, did he imagine his followers living long enough to establish an ongoing fellowship, and did he ever imagine it turning into the highly developed and organized institution that it became? The answer to the latter question may well be "no," but he probably *did* envisage a community of his followers that would outlive him and carry on his mission for a considerable time. In Judaism, a Messiah implied a messianic community, a new or renewed Israel. The Greek word for "church" *(ekklēsia)* translates the Hebrew *qahal*—the standard Old Testament term for the "assembly" of God's

---

57. Richard Bauckham ("The Coin in the Fish's Mouth," in *Gospel Perspectives*, vol. 6, 219–52) argues that Christ and the disciples are virtually penniless at this point in their ministry. A half-shekel equaled two drachma or denarii and, hence, two days' minimum wage.

58. The most serious challenge to this claim comes from E. P. Sanders, *Jesus and Judaism* (London: SCM; Philadelphia: Fortress, 1985), 264–67, largely on the grounds that the early church would surely have given up the dietary laws more quickly had Jesus clearly abolished them. But Jesus' challenge is characteristically indirect and susceptible to more than one interpretation. Given the disciples' propensity for misunderstanding Jesus' more cryptic utterances, early Christian conservatism on this matter is not at all surprising.

people. The nature of Jesus' ethical teaching—on taxes, divorce, nonretaliation, enemy love, stewardship of wealth, and so on, clearly presupposes some significant interval during which his disciples would have to confront all of the problems of ordinary living. Even the portions of this passage unique to Matthew contain numerous Semitisms that could be a literal translation of Jesus' exact wording—"Son of the living God," the beatitude form ("Blessed are you"), *bar-Jonah* ("son of Jonah"[59]), "flesh and blood" (as an idiom for mortal humanity), the play on Peter's name—Cephas ("rock"), the "gates of Hades" (i.e., the power of death), and the imagery of binding and loosing. So whether or not Matthew is actually prior to Mark at this point or is simply supplementing his standard sources, he is likely relying on historical tradition.[60]

Jesus' subsequent calls to radical discipleship (Mark 8:34–38; 9:33–50 pars.) are among the "hard sayings" not readily invented. Peter's rebuke of Christ and Jesus' response (8:32–33 pars.) are so unflattering that they, too, are likely historical. Jesus' threefold prediction of his passion and resurrection (Mark 8:31; 9:31; 10:33–34 pars.) is more disputed. But even apart from supernatural knowledge, awareness of the precedent of the Maccabean martyrs and of the general tenor of Jewish-Roman relationships in the first century would surely have suggested to Jesus that he was on a collision course with the authorities of his day. Only in Matthew 20:19 is death *by crucifixion* ever actually mentioned; "prophecies" after the fact would surely have been more explicit. But if Jesus anticipated martyrdom, then he presumably expected vindication by God as well. Except among the Sadducees, resurrection was the standard Jewish hope for the age to come, but there was no expectation of a crucified and resurrected Messiah, so again Jesus' predictions fit what is both conceivable and yet distinctive in a Jewish milieu.[61] Finally, Mark 9:1 is a potentially embarrassing verse that nevertheless presupposes something like the transfiguration narrative that follows to make any sense of it. And 2 Peter 1:16–18 claims to provide independent, eyewitness attestation of this event.

Theological Distinctives

Again, each of the synoptists puts his own distinctive stamp on this material. *Mark* 8:27–30 clearly forms the hinge that separates the two halves of Mark's Gospel, transitioning from Christ the glorious miracle-worker to Jesus the suffering servant (recall, above, p. 116). To highlight the disciples' lack of understanding, Mark creates a twofold sequence of feeding miracles, sea crossings, conflicts with the Pharisees, conversations about bread, healings, and confessions of faith (6:31–7:37; 8:1–30).[62] *Matthew* also makes Peter's confession a pivotal point (16:13–20; see above, p. 128) but groups the material leading up to this hinge into parallel cycles of ministry among Jews and Gentiles. Jesus is

---

59. Or more probably, *contra* the NIV, "son of John." *Bariona* could be the contracted form of *bar Johanan*, and John 1:42 and 21:15 both refer to Simon as son of John.

60. Cf. further Gerhard Lohfink, *Jesus and Community* (Philadelphia: Fortress, 1984; London: SPCK, 1985); Leonhard Goppelt, *Theology of the New Testament*, vol. 1 (Grand Rapids: Eerdmans; London: SPCK, 1981), 207–22; Ben F. Meyer, *The Aims of Jesus* (London: SCM, 1979): 185–97.

61. For a thorough defense of the historicity of the passion predictions, see Hans F. Bayer, *Jesus' Predictions of Vindication and Resurrection* (Tübingen: Mohr, 1986).

62. Lane, *Mark*, 269.

the Bread of Life for both groups (14:13–36; 15:1–16:12).[63] *Luke* creates his turning point a little further in his narrative (at Luke 9:51, on which see below, p. 288). As already noted, Luke omits all of Jesus' withdrawal from Galilee for geographical/theological purposes but groups material parallel to Mark in Luke 9:1–50 to form a preview of Jesus' journey to Jerusalem. Here he highlights themes of Christology, especially viewing Jesus as the eschatological prophet, and discipleship.[64]

FOR FURTHER STUDY

Parables

Introductory

Clements, Roy. *A Sting in the Tale*. Leicester: IVP, 1995.

Hunter, A. M. *Interpreting the Parables*. London: SCM; Philadelphia: Westminster, 1960.

Kistemaker, Simon. *The Parables of Jesus*. Grand Rapids: Baker, 1980.

Sider, John W. *Interpreting the Parables*. Grand Rapids: Zondervan, 1995.

Stein, Robert H. *An Introduction to the Parables of Jesus*. Philadelphia: Westminster, 1981.

Wenham, David. *The Parables of Jesus: Pictures of Revolution*. London: Hodder & Stoughton; Downers Grove: IVP, 1989.

Intermediate

Bailey, Kenneth E. *Poet and Peasant* and *Through Peasant Eyes*. [2 vols. bd. as 1] Grand Rapids: Eerdmans, 1983.

Blomberg, Craig L. *Interpreting the Parables*. Downers Grove and Leicester: IVP, 1990.

Dodd, C. H. *The Parables of the Kingdom*. London: Nisbet, 1935; New York: Scribner's, 1936.

Donahue, John R. *The Gospel in Parable*. Philadelphia: Fortress, 1988.

Herzog, William R., II. *Parables as Subversive Speech*. Louisville: Westminster/John Knox, 1994.

Jeremias, Joachim. *The Parables of Jesus*. London: SCM; Philadelphia: Westminster, rev. 1972.

Via, Dan O., Jr. *The Parables: Their Literary and Existential Dimension*. Philadelphia: Fortress, 1967.

Young, Brad H. *Jesus and His Jewish Parables*. New York: Paulist, 1989.

Advanced

Crossan, John Dominic. *In Parables: The Challenge of the Historical Jesus*. New York: Harper & Row, 1973.

Funk, Robert W. *Parables and Presence*. Philadelphia: Fortress, 1982.

Scott, Bernard B. *Hear Then the Parable*. Minneapolis: Fortress, 1989.

Bibliography

Kissinger, Warren S. *The Parables of Jesus: A History of Interpretation and Bibliography*. Metuchen, N.J.: Scarecrow, 1979.

---

63. Cf. Craig L. Blomberg, *Matthew* (Nashville: Broadman, 1992), 210.

64. On which, see David P. Moessner, "Luke 9:1–50: Luke's Preview of the Journey of the Prophet like Moses of Deuteronomy," *JBL* 102 (1983): 575–605; and Robert F. O'Toole, "Luke's Message in Luke 9:1–50," *CBQ* 49 (1987): 74–89.

Miracles

Introductory

Deere, Jack. *Surprised by the Power of the Spirit.* Grand Rapids: Zondervan, 1993.
Moule, C. F. D., ed. *Miracles.* London: Mowbray, 1965.
Richardson, Alan. *The Miracle-Stories of the Gospels.* London: SCM, 1941.
Smedes, Lewis B., ed. *Ministry and the Miraculous.* Pasadena: Fuller Theological Seminary, 1987.

Intermediate

Latourelle, René. *The Miracles of Jesus and the Theology of Miracles.* New York: Paulist, 1988.
Brown, Colin. *Miracles and the Critical Mind.* Grand Rapids: Eerdmans; Exeter: Paternoster, 1984.
Sabourin, Leopold. *The Divine Miracles Discussed and Defended.* Rome: Catholic Book Agency, 1977.
van der Loos, Hendrik. *The Miracles of Jesus.* Leiden: Brill, 1965.

Advanced

Blackburn, Barry L. *Theios Aner and the Markan Miracle Traditions.* Tübingen: Mohr, 1991.
Kee, Howard C. *Miracle in the Early Christian World.* New Haven and London: Yale, 1983.
Theissen, Gerd. *The Miracle Stories of the Early Christian Tradition.* Edinburgh: T. & T. Clark; Philadelphia: Fortress, 1983.
Wenham, David, and Craig Blomberg, eds. *Gospel Perspectives.* Vol. 6, *The Miracles of Jesus.* Sheffield: JSOT, 1986.

Withdrawal from Galilee

Bayer, Hans F. *Jesus' Predictions of Vindication and Resurrection.* Tübingen: Mohr, 1986.
Booth, Roger P. *Jesus and the Laws of Purity.* Sheffield: JSOT, 1986.
Caragounis, Chrys C. *Peter and the Rock.* Berlin and New York: de Gruyter, 1990.
Fowler, Robert M. *Loaves and Fishes.* Chico: Scholars, 1981.
McGuckin, J. A. *The Transfiguration of Christ in Scripture and Tradition.* Lewiston: Mellen, 1986.

QUESTIONS FOR REVIEW

1. What principles should we most keep in mind in interpreting parables? Choose a specific parable and illustrate.
2. Explain Mark 4:10–12.
3. What principles should we most keep in mind in interpreting Jesus' miracles, and particularly his "nature miracles"? Choose a specific miracle and illustrate.
4. Discuss the relationship in the Gospels between miracles and faith.
5. What is the main point of Jesus' "withdrawal from Galilee"? Illustrate from several texts.
6. What is the main point of Peter's "confession"? How does he still not understand?

CHAPTER FIFTEEN

ADDITIONAL TEACHINGS OF JESUS

IN MATTHEW, LUKE, AND JOHN

W̲e have generally been following Mark's outline for the Galilean ministry of Christ. At logical points we have inserted related material from the other Gospels. Now it is time to go back and pick up the pieces we have skipped, before moving to the climactic days of Jesus' life in and around Jerusalem. In Matthew, this includes two major sermons (chaps. 10 and 18), arguably though not necessarily collections of Jesus' teachings from several different contexts. In Luke, this involves all of the unparalleled parts of his large central section (9:51–18:34), most of which are teachings, many of them in parables. In John, we must consider the intermediate visits of Christ to Jerusalem and the controversies with the Jewish leaders in which he became embroiled there (most of chaps. 5–11).

MATTHEW 10 AND 18

The Missionary Discourse (Matthew 9:36–10:42)
[Aland §98–105]

Context (Matt. 9:36–10:4). At some point, roughly midway through his Galilean ministry, Jesus commissioned his disciples to begin replicating his work of preaching, teaching, and healing. The potential harvest was great, but the laborers needed to be multiplied (9:35–38). It is at this point that Matthew names the Twelve (10:1–4), although they have actually been chosen earlier (cf. above, p. 238). The sermon, as Matthew presents it, falls into two main sections: instructions for ministry during Jesus' lifetime (vv. 5–16), followed by a look ahead to coming persecution and circumstances after his death and resurrection

(vv. 17–42).[1] Only the latter section contains instructions that are necessarily generalizable to later generations of disciples.

Message (10:5–42). In the short run, the disciples must restrict themselves to Jewish territory (vv. 5–6) and travel light, dependent on the hospitality of those among whom they minister (vv. 7–16). The apparent harshness of these baggage restrictions and short visits stems from the urgency of getting the message out, not from the limited scope of the mission.[2] As explained above (p. 131), Jesus insists that the Jewish people hear the gospel first, but he will later command the disciples to go to all ethnic groups with their message (28:18–20).[3] In fact, even before his death, he will rescind some of these specific instructions about provisions for the journey (Luke 22:35–38). But the basic task of proclaiming the gospel and healing people clearly continues on into the Book of Acts.

Verses 17–42 divide into three main parts. First, Jesus describes the prospect of future hostility (vv. 17–25). It is inevitable, because of the disciples' attachment to Christ (vv. 24–25), but the Spirit will protect and guide them through it all (vv. 17–23). Indeed, he will give them an opportunity for witness (v. 18). There is a fine balance between being on one's guard (v. 17) and yet not worrying (v. 19). In this section appears one of the more puzzling verses in Matthew's Gospel, as Jesus promises the disciples that they will not have finished going through the cities of Israel "before the Son of Man comes" (v. 23). Had this prediction come in verses 5–16, we might imagine it to be a reference simply to the short-term mission of the disciples, but in this context of future hostility that interpretation does not fit well. More likely, Jesus is predicting the perennially incomplete nature of the Jewish mission and perhaps also hinting at its ongoing priority.[4] Second, the proper reaction to hostility is to fear God, not people (vv. 26–31). Physical death is far less ultimate than eternal punishment. Third, as at the end of the Sermon on the Mount, there are essentially only two options: either to acknowledge Jesus or to reject him (vv. 32–42). Those who want to remain faithful may wind up alienating their families, but God must take a higher priority (vv. 34–39). Yet eventually everyone will be judged on the basis of their reception of Christian witnesses (vv. 40–42), so the seemingly high cost is more than worth it.

The Sermon on Humility and Forgiveness (Matt. 18:1–35) [Aland §166, 168–173]

Not long before Jesus' climactic journey to Jerusalem, Matthew records (compiles?) another extended discourse of Jesus, again for the disciples only.

1. For a helpful literary-critical analysis of the sermon, see Dorothy J. Weaver, *Matthew's Missionary Discourse* (Sheffield: JSOT, 1990).

2. A classic so-called contradiction among Gospel parallels involves whether or not Jesus forbade a staff and shoes altogether or only prohibited the disciples from taking extra ones. For a survey of the various commonly-proposed solutions, see Barnabas Ahern, "Staff or No Staff," *CBQ* 5 (1943): 332–37. For a more recent source-critical explanation, see Craig Blomberg, *The Historical Reliability of the Gospels* (Leicester and Downers Grove: IVP, 1987), 145–46: Matthew's account may be a conflation of the sending of the seventy (-two), described in Luke 10, and of the Twelve, described in Mark 6, in which the commands varied slightly.

3. Cf. Amy-Jill Levine, *The Social and Ethnic Dimensions of Matthean Social History* (Lewiston: Mellen, 1988).

4. See further J. M. McDermott, "Mt. 10:23 in Context," *BZ* 28 (1984): 230–40. For a brief overview of other alternatives, cf. D. A. Carson, "Matthew," in *Expositor's Bible Commentary*, ed. Frank E. Gaebelein, vol. 8 (Grand Rapids: Zondervan, 1984), 250–53.

Having already promised to build his church (Matt. 16:16–19), he here elaborates on some of the foundational principles for this fledgling community. Jesus' "sermon" falls into two main parts: teaching on humility (vv. 1–14) and forgiveness (vv. 15–35).[5] Verses 1–9 outline the humility disciples need. They must imitate childlike dependence on God (vv. 1–5) but avoid anything that might cause even one of the seemingly most insignificant of Christians to stumble (vv. 6–9). Verses 10–14 turn to God's "humility"—what great steps he takes to try to save the wayward. In this context (diff. Luke 15:4–7), the parable of the lost sheep seems to apply primarily to straying church members.[6] Throughout this chapter and elsewhere, "little ones" is a favorite term of Matthew's for fellow believers.

Verses 15–35 turn to the complementary topic of forgiveness. When a flagrantly sinning Christian remains unrepentant, an increasingly severe process of intervention is needed to try to bring a change of heart (vv. 15–18). Here is the classic passage in the New Testament to which churches turn (or should turn) to understand the process of discipline. In extreme cases, excommunication may even be necessary, but it is still in hopes of rehabilitation. To treat someone as a "pagan or tax collector" (v. 17) means that they cannot be admitted to gatherings designed for Christians only, but they should still be treated with the respect and love with which one would try to win a non-Christian to Christ.[7] Verses 19–20 clearly belong in this context. The "two or three" gathered in Jesus' name correspond to the person confronting a fellow Christian in the presence of "one or two" witnesses in verse 16. Jesus is teaching nothing here about his being present with every small prayer group, true as that may be, but everything about the fact that heaven is in accord with properly followed church discipline.

By contrast, Jesus enjoins forgiveness seventy-seven-fold in verses 21–22. The only way not to see a contradiction with verses 15–20 is to assume that here true repentance has occurred. The alternating grace and severity of the king in the appended parable (vv. 23–35) confirms this conclusion (cf. also Luke 17:3–4). Together, verses 21–35 outline the lavishness of forgiveness that should be extended to those who truly repent—who change their behavior rather than just apologize. But where professions of repentance do not produce a forgiving demeanor toward others, judgment may be severe indeed. Verses 34–35 have understandably been viewed as support for believing that God's grace and forgiveness can be retracted, but it may be more helpful to understand, with Ridderbos, that "whoever tries to separate man's forgiveness from God's will no longer be able to count on God's mercy. In so doing he does not merely forfeit it, like the servant in the parable. Rather he shows that he never had a part in it. God's mercy is not something cut and dried that is

5. The most detailed modern treatment of this chapter is W. G. Thompson, *Matthew's Advice to a Divided Community* (Rome: BIP, 1970).

6. Matthew's and Luke's versions of the lost sheep provide a classic test case for identifying a critic's presuppositions. If the similarities between the two versions demand that Matthew and Luke have each modified a common source, then clearly they felt free to take considerable liberties with their traditions. But, given two entirely different settings and applications, why not assume that Jesus himself used one plot in two different ways in two different contexts? See further Craig L. Blomberg, "When Is a Parallel Really a Parallel? A Test Case: The Lucan Parables," *WTJ* 46 (1984): 78–103.

7. On the topic more generally, see J. Carl Laney, *A Guide to Church Discipline* (Minneapolis: Bethany, 1985).

received only once. It is a persistent power that pervades all of life. If it does not become manifest as such a power, then it was never received at all."[8]

Historicity

Whether "M" (see above, p. 92) is a distinct source or the apostle's memory, we must take seriously the likelihood of authentic material in Matthew's unparalleled sections. The Jewish particularism of Matthew 10:1–16, much of it later rescinded, clearly shows that Matthew differentiated historical information from the changed circumstances of his day. Verse 23 is sufficiently cryptic and potentially embarrassing as to be almost certainly authentic. Verses 34–36 and 37–39 are obvious "hard sayings," particularly cutting against the grain of other Jewish and later Christian "family values." The themes and forms of Matthew 18 speak for the authenticity of an important core of that "sermon" as well: two "triadic" parables; Jesus' characteristic themes of forgiveness and repentance, each portrayed with distinctive twists; and a focus on humility, not considered a virtue in most of the Hellenistic world and not well modeled in ancient Jewish or early Christian circles.

LUKE'S CENTRAL SECTION (9:51–18:14) [ALAND §174–237]

Chronology, Geography, and Outline

As noted in our discussion of the outlines of the Gospels (above, part 3), Luke's central section, or travel narrative as it is sometimes called, is made up almost entirely of Q + L material. These comprise almost exclusively *teachings* of Jesus. Although the section begins as though it were going to trace Jesus' itinerary from Galilee to Jerusalem for the fate that he knows awaits him there (9:51), there are fewer indications of chronology or geography in the subsequent nine chapters than in any other section of comparable length in any Gospel. What can be deduced is limited to three passages: (1) In 9:51–56 Jesus is rejected in Samaria and so goes "to another village." This has often been interpreted as implying that Jesus avoided Samaria altogether and followed the popular Jewish route of traveling along the Jordan's east bank through Perea. Yet this is sheer inference, and Jesus may well have proceeded simply to a different Samaritan village. (2) In 10:38–42 he is with Mary and Martha, who lived in Bethany, just outside Jerusalem (but we know this location only from John's Gospel—John 11:1). (3) In 17:11 he is traveling along the border between Samaria and Galilee. Whatever else we conclude, this is certainly no straight-line journey from Galilee to Jerusalem!

Given the topical arrangement of these nine chapters, it is best to see them as Luke's way of gathering together teachings of Jesus, perhaps largely from the climactic phase of his public ministry, as he traveled about in numerous places, but all "under the shadow of the cross" that he knew loomed large in his future (9:51). Indeed the most persuasive attempts to outline this section have virtually nothing to do with chronology at all. Several writers have seen

---

8. H. N. Ridderbos, *Matthew* (Grand Rapids: Zondervan, 1987), 346.

parallels between the sequence of passages beginning in 9:51 and selected teachings from the book of Deuteronomy—further evidence that Luke wanted to portray Jesus as the eschatological prophet Moses predicted.[9] Even more compelling are outlines that see the "travel narrative" as an extended chiasmus, usually with the climactic center in Jesus' solemn pronouncement that he must journey to Jerusalem and be killed there (13:31–35).[10] The most consistently convincing parts of such an outline match pairs of closely parallel parables, thus suggesting a modification of this hypothesis: Luke used a chiastically arranged parables source (either oral or written), around which he grouped topically related teachings of Jesus to create a thematically organized section. The climactic center of this hypothetical source would then come in Luke's great banquet parable and related teachings in 14:7–24, which stress Luke's key themes of coming judgment on unrepentant Israel, the acceptance of the kingdom by the outcasts of Jewish society, and possibly also the foreshadowing of the Gentile mission.

Selected Comments on Individual Passages

Space prohibits consideration of every passage in Luke's central section, so we will concentrate here primarily on passages unique to Luke, and on the overall narrative flow of the text. Most of the Q-passages are already treated elsewhere in this book in discussing material in Matthew.

Contrasting Pictures of Discipleship (9:52–62) [Aland §175–176]. With all of the parallels between Jesus and Elijah earlier in Luke, we are not surprised to read that the disciples propose replicating Elijah's miracle of calling down fire from heaven in order to destroy their enemies (vv. 54–56; cf. 1 Kings. 18:38). But one who is journeying to the cross must be prepared to suffer without retaliation. Thus Jesus stresses the radical commitment required of would-be disciples (vv. 57–62). Burying one's father and saying good-bye to one's family could actually be euphemisms for waiting until relatives were dead before joining up with Jesus, but the harshness of Jesus' call must not be overly muted. "Following him is not a task which is added to others like working a second job. . . . It is everything. It is a solemn commitment which forces the disciples-to-be to reorder all their other duties."[11]

The Mission of the Seventy (-two) (10:1–24) [Aland §177–181]. In one of the rare narrative events of Luke's central section, Jesus sends out seventy (-two) disciples, corresponding to the number of nations listed in Genesis 10.[12] His charge closely parallels his earlier commissioning of the Twelve to preach and heal exclusively among the cities of Israel (Matt. 10:5–15 pars.). If Jesus is indeed in Perea at this time, this would be an explicit Gentile mission; if not, the ministry of this larger band of disciples at least foreshadows it.[13] For this

9. An influential hypothesis first proposed by C. F. Evans ("The Central Section of St. Luke's Gospel," in *Studies in the Gospels*, ed. D. E. Nineham [Oxford: Blackwell, 1955], 37–53) found twenty-two separate parallels matching texts from Luke 10–18 with passages, in sequence, from Deuteronomy 1–26. Other scholars, noting that not all of these parallels are equally close or convincing, have preferred to speak merely of key Deuteronomic themes permeating Luke's central section (see above, p. 146).

10. See esp. Kenneth E. Bailey, *Poet and Peasant* (Grand Rapids: Eerdmans, 1976), 80–82.

11. Robert J. Karris, *Invitation to Luke* (Garden City: Doubleday, 1977), 130.

12. The textual evidence in Luke 10:1, 17 between "seventy" and "seventy-two" is relatively evenly balanced but slightly favors the latter. The same variations in number appear, respectively, between the Hebrew and Greek manuscripts of Genesis 10.

13. Cf. John Nolland, *Luke 9:21–18:34* (Dallas: Word, 1993), 558.

A Chiastic Source of Parables Unique to Luke's Central Section	
A. The Good Samaritan (10:25–37)	A.' The Pharisee and Publican (18:9–14)
(outcasts as heroes; Jewish leaders as bad role models)	
B. The Friend at Midnight (11:5–8)	B.' The Unjust Judge (18:1–8)
(rhetorical question form; bold, persistent prayer)	
C. The Rich Fool (12:13–21)	C.' The Rich Man and Lazarus (16:19–31)
(eternal danger due to misuse of riches)	
D. The Watchful Servants (12:35–38)	D.' The Unjust Steward (16:1–13)
(servant parables; right and wrong use of stewardship)	
E. The Barren Fig Tree (13:1–9)	E.' The Lost Sheep, Coin, Son (15:1–32)
(triad of parallel texts on repentance; two short and one long)	
F. The Great Banquet (14:7–24)	
(climactic center; key Lukan themes of reversal, poor/rich, Christ's return)[a]	

a. Craig L. Blomberg, "Midrash, Chiasmus, and the Outline of Luke's Central Section," in *Gospel Perspectives*, vol. 3, ed. R. T. France and David Wenham (Sheffield: JSOT, 1983), 217–61.

reason, Luke inserts various texts from Q that contrast Jesus' rejection in key Jewish cities with his acceptance by the "nobodies" of this world (vv. 13–16, 21–24). In between, he uniquely stresses how the successful exorcisms performed by his followers demonstrate the vanquishing of Satan which the arrival of God's reign accomplishes (vv. 17–20). Though not yet completely executed, the devil's doom is assured.

On Love of God and Neighbor (10:25–42) [Aland §182–184]. A lawyer trying to trap Jesus asks him about eternal life. Jesus initially gives a classically Jewish answer: love God and neighbor (cf. Deut. 6:5; Lev. 19:18). The lawyer, no doubt thinking ethnocentrically, asks how far the definition of "neighbor" extends, so Jesus tells the parable of the good Samaritan (vv. 25–37). From the Samaritan's example we learn that we must show compassion to all who are in need. From the priest and Levite, we see that religious duty is no excuse for lovelessness. But the climactic and unifying theme of the passage that answers the lawyer's question and explains why the hero is a Samaritan, shocking Jesus' Jewish audience, is that *even one's enemy is one's neighbor.*[14]

Attempts at neighbor love, however, can degenerate into mere busywork and sacrifice appropriate love for God. So Luke juxtaposes the equally challenging encounter between Jesus and the two sisters, Mary and Martha. Flying squarely in the face of societal convention, Jesus proclaims that Mary, who is provocatively acting as though she were equal to the male disciples by sitting at her rabbi's feet to learn from him, has chosen the only thing needed on this occasion. Martha's "typically female" preoccupation with domestic chores, to provide the kind of hospitality for Jesus and his troupe that society expected, misses the point altogether.

Teachings about Prayer (11:1–13) [Aland §185–187]. Distinctive in this context is the little parable of the friend at midnight (vv. 5–8). The imagery and language of this parable teach not so much persistence in prayer (that point will come in 18:1–8) but boldness or shamelessness.[15] In the appended Q-passage (vv. 9–13 par.), Jesus promises that God will give only good gifts to his children in response to their requests. But, unlike Matthew's version, Luke concludes by referring specifically to the Holy Spirit as the preeminent good gift that they will receive. This is probably a use of "synecdoche" (a figure of speech in which a part stands for the whole).

Controversy with the Pharisees (11:14–54) [Aland §188–194]. This section is almost exclusively Q-material and is dealt with in various other places in this book.

Preparing for Coming Judgment (12:1–13:9) [Aland §195–207]. The distinctively Lukan portions of this unit center on various parables. The rich fool (12:13–21) is not condemned for his wealth, but for covetousness (NIV "greed"—v. 15), wholly self-centered accumulation and hoarding (vv. 16–20), and taking no thought for God (v. 21). Still, the danger for most affluent Westerners, including Christians, is that we do not see how much we still resemble this man, even after these various qualifications are made.[16] In 12:35–48, one L and two Q parables are grouped together to demonstrate the watchfulness that is needed for Christ's return. But every attempt to guess the time of the Parousia is misguided: he may come surprisingly late (vv. 35–38), wholly unexpectedly (vv. 39–40), or surprisingly soon (vv. 42–46). To this last parable, Luke adds two unparalleled verses that stress that the severity of judgment will vary according to an individual's knowledge (vv. 47–48). It would seem by this that Jesus is teaching degrees of punishment in hell, which is only fair, since condemnation is based on one's works. Luke 13:1–9 is also unique to this Gospel.

---

14. See esp. Robert W. Funk, *Parables and Presence* (Philadelphia: Fortress, 1982), 29–34, 64–65.

15. Recent editions of the NIV correctly translate *anaideia* in v. 8 as "boldness." The "chutzpah" of the man's request is also reflected in some older translations' use of "importunity," though this also misleadingly reflects the notion of persistence. It is also just possible that the shamelessness refers to the sleeping man, in the sense that he wants to avoid the shame that would accrue to him if word got out to the village that he had failed to provide the necessary hospitality. See further J. D. M. Derrett, "The Friend at Midnight: Asian Ideas in the Gospel of St. Luke," in *Donum Gentilicum*, ed. Ernst Bammel, C. K. Barrett and W. D. Davies (Oxford: Clarendon, 1978), 78–87.

16. Cf. further Craig L. Blomberg, *Give Me Neither Poverty nor Riches: A New Testament Theology of Material Possessions* (Leicester: IVP; Grand Rapids: Eerdmans, forthcoming).

References to two recent national disasters lead to a parable about the impending judgment on the nation of Israel if it does not repent.

Kingdom Reversals (13:10–14:24) [Aland §208–216]. This section falls into two closely parallel units (13:10–35; 14:1–24). Each begins with Jesus healing a person on the Sabbath, proceeds to present a pair of brief, parallel parables, and concludes with a longer discourse on who will and will not enter the kingdom. Put together, the dominant theme of this chapter and a half is the surprising reversal of contemporary expectation concerning kingdom participants. Standard practices of reciprocity are rebuked (14:7–14a), while Christ promises eternal reward only to those who follow him with no desire for repayment (v. 14b, illustrated by vv. 15–24).[17]

The Cost of Discipleship (14:25–35) [Aland §217–218]. Again distinctively Lukan parables form the core of this short section (vv. 28–32). Matthew 10:37 is important in interpreting Luke 14:26—"hating" was a vivid Semitic hyperbole for "loving less." Still, in a contemporary conservative Christianity that often seems to stress commitment to "family values" above radical service for Christ, there are strong warnings here. The medieval church was so challenged by the theme of "counting the cost" that at times it limited the application of these verses to clergy and monastic orders! We may also need to rethink the ease with which we declare people to be Christians who pray a simple prayer of invitation or raise a hand in response to an evangelistic appeal. Only those who persevere over the long haul demonstrate themselves truly to have been saved. Still, verses 28–30 balance the cost of following with the cost of not following (vv. 31–32), and it is clear that the second price is far higher.

The Joy of Repentance (15:1–32) [Aland §219–221]. One might also label this section "three parables about lostness"—the lost sheep, lost coin, and lost sons. The three lessons become clear especially when one reads the parable of the prodigal through the eyes of each of the three characters. (1) Wayward individuals are always invited to repent, no matter how far they have fallen. There is no pit so deep that God is not deeper still. (2) God is always waiting, ready to welcome the sinner home. The father demonstrates lavish love by running in a socially undignified fashion and throwing a party rather than requiring penance. (3) The climactic point, however, again addresses conservative religious folk. Those who consider themselves more upright must never resent such "unworthy" recipients of God's grace. Luke 15:1–3 makes it clear that the father is a symbol for God (and indirectly for Jesus), that the prodigal stands for the tax collectors and sinners, and that the older brother represents the Pharisees and scribes criticizing Jesus. But this means that the shepherd and woman in the preceding two parables are also, in some sense, images for God—striking metaphors in a culture that often despised shepherds and considered women second-class citizens![18]

The Use and Abuse of Riches (16:1–31) [Aland §222–228]. The story of the unjust steward (16:1–13) is perhaps the most perplexing of all of Jesus'

---

17. The three main points of the great banquet parable, associated with its three main (groups of) characters, are well captured by Robert H. Stein, *An Introduction to the Parables of Jesus* (Philadelphia: Westminster, 1981), 89: "The point is that the kingdom of God has come and that those who would have been expected to receive it (the religious elite) did not do so, whereas the ones least likely to receive it (the publicans, poor, harlots, etc.) have."

18. On this whole chapter, cf. esp. Kenneth E. Bailey, *Finding the Lost: Cultural Keys to Luke 15* (St. Louis: Concordia, 1992).

parables. Why does the master praise one who has squandered his possessions and then legally cheated him out of additional money? The simplest and probably the correct answer is because of his shrewdness (v. 8). Jesus ironically comments that God's people are often not nearly as clever as fallen humanity. We must learn to be equally shrewd, *without being unethical*, particularly in the use of our finances. Verse 9 commands us to use our material resources for kingdom priorities so that the men and women who have benefited in their Christian lives from our stewardship will welcome us in the world to come.[19]

Luke 16:19–31 is also unique to this Gospel and furthers the theme of the right use of our riches. This sumptuous feaster is not condemned merely for being rich. The concern he expresses for his family members who have not repented (v. 30) shows that he realized he, too, had never become right with God. Yet the manifestation of that lack of repentance was his daily neglect of a hopelessly poor and suffering person on his doorstep. He had Moses and the prophets—the Hebrew Bible (v. 31)—and knew his responsibility to be generous to the needy, but he altogether ignored them. Similar behavior in any era falsifies any claim of faith in Christ a person may profess to make.[20]

Teachings about Faith (17:1–19) [Aland §229–233]. Unique to Luke here is the short parable of the unworthy servant (vv. 7–10), which excellently expresses in story form the biblical doctrine of salvation by grace through faith alone. The episode of the ten lepers (vv. 11–19) furthers Luke's concern for society's outcasts, including the Samaritans. It also upends expectations of reciprocity. All the Samaritan could do was return and give thanks; the Jews might not have given thanks because they assumed that they owed Jesus a favor in return. But there is nothing we can do to repay Christ for what he does for us, except express our gratitude. As a result, only the Samaritan experiences both physical *and* spiritual healing.

When and How the Kingdom Will Appear (17:20–18:8) [Aland §234–236]. Most of this section appears in Luke's sources, but Luke balances present and future eschatology by adding verses 20–21, that stress the kingdom's presence, to verses 22–25. The NIV margin gives the more likely reading for verse 21: the kingdom is "among" not "within" the Pharisees. Thus this text cannot be used to support a merely spiritual or internal interpretation of the kingdom's arrival, as opposed to one that also includes an external or social dimension. In 18:1–8 Jesus returns to the theme of prayer, this time to argue *a fortiori* (from the lesser to the greater) that if even corrupt human judges can be badgered into

---

19. For this approach and for a full history of interpretation, see Dennis J. Ireland, *Stewardship and the Kingdom of God* (Leiden: Brill, 1992). For a similar perspective, in response to several quite recent alternatives, cf. Dave L. Mathewson, "The Parable of the Unjust Steward (Luke 16:1–13): A Reexamination of the Traditional View in Light of Recent Challenges," *JETS* 38 (1995): 29–39.

20. One misses the point and overinterprets if this parable is used to teach in detail about the nature of the afterlife. Similar stories were known in both Egyptian and Jewish circles, and it is likely that Jesus was deliberately adopting and adapting a well-known story to suit his distinctive purposes. Orthodox Christianity has never used this passage to teach that there are people who want to cross over from Abraham's bosom to Hades (rough Jewish equivalents for what in Christian language has come to be known as heaven and hell)—v. 26. So, despite some claims to the contrary, it is equally inappropriate to use this passage to claim that before the cross there were two separate compartments of the underworld from which people could speak back and forth, and so on. Against the argument that this is not a parable, because one of the characters has a name (Lazarus), note the deliberate symbolism of the meaning of the name ("God helps"). The introductory formula and the overall structure of the passage exactly match those of many other parables, and the passage should be categorized accordingly. Cf. esp. Richard Bauckham, "The Rich Man and Lazarus: The Parable and the Parallels," *NTS* 37 (1991): 225–46.

granting justice, then surely one can expect God to vindicate his chosen children.

The Pharisee and Tax Collector (18:9–14) [Aland §237]. In terms of Luke's overall outline, his central section probably extends a little beyond this passage. But with 18:15 he returns to following Mark's narrative fairly closely, and we will pick up the story line there in our next chapter. The final passage unique to Luke in his travel narrative is this parable with yet another striking reversal of expectation as to who is right with God. Unless we recognize the Pharisee as the one assumed to be more godly, we altogether miss the dynamic of Jesus declaring the tax collector justified rather than the religious leader. But it is only the tax collector who understands the principle that justification comes solely by throwing oneself on the mercy of God.

Historicity

The historicity of the Q-material in Luke's central section is treated elsewhere in this book. Many of these passages present us with an almost unanswerable question: When did Jesus say something more than once, and when has Matthew or Luke (or both) relocated a given saying into a new context? As for Luke's distinctive material, we may observe that it is filled with Jesus' characteristic and challenging parables, along with other succinct, subversive sayings. The occasional miracles that occur cohere with Jesus' behavior elsewhere, as they involve healings on a Sabbath (13:10–17; 14:1–6) or praise for outcasts (17:11–19). Luke 9:57–62 furthers the theme of radical discipleship, while letting the (spiritually) dead bury the (physically) dead is almost universally agreed to be much too harsh to have been invented.[21] The sending of the seventy (-two) (10:1–24) coheres with the sending of the Twelve (Mark 6:7–13 pars.). The reference to mighty works in Chorazin and Bethsaida (Luke 10:13–15) is probably historical because these miracles are not actually described anywhere that could have generated this reference. Jesus' commendation of Mary's learning as a rabbi's disciple at the expense of Martha's domesticity (10:38–42) almost entirely inverts both Jewish and early Christian practice. It, too, is thus surely authentic. Whether or not attested elsewhere, the gruesome event of 13:1 fits well with the ruthless behavior of Pilate described in Josephus. Luke 13:31–35 strikingly juxtaposes harshness and tenderness in Jesus' verbal assault on Herod and poignant lament over Jerusalem, both in the context of the most positive statement about the Pharisees as a group anywhere in the Gospels. None of these features, much less their combination, would have easily been invented. The theme of the "great reversal" that pervades Luke's central section, especially chapters 14–15, meshes well with the overall patterns of the historical Jesus, while 17:7–10 and 11–19 narrate two examples of his characteristically radical grace. Luke 17:20–37 well balances Jesus' distinctive "already but not yet" approach to the arrival of the kingdom. These and similar passages support the hypothesis that Luke relied on tradition or source material even for his unparalleled passages. That tradition also shows numerous signs of historical reliability.

21. See esp. E. P. Sanders, *Jesus and Judaism* (London: SCM; Philadelphia: Fortress, 1985), 252–55.

JOHN 5–11

The only full chapter in John's Gospel that presents material about Jesus' great Galilean ministry, and thus overlaps with the synoptic accounts, is chapter 6 (see above, p. 272). Chapters 5 and 7–11 all describe events in conjunction with Jesus' various trips to Jerusalem at festival time, in between his first and last Passovers there. Because John refers to the various feasts, we are able to develop a rough chronology of Jesus' ministry, but his primary purpose in giving these references is not to enable us to reconstruct a life of Christ. Rather, he wants to show how Jesus fulfills all the major institutions of Judaism.[22] In each case, too, Jesus' claims generate considerable controversy and opposition among his Jewish audiences. In chapter 5, John does not identify the feast at hand (5:1), perhaps because the major controversy here surrounds a healing on the *Sabbath*, which Jesus fulfills. But chronologically, this chapter records events at either a Passover (spring) or a Tabernacles (fall) relatively early in Jesus' ministry. John 7:1–10:21 narrates material related to the Tabernacles of Jesus' last year of ministry. John 10:22–39 is associated with Hanukkah (December) during Jesus' last year. As noted in our discussion of chronology above (pp. 191–193), Jesus' final trip to Jerusalem probably begins in between these two festivals because in John 11, Jesus is still nearby in Bethany. With chapter 12, the final week of Jesus' life ensues, and overlaps between John's Gospel and the Synoptics resume.

Healing the Paralytic on a Sabbath (5:1–47) [Aland §140–141]

John 5:1–18 reminds the reader of Jesus' Capernaum miracle narrated in Mark 2:1–12 and parallels, particularly with Jesus' dramatic command, "Pick up your mat and walk" (John 5:8). But the circumstances vary. Jesus is passing by the Bethesda pool where invalids waited in hopes of a chance to bathe and receive divine healing (vv. 2–3, 7). Interestingly, Jesus singles out only one of many to be a recipient of his grace. He also presupposes a connection between the man's illness and his past sinful behavior (v. 14).[23] As with various Synoptic healings, however, the primary controversy that Jesus' actions generate deals with his "working" on the Sabbath (vv. 9–10, 16). Jesus' defense appeals to the continual working of God, whom he invokes as his Father. But for Jesus to be justified in breaking Sabbath by appealing to God's behavior, he must be tacitly claiming divine prerogatives. The Jewish leaders, hence, again begin to plot his death (vv. 17–18).

As frequently in John, a miracle leads to a discourse. Verses 19–47 supply Jesus' more extended defense of his actions. Verse 19 has sometimes been supposed to have been a miniparable all its own—about an apprentice's son who must always imitate his master—which Jesus is now applying to himself.[24] Beginning with this illustration, Jesus elaborates his "sermon" in two main

---

22. See esp. Charles H. Talbert, *Reading John* (New York: Crossroad, 1992), *passim*.

23. A connection not always adequately grasped. See John C. Thomas, "'Stop Sinning Lest Something Worse Come Upon You'," *JSNT* 59 (1995): 3–20.

24. So esp. C. H. Dodd, "A Hidden Parable in the Fourth Gospel," in *More New Testament Studies* (Manchester: Manchester University Press, 1968), 30–40.

sections: verses 19–30 and 31–47. Verses 19–30 articulate two key themes: (1) Jesus is completely dependent on and subordinate to his Father. (2) The Father entrusts Jesus with all judgment. Together these themes balance what has been called Jesus' *ontological* (or essential) *equality* with God and his *functional subordination* within the Godhead. "The Father initiates, sends, commands, commissions, grants; the Son responds, obeys, performs his Father's will, receives authority."[25] In his equality with God, Jesus stands over against us; in his subordination he stands with us, showing how we, too, must perform God's will in complete dependence on him. Verses 31–47 present four witnesses to corroborate Christ's claims: John the Baptist (vv. 33–35), Jesus' "works" (v. 36), the Father himself (vv. 37–38), and Scripture (vv. 39–47).[26] However, the latter three are not particularly distinct from one another; it is precisely through Jesus' miracles and the Scripture that the Father speaks.

Jesus as Fulfillment of the Feast of Tabernacles (7:1–10:21)

Living Water (7:1–52) [Aland §238–241]. The introductory section of this chapter (vv. 1–13) reminds one of the prelude to the Cana miracle of turning water into wine (2:1–11). Jesus' family members urge him to reveal himself plainly; Christ seemingly refuses but then does so anyway, yet on his own time- table rather than theirs. From verse 14 on, we read of what happens when he does appear publicly in Jerusalem. His discourse takes up where he left off when he was last in town (chap. 5). Verses 14–24 raise again the issue of the origin of Jesus' astonishing teaching and defend the legitimacy of his healing on a Sabbath. As Jesus explains, he alludes to the hypocrisy of those who would try to take his life (recall 5:18, and cf. 7:1, 11, and 13), a plot of which the crowds are ignorant (v. 20). Within the Law, the need to circumcise a child could overrule Sabbath regulations. How much more should one who speaks for the Father himself not be able to supersede them (vv. 22–24)?

Jesus' words leave the crowds divided. Verses 25–31 reflect this debate. Verse 27 alludes to a Jewish tradition that the Messiah would suddenly appear "out of nowhere," whereas the crowds know that this man comes from Naza- reth. Verse 28 should be taken either as an ironic declaration, "You *think* you know me and where I am from," or as a question, "*Do* you know me. . . ?" Either way, it is clear that the crowds do not recognize his true heavenly origin. The Jewish leaders remain dead set against him too (v. 32). Jesus knows all this and predicts his coming departure (by death), though again in sufficiently enig- matic language that his listeners fail to catch on (vv. 33–36).

Verse 37 brings us to the climactic claim of this chapter. For seven days the festival-goers had observed the water-drawing ritual in which priests processed from the pool of Siloam to the temple with a golden pitcher of water, proclaim- ing with trumpet blasts the text of Isaiah 12:3: "With joy you will draw water from the wells of salvation." All the participants then waved palm branches and praised God joyfully. On the eighth and final day the ceremony was not enacted. How dramatic and timely, then, for Jesus himself to stand up and

---

25. D. A. Carson, *The Gospel according to John* (Grand Rapids: Eerdmans; Leicester; IVP, 1991), 251.
26. For elaboration, see Urban C. von Wahlde, "The Witnesses to Jesus in John 5:31–40 and Belief in the Fourth Gospel," *CBQ* 43 (1981): 385–404.

proclaim that *he* was the living water, the provider of salvation, for which the Jews longed.[27] Many modern commentators prefer the NIV margin to the text itself for verses 37–38, so that it is clear that it is Christ alone who is the source of this metaphorical water: "If anyone is thirsty, let him come to me. And let him drink, who believes in me. As the Scripture has said, streams of living water will flow from within him [i.e., Christ]." There is no one Old Testament passage that Jesus is quoting here, but the themes he enunciates appear in such texts as Isaiah 58:11, Zechariah 14:8, and various passages throughout Nehemiah 8–9. John explains, too, that Jesus is speaking about the coming Spirit who will be dispensed, through Christ, to his people after his coming "glorification"—death, resurrection, and exaltation (v. 39). Once more a debate ensues among the crowd, again over Christ's origin (vv. 40–44). They are apparently oblivious to his birth in Bethlehem, the city of David from whose lineage Messiah must come. Once again, also, the Jewish leaders are incensed, though Nicodemus offers a minority defense on Jesus' behalf (vv. 45–52).[28]

Light of the World and the Divine "I AM" (8:12–59) [Aland §243–247]. After we realize that 7:53–8:11 was almost certainly not in what John originally wrote (see above, p. 75), 8:12–59 follows naturally. Still at the Feast of Tabernacles, Jesus now makes a second claim—he is the light of the world. This pronouncement would also have electrified the crowds. Every night of the feast, four huge lamps were lit to accompany joyful singing and dancing. On the last night, the main candelabrum was deliberately left unlit as a reminder that Israel had not yet experienced full salvation. Jesus is now declaring himself to be the one who can provide that salvation (v. 12).

Jesus' claim is immediately challenged by the religious leaders (v. 13). For corroborating witness, he appeals again to his Father and to his coming departure (crucifixion and heavenly return)—verses 14–29.[29] Many at first apparently believe in him (v. 30), but, as the subsequent dialogue demonstrates (vv. 31–59), they have altogether misunderstood him (cf. the description of fickle faith in 2:23–25). Adequate faith will continue to hold fast to Jesus' teaching and provide spiritual liberation (vv. 31–32). Jesus' listeners, however, believe that their ancestral credentials as God's chosen people have already guaranteed that (v. 33), so Jesus and his audience debate who the true spiritual descendants of Abraham really are and who are in fact "children of the devil" (vv. 34–47). When reason fails, the authorities resort to name-calling and abuse (v. 48). Tensions heighten as Jesus further defends his claims in language that makes him out to be, first, greater than Abraham; second, preexisting from before the time of Abraham; and, finally, worthy of the very divine name of Exodus 3:14—"I AM" (vv. 49–58).[30] The authorities are so outraged that they

---

27. Cf. further George R. Beasley-Murray, *John* (Waco: Word, 1987), 113–14. For two often overlooked rabbinic references that illuminate this background further (*Pesikta Rabbati* 52:4, 6; *t. Sukkoth* 3:3–12), see Bruce H. Grigsby, "'If Any Man Thirsts . . .': Observations on the Rabbinic Background of John 7,37–39," *Biblica* 67 (1986): 101–8.

28. For a good treatment of the narrative flow of chap. 7, see Harold W. Attridge, "Thematic Development and Source Elaboration in John 7:1–36," *CBQ* 42 (1980): 160–70.

29. Indeed, the entire chapter is couched as a trial in which Jesus judges his audience. The core of this process involves a five-fold cycle of statement, misunderstanding, and explanation in vv. 32–58. See Jerome H. Neyrey, "Jesus the Judge: Forensic Process in John 8,21–59," *Biblica* 68 (1987): 509–42.

30. This explains the otherwise "bad grammar" in "Before Abraham was, I am" (v. 58). The Greek for "I am" (*egō eimi*) could also reflect dependence on passages like Isa. 41:4—"I, the Lord—with the first of them and with the last—*I am he*" (italics added). Cf. further Philip B. Harner, *The "I Am" of the Fourth Gospel* (Philadelphia: Fortress, 1970).

initiate mob violence and attempt to stone Jesus (v. 59). Jewish law commanded the stoning of a blasphemer, though under Rome, Jews were forbidden most forms of capital punishment (cf. John 18:31). In the emotion of the moment, the law apparently did not matter.

More Light for the World: The Healing of the Man Born Blind (9:1–41) [Aland §248]. Jesus' next miracle seems to occur shortly after Tabernacles, before Jesus left Jerusalem with the rest of the festival pilgrims and returned home to Galilee one last time. The miracle invites comparison and contrast with 5:1–15. Again, Jesus deliberately selects a Sabbath on which to do his good work (v. 14) and employs an unusually elaborate method—mixing mud and saliva to put on the blind man's eyes (v. 6). Thus he can be accused of violating the Pharisaic Sabbath laws against kneading and the use of spittle. Once again washing in a Jerusalem pool is instrumental in the healing. Rabbinic traditions about the eschatological dimensions of Siloam may suggest deliberate symbolism here.[31] On the other hand, this time Jesus makes it clear that no one's sin has directly caused this man's deformity; rather, "this happened so that the work of God might be displayed in his life" (v. 3). We must beware of assuming either that disease or disaster are always a direct result of an individual's sin or that they can never be.

As in 8:12, Jesus declares himself to be the light of the world. Healing a blind man vividly illustrates that principle in the physical realm as well as the spiritual. After the miracle itself (9:1–12), the Pharisees investigate what has happened by interviewing the formerly blind man, then his parents, and finally the man himself again (vv. 13–34). They cannot believe that a Sabbath-breaker can be from God. The man cannot believe that one who has brought such great good into his life is not from God. In this case, experience disproves tradition. But again logic gives way to verbal abuse. The final segment of chapter 9 finds Jesus back with the healed man, eliciting a confession of faith from him while pronouncing judgment on his spiritually blind critics (vv. 35–41).[32] Verse 39 recalls Jesus' reason for speaking in parables (Mark 4:11–12 pars.), on which Bruce comments, "[Jesus'] presence and activity in the world themselves constitute a judgment as they compel men and women to declare themselves for or against him."[33]

The Good Shepherd (10:1–21) [Aland §249–250]. The chapter break indicates no change of time or place, and what follows may be an allegory of the preceding incident. Jesus now shifts to a different metaphor: he is the Good Shepherd. Verses 1–5 employ a quasi-parable (see v. 6), which verses 7–18 proceed to explain and elaborate. This entire section develops the contrast between Jesus, the true and noble leader of his people, and the current Jewish regime

---

31. Bruce Grigsby, "Washing in the Pool of Siloam—A Thematic Anticipation of the Johannine Cross," *NovT* 27 (1985): 227–35. These relate particularly to the arrival of the life-giving water flowing from the temple prophesied in Ezekiel 47.

32. This twofold dimension of physical and spiritual sight vs. blindness thus runs throughout chap. 9 and has formed the basis for the influential thesis of J. Louis Martyn, *History and Theology in the Fourth Gospel* (Nashville: Abingdon, rev. 1979), that John is writing to combat Jews in his day who are excommunicating Christians from their synagogues (cf. esp. v. 22). Verse 22 has also been seen as an anachronism that applied only to John's day, but that is to assume that it refers to an empire-wide pogrom. Probably only a short-lived local policy within Jerusalem is in view. After all, it is the parents of the man rather than the man himself who fear expulsion, and they are not even described as believing in Jesus.

33. F. F. Bruce, *The Gospel of John* (Basingstoke: Pickering & Inglis; Grand Rapids: Eerdmans, 1983), 220.

that has proved false and misleading. Jesus alternates between (a) comparing himself, as the good shepherd who enters the sheep pen by the gate, with robbers who would climb over the wall, and (b) contrasting himself, as the actual gate through whom the sheep enter by listening to their shepherd's voice, with hirelings whose words the sheep cannot recognize.[34] Behind these comparisons and contrasts lies Ezekiel 34 with its prophecies of the messianic shepherd who would save his people from the false shepherds currently guiding them.

What makes Jesus so "good" above all is his willingness to sacrifice his very life for his flock (vv. 11, 15, 17). Jesus also hints here at the coming ministry to the Gentiles when he adds that he has other sheep "not of this sheep pen" (v. 16). To all he offers "abundant life" (v. 10; NIV—"life . . . to the full"), but in context this involves no promises of earthly glory or prosperity but rich, eternal life ("whoever enters through me will be saved"—v. 9). Once again, Jesus' audience is deeply divided over all his remarks (vv. 19–21).[35]

The Feast of Dedication (Hanukkah): Jesus and the Father Are One (10:22–42) [Aland §257–258].

The events of John 10:22–11:54 presumably take place after at least the start of Jesus' Judean ministry (see below, chap. 16). But it makes sense to comment on them here because of their thematic links with the preceding material in John. In December of A.D. 29 (or 32), Jesus is in Jerusalem for the last festival before the Passover in which he will lay down his life (vv. 22–23). Just as he has fulfilled the other main Jewish institutions, so he will provide the true spiritual liberation that corresponds to the physical liberation that Hanukkah commemorated. Jesus' audience, frustrated by his seemingly blasphemous claims during prior forays to Jerusalem, but realizing that all of them were susceptible to a variety of interpretations, demands him to disclose his identity plainly (v. 24). Still he refuses. If they had the eyes of faith, they would have found his words and works more than sufficient; those who do belong to Jesus are already secure in that relationship (vv. 25–29). Again, he climaxes his reply with a claim that is taken as blasphemy (vv. 31–33), while still open to other interpretations: "I and the Father are one" (v. 30).[36]

To refute the charge of blasphemy, Jesus in verse 34 makes one of his more enigmatic appeals to Scripture, citing Psalm 82:6. In this passage, the psalmist refers to the corrupt evil judges of his day (or perhaps to Israel at the time of the giving of the Law) as "gods." If the authoritative Scriptures can call mere mortals "gods," in this limited sense of referring to earthly leaders, Jesus argues, then how much more is it not acceptable for him to apply the term to himself, who is God's unique agent on earth (vv. 35–36)?[37] *Contra* various cults and

---

34. For a fascinating discussion of how realistic all this is, even by the practices of modern Middle Eastern peasant shepherds, see Kenneth E. Bailey, "The Shepherd Poems of John 10: Their Culture and Style," *Near East School of Theology Theological Review* 14 (1993): 3–21. Allowing oneself to be killed merely to protect a few sheep, however, is very rare, and highlights the allegorical meaning and central thrust of Jesus' word pictures.

35. On this chapter more generally, cf. Johannes Beutler and Robert T. Fortna, eds., *The Shepherd Discourse of John 10 and Its Context* (Cambridge: CUP, 1991).

36. J. Ramsey Michaels, *John* (Peabody: Hendrickson, 1989), 187, finds a syllogism here: If vv. 28 and 29 predicate parallel truths about the Son and the Father, then the two must be one.

37. On the "from the lesser to the greater" logic of this passage and its various other implications, see Jerome H. Neyrey, "I Said 'You Are Gods': Psalm 82:6 and John 10," *JBL* 108 (1989): 647–63.

sects, this passage teaches nothing about Christians becoming deified. Jesus again appeals to the testimony of his works, but to no avail. He leaves Jerusalem to avoid further troubles for the moment and goes back across the Jordan to where people will believe (vv. 37–42).

The Raising of Lazarus (John 11:1–54) [Aland §259–261]

The first "half" of John's Gospel climaxes with the most dramatic miracle in all of Jesus' ministry, excluding his own resurrection. He has previously brought people back to life shortly after their deaths, but never a person who had been dead four days and already entombed (11:17). Given the Jewish tradition that one's soul hovered near the body for up to three days after expiry (e.g., *Genesis Rabbah* 100 [164a]), here is an individual who has truly "given up the ghost." Once again Jesus' behavior stresses God's sovereign timing: on hearing of Lazarus's illness, Jesus deliberately delays for two days before leaving for Bethany (v. 6). The result is to magnify the miracle that much more, for the sake of God's glory (v. 4). When the disciples protest that Jerusalem and its vicinity are too dangerous, Jesus explains that he is safe until the appointed time for his tragic destiny (vv. 9–10).

John 11:1–16 thus sets the stage for the miracle; verses 17–44 describe what happens when Christ arrives in town. Parallel conversations with Lazarus' sisters, Martha and Mary (vv. 17–37), highlight some of the same features noted about them in Luke 10:38–42. For example, bustling Martha hurries out to meet him, but reflective Mary stays at home (v. 20). A still more important difference characterizes this encounter with the two women. While Jesus elicits a profession of faith from Martha (v. 27), it remains well within conventional Jewish categories (v. 24). "Christ" and "Son of God" need mean no more than "nationalistic Messiah," as for Nathanael in 1:49. Even if Martha does mean more than this, it is clear that she does not yet envision Lazarus's revivification (v. 24). Martha appears again in John's Gospel only in the context of providing domestic hospitality (12:2). Mary however seems to have understood more fully, as she reappears in the company of those Jews who see Lazarus's return to life and genuinely believe (11:45). In chapter 12 she will be the one to anoint Jesus' body in preparation for his burial, perhaps the first person to grasp completely what kind of Messiah Jesus would be (12:3–8).[38]

The central focus of John 11, of course, is the revivification miracle itself (vv. 38–44). Jesus has shown deep emotion upon arrival at the tomb (v. 35); now tears turn to anger (the more common meaning of the verb *embrimaomai* used in v. 38—NIV "deeply moved"). His strong emotions are responding not only to death's apparent victory but also to his contemporaries' unbelief (v. 37). Jesus' sorrow and anger balance each other in crucial ways. "Grief and compassion without outrage reduce to mere sentiment, while outrage without grief hardens into self-righteous arrogance and irascibility."[39] Christ proceeds to corroborate his claim to be the resurrection and the life (v. 25) by calling Lazarus

---

38. Cf. Francis Moloney, "The Faith of Martha and Mary: A Narrative Approach to John 11, 17–40," *Biblica* 75 (1994): 471–93. Arguably Judas is the other person to catch on most quickly, but he responds in exactly opposite fashion, by turning against the one he believes has betrayed the Jews' cause.

39. Carson, *John*, 416.

forth from the tomb. This is the only miracle in which we have a record of Jesus' praying as a prelude, and he does so audibly. He also explains, however, that this is for the crowd's benefit, not his own (vv. 41–42).

Verses 45–54 describe the aftermath of Lazarus' revivification. Here appear some of the most ironic words in all the Gospels. Caiaphas, the high priest, along with the Sanhedrin, determines that one who can bring someone back to life is too dangerous to be allowed to live. As if they could permanently lay Jesus to rest! In solidifying their plot against him, Caiaphas speaks better than he knows. For him, verse 50 would have meant merely that they must save the Jewish nation from Roman retribution by sacrificing Jesus before he stirred up the masses. But John sees in this statement an unwitting prophecy of Christ's atoning sacrifice.[40] For the time being, however, Jesus retreats from the public eye to a small village, Ephraim, probably about twelve miles northeast of Jerusalem (v. 54).

Even at this late date in his ministry, even in this Gospel most concerned to stress the deity of Christ, Jesus' words and works are left to speak for themselves. There is always another way to explain who he is. God never coerces belief. But the growing polarization of response to Jesus will soon erupt into violence and execution.

Historicity

It is very likely that Jesus the Jew would have made the required pilgrimages to Jerusalem at festival times. Contrary behavior would surely have cropped up in the Synoptic accounts of the debates between Jesus and the Jewish leaders. The Sabbath healings of chapters 5 and 9 cohere in contents and style with the Synoptic healing and conflict stories, most notably Mark 2:1–12 and parallels (cf. esp. Mark 2:9 with John 5:8). The healing of *blind* men and the use of *spittle* (John 9:6) also form striking parallels with what we have seen in the Synoptics. So, too, do specific teachings of Christ in these chapters (cf., e.g., John 5:30 with Luke 22:42; or John 9:39 with Matt. 15:14) as well as general themes (e.g., Jesus' joint concern for both physical and spiritual wholeness and his subordination to the Father as one sent as the Father's agent). Nevertheless, the length and tenor of the dialogues and discourses in these chapters is clearly distinct. Perhaps an initial parable about a son's apprenticeship (5:19–20a) has been elaborated into a discourse (see above, p. 295); perhaps Jesus realized that the stakes were higher in his encounters with the *Jerusalem* officials so that more detailed discussion was needed. In choosing to leave out an entire portion of Jesus' ministry, the synoptists may have omitted one distinctive form of debate and discourse in which Jesus engaged.

John 7 begins with Jesus at odds with his family, much as in Mark 3:31–35 and parallels. We have already noted that the "I am" sayings were probably more cryptic in their original contexts than they seem to us. If Jesus believed himself to be the Light of the World (John 8:12; 9:5), it would be natural for him to tell his disciples to reflect that light (Matt. 5:14). John 7:23 contains the same kind of reasoning about the Sabbath as in Luke 13:15–16 and 14:5. The

---

40. Josephus repeatedly speaks of the belief that the high priest could exercise the gift of prophecy (*Antiquities* 11.8.4, 13.10.3).

Jesus Fulfills Jewish Festivals (John 5–11)

5	6	7	8	9	10	11
"the Feast" (5:1) (Passover?) Sabbath	Passover (6:4)	-----Tabernacles----- (7:2)		Sabbath	Sheep Gate and Good Shepherd (10:7, 11) / Hanukkah (10:22)	The Resurrection and the Life (11:25)
fulfilling water rituals of Judaism (5:2)	Bread of Life (6:35)	Living Water (7:38)	Light of the World (8:12)	Light of the World (9:5)		

harsh accusations by Jesus' opponents (he has a demon—7:20; he is a Samaritan and demon possessed—8:48; he is raving mad—10:20) are too unflattering to have been invented. The slave-son comparison of 8:35 mirrors much of the imagery of the Synoptic parables. Jesus' denial that Abrahamic descent guarantees spiritual freedom (8:37–58) matches John the Baptist's warnings (Matt. 3:8–9 par.). Even Jesus' stunning identification of himself with the divine "I AM" in 8:58 simply makes explicit what is already implicit in Mark 6:50 (see above, p. 273). And the divided responses of the crowd throughout these chapters are exactly what one would expect a radical charismatic to elicit.

The metaphors of John 10 fit well with the Synoptics: Jesus' calling himself the Good Shepherd matches God's role in the parable of the lost sheep (Luke 15:3–7 par.), while calling himself the Door (i.e., gate for the sheepfold) reminds us of his command to enter by the correct gate (Matt. 7:13–14). His promise to lay down his life for his sheep (John 10:11–18) meshes with his passion predictions in the Synoptics. The Jews' plea in 10:24 foreshadows Caiaphas's later question at Jesus' trial (Mark 14:61 pars.). Lazarus's revivification in John 11 is not the first such miracle in the Gospels, even if it may be the most dramatic. As with Jairus's daughter (Mark 5:21–43 pars.), Jesus is delayed in coming, but this serves only to magnify the miracle. And the roles Mary and Martha play (e.g., in John 11:20) perfectly fit their characters as described in Luke 10:38–42. Jesus' very human emotions (John 11:35, 38) distinguish this narrative from later Christian apocrypha, while the wealth of circumstantial detail throughout the account reads like eyewitness testimony. The omission of this "greatest of all miracles" from the Synoptics is probably due to nothing more than their desire not to describe Jesus in or around Jerusalem until his final Passover.

FOR FURTHER STUDY

Luke's Central Section

Bailey, Kenneth E. *Poet and Peasant* and *Through Peasant Eyes*. [2 vols. bd. as 1] Grand Rapids: Eerdmans, 1983.

Drury, John. *Tradition and Design in Luke's Gospel*. London: Darton, Longman & Todd; Atlanta: John Knox, 1976.

Egelkraut, Helmuth L. *Jesus' Mission to Jerusalem*. Frankfurt am Main: Peter Lang, 1976.

Evans, Craig A., and James A. Sanders. *Luke and Scripture*. Minneapolis: Fortress, 1993.

Goulder, Michael D. *The Evangelists' Calendar*. London: SPCK, 1978.

Moessner, David P. *Lord of the Banquet*. Minneapolis: Fortress, 1989.

The Teaching of Jesus

Anderson, Norman. *The Teaching of Jesus*. London: Hodder & Stoughton; Downers Grove: IVP, 1983.

Beck, James R. *The Healing Words of Jesus*. Grand Rapids: Baker, 1993.

Bruce, F. F. *The Hard Sayings of Jesus*. London: Hodder & Stoughton; Downers Grove: IVP, 1983.

Dalman, Gustaf. *The Words of Jesus*. Edinburgh: T. & T. Clark, 1902.

Hunter, A. M. *According to John*. London: SCM; Philadelphia: Westminster, 1968.

Hunter, A. M. *The Work and Words of Jesus.* London: SCM; Philadelphia: Westminster, rev. 1973.

Manson, T. W. *The Sayings of Jesus.* London: SCM, 1957; Grand Rapids: Eerdmans, 1975.

Manson, T. W. *The Teaching of Jesus.* Cambridge: CUP, 1939.

Stein, Robert H. *The Method and Message of Jesus' Teachings.* Louisville: Westminster/ John Knox, rev. 1994.

Vanderlip, D. George. *Jesus of Nazareth: Teacher and Lord.* Valley Forge: Judson, rev. 1994.

QUESTIONS FOR REVIEW

1. As you survey this potpourri of additional teachings of Jesus in Matthew, Luke, and John, review the distinctive theological emphases of each of these three evangelists. How many of them can you find in the material surveyed here? Which ones stand out in particular?

2. Are there any of the exegetical observations about specific passages that strike you as particularly new? as particularly relevant to contemporary Christian living? Itemize a few and explain.

CHAPTER SIXTEEN

JESUS' JUDEAN MINISTRY

T he Synoptics go their separate ways in describing the latter stages of
Jesus' Galilean ministry, but they converge again as Jesus arrives in Judea
for the final phase of his life. Closer verbal parallelism leads to fewer
redactional distinctives among the Gospel writers. This chapter surveys Jesus'
teaching immediately en route to Jerusalem, his final public ministry in Jerusalem
during the last week of his life, and his "sermon" to his disciples on the Mount
of Olives overlooking the town.

IN JUDEA ON THE ROAD TO JERUSALEM
(MARK 10 PARS.; JOHN 11:55–12:11 PARS.)

The episodes narrated in Mark 10 and parallels seem to unfold in mostly chronological order as Jesus draws ever nearer to Jerusalem. They are also united by
reflecting (a) primarily teaching material; (b) a series of controversies, often
"traps," generated by questioners who approach Jesus to engage him in dialogue; (c) Jesus' increasing focus on the demands of discipleship; and (d) his
concern to reverse the patterns of privilege of the powerful, religious males in
his society by expressing concern for women, children, the poor, and the sick.
The anointing in Bethany (John 12:1–11 pars.) takes place the day before Jesus'
"triumphal entry," inaugurating his final week in Jerusalem.

Teaching on Divorce (Mark 10:1–12 par.) [Aland §251–252][1]

A lively debate separated the Pharisaic schools of Shammai and Hillel, two
leading rabbis a couple of decades older than Jesus. Deuteronomy 24:1 permit-

---

[1]. For details of the subsequent exposition, see Craig L. Blomberg, "Marriage, Divorce, Remarriage and Celibacy: An Exegesis of
Matthew 19:3–12," *Trinity Journal* n.s. 11 (1990): 161–96.

ted a man to divorce his wife if he found "something indecent" about her. Was this limited to sexual unfaithfulness (so Shammai), or could it be applied much more widely (so Hillel)? The Mishnah would later attribute to Hillel the opinion that divorce could occur "for any good cause"—"he may divorce even if she spoil his cooking" (*Gittin* 9:10)! What did Jesus think? These Pharisees may have hoped that he would incriminate himself on the topic the way John the Baptist had by criticizing Herod Antipas.

For once Jesus' reply is more conservative than both camps. In Mark, his prohibition against divorce seems absolute. In Matthew, he allows divorce in the case of adultery (19:9; recall 5:32), but he does not require it as both schools of Pharisaic law did. Many redaction critics argue that Matthew's "exception clauses" are later additions trying to tone down the seemingly impossible and idealistic demands of Christ. A few ultraconservatives have argued that neither Mark's nor Matthew's version permits divorce under any circumstances because the verb *apoluō* can also be translated "to separate." But it is clear from the reference to Deuteronomy 24:1 that the Pharisees were debating divorce, not merely separation, and there is no contextual evidence that the meaning of the word changes in the middle of the passage. More likely, Mark does not spell out the exception to his rule because all Jewish and Greco-Roman opinion of the day recognized that adultery *de facto* severed a marriage, after which divorce and remarriage were both expected. Matthew, writing to a more Jewish-Christian audience, preserves the fuller account of Jesus' words, to position him more explicitly in the midst of the Jewish debate.[2] Yet both versions agree that the predominant pattern to be emphasized is life-long faithfulness to marriage vows, in keeping with God's creation ordinances, and in contrast to a society in which divorce ran rampant.

Numerous other exegetical controversies surround Matthew 19:9 and 5:32. Should *porneia* (NIV "marital unfaithfulness") be translated more broadly than "adultery" to include premarital sexual relations? Should it be translated more narrowly so as to limit it to marriages between close relatives prohibited by Leviticus 18 (as in 1 Cor. 5:1)? Probably neither is correct. Jewish women married so young that premarital sex was rarely a problem, and the word *porneia* is the standard general term in the Greek for sexual sin, so one should not limit it to incest without immediate contextual support. What does "except for adultery/marital unfaithfulness" modify? Just "divorce" or both "divorce and remarriage"? Probably the latter, given that it is sandwiched in between the two[3] and given the cultural assumptions already noted. Admittedly, the majority view in the ancient church was against all remarriage. But this included widows and widowers, whom the Bible at times encourages to remarry, and was heavily

---

2. William A. Heth ("Divorce and Remarriage: The Search for an Evangelical Hermeneutic," *Trinity Journal* n.s. 16 [1995]: 63–100) argues that we should not assume Jesus followed cultural convention here and maintains that Jesus *never* permitted remarriage after any kind of divorce, since he was countercultural in so many other respects. But in other instances where Jesus goes against the prevailing morals of his day, he makes it clear that he is doing so. Were Jesus (or the Gospel writers) to have intended for us to understand that he was forbidding all remarriage in Matt. 19:9 or 5:32, they would surely have had to have been far clearer than they in fact were.

3. The syntax is admittedly ambiguous. But putting the exception clause before the first verb or after the last verb would have made it even more likely that it would have been meant to modify only the most immediately adjacent verb. For details, see Phillip H. Wiebe, "Jesus' Divorce Exception," *JETS* 32 (1989): 327–33; and cf. the caveats raised by Stanley E. Porter and Paul Buchanan, "On the Logical Structure of Matt. 19.9," *JETS* 34 (1991): 335–39.

influenced by an unbiblical asceticism that increasingly crept into the Greek and Latin churches in sexual matters more generally. (Hence, the later Roman Catholic insistence that clergy and monastic orders be celibate.)

Application of Jesus' teaching on divorce for today requires a fair amount of exegetical sophistication and pastoral sensitivity. At least five points merit consideration: (1) *God's primary intention for marriage remains no separation of any kind.* Christians who are contemplating marriage, or who are still married to their first spouse, should move heaven and earth to stay faithful to one another. (2) In a radically countercultural move, *Jesus puts the husband's and wife's rights (and sins!) on an equal footing* (Mark 10:11–12). (3) *Some Christians may never marry, and they dare not be treated as second-class citizens.* Indeed, celibacy can be a gift from God, like other spiritual gifts (Matt. 19:10–12; 1 Cor. 7:7). ("This word" of verse 11 most likely refers back to verse 10; hence, not all have this gift but some do.) If Catholicism has historically overemphasized the value of celibacy, Protestantism has historically underemphasized the value of the holy, single life.

(4) Additional, crucial teaching appears in 1 Corinthians 7, including *a second exceptional situation in which divorce may be permitted: desertion by an unbeliever* (vv. 15–16). It is instructive to note what this exception has in common with Matthew's. Each ruptures half of the marriage relationship as defined by Genesis 2:24 ("A man will leave his father and mother and be united to his wife, and they will become one flesh"). Part one refers to intimate, interpersonal loyalty; part two, to the consummation of the bond with sexual intercourse. Desertion makes it impossible to continue the interpersonal allegiance; infidelity destroys the exclusivity of the sexual relationship. Perhaps the way to answer the question if any other circumstances ever make divorce permissible in God's eyes is to ask if anything else so undermines an actual marriage. Decisions may need to be settled on a case-by-case basis but always leaning on the side of caution to help keep marriages intact.

(5) Finally, where divorce is already an accomplished fact, we need *the right balance of compassion and firmness.* Where sorrow for sin and repentance for whatever fault one party had in the breakup of a marriage has not adequately occurred, consistent discipline requires that a Christian not be allowed to carry on with church membership or ministry as if nothing had happened. Where such contrition has occurred, where a person has demonstrated a proven track record over time of celibacy in singleness or faithfulness to a second spouse, divorce must not be treated as an unforgivable sin. Neither church membership in good standing nor opportunities for ministry are necessarily forfeited.[4]

---

4. "The husband of but one wife" in 1 Tim. 3:2 cannot exclude the divorced unless it also excludes the widowed (i.e., if the verse refers to someone literally married only once, then it does not distinguish between reasons for a second marriage). But Paul elsewhere counsels widows and widowers to remarry under certain circumstances (1 Tim. 5:14; 1 Cor. 7:9), and it is unlikely he would do this if he knew such people were thereby disqualifying themselves from church office. All the other criteria of 1 Tim. 3:1–7 refer to the settled, current behavior of candidates for the eldership, not to things they may have done a long time ago. "Husband of but one wife" should thus be understood as someone who is (and has been) faithful to his or her current spouse, if married—a mature, committed, family person—nothing more and nothing less. Cf., e.g., Thomas D. Lea and Hayne P. Griffin, Jr., *1, 2 Timothy, Titus* (Nashville: Broadman, 1992), 109–10; following Ed Glasscock, "'The Husband of One Wife' Requirement in 1 Timothy 3:2," *BSac* 140 (1983): 244–58.

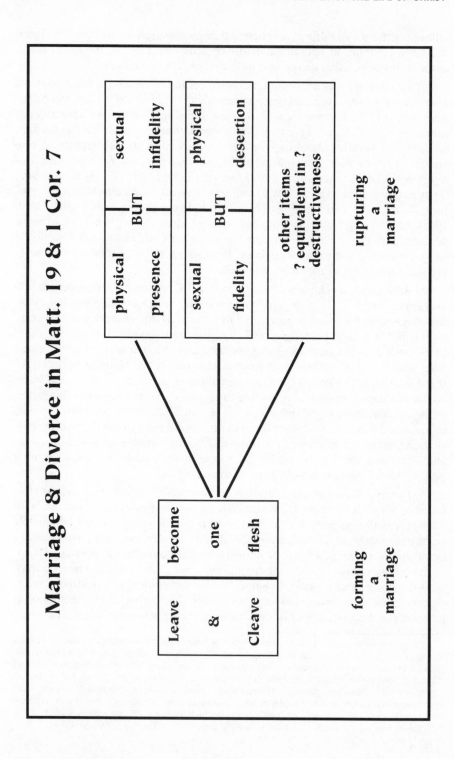

Marriage & Divorce in Matt. 19 & 1 Cor. 7

physical presence   BUT   sexual infidelity

sexual fidelity   BUT   physical desertion

other items
? equivalent in ?
destructiveness

rupturing a marriage

Leave & Cleave   become one flesh

forming a marriage

Jesus Blesses the Children (Mark 10:13-16 pars.) [Aland §253]

After discussing marriage and divorce, the topic of children follows naturally. Rabbis were often asked to bless boys and girls in the ancient Jewish world, and they would pray for God's favor to rest on them. Jesus' disciples reflect a common low view of children in antiquity as they snub some who were seeking Jesus' blessing. The episode turns into a "pronouncement" or "controversy" story with Jesus' climactic declaration that one must enter the kingdom like these little children. As in Matthew 18:3-4, Jesus is not commending childishness, but childlikeness. Just as children recognize their absolute dependence on the adult world, whether they like it or not, so would-be believers must come to God recognizing their utter dependence on him.[5] Jesus' blessing the children has sometimes been used to promote infant baptism, but it may suffice to point out that neither infants nor baptism appears anywhere in the passage.[6]

The Rich Young Ruler and Related Incidents (Mark 10:17-31 pars.; Luke 19:1-27) [Aland §254-255, 265-266]

The next person to approach Jesus on the road is a well-to-do synagogue official (called a "ruler" in Luke 18:18). Like the lawyer in Luke 10:25, this man asks about how to inherit eternal life. Jesus gives a strange rebuff. In Mark, he inquires as to why the man calls him a *good* teacher, since only God is good (Mark 10:18). Is Jesus denying that he is good? Is he implying that he is God? Matthew's redaction makes it less likely that one would come to the former conclusion (Matt. 19:17). Perhaps Jesus is merely diverting attention from the man's inadequate criterion ("What must I *do*?) to focus instead on the divine standard of goodness. Christ goes on to quote key commandments from the Decalogue, but the man insists he has kept these (Mark 10:19-20). Yet he still senses a lack (Matt. 19:20). Jesus puts his finger on it by commanding him to sell his many possessions, give to the poor, and follow him in discipleship (Mark 10:21). These commands must be taken as a package: altruism or humanitarian aid without commitment to Christ counts for nothing in eternity.

Does Jesus make so stringent a demand of all would-be followers? No, as Luke's outline at this point demonstrates most clearly. Luke will shortly juxtapose the story of Zacchaeus' conversion (Luke 19:1-10) and the parable of the pounds (vv. 11-27). The former describes the about-face of a chief tax collector (one of the "publicans" who worked directly for Rome) who voluntarily gives up half his goods to the poor and restores fourfold to those he has cheated in his tax business.[7] Rabbinic law normally discouraged someone from ever giv-

---

5. Cf. James L. Bailey, "Experiencing the Kingdom as a Little Child: A Rereading of Mark 10:13–16," *Word and World* 15 (1995): 58–67, who stresses the element of vulnerability; with Stephen Fowl, "Receiving the Kingdom of God as a Child: Children and Riches in Luke 18.15ff," *NTS* 39 (1993): 153–58, who highlights the characteristic of a single-minded, unrelenting pursuit of a desire.

6. The argument is often based on the observation that the language, "do not hinder them" (Mark 10:14), appears elsewhere in explicitly baptismal contexts (Matt. 3:14; Acts 8:36; 10:47; 11:17). But this must be balanced with the observation that these words also appear in several contexts where baptism is clearly not present (Luke 6:29; Acts 24:23; 1 Cor. 14:39).

7. A vigorous debate has ensued over whether this is a *conversion* story or a *defense* story (in which Luke 19:8 would be describing Zacchaeus's *characteristic* practice, not behavior he was just about to begin). The former is more likely; cf. John Nolland, *Luke 18:35–24:53* (Dallas: Word, 1993), 906.

ing away more than 20 percent. So Zacchaeus is clearly going well beyond the call of duty, but still he retains a fair amount of his wealth. The parable of the pounds commends the faithful servants who invest their wealth and make more money, but all of it reverts back to the master for his service and use.[8] Obviously, there are many different ways to be good stewards of the material possessions God gives us. However, if wealth ever stands in the way of our wholehearted allegiance to Christ, then we must divest ourselves of it. As Gundry remarks, "That Jesus did not command all his followers to sell all their possessions gives comfort only to the kind of people to whom he *would* issue that command."[9]

After the rich young ruler goes away sorrowfully, Jesus astonishes his audience by stressing how hard it is for rich people in general to enter the kingdom (Mark 10:23–24). Using a dramatic hyperbole, he likens the situation to a camel going through the eye of a needle—the largest Palestinian animal passing through the smallest common opening (v. 25)! The disciples recognize the literal impossibility involved. And given the prominent Old Testament mind-set that recognized riches as a blessing from God for faithfulness, they wonder how anyone could ever be saved (v. 26). Jesus' reply makes it clear that by God's grace the humanly impossible becomes possible (v. 27). What then of the disciples who have left many of their possessions behind to go on the road with Christ (v. 28)? Jesus promises them a hundredfold recompense. It is impossible to spiritualize verses 29–30 or limit them to heavenly rewards, since Jesus speaks also of persecutions. Rather, the hundredfold homes and fields the disciples receive come the same way they acquire more brothers, sisters, mothers, and children. All members of the community of God's people are family and share with each other as anyone has need.[10] Matthew's version adds a promise seemingly just for the Twelve: they will sit on thrones judging Israel when the new age arrives in all its fullness (Matt. 19:28). But 1 Corinthians 6:2–3 speaks of all Christians judging the whole world and even angels, so this privilege is somewhat relativized.

The Parable of the Laborers in the Vineyard (Matt. 20:1–16) [Aland §256]

Matthew uniquely appends a parable of Jesus that stresses the equality of all disciples in a world preoccupied with privilege. The three points associated with the master, the first workers and the last workers are aptly captured in Matthew 20:13–16. From those hired first, we learn that God treats no one unfairly (vv. 13–14). From those hired last, we discover that he chooses to treat some quite generously (v. 15). From verse 16, interpreted in light of the imagery of the parable, we recognize the fundamental equality of all disciples in

---

8. This parable is often seen as a later allegorical elaboration of Matt. 25:14–30 and a conflation of the Matthean parable with a "throne claimant parable" (the story of the nobleman going to receive a kingdom opposed by an embassy of his citizens). But the Lukan context (increased misunderstanding and opposition on the road to the cross) makes Jesus' parable here intelligible on its own. In Matthew, the emphasis is on the appropriate response of disciples; in Luke, on the horrible fate of opponents.

9. Robert H. Gundry, *Matthew: A Commentary on His Handbook for a Mixed Church under Persecution* (Grand Rapids: Eerdmans, rev. 1994), 388.

10. See esp. David M. May, "Leaving and Receiving: A Social-Scientific Exegesis of Mark 10:29–31," *PRS* 17 (1990): 141–54.

Luke on Wealth & Stewardship

18:18-30	19:1-10	19:11-27
Jesus & the Rich Young Ruler	Zacchaeus's Conversion	The Parable of the Pounds
"Sell all that you have and distribute to the poor."	"The half of my goods I give to the poor, and if I have defrauded any one of anything, I restore it fourfold."	"Why then did you not put my money into the bank, and at my coming I should have collected it with interest?"
(v. 22)	(v. 8)	(v. 23)

(RSV)

God's eyes. First are last and last are first in this context because all roles are interchangeable. This parable is one of the clearest teaching passages in Scripture against the notion of degrees of eternal reward in heaven. After all, what can improve on perfection?[11]

The Third Passion Prediction and the Disciples' Misunderstanding (Mark 10:32–45 pars.) [Aland §262–263]

To further underline his commitment to servanthood rather than privilege, Jesus predicts his suffering, death, and resurrection yet once more (recall Mark 8:31; 9:31 pars.), this time in the greatest detail of all (10:32–34). Creating a striking contrast, Mark immediately juxtaposes the incident in which two of the disciples request positions of power in Jesus' kingdom (vv. 35–37). Jesus makes it plain that all he can share with them is the right to suffer (vv. 38–41) and proceeds to redefine true spiritual leadership as ruling through selfless service rather than authoritarian power-broking. The latter is a pagan, not a Christian approach (vv. 42–45). The passage culminates with a rare and important statement by Jesus about the substitutionary, atoning nature of his coming death: "the Son of Man did not come to be served, but to serve, and to give his life as a ransom for many" (v. 45). The language of ransom mirrors that of the slave market—the price paid to buy a slave's freedom. An allusion to Isaiah 53:10 or 12 about God's suffering servant is probably present, especially in light of Jesus' explicit use of verse 12 in Luke 22:37. And the Greek word for "for" (*anti*) is probably best rendered here "instead of" or "in place of," hence, the substitutionary nature of the sacrifice.[12]

Healing Blind Bartimaeus (Mark 10:46–52 pars.) [Aland §264]

By now Jesus is in Jericho, just fifteen miles from his destination in Jerusalem.[13] The final full-fledged miracle-narrative of the Gospels ensues. Blind Bartimaeus cries out to the one he acknowledges as Messiah ("Son of David") to help him see.[14] Jesus cures him and for the last recorded time in the Gospels

---

11. See further Craig L. Blomberg, "Degrees of Reward in the Kingdom of Heaven?" *JETS* 35 (1992): 159–72. Millard J. Erickson (*Evangelical Interpretation* [Grand Rapids: Baker, 1993], 92–94) correctly points out that perfection is relative to that which is perfected—even in the eternal state, believers are not deified. But to eliminate my concern that seeking after rewards becomes unduly competitive, he suggests, on the basis of the parable of the talents, that rewards may come as a surprise. Paradoxically, this could now occur only for someone who holds my view, not his, since I do not believe in degrees of reward and would be surprised by them! Far better, if there is no compelling *exegetical* reason for maintaining the doctrine, to err on the side of caution and not postulate any eternal differences among believers beyond the admittedly unique experiences each of us will have standing before God on Judgment Day. The origin of the doctrine of eternal rewards lies actually in the non-Lutheran wings of the Reformation that carried over something of the Roman Catholic notion of purgatory; see Emma Disley, "Degrees of Glory: Protestant Doctrine and the Concept of Rewards Hereafter," *JTS* 42 (1991): 77–105.

12. On the meaning and authenticity of this saying, see esp. Sydney H. T. Page, "The Authenticity of the Ransom Logion (Mark 10:45b)," in *Gospel Perspectives*, vol. 1, ed. R. T. France and David Wenham (Sheffield: JSOT, 1980), 137–61.

13. Mark and Matthew place this story as Jesus is leaving Jericho (Mark 10:4; Matt. 20:29). Luke seems to locate it before they arrive in town (Luke 18:35). But "drawing near" may refer more generally to "being in the vicinity" (see Stanley E. Porter, "'In the Vicinity of Jericho': Luke 18:35 in the Light of Its Synoptic Parallels," *BBR* 2 [1992]: 91–104). Or Luke may be simply abbreviating his material, creating the illusion of a contradiction by omitting intervening information (cf. Craig Blomberg, *The Historical Reliability of the Gospels* [Leicester and Downers Grove: IVP, 1987], 128–30).

14. As in Matt. 9:27–31, Matthew's version refers to two blind men (20:30). Perhaps Bartimaeus was the primary speaker, or perhaps he was the one who subsequently distinguished himself in discipleship.

repeats the refrain "your faith has healed you" (v. 52)—spiritually as well as physically. Previously, Jesus told the recipients of his miracles to say nothing or to return home and witness to their families. Now, however, the appropriate response is to follow Jesus along the road because it is the road to the cross. Bartimaeus' physical and spiritual sight contrasts with the disciples' continuing lack of vision, most recently evidenced in their jockeying for positions of power.

The Anointing in Bethany (John 11:55–12:11; Mark 14:3–9 par.) [Aland §261, 267–268]

Only John gives an explicit statement of when this event happened—six days before the Passover (12:1)—that is, the Saturday before what we now call Palm Sunday. Mark and Matthew relocate this passage topically, because of the symbolism of preparing Jesus for his burial, sandwiching the narrative between a reference to the later plot of the Jewish leaders to arrest Jesus (Mark 14:1–2 par.) and Judas' arrangement to betray him (vv. 10–11 par.). There are other noteworthy differences between John and Mark/Matthew, though none of them needs be viewed as a contradiction.[15] At any rate, Mary lavishes her affection on Jesus by pouring over him a jar of perfume worth about a year's wages (John 12:3). Judas protests at the "waste," but we are told that he was used to pilfering from the disciples' treasury (vv. 4–6).

Jesus' reply answers the similar objection even of a well-meaning individual with a developed social conscience. There are times for one-of-a-kind, unrepeatable, costly acts of devotion to Christ. But the words "You will always have the poor among you" (v. 8) afford no excuse for general inaction. Mark's fuller account of Jesus' reply continues to explain, "and you can help them any time you want" (Mark 14:7). His words actually allude to Deuteronomy 15:11 ("There will always be poor people in the land"), a verse that immediately goes on to declare, "Therefore I command you to be openhanded toward your brothers and toward the poor and needy in your land." But in this unique context Mary's "waste" was appropriate. As Bruce explains, "Unusual expense at a funeral was not regarded as unseemly; why should anyone object if the ointment which would otherwise have been used to anoint his dead body in due course was poured over him while he was still alive and able to appreciate the love which prompted the action?"[16]

Historicity

Jesus' pronouncements in this section continue to differ from both Judaism and early Christianity: his stringent rejection of divorce by appealing to creation ordinances rather than legal casuistry, his exaltation of children as a paradigm of the humble, and his demanding teachings on stewardship of wealth. In addi-

---

15. Was the home Simon's or Lazarus's? Probably Simon's, with Lazarus and his family as the invited guests and servers. Was Jesus anointed on the head or the feet? Probably both, since the quantity of spikenard involved could easily have covered his whole body. In John, moreover, Mary and Judas replace otherwise unnamed characters in Mark, and additional information is given about their motives. Cf. further D. A. Carson, *The Gospel according to John* (Grand Rapids: Eerdmans; Leicester: IVP, 1991), 426–27.

16. F. F. Bruce, *The Gospel of John* (Basingstoke: Pickering & Inglis; Grand Rapids: Eerdmans, 1983), 257.

tion, Mark 10:18 contains potentially embarrassing Christology; verses 23–25, Jesus' characteristic hyperbole. Matthew 19:28 goes to the heart of Jesus' intentions to constitute a new or renewed Israel, despite being largely unparalleled.[17] Other distinctively Matthean material is primarily parabolic and generally held to be authentic. The saying about Jesus' death as a ransom (Mark 10:45) is more disputed. Still, like the passion predictions more generally, this verse seems to be a natural outgrowth of Jesus' meditation on Isaiah 52–53 and the model of the Maccabean martyrs, yet with a distinctive Messianic application not characteristic of the Judaism of Jesus' day. The healing of blind Bartimaeus coheres with other miracles of healing the blind we have previously discussed. At the anointing in the house of Simon the leper, both Mary's and Judas' behavior proves embarrassing, even if in different ways. Interestingly, one of the Dead Sea scrolls confirms that the vicinity of Bethany was home to one of the leper colonies of that day (11QTemple 46:16–18).

JESUS IN JERUSALEM: FINAL DAYS OF PUBLIC MINISTRY (MARK 11–12 PARS.)

With Jesus' arrival in Jerusalem, anticipation and conflict both grow to a fever pitch. The events covered in this section span the Sunday through Tuesday prior to Christ's execution. Three prophetic "object lessons" all portend Israel's ominous future. Then Jesus teaches in the temple, evading verbal traps set by the Jewish leaders, and concludes by pronouncing judgment on them instead.

Actions of Judgment (Mark 11:1–26 pars; John 12:17–50)

Entrance into Jerusalem (Mark 11:1–10 pars.; Luke 19:41–44) [Aland §269–270, 302–304]. This story is usually called the "triumphal entry" and has been celebrated throughout Christian history on "Palm Sunday," one week before Easter. But it might better be labeled the "a-triumphal entry." This ragtag band of followers accompanying a Galilean peasant riding a donkey would have looked like a parody of the standard welcome and fanfare for governors and generals astride their white horses with a retinue of soldiers. Still, Jesus is making deliberate messianic claims. His behavior enacts the prophecy of Zechariah 9:9, which both Matthew and John spell out (Matt. 21:5; John 12:15). He orders the animal commandeered in kingly fashion (Mark 11:2–3). The colt must be unridden, thus still "pure" and suitable for sacred purposes.[18] And Jesus is acknowledged by the crowds of Galilean pilgrims in a manner reminiscent of the greetings for rulers in Old Testament and intertestamental times (cf. 2 Kings 9:13; 1 Macc. 13:51). They line the road with their garments and palm branches from nearby Jericho (Mark 11:8; John 12:13) and cry "Hosanna" (Hebrew, "God save us"), using messianic language from the pilgrims'

---

17. See esp. E. P. Sanders, *Jesus and Judaism* (London: SCM; Philadelphia: Fortress, 1985), 98–102.

18. It is often alleged that Matthew has garbled the picture by speaking of Jesus astride two donkeys (Matt. 21:5, 7). But v. 5 is a case of synonymous parallelism, while the antecedent in the Greek for the final "them" of v. 7 is more naturally the cloaks, not the animals. That a mother would be needed along with her colt to make the younger animal willing to be ridden (and the text does not say that the animal had never previously carried *any* kind of pack) is only to be expected. See Gundry, *Matthew*, 409.

Jesus' Final Week

Sat.	Sun.	Mon.	Tues.	Wed.	Thur.	Fri.	Sat.	Sun.
anointing in Bethany	triumphal entry	temple cleansing & fig tree (1)	fig tree (2) & teaching in temple/ Mt. of Olives	?	prep. for Passover, Last Supper & Gethsemane	trial(s), sentence, & execution		resurrection!

Psalm 118 (vv. 25–26), which was customarily sung during their ascent to the Temple Mount.

The crowds still do not understand, however, that Jesus has come to his nation's capital to die and that reigning as king must await a future day. Unlike the war horse, the donkey is an animal of peace and humility. No Romans will be conquered this week. Luke's immediately preceding parable of the pounds was told to dispel the notion that the kingdom would come in power at once (Luke 19:11). Luke also adds Jesus' lament that the people did not recognize his overtures for peace. As a result the city can look forward only to its coming destruction, in A.D. 70 (19:41–44), about which Jesus will have more to say later on the Mount of Olives. Little wonder that some of these cheering Jesus would join the native Jerusalemites in their disenchantment only five days later and call for Jesus' crucifixion.[19]

As he often does, John makes it clear that even the disciples did not understand the significance of these events until after his resurrection (John 12:16). Typically, too, John appends a discourse of Jesus on the theme at hand: here, the glorification of the Son of Man (12:23–50). It is impossible to determine when this was given; any time between Sunday and Thursday would fit. For John, however, these words form an appropriate conclusion to Jesus' public ministry. They are triggered by the desire of some Greeks (i.e., Gentiles) to see Jesus (vv. 20–22). In essence, Jesus replies that now is not the time for an audience but rather for the event that would provide salvation for all peoples, Greeks included. After frequently declaring that his hour had not yet come (2:4; 7:30; 8:20), John now has Jesus climactically announce that it has arrived (12:23; cf. 13:1; 17:1). Death must precede victory, as it seems to with seeds and as it will with disciples (vv. 24–26). Jesus' message is accompanied by the divine voice of attestation (vv. 27–30), and his audible prayer recalls his language at Lazarus's tomb (11:41–42). His death will bring judgment against his opponents but the opportunity of salvation for all who will allow themselves to be drawn to him (12:31–32).[20] The "lifting up" in verse 32 suggests a classic Johannine double meaning: the crucifixion will also lead to Christ's exaltation. The crowds continue not to grasp Jesus' intent (vv. 33–36), which he recognizes as further fulfillment of Isaiah 6:10 (vv. 37–43). Verses 44–50 conclude the discourse by reiterating the twofold power of Christ's mission—both to judge and to save—in complete accordance with the Father's will.

The Withered Fig Tree (Mark 11:12–14, 20–25 par.) [Aland §271–272, 275]. Part of the anticlimax of Jesus' "triumphal entry" into Jerusalem is that he goes to the temple, looks around, and does nothing (Mark 11:11). After lodging overnight in nearby Bethany, he heads again for the temple the next morning. En route, he finds a fig tree with leaves but no fruit and pronounces a curse on it (vv. 12–14). By the next day it has completely withered (vv. 20–21). This second Gospel miracle of destruction is clearly filled with symbolism. Mark

---

19. For help on interpreting this episode with its triumphal and a-triumphal, conventional and yet subversive overtones, see Brent Kinman, "Jesus' 'Triumphal Entry' in the Light of Pilate's," *NTS* 40 (1994): 442–48; and Paul B. Duff, "The March of the Divine Warrior and the Advent of the Greco-Roman King," *JBL* 111 (1992): 55–71.

20. "There is no limit to Jesus' saving power—except the resistance of unbelief. In spite of the universalistic overtone and intent of the statement, faith is still included as a condition." (Rudolf Schnackenburg, *The Gospel according to St. John*, vol. 2 [London: Burns & Oates; New York: Seabury, 1980], 393).

deliberately sandwiches the two parts of its narrative around the story of the "temple cleansing" (vv. 15–19).[21] The two events are meant to be interpreted together. Just as the land producing no fig trees often stood for judgment against Israel in Jewish literature (esp. Micah 7:1; Jer. 8:13), and just as Jesus had earlier told a parable of a fig tree threatened with destruction (Luke 13:6–9), so now he uses an enacted parable or object lesson to demonstrate the imminent doom of the current Jewish nation if it does not repent.[22]

The disciples marvel, and Jesus uses the occasion to teach a related point about faith (Mark 11:22–25). These verses are often taken out of context and generalized in ways that the text does not permit. Although language about faith moving mountains was proverbial in antiquity (cf. 1 Cor. 13:2), here Jesus specifically promises that "if anyone says to *this* mountain" that it be cast into the sea, it will happen (Mark 11:23, italics added). As the disciples walked from Bethany to the temple, "this" mountain would most naturally refer either to the Mount of Olives or to Zion, the Temple Mount. Given the eschatological symbolism of the Mount of Olives being split in two (Zech. 14:4) and given the symbolism of the withered fig tree and the related incident in the temple, it is far more likely that Jesus is calling his disciples to trust in his promises that a new world order replacing the temple is imminent. Verses 24–25 are probably to be taken in this context, too, although it remains true theologically that "when prayer is the source of faith's power and the means of its strength, God's sovereignty is its only restriction."[23]

"Cleansing" the Temple (Mark 11:15–19 pars.) [Aland §273–274]. Jesus' action in the temple has traditionally been called a "cleansing," on the assumption that, by ridding its precincts of the money changers and vendors of sacrificial animals, Jesus was purifying the building and restoring its original purpose as a house of prayer. An element of cleansing is no doubt present, but it seems that it is too late in Jesus' ministry and that the Jewish leaders are too entrenched in their opposition to him for his behavior to have any enduring positive effect. He may indeed be offering one last chance at repentance, but the outcome is all but certain. Not surprisingly, this event becomes the final catalyst in prodding on those who are plotting his death (Mark 11:18; Luke 19:47–48). Quite likely, an element of prophetic symbolism is also present throughout. As with the fig tree, the temple and all it stands for will soon be destroyed. The literal building will not fall until A.D. 70, but the sacrificial

21. In his desire to create a neater literary narrative, Matthew puts both parts of the fig tree story together, creating the illusion that it all took place on one day (Matt. 21:18–22). But Matthew never says this in so many words, and the language of "immediate" withering (v. 19) is still appropriate even if it took place over several hours. Trees normally take far longer to decay!

22. It is sometimes argued that the presence of leaves suggested that there should be fruit. Similarly, the Jewish leadership manifested all the outward signs of following God, yet failed to yield a true spiritual harvest. The last clause of Mark 11:13, however, makes this interpretation unlikely. Probably this reminder that it was not the season for figs is Mark's way of ensuring that the reader will take the narrative entirely symbolically. Just as the destruction of the swine by the Gadarene demons seemed an unjust loss of life, so too the withering of the fig tree may well have been a "gratuitous" sacrifice for the sake of Jesus' lesson. Animals and plants are not equal to people in God's eyes. But, of course, this offers no precedent for the rape of our environment, since these were exceptional situations. For a similar approach and full history of interpretation, see William R. Telford, *The Barren Temple and the Withered Tree* (Sheffield: JSOT, 1980).

23. William L. Lane, *The Gospel according to Mark* (Grand Rapids: Eerdmans, 1974; London: Marshall, Morgan & Scott, 1975), 410. For a full study of *Prayer, Power, and the Problem of Suffering: Mark 11:22–25 in the Context of Markan Theology*, see the work so-entitled by Sharyn E. Dowd (Atlanta: Scholars, 1988).

system will be outmoded and superseded as soon as Christ dies and is raised again (though Jesus' followers would not recognize that fact immediately). Only in Jesus will forgiveness of sins then be available. That explains why on the very next day Jesus will leave the temple for the last time, declaring "Your house is left to you desolate" (Matt. 23:38). There is also a contrast between the intended use of the court of the *Gentiles* and its Jewish transformation into a "nationalist stronghold." God's salvation in Jesus will be equally accessible to all people.[24]

Teaching in the Temple (Mark 11:27–12:44 pars.)

On Tuesday morning Jesus and his disciples return to the temple for the third straight day. All three Synoptics report how he encounters a series of questioners from among the Jewish leaders trying to make him incriminate himself. Each question aptly fits the category of person who asks it. In Mark, these conflict stories create an inclusio with the similar set of conflicts narrated in 2:1–3:6. The four episodes in Mark 12:13–37 interestingly correspond to the four questions of the ancient Passover liturgy: (a) a question regarding a point of law (on paying taxes—vv. 13–17); (b) a question with a note of scoffing (on the resurrection—vv. 18–27); (c) a question by a person of "plain piety" (the scribe asking about the greatest commandment—vv. 28–34); and (d) a question by the father of the family at his own initiative (Jesus asking about David's son—vv. 35–37).[25] Do the evangelists by this device intend to point out Jesus as the true fulfillment of the Passover?

The Question about Jesus' Authority (Mark 11:27–33 pars.; Matt. 21:28–32; Mark 12:1–12 pars.; Matt. 22:1–14) [Aland §276–279]. The three groups comprising the temple authorities understandably approach Jesus to ask first by what authority he created the previous day's chaos (Mark 11:27–28). In common rabbinic fashion, Jesus answers the question with a question. His ploy in forcing them to respond to the issue of John the Baptist's identity is clear; his authority comes from the same source as John's (God). But the leaders cannot affirm this in good conscience, yet they dare not deny it publicly. So the trap gets them nowhere (vv. 29–33).

Jesus, however, keeps talking. All three Synoptics narrate the parable of the wicked tenants, which contains a clear jab at the leaders' own authority. Matthew uniquely includes this as the middle of a series of three parables that narrate, metaphorically, the trial—"verdict," "sentence," and "execution"— of the present Jewish leadership.[26] The parable of the two sons portrays outcasts and sinners entering the kingdom before (or "instead of") the religious authorities. Performance takes priority over promise (Matt. 21:28–32).

The parable of the wicked tenants narrates the results of the leaders' disobedience: the kingdom will be taken away from them and given to a people (i.e., Jesus' followers of any ethnic background) who do produce the appropriate

---

24. On the entire incident, cf. Craig A. Evans, "Jesus' Action in the Temple: Cleansing or Portent of Destruction?" *CBQ* 51 (1989): 237–70; Morna D. Hooker, "Traditions about the Temple in the Sayings of Jesus," *BJRL* 70 (1988): 7–19; and Sanders, *Jesus and Judaism*, 61–76.

25. David Daube, *The New Testament and Rabbinic Judaism* (London: Athlone, 1956), 158–69.

26. Eduard Schweizer, *The Good News according to Matthew* (Richmond: John Knox, 1975; London: SPCK, 1976), 402.

fruit (Matt. 21:33–46, see esp. v. 43). Three clear points associated with the main characters of this parable emerge: God's patience, the eventual destruction of the rebellious, and the replacement of Israel with the church as the locus of God's saving activity. But the role of the son suggests a fourth point, however muted. Like the son, Jesus will soon be killed, but like the stone of Psalm 118:22–23, he will subsequently be honored and inflict damage on those who oppose him. Whether or not Jesus' opponents understood this veiled christological claim, they definitely recognized their role in his allegory and left all the more convinced to do him in (Mark 12:12).[27]

Matthew 22:1–14 brings this triad of parables to a climax. On the debate about whether verses 6–7 are a "prophecy after the fact," see above, p. 134. Jesus may be looking beyond the Roman suppression of the Jewish rebellion in A.D. 70 to final judgment. Again three key points appear. Two are reminiscent of Luke's great banquet parable (Luke 14:16–24): God invites all kinds of people into his kingdom, and rejection of the invitation leads to exclusion for the original guests and the invitation of replacements. But the distinctive, climactic focus of Matthew's parable involves the curious episode of a man without a wedding garment (vv. 11–13). Perhaps the ancient tradition of a host providing festive attire is presupposed; the man would thus have deliberately refused it. At any rate, Jesus seems to be stressing that all who would come to him must come on his terms and not their own.

On Tribute to Caesar (Mark 12:13–17 pars.) [Aland §280]. Jesus' next group of interrogators are sure they have him trapped. Pharisees resented paying taxes to Rome, while Herodians supported the status quo. However Jesus answers their question, one group will be irate. He avoids their "catch-22" situation by affirming part of each of their views. Human governments have a legitimate but limited scope. The Jews are happy to use Roman coinage minted with the impression of Caesar's image when it serves their financial purposes, so they should pay the tribute even when those purposes seem not to be served. However, God demands the primary loyalty—if his mandates conflict with human regulations, the latter must always give way. This passage has understandably been central in the Lutheran, Baptist, and later American convictions that political and religious "kingdoms" be kept separate. And if Jesus could issue this command to oppressed peoples living under a foreign totalitarian regime, how much more ought Christians in modern democratic contexts work lawfully within the system whenever possible![28]

Ridiculing the Resurrection (Mark 12:18–27 pars.) [Aland §281]. The Sadducees did not believe in resurrection from the dead, for they did not find it taught in the five books of Moses (recall, above, p. 48). To ridicule the doctrine and to try to trap Jesus where the other Jewish leaders failed, they imagine an unusual situation in which a woman has had seven different brothers for husbands. The scenario builds on the Old Testament levirate laws in which brothers were required to marry and raise up children for childless, widowed

---

27. For an excellent detailed study of the parable overall, see Klyne R. Snodgrass, *The Parable of the Wicked Tenants* (Tübingen: Mohr, 1983).

28. Cf. Robert H. Stein, *Luke* (Nashville: Broadman, 1992), 496. The view that sees God's claims as so all-encompassing as to cancel out the first part of Jesus' statement ("give to Caesar . . . ") is improbable, not least because it destroys the delicate balance of Jesus' answer in fully satisfying neither Pharisee nor Herodian.

sisters-in-law (cf. Deut. 25:5; Gen. 38:8). Jesus' reply accomplishes two things: it refutes the Sadducees' mistaken notion that the age to come would preserve the institution of marriage and procreation as we know it, and it demonstrates the existence of resurrection life from the Torah. Jesus' appeal to the implicit present tenses of Exodus 3:6 ("I *am* the God of Abraham," italics added) does not seem to demand his conclusion, at least by modern standards of exegesis, but it does closely parallel ancient Jewish methods of interpretation (cf. esp. *b Sanhedrin* 90b, deriving the resurrection from Num. 18:28). Perhaps our modern hermeneutics are at times overly restrictive![29]

The Greatest Commandment (Mark 12:28–34 par.) [Aland §282]. A lawyer now takes his turn in the line of questioners. He naturally asks about the greatest law, a topic of lively Jewish debate already. Jesus' answer is thoroughly orthodox. Love of God was commanded immediately after the *Shema* ("Hear, O Israel: The Lord our God, the Lord is one"—Deut. 6:4–5) and seen as fundamental to all of life. Hillel had already summarized the Law via Leviticus 19:18, and Akiba would later agree (b. Shabbat 31a; Sifra 89b). But Jesus fuses together the commands to love God and neighbor in a way that makes claims of doing one without the other nonsensical. And, although the lawyer concurs with Jesus' summary, Christ still criticizes him as outside (though not far from) the kingdom (Mark 12:34). Because the man is not yet a disciple of Jesus, he cannot adequately fulfill either commandment.

The Question about David's Son (Mark 12:35–37 pars.) [Aland §283]. The questioners have been silenced, so Jesus turns the tables on them. How can they view the Messiah as a merely human, royal, nationalist descendant of David? To press home his point, he calls attention to Psalm 110, widely believed in his day to be Davidic. In it, two "lords" appear: Yahweh God and another "lord" (*adonai* in Hebrew). Were the speaker anyone other than David, king of Israel, the second "lord" could be some earthly master. But there is no human higher than David in Israel. The lord must be the Messiah, and he must be higher than David. The logic seems irrefutable, and the crowds marvel. Not surprisingly, Psalm 110 came to be the most widely quoted Old Testament passage in all of the New Testament.[30]

Warnings and Woes against the Jewish Leaders (Matthew 23 pars.) [Aland §284–285].[31] Jesus culminates his teaching in the temple with vituperative denunciations of select Pharisees and scribes. Mark gives only a brief account of this invective; Matthew goes into gruesome detail. Jesus' woes at the beginning of the last sermon Matthew records create an inclusio with the beatitudes at the beginning of his first sermon (Matt. 5:3–12). Matthew 23 has been called the most anti-Semitic chapter in the New Testament, but this label is unfair: (1) Jesus and all his first disciples were also Jewish. (2) Jesus is not denouncing all Jews, not even all Jewish leaders. (3) Jesus' words are no more harsh than long sections of Old Testament prophecy, most notably Jeremiah, in which

29. Most attempts to make sense of Jesus' logic focus on the love relationship or covenant God established with the patriarchs, which many Jews, over time, came to believe even death could not break. For a representative study, see John J. Kilgallen, "The Sadducees and Resurrection from the Dead: Luke 20,27–40," *Biblica* 67 (1986): 478–95.

30. On its various uses and their interrelationships in the church's developing Christology, see Martin Hengel, *Studies in Early Christology* (Edinburgh: T. & T. Clark, 1995), 119–225.

31. On this entire chapter, see esp. David E. Garland, *The Intention of Matthew 23* (Leiden: Brill, 1979).

God was particularly displeased with his people and their rulers. (4) Jesus ends his polemic with a poignant lament, demonstrating how grieved he is about this state of affairs (vv. 37–39). (5) Matthew's application of this material to his community probably has conservative legalistic *Christians* in his church primarily in view (cf. vv. 8–12).

There are hypocrites in every religious community, so Jesus' charges are not historically implausible. At the very beginning of his denunciations, he acknowledges that even these teachers should be followed when they promote that which is consistent with Torah (vv. 2–3).[32] But then he proceeds to castigate them for several serious inconsistencies. They are motivated by the desire for human praise and status (vv. 5–12) and misguided in their proselytizing zeal (vv. 13–15). They have inverted priorities in oath-taking and tithing (vv. 16–24) and are more concerned for ritual cleanliness than moral purity (vv. 25–28). Worst of all, they reenact the behavior of their rebellious forefathers by condemning and murdering the spokesmen God sends them (vv. 29–36). These climactic verses are steeped in bitter irony. The Good News Bible captures the sense of verse 32: "Go on, then, and finish up what your ancestors started!" Yet, despite the fact that the sins of generations of Israelites are coming to a head at this moment in history, there is nothing here to suggest the permanent damnation of a race. From Jesus' death to the fall of Jerusalem was forty years—exactly one generation. Does verse 36 imply that after that period, judgment is complete and restoration possible? Verse 39 at least hints at such a day, described as one in which Israel will finally honor Jesus as its Messiah.[33]

The Widow's Mite (Mark 12:41–44 par.) [Aland §286]. As a fitting contrast with the denunciation of the well-to-do and influential within Israel, Mark concludes Jesus' time in the temple with the praiseworthy example of a widow who gave an extraordinarily generous offering to the temple treasury. The quantity was miniscule, but the percentage of her gift enormous in comparison with the seeming generosity of the wealthy. Jesus is not impressed with how much we give but with how much we sacrifice. There may also be an implied critique here of the system that tolerated such disparity.[34]

Historicity

The merely "implicit" Christology of this entire section speaks strongly for its authenticity. Jesus acts out Zechariah's prophecy but makes no explicit messianic claims as he enters Jerusalem and, indeed, subverts conventional expectation concerning a "triumphal entry." His enacted parables of the temple's coming destruction directly challenge prevailing Jewish beliefs, yet do not lead immediately to early Christian abandonment of the temple as a place of prayer and witness. His teaching in the temple involves further distinctive pronouncement stories in which he characteristically and cleverly evades the seemingly foolproof traps set for him. The parable of the wicked tenants suggests that he views himself as God's son, but that is only a subordinate motif in the story.

32. On these puzzling verses, see esp. Mark A. Powell, "Do and Keep What Moses Says (Matthew 23:2–7)," *JBL* 114 (1995): 419–35.

33. On which, see esp. Dale C. Allison, Jr., "Matt. 23:39 = Luke 13:35b as a Conditional Prophecy," *JSNT* 18 (1983): 75–84.

34. For a good survey of recent approaches to this passage with several helpful insights, see Elizabeth S. Malbon, "The Poor Widow in Mark and Her Poor Rich Readers," *CBQ* 53 (1991): 589–604.

The question about how David's son could also be his Lord points in the same direction but remains equally indirect. His praise for the widow's offering reflects a perspective on almsgiving little imitated in any ancient religion.

The extensive woes against the scribes and Pharisees prove more difficult. But the arguments given above for not seeing anti-Semitism here (p. 313) work well only if at least a substantial core of these sentiments are historical. If they are purely the invention of the later church to blindside the Jewish leaders in the second generation of Christianity, it is hard not to see them as a mere blanket condemnation of (non-Christian) Judaism. But if they are limited to certain Jewish leaders and members of crowds on fixed historical occasions, they are more understandable. Additional evidence that the synoptists are constrained to write what actually happened here include the unusually positive acknowledgment of the scribes' and Pharisees' authority in Matthew 23:2–3a; the intra-Jewish nature of the debates over phylacteries, tassels, titles, proselytes, oaths, cups, tombs, and so on (vv. 5–30); the possibility of interpreting verse 39 as holding out a future hope for Israel; and Paul's seeming awareness of the tradition behind verses 31–36 in 1 Thessalonians 2:14–16.

The latter part of John 12 includes another "parable" possibly expanded into a discourse (the "kernel of wheat" in vv. 24–26)[35] and Jesus' inner turmoil, reminiscent of Gethsemane (vv. 27–28). The use of Isaiah 6:10 in v. 40 closely resembles Jesus' words in Mark 4:12 and parallels. In each case, the similarities with the Synoptic tradition enhance the case for authenticity.

THE OLIVET DISCOURSE (MARK 13; MATT. 24–25; LUKE 21:5–38)

Jesus leaves the temple and heads east across the Kidron Valley and up the slopes of the Mount of Olives. As they walk, the disciples understandably marvel at the temple's beauty. To their astonishment Jesus predicts its coming destruction (Mark 13:1–2 pars.). The disciples reply by asking two questions: when will this be, and what will be the sign that it is imminent (vv. 3–4)? In light of Jesus' subsequent answer, it is clear that Matthew has interpreted these as separate questions: when will the temple be destroyed, and what will be the sign of Christ's coming and the end of this age (Matt. 24:3)? In the disciples' minds, the two events were undoubtedly one and the same. Jesus' answer will make plain that they are different issues.

This answer, also known as the Eschatological Discourse, has received a myriad of interpretations through history. Some of the most popular approaches at the grassroots Christian level are among some of the least defensible via sound hermeneutics. The following brief exposition sketches a major, scholarly evangelical perspective that is not as well known as it should be.[36]

---

35. C. H. Dodd, *Historical Tradition in the Fourth Gospel* (Cambridge: CUP, 1963), 366–69.

36. For elaboration, with minor variations in detail, see the commentaries by Carson on Matthew and by Lane and Cranfield on Mark, all *ad loc.* For a thorough history of the interpretation of this passage, followed by a similar exposition, see George R. Beasley-Murray, *Jesus and the Last Days* (Peabody: Hendrickson, 1993). For a brief survey and critique of the four major contemporary evangelical approaches, see David L. Turner, "The Structure and Sequence of Matthew 24:1–41: Interaction with Evangelical Treatments," *GTJ* 10 (1989): 3–27.

When Will the Temple Be Destroyed? (Mark 13:5–23 pars.) [Aland §287–291]

Events Which Must Not Be Interpreted as Overly Significant (vv. 5–13). Trying to calm the eschatological fervor of the day, Jesus answers this first question, in essence, by saying, "not immediately." Verses 5–13 itemize events which must take place without necessarily heralding the end (see vv. 7, 8, 10, 13). These include: (1) the rise of false Messiahs (vv. 5–6, cf. vv. 21–23; "in my name" in v. 6 likely refers to "Christ," not necessarily "Jesus"); (2) wars and rumors of wars (v. 7); (3) earthquakes, famines, and related natural disasters (v. 8; cf. Luke 21:11); (4) persecution from governments and family members (vv. 9, 11–13); and (5) preaching the gospel to all nations (v. 10). Items (1) through (4) were clearly all fulfilled in the years between the crucifixion and the destruction of the temple (A.D. 30–70). Acts 5:36 mentions from this time period the messianic pretender, Theudas, while Josephus narrates the rise of several other would-be Christs (*Antiquities 20*. 97–99, 160–72, 188). Sporadic fighting presaged the Jewish revolt in 67, which itself was the major war leading to the temple's downfall. Laodicea and Pompeii suffered devastating earthquakes in the early 60s, and a significant famine hit parts of the Roman empire, especially Judea, in the late 40s (cf. Acts 11:28). The Book of Acts repeatedly documents the persecution that dogged the early church (cf. also the poignant catalogue of Paul's sufferings in 2 Cor. 11:23–12:10). Even (5) seems to have been fulfilled at least once, given Paul's comments in Romans 10:18; Colossians 1:6, 23; and 1 Timothy 3:16, with "preaching to all the nations" being equivalent to "representative witness throughout the Roman empire" (the Greek *oikoumenē*, often translated "whole world," in fact regularly referred to the known limits of imperial domination).[37]

These five activities, of course, have recurred repeatedly throughout church history. The Book of Revelation depicts similar "end-time horrors." But the application of Jesus' words to the debate about the end of the age would be the same as to the disciples' questions about the timing of the temple's demise. "Such things must happen, but the end is still to come" (Mark 13:7). On the other hand, precisely because all these predictions were at least in some sense fulfilled by A.D. 70, the church in every subsequent generation has been able to believe that the end could come at any time. The challenge for believers, however short or long the interval before Christ's return, is to stand firm, avoid apostasy or lovelessness, be prepared even for martyrdom if necessary, and so be (spiritually) saved (Matt. 24:9, 12–13).

Events Immediately Surrounding the Temple's Destruction (vv. 14–23). Verse 14 brings us to the threshold of A.D. 70. Appropriating the terminology of Daniel 9:27; 11:31; 12:11; and 1 Maccabees 1:54; 6:7, Jesus alludes to the "abomination that causes desolation" (see above, p. 15). Something as bad as or worse than Antiochus Epiphanes' desecration of the temple will occur again. Mark adds parenthetically, "let the reader understand," indicating that the language is deliberately cryptic, perhaps to keep any government official who

---

37. Cf. esp. Robert H. Gundry, *Mark: A Commentary on His Apology for the Cross* (Grand Rapids: Eerdmans, 1993), 739, who lists other texts as well.

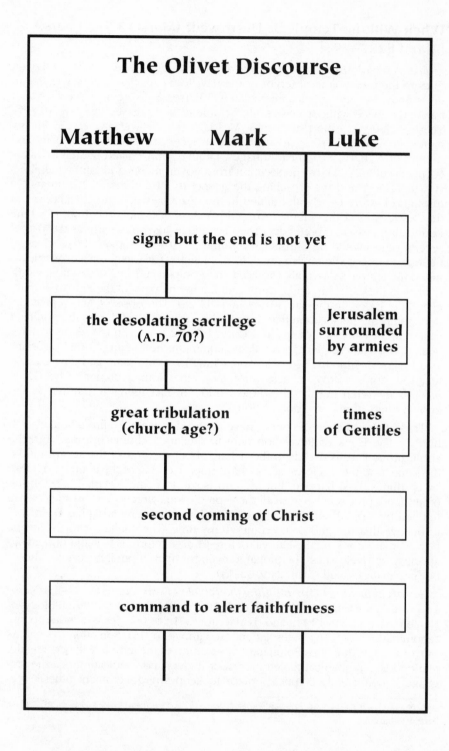

The Olivet Discourse

Matthew	Mark	Luke

signs but the end is not yet

| the desolating sacrilege (A.D. 70?) | Jerusalem surrounded by armies |

| great tribulation (church age?) | times of Gentiles |

second coming of Christ

command to alert faithfulness

might read this Gospel from being able to accuse the Christians of anti-Roman propaganda! The awful conditions surrounding this "abomination" include uniquely first-century Jewish and Judean concerns—living on rooftops and traveling on the Sabbath (Mark 13:15; Matt. 24:20). Luke makes it completely explicit that the event in view is the destruction of Jerusalem (Luke 21:20, 24), which will initiate a period of Jewish captivity and dispersion, during which the city itself will be overrun by Gentile inhabitants. This is exactly what happened after A.D. 70 for nearly 1,900 years.

In this same context, Jesus speaks of unparalleled tribulation (Mark 13:19). It would be hard to prove, historically, that suffering in first-century Jerusalem eclipsed that of all the rest of human history (though recall above, p. 25). But it also makes no sense to limit this suffering to some event just prior to the return of Christ, for then it would be so obvious as to be silly for Jesus to have said there would never again be such suffering. Luke clearly sees this tribulation beginning in A.D. 70, but Matthew just as clearly sees the events portending Christ's return as happening "immediately" after the tribulation (Matt. 24:29). So it seems best to understand Jesus' prediction as referring to the entire period between the destruction of the temple and his return as the "days of distress unequaled." This does not mean that all true Christians have led unpleasant lives filled with persecution, but it does mean that Jesus, like New Testament writers more generally, does *not* see the earthly lot of believers, who faithfully follow their Lord and proclaim his message, to be one of fame or fortune (cf. esp. 2 Tim. 3:12)! It *is* arguable, historically, that the bold articulation and consistent application of the tenets of orthodox Christian faith tend to arouse more animosity than does the comparable practice of any other world religion or ideology.[38]

What Will Signal the End of the Age? (Mark 13:24-32 pars.) [Aland §292-293]

Jesus' answer to this second question is, in essence, "nothing conclusive" or "Don't worry, when it comes you won't miss it!" At some unspecified time after the destruction of the temple, Christ will come back (vv. 24–27). The cosmic distress described is common in apocalyptic literature as metaphorical language for the dramatic, widespread, political and religious turmoil and upheavals that will be brought on by the shift in the ages of human history (cf. Isa. 13:10; 34:4; Ezek. 32:7; Dan. 8:10; Joel 2:10; Hag. 2:21).[39] The only time the word "sign" appears in Jesus' discourse is in Matthew 24:30. But this "sign of the Son of Man" in heaven, whatever it may be,[40] appears too late for those

---

38. The language of Revelation and the frequent pattern in Scripture of multiple fulfillments of prophecy suggest that there may be a particular intensifying of "tribulation" at the very end of the church age. But Jesus, *in this context*, is probably not limiting his use of the term just to that final period of human history.

39. N. T. Wright (*Jesus and the Victory of God* [London: SPCK; Minneapolis: Fortress, 1996]) goes even further to argue that the return of the Son of man itself is equally metaphorical. At least for Luke, Acts 1:9 and 11 seem decisive against this view.

40. Jonathan A. Draper ("The Development of 'the Sign of the Son of Man' in the Jesus Tradition," *NTS* 39 [1993]: 1–21) argues plausibly that the sign, often interpreted as an ensign or military standard, is more specifically the "totem" erected for tribes to gather for war (see esp. Jer. 51:27). This heavenly sign then heralds the fact that Christ will return as king, conqueror, and judge; no longer as suffering servant.

who want to interpret contemporary events and make confident predictions about the time of Christ's return. Rather it is part of the very return (*parousia*) of Jesus itself that is described in this paragraph. And this return will be a public, worldwide, universally visible event (Matt. 24:30–31), disproving the claims of all who have pretended to be Christ incognito (recall Mark 13:21–23).[41]

The second part of Jesus' remarks on the timing of the end of the age is the little parable of the budding fig tree (vv. 28–31). Its point is simply that as leaves on the tree show that summer is near, so the fulfillment of "all these things" demonstrates that Christ's return is near. But what does verse 30 mean by declaring that "this generation will certainly not pass away until all these things have happened"? Many have speculated that Jesus thought he would come back within his disciples' lifetime but was mistaken. Others have translated *genea* not as "generation" but as "race," referring to the Jews. A modern, dispensationalist alternative has been to suggest that "this generation" refers to the end-time generation: from start to finish the events portending Christ's return (sometimes taken to have begun with the reestablishment of the state of Israel in 1948) will last a generation.[42]

None of these options is plausible. In light of its consistent use elsewhere in the Gospels, "this generation" can refer only to a roughly forty-year period of time beginning in Jesus' day (in Matthew alone, cf. 11:16; 12:39, 41, 42, 45; 16:4; 17:17; and esp. 23:36).[43] But careful attention to the immediate context demonstrates that Jesus is not claiming to be coming back in "this generation." "All these things" in verse 30 must be the same as "these things" in verse 29. But the things in question in verse 29 are those things that will show that the end is near. Furthermore, it makes no sense to say that Christ's return demonstrates that the end is near; by that time it will have already arrived! So "these things" must be all the events of verses 5–23, which indeed have already happened and did at least initially occur even before A.D. 70. In other words, nothing stands in the way of Christ's return. But neither does Jesus give any "sign" by which we might be able to predict the time of his coming.

Mark 13:32 now makes that point explicitly. Not even the Son, in his voluntarily accepted limitations on his divine omniscience while a human being, knew the time of his return. How dare any of us claim to know what Jesus himself did not! Nor will it do to claim to know the week or month or year or era because Jesus said merely that he didn't know "the day or hour." These are terms regularly used in Scripture for indefinite periods of time, and Acts 1:7 is even more general: "It is not for you to know the times or dates the Father has set by his own authority."[44]

41. Thus rendering implausible the view that limits the "coming" of the Son of man here to Christ's invisible coming in judgment against the temple in A.D. 70. The consistent use of *parousia* elsewhere also militates against this view. See further Beasley-Murray, *Jesus and the Last Days*, 430.

42. No one has made this view more popular than Hal Lindsey (*The Late Great Planet Earth* [Grand Rapids: Zondervan, 1970], 43), who notes how often fig trees represent Israel in Jewish literature. But Lindsey goes on to equate a generation with a forty-year period of time, suggesting that 1988 should be about the longest one would have to wait for the parousia. How much longer will Bible-believing Christians wait before recognizing Lindsey's approach as simply altogether misguided?

43. Cf. D. A. Carson, "Matthew," in *Expositor's Bible Commentary*, ed. Frank E. Gaebelein, vol. 8 (Grand Rapids: Zondervan, 1984), 507.

44. Cf. further the helpful popular level work by B. J. Oropeza, *99 Reasons Why No One Knows When Christ Will Return* (Downers Grove: IVP, 1994).

The Appeal to Wakefulness (Mark 13:33–37 par.; Matt. 24:37–25:46) [Aland §294–300]

How should we then live? If we are not to try to set dates, not to try to read the "signs of the times" from contemporary events, what do Christ's appeals to alert and wakeful living mean? Quite simply: be ready; be prepared. Be about the business of the kingdom so that whenever the end comes, however unexpectedly, you are ready. Mark, briefly, and Matthew, in much greater detail, record how Jesus proceeded to make this point by means of a variety of parables.

The parable of the doorkeeper (Mark 13:33–37 par.) captures the concept succinctly: stay awake for the master's return, lest he come during any one of the four standard watches (three-hour divisions) of the night. Matthew 24:37–42 and 43–44 reinforce this command with illustrations about the unexpectedness of the flood in Noah's day and of burglars in any day.[45] The parables of 24:45–51 and 25:1–13 then contrast scenarios in which the master returns surprisingly early and surprisingly late. Clearly, disciples are being instructed to be ready for every eventuality. The parable of the talents elaborates what we are to be doing during the interval between Christ's advents, however long or short: we must use all the resources with which he has entrusted us for kingdom purposes. All persons will be called to account for their behavior, and those who have done nothing for the Lord demonstrate that they are no kind of disciple at all and, hence, are eternally condemned (Matt. 25:14–30).[46]

The Olivet Discourse ends with one more quasi-parabolic illustration. The events of Judgment Day, already depicted in the parable of the talents, will resemble a flock herder who separates his sheep from his goats (Matt. 25:31–46). Jesus, the coming king, will divide his followers, who will enjoy his presence forever, from those who are to be condemned to everlasting punishment. But what is the criterion for making this separation? At first glance it seems to be good deeds done for the poor and needy of this world (feeding the hungry, clothing the naked, etc.). Is Jesus teaching salvation by works? Almost certainly not (recall Mark 5:34; 10:52; Luke 7:50; 11:17–19; 18:10–14; etc). Is he then teaching that the true righteousness a disciple exhibits will include such works? This is the most popular contemporary interpretation, but it has not been the dominant view throughout church history[47] nor is it the most plausible. Every other use of "brother(s)" in Matthew, when not meaning biological siblings, refers to spiritual kin—fellow Jews or fellow disciples of Jesus (Matt. 5:22–24, 47; 7:3–5; 12:48–50; 18:15, 21, 35; 23:8; 28:10). The term "least" of these (25:40, 45) uses the superlative form of the adjective "little one," which is one of Matthew's unique ways of referring to Christians (10:42; 18:6,

---

45. Matt. 24:40–41 (par. Luke 17:34–35) is often taken to teach a secret rapture: believers will suddenly disappear from this world as Christ returns before the tribulation and before his universal, public Parousia, leaving behind only unbelievers. But, in context, being "taken away" would have to mean taken away for judgment (parallel to the flood in Matt. 24:39 that "took away" all the unrepentant). Whatever one's position on the rapture, it is best not derived from this passage. Cf. further John F. Walvoord, *Matthew: Thy Kingdom Come* (Chicago: Moody, 1974), 193.

46. For the main points of each of these passages and further exposition of their detail, cf. Craig L. Blomberg, *Interpreting the Parables* (Downers Grove and Leicester: IVP, 1990), *ad loc.*

47. For a full history of interpretation, see Sherman W. Gray, *The Least of My Brothers: Matthew 25:31–46—A History of Interpretation* (Atlanta: Scholars, 1989).

10, 14; cf. 5:19; 11:11). Matthew 10:40–42 offers a close parallel with its promise of reward for those who offer even small acts of kindness to itinerant disciples. So it seems most likely that Jesus is referring to deeds of compassion done for suffering, persecuted Christian emissaries. Because one has accepted the message of the gospel, one is concerned to care for its messenger. Moreover, these "sheep" are not, as it is sometimes alleged, surprised that they are accepted as Christ's followers (the "anonymous Christian" theory); they are surprised only when they are told that they ministered directly to Jesus, since he no longer lives on earth in incarnate form. But Jesus assures them that he is present in every one of his followers to whom they *have* ministered. None of this absolves us of the responsibility to care for the *non*-Christian needy of our world; we simply have to turn to other texts for that teaching.[48]

Historicity

Although it is usually assumed that this discourse is a composite created from the standard Synoptic sources, a good case can be made for a pre-Synoptic "sermon" that Matthew, Mark, and Luke have each in their own ways abbreviated.[49] The fact that Jesus never directly answers the questions with which the discourse begins (Mark 13:4 pars.) speaks for the sermon's authenticity, as does the generally cryptic nature of the discourse itself—most notably the reference to the desolating sacrilege (Mark 13:14 pars.). Jesus' insistence on preliminary signs—"but the end is still to come" (v. 7)—would be superfluous if this teaching were being created after or just before the destruction of the temple. Jesus' ignorance of the day and hour of his return (13:32 pars.) presents potentially embarrassing Christology. Yet given the frequent refrain of the Old Testament prophets that the Day of the Lord was at hand and in light of the proliferation of apocalyptic speculation in first-century Judaism, it would be extraordinary if Jesus had never addressed the topic of the end-times in something like this fashion. 1 Thessalonians 4:16–17; 5:2; and 2 Thessalonians 2:3–6 all betray awareness of similar early "Jesus-traditions." And the distinctively Matthean additions to the discourse are virtually all parables that cohere with the form and contents of the paralleled parables that are almost universally admitted to be authentic.

FOR FURTHER STUDY

In Judea on the Road to Jerusalem

Jesus and Divorce

Atkinson, David. *To Have and to Hold*. London: Collins, 1979; Grand Rapids: Eerdmans, 1981.

Cornes, Andrew. *Divorce and Remarriage: Biblical Principles and Pastoral Practice.* London: Hodder & Stoughton; Grand Rapids: Eerdmans, 1993.

---

48. For this line of interpretation, cf., e.g., George E. Ladd, "The 'Parable of the Sheep and the Goats' in Recent Interpretation," in *New Dimensions in New Testament Study*, ed. Richard N. Longenecker and Merrill C. Tenney (Grand Rapids: Zondervan, 1974), 191–99; and John R. Donahue, "The Parable of the Sheep and the Goats: A Challenge to Christian Ethics," *TS* 47 (1986): 3–31.

49. David Wenham, *The Rediscovery of Jesus' Eschatological Discourse* (Sheffield: JSOT, 1984).

Garland, David, and Diana Garland. *Marriage: For Better or For Worse?* Nashville: Broadman, 1989.

Heth, William A., and Gordon J. Wenham. *Jesus and Divorce.* London: Hodder & Stoughton, 1984; Nashville: Nelson, 1985.

House, H. Wayne, ed. *Divorce and Remarriage: Four Christian Views.* Downers Grove: IVP, 1990.

Keener, Craig S. . . . *And Marries Another: Divorce and Remarriage in the Teaching of the New Testament.* Peabody: Hendrickson, 1991.

Luck, William F. *Divorce and Remarriage.* San Francisco: Harper & Row, 1987.

Jesus and Riches

Hengel, Martin. *Property and Riches in the Early Church.* London: SCM; Philadelphia: Fortress, 1974.

Moxnes, Halvor. *The Economy of the Kingdom.* Philadelphia: Fortress, 1988.

Pilgrim, Walter E. *Good News to the Poor.* Minneapolis: Augsburg, 1981.

Schmidt, Thomas E. *Hostility to Wealth in the Synoptic Gospels.* Sheffield: JSOT, 1987.

Seccombe, David P. *Possessions and the Poor in Luke-Acts.* Linz: Studien zum Neuen Testament und seiner Umwelt, 1982.

Other

Carter, Warren. *Households and Discipleship: A Study of Matthew 19–20.* Sheffield: JSOT, 1994.

Via, Dan O., Jr. *The Ethics of Mark's Gospel—In the Middle of Time.* Philadelphia: Fortress, 1985.

The Olivet Discourse

Beasley-Murray, George R. *Jesus and the Last Days.* Peabody: Hendrickson, 1993.

Geddert, Timothy J. *Watchwords: Mark 13 in Markan Eschatology.* Sheffield: JSOT, 1989.

Giblin, C. H. *The Destruction of Jerusalem according to Luke's Gospel.* Rome: BIP, 1985.

Hartman, Lars. *Prophecy Interpreted.* Lund: Gleerup, 1966.

Wenham, David. The Rediscovery of Jesus' Eschatological Discourse. Sheffield: JSOT, 1984.

QUESTIONS FOR REVIEW

1. From Jesus' Judean ministry, what do we learn about his views on divorce? on the right use of riches? How should the passages dealing with these two particularly sensitive topics be applied today?

2. Walk through each of the main episodes of Mark 11:1–26 and demonstrate how they are "actions of judgment."

3. Proceed through the various pericopae of Mark 11:27–12:44 as Jesus teaches in the temple. What is the main point of each passage? How is it important to recognize who his specific conversation partners are in each instance?

4. Summarize the main contours of the structure and interpretation of Jesus' Olivet Discourse as presented in this chapter. If this approach is at all on target, what implications does it have for contemporary Christian living as we continue to await Christ's return?

CHAPTER SEVENTEEN

PASSION, CRUCIFIXION, AND RESURRECTION

T he final events of the Gospel narratives quickly unfold. Nothing that has been recorded can be confidently ascribed to Wednesday of Jesus' final week. The plotting of Jesus' death by the Jewish leaders (Mark 14:1–2 pars.; Aland §305) probably takes place on Tuesday. They want to avoid conflict with the crowds, with whom Jesus is still popular. That they arrested him during the Passover feast anyway, though with stealth and by night, could reflect a change in plans—or else Mark 14:2a should be translated, "apart from the festal crowds." We pick up the action on Thursday night with Jesus' last supper with the Twelve, their departure for the Garden of Gethsemane, and his arrest. His conviction, execution, and resurrection from the dead will follow shortly.

THURSDAY NIGHT: THE UPPER ROOM AND GETHSEMANE

The Last Supper (Mark 14:10–26 pars.) [Aland §307–16]

Preparation (vv. 10–16 pars.). Two plots are intertwined here. Judas is scheming with the Jewish leaders to betray Jesus (vv. 10–11), while Jesus himself, fully aware of what is going on, is preparing to celebrate his last meal, a Passover feast, with his disciples (vv. 12–16). Matthew characteristically adds information that enables us later to see a fulfillment of prophecy: Judas agrees to betray Jesus for thirty pieces of silver (Matt. 26:15; cf. 27:9). His motives are never explained. Suggestions have ranged from pure greed (but the price was not that high) to a desire to force Jesus' hand and make him act like the military king people hoped he would become. Neither of these is probable, but it is likely that Judas had become disenchanted with the "suffering servant" focus of Christ's mission. The first day of Unleavened Bread (Mark 14:12) informally marked the beginning of the week-long Passover festival, as Jews cleaned all yeast out of their homes. Jesus' directions about preparing for their meal suggest prearranged signals to avoid public scrutiny and the danger that was lurking so close behind (vv. 13–16).

The Passover Meal (vv. 17–26 pars.). For most Jews, the Passover was the favorite feast of the year. Commemorating their escape from Egypt (see Exodus 12), and performed according to the laws God had commanded them (cf. Lev. 23:4–8; Num. 9:1–14; Deut. 16:1–8), this was the one annual festival celebrated primarily in family units. Jesus presides at table with his disciples like the father of a family. The men would have reclined on couches arranged in a square U-shaped configuration. Jesus, as host, would have been second from one end, with Judas on his left and John on his right. Peter may have sat directly across from John, in the position of the humble servant.[1] Together the thirteen men would have begun to reenact the Passover "haggadah" or liturgy. With each of four cups of wine, a portion of Exodus 6:6–7a was recalled. The elements of the ceremony as it had developed, in their probable sequence, would have included:

A blessing and the first cup of wine ("I will bring you out . . .")

The serving of the meal: unleavened bread, bitter herbs, greens, stewed fruit, and roast lamb, each symbolizing details of the first Passover

The youngest son asks, "Why is this night different from other nights?" and the story is retold

Second cup of wine ("I will free you from being slaves to them")

Hallel ("praise") Psalm 113 (or 113–114) sung

Breaking of bread and the eating of the meal

Third cup of wine at end of meal ("I will redeem you")

Hallel ("praise") Psalms 114 (or 115)–118 sung

Fourth cup of wine ("I will take you as my own people, and I will be your God")[2]

The three Synoptic Gospels all clearly allude to various portions of this liturgy. Jesus is proclaiming that a new Passover will now be available through

---

1. Cf. further Leon Morris, *The Gospel according to John* (Grand Rapids: Eerdmans, rev. 1995), 555–58, for the details of seating and conversation.

2. Graham N. Stanton, *The Gospels and Jesus* (Oxford: OUP, 1989), 257. On the primary sources for the Passover haggadah, see Gordon J. Bahr, "The Seder of Passover and the Eucharistic Words," *NovT* 12 (1970): 181–202. Cf esp. *Pesahim* 10:1–7.

his coming death. John does not include the details of the meal or Christ's "words of institution," describing instead the "footwashing" that Jesus initiated on this occasion. The prediction of Judas' betrayal apparently occurred next, followed by the meal itself. By then appending Jesus' detailed Farewell Discourse (see below, p. 334), John may be contextualizing his story by describing it as a Greco-Roman "symposium"—an occasion of informal fellowship and serious conversation following a more formal banquet.

John 13:1–20 narrates the *footwashing*. Verses 1–2 preface the account by describing this as an expression of Jesus' uttermost love.[3] Washing the grime from sandal-clad feet that had walked dusty roads was a common courtesy by a host for his meal guests, but it was normally assigned to the most menial of slaves. Jesus takes the initiative, despite his disciples' complaints, to teach a powerful object lesson about servant ministry, all the more appropriate given the death he would soon die. He also wants to teach them about spiritual cleansing (v. 8). Impulsive Peter, when he catches on, then asks for an entire bath! But Jesus replies that one who has previously bathed needs only to wash his feet. Most commentators recognize this as teaching that a person receives salvation (and possibly baptism) in Christ as a nonrepeatable event, but then needs regular opportunities for confession and forgiveness of subsequent sin. A few churches have made footwashing an ordinance or sacrament to be literally imitated in church from time to time. There is nothing inherently objectionable in this, but footwashing does differ from baptism and the Lord's Supper by not building on preexisting religious rituals, merely on a commonplace household courtesy.

Already in verses 1–20, Jesus has recognized that not all of his disciples are spiritually clean (vv. 10, 18), and he proceeds to spell this out (vv. 21–30; cf. Mark 14:18–21 pars.). One of the Twelve will deliver him over to be crucified (the Greek word for "betray" and "deliver up" is identical). Although Jesus knows exactly what is happening, and indeed it has been foreordained, still Judas remains fully culpable for his treachery. This sharp juxtaposition of divine predestination and human responsibility matches Scripture's consistent treatment of these two themes.[4] Although the disciples badger Jesus to tell them who the traitor is, all he replies is that it is one dipping his bread into the sauce with him, something all of the Twelve would have done during the course of the meal. Matthew adds that Judas asked if it was he (Matt. 26:25), but the most literal translation of Jesus' reply is "you said it"—not an unambiguous affirmative! In John, the beloved disciple (i.e., probably John himself; recall above, pp. 170–173) is reclining next to Jesus and finds out specifically that Judas is the betrayer (John 13:26). But this seems to have been a whispered conversation not over-

---

3. John 13:1 is the first of several verses that lead many scholars to think that John wants to portray Jesus as spending his last night with his disciples *before* the Passover, with the crucifixion taking place on the day of the slaughter of the Passover lambs rather than one day afterwards, as in the Synoptics. But all v. 1 says is that before the Passover Jesus knew what was about to happen and was prepared to love his followers to the end. Without any further qualification, the meal described in v. 2 is most naturally understood as the Passover meal, in light of the reference to Passover in v. 1. When Judas leaves in vv. 29–30 to buy provisions for the "feast," the rest of the week-long festival is in view.

4. See esp. D. A. Carson, *Divine Sovereignty and Human Responsibility* (London: Marshall, Morgan & Scott; Atlanta: John Knox, 1979). Charles H. Talbert (*Reading John* [New York: Crossroad, 1990], 196) describes Jesus' overtures of table-fellowship intimacy with Judas here as "love's last appeal to one on the verge of perdition."

heard by anyone else, because, when Judas leaves, the rest of the disciples have no idea why he is going out (vv. 28–29).

Luke gives a fuller account of the Passover meal itself than does Mark or Matthew.[5] Twice Jesus takes a cup of wine and offers solemn pronouncements over it (Luke 22:17, 20). The "cup" in the Old Testament often symbolized the outpouring of God's wrath (e.g., Ps. 75:8; Isa. 51:17). Whether the first reference corresponds to the first or second cup of the liturgy, the second reference, which is paralleled in Mark and Matthew, drunk after the meal had begun, almost certainly corresponds to the third cup of the haggadah. Jesus speaks of his coming death by means of broken bread and spilled blood, in conjunction with the very cup of the Passover service meant to remind the celebrants of God's redemption. Later Christian theology would erect elaborate theological edifices on Jesus' simple words here, debating such issues as transubstantiation, consubstantiation, and so on (i.e., when and how the bread and wine actually become Christ's body and blood). All of this is anachronistic in the historical context, however. No one seeing Jesus physically holding out a loaf of bread or cup of wine would have imagined him to be claiming that they were somehow a literal extension of his anatomy! The Aramaic behind "this is my body" and "this is my blood" most likely would not have even used a verb for "is."[6] Rather Jesus is offering an enacted parable about how these elements of the Passover meal now represent, symbolize, or depict his coming substitutionary, sacrificial death.[7] "For many" (Mark 14:24) probably alludes to the suffering servant's role in Isaiah 53:4, 10, and 12. The "new covenant" clearly harks back to the one that was prophesied in Jeremiah 31:31–34.

Mark 14:25 suggests that Jesus may not have drunk the fourth cup of wine; at any rate he knows he will not be celebrating this festival again until his second coming. The allusion to the future aspect of the kingdom gives each celebration of the Lord's Supper a forward-looking thrust as well as a backward-looking one. We not only memorialize and reenact Christ's atoning death in the Lord's Supper, but we long for and proclaim our belief in his return to establish his kingdom in all its fullness (cf. the reference to the messianic banquet in Rev. 19:9, drawing on the imagery of Isa. 25:6). Luke inserts at this point a brief episode largely parallel to Mark 10:41–45 (cf. Matt. 20:24–28; 19:28): Jesus' teaching on servant leadership in response to the disciples' dispute about greatness, teaching that was countercultural indeed in light of the prevailing authoritarian systems of leadership particularly in Greco-Roman circles (Luke 22:24–30).[8] The little troupe then sings the closing *Hallel* Psalms and leaves the upper room of the Jerusalem house to head for the slopes of the Mount of Olives (Mark 14:26 pars.).

Prediction of Peter's Denial (Mark 14:27–31 pars.; Luke 22:35–38). About the time of their departure, Jesus also predicts that all the disciples will abandon

---

5. A few ancient manuscripts omit Luke 22:19b–20, but the evidence for their inclusion is quite strong.

6. Clearly a form of the copula (the verb "to be") was to be supplied, but it is risky to draw conclusions about the emphatic nature of a concept that is never expressed but only implied.

7. For a brief readable history of the subsequent theological debate, with suggestions for how true Christians of different traditions can come together in the Lord's Supper, see Donald Bridge and David Phypers, *The Meal That Unites?* (London: Hodder & Stoughton, 1981).

8. On which see esp. Peter K. Nelson, *Leadership and Discipleship: A Study of Luke 22:24–30* (Atlanta: Scholars, 1994).

him and that Peter will explicitly deny him three times during the coming night (before the cock crows twice—Mark 14:30[9]). Luke 22:31–32 sees this as Satan's doing. But, as consistently in Scripture, Satan's power is limited by God's sovereign permission. Jesus ensures Peter that his faith will later return, enabling him to lead God's people. Also distinctive to Luke is Jesus' "change of strategy" for the disciples in their postresurrection missionary work (vv. 35–38). Previously they were to go out peacefully, entirely dependent on others' hospitality (recall 9:1–6 pars.; 10:1–12). From now on they must be more self-sufficient, prepared for hostility and persecution. The disciples take Jesus' words overly literally and brandish two swords, to which Jesus replies with exasperation, "It is enough"—almost equivalent to "Never mind; you just don't get it!"[10]

John's account of the prediction of Peter's denial also includes distinctive material: another reminder that the hour of Jesus' glorification is imminent (John 13:31–33) and the giving of a "new" commandment to love—new in the sense that in Christ they would have a new empowerment to obey it (vv. 34–35).[11] This love would offer a dynamic witness to a watching world. Roughly two centuries later, Tertullian confirms this effect by citing the pagan admiration for the character of Christian assemblies: "'Look,' they say, 'how they love one another' (for themselves hate one another); 'and how they are ready to die for each other' (for themselves will be readier to kill each other)" (*Apology* 39.7).

The Farewell Discourse (John 14:1–17:26)

Only John records Jesus' more extended remarks following the Passover meal. Formally, this "discourse" is introduced already at 13:31, but verses 31–38 have been treated in connection with the prediction of Peter's denial above. Despite this gloomy prophecy, Jesus now urges the disciples not to be troubled but to trust in God and in himself (14:1). Chapters 14–17 in various ways resemble the established genre in Jewish literature of a farewell discourse—a famous hero about to die, instructing his followers about how to prepare for life after his departure (cf. esp. the Testaments of the Twelve Patriarchs). Chapters 14–16 contain the body of the discourse proper, while chapter 17 appends a closing prayer. Chapters 14–16 divide naturally into four parts, which form an ABBA structure: on Jesus' departure and return (14:1–31), the disciples' responsibility to love (15:1–17), contrasted with the world's hatred for the disciples (15:18–16:4), and more on Jesus' departure and return (16:5–33).[12]

Jesus' Departure and Return (14:1–31) [Aland §317–319]. This section of Jesus' discourse is unified by the pattern of four questions from four different disciples, each of which elicits a somewhat oblique answer from Jesus that in

---

9. On the textual and interpretive problems of this verse, see David Brady, "The Alarm to Peter in Mark's Gospel," *JSNT* 4 (1979): 42–57.

10. Cf. further I. Howard Marshall, *The Gospel of Luke* (Exeter: Paternoster; Grand Rapids: Eerdmans, 1978), 827.

11. The Latin for "new commandment" (*mandatum novum*) led to this day being called "Maundy Thursday" in the Christian calendar.

12. It is common in scholarly circles to speak of "two farewell discourses" (or more!), because of the apparent literary seam at 14:31—Jesus says, "Come now; let us leave," but keeps on talking as if they are all still in the Upper Room. But the narrative flow of chaps. 14–16 does not fall as neatly into two parts (14, 15–16) as into the four just outlined. These chapters make sense as a unified whole, so hypotheses about stages of redaction, while hard to disprove, may be unnecessary.

turn triggers the next question. Peter has already asked where Jesus is going in 13:36; Jesus continues his answer in 14:1–4. He is returning to the Father to prepare a place for his followers. Verse 2a is best translated as in the NIV: "In my Father's house are many *rooms*" (italics added) (not "mansions" as in the KJV). The most prominent multiroom dwelling in ancient Israel was, of course, the temple.[13] Jesus' language in verses 2–3 also suggests that the life in the presence of the Father to which his disciples can look forward is a spacious home and involves a welcoming fellowship. By claiming that they know the way, he elicits the next question, this time from Thomas.

Verses 5–7 address the issue of the way to the Father. Jesus replies that he is the true and living way (v. 6). In context, the point is that one cannot have the Father without the Son. Those who reject Jesus turn their back on God also. This passage does not address the question of whether anyone who has never heard of Jesus can be saved. If anyone can, however, it would be only on the basis of the cross-work of Christ. Philip nevertheless insists that Jesus show them the Father (v. 8). Jesus' answer comes in two parts. He again calls the Twelve to look at him (vv. 9–14). Then he promises the Holy Spirit as the one to come to replace him (vv. 15–21). Verses 9–14 make four points: (1) The Father and the Son are so closely related that Jesus can talk of each as being "in" the other (vv. 9–10). (2) If people will not believe Jesus' own claims, they should believe on the basis of his miracles (v. 11). (3) Those who do believe will do even greater works than Christ—not qualitatively but quantitatively (v. 12). The Spirit will enable Christians to reach far more people and influence the world in far greater ways than Jesus could during his lifetime, with his human limitations and a ministry largely restricted to Israel. (4) Requests based on Christ's power and authority (the meaning of "name"), and hence in accordance with his desires, will be granted (vv. 13–14).

Verses 15–21 introduce the first of five "Paraclete" passages in the Farewell Discourse. The Greek *paraklētos* is a term that can mean comforter, counselor, advocate, strengthener, or exhorter. In these passages we see the Holy Spirit introduced as just such a person, a replacement for Jesus ("*another* Counselor"—v. 16, italics added), who functions as a helper (14:16), interpreter (14:26), witness (15:26), prosecutor (16:7), and revealer (16:13).[14] In 14:15–21, the Paraclete helps the disciples by not leaving them "orphaned" when Jesus departs. The Spirit is currently *with* them, as he was with Jesus and believers throughout Old Testament times. But, from Pentecost on, he will be *in* them (v. 17), permanently indwelling and empowering his people to demonstrate their love through obedience to Christ's commands (v. 21).

The final question of chapter 14 comes from Jude. Why such exclusivity that God, in Jesus and the Spirit, reveals himself only to believers (v. 22)? Jesus' answer basically affirms that people must choose for themselves but that the Triune God will make his "home" with anyone willing to love and obey (vv. 23–24). Verses 25–31 summarize the chapter. The purpose of this discourse is to help the disciples make sense of coming events, particularly Jesus'

---

13. For a survey of the temple motif throughout John, in defense of the thesis that Jesus has temple imagery in mind here, too, see James McCaffrey, *The House with Many Rooms: The Temple Theme of John 14, 2–3* (Rome: BIP, 1988).

14. F. F. Bruce, *The Gospel of John* (Basingstoke: Pickering & Inglis; Grand Rapids: Eerdmans, 1983), 302.

death and resurrection, after they have happened. The Spirit will help them interpret his ministry (v. 26), so that they can experience an inner peace different from the mere cessation of external hostility that the world tries to promise (v. 27). Verse 28 offers a balance to the previous statements that stressed the equality of Father, Son, and Holy Spirit. There is still a hierarchy of persons that is irreversible.[15] The puzzling reference at the end of verse 31 may refer to the time at which the disciples followed Jesus out of the Upper Room and headed toward Gethsemane. The rest of the discourse could well have been spoken en route; certainly the imagery of vine and branches might easily have been suggested as they passed the vineyards near the temple and headed for the slopes of the mount covered with olive trees (cf. above, p. 173).

The Vine and the Branches (15:1–17) [Aland §320–321]. This section falls into two parts. Verses 1–8 exhort Jesus' followers to remain in him. Verses 9–17 command them to love each other. This love flows organically from abiding in Christ, just as a branch must remain attached to the vine in order to keep growing and bearing fruit. Verses 1–8 present only two alternatives: remaining (growing and bearing fruit) or not remaining at all. Certain branches (faithful believers) are pruned (disciplined) so as to bear more fruit (all the marks of Christian obedience). They receive whatever they ask for (but, by remaining in Christ, such requests by definition fit in with his will—v. 7; cf. v. 10). Others are cut off and burned (vv. 2, 6). This category of person is best interpreted by another Johannine passage: "They went out from us, but they did not really belong to us. For if they had belonged to us, they would have *remained* with us; but their going showed that none of them belonged to us" (1 John 2:19, italics added). In this context, Judas is the most obvious example of someone who did not "remain" (John 13:18). Jesus' use of the vine metaphor may also suggest that he is presenting himself here as the new Israel.

John 15:9–17 elaborates on the theme of love.[16] By loving obedience, Christians' joy will be perfected (v. 11). The greatest example of love is willingness to die for a friend, as Jesus will soon do for his (v. 13). By no longer calling them servants but friends, he is indicating their privileged position with respect to receiving the Father's revelation (v. 15). But this privilege is nothing in which they can boast, for it was entirely initiated by God (v. 16).

Hatred from the World (15:18–16:4) [Aland §322–324]. The disciples may love each other, but they can expect at least some outsiders to hate them. This thought is unpacked via four subpoints: (1) They will be hated because Jesus was hated (15:18–21). This is the context for the proverb, "No servant is greater than his master" (v. 20), which in other contexts might prove false. But, in any era, no loyal follower of the one who was crucified by hatred can expect lifelong exemption from opposition. (2) Such hatred is inexcusable because people can know about Jesus' good teachings and mighty deeds (15:22–25). Nevertheless it will often persist, typologically fulfilling Scripture, much like King David was hated irrationally (v. 25; cf. Ps. 35:19; 69:4). (3) The Spirit will empower them for bold testimony in the midst of persecution (15:26–27). Acts 5:29–32 narrates one dramatic fulfillment of this promise. (4) All these warnings

---

15. See esp. C. K. Barrett, *Essays on John* (London: SPCK; Philadelphia: Westminster, 1982), 19–36.

16. For further elaboration, see esp. Fernando F. Segovia, *Love Relationships in the Johannine Tradition* (Chico: Scholars, 1982).

are prophylactic, so that the disciples can be ready for what happens (16:1–4). Persecution for Jewish Christians will extend even to excommunication from the synagogue (v. 2; recall 9:22). This policy at first developed only sporadically, but by the end of the first century it was widespread throughout the empire (see above, p. 25).

More on Jesus' Departure and Return (16:5–33) [Aland §325–328]. Again four subsections may be identified. To begin with, Jesus outlines further work of the Holy Spirit (vv. 5–15). This section begins with a puzzling apparent contradiction, as Jesus chastises the disciples for not asking where he is going (v. 5; but see 13:36; 14:5). Perhaps his point is that now, after all this talk of hatred, is the more appropriate time to ask the question, as they grieve over his departure (v. 6).[17] But unless Jesus leaves, the Spirit cannot replace him (v. 7). And the Spirit's ministry will be powerful indeed. He will convict unbelievers of their sin, sham righteousness, and coming judgment (vv. 8–11).[18] Through his disciples, the Holy Spirit will guide believers "into all truth" (vv. 12–15; see esp. v. 13). No doubt this included the writing of the Gospel of John itself and the other New Testament documents, but there is nothing in the context to limit this prophecy to the canon of Scripture. God may not grant revelation today *on a par with* Scripture, but the Spirit is still in the business of illuminating his Word and his will for his people.[19]

Second, the disciples' grief will turn to joy (vv. 16–22). This section revolves around Jesus' enigmatic declaration that in a little while the Twelve would no longer see him, but then, shortly afterwards, they would see him again (v. 16). Jesus' departure and return can be interpreted as referring to his death and resurrection but also to his ascension and second coming. In each case, happiness will follow the sorrow produced by the temporary "absence" of Christ. But, third, even in his absence the disciples can ask and receive many things from the Father in Christ's "name" (vv. 23–28). Now they can make requests of Jesus directly; later they will ask more indirectly. But asking through Christ and by his power and authority (and so, again, in accordance with his desires) will have a mighty effect.[20]

Finally, and fourthly, the disciples claim to understand. But Jesus' response shows the claim to be premature (vv. 29–33). They are still not prepared for his departure. But, with God's presence, they will "rebound." Despite the persecutions the church age will inflict, they will have peace with God. Knowing that he has overcome the world and made their eventual victory certain, they will persevere.

---

17. Cf. C. K. Barrett, *The Gospel according to St. John* (London: SPCK; Philadelphia: Westminster, rev. 1978), 485.

18. D. A. Carson ("The Function of the Paraclete in John 16:7–11," *JBL* 98 [1979]: 547–66) stresses that it is most natural to take all three adjectives as attributes of the fallen world. An alternate, more common interpretation takes the middle term (righteousness) as referring to what Christ bestows on believers.

19. Cf. Bruce, *John*, 320: "As the Messiah was expected to bring out plainly the fuller implications of the revelation that had preceded his coming, so the Paraclete will bring out plainly the fuller implications of the revelation embodied in the Messiah and apply them relevantly to each succeeding generation."

20. Alternately, the contrast between vv. 23a and 23b may be between asking questions for information (as the disciples have been doing on this occasion) and making other requests (because the desired information will have been supplied by the Spirit). Cf. J. Ramsey Michaels, *John* (Peabody: Hendrickson, 1989), 276.

The True "Lord's Prayer" (17:1–26) [Aland §329]. Jesus closes his Farewell Discourse with a poignant prayer for himself (vv. 1–5), for his disciples (vv. 6–19), and for coming generations of followers (vv. 20–26). Because of its intercessory function, it has often been called Jesus' high-priestly prayer. Had the prayer he modeled for his disciples not have come to be known as the Lord's Prayer, that label might have stuck here instead. Once again, Jesus acknowledges that the hour for his departure has come (v. 1). His prayer for himself is that he might complete the work for which the Father sent him. This would bring glory to him, but he would merely reflect that glory back to the Father (vv. 1, 4–5).

The main request for his disciples is for spiritual protection in the midst of the predicted adversity. On the basis of their eternal security (vv. 6–14), Jesus prays that they might be shielded from being overpowered by the devil in this life, and be sanctified (growing in holiness) instead (vv. 15–19). Verse 9 surprises us as Jesus says he is not praying for unbelievers. That does not mean he never prays for them, merely that he is not praying for them here. But as he prays for his followers who will spread his message, he is clearly demonstrating concern for the lost.[21] Verse 12 is not an exception to the principle of eternal security, but it stresses that the one who would betray Christ was a "son of perdition" from the start. Verse 15 has massive implications for Christian living in any culture. Jesus never promoted isolationism or monasticism, nor did he promise relief from great tribulation. But he did pray for, and we can be assured of, protection in the midst of the sin and suffering of the world.[22] It is from verses 14–16 that we get the abbreviated summary that Christians are to be "in the world but not of it."

Included in Jesus' prayer for his disciples is the request for unity (v: 11). In his intercession for those who would come to belief through the apostles' ministry, unity becomes the dominant theme (vv. 21–23). An important reason for desiring unity is its evangelistic impact (vv. 21b, 23b). How impotent much subsequent Christianity has become through its rampant factionalism and denominationalism! The evangelical parachurch movement of our day has demonstrated the potential of Bible-believing Christians of numerous theological traditions working together for kingdom objectives. How long will it be before the established churches and denominations catch on and stop refusing to fellowship with one another but rather cooperate in joint ventures to reach a lost world for Christ?[23] As amazing as anything in this section of Jesus' prayer is his concern that our unity in some sense reflect the unity of the Triune Godhead (vv. 21a, 22, 24). This does not mean that believers are deified, but it

---

21. Cf. esp. George R. Beasley-Murray, *John* (Waco: Word, 1987), 298.

22. Interestingly, the identical two Greek words for "protect from" (the verb *tēreō* plus the preposition *ek*) recur in Rev. 3:10, in which John quotes Jesus as promising the faithful church of Philadelphia that he will "keep them from" the hour of trial about to come on the whole world. Therefore, if this verse refers to the great tribulation at the end of the church age (and it may not), it fits a post-tribulational view (protection in the midst of trial) better than a pre-tribulational one (exemption from the tribulation altogether).

23. Ben Witherington III, *John's Wisdom: A Commentary on the Fourth Gospel* (Louisville: Westminster/John Knox, 195), 274, notes: "Protestantism has tended to hold up Truth, with a capital *T*, while intoning unity with a lowercase *u*, with the end result that Protestant churches and denominations have proved endlessly divisive and factious. On the other hand, Catholicism and Orthodoxy have held up Unity with a capital *U*, and at least from a Protestant viewpoint this has been at the expense of Truth. In other words, no part of the church has adequately gotten the balance between truth and unity right, it would seem."

means we have access to the very revelation of God (vv. 25–26). 1 Corinthians 2:10–16 offers an apt commentary.

Prayer and Arrest in the Garden (Mark 14:32–52 pars.) [Aland §330–331]

Eventually Jesus and the disciples arrive at the Garden of Gethsemane (from the Hebrew, "oil press") on the western slopes of Olivet, overlooking the Kidron ravine and the temple in Jerusalem (Mark 14:32–42 pars.). Jesus asks all his followers to wait for him but takes the inner three to a separate place and commissions them to pray fervently that *they* might not succumb to temptation. As he goes a little further on, he prays for himself, "Abba, Father. . . . Take this cup from me. Yet not what I will, but what you will" (v. 36). Here we see Jesus' close personal intimacy with the Father (on *Abba*, see above, p. 253). Jesus' full humanity is disclosed, conjoined with his perfect obedience to God. No one should ever want to endure the agony Christ knew lay ahead, but he was prepared to submit to God if there was no other way. This is also a perfect example of a prayer not answered in the manner preferred by the person making the request, but through no fault of the pray-er! Hebrews 5:7 will later reflect on this text and insist that Christ "was heard because of his reverent submission." But the answer to Jesus' prayer was resurrection after death, not exemption from it. God may often answer our most fervent prayers to be spared hard times in the same way.[24]

After a while, Judas arrives leading Jewish (and perhaps Roman) authorities to seize Jesus (Mark 14:43–52 pars.). Christ has had to rouse his sleeping disciples who were unable to stay awake and pray (vv. 41–42). Judas greets him with the conventional sign of friendship—a kiss (vv. 43–46). Why did Jesus need to be identified at all to the authorities? Perhaps because it was dark, and perhaps Jesus looked very much like several others in his little group. The presence of people with clubs and swords shows that they feared the disciples might be numerous and armed. Peter, in fact, does briefly resist, cutting off the ear of the high priest's slave, Malchus (John 18:10). But Jesus rebukes him, demonstrates forgiveness for his enemies by healing the ear (Luke 22:51), and reiterates that this is not the time for violent rebellion (Matt. 26:52–56). John, more than any of the other Gospels, highlights how Jesus is in control of the situation. At first, the soldiers fall to the ground in his presence, unable to arrest him (John 18:4–9). But he proceeds to submit, because this is their "hour," they who belong to the power of darkness (Luke 22:53). In stark contrast, the disciples all flee, including a young man who leaves behind his linen undergarment and runs away naked (Mark 14:51–52). This latter reference, unique to Mark, has often been viewed as his ignominious signature to the Gospel. (We know from Acts 12:12 that the disciples later met in Mark's home in Jerusalem; could this have been the site of the Last Supper as well?)

---

24. There is no justification for the view that Christ prayed in the garden to be spared premature death on the spot. Luke 22:43–44 are not in several of the oldest and most reliable manuscripts and are therefore not necessarily historical. Even if they are, they say merely that Jesus' sweat was so profuse that it was *"like* great drops of blood falling on the ground."

Whoever the young man was, he, too, abandoned Christ. All of his followers had now left.[25]

Historicity

The unusually close similarities between John and the Synoptics from here on in the Gospel accounts have suggested to many the concept of an early, written source containing most or all of the passion narrative. The betrayal, denial, and flight of the disciples are all too embarrassing to have been invented. The same is true of the temptation of Jesus in the Garden of Gethsemane, an episode that is also attested in Hebrews 5:7–10. Jesus' submission to his Father's will nicely matches the petition from the Lord's Prayer, "Thy will be done." The Last Supper finds detailed corroboration in the "words of institution" passed on as sacred tradition by Paul in 1 Corinthians 11:23–26. The rest of the events of that Passover meal fit perfectly into the details of the Jewish ceremony, yet they receive Jesus' characteristic and surprising reinterpretations. The entire account also has an unusual concentration of Semitisms.[26]

John 13–17, as with most passages in the Fourth Gospel, proves more complex. It contains overlaps with the Synoptic accounts of Thursday night, most notably the predictions of Peter's denial and Judas's betrayal. We have already noted that John would have had reason to omit the words of institution over the bread and wine (see above, p. 166). The footwashing scene that he describes instead fits well with the emphases of that evening on humility, self-sacrifice, and selfless love (cf. Luke 22:24–27 in particular), however much John's idiom may have transformed it. Various other individual verses find close parallels in the Synoptics (e.g., John 13:20 and Matt. 10:40; John 14:13–14; 16:23–24; and Matt. 7:7–11). Jesus' advance predictions of his death, resurrection, and return permeate both the Farewell Discourse and the Synoptic narratives. John 14:6 ("I am the way") could explain why the first Christians were called "the Way" (e.g., Acts 9:2), while John 15 again seems to rely on parable-like sayings for its core imagery (vine, vinedresser, fruitbearing, etc.). The warnings about the world's hatred, especially prominent in 15:18–16:4, echo many of the predictions of Matthew 10:17–42. John 13:16 and Matthew 10:24 parallel each other particularly closely in this respect. The theme of coming tribulation also ties in with the Olivet Discourse (cf. esp. the repeated imagery of a woman in labor in John 16:21 and Mark 13:8). As noted previously (p. 158), the promises about the ministry of the coming Paraclete (14:26; 15:26) may explain some of the freedom John felt to write his Gospel the way he did. But the very fact that he distinguishes this role of the Spirit as future from what Jesus was saying on the last night of his life further confirms that the past and present ministry of the Spirit are not being confused with each other. John 17, finally, may be read as an expansion of the main thoughts of the Lord's Prayer in Matthew 6:9–13.

25. And this may be the only point Mark is trying to stress here. See Harry Fleddermann, "The Flight of a Naked Young Man (Mark 14:51–52)," *CBQ* 41 (1979): 412–18; Michael R. Cosby, "Mark 14:51–52 and the Problem of Gospel Narrative," *PRS* 11 (1984): 219–31.

26. See Joachim Jeremias, *The Eucharistic Words of Jesus* (Oxford: Blackwell; New York: Macmillan, 1955), 120–27.

FRIDAY: THE TRIALS AND CRUCIFIXION OF JESUS

Jesus before the Sanhedrin (Mark 14:53–15:1 pars.) [Aland §332–35]

After his arrest, Jesus is brought before the Jewish leaders in three phases: an informal hearing before Annas, a more formal trial before Caiaphas and the Sanhedrin while it is still dark, and a brief early morning "rubber-stamping" of the nighttime verdict by the same court, perhaps to create an aura of legality.

Before Annas (John 18:12–14, 19–23). Though Caiaphas had been legally installed as high priest in A.D. 15, Annas, his father-in-law and predecessor in office (A.D. 6–15), would still have been considered by Jews as the rightful man for the position since Jewish law declared it a role to be held for life. It is not at all implausible, therefore, that the arresting leaders would pay respect to Annas by granting him this brief hearing of the celebrated Jesus. If Annas thought he might learn something new and surprising, Jesus assured him that what he stood for was nothing that he had not regularly proclaimed in the open. For his blunt uncooperativeness he is struck, but he quickly points out the injustice of the slap. In John's Gospel especially, even though Jesus is literally on trial before both Jewish and Roman authorities, it repeatedly becomes clear at a spiritual level that they are on trial before him![27]

Before the Sanhedrin at Night: The Scene Inside—Jesus' Confession (Mark 14:53–65 pars.). All four Gospels agree that Jesus was next arraigned before Caiaphas (although in John the episode is merely implied in 18:24, 28a). The Synoptics make it clear that the Sanhedrin had no legitimate charge against Jesus; they could not even get *false* witnesses to agree (Mark 14:56)! The closest they come is a garbled accusation that Jesus had claimed he would destroy the temple: either a reference back to his prophecies of its coming destruction (by others) or possibly an allusion to John 2:19 ("Destroy this temple, and I will raise it again in three days"). Caiaphas finally has to put the question to Jesus directly, "Are you the Christ, the Son of the Blessed One?" (Mark 14:61). He wants to know if Jesus really claims to be the Messiah. All this is strong evidence that Jesus had not previously made regular unambiguous affirmations of his Messiahship among his opponents.

At last he answers. Mark records his words as simply, "I am" (v. 62a). Matthew and Luke give more evasive replies (Matt. 26:64; Luke 22:67, 70). "You say that I am" or "You have said it" may be the more literal translation of what was a cautious or circumlocutory affirmative.[28] Jesus may even be indicting his interrogators by this way of phrasing things. But he does not stop here. He goes on to add, "and you will see the Son of man sitting at the right hand of Power, and coming with the clouds of heaven" (Mark 14:62b, RSV). This reply combines allusions to Daniel 7:13 and Psalm 110:1. In this context, "Son of man" means far more than a simple human being. Jesus is describing himself

---

27. D. A. Carson, *The Gospel according to John* (Grand Rapids: Eerdmans; Leicester: IVP, 1991), 585, adds: "Jesus did not call anyone names; he had nothing for which to apologize. Nor was he refusing to 'turn the other cheek': that ought to be clear from the cross itself. But turning the other cheek without bearing witness to the truth is not the fruit of moral resolution but the terrorized cowardice of the wimp."

28. See esp. David R. Catchpole, "The Answer of Jesus to Caiaphas (Matt. XXVI.64)," *NTS* 17 (1970–71): 213–26.

Jesus' Final Hours

Thursday

AFTER SUNDOWN

LAST SUPPER
PRAYER IN GARDEN
BETRAYAL AND ARREST

Thurs.-Friday

NIGHTTIME

CUSTODY
HEARING BEFORE ANNAS
TRIAL BEFORE CAIAPHAS
PETER'S DENIAL

Friday

EARLY MORNING

SANHEDRIN COMPLETES
    DELIBERATIONS
JESUS SENT TO PILATE
HEARING BEFORE PILATE
JESUS SENT TO HEROD
RETURN TO PILATE

LATE MORNING/NOON

JESUS NAILED TO CROSS

MIDAFTERNOON

JESUS DIES

NEAR SUNDOWN

JESUS BURIED

as the "one like a son of man, coming with the clouds of heaven" who "approached the Ancient of Days and was led into his presence" and given authority and power over all humanity, leading to universal worship and ever-lasting dominion (Dan. 7:13–14). This claim to be far more than a mere mortal is probably what elicited the verdict of blasphemy from the Jewish high court. Notwithstanding the diversity of expectation, they could not automatically con-demn every messianic pretender or they would never get a Messiah! But, in their eyes, one who too closely associated himself with God the Father in this fashion had blasphemed and was worthy of death.[29]

The language of sitting at God's right hand echoes Psalm 110:1, which Jesus had already utilized in his previous teaching in the temple (Mark 12:35–37 pars.). Perhaps that is why Luke adds Jesus' words that, "If I tell you, you will not believe me, and if I asked you, you would not answer" (Luke 22:67–68). That Jesus "sits" before he "comes" makes it highly probable that he has in mind his exaltation to the Father followed by his return to earth, not some other kind of "coming" (such as coming to the Father to receive authority or coming invisibly in judgment on Jerusalem in A.D. 70). Once the Sanhedrin has passed its death sentence, some begin to revile him. They blindfold him and ask him to "prophesy" who is striking him (Mark 14:65), possibly drawing on an interpretation of Isaiah 11:3. There the Messiah will not judge by what he sees or hears but will "delight in the fear of the Lord." The word "delight" could also mean "smell," so the tradition arose that the Messiah would be able by smell to detect who was doing what to him (*b. Sanhedrin* 93b).

Before the Servants near the Fire: The Scene Outside—Peter's Denial (Mark 14:66–72 pars.). As is his custom elsewhere, Mark starkly juxtaposes two events in sandwich fashion, this time inserting the story of Jesus' confession between the two parts of the account of Peter's denial (Mark 14:54, 55–65, 66–72). The contrast between episodes could scarcely be harsher: Jesus courageously admitting his identity, even though he would be condemned to die vs. Peter timidly fearing to admit his identity as a disciple of Jesus even to the lowliest of servants.[30] In so doing, Peter fulfills Jesus' earlier prophecy (vv. 27–31). Hearing the rooster crow, he remembers Christ's words and weeps bitterly (Matt. 26:75). We are meant to understand these as tears of repentance, partic-ularly in Matthew, who alone goes on to add the story of Judas' suicide (27:3–10; though cf. Acts 1:18–19). Judas, too, is filled with remorse and even seemingly confesses his sin (v. 4).[31] Yet instead of returning to Jesus, he appeals to Christ's enemies who can offer him no help. So Peter contrasts unfa-

---

29. Ironically, popular Christian usage today regularly assumes that "Son of man" means Jesus in his complete humanity and "Son of God" refers to his full deity. In this context, the usage is almost exactly the opposite. "Son of man" makes Jesus so divinely exalted a Messiah that the Sanhedrin is scandalized, whereas "Son of God" (Matt. 26:63) is simply another expression for the mili-tary-political ruler many people were awaiting. Cf. the similar use of this title in the newly translated Dead Sea fragment 4Q246. A slightly different way of understanding Caiaphas's question is to take him as asking Jesus if he were the "Son-of-God type" of Messiah rather than the political kind (i.e., more divine than merely mortal); see Joel Marcus, "Mark 14:61: 'Are You the Mes-siah-Son-of-God?'" *NovT* 31 (1989): 125–41.

30. It would seem from comparing the parallel accounts that more than three people asked Peter if he were one of Jesus' followers. But there are no grounds for assuming Peter replied more than three times. For the redactional and stylistic elements illustrated in the diversity of the four accounts, see esp. Neil J. McEleney, "Peter's Denials—How Many? To Whom?" *CBQ* 52 (1990): 467–72.

31. Some translations of Matt. 27:3 read that Judas even "repented." But the verb is *metamelomai* not *metanoeō* (the standard New Testament word for "repent"), so the NIV "seized with remorse" seems better in this context. Matthew, characteristically, finds in Judas' death a fulfillment of Scripture. While referring only to Jeremiah, he obviously has texts from both Jeremiah 19 (vv. 1, 4, 6, 11) and Zechariah (11:12–13) in mind. Cf. further Douglas J. Moo, "Tradition and Old Testament in Matt. 27:3–10," in *Gospel Perspectives*, vol. 3, ed. R. T. France and David Wenham (Sheffield: JSOT, 1983), 157–75.

vorably with Jesus but favorably with Judas. There are no unforgivable sins except refusing to come (or come back) to Christ.

Before the Sanhedrin in the Morning: Jesus Is Taken Away (Mark 15:1 pars.). In Luke it appears as if the entire trial before the Sanhedrin takes place after daybreak (Luke 22:66). However Mark and Matthew clearly locate the proceedings during the night, with merely a final "consultation" occurring in the morning before Jesus is taken to Pilate (Mark 15:1; Matt. 27:1–2). This latter chronology would seem to be the more precise, since legal verdicts probably could not be reached during the night. Luke may have streamlined the story for literary purposes and even recognized that the more elaborate nighttime proceedings would have had to be repeated, however perfunctorily, come daylight.[32]

All this raises the question of other seeming illegalities surrounding the Sanhedrin's proceedings. A comparison with Mishnaic law on capital trials (in the tractate *Sanhedrin*) discloses so many irregularities that many scholars find it impossible to accept the historicity of the Gospel accounts.[33] These include a trial on the eve of a Sabbath, on a feast day at night, without witnesses on behalf of the accused, and with the high priest speaking before those of lesser authority. Some of these details may have been present but not narrated; others are clear violations. On the other hand, (1) there is no evidence that all of these later laws for the second- and third-century Jewish court, the *beth din*, were in force in Jesus' day. (2) Those that were current would have been supported by Pharisees but not by the Sadducees who dominated the council. (3) Even the later Jewish literature allows for trials during festivals in the cases of seducers to idolatry or false prophets (*t. Sanhedrin* 10:11 and 11:7). And (4) desperate men will often manipulate the law if they perceive a higher cause is at stake.

Closely related is the question of whether the Gospels are anti-Semitic in their assigning the primary blame for Jesus' execution to Jewish hands. Surely this charge is unfounded. Jesus and all his first followers were Jews too. The Gospels describe an intra-Jewish debate, at least at the earliest stages. Even as strong and severe a statement as the Jerusalem crowd's cry, "Let his blood be on us and on our children" (Matt. 27:25) does not indict all Jews for all time. It merely means that one group of Jewish leaders in Jerusalem and the followers they whipped up into a temporary frenzy accepted responsibility for Jesus' death. Matthew may well have seen in the addition, "and on our children," a reference to the generation from A.D. 30–70, culminating in the destruction of Jerusalem. We must also remember that the very death for which these crowds clamored made possible their later forgiveness, at least for those who accepted the offer (cf. Acts 2:37; 6:7; 21:20). Although Pilate will try to excuse himself, he, representing Rome, must take equal responsibility for the crucifixion. Furthermore, from a more theological perspective, every one of us must admit that, because of our sins, *we* crucified Christ.[34]

---

32. Cf. further A. N. Sherwin-White, "The Trial of Christ," in *Historicity and Chronology in the New Testament*, ed. D. E. Nineham, and others. (London: SPCK, 1965), 97–116.

33. For a succinct catalogue, see Raymond E. Brown, *The Death of the Messiah*, vol. 1 (New York and London: Doubleday, 1994), 358–59. The best detailed defense of the historicity of numerous elements in the trial narrative often thought suspect is Josef Blinzler, *The Trial of Jesus* (Cork: Mercier, 1959).

34. Cf. further Joseph A. Fitzmyer, "Anti-Semitism and the Cry of 'All the People' (Mt. 27:25)," *TS* 26 (1965): 667–71; Timothy B. Cargal, "'His Blood Be upon Us and upon Our Children': A Matthean Double Entendre?" *NTS* 37 (1991): 101–12; John P. Heil, "The Blood of Jesus in Matthew: A Narrative-Critical Perspective," *PRS* 18 (1991): 117–24.

Jesus before the Roman Authorities (Mark 15:2–20a) [Aland §336–42]

John 18:31 explains that, under Rome at this time, the Sanhedrin does not have the right to inflict capital punishment.[35] Therefore the Jewish authorities must contextualize their complaints against Jesus in a way that will catch the Roman governor's attention. Since in many Jewish hopes the Messiah would be an earthly king, this is the natural charge to bring before Pilate—it would then imply a threat against Rome. Jesus replies to Pilate as circuitously as he did to the Sanhedrin (Mark 15:2), and later he remains altogether silent. In all four Gospels, Pilate is not convinced that Jesus has done anything deserving of death. Luke, in particular, highlights the theme of Jesus as innocent sufferer (Luke 23:4, 13–16, 22). Only Luke explains that Pilate pawns Jesus off on Herod Antipas (in town from Galilee for the Passover) in hopes that he will render a verdict and get Pilate off the hook (vv. 6–12). Matthew uniquely adds the dream that Pilate's wife had, warning her against dealing with "that innocent man" (Matt. 27:19). John arranges his account in seven scenes so that Pilate alternates between interrogating Christ inside his palace and going outside to try to dissuade the Jews of their heinous plot (John 18:28–19:16). Only in John does Jesus clarify that his kingship is not of this world (18:36). This does not mean that he was no political threat or that God's reign has no sociopolitical effect on the authorities and structures of this age. Rather, "John certainly expects the power of the inbreaking kingdom to affect this world," but "theirs is the sort of struggle, and victory, that cannot effectively be opposed by armed might."[36]

Pilate tries to find a final way out by offering to release one prisoner to the crowd, according to a Passover custom. He pits Jesus against Barabbas, a notorious insurrectionist or terrorist (Mark 15:7). An early scribal tradition in Matthew 27:17 calls Barabbas "Jesus Barabbas," which may reflect his actual name (esp. since "Barabbas" is not a proper name but a nickname, meaning "son of a father"—*bar-abba*). How ironic that the crowds opted for crucifying the true Son of their heavenly Father and called for the freedom of this murderous Barabbas. Because Pilate recognizes that he dare not alienate the Jews too much and risk a riot that would discredit him in Rome's eyes (cf. esp. John 19:12), he finally accedes to the mob's requests. Jesus is flogged, traditionally understood to be the wretched Roman *verberatio*—an unspecified number of lashes with a metal-tipped rope that opened gaping wounds in the skin and muscles of a victim's back and so weakened the accused criminal that it was itself at times fatal. Then Jesus is delivered over to be nailed to a cross. Before they lead him off, they add insult to injury by dressing him up with a mock crown, royal robe, and scepter (Mark 15:17–20a).

---

35. Possible striking corroboration of this claim appears in *p. Sanhedrin* 1:1; 7:2, where it is said that this privilege was taken from Israel forty years before the destruction of the temple. For details of this and other disputed elements unique to John's trial narrative, see F. F. Bruce, "The Trial of Jesus in the Fourth Gospel," in *Gospel Perspectives*, vol. 1, ed. R. T. France and David Wenham (Sheffield: JSOT, 1980), 7–20. There seem to have been exceptional situations, however, in which Jews were allowed to execute their own offenders. See Bruce Corley, "Trial of Jesus," in *DJG*, 850.

36. Carson, *John*, 594.

Crucifixion (Mark 15:20b–47 pars.) [Aland §343–51]

The Nature of the Punishment. Death by crucifixion was one of the cruelest forms of execution humanity ever devised.[37] It was also one of the most shame-filled punishments of antiquity. Roman citizens were mostly exempt from this kind of torture; it was generally reserved for the worst of slaves and criminals. Someone condemned to die in this way typically carried his own crossbar, onto which his arms were eventually affixed either with nails through his wrists or by tying them with ropes. The ankles could be similarly attached to the vertical wooden beam. Sometimes footrests or seats were added, not for comfort but to keep the individual alive longer and prolong the torture. Crosses were occasionally X-shaped but usually resembled a capital "T" or lowercase "t" in shape. The earliest Christian testimony is divided as to which of these last two was employed for Jesus, although later Christian art has almost unanimously opted for the latter.

Death usually proceeded slowly, often over a period of several days, and the typical cause was eventual suffocation. The victim became so weakened as to be unable to lift his chest and breathe. Jesus died unusually quickly, perhaps because of his previous flogging and perhaps because of the use of nails rather than ropes. The Gospels also suggest that he died voluntarily, at his chosen time. After all, he had enough strength at the end to cry out with a loud voice and enough will to entrust himself to God. Jews interpreted death by crucifixion as equivalent to "hanging on a tree" and thus concluded that anyone so punished was accursed by God (Deut. 21:22–23). This explains why the Christian message of a crucified Messiah later scandalized so many Jews (1 Cor. 1:23).

Exegetical Observations. Sometime between midmorning and noon on the eve of the Sabbath of Passover week, Pilate delivers Jesus to the soldiers to have him crucified.[38] They take him through the narrow, crowded streets of Jerusalem, memorialized today as the Via Dolorosa ("Sorrowful Way"). The "parade" becomes a macabre parody of the triumphal marches of visiting emperors.[39] Because he was already weak and close to death, he is unable to carry his crossbeam far, so a passerby, Simon of Cyrene, is conscripted to take it the rest of the way for him (Mark 15:20b–21). Various women in the crowd bewail his fate, but he musters enough strength to warn them instead to bemoan God's coming judgment on Jerusalem instead (Luke 23:27–31). When the entourage arrives at Golgotha,[40] probably a busy intersection chosen to heighten the effect of the execution as a public deterrent to similar "crimes,"

---

37. For a thorough study, see Martin Hengel, *Crucifixion* (London: SCM; Philadelphia: Fortress, 1977). For a modern scientific analysis, see William D. Edwards, Wesley J. Gabel, and Floyd E. Hosmer, "On the Physical Death of Jesus Christ," *Journal of the American Medical Association* 255 (1986): 1455–63.

38. Mark's "third hour" (9:00 A.M.; Mark 15:25) and John's "about the sixth hour" (12:00 P.M.; John 19:14) are probably best taken as approximate designations in a culture that often did not refer to time more precisely than by quarters of the day or night. John 19:14 and 31 both refer to "the day of Preparation" of the Passover, which probably does not contradict the Synoptics by implying "Passover eve." Instead, it more likely means the day of preparation *for the Sabbath* in Passover week. Even today, "Preparation" (*paraskeuē*) remains the standard name in Greek for Friday.

39. Thomas E. Schmidt, "Mark 15.16–32: The Crucifixion Narrative and the Roman Triumphal Procession," *NTS* 41 (1995): 1–18.

40. Quite likely the site currently occupied by the Church of the Holy Sepulchre, but probably then more similar in appearance to the skull-shaped rocks visible in the hills at the location known today as Gordon's Calvary.

Jesus is hoisted onto his cross between two *lēstai* (insurrectionists—not thieves—Mark 15:27) and left to die.

The Gospels recount the roughly three hours Jesus hung alive on the cross, by means of two primary narrative devices: the reactions of those who saw him and Jesus' final remarks. Putting all the Gospels together reveals seven sayings of Jesus from the cross, made famous in the history of Christian liturgy as Christ's seven last "words." The reactions of the onlookers all add to the indignity of Jesus' fate. The soldiers offer him an exotic perfumed wine (Mark 15:23). Though possibly a mild painkiller, this is a continuing part of the mockery of the one who they believe traitorously claimed to be king (cf. v. 26). They gamble for his clothes; he may well have been left to hang naked, a major disgrace in Jewish eyes (v. 24). John 19:24 finds in this a typological fulfillment of Psalm 22:18. In fact echoes of Psalm 22 and various other Old Testament texts appear throughout the Passion narratives.[41] The titulus affixed above the cross in three languages for all to read refers to the kingship that his death so ingloriously appears to discredit (John 19:20). Various passersby taunt him to demonstrate his power and come down off the cross (Mark 15:29–32). Ironically, if he saved himself he would be unable to save anyone else, including his tormenters. The criminals crucified with him revile him as well, though one apparently has a change of heart when he sees the noble way in which Jesus is dying (Luke 23:39–42).[42]

The significance of Jesus' death, however, is arguably best brought out by a focus on what Jesus spoke while he died. In the probable order of their utterance, Jesus' seven last words were: (1) "Father, forgive them, for they do not know what they are doing" (Luke 23:34). He who had taught love for one's enemies models it even as they kill him. Jesus' prayer does not mean that all the Jewish and Roman leaders involved in his death *will* be saved, but it paves the way for their forgiveness should they repent.[43] (2) "I tell you the truth, today you will be with me in paradise," he declares to the criminal on the cross (Luke 23:43). The doctrine of the descent into hell is a later Christian creation, not conclusively supported by any text of the New Testament.[44] Here Jesus affirms that heaven is available to believers immediately upon death and that he will go there at once in spirit to be with this one "deathbed" convert. (3) Speaking first to Mary and then to John, Jesus declares, "Dear woman, here is your son," and "Here is your mother" (John 19:27). These words strongly suggest that Joseph has died. Jesus demonstrates a concern for those closest to him (just as he did for his enemies) and a commitment to incorporating his biological family into his spiritual family.

(4) "My God, my God, why have you forsaken me?" (Mark 15:34; cf. Ps. 22:1). The best interpretation of these words is the most literal. Jesus senses

---

41. On which, see esp. Douglas J. Moo, *The Old Testament in the Gospel Passion Narratives* (Sheffield: Almond, 1983).

42. On this theme, see esp. John J. Pilch, "Death with Honor: The Mediterranean Style Death of Jesus in Mark," *BTB* 25 (1995): 65–70.

43. E. Earle Ellis, *The Gospel of Luke* (London: Oliphants, 1974; Grand Rapids: Eerdmans, 1981), 267: "The prayer is answered by his death, which brings the forgiveness of sins (Ac. 2:38)."

44. First Peter 3:18–21 is the most commonly cited passage in support of a descent into hell. But it probably teaches Jesus' announcement of victory over the demonic realm as part of his ascension. For a full history of interpretation, see William J. Dalton, *Christ's Proclamation to the Spirits* (Rome: BIP, rev. 1989).

divine abandonment.[45] The close, unbroken communion with the Father he had experienced throughout his life has been suddenly interrupted. Other New Testament writers understood this as the moment that he bore the sins of the world and experienced the wrath of God that we deserved instead (e.g., 2 Cor. 5:21). Later Christian theologians wrestled with numerous other questions about the relationship between Christ's human and divine natures that this text refuses to answer. Suffice it to say, Jesus died as still the same psychosomatically whole individual that he had been throughout his life. John, writing against incipient Gnosticism and docetism (see above, p. 168), stressed this by describing the spear thrust that proved that a truly human Jesus had expired (John 19:34–35).

(5) "I am thirsty" (John 19:28). No doubt literally true, this statement probably struck John as even more significant, spiritually speaking. One more attempt at offering a mild sedative is rebuffed; Jesus will endure the worst until the end. (6) "It is finished" (John 19:30). Christ will drink little if any of the wine vinegar, but again the spiritual import of Jesus' words proves more crucial. His life is over, but so is the crowning accomplishment of his career—dying an atoning death for the sins of humanity. (7) "Father, into your hands I commit my spirit" (Luke 23:46; cf. Ps. 31:5). Strikingly, he who has just experienced divine abandonment echoes this prayer of trust in his seemingly absent heavenly Father that would later become the standard Jewish child's bedtime prayer. With these words, he breathes his last.

The Events Immediately after Jesus' Death. The Synoptics tell us that already from noon until 3 P.M. on the day we now know as Good Friday a preternatural darkness had fallen upon the land (Mark 15:33 pars.). Whatever its cause, it is clear that "nature" was in sympathy with the horror of the Son of God being put to death. Apocalyptic signs continue as the veil of the temple is rent from top to bottom (v. 38). It is impossible to resolve every question surrounding these symbolic actions (Did the veil rip just before or just after Jesus' expiry? Was it the inner or outer veil? Are the later ideas of Eph. 2:14–16 and Heb. 4:14–16 implied—with people now having immediate access to God?). But the veil's splitting fits the whole scene. The temple, the city, and all those loyal to its corrupt system are being condemned, even as they think they are condemning Jesus.

The Gentile centurion supervising the proceedings, observing these signs and how Jesus died, becomes convinced of Christ's innocence.[46] Further apocalyptic portents shake the area, most notably a significant earthquake (Matt. 27:51). Probably the strangest episode of all appears only in Matthew (vv. 52–53)—tombs were opened and certain "saints" were raised to life. The punctuation of many translations makes it appear as if these resurrections occurred before Jesus' own. But the text should probably be rendered, "the tombs broke open. And the bodies of many holy people who had died were

---

45. The hearers mistake Jesus' (slurred?) speech for a cry for Elijah, the prophet who was to prepare the way of the Lord. "Ironically, while Elijah will not intervene on Jesus' side, soon God will, and in a very visible way that all shall see" (Brown, *Death*, vol.2, 1063).

46. Luke 23:47 has him say, "Surely this was a righteous (or innocent) man." Mark 15:39 and Matt. 27:54 are quite different, making him proclaim Jesus as a S/son of God. Perhaps his literal words were something like, "He was a good man, and quite right in calling God his Father" (Alfred Plummer, *A Critical and Exegetical Commentary on the Gospel according to S. Luke* [Edinburgh: T. & T. Clark, 1896], 539). But Mark and Matthew see a second level of meaning as well—a confirmation of Jesus' true divine sonship.

raised to life, and, having come out of the tombs *after* Jesus' resurrection, they went into the Holy City."[47] Again, there are many unanswerable questions surrounding this mysterious scene (Who were the holy people? How long did they make appearances? What happened to them next?). But Matthew's point is similar to Paul's: Jesus' resurrection is the "firstfruit" of the resurrection of all believers of both old and new covenant times (cf. 1 Cor. 15:20). A few got to be raised not at the end of the world but with Jesus as a dramatic testimony to that fact.

The Passion accounts in the Gospels conclude with the story of Jesus' burial. Joseph of Arimathea, a member of the Sanhedrin, asks Pilate for permission to bury the corpse (Mark 15:42–47). The story is credible, if only because of Jewish scruples that the land not be defiled with a dead body during the Sabbath that began with nightfall. Luke, however, adds that Joseph was a good man who had not consented to the council's verdict (Luke 23:50–51), while Matthew and John describe him as a (secret) disciple of Jesus (Matt. 27:57; John 19:38). In John, Nicodemus accompanies Joseph as well, although his motives are never spelled out. Later Christian legends insist that he, too, had become a believer, but we really have no way of knowing (v. 39). At any rate, the men give Jesus the decent burial he deserved in a newly-hewn rock tomb with a massive quantity of embalming spices. A group of women, including Jesus' mother who had been watching the public events all day long, sees where he is laid so that they can return after the Sabbath and complete the process of caring for the body (Mark 15:40–41, 47 pars.).

Unique to Matthew is the account of the Jewish leaders securing permission from Pilate to seal the tomb and set a guard lest Jesus' disciples should come, steal his body, and declare that he had been raised as he had predicted (Matt. 27:62–66). This episode clearly prepares the reader for a second paragraph found only in Matthew, as part of the resurrection narrative, that explains how the same authorities later tried to use the story of a stolen body as *their* explanation for the empty tomb (28:11–15). But for now, disciples and opponents alike think Jesus is gone for good. To their astonishment, they will soon learn how wrong they are.

Historicity

Jesus' lack of resistance at his arrest and his concern for his enemies (most notably Malchus) both pass the double dissimilarity test. Even John's more dramatic threefold, "I am he" (John 18:5, 6, 8) coheres with similar Synoptic statements suggestive of a double meaning—"It is I" and the divine "I AM" (Mark 6:50; 13:6). The trial before Annas, unique to John, gains plausibility from the Lukan reference to this former high priest in conjunction with his son Caiaphas (Luke 3:1). We have already responded to charges of illegalities (or historical improbabilities) at the trial before the Sanhedrin (above, p. 344). Here we may add, positively, that the later Talmudic tradition confirms that Jesus was condemned by the Jewish leaders for blasphemy (*b. Sanhedrin* 43a)—probably not for explicitly pronouncing the divine name but for equat-

---

47. Cf. esp. John W. Wenham, "When Were the Saints Raised?" *JTS* 32 (1981): 150–52.

ing himself with the Son of Man who could enter into the divine presence. This could have been taken as equivalent to entering the Holy of Holies on earth and thus would have placed Jesus above the Jewish leaders.[48] That Jesus refers to the Son of Man sitting at God's right hand first and then coming on the clouds (rather than the reverse sequence as in Dan. 7:13) makes it clear that the Old Testament was not simply mined to create a saying of Jesus.

The whole picture of subsequent abuse—mockery, flogging, and crucifixion, culminating in the cry of divine abandonment—is far too humiliating for early Christians to have invented, especially without significant Jewish precedent for a crucified Messiah. The flogging of Christ closely resembles that unleashed on Jesus ben Ananias a generation later (Josephus, *Jewish War* 6.5.3). Pilate's ruthlessness combined with a certain cowardice also fits Josephus's description of his behavior elsewhere (*Antiquities* 18.3.1; 18.3.2; 18.4.1–2). The release of Barabbas based on an annual Passover custom has not been conclusively documented elsewhere but resembles offerings of amnesty described in *Pesahim* 8:6a and later texts commenting on this passage. The crucifixion itself, of course, is amply attested by non-Christian writers (Josephus, *Antiquities* 18.3.3; Tacitus, *Annals* 15.44; *b. Sanhedrin* 43a [referring to the death as a hanging]). The atoning significance of Jesus' death was accepted early in Christian history, as witnessed by its presence in a pre-Pauline credal formula (1 Cor. 15:3). Johannine distinctives also demonstrate Jewish backgrounds—the Aramaic expression *Gabbatha* (John 19:13), a testamentary disposition from the cross (19:26–27),[49] the expression "the day of Preparation of Passover Week" (19:14)—and reflect even more directly on eyewitness testimony (19:35).

Other events accompanying Jesus' death also show signs of historical trustworthiness. Judas' death (Matt. 27:3–10) fits the Old Testament fulfillment quotations attached to it so awkwardly that the details must have been accurately narrated. The same is true of the proliferation of Old Testament quotes throughout the Passion narratives more generally.[50] Darkness and an earthquake are cited by the Roman historian Thallus, as quoted by Julius Africanus (*Greek Papyri* 10.89). Burial of Jesus' corpse by Joseph of Arimathea seems probable in light of Jewish scruples against desecrating the Sabbath. That it was an unused tomb would make it unlikely that Jesus' followers would mistakenly go anywhere else after the Sabbath, especially since the same women who had observed the burial went first. The story about the posting of a guard at the tomb cannot plausibly be ascribed to Christian invention since it has a built-in loophole in it: had the disciples wanted to steal Jesus' body and falsely claim him to be resurrected they still would have had all night to do so before the guard ever arrived (cf. Matt. 27:57–61 with 62–66).

---

48. See esp. Darrell L. Bock, "The Son of Man Seated at God's Right Hand and the Debate over Jesus' 'Blasphemy'," in *Jesus of Nazareth: Lord and Christ*, ed. Joel B. Green and Max Turner (Grand Rapids: Eerdmans; Carlisle: Paternoster, 1994), 181–91.

49. Ethelbert Stauffer, *Jesus and His Story* (London: SCM; New York: Knopf, 1960), 136–38.

50. Joel B. Green, "Passion Narrative," in *DJG*, 602–603.

Theological Distinctives

Redactional distinctives again come to the fore in the passion narratives. For *Mark*, Jesus' crucifixion culminates his ministry as suffering servant; he gives his life as a ransom for many (recall Mark 10:45; 14:22–25). The theme of the disciples' failure and misunderstanding also comes to a climax: they deny, betray, and flee, all as Jesus predicted. For the Jews, the temple and the system for which it stands are now doomed, awaiting imminent judgment and destruction. The crucifixion, however, confirms Jesus as the Son of God (15:39). Anyone who wants to follow Jesus and receive similar vindication must also first follow the road of suffering and rejection.

Matthew gives the Jewish leaders a higher profile and the Jewish people in general a greater responsibility for Jesus' death, highlighting the motif of blood-guilt (Matt. 26:3, 57; 27:25). Rome, on the other hand, is more clearly portrayed as recognizing Jesus' innocence (27:19–24). This is the moment of the passing of the kingdom from the Jewish leadership to those in any nation who will follow Jesus (recall 21:43). Additional Scriptures are fulfilled, most notably with respect to Judas (26:14–25, 50; 27:3–10). The crucifixion itself is narrated, first by successive scenes of mocking (27:39–40, 41–43, 44) and then by a heightened emphasis on the cosmic signs that vindicate an apocalyptic interpretation of Christ's death (27:51–53).

For *Luke*, the passion is a time of the resumption of intense demonic activity (Luke 22:3, 31, 53b; recall 4:13). The innocence of Jesus is heightened; he is a righteous sufferer who forgives his enemies (23:2, 4, 6–16, 34, 43, 47). Jesus eschews violence (22:38, 51–53) and weeps over Jerusalem, lamenting her fate (23:27–31; recall 19:41–44). He trusts completely in God, right up to his death, and he is the "prophet-martyr" who fearlessly proclaims God's justice even in the face of rejection and execution.

In *John*, Jesus is consummately in charge, nowhere more strikingly than when he is arrested (John 19:4–6). He speaks the truth, which the authorities reject (19:23, 37). He dies as a fully human being, refuting every form of docetism (19:31–37). His death is the ultimate act of self-revelation, mutual glorification of the Father and the Son, and love for others (chaps. 13–17). It is also the shepherd's sacrifice. On the cross, he triumphs over the cosmic powers of darkness, manifest in the world, whose "hour" has temporarily held sway. In returning to the Father who sent him, he makes a similar "homegoing" possible for all who will be his disciples.

RESURRECTION

Philosophical and Historical Issues

The resurrection brings us to the heart and climax of the Gospel stories. Jesus of Nazareth was seen alive again after his crucifixion! In the Book of Acts, it is consistently the resurrection that forms the central topic of early Christian preaching (e.g., 2:22–36; 17:18; 26:6–8). Although Paul can be viewed as focusing more on the crucifixion than does Luke (see esp. 1 Cor. 2:2), he can also devote lengthy teaching passages to the resurrection as the necessary sequel to the cross (1 Cor. 15; cf. Eph. 1:15–2:10; Col. 3:1–4; and 1 Thess. 4:13–18). The resurrection vindicates the claim that Jesus is both Christ (Messiah) and Lord (Acts 2:36). It gives meaning and purpose to his life and death—a successful revelation of God to the world (the thrust of John) and an atoning sacrifice for its sins (the thrust of the Synoptics). And it ensures that God's plan and purposes for the cosmos will ultimately triumph, among them the resurrection and glorification of all of God's people throughout history (1 Cor. 15:20–28).[51] If Christ's bodily resurrection should turn out not to be true, Christians, Paul declares, would be of all people most to be pitied (v. 19).

But can the resurrection stories be believed? It is often claimed that modern, scientific people know full well that dead people are never again raised to life. In fact, the ancients knew that resurrections were seemingly impossible also, and many early Christian apologists had to address the same skepticism that remains in our age. The nineteenth century saw the rise of many rationalistic explanations of the resurrection, which occasionally reappear in popular-level writings today. Some argued that Christ never fully died on the cross, but revived in the tomb, managed to escape, and appeared to his disciples before dying some time later. Others echoed the original counterclaim of the Jewish authorities that Jesus' disciples stole the body (Matt. 28:13). Or perhaps they went to the wrong tomb, thus finding it empty. Or maybe all the witnesses to the resurrection experienced some kind of mass hallucination.[52]

Most contemporary scholars rightly reject these explanations as harder to believe than the resurrection itself. The gruesome details of the crucifixion, the length of time of burial, and the size of the stone covering the tomb all preclude the idea that Jesus somehow survived this ordeal. If the disciples stole the body, then their entire lives (and in many cases their deaths by martyrdom) were in the cause of a known fraud—a highly unlikely hypothesis, psychologically speaking. Had the disciples or the women originally gone to the wrong tomb, the right one, with body intact, could easily have been produced by Christianity's opponents. And mass hallucinations are not known to occur to more than five hundred people (1 Cor. 15:6) over a forty-day period (Acts 1:3), in different places, who are known to be defeated in outlook and not expecting anything miraculous to happen (John 20:19).[53]

It is far more common, therefore, among scholarly skepticism to promote the idea that the Gospel stories of the resurrection are primarily legendary. Many posit that the disciples had some kind of spiritual experience of God in which they became convinced that the cause of Christ lived on. A number are willing to grant that Jesus' immortal *spirit* did continue to live and may even have been experienced by his followers. It is a literal *bodily* resurrection that continues to be the stumbling block for most. Not surprisingly, it is often postulated that only at a late stage of the tradition did the story of Jesus' continuing

51. For a good study of the theme of resurrection in the various New Testament writers, see John F. Jansen, *The Resurrection of Jesus Christ in New Testament Theology* (Philadelphia: Westminster, 1980).

52. The only recent scholarly defense of any of these views appears in Gerd Lüdemann, *What Really Happened to Jesus?* (Louisville: Westminster/John Knox, 1995), who argues that Peter and Paul were both psychologically ripe for a vision (i.e., hallucination) of a resurrected Jesus, and their enthusiasm infected all the others who subsequently claimed similar experiences.

53. For more detailed refutation of these various theories, see George E. Ladd, *I Believe in the Resurrection of Jesus* (Grand Rapids: Eerdmans; London: Hodder & Stoughton, 1975), 132–42.

to live in some spiritual fashion become "mythologized" in the garb of a bodily resurrection. Sometimes parallels in other religions of the day are cited as support for this line of development: the Gnostic redeemer myth of a descending and ascending heavenly Man or the fertility cults' myths of nature gods who die and rise annually.

But the full-blown Gnostic myths are too late to have influenced early Christianity (see above, p. 36), and the parallels with pagan fertility rites are really quite remote. Had Christianity been born in Greece and later migrated to Israel, one might find more credible the story of a spiritual rebirth later being reclothed in the language of a bodily resurrection. But most Jews had always believed in a very literal reenfleshment of skeletons (cf., e.g., Ezek. 37), while it was the Hellenistic world that accepted only the immortality of the soul. So for a religion born in Judaism and later transplanted into the Greco-Roman world, the hypothesis of development from spirit to body turns out to run backwards. What a truly mythological account of a resurrection would look like is amply illustrated in the docetic, apocryphal Gospel of Peter 10:39–40: Christ appears striding across the earth with his head towering above the clouds of heaven!

Numerous other details suggest that the earliest accounts of the resurrection were not fictitious. Deuteronomy 21:23 demonstrated to first-century Jews that anyone executed by crucifixion was accursed by God, so it would have been enormously difficult for them to create the story of the resurrection of a "crucified Messiah" unless it had really happened. All four Gospels agree that the first primary witnesses to the resurrection were women, another detail unlikely to have been invented, inasmuch as their testimony, because of their gender, would have been inadmissible in a court of law. The empty tomb seems almost certainly to be a historical fact, since no one ever produced a body and no gravesite was ever venerated in early Christianity. Further, something dramatic must have happened on that first Sunday to cause Christians to stop resting and worshiping on the Sabbath, the day commanded by God from the time of the Ten Commandments onward to be set aside as holy, and replace it with Sunday observance (Acts 20:7; 1 Cor. 16:2; Rev. 1:10). Indeed, it is arguable that nothing short of the bodily resurrection of Jesus can adequately explain the rise of "post-Easter" Christian faith more generally.[54]

We may also point to the diversity of witnesses in a variety of places over a forty-day period, the relative anonymity of many of those witnesses (Cleopas and an unnamed disciple, five hundred otherwise unknown), the apparent aimlessness of the disciples even after several appearances (John 21:2–3),[55] the lack of immediate recognition and acceptance by the various observers in several of the resurrection accounts, the early pre-Pauline tradition of several of those appearances (1 Cor. 15:4–8), the use of "the first day of the week" in Mark 16:2 (rather than the later, more conventional "after three days"), and the

---

54. For these and similar arguments, cf. further Craig Blomberg, *The Historical Reliability of the Gospels* (Leicester and Downers Grove: IVP, 1987), 100–110; and William L. Craig, "Did Jesus Rise from the Dead?" in *Jesus under Fire*, ed. Michael J. Wilkins and J. P. Moreland (Grand Rapids: Zondervan, 1995), 141–76; and the literature cited in both works.

55. For this and other signs of historicity in John 21 in particular, see esp. Grant R. Osborne, "John 21: Test Case for History and Redaction in the Resurrection Narratives," in *Gospel Perspectives*, vol. 2, ed. R. T. France and David Wenham (Sheffield: JSOT, 1981), 293–328.

virtual impossibility of proclaiming the resurrection *in Jerusalem* in the face of unbelieving Jewish opposition if the grave (identifiable by the Sanhedrin through Joseph of Arimathea) were not in fact empty.

But what of the scientific and philosophical objections? Of course, if one refuses to believe in the possibility of miraculous occurrences altogether, the resurrection will seem an absurdity. But large numbers of "modern, scientific" people recognize that science itself is merely descriptive rather than prescriptive. If a God exists, it is only natural to expect him to have powers beyond that which science has discovered or can explain and to be able to use them for his purposes.[56] It is arguable that of all the alleged miracles in ancient history, the resurrection is actually the one with far and away the *most* historical support.

A different kind of objection argues that the Bible does not *claim* that Jesus rose bodily. Here, scholars often appeal to 1 Corinthians 15:35–58. Paul talks of a "spiritual" body (vv. 44, 46) and insists that "flesh and blood cannot inherit the kingdom of God" (v. 50). Perhaps what the disciples first saw was indeed real, but a real vision, not a real physical resurrection. This, of course, is hard to square with Jesus' insistence that Thomas touch him and see his scars (John 20:27) or with his ability to eat fish as a demonstration of the corporeality of his presence (Luke 24:40–43). In fact, Paul's language in 1 Corinthians 15 should be understood differently. "Spiritual" is best taken as "supernatural," not "noncorporeal," while "flesh and blood" (*not* "flesh and bones" as in Luke 24:39) was a Semitic idiom for frail, fallen, mortal humanity.[57] At the same time, it is clear that the resurrection involved far more than a resuscitated corpse. Jesus could appear and disappear, pass through locked doors, and not be recognized for some time. We should hope that glorified, perfected bodies will be considerably different than our present ones! There will be substantial discontinuity of form as well as significant continuity of personal identity.

Exegetical Issues (Mark 16; Matthew 28; Luke 24; John 20–21) [Aland §352–367]

Chronology of Events. The four Gospels prove remarkably divergent as to what they include about Jesus' resurrection. Still they agree on the basics to such an extent that they constitute considerable corroboration of the historicity of the event itself.[58] A plausible harmony of the accounts and sequence of events is as follows: (1) A group of women come to the tomb near dawn, with Mary Magdalene possibly arriving first (Matt. 28:1; Mark 16:1–3; Luke 24:1; John 20:1). (2) Mary and the other women are met by two young men who in reality

---

56. On the large numbers of "modern" people who do in fact believe in miracles, see John P. Meier, *A Marginal Jew: Rethinking the Historical Jesus*, vol. 2 (New York and London: Doubleday, 1994), 509–34. On the scientific question, see esp. Peter Medawar, *The Limits of Science* (San Francisco: Harper & Row, 1984). For a philosophical apologetic for the resurrection given the presuppositions of a theistic worldview, see Stephen T. Davis, *Risen Indeed* (Grand Rapids: Eerdmans, 1993).

57. Cf. further Craig L. Blomberg, *1 Corinthians* (Grand Rapids: Zondervan, 1994), 316–22.

58. Cf. the comments of German classical historian H. E. Stier, cited and translated in Hugo Staudinger, *The Trustworthiness of the Gospels* (Edinburgh: Handsel, 1981), 77: "The sources for the resurrection of Jesus, with their relatively big contradictions over details, present for the historian for this very reason a criterion of extraordinary credibility. For if that were the fabrication of a congregation or of a similar group of people, then the tale would be consistently and obviously complete." We would wish to insert the word "apparent" before Stier's use of the term "contradictions."

are angels, one of whom acts as the spokesman and announces Jesus' resurrection (Matt. 28:2–7; Mark 16:4–7; Luke 24:2–7). (3) The women leave the garden with a mixture of fear and joy, at first unwilling to say anything but then resolving to report to the Twelve (Matt. 28:8; Mark 16:8). Mary Magdalene may have dashed on ahead, telling Peter and John in advance of the arrival of the other women (John 20:2). (4) Jesus meets the remaining women en route and confirms their commission to tell the disciples, with the reminder of his promise of meeting them in Galilee. The women obey (Matt. 28:9–10; Luke 24:8–11).

(5) Peter and John meanwhile have returned to the tomb, having heard the report by Mary Magdalene, and discover it to be empty (John 20:3–10; Luke 24:12). (6) Mary also returns to the tomb after Peter and John have left. She sees the angels and then Jesus, although at first supposing him to be a gardener (John 20:11–18). (7) Later that afternoon, Jesus appears to Cleopas and his unnamed companion on the road to Emmaus and, in a separate incident, to Peter (Luke 24:13–35). (8) That same Sunday evening, Jesus appears to the ten (the Twelve minus Judas and Thomas) behind locked doors in Jerusalem (Luke 24:36–43; John 20:19–23). (9) A week later he appears to the eleven at the same venue, with Thomas now present (John 20:24–29). (10) Further appearances take place over a forty-day period, including in Galilee, with over five hundred seeing him altogether (Acts 1:3; John 21; 1 Cor. 15:6). (11) A climactic commissioning in Galilee instructs the disciples to spread the news throughout the world (Matt. 28:16–20). (12) Perhaps only shortly thereafter, Jesus gives his parting instructions to await the coming Holy Spirit and ascends into heaven (Luke 24:44–53; Acts 1:4–11).[59]

Redactional Emphases. Each evangelist, of course, did not have a harmony of the Gospels in mind but was concerned to communicate distinctive theological interests. Perhaps nowhere do these emerge more clearly than in the resurrection narratives.[60] *Mark's* brief account focuses on the women's discovery of the empty tomb and the announcement by the young man that the disciples will meet Jesus in Galilee. Perhaps Mark thinks of them as beginning again. "They have failed Jesus, failed to take up their crosses and follow him to crucifixion, but now they are being summoned once again to follow him, and to learn once again what discipleship means."[61] More striking is Mark's abrupt ending in 16:8 on what seems to be a very discordant and unsatisfying note.[62] But this fits with Mark's portrayal of Jesus' disciples throughout his Gospel. As Lane concludes, "Fear is the constant reaction to the disclosure of Jesus' transcendent dignity in the Gospel of Mark." Again, "the focus upon human

---

59. For a similar harmony, with elaboration, see Ladd, *Resurrection*, 91–93. In great detail, cf. John Wenham, *Easter Enigma* (Exeter: Paternoster; Grand Rapids: Zondervan, 1984).

60. Cf. esp. Grant R. Osborne, *The Resurrection Narratives: A Redactional Study* (Grand Rapids: Baker, 1984); idem, "Resurrection," in *DJG*, 673–88.

61. Morna D. Hooker, *The Gospel according to Saint Mark* (London: A & C Black; Peabody: Hendrickson, 1991), 386, although she goes on to suggest that the simpler explanation is merely that Mark may have wanted to account for why the disciples did in fact return to Galilee.

62. On the unlikelihood that what some Bible translations include as vv. 9–20 reflects what Mark originally wrote, see above, p. 75. A few writers have argued that we simply have lost the original ending to this Gospel, but a sizable consensus agrees today that Mark intended to end with v. 8. Later scribes, not understanding the reason for his ending the way he did, tried to provide what they believed was a more appropriate conclusion.

inadequacy, lack of understanding and weakness throws into bold relief the action of God and its meaning."[63]

But verse 8 must be kept together with verse 7. The resurrection has been repeatedly predicted, and Jesus has proven himself to be a reliable predictor. Even someone entirely unfamiliar with the Gospel story, having read this much of Mark, should recognize that Mark believed verse 7 would be fulfilled. The original Christian readers would of course have already heard the story of the resurrection as the core of the preaching that brought them to faith; Mark does not need to tell the story again here. The reason he does not may be to keep in balance the tension of Christian living before Christ's return: "The word of promise and the failure of the disciples, and yet the word of promise prevailing despite human failure."[64]

Matthew begins with material largely parallel to Mark, though heightening the cosmic signs a bit, as in the Passion narrative—here appears another earthquake; the young man becomes an angel; the white robe is like snow (Matt. 28:2–3). But Matthew, who consistently portrays Jesus' followers somewhat more positively than Mark, has the women conquer their fear and report back to the disciples (v. 8), even meeting Jesus himself en route (vv. 9–10). Verses 11–15 further the theme of Jewish apologetic, countering the earliest Jewish attempt to explain away the resurrection. Verses 16–20 bring Matthew's resurrection narrative, and indeed the whole Gospel, to a climax with the well-known Great Commission. Here appear in summary form several of Matthew's key themes: the universal mission of the church, the importance of discipleship, Jesus' followers' mixture of faith and doubt, his commandments as the center of God's will for Christians, and the abiding and authoritative presence of Jesus as teacher.[65]

The words "go and make disciples" (v. 19) have been the subject of countless expositions. It is important to realize that the only imperative verb in the Greek is "make disciples." Nevertheless, the circumstantial participle "go," by being linked with the main verb, functions derivatively as a mild imperative. The main command is to duplicate Christian followers wherever one is, but there is a subordinate emphasis on going into the whole world. "All nations" could also be translated "all the Gentiles," and some see here an end to the Jewish mission. But the Greek word (*ethnē*) has been used in the more inclusive sense of "ethnic (or people-) groups," including Jews, in the most recent occurrences of the term (24:9, 14; 25:32) and should probably be viewed similarly here.[66] Making disciples is defined as "baptizing them" and "teaching them to obey everything" Christ had commanded. This makes it clear that Jesus' commission is not primarily about initial evangelism but about the lifelong process of bringing people to faith and nurturing them in the will of God.

---

63. William L. Lane, *The Gospel according to Mark* (Grand Rapids: Eerdmans, 1974; London: Marshall, Morgan & Scott, 1975), 591, 592.

64. A. T. Lincoln, "The Promise and the Failure: Mark 16:7, 8," *JBL* 108 (1989): 292. On the positive role of the end of Mark more generally, see J. Lee Magness, *Sense and Absence: Structure and Suspension in the Ending of Mark's Gospel* (Atlanta: Scholars, 1986).

65. For a thorough study, see Benjamin J. Hubbard, *The Matthean Redaction of a Primitive Apostolic Commissioning: An Exegesis of Matthew 28:16–20* (Missoula: Scholars, 1974).

66. See esp. John P. Meier, "Nations or Gentiles in Matthew 28:19?" *CBQ* 39 (1977): 94–102.

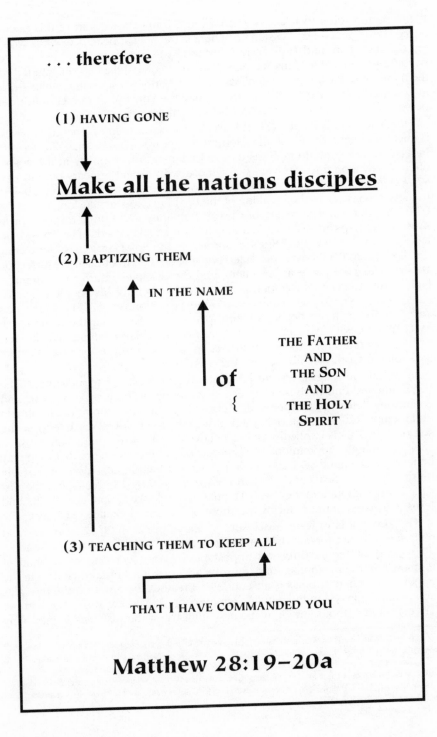

... therefore

(1) HAVING GONE

Make all the nations disciples

(2) BAPTIZING THEM

IN THE NAME

of {

THE FATHER
AND
THE SON
AND
THE HOLY
SPIRIT

(3) TEACHING THEM TO KEEP ALL

THAT I HAVE COMMANDED YOU

Matthew 28:19–20a

Baptism, according to Jesus, is a crucial and foundational part of this obedience. The Trinitarian expression used here is the only appearance of this wording ("Father, Son, and Holy Spirit") in the Gospels and probably has not yet become a technical formula (cf. Acts 2:38, in which baptism is commanded "in the name of Jesus"). What is significant is that Matthew uses one definite article to cover all three names; at least by his day the concept of one God in three persons had already taken root in Christian thinking.[67]

Luke's account is longer still. At least six distinctive themes emerge: (1) Jesus is the fulfillment of all of the Hebrew Scriptures (Luke 24:26–27, 44–48). Indeed, Luke's central emphasis on the fulfillment of prophecy in the gospel offer of salvation and forgiveness for those who repent appears here too (v. 47). (2) Jesus is made known in table fellowship among his people (vv. 30–35). In these references to the breaking of the bread may be an allusion, too, to the Lord's Supper. (3) The reality of Christ's humanity and bodily resurrection is stressed, perhaps against incipient docetic trends in Luke's day (vv. 36–43). (4) Luke's interest in the Holy Spirit continues as the Spirit's role in empowering the disciples at Pentecost is predicted (vv. 48–49). (5) All of Luke's resurrection appearances take place in Jerusalem, and the disciples return to the temple, highlighting the central role of this city in God's plans for his people (cf. v. 47, 52–53; Acts 1:8). (6) Only Luke narrates the ascension (vv. 50–51), which Acts will describe in more detail as taking place forty days after the resurrection (Acts 1:9–11). We have commented already on the chiastic outline of Luke-Acts with the central role of the resurrection and ascension for Luke's entire two-volume work (see above, pp. 142–144)[68]

John has the longest resurrection narrative of all, a full two chapters. The beginning and end of these chapters frame John's account by comparing and contrasting Peter and the beloved disciple. Together they run to the tomb and find it empty (20:3–7), but only John (if we take the beloved disciple to be the son of Zebedee) is explicitly said to believe (v. 8). At the end of the Gospel, after a seemingly ignominious fate is predicted of Peter, we learn that John may be let off more lightly (21:20–23). In between, attention falls more exclusively on three scenes: Jesus and Mary in the garden (20:10–18); Jesus and the disciples, first without and then with Thomas, in the locked room (20:19–29); and Jesus' reinstatement of Peter by the shore of the Sea of Galilee (21:1–19).

The key words in Jesus' disclosure to Mary appear in 20:17: "Do not hold on to me" is better rendered, "Stop clinging to me." Jesus has not yet ascended; the period of the resurrection appearances is not yet one of permanent reunion.[69] In the meantime, Mary must be a witness for her Lord (v. 18). In the upper room when Thomas is absent, Jesus breathes the Spirit on the disciples and commissions them in language reminiscent of Matthew 16:19. But without Thomas, and without any dramatic new ministry of the disciples immediately

---

67. Granville Sharp's rule of Greek grammar: two singular personal nouns in the same case governed by a solitary definite article refer to the same person. D. A. Hagner (*Matthew 14–28* [Dallas and London: Word, 1995], 883) notes that it is easier to imagine this exalted formula on the lips of the *resurrected* Jesus precisely because he has now left behind his earthly limitations.

68. On the conjunction of Lukan themes in the Emmaus narrative, see further B. P. Robinson, "The Place of the Emmaus Story in Luke-Acts," *NTS* 30 (1984): 481–97; on the closing paragraphs of the Gospel, see esp. Mikeal C. Parsons, *The Departure of Jesus in Luke-Acts* (Sheffield: JSOT, 1987).

69. Cf. Michaels, *John*, 339.

afterwards, this is not likely to be John's equivalent of Pentecost. Still, it seems to be more than just a foreshadowing of that later event; it indicates the fulfillment of John's previous promises about the Paraclete. We should probably imagine a two-stage event (combining John 20 and Acts 2), somewhat analogous to the reception of the Spirit followed by the filling of the Spirit.[70] But because these are transitional, nonrepeatable experiences at the time of the shift from old to new covenants, nothing can be deduced from the apostles' experiences here regarding how the Spirit empowers believers today.

A week later when Thomas is with the ten, Jesus demonstrates the reality of his resurrection. Thomas cries out, "My Lord and my God!" (John 20:28). Here is another key text in support of Jesus' deity. But Jesus' reply also reminds us of John's twofold emphasis on the role of signs—they should stimulate faith but they should not be necessary for faith: "Because you have seen me, you have believed; blessed are those who have not seen and yet have believed" (v. 29). John 20:30–31 reads as if the Gospel is coming to an end and clearly articulates John's purpose in writing. But the manuscripts are evenly divided between a present and aorist subjunctive for the verb "you may believe." The former would imply continued belief and point to a Christian readership; the latter would leave the door open to first-time belief and an evangelistic purpose for the Gospel. It may well be that John had both functions in mind (cf. above, p. 169).

The importance of Peter's reinstatement in chapter 21 makes it unnecessary to attribute this chapter to a later redactor, as is commonly done, even if its literary genre is something of an "appendix." This chapter creates an inclusio with Peter's threefold denial of Jesus (18:15–18, 25–27) as well as with his original calling (1:41–42).[71] The accompanying miracle (21:4–14) is strikingly reminiscent of the astonishing fish catch that accompanied Peter's original call (Luke 5:1–11); we may aptly label the second event his "recall." Jesus solicits a threefold affirmation of Peter's love (21:15–19), balancing out his earlier threefold denial. Despite many popular sermons distinguishing between Jesus' word for love (*agapaō*) and Peter's (*phileō*), this is probably mere stylistic variation. John also uses two different Greek words for "sheep" in this passage and two for "tend," without implying any significant distinctions. While *in certain contexts* biblical writers use *agapaō* for a divine love and *phileō* for a brotherly love, in other places the distinction is not observed (e.g., 2 Sam. 13:4; John 5:20; 2 Tim. 4:10; 1 John 2:15).[72] With nothing in this context to demand the distinction, it is risky to assume it is present.

The Gospel closes with testimony to the veracity of the book's author (vv. 24–25). On the implications of these verses for the Gospel's composition, see above (pp. 173–174). The change of person (to "we" and then to "I") shows that at least some minimal final redaction of the Gospel has occurred. This leaves the door open for theories of more widespread editing, however unverifiable they may be. The suggestion that this editing occurred just after John's

---

70. Cf. Bruce, *John*, 397, n. 18; Thomas R. Hatina, "John 20,22 in Its Eschatological Context: Promise or Fulfillment?" *Biblica* 74 (1993): 196–219.

71. Paul S. Minear, "The Original Functions of John 21," *JBL* 102 (1983): 85–98.

72. D. A. Carson, *Exegetical Fallacies* (Grand Rapids: Baker, rev. 1996), 31–32, 51–53.

death, which had necessitated the clarification of verse 23, remains an attractive hypothesis but is also unprovable.

FOR FURTHER STUDY

The Upper Room and Gethsemane

The Last Supper

Chilton, Bruce. *A Feast of Meanings: Eucharistic Theologies from Jesus through Johannine Circles.* Leiden: Brill, 1994.

Jeremias, Joachim. *The Eucharistic Words of Jesus.* Oxford: Blackwell; New York: Macmillan, 1955.

Léon-Dufour, Xavier. *Sharing the Eucharistic Bread.* New York: Paulist, 1987.

Marshall, I. Howard, *Last Supper and Lord's Supper.* Grand Rapids: Eerdmans; Exeter: Paternoster, 1980.

Perry, J. M. *Exploring the Evolution of the Lord's Supper in the New Testament.* Kansas City: Sheed and Ward, 1994.

Thomas, John C. *Footwashing in John 13 and the Johannine Community.* Sheffield: JSOT, 1991.

The Farewell Discourse

Carson, D. A. *The Farewell Discourse and Final Prayer of Jesus.* Grand Rapids: Baker, 1980 [=*Jesus and His Friends: His Farewell Message and Prayer in John 14 to 17.* Leicester: IVP, 1986].

Segovia, Fernando F. *The Farewell of the Word: The Johannine Call to Abide.* Minneapolis: Fortress, 1991.

White, R. E. O. *The Night He Was Betrayed.* Grand Rapids: Eerdmans, 1982.

Trials and Crucifixion of Jesus

Introductory

Kiehl, Eric H. *The Passion of our Lord.* Grand Rapids: Baker, 1990.

Matera, Frank J. *Passion Narratives and Gospel Theologies.* New York: Paulist, 1986.

Morris, Leon. *The Cross of Jesus.* Grand Rapids: Eerdmans; Exeter: Paternoster, 1988.

Senior, Donald P. *The Passion of Jesus in the Gospel of John.* Collegeville, Minn.: Liturgical, 1991.

Senior, Donald P. *The Passion of Jesus in the Gospel of Luke.* Wilmington: Glazier, 1989.

Senior, Donald P. *The Passion of Jesus in the Gospel of Mark.* Wilmington: Glazier, 1984.

Senior, Donald P. *The Passion of Jesus in the Gospel of Matthew.* Wilmington: Glazier, 1985.

Intermediate

Crossan, John Dominic. *Who Killed Jesus?* San Francisco and London: HarperCollins, 1995.

Hendrickx, Herman. *The Passion Narratives of the Synoptic Gospels.* London: Geoffrey Chapman, 1984.

Hengel, Martin. *Crucifixion.* London: SCM; Philadelphia: Fortress, 1977.

Rivkin, Elias. *What Crucified Jesus?* Nashville: Abingdon, 1984.

Sherwin-White, A. N. *Roman Society and Roman Law in the New Testament.* Oxford: OUP, 1963.

Sloyan, Gerard S. *The Crucifixion of Jesus: History, Myth, Faith.* Minneapolis: Fortress, 1995.

Stott, John R. W. *The Cross of Christ.* Leicester and Downers Grove: IVP, 1986.

Advanced

Bammel, Ernst, ed. *The Trial of Jesus.* London: SCM; Naperville: Allenson, 1976.

Blinzler, Josef. *The Trial of Jesus.* Cork: Mercier, 1959.

Brown, Raymond E. *The Death of the Messiah.* 2 vols. New York and London: Doubleday, 1994.

Carroll, John T., and Joel B. Green. *The Death of Jesus in Early Christianity.* Peabody: Hendrickson, 1995.

Catchpole, David R. *The Trial of Jesus.* Leiden: Brill, 1971.

Green, Joel B. *The Death of Jesus: Tradition and Interpretation in the Passion Narrative.* Tübingen: Mohr, 1988.

Winter, Paul. *On the Trial of Jesus.* Edited by T. A. Burkill and Geza Vermes. Berlin and New York: de Gruyter, rev. 1974.

Bibliography

Garland, David E. *One Hundred Years of Study on the Passion Narratives.* Macon: Mercer, 1989.

Resurrection

General

Harris, Murray J. *From Grave to Glory.* Grand Rapids: Zondervan, 1990.

Ladd, George E. *I Believe in the Resurrection of Jesus.* Grand Rapids: Eerdmans; London: Hodder & Stoughton, 1975.

Lapide, Pinchas. *The Resurrection of Jesus: A Jewish Perspective.* Minneapolis: Augsburg, 1983.

O'Collins, Gerald. *Jesus Risen.* New York: Paulist, 1987.

Perkins, Pheme. *Resurrection.* Garden City: Doubleday, 1984; London: Geoffrey Chapman, 1985.

Philosophical-Apologetic

Carnley, Peter. *The Structure of Resurrection Belief.* Oxford: Clarendon, 1987.

Craig, William L. *Assessing the New Testament Evidence for the Historicity of the Resurrection of Jesus.* Lewiston: Mellen, 1989.

Davis, Stephen T. *Risen Indeed.* Grand Rapids: Eerdmans, 1993.

Habermas, Gary R. *The Resurrection of Jesus.* Grand Rapids: Baker, 1980.

Morison, Frank. *Who Moved the Stone?* London: Faber & Faber, 1930.

Wenham, John. *Easter Enigma.* Exeter: Paternoster; Grand Rapids: Zondervan, 1984.

Theological-Exegetical

Harris, Murray J. *Raised Immortal.* London: Marshall, Morgan & Scott, 1983; Grand Rapids: Eerdmans, 1985.

Hendrickx, Herman. *Resurrection Narratives.* London: Geoffrey Chapman, rev. 1984.

Jansen, John F. *The Resurrection of Jesus Christ in New Testament Theology.* Philadelphia: Westminster, 1980.

Moule, C. F. D., ed. *The Significance of the Message of the Resurrection for Faith in Jesus Christ.* London: SCM; Naperville: Allenson, 1968.

Osborne, Grant R. *The Resurrection Narratives: A Redactional Study.* Grand Rapids: Baker, 1984.

Perrin, Norman. *The Resurrection according to Matthew, Mark, and Luke.* Philadelphia: Fortress, 1977.

QUESTIONS FOR REVIEW

1. How does interpreting the Last Supper against its Passover background illumine this event?

2. What are the key themes that John stresses in John 13–17?

3. What is the theological significance of Jesus' time in the Garden of Gethsemane?

4. What are the most acute historical problems surrounding Jesus' trial and execution? What are some possible solutions to these problems?

5. What are the main theological distinctives of each evangelist in the Passion narratives?

6. What are the most acute historical problems surrounding Jesus' resurrection? What are some possible solutions to these problems?

7. What are the main theological distinctives of each evangelist in the Resurrection narratives?

PART FIVE

HISTORICAL AND THEOLOGICAL SYNTHESES

I t is time to draw together the many threads of this study. We have already commented in numerous places on the historicity of the gospel tradition in general and of specific passages and themes in particular. We must briefly review these discussions and then proceed to deal with additional *external* evidence for the Gospels' reliability. This will occupy our attention in chapter 18. But a theological synthesis is needed as well. If the main contours of the gospel data surveyed here can be trusted, what do they disclose about the primary themes and intentions of Jesus? What was the heart of his message, and how may we categorize the kind of religious teacher that he represented? Answers to these questions will form the core of chapter 19.

CHAPTER EIGHTEEN

THE HISTORICAL
TRUSTWORTHINESS OF
THE GOSPELS

A n investigation of the historicity of any ancient document must begin with the discipline of *textual criticism*. Do we even have reliable copies of what the original author of that document wrote? We have already noted briefly above that the evidence in the case of the Gospels is overwhelming in this respect (see pp. 74–75). More than five thousand ancient manuscripts, from fragments to whole books, contrast dramatically with the available material for any other document from antiquity.[1] Second, we must consider questions of *authorship and date*. Even the critical consensus places all four Gospels in the first century and assumes authorship by orthodox Christians who were in touch with apostolic tradition. But we have argued in chapters 6 through 9 that a good case can still be made for Matthew, Mark, Luke, and John as the authors of the Gospels that have traditionally been attributed to them, and that at least the three Synoptics may have been completed by the decade of the 60s, little more than thirty years after Jesus' life and death. These

---

1. E.g., for Caesar's *Gallic War* (written ca. 50 B.C.) there are only about ten good manuscripts, none earlier than the ninth century A.D. From roughly the same period, only 35 of Livy's 142 books on Roman history survive; from 20 major manuscripts, only one is as old as the fourth century. Of Tacitus' 14 volumes of *Histories* (early second century A.D.), 4 1/2 remain; of 16 volumes of his *Annals*, 10 remain plus a few fragments. And the oldest manuscripts (each a single copy) for each of these works are ninth and eleventh centuries! See F. F. Bruce, *The New Testament Documents: Are They Reliable?* (London and Downers Grove: IVP, rev. 1960), 16.

conclusions would clearly put the Gospel authors in touch with eyewitness data within one generation of the events they narrate. The presence of hostile opposition that also witnessed many of the public events of Jesus' life makes it unlikely that widespread fabrication of gospel tradition could have survived without refutation.

Third, we must ask questions of *intention* and *genre*. Again, we have given reasons why the early church probably wanted to preserve accurate history, was in a position to do so (given the emphasis on memorization in the oral culture), and used literary genres that express such a historical intention, though obviously with theological motivations as well (see above, pp. 84–86, 107–108). Throughout our survey of Christ's life, we have pointed to a variety of arguments that suggest the evangelists were concerned to distinguish the events of Jesus' lifetime from later theological convictions of the church and indeed generally succeeded in keeping these periods separate in their thought and writing. The so-called "contradictions" among Gospel parallels all turn out to have plausible harmonizations or resolutions, and we have highlighted some of the most significant of these as well.

Fourth, we have applied the *criteria of authenticity* to each of the main stages of Jesus' ministry, showing how numerous themes and details demonstrate dissimilarity from ancient Jewish or early Christian thought, are multiply attested, fit an early first-century Palestinian environment, and so on.

But what of specific *external evidence*? What *archaeological* evidence impinges on the historicity of the gospel traditions? Or again, what do other ancient writings besides the four Gospels say about these events? We may divide this latter question into three parts: (1) What evidence is there for the life of Jesus from ancient *non-Christian* writers? (2) How are our assessments affected by early *noncanonical Christian* writers? (3) What about the evidence of the *rest of the New Testament* itself, apart from the four Gospels? For some, question (1) is the most significant of the three. It is argued that only writers not already committed to the Christian movement can be trusted to be objective in their presentations. This argument however is seriously flawed. There is no necessary connection between supporting a movement and one's ability to tell the truth. We have already drawn attention to the modern analogy of Jewish historians of World War II and noted that in the ancient world *all* history and biography was narrated for ideological purposes. Detached objectivity was largely unknown and would have been considered pointless. We must also remember that many early Christians converted to this fledgling religion from Jewish or Greco-Roman backgrounds precisely because they were convinced by the evidence supporting it. So we insist on the importance of surveying *both* non-Christian *and* Christian testimony outside the Gospels.

ARCHAEOLOGY

In a world without photography or tape recorders, the vast majority of the deeds and sayings of Jesus disappeared without any physical remains. It is unrealistic, therefore, to turn to archaeology for corroboration or refutation of most of the Gospel data. Nevertheless, a remarkable amount of circumstantial detail does receive support of one kind or another from the excavations that dot the Middle Eastern landscape. Most of these serve merely to enhance our understanding of the historical, religious, cultural, and social background of the world of Jesus, as discussed in our opening three chapters—Herod's building projects, the layout and function of the temple, the size and contents of the typical Palestinian home, the nature of Roman roads, and so on. Some findings give insights into specific imagery Jesus used in his teaching. For example, the millstone was a huge, round rock attached by a pole to a beast of burden (like a donkey) who repeatedly walked around a circular birdbath-shaped stone structure into which grain or olives were poured. As the heavy wheel was dragged around, the produce was easily crushed. Little wonder, then, that putting a millstone around someone's neck and throwing that person into the open sea would insure instant drowning (cf. Matt. 18:6). Or again, foundation stones still standing in the Herodian parts of the outer wall surrounding the temple precincts in Jerusalem measure up to 40 feet long, 3 feet high, and 8 feet thick, estimated at 50 tons apiece.[2] If Jesus referred to himself as a cornerstone (Mark 12:10 [NIV mg]), there would have been little doubt as to how solid a foundation he was describing! Still other findings disclose the Jewish practice of baptism by immersion (the mikveh pools), "Moses' seat" in the Chorazin synagogue (cf. Matt. 23:2), houses with thatched roofs that a person might dig through (cf. Mark 2:4), and the style of ancient winepresses (cf. Luke 6:38).

In some instances, however, actual sites described in the Gospels seem likely to have been unearthed—the synagogue in Capernaum, possibly Peter's home there, Jacob's well at Sychar where Jesus met with the Samaritan woman, the pool of Bethesda with its five porticoes near the Sheep Gate in Jerusalem, the pool of Siloam also in Jerusalem, and possibly the paving stones (*Gabbatha* or *Lithostrotos*—see John 19:13) outside Pilate's Jerusalem headquarters (assuming this to have been the Antonia Fortress).[3] The same is true for the location of cities. A first-century mosaic of a fishing boat with the inscription "Magdala" helped lead to the discovery of the hometown of Mary the Magdalene, while ruins of an ancient Byzantine church east of the Sea of Galilee may point to the site of Khersa, near which the demon-possessed pigs ran over the cliff. Still other natural features of the landscape remain above ground—a garden with olive trees on the ancient site of Gethsemane on the western slopes of the Mount of Olives, the rugged Judean wilderness where one can easily imagine the need for an ascetic lifestyle like that of John the Baptist, or Mt. Gerizim in the center of Israel, still home to a small Samaritan sect. Present-day tourists can quite literally eat lunch in "hell"—*Gehinnom* in Hebrew and *Gehenna* in Greek—the valley to the west and south of Mt. Zion, that later traditions described as a perpetually burning garbage dump, which was the site of child sacrifice by Canaanites to the god Molech in Old Testament times.

---

2. Jack Finegan, *The Archeology of the New Testament: The Life of Jesus and the Beginning of the Church* (Princeton: Princeton University Press, rev. 1992), 205.

3. The last of these is the most disputed, in view of a strong case that can be made for Pilate staying at Herod's palace on the west side of town near the present-day Jaffa Gate. This would then locate the *Via Dolorosa* and Christ's "stations of the cross" in almost the exact opposite direction from where they have traditionally been identified.

Some finds are quite recent. Not until 1961 was inscriptional evidence unearthed (at Caesarea Maritima) corroborating Pilate as prefect of Judea during Tiberius' reign. In 1968 an ossuary (bone box) of a crucified man named Johanan confirmed for the first time that nails could be driven through the feet or anklebones of executed victims. A first-century fishing boat from the mud beneath the Sea of Galilee was found as recently as 1986, when a drought caused the coastline to recede more than at any time in recent memory. In 1990, the tomb of what seems likely to be the high-priest Caiaphas was first discovered.[4] The most recent center of archaeological activity has been Bethsaida. Although to date nothing dramatic has emerged, many small artifacts, including numerous items relating to the fishing industry, have been dug up. Who knows what yet lies buried there or elsewhere awaiting excavation?

Frequently, archaeology provides good "object lessons" for the interested Bible reader. In other words, sites that are not the actual locations of biblical events closely resemble what the real sites probably looked like. Thus, with respect to the Gospels, the location now occupied by the Church of the Holy Sepulchre in Jerusalem is far more likely to be the actual place of the crucifixion than "Gordon's Calvary." Yet the latter, a skull-shaped outcropping of rock just above the modern-day Jerusalem city bus station, is so characteristic of the terrain that it probably looks something like the original site of Golgotha. So, too, a circular tomb entrance—complete with sloping pathway and rolling stone—discovered near Bethphage may resemble the very gravesite of Jesus, even though it is several miles from any place Joseph of Arimathea is likely to have used. Or again, tourists are regularly shown a small plateau a few hundred feet up from the northwest shore of Galilee and beneath the traditional "Mount of Beatitudes," where the natural acoustics allow one speaker standing on the slopes to be heard by a large crowd. This could be where Jesus preached his great sermon, but we simply have no way of telling.

Other discoveries of this nature include caves under and around the Church of the Nativity in Bethlehem (was one of these where Jesus was born?) and a decree in Nazareth threatening capital punishment for grave robbers (similar to the seal placed over Jesus' tomb outside Jerusalem?). Or one can imagine Jesus looking across to the east of the sea of Galilee to the hilltop city of Hippos, whose torchlights at night could be seen around the entire lake, when he declared, "A city on a hill cannot be hidden" (Matt. 5:14). And was he looking down into the Kidron Valley to many of the beautifully ornate graves and mausoleums there, relatively recently built in his day, when he compared the hypocritical scribes and Pharisees to "whitewashed tombs" (Matt. 23:27)?

Excavated artifacts can often give insights into specific words or customs. The single word *corban*—dedicated to God—has been found on a Jewish sarcophagus as a guard against grave robbers. We know from the shape of the temple mount in Jerusalem that it had no "pinnacles," only "porticoes"—flat, porch-shaped structures. Yet the southeast portico overlooking the Kidron val-

---

4. This conclusion has been challenged by the very cautious and respected scholar William Horbury, based on questions about the spelling of the name Caiaphas, arguably to be transliterated *Qopha* ("The 'Caiaphas' Ossuaries and Joseph Caiaphas," *PEQ* 126 [1994]: 32–48), but to date this opposition has not caught on in any widespread fashion. There are too many other striking pieces of circumstantial evidence—the signs of wealth, priestly and temple connections, other family names, location in the general area tradition had assigned to the tomb, etc.—to dismiss the identification quickly.

ley would still have been a sufficiently fear-inspiring referent for the devil's temptation in Matthew 4:5–6. Coins in abundance confirm the custom of minting Caesar's image on them and also help archaeologists date other items in which they are embedded.

Ancient traditions, perhaps as old as the fourth or fifth century, often equate certain sites with events from the Gospels, even though there are good reasons for doubting the locations. For example, Mount Tabor was probably not remote or high enough for the Transfiguration; modern-day Cana is in the wrong place to be the ancient city by that name; and the traditional site of Caiaphas's headquarters is built over ancient Jewish graves—not where a high priest would have made his home. The feeding of the five thousand was not likely near Tabgha on the west bank of Galilee, as some tour guides allege, because John 6:17 describes the disciples departing from the site of that miracle by boat to head "across the lake" for Capernaum, which was also on the western shore.[5] In other cases there is simply not enough information, inside or outside the Gospels, to prove or refute certain traditions—Ain Karim in the Judean hill country as John the Baptist's birthplace, the alleged tomb of Lazarus in Bethany, the supposed "upper room" on Mt. Zion, the *Dominus Flavit* chapel as the place Jesus wept over Jerusalem on the Mount of Olives, or the Church of the Annunciation in Nazareth as the place of Gabriel's appearance to Mary. Indeed, doubts of various kinds surround even many of the locations we have mentioned above as probably authentic. This simply reflects the uncertainty that characterizes the disciplines of archaeology and historical geography in general.

A different kind of uncertainty results when archaeology provides multiple options in trying to resolve a thorny historical problem. There are at least two, possibly three, plausible locations for Emmaus. We have still not solved the problem of Quirinius's census (see above, p. 188), even though we have discovered some ambiguous evidence that may suggest censuses on fourteen-year cycles throughout the Roman empire, a possible joint-governorship of some kind for Quirinius before his one clearly documented term beginning in A.D. 6, and evidence from Egypt that those who were residing away from property of their family of origin had to return to their homes for a census. It seems premature, therefore, to accuse Luke of a definite error in attributing a census to a reign of Quirinius in about 6 B.C., as so many have, even though we have no demonstrable vindication of Luke's accuracy either.[6]

Archaeology further holds the potential for illuminating the silences of the Gospels. Much recent excavation has centered on Sepphoris, the original Herodian capital of Galilee before the construction of Tiberias in the mid-20s, and a center of much building and trade during Jesus' youth and early adulthood. As it was less than five miles from Nazareth, can we imagine Jesus not having visited this center of Greek culture, complete with its theater? Might he have been employed in town? Is that where he learned about "hypocrites"

---

5. One possible way around this "contradiction" is suggested by Bargil Pixner ("The Miracle Church at Tabgha on the Sea of Galilee," *BA* 48 [Dec. 1985]: 196–206), but the hypothesis requires taking John's narrative as a conflation of the independent, separately located feedings of the five thousand and four thousand known from the Synoptics, and it is probably not very likely.

6. So, too, Gary R. Habermas, *Ancient Evidence for the Life of Jesus* (Nashville: Thomas Nelson, 1984), 152–53.

(Greek for "playactors"), a term he later used with such rhetorical power against various Jewish leaders? Conversely, may we assume from the silence of the Gospels about Sepphoris that Jesus' later adult ministry deliberately avoided this least Jewish of Galilean locales precisely because of his commitment to go to the Jew first (cf. our discussion above, p. 132)? None of these hypotheses can be demonstrated, but all are plausible and worth considering.[7]

Archaeological evidence can, however, be abused. Implausible harmonizations of difficult problems can be too easily proposed. For example, it is well known that there are ruins of two different cities within two miles from each other: Old Testament Jericho and New Testament Jericho. A popular solution to the problem of Mark having Jesus heal blind Bartimaeus as he was leaving Jericho (Mark 10:46), while Luke seems to think this happened en route to Jericho (Luke 18:35), has been to postulate that Jesus was in between the *two* Jerichos. But there is no evidence that any reader of a New Testament account of an otherwise unspecified Jericho would ever assume it to be the old city now in ruins, so other solutions to this problem will have to be sought.[8] Nor is it always remembered that the parable of the good Samaritan was precisely that—a parable—so that debates over the authenticity of ruins of an inn on the Jericho road prove irrelevant. Jesus may have had no real-life site in mind at all as he told his story!

One ancient artifact of a quite different nature deserves brief comment. Small fragments of the Shroud of Turin, carefully guarded for centuries by Italian Catholic authorities, and traditionally believed to be the very graveclothes of Jesus, were subject to a battery of scientific tests in 1988 at three different laboratories around the world. All the results independently concurred that this was an eleventh or twelfth-century piece of cloth, much too recent to have belonged to Christ. There is still no convincing explanation of the origin of the striking impression of a crucified man imprinted on this cloth, but nothing is to be gained by arguing any longer for its authenticity.[9] Notwithstanding "reversals" of this nature, the ancient physical remains that impinge on the life of Jesus as narrated in the canonical Gospels continue to vindicate its substantial historicity time and again in those areas that can be tested. We should welcome all further investigations with the confidence that such corroboration will continue to emerge.

OTHER ANCIENT SOURCES

Non-Christian Writers

It is occasionally doubted if Jesus even existed.[10] This claim can be decisively refuted without once appealing to Christian evidence. The non-Christian

7. See further Richard A. Batey, *Jesus and the Forgotten City* (Grand Rapids: Baker, 1991).

8. See Craig Blomberg, *The Historical Reliability of the Gospels* (Leicester and Downers Grove: IVP, 1987), 128–30; alternately, cf. Stanley E. Porter, "'In the Vicinity of Jericho': Luke 18:35 in the Light of Its Synoptic Parallels," *BBR* 2 (1992): 91–104.

9. See further Graham N. Stanton, *Gospel Truth? New Light on Jesus and the Gospels* (London: HarperCollins; Valley Forge: TPI, 1995), 119–20.

10. The only serious scholar to defend this view in the past generation is G. A. Wells in a trilogy of works: *The Jesus of the Early Christians* (London: Pemberton, 1971); *Did Jesus Exist?* (London: Pemberton; Buffalo: Prometheus, 1975); and *The Historical Evidence for Jesus* (Buffalo: Prometheus, 1982).

testimony from antiquity may be divided into Greco-Roman and Jewish sources.

Greco-Roman Sources. Four ancient Roman historians that we know of referred to Jesus.[11] The briefest and least significant reference comes from the early third-century historian Julius Africanus, who cites a certain Thallus who wrote a chronicle of world history in Greek in the first century. In that document, Thallus referred to the darkness that occurred at the time of the crucifixion (*Chronography,* frag. 18), attributing it to an eclipse of the sun, an interpretation Africanus disputes. Pliny the younger, a Roman legate from the early second century, wrote to the emperor Trajan requesting advice on how to deal with Christians who refused to worship the emperor. Pliny noted that these Christians met regularly and sang hymns "to Christ as if to a god" (*Letters* 10:96.7). This expression suggests that Pliny knew Jesus was a historical figure and so was reluctant to call him divine.

The third Roman source is Suetonius, also an early second-century writer, who describes the expulsion of Jews from Rome under the emperor Claudius as due to rioting "at the instigation of Chrestus" (*Claudius* 25:4), a remark usually interpreted as a garbled reference to Jewish followers of Christ (Latin, *Christus*). The reference nevertheless points to Jesus as the leader of a group of Jewish dissidents and perhaps even the founder of Christianity. The one really substantive and decisive piece of Roman testimony, however, comes from a contemporary of Suetonius, the historian Tacitus. In his *Annals* 15:44, he wrote that Christians received their name from "Christ who had been executed by sentence of the procurator Pontius Pilate in the reign of Tiberius," details which mesh perfectly with the information found in the New Testament.

One additional scrap of testimony comes from the Greek satirist Lucian of Samosata, writing in the mid–second century. In describing a recently deceased philosopher Peregrinus, who apparently made some profession of Christian faith, Lucian likened him to "that other whom they still worship, the man who was crucified in Palestine because he introduced this new cult into the world." Later Jesus is called Christians' "first lawgiver," who persuaded his followers that they were all "brothers of one another," as well as "that crucified sophist" (*Peregrinus,* 11, 13). Categories of law and wisdom are exactly what one would expect a non-Christian Hellenist to use in describing Jesus.

Jewish Sources. A letter written in Syriac some time after the fall of Jerusalem refers to a "wise king" whom certain Jews apparently killed (*Mara bar Serapion*). The downfall of the Jews in A.D. 70 is attributed to this behavior. But this writer, with a Jewish name, cannot have been a Christian because he puts Jesus on a par with Socrates and Pythagoras, noting how the murders of all three did not stamp out the movements each began. It is interesting, too, how Jesus himself linked his rejection and demise to the coming Roman invasion of Jerusalem (esp. Matt. 23–25).

Of only slightly more help are scattered references throughout the voluminous rabbinic literature. It is difficult to know where, if ever, these references represent independent or accurate historical information. Rabbinic literature

---

11. Cf. further Murray J. Harris, "References to Jesus in Early Classical Authors," in *Gospel Perspectives*, vol. 5, ed. David Wenham (Sheffield: JSOT, 1985), 343–68.

372 HISTORICAL AND THEOLOGICAL SYNTHESES

progressively excised mention of Jesus and Christianity and became increasingly polemical against its rival faith. None of the references comes in the Mishnah or early midrashim (late first- through early–third century) but only in later Jewish sources. Nevertheless, their contents are intriguing.[12] In the Palestinian Talmud, the third-century Rabbi Abbahu says, "If a man says to you 'I am (a) God,' he is a liar; 'I am (a) Son of Man,' he will regret it; 'I go up to heaven,' he has said it but he will not be able to do it" (*p. Ta'anith* 65b). However derivatively, the passage reflects Christian claims about who Jesus said he was. Interestingly, no attempt is made to deny the claims, only a person's power to fulfill them.

As already noted above (p. 241), the same situation recurs with rabbinic commentary on Jesus' miracles and exorcisms. Plenty of ancient writers knew how to dispute claims of extraordinary ability, but the consistent Jewish witness was merely to question the *source* of Jesus' admitted powers. Thus *b. Sanhedrin* 103a likens a rebellious disciple to one "who publicly burns his food like Jesus of Nazareth"—a metaphor for distorting Jewish teaching. In the same tractate, we read that "Jesus the Nazarene practiced magic and led Israel astray" (43a; cf. 107b).[13] Several sources refer to Jesus as the son of "Pandera" (or Pantera or Panthera), a Roman soldier, hinting at the unusual circumstances surrounding his birth. As already suggested in the Gospels (John 8:41), Jewish polemic against Christ's virginal conception argued that he was merely an illegitimate child. Actually Pandera may be a corruption of the Greek *parthenos* or virgin.

Yet another rabbinic tradition speaks of Jesus as having five disciples named Matthai, Naqai, Nezer, Buni, and Todah (*b. Sanhedrin* 43a). Matthai, Naqai, and Todah could be corrupt spellings of Matthew, Nicodemus, and Thaddaeus, while Nezer probably refers to an unnamed "Nazarene." Buni might just be a corruption of the Hebrew for John, but all this is guesswork. The most substantial testimony in a later Jewish source probably remains the statement in this same section of the Babylonian Talmud that Jesus was hanged on the eve of the Passover. But this section also contains a reference to his being stoned and to a herald who announced the execution for forty days before it took place. Since both of these statements seem historically groundless, it is hard to know whether any of the text relies on accurate tradition.

Other information is of even more dubious worth. One possible reference to Jesus (but the individual in question is referred to only as a well-known heretic *à la* Balaam) states that he was thirty-three or thirty-four when he died (*b. Sanhedrin* 106b). Another describes a dialogue between a putative disciple of Jesus and Rabbi Eliezer, in which Jesus is quoted as having taught that a latrine could be bought with the wages of a harlot (*b. Abodah Zarah* 16b–17a). Numerous passages refer to anonymous heretics, some of which could be speaking of Jesus. A widely read medieval Jewish source, perhaps as old as the eighth century, called the *Toledoth Jesu* ("The Generations of Jesus"), describes

---

12. Cf. further Graham H. Twelftree, "Jesus in Jewish Traditions," in *ibid.*, 289–341.

13. On the pervasiveness and significance of this latter tradition, see Graham N. Stanton, "Jesus of Nazareth: A Magician and a False Prophet Who Deceived God's People?" in *Jesus of Nazareth: Lord and Christ*, ed. Joel B. Green and Max Turner (Carlisle: Paternoster; Grand Rapids: Eerdmans, 1994), 164–80.

the illegitimate child Jesus growing up to disrespect his teachers, performing miracles, attracting a following, and eventually being executed. The story then describes the discovery of an empty tomb followed by the recovery of Jesus' corpse. All in all the work is nothing but a late, polemical revisionist attempt by certain Jews to discredit the classic claims of Christian origins.

The only truly valuable Jewish testimony to the life of Christ thus comes not from the rabbinic literature but from the first-century Pharisee and defeated freedom-fighter-turned-historian, Josephus. In *Antiquities* 20.9.1, Josephus describes the martyrdom of James, "the brother of Jesus—the one called Christ." This passing reference alone serves to substantiate the historicity of Jesus per se, but it seems to presuppose more detailed, prior knowledge of this individual. This information was in fact provided in 18.3.3. The text as it stands reads:

> About this time there lived Jesus, a wise man, if indeed one ought to call him a man. For he was one who wrought surprising feats and was a teacher of such people as accept the truth gladly. He won over many Jews and many of the Greeks. He was the Messiah. When Pilate, upon hearing him accused by men of the highest standing amongst us, had condemned him to be crucified, those who had in the first place come to love him did not give up their affection for him. On the third day he appeared to them restored to life, for the prophets of God had prophesied these and countless other marvellous things about him. And the tribe of the Christians, so called after him, has still to this day not disappeared.

Because the rest of his writings make it clear that Josephus never became a Christian, it seems impossible that he (1) should have questioned Jesus' humanity, (2) called Jesus the Messiah, or (3) affirmed the resurrection. As a result some scholars have wondered whether or not this entire passage is a later Christian "interpolation" into the works of Josephus, since it was largely in Christian circles that his writings came to be preserved. But if we excise these three parts, the rest of Josephus' testimony flows smoothly, fits his style, and seems likely to be authentic. Perhaps, as in section 20, he originally wrote "the one called Messiah." A later Arabic version of Josephus in fact closely resembles this abridged reconstruction of his original text, with the latter two supposed interpolations combined at the end of the paragraph. This would seem to confirm our hypothesis about the original form of Josephus's testimony.[14] Other passages in *Antiquities* describe the ministry and execution of John the Baptist, and the lives and times of the various Herods, the Roman governors, and the Jewish high priests, including Pilate and Caiaphas, respectively.

To some this may all seem like precious little non-Christian corroboration of the Gospel narratives. But we have to remember that in the ancient world, history was almost exclusively the chronicle of the deeds of politicians, warriors, and holders of high religious office. Other figures were mentioned only if they spawned widespread, long-term, public followings. Jesus and Christianity fit

---

14. Cf. esp. John P. Meier, *A Marginal Jew: Rethinking the Historical Jesus*, vol. 1 (New York and London: Doubleday, 1991), 56–88. For the significance of Josephus for New Testament studies more broadly, cf. Steve Mason, *Josephus and the New Testament* (Peabody: Hendrickson, 1992).

none of these categories at this early date. So it is arguable that it is both surprising and significant that they even got as much press as they did![15]

Post–New Testament Christian Writers

Unorthodox Sources. We have already noted how the Coptic Gospel of Thomas has been alleged to preserve reliable, independent tradition about the sayings of Jesus, even though its origin cannot be demonstrated to predate the mid-second century and even though it contains numerous sayings attributed to Jesus that are thoroughly Gnostic in character (above, pp. 35–36). While Thomas is by far the most commonly cited heterodox Christian document that some think may illuminate the gospel tradition, other works have at times been appealed to in this respect as well.[16] From the Nag Hammadi collection of primarily Gnostic texts comes also the Apocryphon of James, with various new parables and kingdom sayings attributed to Jesus. A large number of "Gospels" are made up primarily of lengthy dialogues attributed to the resurrected Jesus, who imparts secret (i.e., Gnostic) revelation to various disciples. Two that occasionally have sayings more akin to the canonical Gospels are the Gospel of Philip and the Gospel of Truth. Yet careful studies have demonstrated that all these works are in fact later than and dependent on the collected canonical Gospels and add nothing to our knowledge about the historical Jesus.[17]

Other Apocrypha. A very different type of document that some have appealed to as a primitive Gospel source is the Gospel of Peter, a narrative that deals largely with the passion and resurrection of Christ. This work is clearly "docetic" in nature, that is, Christ only *seems* (from Greek, *dokeō*) to be human. Thus 4:10b states that during his crucifixion Jesus "was silent, as if having no pain." As already noted, in the account of Christ's resurrection, even more obviously legendary elements appear: three men emerge from the tomb, "two sustaining the one, and a cross following them, and the heads of the two reaching to heaven, but that of him who was led by them by the hand going beyond the heavens" (10:39–40). Notwithstanding this ethos, J. D. Crossan has attempted to reconstruct an underlying "Cross Gospel" behind the Gospel of Peter, which he postulates as the sole pre-Markan source for the canonical passion narratives.[18] Far more brief and fragmentary is Papyrus Egerton 2, the so-called "Unknown Gospel," which comprises four scraps of Gospel-like accounts, including a dialogue between Jesus and the Jewish rulers similar to those in John 5 and 9–10, the story of a cleansing of a leper, the question for Jesus about paying taxes, and an apparent miracle of quickly growing seed that has no exact canonical parallel. With both the Gospel of Peter and the Unknown Gospel, however, painstaking comparisons with the canonical narratives make it far more probable that the New Testament accounts generated the later additions and "revisions" than that the reverse sequence obtained.[19]

15. Cf. further Paul Barnett, *Is the New Testament History?* (London: Hodder & Stoughton, 1986), 159–63.
16. See esp. throughout John Dominic Crossan, *The Historical Jesus* (San Francisco: HarperSanFrancisco, 1991).
17. See esp. C. M. Tuckett, *Nag Hammadi and the Gospel Tradition* (Edinburgh: T. & T. Clark, 1986).
18. John Dominic Crossan, *The Cross That Spoke* (San Francisco: Harper & Row, 1988).
19. David F. Wright, "Apocryphal Gospels: The 'Unknown Gospel' (Pap. Egerton 2) and the *Gospel of Peter*," in *Gospel Perspectives*, vol. 5, 221–227. The other main narrative that resembles the Gospel of Peter is the Gospel of Nicodemus, containing an account of Christ's passion and of his descent into hell. The first part of this work is also called the Acts of Pilate. Here virtually all scholars agree on the worthlessness of this document for historical Jesus research.

Even more blatantly legendary are the apocrypha that try to fill in the gaps in the canonical Gospels concerning Christ's "hidden years"—his childhood and young adulthood. The Protevangelium of James is important as the source for Roman Catholicism's dogma of *Mary's* sinlessness, describing among other things Jesus' emerging from the womb without breaking Mary's hymen (see above, p. 209). The Infancy Gospel of Thomas, not to be confused with the Coptic Gnostic document by the same name, describes Jesus the child miracle-worker and carpenter prodigy (p. 207). But neither document shows any signs of preserving independent historical traditions about Christ.

Jewish-Christian Gospels. This category of literature is known to us solely from quotations that have been preserved in the various Church Fathers. Apparently there were at least three different documents, all perhaps bearing some resemblance to the Gospel of Matthew—an Ebionite Gospel, the Gospel of the Nazoreans, and an Egyptian Gospel of the Hebrews. These traditions are of interest because of the recurring testimony within early Christianity that Matthew compiled something in the Hebrew language before the appearance of the canonical Greek Gospel that bears his name. Certain patterns emerge in the scattered references to these Gospels that remain: Jesus is cast in terms of Wisdom and Law, there are ascetic tendencies, and James the brother of Jesus plays a prominent role. All of these fit with what we know of second-century Jewish Christianity. As with the Coptic Gospel of Thomas, it is possible that in isolated places these documents preserve otherwise unknown but authentic sayings of Jesus. Still, as with the other documents surveyed in this section, there is also plenty of evidence of dependence on the canonical tradition.[20]

Later Legends. The unsuspecting modern reader may pick up "New Age" or similar literature that refers to still more extracanonical documents. Often, this literature does not disclose that the works it treats were not even composed until the Middle Ages or later. In such works, one can read about Pilate's correspondence, Jesus as an Essene, or Christ traveling to India to study with the great gurus there. Muslims often appeal to the Gospel of Barnabas, a document that has Judas replacing Jesus on the cross at the last minute and that denies Christ's divinity, even though it was not composed until after the birth of Islam and the oldest known copy is an eighteenth-century Italian manuscript. Modern-day forgeries even pass off Jesus as an alien from outer space! All of this literature is worthless for an analysis of the Jesus of history, regardless of the misleading claims of some of the books that reproduce this material.[21]

The Apostolic Fathers. Substantially more valuable testimony comes from the second-century orthodox Christian writers known as the Apostolic Fathers.[22] Within less than a hundred years from the completion of the books we now know as the New Testament, quotations and allusions from sizable portions of those books were showing up in other Christian literature. Polycarp, Ignatius,

---

20. For the fullest analysis and presentation of texts, see A. F. J. Klijn, *Jewish-Christian Gospel Tradition* (Leiden: Brill, 1992).

21. A convenient sampling of a representative portion of this literature appears in Per Beskow, *Strange Tales about Jesus* (Philadelphia: Fortress, 1983); cf. more briefly Douglas Groothuis, *Jesus in an Age of Controversy* (Eugene, Ore.: Harvest House, 1996), 119–51. The UFOlogist in question is James W. Deardorff (*Celestial Teachings: The Emergence of the True Testament of Jmmanuel [Jesus]* [Tigard, Ore.: Wild Flower Press, 1991]).

22. A standard edition of their collected works is *The Apostolic Fathers*, trans. J. B. Lightfoot and J. R. Harmer, ed. & rev. Michael W. Holmes (Grand Rapids: Baker, 1992).

and Clement alone betray awareness of twenty-five of the twenty-seven New Testament documents. Ignatius recognizes, too, that the end of an era has come. In his early second-century letter to the Trallians, for example, he admits, "I did not think myself competent for this, that . . . I should order you as though I were an apostle" (3:3). The Gospels, and the sayings of Jesus in particular, were the most popular part of the New Testament documents to receive citation by these early Church Fathers, and Matthew was the most popular Gospel of all. (John would later receive the special attention of the heterodox or Gnostic works because of passages that could be twisted or taken out of context to support that theological system.)

Indeed, it is important to stress that one of the significant contributions of the Apostolic Fathers is to corroborate the widespread influence of a substantial portion of the Gospel tradition. Clearly all four canonical Gospels, circulating together by at least the early second century, had a profound influence on the developing church. But whereas various critics have put forward relatively specious arguments for the Nag Hammadi and other heterodox literature relying on early, independent tradition, the case is different with the Apostolic Fathers. The Coptic Gospel of Thomas discloses parallels to every single canonical Gospel and every putative Gospel layer of tradition or redaction, even the relatively rare material unique to Mark. But several of the Apostolic Fathers are far less balanced in their use of canonical Gospel material. The *Didachē* (or "Teaching of the Twelve Apostles"), written probably as early as the 90s, is filled with references to teachings of Jesus paralleled in Matthew's Gospel but never when Matthew is identical to Mark. Given Matthew's widespread dependence on Mark, this is a striking coincidence if this document were relying on the final form of the Gospel. But it could be evidence that the *Didachē* knew and used something like Q—an underlying Gospel source. So, too, Ignatius also cites texts from Matthew in abundance, but *three*-fourths of his quotations or allusions come from "M" (uniquely Matthean) material, whereas "M" comprises no more than *one*-fourth of the overall Gospel. In some cases these references involve material previously thought to be Matthew's own redaction (e.g., Matt. 3:15 in Ignatius's letter to the Smyrneans 1.1). So perhaps there is actually evidence here for the persistence of underlying oral or written source material to which later Christian writers referred. First Clement and Polycarp independently reproduce collections of gospel traditions that resemble one another in ways that also suggest common, noncanonical source material. None of this proves the historical trustworthiness of the details cited, but it all suggests that early sources continued to influence Christian writers even after the four Gospels were compiled. And the earlier the source, the more likely it was in touch with authentic tradition.[23]

Authentic Agrapha? When we amass all of the evidence of these post-canonical Christian writers, do we discover potentially reliable information about Jesus that we would not have known from Matthew, Mark, Luke, or John? The question is legitimate, for even the Book of Acts quotes a saying of Jesus not found in any of the Gospels ("It is more blessed to give than to

---

23. For more details on the data of this paragraph, see Craig Blomberg, *The Historical Reliability of the Gospels* (Leicester and Downers Grove: IVP, 1987), 204–8, and the literature there cited.

receive"—Acts 20:35). And John reminds us, however hyperbolically, that many other things Jesus said and did were never written down (John 21:25). A famous study called *Unknown Sayings of Jesus,* by the relatively conservative German scholar Joachim Jeremias, identified eighteen such *agrapha* (from the Greek for "unwritten things"—i.e., not written down in the canonical Gospels but found in other early Christian literature.)[24] More recent studies have been skeptical of accepting even this many.[25] A sample of those that might conceivably pass the standard criteria of authenticity and the sources in which they are found include:

> On the same day Jesus saw a man working on the sabbath, and said to him, "Man, if you know what you are doing, you are blessed; but if you do not know, you are cursed and an offender against the law." (an addition to Luke 6:5 in Codex Bezae [D])
> No one will reach the kingdom of heaven without being tempted. (Tertullian, *On Baptism,* 20)
> Ask for great things, and the little things will be added to you. (Clement of Alexandria, *Stromateis* 1.24)
> Be approved money-changers. (Origen, *Commentary on John,* 19.7; and several other sources)
> But the rich man began to scratch his head, and it pleased him not. And the Lord said to him: "How can you say, 'I have kept the law and the prophets?' For it is written in the law: 'You shall love your neighbor as yourself,' and lo, many of your brothers, sons of Abraham, are clad in filth, dying of hunger, and your house is full of many good things, and nothing of it goes out to them." (Gospel of the Nazoreans 16, as quoted by Origen, *Commentary on Matthew 15.14*)
> Whoever is near me is near the fire; whoever is far from me is far from the kingdom. (Gospel of Thomas 82)
> And never be joyful, save when you look upon your brother in love. (Gospel of the Hebrews 5, as quoted by Jerome, *Commentary on Ephesians 3*)
> Woe to you blind who see not! You have washed yourself in water that is poured forth, in which dogs and swine lie night and day, and washed and scoured your outer skin, which harlots and flute girls also anoint, bathe, scour, and beautify to arouse desire in men, but inwardly they are filled with scorpions and with all manner of evil. But I and my disciples, of whom you say that we have not bathed, have bathed ourselves in the living and clean water, which comes down from the father in heaven. (pOxyrhynchus 840.2)

Whether or not any of these sayings is authentic, the overwhelming conclusion at the end of this survey of post–New Testament Christian writers is that very little if anything emerges to supplement or alter the picture of Jesus we receive from the canonical Gospels. On the other hand, widespread citation demonstrates that at least the early Christian church was convinced of the truthfulness and relevance of a sizable portion of the contents of Matthew, Mark, Luke, and John.

---

24. (London: SPCK, rev. 1964). The texts of 266 agrapha appear in William D. Stroker, *Extracanonical Sayings of Jesus* (Atlanta: Scholars, 1989). The vast majority of these stand no chance of reflecting independent authentic gospel tradition.

25. See esp. Otfried Hofius, "'Unknown Sayings of Jesus'," in *The Gospel and the Gospels,* ed. Peter Stuhlmacher (Grand Rapids: Eerdmans, 1991), 336–60.

The Testimony of the Rest of the New Testament

It is sometimes argued that the rest of the New Testament shows so little awareness of the Jesus-tradition that it could not have been well known in the first generation of Christianity. In extreme instances, Paul and not Jesus is treated as the founder of this new religion![26] On the one hand, it is true that the Acts and the epistles do not regularly quote sayings of Jesus and that episodes from his life are rarely mentioned. But there are several plausible reasons for this. None of these documents represents the initial evangelistic outreach of the church; all are written to well-established Christian communities for specific reasons (usually "in-house" concerns) that do not require a first-time presentation of the life of Christ. Luke, of course, has already narrated his Gospel when he writes the Acts. Paul and the other epistle writers may equally presume that the core *kerygma* (proclamation) of the church is well known, so that they can proceed to build upon it. Moreover, Christian theology became quickly convinced that the most important things about Jesus' life were his death and resurrection. Important as his teachings and other deeds were, they did not put into effect God's plan of atonement for the sins of the world, and so they came to take second place in overtly theological presentations of Christ's significance.

On the other hand, it is easy to underestimate the extent to which the Jesus-tradition *did* influence Acts and the epistles. There are actually quite a number of places where direct quotations or references to various sayings or events from Jesus' life appear, and numerous additional allusions, although it becomes difficult to know when certain references actually allude to teachings of Jesus rather than referring to common illustrative material in ancient religious thought more generally. We will briefly survey some of the more secure and significant quotations and allusions here.

Acts. In Acts 13:24–25, Paul's sermon in Pisidian Antioch includes reference back to John the Baptist and specific teaching from John about his unworthiness even to untie the sandals of the one coming after him. In 20:35, as noted above, we have an otherwise unknown saying of Jesus. But the most important reference in Acts back to the Gospel tradition is the summary of Jesus' life in Peter's words to Cornelius in 10:36–41:

> This is the message God sent to the people of Israel, telling the good news of peace through Jesus Christ, who is Lord of all. You know what has happened throughout Judea, beginning in Galilee after the baptism that John preached—how God anointed Jesus of Nazareth with the Holy Spirit and power, and how he went around doing good and healing all who were under the power of the devil, because God was with him. We are witnesses of everything he did in the country of the Jews and in Jerusalem. They killed him by hanging him on a tree, but God raised him from the dead on the third day and caused him to be seen. He was not seen by all the people, but by witnesses whom God had already chosen—by us who ate and drank with him after he rose from the dead.

---

26. One of the most famous examples is the essay by the celebrated English writer and outspoken critic of Christianity, George Bernard Shaw, "The Monstrous Imposition upon Jesus," in *The Writings of St. Paul,* ed. Wayne A. Meeks (New York: Norton, 1972), 296–302 [orig. 1913].

A summary like this was what led C. H. Dodd to suggest that the Gospels themselves fleshed out the outline of early Christian preaching (see above, p. 117).

Paul.[27] Because most if not all of the Pauline epistles were written before the first Gospel was ever published, Paul's testimony proves even more significant, demonstrating the existence of information being circulated about the life of Christ within the first twenty years or so of Christian history. Upon careful inspection, a fairly full summary of the main contours of Jesus' life can in fact be pieced together from Paul's writings: his descent from Abraham and David (Gal. 3:16; Rom. 1:3); upbringing in the Jewish Law (Gal. 4:4); gathering together disciples, including Cephas (Peter) and John; having a brother named James (Gal. 1:19; 2:9); an impeccable character and exemplary life (Phil. 2:6–8; 2 Cor. 8:9; Rom. 15:3, 8); the Last Supper and betrayal (1 Cor. 11:23–25); and numerous details surrounding his death and resurrection (Gal. 3:1; 1 Thess. 2:15; 1 Cor. 15:4–8).

Even more noteworthy are various quotations of or references to Jesus' teaching. Romans 12:17–19 includes a cluster of allusions to the Sermon on the Mount and the principles of enemy love (cf. esp. Matt. 5:38; Luke 6:27, 33). Romans 13:7 seems familiar with Jesus' famous teaching on paying taxes (cf. Mark 12:17 pars.). Romans 14:20 apparently relies on Jesus' abolition of the kosher laws (cf. Mark 7:19).[28] 1 Corinthians contains three direct references: 7:10 on marriage and divorce (cf. Matt. 19:1–12), 9:14 (cf. also 1 Tim. 5:18) on a worker deserving his wages (cf. Luke 10:7), and 11:23–25 with its detailed knowledge of the teaching of Jesus about the Passover bread and wine (cf. esp. Luke 22:19–20). Other probable allusions include 9:18 (on Paul's preaching the gospel free of charge) to Matthew 10:8, and 13:2 (on faith moving mountains) to Mark 11:23 and parallels. Second Corinthians 1:17 seems to hark back to Matthew 5:37—letting one's yes be yes and one's no be no. 1 Thessalonians again contains three clear clusters of references to Jesus' teachings: 2:14–16 resembles selections of Matthew 23:29–38, with its invective against the Jewish leaders; 4:15–17 refers to a word of the Lord concerning his return and contains several echoes of the Olivet Discourse (Mark 13 pars.); and 5:2–4 refers specifically to the Day of the Lord coming like a thief, in dependence on the parable in Matthew 24:43–44 and Luke 12:39–40. More generally, 2 Thessalonians 2:3–4 refers to belief in a coming Antichrist reminiscent of Jesus' teaching about the "abomination that causes desolation" (Mark 13:14 pars.).

Other references are less definite and yet seem still to betray some awareness of the Jesus-tradition. Paul's mention of the Jerusalem apostles as "pillars" of the church (Gal. 2:9) could allude back to Jesus' promises to Peter and his companions in Matthew 16:17–19 and 18:19–20. Echoes of the parable of the sower may be heard in Colossians 1:6; 1 Thessalonians 1:6; or 2:13. It would be striking for Paul to have described God the Father as *Abba* (almost "Daddy") in Galatians 4:6 and Romans 8:15 had he not known about Jesus' own

---

27. By far and away the most important study and collection of possible citations and use of the Jesus-tradition in Paul is David Wenham, *Paul: Follower of Jesus or Founder of Christianity?* (Grand Rapids and Cambridge: Eerdmans, 1995).

28. On Romans' use of the Jesus-tradition, see esp. Michael B. Thompson, *Clothed with Christ: The Example and Teaching of Jesus in Romans 12.1–15.13* (Sheffield: JSOT, 1991).

distinctive use of the term (see esp. Mark 14:36). Paul's understanding of
Christ's redemptive death (e.g., Rom. 3:24) may well depend in part on Jesus'
ransom saying in Mark 10:45 and parallel. Key themes in Paul's theology, as
different as it superficially seems to be from Jesus' own thought, also suggest
stronger lines of continuity: several references to "kingdom," though substantially diminished in frequency from the Gospels; the sequence of going first to
Jew and then to Gentile with the gospel; Jesus as the fulfillment of the Law,
implying freedom from slavish obedience to its "letter" coupled with the need
to adhere to its abiding moral demands; the summary of the Old Testament in
the love-command; the flesh-Spirit contrast as in Mark 14:38; and justification
by grace through faith as in Luke 18:10–14.

The General Epistles. James and 1 Peter, too, seem to rely on a form of the
Jesus-tradition that would have circulated prior to the first written Gospels. The
evidence from James may prove particularly significant if, as many scholars
suspect, that letter was the earliest New Testament document written, perhaps
in the late 40s. Then the oral tradition on which James relied would be barely
more than fifteen years removed from the events themselves. James has one
direct quotation of Jesus' words (again on letting one's yes be yes and one's
no, no—James 5:12; cf. Matt. 5:37) but numerous allusions, especially to the
Sermon on the Mount. Compare, for example, 1:2 with Matthew 5:11–12; 1:4
with Matthew 5:48; 1:5 with Matthew 7:7; 1:6 with Mark 11:23; and so on.[29] First
Peter, on the other hand, even if dated as early as about 64 (during Peter's lifetime and just at the onset of Nero's persecution), could have known the final
forms of Matthew, Mark, or Luke. But interestingly, some of Peter's clearest
allusions to Gospel tradition resemble uniquely Johannine material, perhaps
not written down until the 90s. Thus, 1:3 speaks of being born anew (cf. John
3:3); 1:8, of loving Jesus without having seen him (cf. John 20:29); and 2:9, of
being called out of darkness into light (cf. John 8:12). So again there may be
evidence for the oral transmission at an earlier date of what was only later written down in our canonical Gospels.[30]

Early Christian Creeds. A final piece of evidence may push back the existence
of the oral traditions about Jesus to an astonishingly early date. There are various
passages in the epistles that have frequently been identified as poetic, even hymnic, in structure and form, that are filled with christological teaching in a style
reminiscent of later Christian creeds.[31] There are often signs, too, that these predate the New Testament authors who use them, because of key words or phrases
reflecting those authors' distinctive theologies that interrupt the structure or symmetry of the "creeds." If this is the case, then we have evidence in these passages
for what Christians confessed about Jesus at a very early date. Remarkably, these
passages include some of the "highest Christology"—the most lofty and exalted

---

29. For the dating of James and a listing and discussion of allusions to the Jesus-tradition, see esp. Peter H. Davids, *The Epistle of
James* (Exeter: Paternoster; Grand Rapids: Eerdmans, 1982), 2–22, 47–51.

30. Cf. further Robert H. Gundry, "'Verba Christi' in 1 Peter: Their Implications Concerning the Authorship of 1 Peter and the
Authenticity of the Gospel Tradition," *NTS* 13 (1966–67): 336–50; idem, "Further *Verba* on *Verba Christi* in First Peter," *Biblica* 55
(1974): 211–32.

31. For an introductory discussion, see Ralph P. Martin, *New Testament Foundations*, vol. 2 (Grand Rapids: Eerdmans; Exeter,
Paternoster, 1978), 248–75. For a good list of criteria for recognizing traditional material embedded in New Testament epistles, see
Markus Barth, *Ephesians 1–3* (Garden City: Doubleday, 1974), 6–10.

statements about the person and work of Christ—found anywhere in the New Testament (e.g., Phil. 2:5–11; Col. 1:15–20; Rom. 1:3–4; and 1 Tim. 3:16). Peter clearly makes reference to the exemplary life and redemptive death of Jesus in similar confessional passages (1 Pet. 1:20–21; 2:21–25; 3:18–22). In perhaps the most significant creed of all, Paul cites tradition that had been passed on to him about the eyewitnesses to Jesus' resurrection (1 Cor. 15:3–7). The language here is technical Jewish terminology for the transmission of sacred tradition. Given that the reality and significance of Jesus' death and resurrection would have no doubt been one of the first things other Christians would have taught Paul as a new convert, it is plausible to date this information to the year of Paul's conversion, perhaps as early as A.D. 32. Thus, based on all these lines of evidence, within at least two years of Jesus' death, Jewish Christians may well have been confidently proclaiming his bodily resurrection.[32] What a far cry from revisionist reconstructions of Christian origins that assign all this to late, second-generation Hellenistic perversions of the story of Jesus!

CONCLUSION

In various places in this book we have seen evidence for (1) the general care the early Christians took to preserve accurate information about Jesus and (2) the authenticity of a broad cross-section of selections from the Gospel texts themselves. In this chapter we have focused primarily on (3) the testimony of other evidence outside the Gospels—the physical remains of archaeology and historical geography and the written references in other Christian and non-Christian authors. None of this adds up to proof for the total trustworthiness of the Gospel tradition. Neither does it demonstrate inspiration or inerrancy. Those who believe these theological affirmations of faith *deduce* them from other convictions about the nature of God and his revelation. There is a proper time and place for such affirmations, but they cannot be of much help in discussion with those who do not already share certain common presuppositions. This book has focused primarily on more *inductive* observations about the nature of the Gospel texts themselves, interpreted in light of a wide diversity of other ancient historical, theological, and literary data. Whatever else one may or may not believe by faith, on sheer historical grounds alone there is substantial reason to believe in the *general* trustworthiness of the Gospel tradition. Those who then go on by a "leap of faith" to accept the *entire* trustworthiness of that material do so not by flying in the face of the bulk of the evidence but by moving in a direction in which the evidence was already pointing.

FOR FURTHER STUDY

Archaelogy

Introductory

Blaiklock, E. M. *The Archaeology of the New Testament.* Nashville: Thomas Nelson, rev. 1984.

---

32. Cf. further Peter J. Kearney, "He Appeared to 500 Brothers (1 Cor. XV 6)," *NovT* 22 (1980): 264–84.

Blaiklock, E. M., and R. K. Harrison, eds. *The New International Dictionary of Biblical Archaeology.* Grand Rapids: Zondervan, 1983.
Riesner, Rainer. "Archeology and Geography," in *DJG*, 33–46.

Intermediate

Arav, Rami, and John J. Rousseau. *Jesus and His World: An Archaeological and Cultural Dictionary.* Minneapolis: Fortress, 1995.
Free, Joseph P. *Archaeology and Bible History.* Rev. & expd. by Howard F. Vos. Grand Rapids: Zondervan, 1992.
McRay, John. *Archaeology and the New Testament.* Grand Rapids: Baker, 1991.
Shanks, Hershel, and Dan P. Cole, eds. *Archaeology and the Bible: The Best of Biblical Archaeology Review.* 2 vols. Washington, D.C.: Biblical Archaeological Society, 1990.

Advanced

Finegan, Jack. *The Archeology of the New Testament.* Princeton: Princeton University Press, rev. 1992.

Other Ancient Sources

Introductory

Barnett, Paul. *Is the New Testament History?* London: Hodder & Stoughton, 1986.
Dunn, James D. G. *The Evidence for Jesus.* London: SCM; Philadelphia: Westminster, 1985.
Evans, Craig A. "Jesus in Non-Christian Sources," in *DJG*, 364–68.
France, R. T. *The Evidence for Jesus.* London: Hodder & Stoughton; Downers Grove: IVP, 1986.
Habermas, Gary R. *Ancient Evidence for the Life of Jesus.* Nashville: Thomas Nelson, rev. 1984.

Intermediate

Jeremias, Joachim. *Unknown Sayings of Jesus.* London: SPCK, rev. 1964.
Mason, Steve. *Josephus and the New Testament.* Peabody: Hendrickson, 1992.
Stroker, William D. *Extracanonical Sayings of Jesus.* Atlanta: Scholars, 1989.
Wenham, David., ed. *Gospel Perspectives.* Vol. 5, *The Jesus Tradition outside the Gospels.* Sheffield: JSOT, 1985.
Wenham, David. *Paul: Follower of Jesus or Founder of Christianity?* Grand Rapids and Cambridge: Eerdmans, 1995.

Advanced

Charlesworth, James H., and Craig A. Evans. "Jesus in the Agrapha and Apocryphal Gospels." In *Studying the Historical Jesus.* Ed. Bruce Chilton and Craig A. Evans. Leiden: Brill, 1994.
Evans, Craig A. "Jesus in Non-Christian Sources." In *Studying the Historical Jesus.* Ed. Bruce Chilton and Craig A. Evans. Leiden: Brill, 1994.
Klijn, A. F. J. *Jewish-Christian Gospel Tradition.* Leiden: Brill, 1992.
Meier, John P. *A Marginal Jew: Rethinking the Historical Jesus.* Vol. 1. New York and London: Doubleday, 1991.
Tuckett, C. M. *Nag Hammadi and the Gospel Tradition.* Edinburgh: T. & T. Clark, 1986.

Index

Evans, Craig A., Robert L. Webb, and Richard A. Wiebe. *Nag Hammadi Texts and the Bible: A Synopsis and Index.* Leiden: Brill, 1993.

Bibliography

Evans, Craig A. *Jesus.* IBR Bibliographies #5. Grand Rapids: Baker, 1992.

QUESTIONS FOR REVIEW

1. Itemize each of the main steps in constructing a case for the general historical trustworthiness of the Gospels.

2. Which of these steps seem most persuasive to you? least persuasive? Why? (Give reasons for each evaluation.)

CHAPTER NINETEEN

THE THEOLOGY OF JESUS

We have had neither the space nor adequate comparative data to argue for the authenticity of every portion of the Gospel tradition. But based on a presumption of the general trustworthiness of the major contours of the Gospels, particularly the Synoptics, and based more narrowly on those specific sayings, deeds, and themes of Jesus' ministry for which good arguments for their reliability can be marshaled, what may we conclude with reasonable probability about Jesus' own agenda and intentions? The answers to this question fall into several broad headings: Jesus announced the arrival of the kingdom, promoted high ethical standards for those who would be his followers, particularly in the area of social concern; and challenged many prevailing interpretations of the Law with a gospel ("good news") that was based fundamentally on his direct understanding of God's will rather than the written Scriptures of Israel (see below, pp. 392–396). While resembling other Jews of his day in a variety of ways, the specific mix of views and claims he put forward meshes neatly with no other known sect or party from the first century. Central to Jesus' distinctives were his convictions that he must die for the sins of the world and be vindicated by a subsequent resurrection and future return to earth in glory. Jesus' self-understanding is disclosed both by implicit claims and actions—suggesting a very high view of himself as God's unique agent mediating God's will to humanity—and by his use of and response to various christological titles—most notably Son of Man, Son of God, Lord, and Messiah. His reticence to accept acclamation with several of these does not diminish his strong self-image but reflects conventional stereotypes attached to the titles that did not characterize Jesus' own understanding of his mission.

Whether as a historian or as a believer, the diligent student of this first-century Jew from Nazareth is confronted with a man who fits no conventional religious categories. It quickly becomes clear why the Gospel writers (most notably John) and Christians in the next several centuries came to the conviction that Jesus was the unique God-man who made salvation available for all, but who required a response from every person, on which his or her eternal destiny would hinge.

KINGDOM

It is widely agreed that the heart of Jesus' authentic message centers on the *kingdom of God*. The term never appears in the Old Testament, but the concept of God as king and sovereign is pervasive throughout it, especially among the promises to David and in the Book of Daniel. In the intertestamental period, the term was frequently used to refer to God's regal power, often in the context of some kind of hope for the restoration of a literal Davidic kingship to Israel. Jesus developed the idea of the kingdom as the *in-breaking of God into history to realize his redemptive purposes* but dissociated his current ministry from the establishment of a politically free Israel. For Jesus the kingdom was a reign more than a realm, a power rather than a place. Yet inasmuch as he created a community of his followers, one may speak of the kingdom particularly manifested in the group of disciples that would form the nucleus of the church. Perhaps the English word "dominion" best captures the implied combination of sovereign authority with a group of subjects confessing allegiance to their sovereign.[1]

Jesus' teachings about the kingdom can be variously categorized. E. P. Sanders identifies six groups of sayings, with the kingdom described as (a) a covenant into which one enters; (b) a future entity yet to be fully established; (c) an unexpected coming event separating the righteous from the wicked; (d) the establishment of a recognizable social order; (e) a present experience of Jesus' words and deeds; and (f) a characteristic of God and his reign as kingly.[2] Most scholars simplify the discussion, comparing and contrasting merely *the present and future aspects of God's reign*. This consensus has emerged after several previous periods of scholarship. The nineteenth century's various sociopolitical interpretations of the kingdom gave way to Albert Schweitzer's "consistent eschatology"—the kingdom as entirely future—at the beginning of the twentieth century. In the 1930s, C. H. Dodd swung the pendulum to the opposite extreme, arguing for entirely "realized eschatology"—the kingdom as fully present. But today, most follow Joachim Jeremias' "eschatology in the process of being realized," and admit both present and future dimensions to the kingdom.[3] "Already but not yet" is a helpful slogan that encapsulates this combination of perspectives.

---

1. Cf., e.g., Ben Witherington III, *The Christology of Jesus* (Minneapolis: Fortress, 1990), 197–98.

2. E. P. Sanders, *Jesus and Judaism* (London: SCM; Philadelphia: Fortress, 1985), 141–50.

3. For a full survey of these various developments, see Wendell Willis, ed., *The Kingdom of God in 20th Century Interpretation* (Peabody: Hendrickson, 1987). As noted above, p. 233, n. 2, there is a more avant-garde school of interpretation that favors a non-eschatological view of the kingdom. Some in their midst even argue that they have now attained a consensus (e.g., Marcus Borg, *Jesus in Contemporary Scholarship* [Valley Forge: TPI, 1994], esp. 47–96), but in fact they would still seem to be in a small minority. Borg has demonstrated that few still believe in an interpretation of Jesus' teaching exactly like Schweitzer's, i.e., that the kingdom's full establishment was so imminent for Jesus that he turned out to be mistaken. But rejecting Schweitzer by no means implies that most have rejected all forms of apocalyptic or eschatology as central to Jesus' message in general or kingdom teaching in particular.

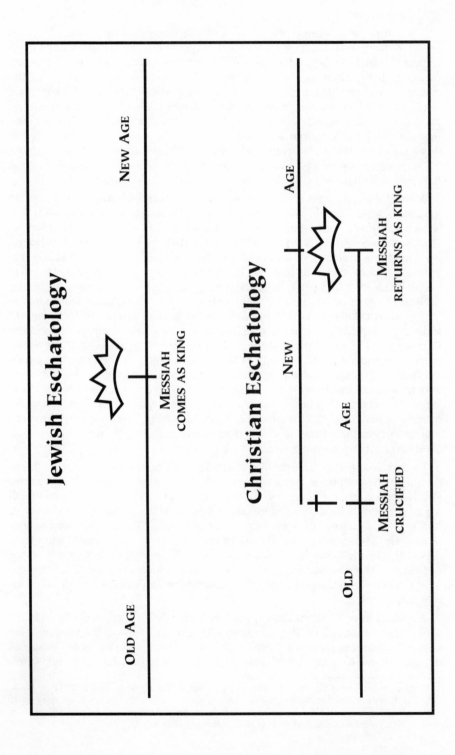

The future dimensions of the kingdom for Jesus most closely match previous Jewish expectation. The Last Supper foreshadows the messianic banquet envisioned in Isaiah 25:6–9, which is also depicted in Jesus' parables of feasting (Matt. 22:1–14; Luke 14:15–24). Jesus teaches his disciples to pray for the coming kingdom (Matt. 6:10). He promises to give his "little flock" a kingdom, when they will judge the twelve tribes of Israel (Luke 12:32; 22:28–30) and warns the crowds against a belief in its immediate appearance (19:11). He contrasts entering the kingdom with being thrown into hell as two possible future destinies (Mark 9:47). Enjoying God's reign is likened to an inheritance (Matt. 5:20) or a future state into which one enters (Matt. 25:31–46). It is part of what happens at Judgment Day (Matt. 7:21–23; 25:1–13; Luke 21:31).

More striking, however, are the present dimensions of Jesus' teaching on the kingdom, which would have stood out against his Jewish background. The "headline" of his entire ministry is the call to repent because the kingdom of God is at hand or has drawn near (Mark 1:15; Matt. 4:23; Luke 4:43). It is bound up with Jesus' ministry of exorcism and the vanquishing of Satan (Luke 9:1; 10:18–19), demonstrating that the kingdom has come upon those in Jesus' audience (Matt. 12:28 par.). In Jesus' person, God's reign appears even in the midst of his enemies (Luke 17:20–21). One can enter it, in part at least, already in the present (Luke 16:16), by humbling oneself as a child (Mark 10:15 pars.).[4] Indeed the kingdom era has been present ever since the ministry of John the Baptist (Matt. 11:11–12 par.). More general statements speak also of the fulfillment of prophecy in the ministry of Jesus as a pointer to the arrival of a new era (Luke 4:21; Matt. 11:4–6 par.), into which certain Pharisees and scribes prevent many from entering (Matt. 23:13). In short, with the coming of Jesus a new stage of God asserting his power over the cosmos had arrived. God's people, namely Jesus' disciples, were thus given a greater and more permanent empowerment than Israel of old had received. Still, the full purposes of God for us and for the universe await future fulfillment.

Understanding this combination of future and present elements of the kingdom gives us both hope and a certain realism about the Christian life and task. On the one hand, we dare not underestimate how much we can accomplish for God when yielded to his Spirit. He wants to create an outpost or colony of heaven—of the world to come—in our lives individually and corporately now in this age. Thus we become the salt of the earth and light of the world (Matt. 5:14–16). On the other hand, we dare not underestimate the strength of the opposition. We will not Christianize the earth or establish God's righteousness in any wholesale way in this life; that remains for Jesus himself to do after his return.[5]

A related topic involves the expression Jesus uses in Mark 4:11–12 and parallels—the "mystery" of the kingdom. A popular old-line dispensationalist approach that still has widespread influence at the grassroots level imagines that Jesus came to offer a literal, earthly, sociopolitical kingdom to Israel. When

---

4. On the recurring theme of "entering the kingdom," see esp. Joel Marcus, "Entering into the Kingly Power of God," *JBL* 107 (1988): 663–75, who shows how frequently this expression refers to human participation in God's already present activity in the world.

5. For detailed application of these themes to one area in which many readers of this book will be involved, see Craig L. Blomberg, "The Kingdom of God and Evangelical Theological Education," *Didaskalia* 6.2 (1995): 14–35.

the nation rejected that offer, God fell back on "plan B" as it were—the "mystery form of the kingdom"—that is, the multiethnic church. From this point on, Jesus spoke to the crowds only in parables, so that they might not understand (Matt. 13). But one day, after his return, Jesus will again literally establish Israel as a nation under his kingship.

This view, however, does not do justice to the data of the Gospels, as most contemporary dispensationalist scholars themselves are admitting.[6] Jesus came first of all to die a redemptive death for humanity; establishing an earthly kingdom for Israel would have short-circuited this necessary prerequisite. In context, the mystery of the kingdom is elucidated by the parables of Mark 4 and Matthew 13 that describe the surprising endings that come from inauspicious beginnings (the so-called parables of growth). Jesus does not speak in parables for the first time here (cf. Matt. 7:24–27), while as late as the last week in his life his opponents are still understanding his parabolic claims quite well, at least at the cognitive level (Mark 12:12). Jesus' calling of twelve apostles suggests that he intended to create a "new Israel" out of the community of his followers from the outset. It is best, therefore, to recognize the mystery of the kingdom—the secret now revealed—as nothing more and nothing less than the fact that *the kingdom of God is present in the ministry of Christ but not with irresistible power.*[7]

A final reminder that the kingdom does not refer primarily to a future Jewish realm comes with Paul's use of the term in letters to predominantly Gentile Christians about the blessings of the Christian life presently available: righteousness, peace, and joy in the Holy Spirit (Rom. 14:17); spiritual power (1 Cor. 4:20); departure from the kingdom of darkness (Col. 1:13); and cooperative work with the apostles (Col. 4:11).

Nor does the old supposed distinction between "kingdom of God" and "kingdom of heaven" withstand any careful exegetical scrutiny. "Heaven" was a well-known Jewish euphemism for "God" (cf., e.g., Luke 15:21). The two terms are used interchangeably (along with inheriting "eternal life" and being "saved") in Matthew 19:23 and 24 (cf. vv. 16, 25). And numerous passages in Matthew (the only Gospel to use "kingdom of heaven") are exactly paralleled in Mark or Luke with no substantive differences save the expression "kingdom of God" (cf., e.g., Matt. 4:17 with Mark 1:14–15; Matt. 5:3 with Luke 6:20; Matt. 8:11 with Luke 13:29; Matt. 13:11 with Mark 4:11; Matt. 13:31 with Mark 4:30; Matt. 19:14 with Mark 10:14; and Matt. 19:23 with Mark 10:23.

The kingdom of God (or heaven) is thus not identical to the church—the *kingdom is a power; the church is a people.* That explains how Jesus can describe the field in the parable of the wheat and the weeds alternately as the "world" and the "kingdom" (Matt. 13:38, 41). God's sovereign power extends over all the cosmos, even though not all persons and powers in the universe yet acknowledge that fact. But there remains substantial overlap between the two entities, inasmuch as the church is the collection of persons who individ-

---

6. See esp. Robert L. Saucy, *The Case for Progressive Dispensationalism* (Grand Rapids: Zondervan, 1993); Craig A. Blaising and Darrell L. Bock, *Progressive Dispensationalism* (Wheaton: Victor, 1993).

7. George E. Ladd, *The Gospel of the Kingdom* (Grand Rapids: Eerdmans; Exeter: Paternoster, 1959), 56. Against the postponed kingdom theory more generally, see idem, *Crucial Questions about the Kingdom of God* (Grand Rapids: Eerdmans, 1952), 101–17.

ually submit to God's reign. Ladd aptly summarizes the relationship under five headings: the church is not the kingdom; the kingdom creates the church; the church witnesses to the kingdom; the church is the instrument of the kingdom; and the church is the custodian of the kingdom. He also notes the resultant picture of the God of this kingdom: a father who seeks, invites, and yet judges.[8]

ETHICS

General Principles

The combination of petitions in the Lord's Prayer, "Thy kingdom come, thy will be done," shows how closely the topics of kingdom and ethics are related. God's kingly rule is fully established on earth precisely when his righteous standards are implemented. The ethics of the kingdom thus refer to *the accomplishment of God's will in every area of life.* The believers' task is to seek first his kingdom and its righteousness; then all their needs will be met (Matt. 6:33 par.).

Does this then lead to works-righteousness? There are two seemingly competing strands of thought in Jesus' teaching about his followers' behavior. On the one hand, many passages command us to do good—to pursue righteousness, live a life of discipleship, and imitate Jesus. The Sermon on the Mount is summed up in the righteousness demanded of us that is greater than that exhibited by the Jewish leaders (Matt. 5:20). We are told to enter by the narrow gate, anticipating the stringency of this life of discipleship (Matt. 7:13). God's forgiveness of us is in some way contingent on our forgiveness of others (Matt. 6:12, 14–15). And we must be prepared to sacrifice everything (Matt. 13:44–46) in unqualified commitment to the gospel (Luke 14:25–33).

On the other hand, Jesus makes it equally clear that a life of discipleship is a life of faith. The starting point is repentance that leads to belief in the good news Jesus preaches (Mark 1:15). We confess this belief publicly (Luke 12:3) and receive God's kingdom as a gift (v. 32). Frequently Jesus praises the faith of those who come in trust to him—most notably the centurion with a sick servant (Matt. 8:10), but also several others who believe Jesus can heal them or their loved ones (Matt. 9:22, 29; 15:28). Indeed, the refrain "your faith has made you whole" appears in four different contexts in the Gospels to refer to a combination of physical and spiritual healing (Mark 5:34 pars.; Mark 10:52 par.; Luke 7:50; 17:19).[9] The little parable of the unprofitable servant beautifully summarizes a theology of grace (Luke 17:7–10), while the story of the Pharisee and tax collector anticipates Pauline language about justification by faith (18:9–14). The parable of the laborers in the vineyard makes it clear that believers do not work for a wage and that heavenly reward is the great equalizer, but it is the equality of perfection![10] Finally, the thief on the cross stands as the

---

8. *Idem, A Theology of the New Testament,* rev. Donald A. Hagner (Grand Rapids: Eerdmans, 1993), 109–17, 80–88.

9. For elaboration, cf. Craig L. Blomberg, "'Your Faith Has Made You Whole': The Evangelical Liberation Theology of Jesus," in *Jesus of Nazareth: Lord and Christ,* ed. Joel B. Green and Max Turner (Carlisle: Paternoster; Grand Rapids: Eerdmans, 1994), 75–93.

10. On which, cf. further *idem,* "Degrees of Reward in the Kingdom of Heaven?" *JETS* 35 (1992): 159–72.

crowning example of one who didn't have time to do good works by which he might try to merit salvation.

How do we resolve the potential tension between these two strands of texts from Jesus? Precisely by recognizing the context of the demands Jesus makes. In most instances, as with the Sermon on the Mount, these are addressed primarily to those who have already begun to follow him in discipleship. Character precedes conduct (Matt. 7:16–20). Recognition of the forgiveness God gives enables us to forgive others (Luke 6:36; Matt. 18:23–35). The greater righteousness Christ demands is not an entrance requirement to get into the kingdom but *a lifestyle characteristic that God enables those who come to him in Christ increasingly to approximate.*[11] Thus, paradoxically, he can speak of his requirements as an easy yoke and a light burden (Matt. 11:30). The foundational motive for obeying Jesus thus becomes one of profound gratitude for what he has done for us that we could never have performed or deserved on our own. This leads to a radical commitment, a renunciation of our own rights (Mark 8:34–38 pars.), where the only rewards that are given are to those who are not looking for them (Luke 14:7–14).

The centerpiece of Jesus' ethic is love: the twofold command to love God and neighbor (Mark 12:29–31 par.) and the reminder that neighbors include even our enemies (Luke 10:25–37; cf. Luke 6:35). The gospel calls us to confront all tribalism, nationalism, or ethnocentrism that would value allegiance to human groups above cross-cultural *agapē* for all people and especially all fellow Christians. Unlike various negative prohibitions, the positive command to love can never be said to have been perfectly kept. Modeling our love upon God's leads us to reject every form of judgmentalism (Matt. 7:1) and to treat others exactly as we, in our best moments, would want to be treated (v. 12). Whether or not enemy-love leads to full-fledged pacifism, it certainly should stir us to move heaven and earth to promote "just peacemaking," that is, doing everything within our power to reconcile alienated persons to God and to one another.[12] In short, our lives are lived in loving service for others, at the risk of suffering and, if necessary, to the point of death (John 15:12–13).

Numerous topics receive concentrated focus in Jesus' ethical teaching. One involves "family values."[13] On the one hand we are commanded to unswerving, lifelong loyalty and faithfulness to our spouses and children if we have them. Jesus gives wives and children a dignity unparalleled in his culture (Mark 10:1–16 pars.). On the other hand our love for our families is to seem like hate in comparison with our love for God (Luke 14:26 par., Mark 3:31–35 pars.), and singleness may also be a gift from God (Matt. 19:10–12). Other topics that receive extended attention include personal integrity (Matt. 5:33–37; 7:1–6; 23:1–39); bold, persistent, faith-filled prayer (Luke 11:1–13; 18:1–14; Mark 11:22–25); humility, considered more a vice than a virtue in Greco-Roman society (Matt. 18:1–5; Mark 9:33–37; 10:13–16; Luke 17:7–10);[14] paying taxes, though neither Jewish nor Roman claims may be considered absolute

---

11. Cf. further Robert A. Guelich, "The Matthean Beatitudes: 'Entrance-Requirements' or Eschatological Blessings?" *JBL* 95 (1976): 415–34.

12. See esp. Glen H. Stassen, *Just Peacemaking* (Louisville: Westminster/John Knox, 1992).

13. Cf. esp. Stephen C. Barton, *Discipleship and Family Ties in Mark and Matthew* (Cambridge: CUP, 1994).

14. On which, see esp. Craig A. Evans, "Jesus' Ethic of Humility," *Trinity Journal* n.s. 13 (1992): 127–38.

(Matt. 17:24–27; Mark 12:13–17 pars.); and rejecting the Jewish rituals that served as badges of national identity (see below, p. 394). But eclipsing all these is a cluster of topics united under the theme of social concern: mercy, justice, stewardship, and the like.

Social Concern

Jesus was never overtly political in the sense that he attempted to wield or usurp earthly power or promote a particular political party or socioeconomic program. When his followers tried by force to make him king, he fled (John 6:15). When his teachings about preparation for danger were misinterpreted in Gethsemane, he healed the wound that Peter's sword had inflicted (Luke 22:51). Although he cleared the temple, this was a minor protest with no lasting effect, intended more to portend the temple's doom than create systemic change. Hence, he was neither a social revolutionary nor a reformer in the contemporary senses of those terms. Partly, this was because he knew the climactic focus of his mission was to die for the sins of the world. But partly it was also because he was too radical to settle for a *merely* structural reform; he knew regenerated hearts were the prerequisite to lasting social or economic redistribution of resources. Nevertheless, he called his listeners to observe the weightier matters of the Law, which he defined, à la Micah 6:8, as justice, mercy, and faithfulness (Matt. 23:23)—the epitome of social concern. We misrepresent his ethic of nonviolence and nonretaliation if we label it one of passivity; he is better likened to the Old Testament prophets whose strong denunciations of the injustice they saw called on others to practice God's righteous standards.[15]

In rejecting institutional power, Jesus called on his followers to lead as servants, not in the authoritarian fashion of the Roman world around them (Luke 22:25–27). He promoted "the upside-down kingdom,"[16] seeking to save the lost and outcast of his society and calling his followers to do the same. Nevertheless, he never endorsed the state uncritically (cf. his two major injunctions on the Jewish and Roman tax just noted). But he saw the possibility of lasting change for the better in this world not through government, not even through individuals, but through the collective body of his followers that came to be known as the church. Hauerwas and Willimon put it succinctly: "The church does not have a social strategy, the church *is* a social strategy."[17] In the history of Protestantism, we have seen attempts at creating a Christian state (esp. through Calvinism) and a focus on individual repentance and Christian living (esp. through Luther), but it is the Anabaptist vision of *the church corporately as the model of implementing the ethics of God's kingdom* that best approximates the contexts and intentions of Jesus' teachings.

In Jesus' world, his option was a *via media* between the retreatism of the Essenes and the revolutionary fervor of the Zealots. In his objectives he was probably closest to the Pharisees—wanting God's people to live their entire lives by his will—but Jesus' methods differed sharply. Although the categories are Paul's,

---

15. See, e.g., Walter Wink, "Neither Passivity nor Violence: Jesus' Third Way (Matt. 5:38–42/Luke 6:29–30)," *Forum* 7 (1991): 5–28.

16. The title of an outstanding little book on the topic by Donald B. Kraybill (Scottdale: Herald, 1978).

17. Stanley Hauerwas and William H. Willimon, *Resident Aliens* (Nashville: Abingdon, 1989), 43.

they fit Jesus' life as well: empowerment not by the Law but by the Spirit. When any community catches the vision for the possibilities of living this way, the established political and religious leaders will often be threatened because their impotence to create similar improvements is highlighted by contrast.

Mercy and justice were key concerns throughout Christ's life. John's and Jesus' ministries had been predicted to be ones of reconstituting Israel along the lines of these attributes (Luke 1:17, 50, 72), and John's own teaching on these topics ultimately cost him his life (Luke 3:10–14, 19). Jesus' inaugural sermon in Nazareth outlined his manifesto: good news to the poor, release to the captives, sight to the blind, liberty to the oppressed, and a declaration of the year of jubilee (Luke 4:16–21). His holistic ministry of healing spirit and body concentrated in particular on the social outcast, the poor, Samaritans, Gentiles, women, children, and the sick (especially the "untouchable" lepers). His parables highlighted God's grace and mercy (Luke 15:1–32) but also God's desire for social justice (Luke 18:1–8) that transcends all cultural distinctions (Luke 10:25–37; John 4:1–42).

Yet the area about which he taught most was that of *stewardship of our material possessions*.[18] One cannot serve both God and money (Matt. 6:19–34 par.). Blessed are those materially poor whose poverty drives them to utter dependence on God (Luke 6:20; Matt. 5:3). Beware of covetousness or needless accumulation of wealth (Luke 12:13–21) and of living in luxury while the poor of the world go begging (Luke 16:19–31). Use worldly wealth for eternal purposes (Luke 16:1–13). No one percentage for giving is established (recall the trio of passages in Luke 18:18–30; 19:1–10, 11–27), but in every instance all possessions are ultimately the Lord's. Doubtless the most haunting question of all comes in Mark 8:36: "What good is it for a man to gain the whole world, yet forfeit his soul?"

Implementing Jesus' kingdom ethics, especially his ethics of social concern, particularly in a modern democratic society unlike the first-century Roman world, requires considerable sensitivity and sophistication. Surely we have the right and responsibility as much as anyone to pursue what we believe will promote our "common good," but we dare never count on legislation or political parties to accomplish what only God's people functioning as the church can do. We must seek a completely pro-life agenda, trying to prevent abortion and to avoid endorsing sexual sin or glamorizing dysfunctional family life, but at the same time we must work for the best quality of life for those already born, including adequate health care for the poor, housing for the homeless, jobs for the unemployed, and positive alternatives for those lured by a life of crime.[19] We must demonstrate genuine concern for the rape of the environment, which is also God's creation. In societies, including our own, where racism, sexism, classism, and ethnocentrism still alienate millions of people from one another and do not give everyone equal opportunities for basic human rights, we must oppose injustice and promote the liberation of the oppressed. But we dare

18. On which see further Craig L. Blomberg, *Give Me Neither Poverty Nor Riches: A New Testament Theology of Material Possessions* (Leicester: IVP; Grand Rapids: Eerdmans, forthcoming).
19. Cf. Ronald J. Sider, *Completely Pro-Life* (Downers Grove: IVP, 1987).

never assume that these are ends in themselves, lest people gain earthly freedoms without being prepared for eternity by being followers of Jesus Christ.[20]

LAW AND GOSPEL

It is clear from our discussions throughout this book that all of Jesus' ethical
teachings need to be understood in their historical context. All contain timeless
principles, but not all may be applied in our world today in the identical way
they were in his. But what of the relationship between Jesus' teaching and the
Old Testament Scriptures? Here, too, radical changes took place. Although
Jesus clearly stands for various abiding moral absolutes, he has not given us a
new Law. Although many of the principles of the Torah carry over into the
New Testament age, we cannot take any command of Moses and assume that
it applies to believers until we understand how it has been fulfilled in Christ.
It is striking how rarely Jesus ever invokes the Hebrew Scriptures as his authority; indeed, most of the time he cites the Old Testament merely as a foil or contrast for his own teaching! All of these observations now require some
unpacking.

The relationship between Jesus' teaching and Old Testament Law has been
variously categorized. Some have indeed spoken of him creating a new law;
others of him abrogating the old. Mediating positions suggest that Jesus transcends, expounds, obeys, radicalizes, intensifies, or internalizes the Law. All of
these approaches can find support in certain passages but run afoul of others.
The most consistent and valid approach would seem to follow from Jesus' own
words in Matthew 5:17: *he came to fulfill the Law*—"by teaching the eschatological will of God which the Law anticipated."[21] For the Christian to apply any
passage of the Old Testament today requires filtering it through the grid of how
Jesus' teaching and ministry did or did not change the nature of God's demands
on his people.[22]

Jesus' appeals to the Old Testament are neither systematic nor anything like
a representative cross-section of its contents. We have noted above that in the
six antitheses of the Sermon on the Mount (Matt. 5:21–48), he internalizes and
intensifies the commands about murder, adultery, and enemy love, yet seemingly abrogates certain parts of the stipulations about divorce, oaths, and retaliation (p. 250). In every case, however, Jesus shows himself to be the Law's
sovereign and authoritative interpreter (cf. 7:28–29). There is no evidence that
Jesus ever actually broke one of the written laws of the Pentateuch or taught

---

20. At its best moments, liberation theology has captured this balance; one can even speak of an evangelical liberation theology.
Cf., e.g., Thomas D. Hanks, *God So Loved the Third World* (Maryknoll: Orbis, 1983). More often than not, however, in reacting against
an excessive spiritualization of the gospel, it has swung the pendulum in the opposite direction in favor of an excessive politicization.
But who are we to say that we might not (or even should not) react in the same way if we found ourselves in the desperate physical
plight of many in today's Third World, as well as America's inner cities? For a good survey of representative perspectives about Jesus in
liberation theology, see Claus Bussmann, *Who Do You Say? Jesus Christ in Latin American Theology* (Maryknoll: Orbis, 1984). For
a survey of perspectives around the entire world, cf. Priscilla Pope-Levison and John R. Levison, *Jesus in Global Context* (Louisville:
Westminster/John Knox, 1992).

21. For both categories and conclusion, see Douglas J. Moo, "Jesus and the Authority of the Mosaic Law," *JSNT* 20 (1984): 3–49.

22. Cf. further William W. Klein, Craig L. Blomberg, and Robert L. Hubbard, Jr., *Introduction to Biblical Interpretation* (Dallas
and London: Word, 1993), 278–83; David A. Dorsey, "The Law of Moses and the Christian: A Compromise," *JETS* 34 (1991): 321–34.

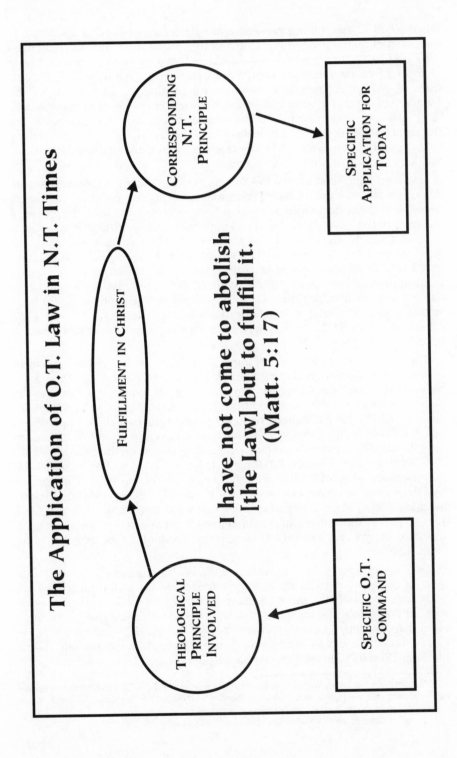

The Application of O.T. Law in N.T. Times

CORRESPONDING N.T. PRINCIPLE

SPECIFIC APPLICATION FOR TODAY

FULFILLMENT IN CHRIST

I have not come to abolish [the Law] but to fulfill it. (Matt. 5:17)

THEOLOGICAL PRINCIPLE INVOLVED

SPECIFIC O.T. COMMAND

others to do so, but still the impression we get is far more one of discontinuity than of continuity between the Law and the gospel. Certainly he challenged the better part of the "traditions of the elders," so dear to the Pharisees. Those areas in which he seemingly kept various parts of the oral law—specific features of synagogue attendance and festival pilgrimage, the wearing of the fringes, and various prayers and postures at mealtimes—seem to involve standard Jewish custom more than adherence to specific Pharisaic practice.[23] But the ritual badges of Jewish nationalism came under strong attack, particularly Sabbath and kosher laws, and other traditions that ostracized certain persons and kept them as second-class citizens.

Jesus' teachings concerning the Sabbath are particularly important because this command was one of the "Ten Commandments" on which all the others rested. It will not do simply to say that Jesus complained about the abuse of the spirit of the Sabbath by the nitpicking Pharisaical *halakah*, for he appeals to more foundational principles in his criticism: "The Sabbath was made for man" (Mark 2:27), "The Son of Man is Lord even of the Sabbath" (v. 28), and "It is lawful to do good on the Sabbath" (Matt. 12:12). Christians in the coming generation would interpret Jesus as having abolished the need for a mandatory day of the week in which they had to stop working. The Sabbath was fulfilled as they rested "in Christ" throughout their Christian lives (Col. 2:16–17; Heb. 4:1–11). Matthew 11:28–30 may well have set the precedent for this perspective.[24]

The same kind of far-reaching implications stem from Jesus' treatment of handwashing, kosher, and *corban* laws (Mark 7:1–23 par.). At least Mark believed that the later Christian conviction that all foods (and therefore all people) were now clean stemmed from Jesus' own mandate in these controversies with the Jewish leaders, however poorly understood the implications may have been at the time (v. 19b). Jesus seems even to go out of his way to provoke such controversies, deliberately healing people on the Sabbath whose lives were not at risk (Mark 3:1–6 pars.; Luke 13:10–17; 14:1–6; John 5:1–18; 9:1–41), associating and eating with the ritually unclean in ways that scandalized the scribes and Pharisees (Mark 2:13–17 pars.; Luke 7:36–50; 19:1–10), and touching a leper to heal him when a spoken word might have sufficed (Mark 1:40–45 pars.). The attitude that enabled Jesus to act in such a "cavalier" fashion was apparently a very exalted self-image: "one greater than the temple is here" (Matt. 12:6).

The Gospel writers, too, regularly see the events of Jesus' life as the fulfillment of Scripture, particularly in the clusters of details surrounding his birth and death. Occasionally, these are the relatively direct fulfillments of straightforward prediction (the birth in Bethlehem or the triumphal entry), but more often than not they employ typology (see above, pp. 199–200). Jesus is likened—though viewed as superior—to Jonah, Solomon, David, the priesthood, Elijah and Elisha, and Israel as a whole (esp. in his temptations, suffering, and

---

23. Cf. Robert Banks, *Jesus and the Law in the Synoptic Tradition* (Cambridge: CUP, 1975), 237: Jesus' observation or nonobservation of customary practices did not arise from an attitude of reverence or lack of reverence to the practices themselves. It derives from the compatibility or incompatibility of such with the purposes of his ministry.

24. Cf. esp. D. A. Carson, ed., *From Sabbath to Lord's Day* (Grand Rapids: Zondervan, 1982).

resurrection on the third day). Disciples are viewed typologically, too, as in the employment of Psalm 37:11 in Matthew 5:5; the same is true of Jesus' opponents (cf. Mark 4:12 with Isa. 6:9–10). Jesus' messianic image is taken from Scripture as well—the Good Shepherd, the Son of Man, the Suffering Servant.[25]

At least some of the inspiration for the evangelists' use of Scripture came from Jesus himself. Among the more indisputably authentic parts of the Jesus-tradition are the parable of the wicked tenants (Mark 12:1–12, reapplying Isaiah's vineyard metaphor—Isa. 5:1–7), his question about how David's son could also be his lord (Mark 12:35–37, based on Ps. 110:1), and his summary of the heart of the Law with the double love-command (Mark 12:28–34, citing Deut. 6:4–5 and Lev. 19:18). But often his use of the Old Testament is creative and polemical—finding the resurrection in the Pentateuch (Mark 12:26–27, citing Exod. 3:6), labeling the temple a den of robbers (Mark 11:17, citing Jer. 7:11), or reapplying Daniel's "abomination of desolation" to the destruction of that very edifice (Mark 13 pars.).

So, too, the *form* of Jesus' teaching often closely approximates standard Jewish conventions, even while the *contents* may vary noticeably. Thus Christ uses a large array of Jewish exegetical techniques, prefers parables and related metaphors, and interprets Scriptures as messianic that usually have some Jewish precedent of being taken this way, even if only among a minority of interpreters. Yet the heart of his message is not the exegesis of Scripture but the announcement of the arrival of God's reign and his Messiah. And the nature of his ethical teachings differs radically from Law, which is characterized by apodictic or casuistic rules and regulations.[26] Strikingly, it is seldom possible to claim that (or even to know if) one has obeyed one of Jesus' mandates because of its open-ended, wide-ranging, principial nature—love your enemies, do good on the Sabbath, use your money for kingdom purposes, and so on. To the extent that Jesus has brought a new covenant "written on the heart," formerly external statutes have been internalized. To the extent that Jesus brought a new empowerment—the Holy Spirit—the laws have become personalized. Thus Douglas Moo can define the "law of Christ" (as in Gal. 6:2) as *not* "legal prescriptions and ordinances," *but* "the teaching and example of Jesus and the apostles, the central demonstration of love, and the guiding influence of the indwelling Holy Spirit."[27]

Yet, although no teaching of Jesus is ever called *nomos* (law) in the Gospels, his ethical instructions are referred to, especially in John, as *entolai* (commandments). Jesus still believes in moral absolutes. As Stephen Westerholm explains: "[Jesus] found the will of God not in statutes but in a heart in tune with the divine purposes. . . . [Nevertheless] certain activities are in themselves so utterly opposed to the divine intention that it is impossible for one whose heart is sensitive to it to engage in them."[28]

---

25. For a comprehensive list of these various direct and typological uses of the Old Testament, see R. T. France, *Jesus and the Old Testament* (London: Tyndale; Downers Grove: IVP, 1971).

26. Apodictic laws are the "thou shalts" or "thou shalt nots." Casuistic laws refer to specific cases ("if such-and-such, then do this-or-that").

27. Douglas J. Moo, "The Law of Christ as the Fulfillment of the Law of Moses: A Modified Lutheran View," in *The Law, the Gospel, and the Modern Christian: Five Views*, ed. Wayne G. Strickland (Grand Rapids: Zondervan, 1993), 343. The book more generally is an outstanding tool for comparing five major Christian approaches to the relationship between Law and Gospel.

28. Stephen Westerholm, *Jesus and Scribal Authority* (Lund: Gleerup, 1978), 91, 124.

But these activities are not the external dos and don'ts of so many contemporary "Christian" lists, but foundational principles such as spouses loving each other until death parts them, consistent stewardship of one's treasures, and reconciling previously estranged groups of people, especially within Christian fellowship.

It is clear, finally, that Jesus' attitude to the Law cannot be summed up merely in the popular Christian categorization that claims he kept the moral law while abolishing the ceremonial or civil law. Jesus continues to be concerned for every arena of life—he, too, promoted rituals or ceremonies (baptism and the Lord's Supper) and recognized a legitimate role for governments (in levying taxes). In overturning a literal implementation of the Sabbath he challenged the heart of Israel's moral law, yet the gospel is fundamentally moral itself. On the other hand, one can, with Jesus, speak of weightier matters of the Law that should be given priority—justice, mercy, and faithfulness (Matt. 23:23). So, in the end, there is profound truth to the saying made famous by Augustine, Luther, and many others that the demands of the gospel boil down to "love God and do as you please." When one truly loves God, having been born again and choosing to yield oneself to the empowerment of the Spirit, one will do what pleases him.

JESUS AND JUDAISM

The previous section has already pointed out several similarities and differences between Jesus and other Jews of his day. The topic deserves further attention, however. The last generation of scholarship has seen a considerable resurgence of interest by both Christian and Jewish scholars in the topic, "Jesus the Jew."[29] A renewed scrutiny of ancient Jewish literature coupled with a flurry of archaeological discoveries has increasingly demonstrated the diversity of Judaism in the time of Jesus. On the one hand, it has become clear just how thoroughly Jewish Jesus and his disciples were. Hebrew or Aramaic idiom can be reconstructed behind a substantial percentage of Jesus' teachings. Christ used many of the identical teaching methods and observed many of the same customs of his culture. Parallels to numerous individual teachings of Jesus can be found in other Jewish literature, and, as noted above (pp. 182–182), his itinerant ministry of healing resembled that of various other "charismatic" Jewish miracle-workers and exorcists of his day.[30] Our appreciation of how previous Christian portrayals of the Pharisees and other Jewish leaders have often relied on caricature and overgeneralization (above, pp. 47–48) also helps to narrow the gap between Jesus and other Jewish teachers of his time.

A considerable amount of Jesus-scholarship narrows this gap further, however, by jettisoning substantial portions of the Gospels as inauthentic. If one accepts the general trustworthiness of the gospel tradition, we must admit

---

29. For an excellent survey from an evangelical perspective, see Donald A. Hagner, *The Jewish Reclamation of Jesus* (Grand Rapids: Zondervan, 1984). For an update from a more ecumenical perspective, cf. James H. Charlesworth, ed., *Jesus' Jewishness* (New York: Crossroad, 1991).

30. Irving Zeitlin (*Jesus and the Judaism of His Time* [Oxford: Blackwell, 1988], 61) uses the label "charismatic religious virtuoso." Cf. further Geza Vermes, *Jesus the Jew* (London: Collins, 1973; Philadelphia: Fortress, 1974).

significant differences between Jesus and his contemporaries as well. Not only did he make indirect and direct messianic claims, in and of themselves not always unique, but he also linked himself with God as his Father more closely than most of the religious leadership could tolerate (see below, pp. 401–407). Yet Jewish monotheism was defined flexibly enough at that stage to permit even this, in principle, which explains how Jesus came to have *any* Jewish followers at all (recall p. 42).

The way for scholarship to progress in this arena is to recognize that one can accept the Gospels' portrait of Jesus as it stands *and still* see Jesus as thoroughly Jewish, however unconventional or surprising a form of Judaism he at times manifested. There is no evidence that Jesus ever intended to found a new religion. But he certainly did intend to shatter the ethnocentric boundaries of his day, to set the stage for the Gentile mission, in keeping with the Old Testament theme of Israel as a light to the nations (Isa. 42:6), which began already with the promise to Abraham that by his seed all nations would be blessed (Gen. 12:1–3).[31] Indeed, a considerable impetus for the "parting of the ways" between Judaism and early Christianity came after the destruction of the temple—as Rabbinic Judaism began to emerge from the Pharisaic movement as the sole, main survivor among the much greater diversity of pre-70 *Judaisms*, and was noticeably less willing to accept the Jesus-movement as an authentic expression of Judaism than many pre-70 Jews (including Christian Jews) had been.[32]

How did Jesus compare with the various Jewish sects? There are similarities and differences with each, as well as scholars who have attempted to identify Jesus with each. Possible links with *Essenism* include Jesus' techniques of biblical interpretation, apocalyptic focus, rejection of the rest of Judaism as corrupt, dissociation from the temple, and formation of a new community as the true Israel carrying out the will of God. Yet Jesus' emphases directly opposed the Essenes' austerity, monasticism, and passion for the Law.

Was Jesus a *Zealot?*[33] It is true he gathered his followers in the wilderness, had a Zealot (Simon) as a follower, staged a triumphal entry to Jerusalem, and told them to take up swords and expect opposition, but too many differences remain for this identification to work either. His ethic was one of nonviolence: he healed Malchus' wound after Peter attacked him in Gethsemane, adopted no overtly political strategies or agendas (see above, p. 390), taught consistently about suffering and self-renunciation, and gave his life rather than fight back.

What about the *Sadducees?* In common with them, Jesus rejected the oral Torah and believed in the abiding authority of the written Scriptures. Presumably this is why later Christians (esp. the author of Hebrews) saw the need for a literal sacrifice for sins when Pharisaism/early Rabbinic Judaism substituted prayer, repentance, and good works. But Christ also saw the coming demise

31. A theme helpfully surveyed in Roger E. Hedlund, *The Mission of the Church in the World: A Biblical Theology* (Grand Rapids: Baker, 1991).

32. This area has been the subject of a flurry of recent interest. See esp. J. D. G. Dunn, ed., *Jews and Christians: The Parting of the Ways* (Tübingen: Mohr, 1992); idem, *The Parting of the Ways between Christianity and Judaism and Their Significance for the Character of Christianity* (London: SCM; Philadelphia: TPI, 1991).

33. By far and away the most famous attempt to make this case remains S. G. F. Brandon, *Jesus and the Zealots* (Manchester: Manchester University Press, 1967).

of the current temple, which no Sadducee could have welcomed, and sought to abolish nationalism (esp. in John 4) and the badges of religious ethnocentrism that went along with it.

Paradoxically, it was probably the *Pharisaic* movement, with whom Jesus was most at odds, that he also most closely resembled.[34] Both Jesus and the Pharisees had a passionate commitment to apply God's will to every area of life. Jesus' teachings focused on the same topics the Pharisees debated. Sometimes he resembled the more conservative Shammai (as on the divorce question); other times he echoed the words of the more liberal Hillel (as with the double love-command and "golden rule"). With the Pharisees and against the Sadducees, he believed in the resurrection and in angels. But again, Jesus' ethics were not Law-centered. And against *all* the major Jewish sects, Jesus focused far more on morality than on ritual, announced the arrival of the kingdom, stressed love for all peoples, even one's enemies, and claimed that he was the Messiah who was one with God.[35]

In this post-holocaust age, Christians and Jews are (or should be) very sensitive about anything that smacks of anti-Semitism. Was Jesus (or any Gospel writer) anti-Semitic? There are certainly harsh invectives against various Jewish individuals and even wholesale broadsides against "the Jews," especially in the Fourth Gospel. We have already commented on this problem in conjunction with specific texts and themes above (e.g., p. 313). By way of review and synthesis, however, it is important to stress that: (1) Nothing in the Gospels is any stronger than the denunciatory polemic canonized in the Hebrew Scriptures, particularly in the Prophets, by various Jewish spokesmen against their own people. (2) Jesus and the evangelists are in-house critics; this is an *intra*-Jewish debate as to which forms of religion may or may not still call themselves Jewish and comprise the true people of God.[36] (3) It is not anti-Semitic to claim Jesus as the one, true fulfillment of Old Testament promises; rather, it is *exclusivist*. Jesus and the Gospels were clearly making claims of uniqueness for Jesus, but that is quite different from expressing hostility against an entire people. (4) Even the seemingly sweeping references to "the Jews" in various pejorative contexts never embrace every ethnically Jewish person in Jesus' day, since Jesus and all his first followers were Jews. Rather, as noted above (p. 167), depending on the context, they may refer to all Jews who rejected Jesus, a prevailing group of opponents among the crowds, certain Jewish leaders, various Judeans, or select Jerusalemites.[37]

Genuine Christians must surely denounce the past atrocities that have been committed against Jews, often in the name of Christ, and do their best to see that they are never replicated. Ecumenical dialogue can help ensure that we avoid perpetuating the false stereotypes and sweeping generalizations that

---

34. An excellent illustration, though overstated, is Harvey Falk's *Jesus the Pharisee* (New York: Paulist, 1985).

35. For helpful nuancing of these various "transformations," see John Riches, *Jesus and the Transformation of Judaism* (London: Darton, Longman & Todd, 1980).

36. A point increasingly recognized in helpful studies of "formative" Judaism such as J. Andrew Overman, *Matthew's Gospel and Formative Judaism* (Minneapolis: Fortress, 1990); and Anthony J. Saldarini, *Matthew's Christian-Jewish Community* (Chicago and London: University of Chicago Press, 1994).

37. The two best studies of supposed anti-Semitism in the New Testament, both collections of essays, are (from an evangelical perspective) Craig A. Evans and Donald A. Hagner, eds., *Anti-Semitism and Early Christianity* (Minneapolis: Fortress, 1993); and (from an ecumenical perspective) Peter Richardson, David Granskou, and Stephen G. Wilson, eds., *Anti-Judaism in Early Christianity*, 2 vols. (Waterloo, Ontario: Wilfrid Laurier, 1986).

most conservative Christian preaching still puts forward about "the Jews." As simple a move as remembering every time one is talking about Jesus and his first-century opposition to say something like, *"certain* Jews" or "many of the Jewish *leaders"* can go a long way toward this end (and toward ensuring historical accuracy). Still, it is questionable whether a Christian can remain faithful to the biblical data or to history without at some point raising the problem of exclusivity. If Jesus claimed that he was the only way to the Father (John 14:6), then we dare not categorize non-Christian Jews as any more *soteriologically* privileged than any other non-Christians.[38] We can still carry on irenic dialogue, but we accomplish little by sidestepping altogether the most foundational issues that separate us.[39] But we also dare not lose sight of the future hope for Israel that Jesus holds out in texts like Matthew 23:39 and Luke 21:24, after the time of Gentile dominance has run its course (esp. in light of Rom. 11:25–26). Finally, we must remember to apply Jesus' harsh polemic in a similar "in-house" fashion in our day and age—to those who corrupt and pervert *Christianity* in a legalistic direction.

REDEMPTION AND VINDICATION

We have thus far focused primarily on Jesus' teaching—his announcement of God's reign, the ethics that follow for his disciples, the comparison between Law and gospel, and the resulting similarities and differences between Jesus and the rest of Judaism. But the first generation of Christians was profoundly convinced that the most important elements of Jesus' life were his death and resurrection. Given our conviction of the general trustworthiness of the Gospel tradition, what can we learn from it about Jesus' own understanding of these crucial events in his ministry?

To begin with, they were long anticipated. From the outset of his ministry, the devil tempted Jesus to bypass the way of the cross, but Christ remained unyielding. In an early pronouncement story, Jesus acknowledged that the days were coming when the "bridegroom" would be taken away (Mark 2:20 pars.). Ominous portents appear elsewhere when Jesus speaks of the violence surrounding the arrival of the kingdom (Matt. 11:12 par.), the struggle between God and Satan (Mark 3:27 pars.), and the "sword" that would divide families (Matt. 10:34 par.). But the key turning point in Jesus' career comes after Peter's confession on the road to Caesarea Philippi. Then Jesus speaks explicitly of his coming death and resurrection in his three passion predictions, using the language of divine necessity (Mark 8:31; 9:31; 10:33–34 pars.). Then Jesus "sets his face" to go to Jerusalem (Luke 9:51), knowing full well the fate that awaits him there (13:32–33).

As the time draws close he speaks of having to drink "the cup," a common Old Testament metaphor for judgment and God's wrath (Mark 10:38; cf. Luke 12:50). The cup image appears again as Jesus struggles in Gethsemane to come to grips with God's will. In Mark 10:45 and parallel appear a cluster of concepts

---

38. E.g., in the "two-covenants" theology that holds that Jesus is Savior for the Gentile world, while Jews may still be saved by faithfulness to the Mosaic covenant.

39. A salutary example of irenic dialogue that *does* deal with foundational issues is the Jewish-Christian interchange in Pinchas Lapide and Ulrich Luz, *Jesus in Two Perspectives: A Jewish-Christian Dialogue* (Minneapolis: Augsburg, 1985).

that disclose Jesus' understanding of his death in even more detail. It will be a "ransom"—the price paid for a slave's freedom, *anti* ("in the place of") many—a substitutionary sacrifice, alluding to language from Isaiah's suffering servant prophecies (cf. Isa. 53:12).[40] John 10:11–18 refers to a similar sacrificial death—Jesus is the Good Shepherd who lays down his life for his sheep. Jesus predicts the demise of the current temple and seems to imply that his resurrected body will function as a new temple (John 2:19), providing further support for his death as an *atoning sacrifice*.

The Lord's Supper repeats a number of these concepts. As a Passover meal it suggests the typology of Jesus as the Paschal lamb. The broken bread and cup of wine reiterate the allusions to life-bringing death and God's wrath being placated. The "blood" also symbolizes a life for a life, and Jesus declares it to be "poured out *for many*" (Mark 14:24), again a probable allusion to Isaiah 53:12. His death inaugurates a new covenant for the forgiveness of sins (Luke 22:20, echoing the prophecy of Jer. 31:31–34), and the memorial of that death in the Lord's Supper also looks forward to the coming of the kingdom in all its fullness (Mark 14:25 pars.).[41] The Passion narrative itself poignantly illustrates Jesus' selfless, suffering love as he forgives his persecutors, tends to his family and followers, senses divine abandonment, and yet entrusts himself to his Father in his dying gasps. Second Corinthians 5:21 is the natural interpretive outgrowth of these scenes: "God made him who had no sin to be sin for us, so that in him we might become the righteousness of God."

But what of the aftermath? In every one of Jesus' Passion predictions he also promised a resurrection. He consistently said this would take place "on the third day," a probable allusion to Hosea 6:2 (and the experience of Jonah), enabling Paul later to stress that this chronology was "according to the Scriptures" (1 Cor. 15:4). Jesus clearly believed in the general resurrection of "saints" at the end of time (Mark 12:18–27 pars.; cf. Luke 14:14), as well as the personal presence of believers with himself immediately upon their deaths (Luke 23:43). But belief in the resurrection of a single individual in advance of the general resurrection at Judgment Day was unheard of. Almost certainly, then, Jesus viewed his resurrection as at the very least *inaugurating* the last days, bringing in the new age to overlap with the old, even if all of God's plans for history were not yet fulfilled. He would have also seen it as *vindication* of his life and death, validating his claims to be the divine Messiah (see below, pp. 401–412) who offered the atoning sacrifice for the sins of humanity.[42] Jesus' ministry with his disciples during the forty-day period of resurrection appearances offered opportunity for further instruction on how the Scriptures were fulfilled in him and on the nature of the kingdom (Luke 24:45–49; Acts 1:3). It gave all the disciples a chance to be forgiven, reinstated (John 21:15–23), and recommissioned (Matt. 28:16–20). But Jesus' vindication was not complete until after his ascension, exaltation, and return to the right hand of the Father (Acts 1:9–11).

---

40. This allusion is disputed, but see esp. France, *Jesus and the Old Testament*, 110–35. The cumulative effect of all the passages in which similar suffering servant allusions may be present makes the motif that much more likely in any one instance.

41. On the authenticity and significance of these various elements, see esp. I. Howard Marshall, *Last Supper and Lord's Supper* (Exeter: Paternoster; Grand Rapids: 1980), 30–56, 76–106.

42. How different this was from conventional Judaism is demonstrated by the work of the German rabbi, Pinchas Lapide. Lapide stunned the scholarly world in the early 1980s by arguing that Jesus was truly bodily resurrected from the dead. But he was still not prepared to accept him as the Jews' Messiah because not all of the prophecies of the Old Testament were fulfilled following the resurrection. See his *The Resurrection of Jesus* (Minneapolis: Augsburg, 1983).

And the decisive moment for the empowerment of the disciples for their mission would not come until Pentecost (Acts 2).

But what would come after that? Did Jesus really anticipate a prolonged interval between his resurrection and his return? Three texts have convinced many that he anticipated his return within the lifetimes of his disciples but was mistaken (Matt. 10:23; Mark 9:1 pars.; Mark 13:30 pars.). But we have seen above that none of these texts is best taken to teach this. Rather they refer, respectively, to the perennially incomplete mission to the Jews, to the transfiguration as a foretaste of the Parousia, and to events *preceding* Christ's return that would in fact take place by A.D. 70 (see above, pp. 286, 279, and 326). Parables like the pounds (see esp. Luke 19:11) and the ten bridesmaids (Matt. 25:1–13) do indeed anticipate a possible delay, and the "bottom line" is that we simply cannot know when Christ will come back, for he himself in the limitations of his incarnation did not know (Mark 13:32 pars.).[43]

What we can know about the interval between Christ's first and second comings is that there will be a period of unspecified length for the church to carry out its work, most notably evangelizing the nations (Mark 13:10 par.), and that tribulations will intensify near the end, culminating in a reenactment of some kind of desecration reminiscent of the sacrilege of Antiochus Epiphanes (see above, pp. 324–325) that Jesus called "the abomination that causes desolation" (v. 14 par.). It is conceivable that there will be an influx of Jewish believers after this period. Christ will then return in a universal, visible, glorious fashion (vv. 24–27 pars.; cf. 14:62 pars.), gathering together his elect and assembling all humankind for the final judgment (Matt. 25:31–46). People will be assigned to one of two fates—everlasting, conscious bliss with God or unending, conscious agony separate from him (cf. also Matt. 19:28; John 5:24–30). The perfect fellowship and intimacy of believers with one another and with God in Christ is frequently depicted as a joyous banquet (Matt. 8:11 par.; Matt. 22:1–14; Luke 14:16–24), while "hell" is consistently described as a place of "weeping and gnashing of teeth" (Matt. 8:12; 13:42, 50).[44] Questions about a rapture or a millennium are not clearly addressed in any texts from the Gospels; they will have to be answered by analysis of other parts of Scripture. Instead of speculating about the details and timing of the end, Christ calls us to *vigilant obedience* whenever the end may come (Matt. 24:37–25:46).

CHRISTOLOGY

What was Jesus' self-understanding? Did it progress? Was it consistent with the evangelists' later Christology? With questions like these we come to the most important issues of all concerning Jesus' theology as we attempt to answer for ourselves the question of his identity.

---

43. Cf. further Arthur L. Moore, *The Parousia in the New Testament* (Leiden: Brill, 1966), 190, who concludes that the end for Jesus "was *in some sense* near but that evidence is lacking that he held to a delimited hope."

44. The other two primary metaphors for hell in the Gospels—unquenchable fire and outer darkness—if taken literally, contradict one another. Cf. George E. Ladd, *A Theology of the New Testament*, rev. Donald A. Hagner (Grand Rapids: Eerdmans, 1993), 196. But the fact that Jesus uses symbols rather than a literal description of eternal punishment should not lead us to play down the awfulness of the reality so depicted.

Phases of Jesus' Mission

Much speculation has gone into the questions of whether Jesus ever knew himself to be the Messiah or to be divine, and if he did whether it was a notion he always had or if it grew on him over time. There is actually very little information in the Gospels to help us answer these questions definitively. On the one hand, Luke 2:49 ("Didn't you know I had to be in my Father's house?") suggests some awareness by the boy Jesus that he had a special relationship with God. On the other hand, the silence of the Gospels concerning most of Jesus' childhood and young adulthood suggests there was nothing *too* special about these years. Clearly Jesus' baptism by John marked a dramatic new stage in his life as he was commissioned by God for ministry (Mark 1:9–11 pars.). The heavenly voice echoed Old Testament texts and linked Jesus with both royal Messiah and suffering servant (see above, p. 222). We have already spoken of a broad outline of Jesus' ministry in terms of stages of obscurity, popularity, and rejection, but beyond that it is difficult to trace any clear lines of development.

At some point, Jesus definitely begins to give clearer public indications of the need for him to follow the way of the cross. John the Baptist's death certainly sends signals about the potential danger of Jesus' ministry. Matthew 11–12 portray a "miniclimax" of hostility against Jesus, with chapter 13 as a modest turning point in which Jesus begins to focus more on outsiders and on disciples than on the general Jewish populace or its leadership. In the Synoptics, Peter's confession on the road to Caesarea Philippi brings a new stage in christological understanding, but one that still needs substantial correction (Mark 8:27–30 pars.). From here on, Jesus teaches much more explicitly and consistently about his coming suffering. Luke 9:51 introduces a lengthy period of Jesus' itinerant teaching under this very shadow of the cross.

The "triumphal" entry initiates the last phase of Jesus' mission, climaxing the crowds' anticipation but also their misunderstanding of Jesus. Euphoria will quickly give way to hostility and to crucifixion. Jesus' clearest public self-disclosure will come before the Sanhedrin (Mark 14:62 pars.); his most extensive private self-disclosure, in the Upper Room (John 13–17). Both take place on the last night of his life, and in both cases his audiences still misunderstand. True understanding of Christ's identity is possible, whether for "insider" or "outsider," only after the resurrection (Mark 9:9; John 2:22).[45]

Indirect Evidence

But what was that identity? We will look below at the specific titles that Jesus or others used to speak of him, but it is important not to neglect what is often called "nontitular" or "implicit" Christology. Precisely because these data often emerge in contexts that are not explicitly addressing the question of who Jesus is, they prove all the more valuable in the quest for the historical Jesus' self-understanding. We may cite twelve such categories of data here.

---

45. Cf. further Ben F. Meyer, "'Phases' in Jesus' Mission," *Gregorianum* 73 (1992): 5–17.

1. *Jesus' Relationships.*[46] In the ways Jesus interacted with and spoke about others, the impression one gets is that he was always "in charge." Even while speaking humbly, he makes statements that disclose a remarkable self-estimation. Jesus declares that John the Baptist was the greatest of all previous people, yet Jesus ushers in the kingdom that will make its subjects greater still (Matt. 11:11–12 par.). He calls John the Elijah who was to come (Matt. 17:11–13 par.), but that leaves only a messianic "job description" open for Jesus, his successor. Jesus similarly challenges the Jewish leaders with an authority that transcends even the written Law, and he calls his disciples to form the nucleus of a new, spiritually liberated Israel, tasks traditionally reserved for God or at least his appointed spokespersons.

2. *Accepting Worship, Prayer, and Faith.* Repeatedly people fall down before Jesus with their requests. English translations may at times translate *proskuneō* with the term "worship," but *proskuneō* also means to "prostrate" oneself before an individual, a customary posture in the ancient world for someone to use when beseeching an authority figure. Still, there are times when more seems implied. After Jesus walks on the water and climbs into the disciples' boat, they "worship" him, saying "Truly you are the Son of God" (Matt. 14:33). Jesus commands his followers to pray to the Father *in his name*—that is, by his power or authority (John 16:23–24; 14:13–14), and it is faith in him that repeatedly brings people physical and spiritual healing (Mark 5:34 pars.; 10:52 par.; Luke 7:50; 17:19). Later the disciples (and even angels!) would rebuke people who treated them that way (e.g., Acts 14:14–15; Rev. 22:8–9), but Jesus actually encourages such behavior (cf. also John 14:1).

3. *God's Final Eschatological Agent.* In Mark 8:38 and parallels, Jesus declares that one's response to him determines his or her eternal destiny. Luke 12:8–9 puts it even more bluntly: "I tell you, whoever acknowledges me before men, the Son of Man will also acknowledge him before the angels of God. But he who disowns me before men will be disowned before the angels of God." Apparently, Jesus thinks he will be God's helper on Judgment Day (cf. also Matt. 7:21–23; 25:31–46)! Even now, actions done to him are equivalent to those done to God (Matt. 10:40; Mark 9:37).

4. *Authority to Forgive Sins.* Mark 2:10 and parallels astounded its original audience as Jesus claimed to forgive the paralytic's sins. Of course, priests in a variety of religions have claimed to mediate forgiveness, although Jesus was not of priestly lineage. But his reply suggests something more, a heavenly origin: "But that you may know that the Son of Man has *authority* on earth to forgive sins" (italics added). And his miraculous cure of the man demonstrates the power to back up his claim (cf., Luke 23:43 for Jesus' ability to promise the crucified "robber" immediate forgiveness and presence in Paradise).

5. *Metaphors Applied to Yahweh in the Old Testament.* In a series of passages, particularly in the Synoptic parables, Jesus applies to himself metaphors from the Old Testament that were often reserved for God. Any one of these by itself is scarcely conclusive, but the cumulative effect is significant: Jesus refers to himself, often indirectly, as bridegroom, rock, director of the harvest, sower, shepherd, father, giver of forgiveness, vineyard owner, and king. The combined

---

46. Cf. esp. Witherington, *Christology,* 33–143.

effect goes even beyond indicating Jesus as Messiah to pointing out one who is God himself, a theme which otherwise only John, among the Gospels, introduces explicitly.[47] Other ways in which Jesus associates himself with functions of Yahweh include receiving children's praise (Matt. 21:16; cf. Ps. 8:2), seeking the lost (Luke 19:10; cf. Ezek. 34), and experiencing rejection as the cornerstone that becomes a stumbling stone (Luke 20:17–18; cf. Isa. 8:14–15).

6. *Miracles and the Kingdom.* We have noticed above how Jesus' miracles were not arbitrary or capricious but dovetailed with his announcement of the arrival of God's kingdom and fulfilled Old Testament and intertestamental Jewish expectation of what would happen when the messianic age arrived (pp. 267–268). But if the kingdom or messianic age has arrived, then the king or Messiah must also be present.

7. *Abba.* Although its significance can be exaggerated, Jesus' sense of filial consciousness should not be ignored (see further below, pp. 407–408). The intimate Aramaic *Abba* (not exactly but almost "Daddy") is not quite as unparalleled in Jewish literature as once was thought but it is still highly provocative. Found in transliteration in the Gospels in Mark 14:36, it presumably lies behind other uses of the Greek *patēr* ("father") and explains Paul's use of the term in Romans 8:15 and Galatians 4:6 for the new intimacy all believers can have with God through Christ.[48]

8. *Amēn.* A second Semitic term preserved in Greek transliteration is *Amēn,* often translated into English as "verily" or "truly." Jesus begins numerous solemn pronouncements with this forceful introduction (in John, it is often doubled—"truly, truly"), followed by "I say to you" (e.g., Matt. 5:18, 26; 6:2, 5, 16; 8:10; Mark 3:28; 8:12; 9:1, 41; Luke 4:24; 11:51; 13:35; cf. John 1:51; 3:3, 5; 5:19, 24, 25; etc.). Unlike the prophets, Jesus does not declare what the Lord God says, but what he himself says, yet in contexts of equally authoritative claims.

9. *The Messianic Demonstrations of the Final Week.* The "triumphal" entry consciously reenacts messianic prophecy (Zech. 9:9); the cursed fig tree and "cleansed temple" portend the dissolution of "the Old Testament age"; and Jesus' teaching in and concerning the temple during the last week of his life reinforces the conviction that the last chance for repentance for the current regime in Israel will soon pass. But who can declare without further support that such apocalyptic upheavals have begun who is not much more than a typical prophet?

10. *"Something Greater" Is Here.* The same kind of logic lies behind several statements of Jesus that show him to be greater than David or the temple or Solomon or Jonah (Matt. 12:3–6, 41–42). There are no obvious intermediate categories short of "the Messiah" for which such labels can qualify. The same is true of other "quasi-titles" in the Gospels such as John the Baptist's reference to "the coming one" (Mark 1:7 pars.) or Jesus as "wisdom" (Matt. 11:19 par.).[49]

---

47. Cf. further Philip B. Payne, "Jesus' Implicit Claim to Deity in His Parables," *Trinity Journal* n.s. 2 (1981): 3–23; Daniel Doriani, "The Deity of Christ in the Synoptic Gospels," *JETS* 37 (1994): 333–50.

48. Cf. further Witherington, *Christology*, 216–21.

49. On which, see esp. Ben Witherington III, *Jesus as Sage* (Minneapolis: Fortress, 1994).

11. *Shaliach*. In the Synoptics, Jesus often uses the expression, "I have come to . . . " (e.g., Matt. 5:17; 9:13; 10:34–35; cf. Luke 19:10). In John, his speech often refers to "[the one] who sent me" (John 4:34; 5:23–24, 36–37; 6:38–40; 7:16; etc.). Both forms suggest that he is on a mission from God. The language hints at, though does not require, the idea that his origin is otherworldly. It also conforms to one of the clusters of concepts at times associated with the Jewish Messiah—the *shaliach* (Greek *apostolos* or apostle—cf. John 13:16)—the one sent out from Yahweh on a mission to reveal himself to and redeem his people.[50]

12. *Jesus' Seemingly Supernatural Insight*. On several occasions, Jesus appears to be able to read people's minds or sense their deepest needs (e.g., Mark 10:21; 12:24 pars.). He can predict the future (his passion, resurrection, the coming destruction of Jerusalem). And he can refer to seemingly incidental details of coming events in ways that leave it unclear if he has supernatural knowledge or is simply staging somewhat cryptic or secretive activities (e.g., in his instructions to the disciples to find a man carrying a water jar as the rendezvous person for arranging the final Passover—Mark 14:13–15 pars.; cf. also the episode with the colt for "Palm Sunday" in Mark 11:2–3 pars.).[51]

Son of Man

From implicit Christology, we turn to the explicit titles used of Jesus. The most common one that he himself employed was "Son of Man." The term is used eighty-two times, well distributed among the four Gospels. It is always on the lips of Jesus, except in John 12:34 where the crowd uses the term in reply to Jesus' previous use of it. Outside the Gospels, however, it appears as a title only in Acts 7:56 when the dying Stephen addresses Jesus (cf. also the uses without the definite article in Rev. 1:13 and 14:14). Jewish backgrounds are greatly disputed since there is no exact parallel to Jesus' uses of the term. The expression thus passes the dissimilarity criterion of authenticity with flying colors.

But what did Jesus mean by it? An older view, often associated with Bultmann and some of his followers, wondered whether Jesus, at times at least, was talking about someone other than himself—a *coming* Son of Man or Messiah. But this view is now largely abandoned. In recent years, much linguistic study has given rise to hypotheses that the expression evolved from the frequent Old Testament use of the address "son of man" as an equivalent to "mortal human" (e.g., Ps. 8:2 and throughout Ezekiel). Based on various later Aramaic usages of *bar (e)nash(a)*, it has thus been taken generically to mean "a man," or as a circumlocution for "I," or as a categorical reference to "a man like me" or "a man in my position."[52] These interpretations work reasonably

50. Cf. A. E. Harvey, "Christ as Agent," in *The Glory of Christ in the New Testament*, ed. L. D. Hurst and N. T. Wright (Oxford: Clarendon, 1987), 239–50.

51. For a succinct list and discussion of several of the above implicit indicators of Christology, see R. T. France, "The Worship of Jesus: A Neglected Factor in Christological Debate?" in *Christ the Lord*, ed. H. H. Rowdon (Leicester: IVP, 1982), 28.

52. See, respectively, Maurice Casey, *Son of Man* (London: SPCK, 1979); Geza Vermes, *Jesus the Jew* (London: Collins, 1973; Philadelphia: Fortress, 1974), 160–91; Barnabas Lindars, *Jesus Son of Man* (London: SPCK; Grand Rapids: Eerdmans, 1983). More recently, Casey has largely agreed with Lindars' positions.

well in texts like Matthew 8:20 ("The Son of Man has no place to lay his head") or 12:32 ("Anyone who speaks a word against the Son of Man will be forgiven"), but less so in those that depict Jesus as more exalted. Proponents of this view usually argue, therefore, that a core of authentic "Son of Man" texts have been elaborated with additional, inauthentic ones. They are hard pressed to explain how the expression became titular (or at least articular) in all its Greek references in the Gospels: *ho huios tou anthrōpou* ("*the* Son of Man"). There is no doubt, however, that in *certain* texts even the Gospel writers recognized the interchangeability of Son of Man with "I" (cf., e.g., Luke 6:22 with Matt. 5:11; Mark 8:27 with Matt. 16:13; or within Luke 12:8).

It is not likely, though, that this explanation can account for all or even a majority of the uses of this term. Daniel 7:13 probably provides more directly relevant background. In his vision, Daniel sees "one like a son of man," that is, one who is apparently human. Yet this individual was "coming with the clouds of heaven." He approached the Ancient of Days and was led into his presence: "He was given authority, glory and sovereign power; all peoples, nations and men of every language worshiped him. His dominion is an everlasting dominion that will not pass away, and his kingdom is one that will never be destroyed" (vv. 13–14).

On the basis of verse 18 ("The saints of the Most High will receive the kingdom and will possess it forever"), many Jews interpreted this vision as a prophecy of the collective future and glory of Israel. But verses 13–14 seem to suggest more than this—that Israel will be led by a representative who is described as a heavenly figure worthy of universal worship (an unlikely attribute for monotheistic Jews to ascribe to themselves as a whole!). In 1 Enoch and 4 Ezra, Jewish pseudepigraphal works written no later than the end of the first century, the Son of Man appears clearly as an individual and a messianic figure. Demonstrably pre-Christian works also point to at least a minority voice within Judaism that would have agreed (cf. esp. Ezekiel the Tragedian and 11Q Melchizedek from Qumran).[53] The Greek definite article may function as a demonstrative: "this 'Son of Man'," that is, "the one described in Daniel."[54]

Most scholars have grouped Jesus' Son of Man sayings into three categories: those that refer to his earthly ministry, those that portend his coming suffering, and those that allude to his future, exalted state. Seeing a Danielic background for the title allows one to accept sayings in all three categories as authentic. The vision of a heavenly man clearly fits the exalted sayings (e.g., Matt. 10:23; 19:28; Mark 8:38; 9:1). The references to oppression and war against the saints in Daniel 7:21, 25 could have suggested the link with suffering (as in Mark 8:31; 14:21; or Luke 12:40). Even in the sayings that seem least dependent on a Danielic background, hints of either suffering or exaltation seem present. For example, when the Son of Man has nowhere to lay his head, the ignominy of Jesus' itinerant ministry is highlighted. When he demonstrates authority to forgive sins on earth (Mark 2:10) or shows that he is Lord of the Sabbath (2:28), a certain transcendence seems present. If it is difficult to see how Ezekiel's "son

---

53. For these and related references, see William Horbury, "The Messianic Associations of 'The Son of Man'," *JTS* 36 (1985): 34–55.
54. Seyoon Kim, *The Son of Man as the Son of God* (Grand Rapids: Eerdmans, 1985).

of man" (a mere mortal) could have given rise to the exalted titular passages in the Gospels, it is not hard to see how a Danielic, messianic, suffering Son of Man could lurk in the background of even the less explicitly titular Gospel references.[55]

The upshot of all of this is that, contrary to popular contemporary Christian (mis-)conceptions, "Son of Man" winds up being a very exalted title for Jesus. *It does not primarily focus on his true humanity but on his heavenly enthronement* (cf. also the plural "thrones" of Dan. 7:9). It is more of a synonym than an antonym of "Son of God." But it remains ambiguous enough that Jesus was able to invest the term with his own meaning and clarifications.[56] It was not susceptible to the political misunderstandings surrounding the term "Messiah" itself (see below, pp. 409–411). The possibility of linking it with suffering was not one that pre-Christian Jews had clearly exploited. And whereas Daniel's Son of Man travels on the clouds *to* the very throne room of God, Jesus uses this imagery to describe his return *from* heaven to earth in glory (Mark 14:62 pars.).

Son of God

The title "Son of God" is much less common in the Gospels than "Son of Man." It is used mostly by others of Jesus. The angels predict that Jesus will be called Son of the Highest and Son of God (Luke 1:32, 35). The voice from heaven declares Jesus to be his Son, alluding to Psalm 2:7, at both Christ's baptism and his transfiguration (Mark 1:11; 9:7 pars.). Frequently the devil and his demons acknowledge Jesus as God's Son, as part of spiritual warfare (e.g., Matt. 4:3, 6; Mark 3:11; 5:7). The centurion at the cross recognizes Jesus as the Son of God (Mark 15:39), but this need mean nothing more than a "divine man"—a human deified upon death—after the typical Greco-Roman conception (cf. the parallel in Luke 23:47 in which the centurion declares Jesus merely to be innocent). Indeed, even in Jewish backgrounds the term "son of God" could refer to powerful influential humans, charismatic teachers and rabbis, angelic or demonic beings, or the Messiah (see now esp. the recently translated Dead Sea fragment 4Q246; and cf. 1QSa 11–12 and 4QFlor 10–14 on 2 Sam. 7:11–14).[57]

In several strategic places, however, the stakes seem to be higher. Gabriel tells Mary that the child she will conceive will be called "the Son of God" (Luke 1:35). After Jesus walks on the water, the disciples, at least in Matthew's account, worship him and declare him to be Son of God (Matt. 14:33). Yet this understanding is apparently still not as appropriately nuanced as Peter's later confession of Jesus as "Son of the living God," which Jesus attributes to supernatural influence (Matt. 16:16). Even here the immediate context makes it clear that Peter does not understand as he will after the death and resurrection about the need for the Son of God to suffer. Since neither of these passages uses the title "Son of God" in their Markan parallels (the earliest written forms of the tradition), it is not until we get to Jesus' trial before the Sanhedrin that we can

55. For a succinct but incisive critique of the Casey-Vermes-Lindars tradition in favor of the views set forth here, see Delbert Burkett, "The Nontitular Son of Man: A History and Critique," *NTS* 40 (1994): 504–21.

56. Cf., e.g., F. F. Bruce, "The Background to the Son of Man Sayings," in *Christ the Lord*, 50–70.

57. For a good list of uses, see Jarl Fossum, "Son of God," in *ABD*, vol. 6, 128–37.

get a secure read on Jesus' own estimation of the label. There he replies with an affirmative, however qualified, to the question of his identity as "Christ, the Son of the *Blessed One*" (a Jewish euphemism for God). Still, he immediately redefines his role in terms of the heavenly Son of Man (Mark 14:61–62 pars.)

More helpful perhaps are references where Jesus speaks of the "son" without qualification. In Matthew 11:27 he uses language very similar to numerous references to the Son or Son of God in John's Gospel when he declares, "All things have been committed to me by my Father. No one knows the Son except the Father, and no one knows the Father except the Son and those to whom the Son chooses to reveal him." Here is a clear expression of Jesus' awareness of a uniquely intimate and revelatory relationship with God as his heavenly Father. This is the logical corollary of his use of *Abba* to address God (see above, p. 253). In the parable of the wicked tenants, the "son" of the landlord emerges as a Christ-figure, anticipating Jesus' crucifixion (Mark 12:6 pars.; cf. the image of the king's son in the parable of the wedding banquet—Matt. 22:2). And in his Olivet Discourse, Jesus describes the limitations of his present knowledge in terms of what the "Son" does not know about his return (Mark 13:32 par.). Only after the resurrection is the term used approximately as in later Trinitarian formulas in which Jesus becomes Son of God in the sense of God's ontological equal and one part of the Godhead itself (Matt. 28:19). Even in John's Gospel, where sonship throughout seems more exalted, there are also statements of functional subordination as radical as Jesus' words, "The Father is greater than I" (John 14:28).

Ironically, therefore, Son of God may often be a slightly less exalted title for Jesus, especially in the Synoptics, than Son of Man. A. E. Harvey's conclusions aptly summarize this "functional" sense of sonship:

> Jesus had indeed shown that absolute obedience to God, had spoken of God with that intimate authority, and had acted with the unique authorization which belonged to God's representative and agent on earth, which would be characteristic of one who was (in the sense usually ascribed to "sonship" in antiquity) in very truth "Son of God"; and the reversal of the world's judgment upon him, which was implied by the event his followers called "the Resurrection," enabled them to describe Jesus with absolute confidence as "the Son," a title which would certainly have been correct in his lifetime, and was presumably acknowledged by supernatural beings, but was too momentous to be openly acknowledged even by those of his followers who had found their way to faith in him.[58]

Clearly even this functional sonship was impressive and unique.

Lord

In the Greco-Roman world, "lord" (Gk., *kurios*) was a title applied to gods, emperors, other human masters, and anyone a person wanted to address respectfully. In the Jewish world, it was one of the titles for Yahweh, God himself (Heb., *adonai*) but could similarly apply to various human masters and authority figures. In most of the uses in the Gospels when somebody addresses

58. A. E. Harvey, *Jesus and the Constraints of History* (London: Duckworth; Philadelphia: Westminster, 1982), 167–68.

Jesus as "lord," therefore, we dare not infer more than a title of respect that recognizes his charisma or authority. Mark 11:3 is a bit more suggestive when Jesus tells his disciples to respond to anyone questioning them about taking the colt for "Palm Sunday" by saying, "The Lord needs it." The average Jew would assume the disciples were speaking of God, but is Jesus thus implicitly linking himself with God by using this title? In Mark 2:28 and parallels, the Son of Man is "Lord" even over the Sabbath. But who has the right to transcend Sabbath law but God? Most significant of all is 12:35–37 and parallels, in which Jesus questions the Jewish leaders in the temple about how David's son (the Messiah) can also be his "Lord." He quotes Psalm 110:1, in which David declares, "The Lord [Yahweh] says to my Lord *[adonai]*" But who is this second "Lord" who is above even the king of Israel if not a Messiah who is more than a mere man?

Still, it is primarily only after the resurrection that "Lord" in its strongest sense can be applied to Jesus. Hence, Acts 2:36 climaxes Peter's Pentecostal sermon with the conclusion that on the basis of the resurrection and exaltation Jesus can be designated "both Lord and Christ." Among the Gospel writers it is only Luke who then retrojects this understanding into his Gospel narrative, not in settings where people approach Jesus but in his larger narrative framework. Elizabeth refers to Mary, before she has given birth, as "the mother of my Lord" (Luke 1:43). The angels proclaim to the shepherds that a Savior is born who is "Christ the Lord" (Luke 2:11). And from time to time Luke refers to Jesus simply as "the Lord" (Luke 7:13, 19; 10:39, 41; 11:39; 12:42; etc.).

Nevertheless, we must not underestimate the significance of the use of "Lord" as a title for Jesus. Even when it means only "master," we are reminded that *we must not conceive of worshiping Jesus as Lord (God) without simultaneously making him our master.*[59] Matthew 7:21 puts it pointedly, "Not everyone who says to me, 'Lord, Lord,' will enter the kingdom of heaven, but only he who does the will of my Father who is in heaven." On the other hand, the use of "Lord" for Jesus as God must have developed quite early in Christian circles because already by the time of the mid-50s Paul could quote the Aramaic *Maranatha* without explanation as a closing prayer for the return of Christ (1 Cor. 16:22). Depending on how the compound word is divided, it means either "Come, O Lord!" or "Our Lord has come" (the former seems more probable). But *mar* was the Aramaic word that regularly was substituted for the Hebrew Yahweh in Old Testament texts and paraphrases. That a title used for God could be applied to Jesus so early in Jewish Christianity suggests it has roots in Jesus' own usage and self-understanding, particularly in light of the Mark 12:35–37 passage.

Messiah

We have saved the most well-known of all the titles of Jesus for last. "Christ" (Gk., *christos*), even within the later New Testament writers, becomes a virtual second name for Jesus, losing its titular sense as the translation of the "Messiah"

---

59. With respect to the "lordship salvation" controversy, particularly helpful and balanced are Darrell L. Bock, "Jesus as Lord in Acts and in the Gospel Message," *BSac* 143 (1986): 146–54; and idem, "A Review of *The Gospel according to Jesus*," *BSac* 146 (1989): 21–40.

(Heb., *Meshiach*) or *anointed one*.[60] The English word "Messiah" itself appears in most translations of the Old Testament only in Daniel 9:25–26. But prophets, priests, and kings were all anointed at various times throughout the Old Testament period. The concept of Messiah came to be associated particularly with the kingly line that Nathan had promised would occupy David's throne in perpetuity (2 Sam. 7:14). And Old Testament kings, present and future, are regularly called "the Lord's anointed." Other influential texts describing this kingship include 1 Samuel 2:10; Isaiah 7:1–9:7; 11:1–9; Micah 5:1–5; Zechariah 9:9–12; and Psalms 2, 45, and 110. Even a pagan Persian ruler could be called God's *meshiach* (Cyrus in Isa. 45:1) when he fulfilled God's purposes in repatriating God's people.

In intertestamental Judaism, one may distinguish at least six different strands of messianic expectation: (1) The Maccabean revolt initially did away with the need in some people's minds for a literal Messiah. As the Hasmonean dynasty moved further away from its original ideals, others came to the conviction that God would no longer bless his people as previously anticipated. We can speak of this strand of thought as the Messianic hope *fulfilled or forfeited*. (2) In the sectarian Judaism represented at Qumran, both *priestly and kingly* Messiahs were anticipated. This hope reflected both the dissatisfaction with the corrupt Hasmonean regime that had combined the two offices and the realization that priest (tribe of Levi) and king (tribe of Judah) could not normally be joined in the same person. (3) A substantial portion of mainstream Judaism looked for a *warrior* king who would help the Jews shake off the shackles of Rome (recall the discussion of the Psalms of Solomon above, p. 17). Hence, we read of the various prophets, bandits, and would-be Messiahs that characterized the initial ragtag stages of the Zealot movement (pp. 50–51).

(4) The parables or similitudes of 1 Enoch equate the Messiah, portrayed as an *apocalyptic* Davidic king, with titles such as "Holy" or "Elect one" and "Son of Man." So, too, does the post-Christian 4 Ezra. Questions about the dating of these documents have led many scholars to wonder whether such expectation was present in Christ's day, but increasing analysis of the Qumran and other little-known pseudepigraphal literature is making this assumption probable.[61] (5) The Samaritans looked for a *Taheb* (a "*restorer*"), who would fulfill the prophecy of a new Moses outlined in Deuteronomy 18:18. While having certain characteristics of a political deliverer, he was viewed more as a teacher than in some of the other traditions. (6) This concept of *teacher or sage* became prominent in the post-Christian rabbinic literature; it is probable that its seeds were at least beginning to germinate in the first century.

Thus we must beware of any glib generalizations about what all or most Jews were looking for at the time of Jesus. Messianic expectations were diverse and in some circles virtually nonexistent.[62] Where they were present, they were

---

60. Indeed, we have regularly used the term that way in this book, in keeping with subsequent Christian convention, but largely to avoid repeating the name "Jesus" quite so much.

61. See esp. John J. Collins, *The Scepter and the Star: The Messiahs of the Dead Sea Scrolls and Other Ancient Literature* (New York and London: Doubleday, 1995).

62. This diversity of expectation is the major theme permeating James H. Charlesworth, ed., *The Messiah: Developments in Earliest Judaism and Christianity* (Minneapolis: Fortress, 1992), even though it is probably somewhat exaggerated. For balance, see I. Howard Marshall, "The Messiah in the First Century: A Review Article," *Criswell Theological Review* 7 (1993): 67–83.

often politicized. This probably explains Jesus' reticence to accept the term without qualification (Mark 8:29; 14:62 pars.), the relative scarcity of occasions in which he uses the term himself, and his concern to silence others at times when they do use it (the "Messianic secret" motif, on which see above, p. 119). One must also take into account belief in certain Jewish circles that it was inappropriate for the Messiah to identify himself as such until after he had fulfilled his ministry.

Nevertheless, there are references to the title "Christ" attributed to Jesus in the Gospels that indicate indirectly that he was prepared to accept the designation, however overlaid those references may be with the evangelists' redaction. In Mark 9:41 he promises a reward to any who give a cup of water "in my name because you belong to Christ." In Mark 12:35 he asks how the Christ can be merely the Son of David. In Matthew 23:10 he reminds the Pharisees that there is only one who is the Christ, and in 24:5, 23 he predicts the coming of false Christs who would imitate him. In John 4:25 he discloses himself more directly to the Samaritan woman as the Messiah. All of these texts set the stage for his postresurrection question, "Did not the Christ have to suffer these things and then enter his glory?" Luke immediately adds, "And beginning with Moses and all the Prophets, he explained to them what was said in all the Scriptures concerning himself" (Luke 24:26–27). Little wonder that the title became the most all-embracing in subsequent Christian thought. But it probably originated with Jesus. As de Jonge explains,

> In view of the fact that David was not only portrayed as a king, and thereby as a political figure, but also as a prophet, a singer of psalms, and an exorcist, it does not seem impossible that Jesus regarded himself as a true Son of David who could properly be called the Lord's anointed—not only in view of his future role when God's rule would reveal itself with power, but already in the present while the kingdom of God manifested itself in his words and actions.[63]

Other Titles

Closely related to Messiah but even more susceptible to political misunderstandings was the title *king*. Jesus is the one, unlike Herod, who is *born* "king of the Jews" (Matt. 2:2). He comes as humble Messianic king at the triumphal entry (Matt. 21:5) and as kingly judge at the end of history (25:34, 40). Jesus is crucified as "king of the Jews" (Mark 15:9, 12, 18, 26, 32), a charge which is accurate but misunderstood. Christ's kingdom is not of this world (John 18:36), but that does not mean it has no sociopolitical overtones (see above, p. 345).

Jesus is also *servant of the Lord* (Mark 10:45; Matt. 12:18–21), interpreting Isaiah's suffering servant prophecies to apply to his own ministry of substitutionary, atoning death (recall above, p. 312).[64] He is a *prophet*, particularly the eschatological prophet *par excellence* like Moses (Deut. 18:18). The crowds hail him as such (Mark 6:15; 8:28; Luke 7:16, 39; 24:19), but it is generally felt

63. Marinus de Jonge, *Christology in Context* (Philadelphia: Westminster, 1988), 211.

64. Cf. further esp. R. T. France, "The Servant of the Lord in the Teaching of Jesus," *TynB* 19 (1968): 26–52. On the possibility of a pre-Christian Jewish linkage between Messiah and suffering servant, see Joachim Jeremias, "παῖς" θεοῦ in Later Judaism in the Period after the LXX," in *TDNT*, vol. 5, 677–700, but his arguments have not proved persuasive for most.

by his followers to be inadequate as a full description of Jesus' identity. He is called *teacher* (Heb., *rabbi*), but particularly in Matthew and John this title is usually used in contexts by people who don't fully grasp Jesus' significance. His own attitude to the title is reflected in Matthew 23:10—"Nor are you to be called 'teacher,' for you have one Teacher, the Christ." Other titles are more distinctive of particular Gospels—Matthew's "Son of David," Luke's "Savior," John's "Lamb of God," "Word," and the Divine "I Am's," and have already been treated above.

CONCLUSION

No matter what level of Gospel tradition one examines—the evangelists' redaction, the developing oral tradition, or the bedrock core of what can securely be assigned to the historical Jesus—one impression remains the same. Jesus, like his earliest followers, was convinced that how one responded to him was the most important decision anyone could make in his or her life. On this response hinges one's eternal destiny. We are called to become Christ's followers, to be subjects of the kingdom, to practice the "greater righteousness" that he demands but also makes possible for those who declare their allegiance to him. We must mirror his compassion for the outcasts and disenfranchised of our world. We dare not turn his teaching into a new law or legalism, but we must be prepared to carry our own crosses, experiencing rejection, hostility, and even martyrdom if necessary. Simply admiring and imitating Jesus, however, is not adequate, unless it stems from our faith in his person as the unique God-man and our reception of the forgiveness of sins that he offers. If this book has enabled its readers to progress towards these goals, in the myriad of fascinating and controversial details that it has explored, then it will have proved worth the effort for both writer and readers.

FOR FURTHER STUDY

Kingdom of God

Beasley-Murray, George R. *Jesus and the Kingdom of God.* Grand Rapids: Eerdmans; Exeter: Paternoster, 1986.

Caragounis, Chrys C. "Kingdom of God/Kingdom of Heaven," in *DJG*.

Chilton, Bruce D., ed. *The Kingdom of God in the Teaching of Jesus.* London: SPCK; Philadelphia: Fortress, 1984.

Chilton, Bruce. "The Kingdom of God in Recent Discussion." In *Studying the Historical Jesus.* Ed. Bruce Chilton and Craig A. Evans. Leiden: Brill, 1994.

Kirk, Andrew. *A New World Coming.* London: Marshall, Morgan & Scott [=*The Good News of the Kingdom Coming.* Downers Grove: IVP], 1983.

Ladd, George E. *The Presence of the Future.* Grand Rapids: Eerdmans, 1974; London: SPCK, 1980.

Marcus, Joel. *The Mystery of the Kingdom of God.* Atlanta: Scholars, 1986.

Marshall, I. Howard. "The Hope of a New Age: The Kingdom of God in the New Testament." *Themelios,* 11 (1985): 5–15.

Perrin, Norman. *Jesus and the Language of the Kingdom.* Philadelphia: Fortress; London: SCM, 1976.

Song, C. S. *Jesus and the Reign of God.* Minneapolis: Fortress, 1993.

Willis, Wendell, ed. *The Kingdom of God in 20th Century Interpretation*. Peabody: Hendrickson, 1987.

Ethics

Jesus' Ethics in General

Chilton, Bruce, and J. I. H. McDonald. *Jesus and the Ethics of the Kingdom*. London: SPCK, 1987; Grand Rapids: Eerdmans, 1988.

Harvey, A. E. *Strenuous Commands: The Ethics of Jesus*. London: SCM; Philadelphia: TPI, 1990.

Hurst, L. D. "Ethics of Jesus," in *DJG*.

Lohse, Eduard. *Theological Ethics of the New Testament*. Minneapolis: Fortress, 1991.

Meeks, Wayne A. *The Moral World of the First Christians*. Philadelphia: Westminster, 1986.

Piper, John. *"Love Your Enemies": Jesus' Love Command in the Synoptic Gospels and in Early Christian Paraenesis*. Cambridge: CUP, 1979.

Schnackenburg, Rudolf. *The Moral Teaching of the New Testament*. New York: Herder & Herder, 1971.

Schrage, Wolfgang. *The Ethics of the New Testament*. Edinburgh: T. & T. Clark; Philadelphia: Fortress, 1988.

Wiebe, Ben. *Messianic Ethics: Jesus' Proclamation of the Kingdom of God and the Church in Response*. Scottdale and Kitchener: Herald, 1992.

White, R. E. O. *Biblical Ethics*. Exeter: Paternoster; Atlanta: John Knox, 1979.

Social Concern

Bammel, Ernst, and C. F. D. Moule, eds. *Jesus and the Politics of His Day*. Cambridge: CUP, 1984.

Cassidy, Richard J. *Jesus, Politics and Society*. Maryknoll: Orbis, 1978.

Hengel, Martin. *Was Jesus a Revolutionist?* Philadelphia: Fortress, 1971.

Ringe, Sharon H. *Jesus, Liberation and the Biblical Jubilee*. Philadelphia: Fortress, 1985.

Segundo, Juan L. *The Historical Jesus of the Synoptics*. Maryknoll: Orbis, 1985.

Sider, Ronald J. *Rich Christians in an Age of Hunger*. Dallas: Word, rev. 1990.

Sobrino, Jon. *Jesus the Liberator*. Maryknoll: Orbis, 1993.

Verhey, Allen. *The Great Reversal: Ethics and the New Testament*. Grand Rapids: Eerdmans, 1984.

Witherington, Ben, III. *Women in the Ministry of Jesus*. Cambridge: CUP, 1984.

Yoder, John H. *The Politics of Jesus*. Grand Rapids: Eerdmans; Carlisle: Paternoster, rev. 1994.

Law and Gospel

Banks, Robert. *Jesus and the Law in the Synoptic Tradition*. Cambridge: CUP, 1975.

Dodd, C. H. *Gospel and Law*. Cambridge: CUP, 1951.

France, R. T. *Jesus and the Old Testament*. London: Tyndale; Downers Grove: IVP, 1971.

Meier, John P. *Law and History in Matthew's Gospel*. Rome: BIP, 1976.

Moo, Douglas J. "Law," in *DJG*.

Sloyan, Gerald S. *Is Christ the End of the Law?* Philadelphia: Westminster, 1978.

Westerholm, Stephen. *Jesus and Scribal Authority*. Lund: Gleerup, 1978.

Jesus and Judaism

Charlesworth, James H., ed. *Jesus' Jewishness*. New York: Crossroad, 1991.

Evans, Craig A., and Donald A. Hagner, eds. *Anti-Semitism and Early Christianity*. Minneapolis: Fortress, 1993.

Flusser, David. *Jesus*. New York: Herder & Herder, 1969.

Hagner, Donald A. *The Jewish Reclamation of Jesus*. Grand Rapids: Zondervan, 1984.

Richardson, Peter, and David Granskou, eds. *Anti-Judaism in Early Christianity*. Vol. 1. Waterloo, Ontario: Wilfrid Laurier, 1986.

Riches, John. *Jesus and the Transformation of Judaism*. London: Darton, Longman & Todd, 1980.

Sanders, E. P. *Jesus and Judaism*. London: SCM; Philadelphia: Fortress, 1985.

Sandmel, Samuel. *Judaism and Christian Beginnings*. Oxford: OUP, 1978.

Vermes, Geza. *The Religion of Jesus the Jew*. London: SCM; Minneapolis: Fortress, 1993.

Young, Brad H. *Jesus the Jewish Theologian*. Peabody: Hendrickson, 1995.

Zeitlin, Irving. *Jesus and the Judaism of His Time*. Oxford: Blackwell, 1988.

Redemption and Vindication

Redemption

Antwi, Daniel J. "Did Jesus Consider His Death to Be an Atoning Sacrifice?" *Interpretation*, 45 (1991): 17–28.

Hengel, Martin. *The Atonement*. London: SCM; Philadelphia: Fortress, 1981.

Hooker, Morna D. *Not Ashamed of the Gospel: New Testament Interpretations of the Death of Christ*. Carlisle: Paternoster; Grand Rapids: Eerdmans, 1994.

Hultgren, Arland J. *Christ and His Benefits: Christology and Redemption in the New Testament*. Philadelphia: Fortress, 1987.

McDonald, H. D. *New Testament Concept of Atonement*. Cambridge: Lutterworth; Grand Rapids: Baker, 1994.

Stott, John R. W. *The Cross of Christ*. Leicester and Downers Grove: IVP, 1986.

Weber, Hans-Ruedi. *The Cross: Tradition and Interpretation*. London: SPCK, 1978; Grand Rapids: Eerdmans, 1979.

Vindication

Allison, Dale C., Jr. *The End of the Ages Has Come: An Early Interpretation of the Passion and Resurrection of Jesus*. Philadelphia: Fortress, 1985.

Beasley-Murray, George R. *Jesus and the Last Days*. Peabody: Hendrickson, 1993.

Conyers, A. J. *The End: What Jesus Really Said about the Last Things*. Downers Grove: IVP, 1995.

Cranfield, C. E. B. "Thoughts on New Testament Eschatology." *Scottish Journal of Theology*, 35 (1982): 497–512.

Meyer, Ben F. "Jesus' Scenario of the Future." *Downside Review*, 109 (1991): 1–15.

Moore, Arthur L. *The Parousia in the New Testament*. Leiden: Brill, 1966.

Witherington, Ben, III. *Jesus, Paul, and the End of the World*. Downers Grove: IVP, 1992.

Christology

In General

Brown, Raymond E. *An Introduction to New Testament Christology*. New York: Paulist, 1994.

Caird, G. B. *New Testament Theology*, compl. & ed. L. D. Hurst. Oxford: Clarendon, 1994.

de Jonge, Marinus. *Christology in Context*. Philadelphia: Westminster, 1988.

Dunn, James D. G. *Christology in the Making*. London: SCM; Philadelphia: Westminster, 1980.

Farmer, William R., ed. *Crisis in Christology: Essays in Quest of Resolution*. Livonia, Mich.: Dove Booksellers, 1995.

Leivestad, Ragnar. *Jesus in His Own Perspective*. Minneapolis: Augsburg, 1987.

Marshall, I. Howard. *The Origins of New Testament Christology*. Leicester and Downers Grove: IVP, rev. 1990.

Moule, C. F. D. *The Origin of Christology*. Cambridge: CUP, 1977.

Pokorny, Petr. *The Genesis of Christology*. Edinburgh: T. & T. Clark, 1987.

Reymond, Robert L. *Jesus: Divine Messiah*. Phillipsburg, N.J.: Presbyterian & Reformed, 1990.

Witherington, Ben, III. *The Christology of Jesus*. Minneapolis: Fortress, 1990.

Son of Man

Burkett, Delbert. *The Son of Man in the Gospel of John.* Sheffield: JSOT, 1991.
Caragounis, Chrys C. *The Son of Man.* Tübingen: Mohr, 1986.
Casey, Maurice. *Son of Man.* London: SPCK, 1979.
Collins, John J. "The Son of Man in First-Century Judaism." *NTS* 38 (1992): 448–66.
Hare, D. R. A. *The Son of Man Tradition.* Minneapolis: Fortress, 1990.
Higgins, A. J. B. *The Son of Man in the Teaching of Jesus.* Cambridge: CUP, 1980.
Horbury, William. "The Messianic Associations of 'The Son of Man'." *JTS* 36 (1985): 34–55.
Kim, Seyoon. *The Son of Man as the Son of God.* Grand Rapids: Eerdmans, 1985.
Lindars, Barnabas. *Jesus Son of Man.* London: SPCK; Grand Rapids: Eerdmans, 1983.
Marshall, I. Howard. "The Synoptic 'Son of Man' Sayings in the Light of Linguistic Study." In *To Tell the Mystery: Essays on New Testament Eschatology in Honor of Robert H. Gundry.* Ed. Thomas E. Schmidt and Moisés Silva. Sheffield: JSOT, 1994.
Slater, Thomas B. "One Like a Son of Man in First-Century CE Judaism." *NTS* 41 (1995): 183–98.

Son of God

Bauckham, Richard. "The Sonship of the Historical Jesus in Christology." *SJT* 31 (1978): 245–60.
Bauer, David L. "Son of God," in *DJG.*
Hengel, Martin. *The Son of God.* London: SCM; Philadelphia: Fortress, 1976.

Lord

Fitzmyer, Joseph A. "New Testament Kyrios and Maranatha and Their Aramaic Background." In *To Advance the Gospel,* pp. 218–35. New York: Crossroad, 1981.
Hurtado, Larry W. *One God, One Lord: Early Christian Devotion and Ancient Jewish Monotheism.* Philadelphia: Fortress, 1988.
Witherington, Ben, III. "Lord," in *DJG.*

Messiah

Charlesworth, James H., ed. *The Messiah: Developments in Earliest Judaism and Christianity.* Minneapolis: Fortress, 1992.
Collins, John J. *The Scepter and the Star: The Messiahs of the Dead Sea Scrolls and Other Ancient Literature.* New York and London: Doubleday, 1995.
Dahl, Nils A. *Jesus the Christ: The Historical Origins of Christological Doctrine.* Ed. Donald Juel. Minneapolis: Fortress, 1990.
de Jonge, Marinus. *Jesus, the Servant-Messiah.* New Haven and London: Yale, 1991.
Hurtado, Larry W. "Christ," in *DJG.*
Neusner, Jacob, William S. Green and Ernest S. Frerichs, eds. *Judaisms and Their Messiahs at the Turn of the Christian Era.* Cambridge: CUP, 1987.
O'Neill, J. C. *Who Did Jesus Think He Was?* Leiden: Brill, 1995.

QUESTIONS FOR REVIEW

1. What are the major topics about which Jesus taught? How would you summarize his main emphases on each topic?

2. What are the categories of data available to us for constructing a Christology of Jesus?

3. What did each of the main christological titles in the Gospels mean in its primary, original contexts?

4. As a result of this chapter (and this book), how would you summarize the mission and identity of Jesus of Nazareth? How are these conclusions relevant to our contemporary world? to your life personally?

Author Index

SUBJECT INDEX

Scripture Index